Serious & Violent Juvenile Offenders

Risk Factors and Successful Interventions

Rolf Loeber
David P. Farrington
EDITORS

SAGE Publications
International Educational and Professional Publisher
Thousand Oaks   London   New Delhi

For information:

SAGE Publications, Inc.
2455 Teller Road
Thousand Oaks, California 91320
E-mail: order@sagepub.com

SAGE Publications Ltd.
6 Bonhill Street
London EC2A 4PU
United Kingdom

SAGE Publications India Pvt. Ltd.
M-32 Market
Greater Kailash I
New Delhi 110 048 India

Printed in the United States of America

Library of Congress Cataloging-in-Publication Data

Main entry under title:

Serious and violent juvenile offenders: Risk factors and successful
    interventions / [edited] by Rolf Loeber, David P. Farrington.
        p. cm.
    Includes bibliographical references and index.
    ISBN 0-7619-1275-4 (cloth: acid-free paper)
    ISBN 0-7619-2040-4 (pbk.: acid-free paper)
    1. Juvenile delinquency—United States—Prevention. 2. Deviant
behavior—United States—Prevention. 3. Violent crimes—United
States—Prevention. 4. Problem youth—Behavior modification—United
States. I. Loeber, Rolf. II. Farrington, David P.
HV9104.S42 1998
364.40973—dc21   97-33930

99 00 01 02 03 04 05 10 9 8 7 6 5 4

Acquiring Editor:	C. Terry Hendrix
Editorial Assistant:	Dale Mary Grenfell
Production Editor:	Diana E. Axelsen
Production Assistant:	Lynn Miyata
Typesetter/Designer:	Danielle Dillahunt
Indexer:	Trish Wittenstein
Cover Designer:	Ravi Balasuriya

Serious & Violent Juvenile Offenders

Contents

PART I DEVELOPMENTAL COURSE AND RISK FACTORS

PART III CONCLUDING OVERVIEW

Foreword

Never Too Early

For decades, scholars have quarreled over whether crime could best be reduced by punishing offenders or treating offenders. In the punishment group were those, including myself, who argued that we knew too little about the causes of crime; that such causes as could be identified were beyond much planned change; and that in any event the results, if any, of those changes would take years, perhaps decades, to appear. In the treatment group were writers who believed that causes could be found; that government could change them significantly; and that the benefits of those changes, even if they took years to appear, would do less harm than the painful effects of punishment. Among those effects, they argued, were the tendency of punishment to confirm people in a life of crime. Prisons were not only costly, they were also schools for crime.

That debate continues, but now, I think, in a somewhat less extreme fashion. The de-fenders of the deterrent and incapacitative effects of punishment still argue (reasonably, I believe) that higher levels of punishment have in fact lowered crime rates in the United States, but they now concede that the financial and human costs of this strategy are, indeed, very large. We have more than a million inmates in state and federal prisons (plus many in jails). Not only has this created a substantial monetary burden, it has also affected racial groups very differently. An Afro-American male born today will, if present imprisonment and crime rates continue, have more than a one in four chance of being in state or federal prison before he dies. It is hard to be sanguine about a policy that produces so profound a racial divide in our society.

The defenders of treatment have become a bit less optimistic about what rehabilitative programs can achieve, are less convinced now that merely increasing the number of jobs or multiplying new government programs will reduce the crime rate, and are more willing than previously to acknowledge the vital importance of early childhood experiences and personal endowments in explaining why some youth commit crimes at such high rates. Moreover, they now are more inclined to admit that community-based alternatives to traditional juvenile prisons must exercise very close supervision if they are to be as effective.

The narrowing of the punishment-versus-treatment policy gulf is best illustrated by the increased attention both sides now give to crime prevention. By *prevention* I mean intervening in a person's life before he or she has become a serious or high-rate offender. This book provides a rigorous synthesis of much that has been learned about such prevention programs.

Though I would draw somewhat different conclusions from the data reviewed in some parts of this book, I am struck by the extent to which so many authors now emphasize early childhood experiences. Crime prevention is less likely to be defined by scholars as trying some bold new program, whether it involves how police are trained or assigned; what prosecutors do; how Neighborhood Watch can make places safe; or why bringing down the unemployment rate, embracing some new rehabilitation program, or mounting innovative high school courses can make our streets much safer.

Instead, the focus is to a greater extent than ever before on several important themes that are supported by research:

- The precursors of crime occur very early in the lives of many serious offenders.
- These precursors involve a complex array of relationships between child and parents.
- Changing those precursors requires a complex intervention that affects parents as well as children and that best occurs early in the life of the youngsters.

Interventions based on these principles are likely to make the most difference for children who display certain risk factors: early use of alcohol and drugs, ties to antisocial friends, early expressions of aggression, poor parent-child relations, low intelligence, and similar factors. Modern criminology has rediscovered arguments made in the 1950s by Sheldon and Eleanor Glueck and soon thereafter rejected by people who wrongly believed that families were of little importance compared with economic opportunity.

Gail Wasserman and Laurie Miller supply us with a good review of what we know about the consequences of programs that attempt to modify family life. Richard Catalano and his colleagues are sufficiently impressed with efforts to alter the factors that put children at risk that they press for "comprehensive," "community-wide" interventions that embody a variety of treatments. Of course, the story is not over once the child becomes a delinquent, as Mark Lipsey and David B. Wilson show in their analysis of interventions on known offenders.

Some early childhood programs do make a lasting difference, just as some rehabilitation programs applied to certain kinds of offenders seem to make a difference. But to expand on these programs some difficult problems must still be overcome.

Very few of the more successful interventions were expressly aimed at reducing the crime rate of serious offenders. Some may have had this effect, but we are not quite certain why. Many of these successful efforts were small-scale programs run by dedicated clinicians employing talented staff, but we have no reason yet to think that these efforts would be as successful as they were for 2 dozen children if they were applied to 2,000 or 200,000 youngsters. We now have a pretty good understanding of the characteristics of children who are at risk of becoming serious offenders, but that knowledge is not so good that we can reliably identify the at-risk children at an early age. Some of the best early interventions were carried out many years ago, before drug use, social disorganization, and high levels of gang violence had become as commonplace as they are now. In short, our growing awareness of the potential value of early interventions rests on replication of those findings in several sites by people other than those who invented the program.

What is impressive about many of the essays in this book is that they reveal a common interest in early intervention involving both parents and children, and they are informed by a shared knowledge of the experimental efforts that seem to have worked.

This common interest should help to further narrow the policy differences among scholars. The choice today is not one between the death penalty or midnight basketball. The real choice is between mounting a serious, large-scale effort to rebuild weak families or continuing a politically attractive but largely sterile debate over how great the maximum sentence should be for convicted felons. Rebuilding weak families is still very much in the pilot project phase: We do not know how to do it on a large scale. We can discuss comprehensive, community-wide projects, but we have virtually no experience with actually producing them. By the same token, making people who commit serious crimes face longer maximum sentences is in part a cheap, symbolic effort, given the fact that most offenders—because of plea bargaining, judicial discretion, or prison crowding—serve only a fraction of these maximum penalties.

Theft and other forms of property crime are, as it turns out, more susceptible to control than violent crime. Our rates of property crime, have, for the most part, gone down since 1980, and now are, for many offenses, lower than they are in England, Sweden, or other European nations. But we are still today, as we have been for generations, the murder capital of the industrialized world. Most troubling, it has been the murder rate among juveniles that has, in recent years, climbed the fastest. If we wish to reduce the murder rate, for example, we must confront the fact that we have only imperfect ways of identifying would-be murderers at any early age (and hence prevention is difficult) and the median murderer released from prison today has probably served after considerable pretrial delay no more than 6 years in confinement (and hence sanctions are both postponed and moderate). We ought to try to improve our performance on both prevention and punishment efforts, but we have a long ways to go before we know how to do either.

Crime prevention, I think, has come face to face with the central social question of our time: How, if at all, can we sustain a healthy family life in a culture that rewards personal self-expression, an economy that no longer is dominated by family labor, and a policy world that provides countless opportunities for living apart from family obligations? Crime control, in short, is now engaged with the issue whose resolution will profoundly affect the future of our culture. This book is a good place to start looking for what we know and what we do not know about why this has happened and what can be done about it.

JAMES Q. WILSON

Foreword

How Criminology Can Be Enhanced by the Study of Serious and Violent Juvenile Offenders

This book brings together new insights and understanding of the origins of criminal careers and the effectiveness of intervention or prevention programs. The task was greatly facilitated by the initiation over the past two decades of major research studies focused on the development of delinquent conduct. The productivity of the Study Group that produced this book was also enhanced by several strategic decisions on the issues to be explored. From the outset a primary concern was to search for explanations of serious and violent conduct by juvenile offenders. This helped to sensitize literature reviews to the factors accounting for such conduct. At the same time it made the search more difficult because serious and violent offending occurs at a low rate among all juvenile offenses. In a number of instances this led to additional analyses of existing data sets focusing more sharply on correlates of such behavior.

Another defining strategy was the primacy given to studies of delinquent and criminal behavior that took a developmental approach involving successive interviews with one or more age cohorts. This approach broadens the range and salience of the questions that can be addressed. For example, it can relate the evidence of early childhood problems to the various pathways leading to serious and violent conduct. It can explore the predictive value of self-reports of offending compared to arrest data at different age levels, and it can determine the relative importance of gang membership as a factor in the development of serious and violent behavior. In fact, each of the chapters in this report provides fresh evidence of the explanatory power gained through the developmental study of age cohorts.

Another major guideline was the constant attention to identifying both risk and protective factors in the progression toward serious and violent conduct. How did these factors vary with age and their relation to other problems of childhood and youth? Finding answers to this type of question was, of course, one of the primary aims in creating the Study Group with the support of the Office of Juvenile Justice and Delinquency Prevention in the U.S. Department of Justice. This agency has also provided support for several developmental research studies represented in the Study Group and was interested in assessing the current state of knowledge in the field in general.

A second aim of the Study Group was to assess the relevance of knowledge gained from the developmental studies for the design of intervention and prevention policies and programs. This interest served to highlight the importance of community institutions, social agencies, and contextual influences on the type and rates of juvenile offenses. It led to a major effort by the Study Group to survey the results and effectiveness of programs of interventions and prevention. The Study Group encountered serious deficiencies in the design and effectiveness of studies because of the complexities in administration and costs of experimental evaluations. It, nevertheless, concluded that the available evidence justified a much greater attention to the role of community influences on juvenile conduct in research studies of risk and protective factors and in the design of intervention and prevention policies and programs.

Throughout the report the Study Group has pointed to gaps and limitations of existing research findings and program development. Taken as a whole they constitute an impressive agenda for further basic research on risk and protective factors and program evaluations. Most of the research studies in recent years have focused on the individual differences in the characteristics and experiences of various types of offenders. Much less attention has been devoted to identifying community and institutional differences that could become major targets for intervention and prevention strategies. In calling attention to these types of deficiencies in our knowledge, the Study Group has underscored the need for more balanced research policies that will assist the development of more effective program designs and evaluations.

The editors of this book have a history of involvement in developmental studies of delinquent youth that spans two decades—and longer, in the studies by Farrington in England. The Office of Juvenile Justice and Delinquency Prevention provided support for three developmental studies that generated comparative data as well as data on different issues. The studies undertaken in Rochester, Denver, and Pittsburgh demonstrated the productivity of developmental research designs in advancing knowledge about the onset, growth, and termination of criminal careers. The studies also stimulated the reanalysis of earlier research findings from such studies as those of Sheldon and Eleanor Glueck prior to World War II and the Cambridge-Somerville treatment study by Joan McCord.

The insights gained from such work have greatly enlarged the range of issues addressed in the various chapters in this book. Without the studies conducted over the past two decades, this book could not have been written. The editors' immersion in these developments provided them with an understanding of the range of issues involved and the persons best equipped to assess them in a critical and constructive manner. The editors and chapter authors are to be congratulated for the scope and depth of their assessments of the state of knowledge and their definitions of the need for continuing research on critical issues. By dealing with the course of development and risk factors in criminal careers and juxtaposing the insights gained with the relevance and potential effectiveness of prevention policies and programs, the authors are helping to transcend a division between research and action. Well-designed evaluations of programs and policies of interventions also contribute to the basic fund of knowledge about what works and why. In producing a report that fosters both types of inquiry, the Study Group and its sponsors in the Office of Juvenile Justice and Delinquency Prevention have created a solid foundation for further growth of research and policy in the years ahead.

LLOYD E. OHLIN

Preface

This volume sets out the conclusions of the Office of Juvenile Justice and Delinquency Prevention's (OJJDP) Study Group on Serious and Violent Juvenile Offenders. The initial idea for the Study Group was broached with James C. Howell, then Director of Research at OJJDP, who enthusiastically endorsed it. Subsequently, the office issued a request for proposals, and Rolf Loeber and David P. Farrington were the successful applicants and became cochairs of the Study Group. Members of the Study Group, who were selected because of their expert knowledge of different aspects of serious and violent juvenile offenders, were David M. Altschuler, Alfred Blumstein, Richard F. Catalano, Julius Debro, David P. Farrington, Peter Greenwood, Nancy G. Guerra, Darnell Hawkins, J. David Hawkins, James C. Howell, David Huizinga, Barry Krisberg, John H. Laub, Marc Le Blanc, Mark W. Lipsey, Rolf Loeber, Walter Miller, Mark H. Moore, Howard N. Snyder, Terence P. Thornberry, Patrick Tolan, and Gail A. Wasserman.

Starting in November 1995, the Study Group met periodically to discuss the main thrust of the report, and later, the drafts that members (some joined by one or more coauthors) prepared. In the process we received valuable guidance from several staff members of OJJDP, including Shay Bilchik, John Wilson, Betty Chemers, Joan Hurley, and Barbara Allen-Hagen. Furthermore, observers from some other agencies assisted in several meetings, including Christy Visher of the National Institute of Justice, Carol Petrie of the National Academy of Sciences, and Jan Chaiken of the Bureau of Justice Statistics. Chapters were reviewed by agency staff members, in addition to the editors and Study Group members, and went through several iterations. OJJDP provided financial support for the project (Grant 95-JD-FX-0018). Points of view or opinions in this document are those of the authors and do not necessarily represent the official position of OJJDP or the Department of Justice.

In Pittsburgh, we received assistance from David Kupfer, Chair of the Department of Psychiatry, School of Medicine, University of Pittsburgh. We are particularly grateful to JoAnn Fraser for her thoughtful and effective administrative guidance to the project, and to Daniel Waschbusch for his help in retrieving source material and checking the manuscript chapters. Most of all, we want to thank the members of the Study Group for their splendid collaboration, writing, and secondary data analyses; for their tolerance of our unreasonable requests for revisions of their manuscript chapters at short notice; and for their collegial assistance in advancing knowledge about serious and violent juvenile offenders.

Executive Summary

■ *Rolf Loeber & David P. Farrington*

We draw a number of key conclusions in this volume about serious and/or violent juvenile (SVJ) offending. Serious violent offenses include homicide, rape, robbery, aggravated assault, and kidnapping. Serious nonviolent offenses include burglary, motor vehicle theft, theft over $100, arson, and drug trafficking.

The two main aims of this volume are to review knowledge about SVJ offenders and about which types of interventions can reduce their level of offending. This volume was inspired by the Office of Juvenile Justice and Delinquency Prevention's (OJJDP) Comprehensive Strategy for Serious, Violent, and Chronic Juvenile Offenders. This strategy emphasized strengthening the family and core socializing institutions, implementing prevention programs targeting key risk factors, identifying early potential offenders, and employing graduated sanctions based on assessments of risks and needs. The Comprehensive Strategy provides an excellent framework for understanding, preventing, and controlling SVJ offending. The present volume uses the Comprehensive Strategy as a springboard and includes detailed quantitative analyses of risk and protective factors and of the effectiveness of prevention and intervention programs for SVJ offenders. It also aims to integrate the risk/protective factor and prevention/intervention program literature, so that programs are based more on research on influential factors, and conclusions about putative causal effects of factors are drawn from knowledge about the effectiveness of programs.

This volume carries two main themes. First, SVJ offenders tend to start displaying behavior problems and delinquency early in life, warranting early intervention. It is our thesis that prevention is never too early. Second, we also maintain that interventions for SVJ offenders can never be too late; effective interventions exist for known SVJ offenders.

The executive summary centers around the following main conclusions:

- SVJ offenders are a distinct group of offenders who tend to start early and continue late in their offending.
- From childhood to adolescence, SVJ offenders tend to develop behavior problems in several areas, including aggression, dishonesty/property offenses, and conflict with authority figures.
- Many potential SVJ offenders below the age of 12 are not routinely processed in the juvenile court, and services in the community for such offenders appear unnecessarily fragmented, leading to a lack of public accountability for young potential SVJ offenders.
- There are many known predictors of SVJ offending that could be incorporated into screening devices for the early identification of SVJ offenders.
- It is never too early: Preventive interventions for young children at risk for SVJ should be implemented at an early age and are known to be effective.
- It is never too late: Interventions and sanctions for known SVJ offenders can reduce their risk of reoffending.
- Evaluations of interventions often are inadequate and usually do not provide information specifically about changes in the rate of offending by SVJ offenders.
- An integrated and coordinated program of research is needed on the development and the reduction of SVJ offending.
- Several key issues about SVJ offenders are unresolved and remain to be addressed through research.

We will now elaborate on each point.

SVJ Offenders Are a Distinct Group of Offenders

- The majority of the SVJ offenders of any race tend to be multiple-problem youth. They often have school problems (truancy, suspension, and dropout), substance use problems, and mental health problems, and they are disproportionally victims of violence.
- SVJ offenders are also distinguishable from non-SVJ offenders in that the majority of the SVJ offenders start offending early in life and continue offending longer than non-SVJ offenders. In addition, the age of onset of nondelinquent behavior problems is much earlier in SVJ offenders than in non-SVJ offenders.
- Chronic offenders account for more than half of all serious crime committed by juveniles. The vast majority of chronic offenders are SVJ offenders.
- Black (African American) youth have higher rates of SVJ offending, but this may be due to community factors such as living in a socially disorganized neighborhood.

Development of SVJ Offending

- From childhood to adolescence SVJ offenders tend to develop behavior problems in several areas, including aggression, dishonesty/property offenses, and conflict with authority figures.
- Typically, SVJ offenders tend to advance simultaneously in each of these areas, with minor problem behaviors preceding the onset of moderately serious problem behaviors, which in turn tend to progress to more serious forms of delinquency.
- As offenders progress in these areas to SVJ offending, they tend to continue to commit less serious delinquent acts at high rates.

Comment. The delinquency careers of SVJ offenders are vastly different according to official records of arrest or referral to the juvenile court compared with self-reported delinquency.

Self-reports show that most persisting serious offenders have an onset of serious offending before age 14, with about half of the persisting SVJ offenders starting their delinquent career before age 12.

SVJ Offenders, Juvenile Justice, and Public Accountability

- Typically, juvenile courts do not routinely deal with delinquency by youth below the age of 12. However, very young offenders, and particularly serious or persisting young offenders, are the most likely group from which SVJ offenders will develop. Presently, no alternative agency in society is held accountable for the early-onset offenders, and as a result there is a fragmentation of services and lack of resources to deal effectively with early-onset offenders.

- Many SVJ offenders, judging from their self-reports, are never arrested, even at a later age.

- At first appearance before the juvenile court, SVJ offenders are often not readily identifiable, because many of them are arrested for less serious delinquent acts. Screening devices, based on legally permissible predictors, need to be improved to identify potential SVJ offenders at their first arrest or first referral to the juvenile court.

- SVJ offenders tend to be persistent offenders, and many of them will be at risk in the community during their peak offending years even if they were apprehended earlier and incarcerated for a short period of time.

- The majority of violent youth commit only one officially recorded violent crime as a juvenile. Therefore, to prevent violence it is important not to wait to intervene before this officially recorded violent crime occurs.

Comment. In evaluating the roles and functions of the juvenile justice system, the mental health system, and child welfare services in addressing SVJ offenders, it is clear that integration of services is often lacking and that gaps exist in who receives sanctions and/or intervention. Also, because each institution is reactive rather than proactive, none of them serves an efficient role in preventing SVJ offending in the community. Most important, it is not clear which institutions or community groups are held accountable for SVJ offenders as they emerge in each generation of youth. This lack of public accountability stands in the way of the development of effective interventions, particularly at the community level. An important priority is to give resources and mandates to agencies that can focus on the prevention of SVJ offending, and to require coordination and public accountability across the different systems of care.

Screening for SVJ offenders has two purposes: the identification of future SVJ offenders for prevention purposes, and the classification of offenders for juvenile justice programming. Screening is most effective using multiple informants, multiple methods, and multiple types of variables. Variables that might be used in a prevention screening instrument include prior delinquency, antisocial peers or parents, and poor school attitudes or performance. Risk assessment instruments are widely used by juvenile court personnel. However, more technical work, and especially validations, needs to be completed before adequate screening instruments, individualized for particular communities, can be confidently recommended to policymakers and practitioners.

Predictors of SVJ Offending

- Persistent precocious behavior problems in children during the elementary school-age years are a warning sign for later SVJ offending.

- Among the strongest, potentially modifiable predictors of SVJ offending evident between ages 6 and 11 are nonserious delinquent acts, aggression, substance use, low family socioeconomic status, and antisocial parents.
- Among the strongest predictors of SVJ offending evident between ages 12 and 14 are lack of strong social ties, antisocial peers, nonserious delinquent acts, poor school attitude and performance, and psychological conditions such as impulsivity.
- Juveniles to whom the strongest predictor variables apply are 5-20 times more likely to engage in subsequent SVJ offending than those without such predictor variables.
- The risk of juveniles engaging in SVJ offending is greatly enhanced when they join a gang or become a drug dealer.
- The higher the number of risk factors, the greater the likelihood of a youth engaging in SVJ offending.

Comment. In general, violent behavior results from the interaction of individual, contextual (family, school, peers), situational, and community factors. Much is known about the predictors of serious and violent offending.

Adolescents who join delinquent gangs are more frequently involved in SVJ offending than non-gang members. Gang members, although representing a minority of the juvenile population, are responsible for the vast majority of serious delinquent acts. Rates of SVJ offending increase after joining a gang and decrease after leaving a gang. Hence, it is important to target gangs to reduce SVJ offending.

Prevention of SVJ Offending

- Early intervention in childhood and early adolescence can reduce the likelihood of young at-risk juveniles becoming SVJ offenders.
- Preventive interventions should be based on public health approaches and should target known risk factors within a comprehensive community-based program in disadvantaged neighborhoods.
- The best preventive interventions are based on an integration of different services, including services provided by the juvenile justice system, schools, mental health, medical health, and child protection agencies.
- Early prevention is important, including home visitation of pregnant women, teenage parents, parent training, preschool intellectual enrichment programs, and interpersonal skills training.
- Important targets for later prevention are reductions in gangs, victimization, gun availability, and drug markets.

Comment. Because SVJ offending is multiply determined, it is unlikely that interventions directed only toward a single source of influence (e.g., individual, family, school, or peers) will be very successful. Multiple-component prevention programs are needed. Therefore, priority should be given to preventive actions that reduce risk factors in multiple domains. Few programs have been evaluated specifically in relation to SVJ offenders. The most successful early prevention programs involve interventions simultaneously in the home and the school. Many of the same risk factors that predict adolescent delinquency and violence also predict substance abuse, dropping out of school, early sexual involvement, and teen pregnancy.

The primary methods of preventing the development of SVJ offenders are through family, school, and community interventions. Public health approaches to offending are desirable that target risk or protective factors and immediate situational influences. For that reason, better routine data collection methods are needed that specify when, where, and how offenses occur and offenders develop. Wide-ranging community-based programs are required in which risk and protective factors are measured and intervention techniques targeting these factors are implemented and their impact measured.

Many preventive actions can best take place in communities. Community mobilization, community policing, and intensive policing strategies can be effective. School-based strategies are also useful, especially those targeted on school organization or on classroom-based curricula emphasizing the reinforcement of prosocial and academic skills. Other targets for community interventions include reducing the availability of firearms and drugs, and enhancing laws and norms favorable to prosocial behaviors. Most of these approaches have been incorporated in the comprehensive Communities That Care preventive strategy, which still remains to be evaluated.

Interventions and Sanctions for Identified SVJ Offenders

- SVJ offenders constitute only a minority of identified offenders in the juvenile court system.
- The reoffending of SVJ offenders can be reduced by appropriate intervention, especially interpersonal skills training and cognitive-behavioral treatment.
- Programs to prevent youth gang violence can be successfully implemented.
- In selecting treatment and sanctions in the juvenile justice system, account should be taken of (a) the severity of the presenting offense; (b) the risk of recidivism for serious offenses; and (c) the individual needs of the juvenile offender, such as academic needs and family support.
- Interventions for SVJ offenders often have to be multimodal to address multiple problems, including law breaking, substance use and abuse, and academic and family problems.
- The administration of multimodal programs requires integration of services of the juvenile justice system, mental health, schools, and child welfare agencies.
- Aftercare programs are essential to reduce the likelihood of reoffending by SVJ offenders.

Comment. A meta-analysis of experimental and quasi-experimental intervention programs for reducing the recidivism of SVJ offenders showed that the most effective programs with noninstitutionalized offenders involved interpersonal skills training, behavioral contracting, or individual counseling. The most effective programs with institutional offenders involved interpersonal skills training, cognitive-behavioral treatment, or teaching family homes programs. Intervention effects were greater where there was a longer duration of treatment.

Three promising programs were identified to prevent youth gang violence. The comprehensive community approach developed by Spergel involves the design and mobilization of community efforts by police, prosecutors, judges, probation and parole officers, corrections officers, schools, employers, community agencies, and grassroots organizations. OJJDP's Comprehensive Strategy also targets youth gang violence through risk-focused prevention and graduated sanctions. Youth gang homicides can be addressed by a multiple-component program combined with restricting access to firearms, enhanced prosecution of gang crimes, with multiagency sanctioning and hospital emergency room intervention.

Most SVJ offenders slow down their rate of offending after correctional interventions. However, alternatives to secure confinement for SVJ offenders are at least as effective as incarceration in suppressing recidivism and are far less costly. Juveniles who are transferred to the adult court are more likely to be incarcerated but also more likely to reoffend. Because of the inadequacy of research designs, the relative effectiveness of juvenile and adult court disposals is unclear.

Intermediate sanctions, including electronic monitoring, house arrest, home detention, drug and alcohol testing, community tracking, intensive supervision, boot camps, day treatment/reporting centers, and community service and restitution, are increasingly being used as alternatives to institutionalization, probation, parole, and aftercare. These sanctions are being used by varying degrees with SVJ offenders. Existing research on intermediate sanctions suggests that treatment availability and participation in treatment are associated with lower recidivism. Unfortunately, many offenders are left untreated. Risk-based treatment services should play a prominent role in the philosophy, design, and implementation of intermediate sanctions.

Evaluation of Interventions

- Better designed evaluations of the effectiveness of programs are needed (e.g., randomized experiments), and studies of the cost-effectiveness of one program compared with others.
- More evaluations need to study the impact of prevention and intervention programs specifically on SVJ offending.
- The effectiveness of transfer to adult court for SVJ offenders compared with the effect of sanctions administered by the juvenile court needs to be evaluated in terms of the risk of reoffending.
- Community-wide programs, such as Communities That Care, need to be evaluated for their efficacy in reducing both community levels of delinquency and SVJ offending.

Comment. Evaluation of intervention programs is essential to identify more effective versus less effective programs. Evaluations are also essential to make cost comparisons between programs and implement programs with the highest yields at lowest cost. However, the evaluation of community-based programs poses many challenges.

Research Priorities

- More studies are needed focusing specifically on risk factors for SVJ offenders and aiming to identify protective factors in disadvantaged neighborhoods where SVJ offenders are especially found.
- Because SVJ offenders commit less serious delinquent acts at a high rate, screening devices need to be developed that can identify potential SVJ offenders on their first arrest or referral to the juvenile court.
- A key research priority is to assess the effects of interventions specifically on SVJ offenders.
- The course of development of SVJ offenders needs to be investigated, not only in inner cities but also in rural communities and for female offenders.
- Annual or biannual surveys are needed, especially in large metropolitan areas, to measure (a) the prevalence of SVJ offenders, and (b) the prevalence of youth at risk for SVJ offending. These surveys can assist in the evaluation of prevention and intervention programs for SVJ offenders.
- Longitudinal studies are needed, in which multiple cohorts are followed up, to draw conclusions about development from birth to the teenage years and into early adulthood.

Comment. Research on risk factors for SVJ offending needs to have a more developmental focus, documenting how they emerge and change in different contexts, and how risk and protective factors affect onset, persistence, escalation, and desistance of offending. There is a need to develop theories that apply not just to juvenile delinquents in general, but also to SVJ offenders. New longitudinal studies should measure a wide range of risk and protective factors. They should be based on high-risk samples incorporating screening methods to maximize the yield of SVJ offenders. Experimental studies are also needed in which multiple-component interventions are used and SVJ offending is measured. The different components should be targeted on different age ranges, and the interventions should be applied to high-risk youth or high-risk communities. In some cases, it is desirable to include interventions in a longitudinal study or to follow up cohorts in an intervention study. Such a coordinated program could dramatically advance knowledge about SVJ offending and ultimately lead to a significant reduction in this troubling social problem in the next decade.

An integrated and coordinated program of data collection, intervention, and research specifically on SVJ offenders should be developed and administered by an appropriate federal agency, advised by scholars from the juvenile delinquency and juvenile justice communities.

CHAPTER 1

Major Aims
of This Book

■ *David P. Farrington & Rolf Loeber*

The main aim of this book is to review knowledge about serious and/or violent juvenile (SVJ) offenders. These are a group of offenders who pose a great challenge to juvenile justice policy, and who are responsible for a disproportionate fraction of all crime. Given population trends, the number of teens in the 14 to 17 age group is anticipated to increase by 20%. If the rate of teen homicide and violence remains at current levels, this will mean a substantial increase shortly in the volume of juvenile violence at the beginning of the next century (Fox, 1996).

This book, the main report of the Office of Juvenile Justice and Delinquency Prevention (OJJDP) Study Group on Serious and Violent Juvenile Offenders, addresses serious and violent juvenile delinquency. The volume aims to integrate knowledge about risk and protective factors and about the development of juvenile offending careers with knowledge about prevention and intervention programs, including interventions in the juvenile justice system, so that conclusions from one area can inform the other. Much of our knowledge about risk/protective factors and prevention/ intervention programs does not apply specifically to SVJ offenders, so the Study Group commissioned specific new analyses that are included in various chapters.

There have been several recent major reports on violence: from the National Academy of Sciences Panel on Violence (Reiss & Roth, 1993), the American Psychological Association Commission on Violence and Youth (Eron, Gentry, & Schlegel, 1994), Harvard Law School (Ethiel, 1996), the Council on Crime in America (Bell & Bennett, 1996), and the University of Maryland Report to the U.S. Congress (Sherman et al., 1997). All of these reports are extremely valuable. Some of the reports cover topics that this volume does not attempt to cover: biobehavioral influences on violence, for example, in the National Academy of Sciences volume (Reiss, Miczek, & Roth, 1994), and the influence of labor markets and places in the University of Maryland Report to the U.S. Congress (Sherman et al., 1997). Also, the present volume does not claim to address larger societal and structural influences on violence (e.g., welfare legislation) or female violence, because of the relative paucity of studies. None of the above studies, however, covers the same ground as this volume, which systematically links risk and protective factors of violence to a wide range of interventions, ranging from early childhood to adulthood, from preventive approaches to aftercare approaches for known violent youth, and from approaches in the home and school to approaches in the juvenile justice system. Thus, the main aim of the present volume is to be more comprehensive in some ways than past works, but also more selective by focusing on serious and violent offenders. As a result, the present volume, by means of the results of expert reviews and newly commissioned meta-analyses, points to many options for advancing knowledge and improving interventions.

■ Definitions

The main focus of this book is on serious violent and serious nonviolent juvenile offenders. Serious violent offenses include homicide, rape, robbery, aggravated assault, and kidnapping. Serious nonviolent offenses include burglary, motor vehicle theft, theft over $100, arson, drug trafficking, and extortion (see Chapter 2 for more details of these definitions). This book aims to establish the overlap between serious violent juvenile offenders and serious nonviolent juvenile offenders.

The Study Group initially intended to focus on serious and/or violent and/or chronic juvenile offenders. Unfortunately, it proved difficult to find a satisfactory definition of chronic (frequent and/or persistent) offending that was equally applicable to court referrals, arrests, and self-reported offending. For example, a criterion of committing three or more serious violent offenses as a juvenile would identify hardly any chronic offenders in court records (Snyder, this volume) but a large number in self-reports (Elliott, 1994). Nevertheless, although chronic offenders are not one of the major concerns of this book, efforts will be made to establish the overlap between SVJ offenders and chronic offenders (defined in various ways), especially in the Appendix by Snyder. Similarly, efforts will be made to specify what proportion of serious violent and serious nonviolent offenses are committed by chronic offenders (defined in various ways).

■ Recent Trends

Snyder, Sickmund, and Poe-Yamagata (1996) and Snyder and Sickmund (1995) have

TABLE 1.1 Juvenile Arrest Rates in the United States: 1975-1995 (arrests of 10- to 17-year-olds/ 100,000 10- to 17-year-olds)

Year	Violent Crime Index	Murder	Forcible Rape	Robbery	Aggravated Assault	Property Crime Index	Burglary	Larceny Theft	Motor Vehicle Theft	Arson
1975	313.5	5.7	14.2	162.2	131.4	2,819.6	910.0	1,630.9	249.2	29.5
1976	302.1	6.1	15.1	145.7	135.3	2,688.5	840.0	1,573.6	244.9	30.0
1977	302.9	6.2	15.7	146.1	134.9	2,719.0	849.7	1,575.6	264.6	29.2
1978	340.6	6.2	16.0	173.4	145.1	2,784.6	884.4	1,600.2	269.1	30.9
1979	331.3	6.5	17.3	158.4	149.1	2,759.8	844.4	1,619.8	262.1	32.9
1980	334.1	6.4	15.9	167.5	144.3	2,562.2	794.2	1,520.9	221.9	25.2
1981	322.6	7.0	16.0	161.4	138.2	2,442.8	752.0	1,484.0	181.7	25.1
1982	314.5	6.6	17.1	151.1	139.7	2,373.3	700.7	1,488.1	162.6	22.0
1983	296.0	5.4	17.4	140.4	132.8	2,244.4	621.2	1,455.8	146.1	21.3
1984	297.5	5.4	19.7	132.4	140.0	2,220.7	568.3	1,473.9	155.7	22.8
1985	303.0	5.7	20.4	129.4	147.5	2,370.7	592.6	1,568.9	185.6	23.6
1986	316.7	6.4	21.2	128.2	160.9	2,427.1	574.8	1,602.8	226.7	22.8
1987	310.6	6.9	20.9	118.9	163.9	2,451.4	555.1	1,621.0	253.3	22.0
1988	326.5	8.5	19.4	117.5	181.1	2,418.7	505.6	1,592.5	296.7	23.9
1989	381.6	10.0	21.1	139.6	210.8	2,433.8	498.7	1,571.9	339.2	24.1
1990	428.7	11.9	21.8	155.4	239.5	2,564.7	513.5	1,678.4	347.2	25.6
1991	461.6	13.1	23.0	175.3	250.2	2,614.8	515.2	1,723.9	347.5	28.3
1992	482.9	12.5	22.0	175.0	273.4	2,526.6	507.8	1,658.4	331.1	29.3
1993	505.2	14.5	22.4	185.1	283.1	2,434.4	477.7	1,599.4	327.6	29.6
1994	527.1	13.2	20.3	199.4	294.1	2,547.6	481.1	1,721.0	311.2	34.2
1995	510.3	11.2	18.4	197.5	283.2	2,454.6	447.8	1,697.5	278.6	30.8

SOURCE: Arrest rates were developed by Howard Snyder at the National Center for Juvenile Justice in 1997 using (a) unpublished, machine-readable, 1975-1995 arrest counts and the arrest sample's total population statistics from the FBI's Uniform Crime Reporting Program, and (b) machine-readable data files of 1975-1995 estimates of the resident population of the United States in single years of age from the U.S. Bureau of the Census.

summarized recent trends in juvenile arrest rates for index offenses. Table 1.1 shows the numbers in detail. Arrests for index violence offenses increased by a remarkable 61% between 1988 and 1994, but arrests for index property offenses stayed virtually constant, increasing by only 5% over the same time period. The juvenile arrest rate for homicide increased by 90% between 1987 and 1991 but has since remained tolerably constant. The juvenile arrest rate for robbery increased by 70% between 1988 and 1994, and the aggravated assault rate increased by a similar 62%. The forcible rape rate has stayed tolerably constant over this time period.

Similar increases in violence are generally not seen in the Monitoring the Future study, which is the major repeated self-report survey based on national samples (of high school students). For example, the percentage of boys who said that they had "hurt someone badly enough to need bandages or a doctor" in the previous year was 20.1% in 1987 and 20.4% in 1995. However, there was an increase in the small proportion who had done this three or more times (from 2.8% to 6.1%). The percentage of boys who said that they had "used a knife or gun or some other thing (like a club) to get something from a person" was 5.1% in 1987 and 5.4% in 1995 (Maguire & Pastore, 1996, Table 3.48).

■ OJJDP's Comprehensive Strategy

The work of the Study Group was inspired by OJJDP's Comprehensive Strategy for Serious, Violent, and Chronic Juvenile Offenders (Howell, this volume; Wilson & Howell, 1993). This is based on five general principles:

1. Strengthen the family in its primary responsibility to instill moral values and provide guidance and support to children.
2. Support core social institutions (schools, religious institutions, and community organizations) in their roles of developing capable, mature, and responsible youth.
3. Promote delinquency prevention as the most cost-effective approach to dealing with juvenile delinquency. When children engage in "acting out" behavior, such as status offenses, the family and community, in concert with child welfare services, must take primary responsibility for responding with appropriate treatment and support services. Communities must take the lead in designing and building comprehensive prevention approaches that address known risk factors and target youth at risk of delinquency.
4. Intervene immediately and effectively when delinquent behavior occurs, to prevent delinquent offenders from becoming chronic offenders or progressively committing more serious and violent crimes. Initial intervention attempts should be centered on the family and other core social institutions.
5. Identify and control the small group of serious, violent, and chronic juvenile offenders who have failed to respond to intervention and nonsecure community-based treatment and rehabilitation services offered by the juvenile justice system.

The Comprehensive Strategy recommends prevention efforts targeting five categories of risk factors:

1. Individual characteristics such as alienation, rebelliousness, and weak bonding to society
2. Family influences such as parental conflict, child abuse, and a family history of problem behavior (criminality, substance abuse, teen pregnancy, school dropout)
3. School experiences such as early academic failure and lack of commitment to school
4. Peer group influences such as friends who engage in problem behavior (including gangs and violence)
5. Neighborhood and community factors such as economic deprivation, high rates of substance abuse and crime, and low neighborhood attachment

The Comprehensive Strategy recommends that communities should identify and understand to what risk factors their children are exposed and should implement prevention programs designed to counteract these risk factors. Communities should also aim to enhance protective factors that promote desirable behavior, health, well-being, and personal success. Recommended prevention programs targeting the five categories of risk factors include the following:

1. Youth service programs, adventure training, mentoring, literacy programs, Head Start, recreational programs
2. Teen pregnancy prevention, parental skills training, family crisis intervention services, family life education for teens and parents
3. Drug and alcohol prevention and education, bullying prevention, violence prevention, alternative schools, truancy reduction, law-related education, afterschool programs for latchkey children
4. Gang prevention and intervention, peer counseling and tutoring, community volunteer service
5. Community policing, Neighborhood Watch, neighborhood mobilization for community safety, foster grandparents

The Comprehensive Strategy aims to improve the juvenile justice system response to delinquent offenders through a system of graduated sanctions and a continuum of treatment alternatives that include immediate intervention, intermediate sanctions, community-based corrections sanctions including restitution and community service, and secure corrections including community confinement and incarceration in training schools, camps, and ranches.

Graduated-sanctions programs should use risk and needs assessments to determine the appropriate placement for the offender. Risk assessments should be based on the seriousness of the delinquent act, the potential risk for reoffending, and the risk to public safety. Needs assessments will help ensure that different types of problems are taken into account when formulating a case plan, that a baseline for monitoring a juvenile's progress is established, that periodic reassessments of treatment effectiveness are conducted, and that a systemwide database of treatment needs can be used for the planning and evaluation of programs, policies, and procedures. Together, risk and needs assessments will help to allocate scarce resources more efficiently and effectively.

■ Aims of the Study Group and This Book

OJJDP's Comprehensive Strategy, the guide to its implementation (Howell, 1995), and the sourcebook (Howell, Krisberg, Hawkins, & Wilson, 1995) provide an excellent framework for understanding, preventing, and controlling serious and/or violent juvenile (SVJ) offending. However, there is a need for more detailed quantitative analyses of risk and protective factors for SVJ offending; most previous reviews focus on delinquency in general rather than on SVJ offenders. Similarly, there is a need for more detailed quantitative analyses of the effectiveness (and cost-effectiveness) of prevention and intervention programs, again focusing on their effects on SVJ offenders.

This book aims to provide reviews of risk and protective factors and prevention and intervention programs focusing especially on SVJ offenders. It also aims to integrate the two different areas, so that knowledge about risk and protective factors is linked to knowledge about prevention and intervention programs, and vice versa. Ideally, prevention/intervention programs should be based on research on risk/protective factors, and conversely, conclusions about causal effects of risk/protective factors might be drawn from knowledge about the effectiveness of prevention/intervention programs. Attempts will be made to compare SVJ offenders with other offenders as well as with nonoffenders.

This book aims to specify the relative importance of different risk and protective factors in the development of SVJ offending, and the relative effectiveness of different prevention/intervention programs with SVJ offenders. It aims to specify what works best with what types of individuals, at what stages of development, and under what contextual conditions. It aims to investigate why some juveniles living in high-risk communities nevertheless do not get involved in SVJ offending. It has a developmental focus, reviewing the effects of risk factors and interventions on different stages of development, including the onset, persistence, escalation, de-escalation, and desistance of serious offending. It also aims to study key transition points in the development of serious delinquency careers, and optimal points for intervention efforts. The book also focuses on the emergence and disappearance of gangs, on the effects of joining or leaving a gang on SVJ offending, and on prevention/intervention programs targeted on gangs.

Key issues to be addressed in this book include

1. The extent to which risk factors are common to a number of problem outcomes or specific to SVJ offending
2. The extent to which SVJ offenders have multiple risk factors and/or multiple-problem outcomes
3. How far interventions targeted on early problem behaviors might reduce SVJ offending, to the extent that early problem behaviors are "stepping stones" in a developmental sequence leading to SVJ offending
4. The optimal timing of interventions, given that predictive accuracy increases and behavioral malleability decreases as children grow older
5. The trade-off between focusing interventions on high-risk populations (who may be responsible for more serious crime) or lower-risk populations (who may be more responsive to interventions)

This book also aims to develop an agenda for future research on SVJ offenders, by identifying gaps in knowledge about risk/protective factors and prevention/intervention programs. It is likely that much of our knowledge about risk/protective factors and prevention/intervention programs does not apply specifically to SVJ offenders. Conversely, the review of risk/protective factors may pinpoint promising prevention/intervention programs that should be implemented and evaluated with SVJ offenders, as well as evaluations whose results may be questionable because of methodological problems.

The key questions and issues that are addressed in the chapters of this book are as follows.

Serious and Violent Juvenile Offenders

The definitions of serious and/or violent and/or chronic offenders are discussed, with empirical analyses of how far these groups overlap (using different definitions). Measurement issues are reviewed, and in particular the different conclusions drawn from official records (of arrests and court referrals) and self-reports. In this chapter and in the Appendix by Snyder, trends over time in serious/violent/chronic offenders are reviewed, and the large proportion of crimes committed by the small population of chronic juvenile offenders (however defined). Special analyses of the juvenile court careers of successive birth cohorts are carried out to investigate how the probability of violent and serious nonviolent offenses increases with the total number of offenses committed. The ages of onset of SVJ offending are also described.

Race and Ethnicity and SVJ Offenders

Differential rates of offending of juveniles in different racial and ethnic groups are discussed, together with trends over time. Arrest, self-report, and victimization data are compared, addressing the key issue of how far police or court processing might be biased against certain racial/ethnic groups. Community- and individual-level explanations of racial/ethnic differences in offending are compared, with special reference to the effects of macrosocial changes on minority communities.

Co-occurrence of SVJ Offending and Other Problems

The co-occurrence of serious and/or violent juvenile offending with substance use (alcohol, marijuana, other illicit drugs) and mental health problems (aggression, hyperactivity, depression) is reviewed. Other co-occurring problems include victimization and school problems (truancy, low achievement, supervision, dropping out). Special analyses of the Denver Youth Survey (Huizinga, Loeber, & Thornberry, 1993) are described, and conditional probabilities of co-occurrence are calculated. An important issue is how far SVJ offenders are multiple-problem youth.

Development of SVJ Offending Careers

The time course of SVJ offending careers is reviewed, focusing especially on the prevalence and frequency of offending, and on ages of onset and desistance. Developmental pathways leading to SVJ offending are reviewed, and especially the role of aggressive and early disruptive problem behaviors in these pathways. Implications for intervention are drawn, and especially the predictive usefulness of age of onset and speed of progression through different onsets. Special analyses of the National Youth Survey (Elliott, Huizinga, & Ageton, 1985) and Chicago Youth Development Study (Tolan, Gorman-Smith, Huesmann, & Zelli, in press) are described, in testing the developmental pathways approach of Loeber and colleagues.

Predictors of SVJ Offending in Adolescence and Early Adulthood

Meta-analytic techniques are used to summarize the results of longitudinal research on predictive risk factors for SVJ offending in adolescence and early adulthood. The analyses aim to identify predictor variables measured at ages 6-11 and 12-14 that are correlated with serious and/or violent offending at ages 15-25. Childhood and adolescent predictors are compared.

Predictors of Youth Violence

The major modifiable individual, family, peer, school, and community risk and protective factors for youth violence are reviewed. Few longitudinal studies provide results specifically for interpersonal physical violence as opposed to delinquency in general. The results of studies that are the most adequate methodologically are described. Protective factors are also discussed, including those that are at the opposite end of the scale to risk factors and those that interact with risk factors. Also, implications for prevention/intervention that can be drawn from knowledge about risk/protective factors are discussed.

Gangs and SVJ Offenders

Gangs and gang membership have increased dramatically in the past 15 years. The links between gang membership and SVJ offending are reviewed, as well as the effect of joining or leaving a gang, and gang activities, on SVJ offending. An important issue is how much SVJ offending is committed by gang members. Youth gang homicide cases are discussed, and risk factors for gang membership. Special analyses of the Rochester Youth Development Study (Thornberry, Huizinga, & Loeber, 1995) are described. Factors influencing the emergence, development, persistence, and disappearance of gangs are reviewed. Implications for intervention are drawn from the links between gang membership and SVJ offending.

Screening of SVJ Offenders

Screening instruments can be developed to identify potential SVJ offenders among a larger youth population, and methods of developing such instruments are reviewed.

Screening instruments have also been developed to assist in detention, probation, parole, and placement decisions in the juvenile justice system, and these instruments are described. Risks and needs assessments are also reviewed. No existing screening instrument is specifically applicable to SVJ offenders. Ethical, legal, and policy issues arising in screening are discussed, and policy recommendations are made.

Prevention of SVJ Offending

Primary prevention programs targeted on parents and families (e.g., parent management training, family preservation), children's social and academic skills, and conflict resolution and peer mediation are reviewed. Many early programs target risk factors for the behavioral precursors of SVJ offending (such as conduct disorder or aggressive behavior) rather than risk factors for SVJ offending. Multicomponent programs are especially described, because it seems likely that they will be more effective than programs containing only a single intervention component (e.g., child, family, or peer group). Programs targeting different development periods (infancy, early childhood, adolescence) and different populations (universal, children at risk, behavior problem youth) are considered.

Community Interventions to Prevent SVJ Offending

The most promising community prevention strategies, adapted from the field of public health, involve reducing risk factors and enhancing protective factors. Community mobilization, situational prevention, intensive policing strategies, and changes in laws are reviewed. School-based strategies are also discussed, including changing school organization and introducing classroom-based curricula emphasizing the reinforcement of skills. Communities That Care, a comprehensive community prevention strategy, is also described.

Promising Programs for Youth Gang Violence Prevention and Intervention

Three types of gang prevention programs are reviewed. The first targets gang problems directly, using community efforts by police, prosecutors, judges, probation and parole officers, corrections officers, schools, employers, community-based agencies, and a range of grassroots organizations. It combines increased supervision and suppression with social services and opportunities for gang youth. The second is based on OJJDP's Comprehensive Strategy. The third specifically targets gang-related homicides, using a variety of measures such as reducing access to firearms, vertical prosecution of gang crimes, hospital emergency room intervention, and counseling drive-by shooting victims.

Effective Intervention for SVJ Offenders

Meta-analytic techniques are used to summarize experimental and quasi-experimental research on the effectiveness of interventions in reducing the recidivism rates of serious offenders aged 12-21. Interventions for both institutionalized and noninstitutionalized offenders are reviewed, including interpersonal skills training, individual and group counseling, employment programs, wilderness challenge programs, restitution, and shock incarceration.

Impact of the Justice System on SVJ Offenders and Prospects for Graduated Sanctions in a Comprehensive Strategy

The effectiveness of the juvenile justice system in handling SVJ offenders is investigated. Studies of the impact of priority prosecution programs and juvenile confinement are reviewed. The relative effects on recidivism of incarceration as opposed to intensive community-based sanctions are studied. Research on the effects of transferring offenders from the juvenile to the adult court is also described.

Intermediate Sanctions and Community Treatment of SVJ Offenders

The rationale for community treatment, intermediate sanctions, and intensive supervision in juvenile probation and parole is reviewed. In most cases, these dispositions are used for less serious offenders. Different types of programs are described, including intensive surveillance and electronic monitoring, house arrest, home detention and curfews, drug and alcohol testing, day treatment/ reporting centers, restitution, community service, shock incarceration and boot camps, victim-offender mediation, job placement, and mentoring. A key issue is how far SVJ offending can be reduced by intermediate sanctions or intensive aftercare, and what is the cost-effectiveness of these programs. Other key issues of program design, management, cost, implementation, and evaluation are discussed.

SVJ Offenders: Gaps in Knowledge and Research Priorities

Key gaps in knowledge and research priorities are identified, including the need for risk/protective factor and prevention/intervention research that focuses specifically on SVJ offenders. Another important gap in knowledge is the relative lack of research on protective factors. The need to identify developmental pathways to SVJ offending, and to forge partnership between researchers and practitioners, is also discussed.

Policy Implications

Policy implications are reviewed. More efforts should be made to construct screening devices to discriminate between SVJ and other offenders. These can assist in risk and needs assessments and in the choice of graduated sanctions. Public health-based prevention approaches are recommended as the most cost-effective way of reducing SVJ offending. The accountability of the juvenile justice, child welfare, and mental health services, especially for very young offenders, is discussed. A research agenda is proposed, focusing on longitudinal and experimental studies.

■ *Subsequent Chapters*

Subsequent chapters of this book expand all these points in great detail, so that this book represents the most extensive and up-to-date survey of current knowledge about serious and/or violent juvenile offenders.

■ *Some Recent Findings*

Since the completion of the main body of this book, news arrived of significant declines in certain indicators of serious delinquency, including juvenile homicide (Sickmund, Snyder, & Poe-Yamagata, 1997). Although such decreases are to be welcomed, it is still unclear which factors cause such change, whether the decreases imply that the proportion and level of offending by current SJV offenders is declining, and whether future generations of offenders will reduce their level of serious and violent offending as well.

Furthermore, the present decrease in juvenile delinquency does not mean offending levels have come down to acceptable levels. Many of the issues reviewed in this volume—development, risk, and successful interventions for SVJ offending—still remain important in addressing a delinquency problem that is too large for the U.S. population.

PART I

Developmental Course and Risk Factors

CHAPTER 2

Serious and Violent Juvenile Offenders

■ *Rolf Loeber, David P. Farrington, & Daniel A. Waschbusch*

Given the importance of understanding serious and violent juvenile (SVJ) offenders (see Farrington and Loeber, Chapter 1, this volume), this chapter examines several basic issues regarding SVJ offenders. A first goal is to offer definitions of SVJ offenses in terms of both official records and in terms of self-report. A second goal is to review serious and violent offending in the context of past classification systems.

A third purpose of this chapter is to examine the extent to which SVJ offenders overlap with chronic offenders, and whether the overlap between violent juvenile offenders and chronic offenders is similar to that between serious nonviolent juvenile offenders and chronic offenders. The issue of overlap is im-

portant because one of the missions of the juvenile courts is to protect society by punishing and discouraging those who are at highest risk of reoffending. Thus, recommendations have been made that the juvenile justice system "should focus its scarce resources on the chronically violent offender" (Fagan & Hartstone, 1984, p. 39). This is particularly needed because chronic offenders constitute a relatively small group who account for half or more of all delinquent offending (see below).

A fourth purpose of this chapter is to examine changes in the prevalence of chronic offending. Many measures of SVJ offending, including arrest, court, and victimization measures, indicate large increases in the levels of SVJ offending in the past decades. However, it is much less clear to what extent the prevalence of chronic offenders has increased as well during the period.

A fifth purpose of this chapter is to examine how knowledge of SVJ offenders depends on the type of data used to examine them. Official records of arrest and/or adjudication of offending produce different insights into the careers of SVJ offenders as compared to self-reports. However, the advantages and limitations of official records and of self-reports remain unclear. Relatedly, this section examines the age of onset of serious offending by juvenile offenders (as evident from self-reports).

A sixth purpose of this chapter is to examine the extent to which chronic juvenile offenders are responsible for the total amount of delinquency committed by juveniles. As we will show, there is a consensus that a small proportion of youth become chronic offenders and that this group is responsible for more than half of all juvenile offenses. However, we will also show that findings vary a great deal from study to study and by ethnicity and gender.

Finally, this chapter examines whether SVJ offenders are concentrated in particular geographical areas. Knowledge of whether SVJ is concentrated in particular geographic areas, such as inner cities and large urban areas, should be directly relevant for the selective allocation of resources to those areas to stem the tide of SVJ offending in these areas. This chapter will examine this question by geographically plotting homicides committed by juveniles in the United States.

■ How Can SVJ Offenders Best Be Defined?

We will first examine definitions of SVJ offenders. Starting with juveniles, it must be

noted that the definition of *juveniles* varies from state to state. In the majority of states, juveniles are defined as boys or girls under the age of 18. This accords with most state statutes that define the upper age for juvenile court jurisdiction in delinquency matters as age 17. However, 10 states define the upper age as 16 (Georgia, Illinois, Louisiana, Massachusetts, Michigan, Missouri, New Hampshire, South Carolina, Wisconsin, and Texas), and 3 states define the upper age as 15 (Connecticut, New York, and North Carolina). Moreover, many states have redefined the criteria for referring juveniles to adult courts for delinquency offenses, with different offense types leading to referral from different ages (Krisberg and Howell, Chapter 14, this volume; Snyder & Sickmund, 1995). It is against this background of a lack of consensus regarding the definition of juveniles that we examine the definition of SVJ offending.

Probably the best summary of issues surrounding the definition of the "toughest kids" has been written by Fagan and Hartstone (1984). Definitions are important because they provide a common language for a summary of findings, formulation of policy, and execution of such policy. To accommodate these different needs, definitions of serious, violent, and chronic juvenile offenders should bring together the perspectives of research, legislation, and intervention (Fagan & Hartstone, 1984).

Serious Offenders

We define serious offenders as those juveniles who have committed one or more of the following offenses:

Violent offenses (see below)	Fraud
Felony larceny/theft	Dealing in stolen
Auto theft	property

Burglary	Embezzlement
Break and enter	Drug trafficking
Carjacking	Arson (other than of an
Extortion	occupied dwelling)
Forgery and	Weapons violation and firearms
counterfeiting	regulations/statutes

Excluded from this definition are status offenses, violations of ordinances, vandalism, drunkenness, malicious mischief, disorderly conduct, and traffic and motor vehicle law violations. In short, serious offenders are defined by their involvement in serious forms of delinquency.

Violent Offenders

We define violent offenders as those juveniles who have committed one or more of the following delinquent acts:

Homicide	Kidnapping
Aggravated assault (including	Voluntary manslaughter
weapons offenses and	Rape or attempted rape
attempted murder)	Arson of occupied
Robbery (including armed	building
robbery)	

Thus, violent offenders, by definition, are a subset of all serious offenders. In concentrating on violent offenders, we exclude minor forms of aggression, such as simple assault and juvenile fist fights, as they rarely lead to prosecution. However, in practice, it is often difficult to agree on the threshold between what is and what is not legally violent. As Fagan and Hartstone (1984) point out, it is not always clear what "excessive" violence is.

Chronic Offenders

There is less agreement among scholars, lawmakers, and juvenile justice professionals on how to best define juvenile chronic offenders. Although it is clear that the key feature distinguishing chronic from nonchronic offenders is the frequency of offending, there is no consensus about the optimal cut-off to distinguish the two groups. For example, state legislation varies considerably regarding the number or nature of prior offenses that make some juveniles qualify for the category of chronic offender (Fagan & Hartstone, 1984). Research also varies considerably in the cut-offs used to define chronic offenders, ranging from five or more arrests (e.g., Shelden & Chesney-Lind, 1993; Wolfgang, Figlio, & Sellin, 1972) to nine or more convictions (Farrington & West, 1993). When self-reported delinquency is the criterion, chronic offenders are often defined as those juveniles repeatedly committing serious offenses (Dunford & Elliott, 1984; Stouthamer-Loeber, Loeber, Huizinga, & Porter, 1997). For example, Huizinga, Esbensen, and Weiher (1994) defined serious delinquents as those juveniles who self-reported three or more serious offenses. There is also controversy about including the persistence of offending over time to define chronic offenders. For example, the Huizinga et al. definition did not require the persistence of serious offenses over more than one measurement window (e.g., more than 1 year), whereas the definition used by Stouthamer-Loeber et al. (1997) did require persistence over time. Thus, researchers have employed a variety of definitions of chronic offenders.

Moreover, it is debatable whether similar definitions of chronic offenders should be used for each gender. Although legal reasons may necessitate the same definition for each gender, research makes it clear that the distribution of the frequency and severity of offending is different for females and males. Specifically, females usually show lower rates of serious forms of offending (e.g., Elliott,

1994; Espiritu & Huizinga, 1996). Given these major distributional differences, it may not make sense to apply the same cut-off (e.g., five or more offenses) to identify chronic-offending males and chronic-offending females. A uniform cut-off will likely identify a minute percentage of females (who probably represent a more extreme group) compared with the percentage of male offenders meeting the same criterion.

Given the major difficulties in defining chronic offenders, this volume will concentrate on serious juvenile offenders and violent juvenile offenders. However, this chapter will also examine the overlap between SVJ offenders and chronic offenders, changes in the prevalence of chronic offenders over time, and how much of the total crime is accounted for by chronic offenders.

Some Cautionary Notes

Most of the terminology about offense types used in the preceding section is based on the terminology used in the Uniform Crime Reports. However, in this volume, we will focus on serious and violent offenders as evident from either official records or self-reports. Unless stated otherwise, self-reported serious delinquency reflects the same serious offense types defined above.

It should be noted that the criteria for the severity of certain forms of delinquency have changed over the past decades. Particularly, drug possession and drug dealing have traditionally been concerned with marijuana and hashish, but in recent years police and courts have put more effort into prosecuting juveniles who deal in cocaine, crack, and other, potentially addictive drugs (Snyder & Sickmund, 1995). Furthermore, even within the category of serious offenses there are different degrees of severity, such as joyriding ver-

sus car theft, that usually lead to different legal sanctions. One should keep in mind that criteria for making these distinctions are dependent on judgment and may change over time.

■ SVJ Offenders as a Separate Category of Offenders

A second purpose of this chapter is to examine SVJ offenders in light of previous classification efforts, particularly those that shed light on the development of SVJ offending. Separating SVJ offenders from general delinquency is in essence a typology and can thus be seen in the light of a strong tradition in criminology of creating typologies of delinquents (see, e.g., Brennan, 1980; Buikhuisen & Jongman, 1970; Chaiken & Chaiken, 1984; Gibbons, 1962, 1975; Huizinga, 1979; Roebuck, 1967). Initially, classifications were mostly theory driven and focused on offense types, such as "the professional thief" or "the amateur shoplifter," and were based on the predominant form of offending (Gibbons, 1975). Later typologies referred to broader behavioral categories. Most of these typologies, often with considerable merit, attempted to classify offenders into mutually exclusive groups, such as property and violent delinquents (Gottfredson, 1975), life-course-persistent versus adolescent limited delinquents (Moffitt, 1993), and overcontrolled versus undercontrolled delinquents (Megargee & Bohn, 1979). However, dichotomies of offenders may be too simple for such a complex phenomenon as SVJ offending.

Several studies have produced evidence that the specialization in offense types is not common among the most serious offenders (e.g., Bursik, 1980; Farrington, Snyder, & Finnegan, 1988; Wolfgang et al., 1972;

Wolfgang, Thornberry, & Figlio, 1987). Farrington et al. (1988) found that the degree of specialization was small but significant and that it increased with the number of referrals to the juvenile court. This indicates that a higher proportion of the chronic offenders were specialized.

Many of the preceding classifications encompassed juvenile and adult offenders. However, several classification schemes focusing exclusively on juvenile offenders have been proposed (Buikhuisen & Jongman, 1970; Jenkins, 1973; Quay, 1964, 1979). Considerable differences in typologies of juvenile offenders exist, depending on whether they are based on official records (Buikhuisen & Jongman, 1970; California Department of Youth Authority, 1982; Shelden & Chesney-Lind, 1993; Smith, Smith, & Noma, 1984), self-reports (Huizinga, 1979; Kulik, Stein, & Sarbin, 1968), or a combination of both (Farrington, 1979).

In recent years, classification schemes have combined features of offense types and offender types. For example, Shelden and Chesney-Lind (1993), using court referrals, distinguished between one-time offenders, nonchronic recidivist offenders, and chronic offenders. Turning to self-report measures, Dunford and Elliott (1984) used a delinquency typology based on frequency and severity of self-reported delinquent acts over a period of years, consisting of (a) nondelinquents, (b) exploratory delinquents, (c) nonserious patterned delinquents, and (d) serious patterned delinquents. This was subsequently modified by Huizinga (1995), who classified juvenile delinquents on the basis of their self-reported delinquency over five annual data waves as either (a) nonoffenders, (b) status offenders, (c) minor offenders, or (d) serious offenders. It should be noted that several criteria used in these classification schemes are correlated, such as offense seriousness, frequency, and variety (e.g., Braithwaite & Law, 1978).

Classifications have also been formed on the basis of empirical data. For example, advances in the collection of onset and offset information in self-reported delinquency measures have made it possible to introduce a typology of delinquents that focused on the beginning, persistence, and ending of delinquency careers. Loeber and colleagues (Loeber, Stouthamer-Loeber, Van Kammen, & Farrington, 1991) proposed a classification of juvenile offenders over time that is based on juveniles' self-reports and parent and teacher reports: (a) stable nondelinquents, (b) starters (i.e., those who made the transition from nondelinquency to minor delinquency), (c) stable moderately serious offenders, (d) escalators (i.e., those who escalated in the seriousness of offenses), (e) stable high serious offenders, (f) de-escalators (i.e., those who de-escalated in the seriousness of their offenses), and (g) desisters (i.e., those who ceased offending in the study period).

These categories are important because they help to shed light on developmental pathways to SVJ offending. Loeber and colleagues found evidence showing that particularly the development of persisting delinquency often is orderly and starts with predelinquent problem behaviors and escalates to serious and violent forms of delinquency in a minority of juveniles. According to their developmental model, there is a convergence in juvenile chronic offenders of serious overt or aggressive behavior patterns and serious covert or concealing behavior patterns (e.g., Loeber, DeLematre, Keenan, & Zhang, in press; Loeber, Keenan, & Zhang, 1997; Loeber et al., 1997). The significance of this development in classification is that it is empirically and theoretically driven, integrates predelinquent behavior problems and delinquent behavior, accounts for offenders who specialize in offending to different degrees, and explains along which paths juveniles escalate to violence, or serious nonviolent forms of offending and which groups eventually become chronic offenders. These developmental pathways are discussed in more detail by Tolan and Gorman-Smith (Chapter 5, this volume).

■ How Much Overlap Is There Between SVJ Offenders and Chronic Juvenile Offenders?

We will consider the overlap between SVJ offenders and chronic juvenile offenders separately for two measurement modes: juvenile court records of delinquent offending and police records of arrest.

Juvenile Court Records

Snyder (Appendix, this volume) analyzed the juvenile court careers of 151,209 youth in a southwestern county of the United States from 1980 through 1995. Careers were defined as one or more court referrals for delinquent acts during the juvenile years (those youth who were transferred to the adult court for disposition were included in the analyses). Out of all the juvenile delinquents, 29.6% could be characterized as serious nonviolent juveniles (e.g., those arrested for burglary, serious larceny, motor vehicle theft, etc.), 8.1% were violent juveniles (e.g., those arrested for murder, kidnapping, violent sexual assault, robbery, and aggravated assault), and 63.9% of juveniles had careers characterized by nonserious offenses.[1] Also, 14.6% were chronic juvenile offenders (i.e., those with 5 or more court referrals).

Table 2.1 and Figure 2.1 show the overlap between the serious nonviolent offenders, violent offenders, and chronic offenders (the latter defined as those with at least four juvenile court referrals). Just under one third (29.0%) of the chronic offenders were also violent offenders, whereas half (52.6%) of the violent offenders were also chronic offenders (i.e., those with five or more police contacts). Of the total sample of juvenile delinquents, 4.2% could be characterized as chronic violent offenders. Out of this group, three quarters (78.3%) also had at least one serious nonviolent referral in their careers. Thus, the typical serious juvenile delinquent career consisted of a serious violent and several serious nonviolent court referrals, whereas the serious juvenile delinquent career with only violent offenses was unusual (see also Farrington, 1991; Mathias, DeMuro, & Allinson, 1984).

Police Records

How do these percentages of overlap compare when police records of delinquency are used? In the Pittsburgh Youth Study, Loeber, Van Kammen, and Fletcher (1996) found that 48.7% of the oldest sample had been arrested for a serious offense by age 18, 13.8% had been arrested for a violent offense, and 17.3% of the boys were chronic offenders (based on three or more episodes of serious offenses). Table 2.1 shows that about a third (35.6%) of the chronic offenders were also violent offenders, but just under half (44.8%) of the violent offenders were also chronic offenders. Moreover, a third (35.1%) of the serious offenders were also chronic offenders.

In summary, there was substantial agreement between the two studies in the overlap between juvenile violent, serious, and chronic offenders, even though court records

TABLE 2.1 Overlap Between Juvenile Violent, Serious, and Chronic Offenders, Using Either Court or Police Records as Criterion

	Snyder (Appendix, this volume) (juvenile court records) in %	*Loeber, Van Kammen, and Fletcher (1996) (police records) in % (N)*
Chronic offenders who were also violent offenders	29.0	35.6 (26/73)
Violent offenders who were also chronic offenders	52.6	44.8 (26/58)
Serious offenders who were also chronic offenders	34.5	35.1 (72/205)

were the criterion in one study (Snyder, Appendix, this volume) and police records were used in the other study (Loeber et al., 1996). About half of the violent juvenile offenders were also chronic offenders, whereas about a third of the chronic offenders were also violent offenders. Moreover, about a third of the serious offenders were also chronic offenders. It should be kept in mind, however, that these percentages are a function of age, and they will vary for younger juvenile populations who have not yet gone through the full risk window.

■ *What Are the Major Trends in the Prevalence of SVJ Offending Over the Past Decades?*

Juvenile delinquency trends over the past decades have shown converging results across different types of records. Victimization surveys indicate that between 1987 and 1991 the risk that juveniles (ages 12-17) became victims of a nonfatal violent crime increased by 17% (Snyder & Sickmund, 1995). Likewise, the proportion of juveniles killed

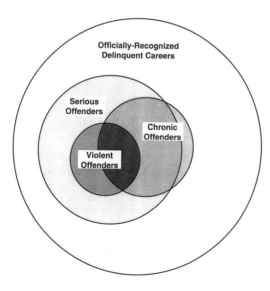

Figure 2.1. Overlap Between Juvenile Delinquents, Serious Delinquents, Violent Offenders, and Chronic Offenders (also see Snyder, Appendix in this volume)

NOTE: The outer circle represents all officially recognized delinquent careers. The portion of the large circle not covered by the chronic, serious, and violent offenders' circles represents careers with fewer than four referrals and no referrals for a serious offense. Overlaps represent careers with multiple attributes. Circles and their overlaps are drawn proportional to the number of careers with those attributes.

by guns has dramatically increased between 1984 and 1991 (Howell, Krisberg, Hawkins, & Wilson, 1995; Snyder & Sickmund, 1995). In Chapter 1 of this volume, we reviewed the major increases in juvenile violence during the past decades. Also, the proportion of prisoners who are juveniles escalated by 46% between 1983 and 1991 (Snyder & Sickmund, 1995). However, it is unclear to what extent changes in these juvenile delinquency indicators represent an underlying increase in the proportion of chronic delinquent juveniles in the general population or changes in police and juvenile (and adult) court practices. In addition, none of the preceding types of indicators reveals changes in the SVJ and/or chronic juveniles. Thus, it is unclear whether the proportion of SVJ and chronic juvenile offenders in the population has remained stable or has increased during the past decades. There are two types of records that may shed light on this question: the age of first arrest for serious delinquency, and changes in the proportion of chronic offenders in different graduating cohorts appearing before the juvenile courts.

First, changes in the proportion of SVJ and chronic offending can be examined using the age of first arrest or referral to the juvenile court. It has been established that the seriousness and chronicity of delinquency is correlated with an earlier age of first arrest (Farrington et al., 1990; Loeber, 1982), and chronic delinquents tend to have an earlier age of referral to the juvenile court than nonchronic delinquents (Farrington & Wikström, 1994; Shelden & Chesney-Lind, 1993). These findings imply that if the average age of first arrest (or court referral) for serious delinquency remains constant in a population, the proportion of chronic offenders is likely to remain constant. However, if the average age of first arrest or court referral becomes earlier over successive age cohorts, this may imply that,

given similar police and court practices, the proportion of chronic juvenile offenders tends to increase over time. Snyder (Appendix, this volume), using data from Maricopa County in Arizona, failed to find a shift in the average first age of referral to the juvenile court for a violent offense in age cohorts between 1980 and 1995 (the average age ranged from 15.6 to 16.1). These findings suggest little or no change in the prevalence of chronic offenders.

Second, changes in the proportion of SVJ and chronic offending can be examined using the proportion of chronic offenders in successive cohorts in the same geographic location. Cohort studies in Philadelphia indicated that the proportion of chronic offenders (more than four arrests) had dramatically increased from the 1945 to the 1958 cohorts (Tracy, Wolfgang, & Figlio, 1985). In addition, Snyder (Appendix, this volume) found that 13% of youth referred to juvenile courts in the 1980s were chronic offenders, but that the proportion of chronic offenders abruptly increased in the early 1990s, averaging 17% of the careers in 1992 through 1995. However, the crime mix committed by chronic offenders (i.e., the proportion of nonserious offenses, serious nonviolent offenses, and violent offenses) remained highly stable across both time periods. These findings, in contrast to age of onset, suggest increases in the prevalence of chronic offenders.

Chronic offenders are known to be responsible for a disproportionally large share of the total volume of delinquency in each age cohort (see below). When the proportion of chronic offenders in a population increases, it is almost inevitable that the total volume of offenses per offender will increase as well. Snyder (Appendix, this volume) reported that "compared to the 1980 juvenile justice graduating class, the typical career in the class of 1995 had not only more referrals per career

(2.36 vs. 2.06), it also had more nonserious (1.76 vs. 1.47) and more violent (0.124 vs. 0.095) referrals per career," but virtually the same number of referrals for serious nonviolent delinquency (0.493 vs. 0.476). A crucial question is, however, to what extent real changes in the prevalence of chronic offenders have taken place, rather than changes in court and police practices, that might explain the results. However, this question cannot be answered at this time.

In summary, there is some evidence suggesting that the proportion of chronic juvenile offenders increased in several locations over the past decades, but the evidence from age of onset is not consistent. Given the absence of good national data, it is not clear whether the proportion of chronic juvenile offenders has dramatically changed in the United States over the past decades. One way to examine this question further would be to examine the proportion of chronic offenders in high-crime inner cities (see below).

■ *How Well Do Official Records and Self-Reports of SVJ Offenders Represent Their Actual Delinquent Involvement?*

To address this question, we will briefly review SVJ offenders according to official records, particularly arrest and adjudication data, and contrast these with the identification of SVJ offenders by means of self-reports of delinquent activities. Specifically, we will address the question of what proportion of self-reported SVJ offenders are known to the police or the juvenile courts. We will also address the advantages and limitations of self-reports of SVJ offending.

Official Records

Studies based on official records have varied much in the types of data used. Many studies have reported arrest data, and a minority have been based on evidence of adjudication. Overall, adjudication is to be preferred because arrests do not necessarily indicate a legal finding of guilt for the offense and, as a consequence, include a significant proportion of innocent juveniles (Wilson & Howell, 1995).

It should be kept in mind that given the reluctance of courts to deal with all but the most serious preadolescent offenders, juvenile delinquency careers as evident from official records usually cover merely 6 years (until age 17). From ages 16 to 18 onward (depending on which state), federal and state legislation concerning juvenile delinquency no longer applies, and juvenile courts no longer deal with these offenders because they are routinely referred to adult courts. The peak period of officially recorded offending for juveniles usually falls between the ages of 14 and 17 (Farrington, 1986). However, as we will show below, the majority of self-reported male juvenile persistent serious offenders show an onset of serious offending between ages 7 and 14.

Self-Reports

Increasingly, self-reports have been accepted as a valid measure of juvenile delinquency (e.g., Elliott, 1994; Elliott, Huizinga, & Ageton, 1985; Farrington, 1973, 1989b; Farrington, Loeber, Stouthamer-Loeber, Van Kammen, & Schmidt, 1996). However, self-reports used to measure SVJ delinquency raise a number of important issues. For example, there is consensus that additive scales of self-reported delinquency cannot capture the distinction between juveniles who commit only a high frequency of minor offenses, and those who commit a high frequency of both minor and major offenses (Cernkovich, Giordano, & Pugh, 1983). Instead, serious offenders need to be identified from self-reports, recognizing that the majority of them also commit minor offenses at a high rate (Cernkovich, Giordano, & Pugh, 1985).

In fact, there is some controversy about whether self-reports sufficiently capture serious offenses for two reasons. First, serious offenders in neighborhood surveys commit delinquency at a lower rate than serious offenders who are institutionalized (Cernkovich et al., 1985). Second, self-report surveys used in schools can miss truants and suspended students, who tend to be more delinquent than nontruants. Furthermore, juveniles' self-reports are not perfect indicators of offending because they are subject to biases (e.g., poor memory, exaggeration, and concealment), and this may be true for juveniles' self-reports of serious and violent offending as well.

In conclusion, both self-reports and official records of SVJ offending have certain limitations. In addition, each measure has biases but not necessarily in the same direction. Therefore, each measure is needed to understand SVJ offending better. Having said that, however, we should address what official records cannot show about SVJ offenders and where self-reports are undeniably essential.

How Do SVJ Offenders Compare in Self-Reports and in Official Records?

The importance of official records to define delinquency is highlighted by the fact that virtually all information in the media (newspapers, television), generated by the FBI, and by agencies concerned with juvenile delinquency (e.g., Office of Juvenile Justice and Delinquency Prevention, Bureau of Justice Statistics, National Institute of Justice, National Center for Juvenile Courts) focuses on official records of delinquency. At the same time, the importance of self-report is highlighted by the fact that only the juveniles themselves have full knowledge of their delinquency. Thus, an important question is what proportion of self-reported SVJ offenders are represented in official records of delinquency?

The answer to this question is particularly important in studying SVJ offenders. If self-reports of SVJ are underrepresented in official records, then official records are not adequate to control crime and to measure changes in community levels of SVJ offending. For instance, if only a proportion of the SVJ offenders show up in official records, assertions about year-to-year changes in offense levels by juveniles are bound to be flawed. Similarly, delinquency reduction programs that solely rely on official indicators of SVJ offenders may not accurately ascertain the actual impact of the program on SVJ offenders not known to the police or the juvenile courts.

Dunford and Elliott (1984) compared self-reports and official records and found that 86% of the juvenile career offenders (defined in terms of high frequency, severity, and persistence of self-reported delinquency) did not have a record of arrest. Huizinga, Esbensen, and Weiher (1996) in the Denver Youth Survey investigated over a period of 5 years the proportion of self-reported violent offenders who had been arrested and for what type of delinquent act. The latter issue is important because (a) violent offenses have a much lower base rate than nonviolent offenses, and (b) those involved in violence tend to commit nonviolent offenses at a high rate. This makes it more probable that violent offenders are arrested for nonviolent delinquent acts.

Huizinga et al. (1996) defined self-reported violent offenders as those who had inflicted relatively serious injury on another person or persons (leading to cuts/bleeding, unconsciousness, or hospitalization). The results showed that 74% of the self-reported violent offenders had been arrested in that period. However, out of this percentage only 6% had been arrested for a serious violent offense, and 15% had been arrested for a minor violent offense. Moreover, the probability that self-reported violent offenders were arrested for nonviolent offenses was quite high (53%). Thus, most of the self-reported violent offenders were arrested for offenses other than violence. Given this pattern of offending and arrest, police and court officials, without knowledge of an arrestee's prior career of offending, often cannot identify violent (or serious) offenders accurately based on the presenting offense (see also Cernkovich et al., 1983).

How Do Self-Reports and Official Records Shed Different Light on the Course of Delinquent Careers?

It is very common that delinquency career studies using self-reports come to different conclusions than studies based on official records. For example, studies using self-reported delinquency often show an escalation in the severity of offending by those who become chronic or frequent offenders (Le Blanc, Côté, & Loeber, 1991; Loeber et al., 1993). However, this is not apparent from longitudinal analyses of police or court records (e.g., Weitekamp, Kerner, Schindler, & Schubert, 1995; Wolfgang et al., 1972; Wolfgang et al., 1987). On the other hand,

both self-reports and official records indicate that the seriousness of delinquency tends to increase with age (Elliott, 1994; Farrington, 1996b; Snyder, 1988; Tracy, Wolfgang, & Figlio, 1990; Wolfgang et al., 1972). Thus, offense seriousness appears to be a consistent indicator across the two types of measurements of juveniles' progression in delinquent acts as they grow older.

Furthermore, an early age of onset of self-reported offending is predictive of chronicity (Loeber, 1982; Tolan, 1987). However, this is less consistently true for court or police records of the first recorded offense. Specifically, although an early age of official offending predicts a larger number of offenses, studies do not consistently show that early-onset offenders display a higher rate of offending during their juvenile delinquency career than late-onset offenders, using official records as a criterion (Hamparian, Schuster, Dinitz, & Conrad, 1978; Loeber, 1982; Mathias et al. 1984; Snyder, 1988; Tracy et al., 1990). However, an early age of onset of offending is associated with more serious delinquency later, even in official records of delinquency (Snyder, 1988).

What do the data show about the age of onset of persistent SVJ offending? OJJDP's Causes and Correlates of Juvenile Delinquency Program in Denver, Pittsburgh, and Rochester addresses this question (Stouthamer-Loeber et al., 1997). Violent persistent offenders were defined as those boys who committed one or more violent acts (strongarming, attack to seriously hurt or kill, forced sex) at more than one assessment over a period of 5 years. Serious nonviolent persistent offenders were defined as those boys who committed one or more serious nonviolent delinquent acts during that period such as breaking and entering, car theft, and selling drugs, but did not commit serious violent acts. At about age 19 about a third of each of

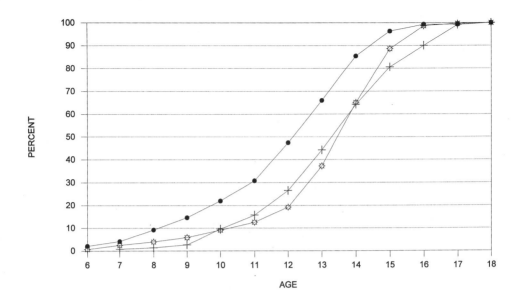

Figure 2.2. Cumulative Ages of Onset of Serious Delinquency for Persistent Juvenile Offenders (Stouthamer-Loeber, Loeber, Huizinga, & Porter, 1997)

the male samples, according to their self-reports, were persistent serious delinquents.

The onset data of persistent serious violence were very similar to the onset data of persistent serious nonviolent offenses, and for that reason were combined. Figure 2.2 shows the age of onset of persistent serious offending and indicates that by age 12 a sizable proportion of boys who eventually became persistent serious offenders had started their first serious delinquent act (27% in Denver, 47% in Pittsburgh, and 19% in Rochester). By age 14, 85% of the persistent serious offenders in Pittsburgh already had committed their first serious offense; in Denver and Rochester, this was about 65%. In summary, the majority of the persistent serious offenders first committed serious nonviolent offenses between the ages of 7 and 14.

These findings can be compared with the hazard rate (i.e., the rate of new cases emerging in the at-risk population) of self-reported serious violent offenders between ages 7 and

27 based on the National Youth Survey (Elliott, 1994). The hazard rate increased for serious violent offenders particularly after age 11 and, although differing somewhat by ethnicity, peaked by age 15. Thus, these findings reinforce the notion that most of the serious juvenile offenders emerge prior to midadolescence and well before the peaking of the age-crime curve for general delinquent populations (Farrington, 1986).

Finally, in 1994 the juvenile courts in the United States processed 1.5 million juvenile offenders, of which 6.5% were juveniles below the age of 12 (N = 97,700). About one quarter (26.1%) of these young offenders were below the age of 10. That a substantial proportion of below age 12 offenders committed relatively serious offenses is evident from the fact that the juvenile courts formally processed about a third (32.2%; N = 31,500) (H. N. Snyder, personal communication, March 1997).

In summary, there is substantial evidence that a large proportion of SVJ offenders have an early onset of offending and that large numbers of juveniles below age 12 are formally processed in juvenile courts. It is not clear, however, what proportion of very young offenders in the community come to the attention of the juvenile courts, and to what extent those who are processed by the juvenile courts are likely to become serious, violent, and chronic offenders. The impact of juvenile court processing on the delinquency careers of very young offenders is also not known.

We should express several caveats about the comparability of results on SVJ offending when based on either self-reports or on official records of delinquency. Comparability between self-reports and official records of offending may be restricted because of different definitions of serious forms of delinquency in each measure. Even acts with the same legal label may be of different seriousness in self-reports and official records. In addition, the ability to identify SVJ persisting offenders in self-reports and official records depends considerably on the length of the measurement window (Huizinga, Esbensen, & Weiher, 1994). However, in contrast to the 6-year interval covered by official records of juvenile delinquency, measures of self-reported delinquency can cover more years of juvenile delinquency careers, such as delinquency prior to age 12 (e.g., Loeber, Stouthamer-Loeber, Van Kammen, & Farrington, 1989).

With these caveats in mind, one of the major complications of arrest or adjudication records of juvenile offending is that such records are the tip of the iceberg of the actual delinquent activities evident from self-reports (Huizinga, 1991). This underrepresentation of actual offenses among the court records has major implications for the juvenile justice system. First, one of the big challenges for case workers is to discriminate between minor offenders and SVJ offenders. This is particularly difficult given that many of the SVJ offenders are arrested for minor delinquent acts (see also Le Blanc, Chapter 9, and Krisberg and Howell, Chapter 14, this volume). Second, it is highly debatable that the juvenile justice system can intercept SVJ offenders at the beginning of their delinquent career, given that a large proportion of these offenders have a very early onset of offending.

■ *How Much of the Total Volume of Crime Do Chronic Juvenile Offenders Account For?*

The pioneering studies by Wolfgang (Wolfgang et al., 1972; Wolfgang et al., 1987) suggested that chronic offenders, although constituting a small proportion of all offenders, commit a majority of all forms of delinquency. This section will examine whether this finding has been replicated since that study, and whether the results apply equally well across ethnic groups and genders.

Table 2.2 summarizes studies relating the contribution of chronic offenders to the total volume of delinquency in populations. Most studies in Table 2.2 concern juveniles, but several also take into account offending during adulthood (e.g., Farrington & West, 1993; Farrington & Wikström, 1994; Shannon, 1988). The studies used a variety of different measures of delinquency, including police arrest data, court data, and convictions. In addition, studies used a variety of definitions of chronicity. Although most studies defined chronicity as more than four official offenses, some studies (particularly the non-U.S. adult studies) defined chronicity as more than eight or even 34 offenses (Farrington & West, 1993; Farrington & Wikström, 1994). Only three studies took self-reported violent delinquency as a criterion (Huizinga, Loeber, & Thornberry, 1995; Thornberry, Huizinga, & Loeber, 1995).

TABLE 2.2 Offending by Chronic Offenders

Study	Sample Location (cohort year)	N (max. age)	% Offenders (source)	% Chronic Offenders (criterion)	% Chronic Offenders/ All Offenders	Chronic Offenders Account for % of the Following Offenses:										
						All	Aggravated Assault	Homicide	Rape	Robbery	Burglary	Motor Vehicle Theft	Drug	Index	Non-Index	Violence
Wolfgang, Figlio, and Sellin (1972); Tracy, Wolfgang and Figlio (1990)	Philadelphia (1945)	9,945 M 2,902 NWM 7,043 WM (17)	35 (P) 50.2 NWM 28.6 WM	6 M 14 NWM 3 WM (> 4)	18 M 29 NWM 10 WM	52 66 34	69 74 47	71 71 —	73 76 50	82[a] 72 93	66 73 54	51 51 45		71 48	63 31	
Wolfgang et al., (1983); Facella (1983); Tracy et al. (1990)	Philadelphia (1958)	13,160 M (17) 6,944 NWM 6,216 WM 14,000 F 7,363 NWF 6,637 WF	33 M (P) 41.8 NWM 22.7 WM	7 M 11 NWM 3 WM 8 NWF 5 WF (> 4)	23 M 27 NWM 15 WM	61 65 49 30 23	65 68 53	60 61 50	75 77 56	73 74 63				70 61	59 41	
Thornberry, Huizinga, and Loeber (1995)	Denver, CO (X̄ = 16)	874 MF	54 (S[b])	14	Upper 25%											82
Thornberry et al. (1995)	Rochester, NY (X̄ = 16.4)	750 M 250 F	58 (S[b])	15	Upper 25%											75
Thornberry et al. (1995)	Pittsburgh, PA	506 M	51 (S[b])	17	Upper 25%											77
Snyder (1988)	Phoenix, AZ	51,900 M 49,700 F	47 M (C) 22 F	18 M 6 F	38 M 26 F	46 M	60 M	54 M	64 M	64 M	61 M	62 M				61
	Utah	53,700 M 51,500 F (17)	45 M 20 F	22 M 11 F (> 3)	48 M 54 F	55 M	64 M	73 M	72 M	72 M	75 M	75 M	68			
Home Office (1989a, 1989b)	England and Wales (1953) (1958) (1963)	341,140 M 327,590 F 371,540 M 354,890 F 416,680 M 396,870 F	33 (C)	7	21 23	65 58										

26

Study	Location (period)	Sample	Prevalence								
Shelden and Chesney-Lind (1993)	Las Vegas, NV (c. 1956-1962)	1,000 MF	100 (C[c])	8 WM / 16 NWM / 0 WF / 5 NWF (>4)							
Shannon (1988)	Racine, WI										
	(1942)	679 M	67 M (P)	42 M	63 M	85 M					
		673 F (33)	25 F	5 F	20 F	41 F					
	(1949)	1,081 M	67 M	35 M	52 M	83 M					
		1,018 F (26)	31 F	8 F	26 F	51 F					
	(1955)	1,369 M	61 M	27 M	44 M	90 M					
		1,397 F (22)	33 F	7 F (>4)	21 F	65 F					
Farrington and West (1993)	London, England (1952-1953)	411 M (32)	37 (C)	6 (>8)	16	49	59	51	45	68	47
Farrington and Wikström (1994)	Stockholm, Sweden (1953)	7,719 M / 7,398 F (25)	32 (CW/P)	2 M (>34)	7	51					
Cernkovich, Giordano, and Pugh (1983)	North-central standard statistical area	942 MF / 462 M / 480 F (19)	56 (S)	14 (>4 major offenses)	27	42				95	47

NOTE: M = male; F = female; NW = nonwhite; W = white; P = police record; C = conviction; S = self-report; CR = court referral; CW = child welfare committee record.
a. 70% according to Weitekamp, Kerner, Schindler, and Schubert's (1994) reanalysis.
b. Self-reported violence.
c. Court-referred sample.

The following are some conclusions about the pattern of offending by chronic offenders based on Table 2.2.

- The percentage of chronic offenders varied much from study to study (7% to 25%), which can only partly be explained by differences in cut-offs for defining chronic offenders.
- The amount of crime accounted for by chronic offenders varied by ethnicity, with nonwhite male chronic offenders accounting for a higher amount of serious delinquency than white male offenders (Tracy et al., 1990). Similarly, nonwhite female chronic offenders accounted for a higher amount of serious delinquency than white female chronic offenders (Facella, 1983; Tracy et al., 1990; Wolfgang, 1983).
- The amount of crime accounted for by chronic offenders varied by cohort in the same location (Shannon, 1988).
- The amount of crime accounted for by chronic offenders varied by offense type, being relatively low when all offenses were taken into account, and somewhat higher for violent offenses, especially robbery (Snyder, 1988; Tracy et al., 1990; Wolfgang et al., 1972), and drug offenses (Farrington & West, 1993). For example, white male chronic offenders in the Wolfgang et al. (1972; Tracy et al., 1990) study accounted for 93% of all robberies, but only 45% of all motor vehicle thefts.

■ What Is the Geographic Distribution of SVJ Offenders?

A final purpose of this chapter is to examine the geographical distribution of serious juvenile delinquency. SVJ offenders do not appear to be randomly distributed across the United States, but instead appear clustered in certain regions and cities. Precise national data for all forms of SVJ offending are somewhat spotty, but geographic distributions for juvenile violent arrest rates in 1992 shows concentrations in the states of New York, Florida, New Jersey, Maryland, and California (Snyder & Sickmund, 1995). Furthermore, recent analyses by Sickmund, Snyder, & Poe-Yamagata (1997) for juvenile homicide offenders also indicate major geographic concentrations (Figure 2.3). The data from this study come from FBI records collected from those counties that made available data on juvenile homicide offenders under the age of 18. The data are somewhat of an underestimate of actual juvenile homicide offenders because all negligent manslaughter and justifiable homicides are excluded, and because a significant portion of reported murders were never solved (or their solution was never reported to the FBI).

Taking these caveats into account, Figure 2.3 shows that 84% of the 3,139 counties in the United States reported no juvenile homicide offenders in 1995. Ten percent of the counties reported a single homicide offender. However, a substantial proportion of juvenile homicide offenders were located in certain locations. Specifically, Sickmund, Snyder, & Poe-Yamagata (1997) found that 25% of all known juvenile homicide offenders were reported in just five counties, all located in major cities, namely, Los Angeles,, Chicago Houston, Detroit, and New York. The nation's estimated 2,300 juvenile murderers in 1995 were geographically concentrated in a small number of jurisdictions.

■ Conclusion

We started out with asking the question, How can serious, violent, and chronic offenders best be defined? We advocated that serious offenders are defined as those juveniles who have committed one or more serious offenses, such as violence, burglary, embezzlement, or drug trafficking. We defined violent offenders as those juveniles who have committed one or more violent offenses, such as homicide, robbery, and rape or attempted

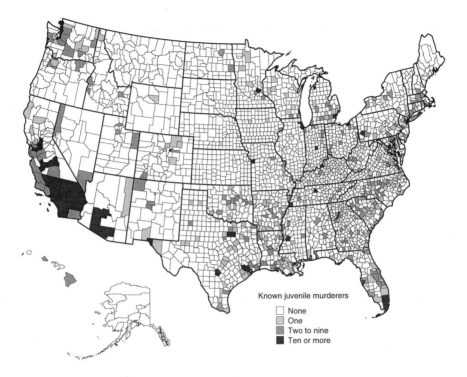

Known juvenile murderers

☐ None
One
Two to nine
Ten or more

Figure 2.3. Geographical Distribution of Juvenile Homicide Offenders in the United States in 1994 (Sickmund, Snyder, & Poe-Yamagata, 1997)

SOURCE: Authors' analysis of the FBI's Supplementary Homicide Report for 1995 (machine-readable data file).
NOTE: Each year, the FBI collects from a large sample of law enforcement agencies across the United States a detailed report on each homicide that occurred in their jurisdictions. In 1995, the FBI estimates that these supplementary homicide reports (SHRs) were submitted on 93% of all homicides. The SHR file was analyzed, excluding all negligent manslaughters and justifiable homicides, to produce a count of known offenders under the age of 18 in each U.S. county in 1995. Most counties with no reported juvenile murders in 1995 actually had no juvenile murderers; some were counties that did not report data. In 38% of murder incidents, offender characteristics were unknown, mostly because the offender(s) were never identified. Therefore, the counts presented in the map represent a slight undercount of known juvenile offenders (the 93% reported homicides). In reality, the map probably presents a large undercount of actual juvenile homicide offenders given that a significant portion of reported murders were never solved or their solutions never reported to the FBI.

rape. We concluded that there is less agreement among scholars about the definition of chronic juvenile offenders. Therefore, we concentrated on SVJ offenders, but wherever possible we related SVJ offending to chronic offending.

The fact that most reporting systems rely on offense data rather than offender data is a serious weakness. Offender-based information systems are needed to allocate resources better to those areas in which SVJ offenders are concentrated, and they are a necessary requirement to gauge the effectiveness of intervention or sanction programs. By presenting the geographic distribution of juvenile homicide data, we demonstrated the high degree to which juvenile homicide and other forms of violence are concentrated in certain inner cities and metropolitan areas, and in certain states. Ultimately, the safety and well-being of citizens in those areas are best served by our ability to reduce not only SVJ offending but particularly the number of SVJ offenders.

■ *Note*

1. The offenses were simple assault, possession of a controlled substance, disorderly conduct, vandalism, nonviolent sex offenses, minor larceny, liquor law offenses, and so forth.

CHAPTER 3

Race, Ethnicity, and Serious Juvenile Offending

■ *Darnell F. Hawkins, John H. Laub, & Janet L. Lauritsen*

This chapter examines the relationship between race and ethnicity and serious juvenile offending through the use of data from the Uniform Crime Reports (UCR) and self-report and victimization surveys. First, we provide a descriptive account of the racial distribution of serious violent offending among juvenile offenders in the United States. Next, information on short-term national and local trends related to offending patterns by race and ethnicity is provided. This is followed by a summary of research findings on race and ethnic differences in chronic or persistent offending.

Since the beginning of the 20th century, researchers have observed differences in rates of serious juvenile and adult offending among the various ethnic and racial groups in the United States. These differences have been the subject of competing theoretical interpretations and much public policy debate. Thus, following our presentation of the data relating to intergroup disparities, we consider the explanations that we think are most useful for understanding race and ethnic differences in serious juvenile offending. We suggest that many of the social ecological correlates of serious and chronic criminal offending have not

AUTHORS' NOTE: We thank Howard Snyder for providing us with key data. We also thank James C. Howell for comments on an earlier version of this chapter. The research assistance of Chris Kenaszchuk is gratefully acknowledged.

been fully incorporated into extant theory and explanation. The omission of other potentially significant correlates is also noted. Based on our review of the theoretical literature, we propose that the research agenda on racial and ethnic differences needs to be reframed and expanded.

Before describing the sources of data that are relevant for examining racial and ethnic differences in serious juvenile offending, it is important to note that our use of the terms to describe America's ethnic and racial groups follows definitions established by the U.S. Census Bureau. For numerous historical reasons, a person's *race* in the United States is indicated by one of five categories that are assumed to be mutually exclusive: (a) white; (b) black; (c) American Indian, Eskimo, or Aleut; (d) Asian or Pacific Islander; or (e) other. *Ethnicity* is considered a separate measure, usually indicating a person's country(s) of ancestral origin. Data on ethnicity available to those who study crime are limited currently to a determination of whether a person is of *Hispanic* origin. According to the Census Bureau, Hispanics are self-identified persons of Spanish-speaking origin who may be members of any one of the above race groups. Current official census records do include other ethnic demarcations, but these are not used in the collection of crime data.

In this chapter we focus predominantly on racial as opposed to ethnic comparisons. The reason stems from a lack of consistency in the crime data that contrasts Hispanics and non-Hispanics. Despite census guidelines, many law enforcement agencies do not routinely gather such ethnicity data. Furthermore, because similar problems frequently affect the collection of crime data for racial groups such as Asians and Native Americans, we focus primarily on comparisons between *blacks* and *whites*. Where available, data reflecting other race and ethnic comparisons are presented.

The numerous sources of data on serious juvenile offending are collected for diverse purposes and thus reveal different things about the nature and extent of serious, violent, and chronic offending among youth. One source of data consists of records generated by criminal justice agencies, such as police, courts, and corrections, and are commonly referred to as *official* data. In contrast, other sources include social surveys conducted independently of criminal justice agencies. Among these are self-reported delinquency surveys and victimization surveys.[1] We briefly describe each of these data sources and highlight some of their major strengths and weaknesses as instruments for the study of ethnic and racial differences in rates of serious offending.

■ *Sources of Data*

Official Data

Criminologists have traditionally used data on arrests to study race, ethnicity and other demographic correlates of offending,[2] although numerous criticisms have been offered regarding the adequacy of these data. One disadvantage of arrest data is that information is collected only for those criminal events that come to the attention of the police through citizen complaints or through their own surveillance activities (Hindelang, 1974). It may be that these events exhibit characteristics that are different from unlawful events that do not come to the attention of authorities. It is possible that ethnic and racial groups differ in their inclinations to report crime, even serious conduct, to authorities (Skogan, 1984). To the extent that they do, officially reported data may produce biased estimates of racial and ethnic differences in actual criminal involvement.

There is also reason to be concerned that police may be biased in their arrest policies against certain groups, particularly those with limited economic and political power (e.g., young, poor, minority males). If so, these groups would exhibit higher rates of offending compared with the general population partly because of differential handling by the police (Chambliss, 1994; Hagan & Peterson, 1995; Hindelang, Hirschi, & Weis, 1981; Mann, 1993). Greater police surveillance and a tendency to arrest rather than to warn or to sanction by means other than arrest those adolescents who are members of low-status groups may contribute to a widening of the gap in official rates of offending between ethnic and racial groups.

Official crime statistics have other major limitations. Because such statistics are incident based rather than person based (Reiss & Roth, 1993), they provide no information regarding the chronicity of individual offending and potential racial and ethnic differences in the length of involvement in crime. Finally, as previously noted, official data such as the UCR can be used to calculate race-specific arrest rates, but cannot provide reliable comparisons of differences within racial groups (e.g., white non-Hispanics vs. white Hispanics or Caribbean blacks vs. native U.S. blacks).

However, Gove, Hughes, and Geerken (1985) offered evidence that the UCR do represent a valid source of data for the study of group differences if analyses are limited to the study of serious crimes like homicide and robbery. Theirs and other studies have shown that rates of offending by characteristics such as age, gender, and race as measured by the UCR are fairly accurate and that systematic biases in the detection and processing of offenders charged with serious crimes may have been overstated (Blumstein, Cohen,

Roth, & Visher, 1986; Hindelang, 1978, 1981; Sampson & Lauritsen, 1997). At the same time there also is evidence that consideration of the race and ethnicity of offenders continues to play a role in juvenile justice decision making (Pope & Feyerherm, 1993; Sampson & Laub, 1993b; Tonry, 1994, 1995). Thus, it is prudent to use official sources of data cautiously when assessing racial and ethnic differences in serious offending among juveniles, and, to the extent possible, these data should be supplemented with data from alternative sources.

Self-Report Offending Data

Fortunately, there are several alternative sources of data of potential usefulness for the study of serious violent offending among juveniles. Self-report surveys were designed, in part, to eliminate some of the weaknesses of official records noted. Data generated from these surveys of the general population of youth are measures of the individual's behavior rather than the response of the criminal justice system. As the name implies, self-report surveys allow juveniles to tell researchers of their own misconduct even if such behavior was not detected by authorities. For this reason, it is believed that self-report data more accurately reflect the true distribution of crime. One of the most widely used self-report surveys is the National Youth Survey (NYS). The NYS is a survey of delinquency and drug use among a national probability sample of 1,725 youth, ages 11 to 17 (Elliott, Huizinga, & Ageton, 1985). The collection of data for this longitudinal survey began in 1977 and individuals were reinterviewed for nine waves (Elliott, 1994).

Unfortunately, self-report surveys have serious limitations when they are used for the study of serious violent offending (Reiss & Roth, 1993). For example, most surveys do not generate enough serious and/or violent offenders for adequate analysis (see Chapter 2). This is due to the typically small sample sizes used in most self-report studies and their subsequent inability to capture truly serious violent offenders (Cernkovich, Giordano, & Pugh, 1985). Consequently, it has been difficult for researchers to assess the racial and ethnic correlates of serious and violent juvenile offending using self-report data alone, although recent data from the Denver Youth Survey, the Rochester Youth Development Study, and the Pittsburgh Youth Study are exceptions to this point.

There is also debate concerning the differential validity of self-reports for blacks and whites (Hindelang et al., 1981, but cf. Huizinga & Elliott, 1986). Early studies found that blacks were more likely than whites to underreport serious misconduct. In the most recent study to date, Farrington and his colleagues (Farrington, Loeber, Stouthamer-Loeber, Van Kammen, & Schmidt, 1996) found no consistent racial differences in predictive validity for self-reported delinquency.

In short, like official data, much self-report data have limitations when used in the study of ethnic and racial differences in serious violent crime by juveniles. However, data drawn from more recent, methodologically sophisticated self-report studies provide an important alternative picture of what is known about offending compared with that derived from official sources of data. The extent to which results based on official data correspond to those based on self-report surveys increases our confidence in findings of ethnic and racial difference.

Self-Report Victimization Data

There also exists a second major alternative or supplement to the UCR—the National Crime Victimization Survey (NCVS). Initi-ated in 1973, the NCVS is an ongoing survey designed to measure the extent of personal and household victimization in the United States. Interviews are conducted at 6-month intervals with respondents 12 years of age and older who live in residential housing units in the United States. Although not designed to study offender characteristics, the NCVS can be used to assess the characteristics of offenders as *perceived* by their victims. Victims are asked to report on the age, race, and sex characteristics of their assailants.

Like the other sources, the NCVS data are not problem free (Skogan, 1981). The NCVS excludes important types of crime and victims. For instance, no information on homicide is available in the NCVS data set. Also, a significant portion of serious violent crime involves victims that are likely to be missed by the NCVS because of their patterns of residential mobility. A large portion of this mobile population consists of blacks, Hispanics, other minorities, and the poor (Loftin & Mercy, 1995). This may account for Cook's (1985) finding that compared with police data, the NCVS undercounts (by a factor of about three) serious assaults involving gunshot wounds. It is also known that victims of personal crimes involving family members or other nonstrangers underreport their victimizations (Skogan, 1981). Finally, with respect to data drawn from victims regarding the characteristics of their assailants, there is little information that can be used to corroborate the accuracy of the victim's reports of offender attributes. And like UCR data, NCVS data cannot be used to calculate the prevalence and incidence of offending (Laub, 1987).

In sum, although no set of data is without problems, assessments of official, self-report, and victimization data suggest that they are all useful for our purposes in this chapter. We know that each of these sources of data underestimates the overall volume of violent crime. Depending on the type of offense (e.g., sexual assault) and the seriousness of the event (e.g., attempted vs. completed crimes, the extent of injury to the victim, the use of weapons), this underestimate of the extent of violent crime could be by a wide margin. Moreover, each of these sources provides relatively little detailed information about the characteristics of offenders and victims of violence and the nature of violent incidents. Data on the social contexts of violence and other covariates are especially lacking in the UCR and NCVS (Loftin & Mercy, 1995). Apart from the cautions noted above, we know of no reasons why these sources of data cannot be used in tandem to provide reasonably reliable estimates of the extent of racial and ethnic differences in serious juvenile offending.

■ Serious Violent Offending by Race and Ethnicity

We start with a description of youth offending patterns in the United States using the most recent available data from the UCR.[3] Arrest data from the 1995 UCR (displayed in Table 3.1) show that race is related to differential rates of official criminal offending. For example, white youth comprised 65% of the (under 18) arrests for index crimes compared with 31% for black youth. American Indian or Alaskan Native and Asian or Pacific Islander accounted for 1% and 2%, respectively, of the arrests for index crimes.[4] Given that black juveniles (ages 0-17) represent 15% of the U.S. juvenile population (Snyder & Sickmund, 1995), they are overrepresented in arrests for index crimes reported to the UCR.

However, the percentage distribution by race varies considerably by crime type. In 1995, black youth accounted for 49% of the (under 18) arrests for violent crime compared with 48% for white youth.[5] Compared to whites, black youth are most overrepresented in arrests for robbery (60% vs. 37%), and least disproportionately involved in serious property arrests (27% vs. 69%).[6]

In general, patterns of differential criminal involvement by race have been consistent over the past several decades (LaFree, 1995). But although racial differences in arrests for violence have been longstanding, there is evidence of a widening racial gap in rates of homicide during recent years. Snyder, Sickmund, and Poe-Yamagata (1996) report that in 1980, 48% of juvenile homicide offenders were white and 46% were black. In 1994, 61% of juvenile homicide offenders were black and 36% were white. Furthermore, over the period from 1983 to 1992, the black juvenile arrest rate for homicide increased 166% compared with a 94% increase for white juveniles (Snyder & Sickmund, 1995).

When serious crime of all types is considered, a somewhat more complex picture of change over time emerges. For example, Snyder and Sickmund (1995) reported that between 1983 and 1992 juvenile arrest rates for all types of violent crimes increased 82% among white youth and 43% among black youth. Again, however, crime-type-specific data reveal a different pattern of change. In Figure 3.1, we display arrest rates for all violent crime among white and black juveniles for the 1983 to 1992 period. Figures 3.2 and 3.3 show comparable arrest rates for murder and robbery, respectively, during the same period. Because of the differences in the rates of increase, Figure 3.1 reveals that the black-white juvenile arrest ratio for violent crimes actually declined over this same time period (from approximately 7:1 to about 5:1).

The largest racial differences exist for the robbery and homicide arrest rates. For instance, the black-white ratios for robbery

TABLE 3.1 Total Arrests, Distribution by Race, 1995

Offense Charged	Arrests Under 18					Percentage Distribution				
	Total	White	Black	American Indian or Alaskan Native	Asian or Pacific Islander	Total	White	Black	American Indian or Alaskan Native	Asian or Pacific Islander
Total	2,081,391	1,439,825	579,875	24,739	36,952	100.0	69.2	27.9	1.2	1.8
Murder and nonnegligent manslaughter	2,558	1,009	1,477	24	48	100.0	39.4	57.7	0.9	1.9
Forcible rape	4,184	2,250	1,868	28	38	100.0	53.8	44.6	0.7	0.9
Robbery	44,498	16,725	26,799	239	735	100.0	37.6	60.2	0.5	1.7
Aggravated assault	64,255	35,981	26,765	652	857	100.0	56.0	41.7	1.0	1.3
Burglary	102,558	74,694	25,068	1,272	1,524	100.0	72.8	24.4	1.2	1.5
Larceny-theft	387,928	271,234	102,854	5,099	8,741	100.0	69.9	26.5	1.3	2.3
Motor vehicle theft	62,471	36,238	23,864	999	1,370	100.0	58.0	38.2	1.6	2.2
Arson	7,823	6,216	1,429	87	91	100.0	79.5	18.3	1.1	1.2
Violent crime	115,495	55,965	56,909	943	1,678	100.0	48.5	49.3	0.8	1.5
Property crime	560,780	388,382	153,215	7,457	11,726	100.0	69.3	27.3	1.3	2.1
Crime Index total	676,275	444,347	210,124	8,400	13,404	100.0	65.7	31.1	1.2	2.0

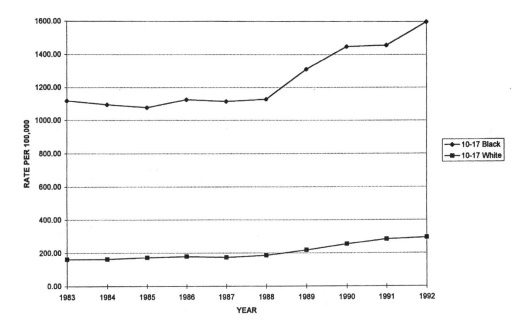

Figure 3.1. Violent Crime Arrest Rates, by Age and Race

ranged from approximately 13:1 to 8:1 over the 1983-1992 period. As was true for juve-nile violent crime arrests, the black-white robbery arrest ratios declined over this 10-

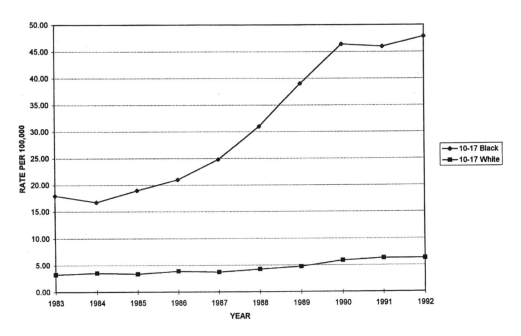

Figure 3.2. Homicide Arrest Rates, by Age and Race

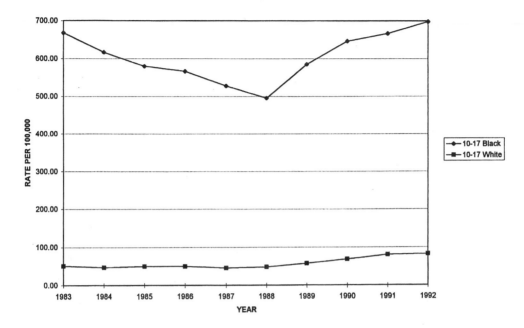

Figure 3.3. Robbery Arrest Rates, by Age and Race

year period. On the other hand, consistent with the findings of Snyder and Sickmund (1995), the racial gap in arrest ratios for juvenile homicide has grown larger over these years, particularly from the mid-1980s on.[7] In 1983 black youth were approximately five times more likely to be arrested for homicide than were white youth; by 1992 the ratio was more than seven to one. Thus, for official data drawn from the UCR, racial differences in offending for serious violent crime appear substantial, but are not invariable over time.

Blumstein (1995) offers insights that might help account for the recent race-specific trends in violence. He attributes the growth in youth homicide since 1985 to the recruitment of young people into illicit drug markets, especially crack cocaine street markets. He hypothesizes that juveniles working in crack markets in inner-city neighborhoods armed themselves for protection and eventually gun carrying and the accompanying use of guns was "diffused" to other teenagers in the larger community. Blumstein presented data showing that the increase in violent crime coincided with an increase in drug arrests among nonwhites in urban areas. According to Blumstein, because there was no apparent increase in the involvement of white juveniles in the drug markets during this time period, yet their homicide rate increased markedly as well, the idea of a gun diffusion process is supported. However, other studies of gangs, drug trafficking, and violence do not support the diffusion hypothesis (Howell, 1997).

The notion of a diffusion process across racial and ethnic lines illustrates the need for more refined group comparisons. We noted earlier the paucity of official data on ethnic as opposed to racial differences in rates of criminal offending. However, a compilation of case studies conducted in several U.S. cities during the 1980s provides some data on rates of violent offending and victimization among youth of Hispanic ancestry.

Rodriguez (1988) showed homicide arrest rates for 10- to 17-year-old Hispanics in New York City to be more than twice those of whites and to be only slightly lower than rates for blacks between 1980 and 1985. Valdez, Nourjah, and Nourjah (1988) found that the homicide death rate for 15- to 24-year-old Latino males in southern California was more than four times the rate for white Anglo males in this age range during 1980. In Chicago during 1980, Latino males between the ages of 15 and 19 had rates of homicide victimization four and one half times greater than those of non-Latino white males. Rates of homicide resulting from assault and robbery were actually higher among 15- to 19-year-old Latinos than among non-Latino blacks (Block, 1988, p. 49). Such findings highlight the importance of taking ethnicity into account when examining official sources of data on youth violence.

Chronic Offenders

Are there racial and ethnic differences in the length of time during which youth are involved in serious crime or in the degree of their involvement? With respect to the chronicity of serious violent offending, data like the UCR are not helpful. But some longitudinal studies using official data have addressed this issue. For example, using police data from the Philadelphia 1945 cohort, Wolfgang, Figlio, and Sellin (1972) found that poor nonwhites were more likely to be frequent offenders and were "most overrepresented in the chronic category" (defined as more than four police contacts; see Table 2.2 in Chapter 2). Race and socioeconomic status were also related to the seriousness of offending; mean seriousness scores were highest for poor nonwhites. These findings were confirmed in the 1958 Philadelphia cohort study by Tracy and his colleagues (Tracy,

Wolfgang, & Figlio, 1985). However, in a reanalysis of the Philadelphia 1945 cohort data, Blumstein et al. (1986) reported that the frequency rates of police contacts of *active* white and black juvenile offenders were similar (ratios under 2:1). Clearly, more data are needed to fully assess the extent to which persistent offending as measured by official data is related to race and ethnicity.

■ Alternative Data Sources

Self-report data. Although early self-report studies (Gold, 1970; Hirschi, 1969) found little difference in rates of delinquency for blacks and whites, studies using more refined measures of delinquency like the NYS show a somewhat different, and more inconclusive, pattern. Using data from the 1976 NYS, Elliott and Ageton (1980) showed that black males were more likely to report involvement in more serious crimes and there were larger proportions of black males among frequent offenders. Similarly, using NYS data from 1976-1980, Elliott, Huizinga, and Morse (1986) found that serious violent offenders in the NYS sample were disproportionately black males. However, these authors found no statistically significant differences in individual violent offending rates by race.

In a recent analysis of the NYS data examining serious violent offending, Elliott (1994) found that at the peak age of offending (17), 36% of black males and 25% of white males report one or more serious violent offenses (i.e., aggravated assault, robbery, or rape). This differential by race is far less than those found in studies using official records (e.g., Wolfgang et al., 1972).[8] Furthermore, there appeared to be little difference by race in the self-reported *ever*-prevalence violent rates (Elliott, 1994).

Interestingly, Elliott (1994) found that almost twice as many blacks as whites continued violent offending into early adulthood. Thus, based on the NYS data, blacks may be more likely than whites to persist in violent offending over the life course. Moreover, these race differences in the prevalence of self-reported violent offending were similar to the race differentials found in official data. Elliott (1994, p. 19) has argued that even though race differences are "small, at best" in the propensity among young males for involvement in violence, for those involved in violence, race becomes more salient in the transition from adolescence to adulthood (see also Anderson, 1990; Sullivan, 1989). Because young blacks are denied full adult status in our society and thus have fewer economic opportunities, they become "more deeply embedded in and dependent upon the gangs and the illicit economy that flourish in their neighborhoods" (Elliott, 1994, p. 19). In this regard, Steffensmeier and Allan's (1995) observation that age-related processes of status attainment in the larger society are reproduced within populations of criminal offenders may well explain some of the racial difference in rates of serious violent crime, as well as lower rates of desistance among blacks.

More recent self-report data from the three projects under the Office of Juvenile Justice and Delinquency Prevention's (OJJDP) Causes and Correlates of Juvenile Delinquency research program shed further light on the issue of ethnic and racial differences in serious offending among whites, African Americans, and Hispanics. For example, Huizinga, Loeber, and Thornberry (1994) reported that in Denver, Pittsburgh, and Rochester whites had a lower prevalence rate for street crimes compared with other racial groups. In Denver, Hispanics had lower prevalence rates than African Americans, but higher rates than whites. However, as dis-

cussed in detail below, the racial/ethnic differences found in Pittsburgh disappeared when residence in underclass neighborhoods was controlled (Peeples & Loeber, 1994).

Victimization data. Analyses of victimization survey data have produced results generally consistent with official records concerning racial differentials in offending (see Hindelang, 1978, 1981). Focusing specifically on juveniles, Laub (1987) found that for the crimes of rape, robbery, assault, and personal larceny, the ratio of black juvenile offending to white juvenile offending was about 4.5:1. Racial differences in offending were particularly pronounced in robbery. More recent NCVS data reveal that victims of personal crime reported that 51% of juvenile offenders were white and 41% were black (Snyder & Sickmund, 1995, p. 47). In the NCVS data, as in official arrest data, blacks are overrepresented as offenders relative to their proportion in the general population. Thus, victimization survey data agree with the patterns found in official and self-report data that the prevalence of serious and violent juvenile offending is higher among blacks than among whites.

■ *Explaining Race and Ethnic Differences in Serious Juvenile Offending*

Although criminologists and other social scientists have long noted the existence of racial and ethnic differences in criminal conduct, including serious juvenile offending, there is a considerable lack of consensus as to how these disparities should be interpreted and explained. None of the dominant theories of the etiology of crime has adequately addressed the question of what accounts for such differences (D. F. Hawkins, 1993, 1995).

Documented racial and ethnic disparities include comparatively high rates of crime and violence found among some white ethnics of the past and among some subgroups of whites and nonwhite minorities living in the United States today. For historical and political reasons, some of these group differences have received greater attention than others (Hawkins, 1994).

Quite surprisingly, criminologists have conducted only a few studies that explore the extent to which socioeconomic disparity accounts for the well-documented differences in rates of violence shown for blacks and whites (Hawkins, in press; Reiss & Roth, 1993). This is unexpected because a common theme in the study of racial differences over the decades has been the question of whether anything remains to be explained when comparisons of social conduct are made between individuals of different races but similar socioeconomic status. It is also surprising because criminologists and other social scientists have tended to attribute high rates of crime among African Americans to their disadvantaged economic status (Tonry, 1995).

There are several reasons for these patterns of omission. The dominant tradition in criminology has been to use individual-level data to search for and document differences between offenders and nonoffenders. This is quite understandable given the rehabilitative ideals that marked the emergence of modern criminology and continue to shape current social policy. However, it is questionable whether individual-centered research protocols alone are useful for improving our understanding of group differences, such as the black-white disparities documented in this chapter. Some have argued that although an examination of the correlates of serious and violent behavior among individuals are valuable and may help identify those persons most likely to offend, such analyses and the interpretations that flow from them may ignore a variety of larger, social structural attributes that distinguish groups (and individuals) in society. For example, the social and developmental life courses of blacks and whites in the United States are products of not only their specific individual experiences but also their membership in historically distinct and unequal social and economic groupings. It is for these reasons that our interpretation of the association between race and ethnicity and serious juvenile offending in this chapter is not based entirely on a review of findings related to traditional individual-level correlates serious crime. Because purely individual-level theories of offense involvement have arguably not provided a very thorough understanding of race and ethnic differences in serious violent juvenile offending, we focus our review on the potential of community-level research and theories to do so.

To begin, we propose that interpretations of group differences inherent in traditional criminological analyses of offending have the tendency of invoking what Sampson and Wilson (1995) call the "individualistic fallacy"—the assumption that individual-level causal relations necessarily generate individual-level correlations. Prior summaries of the literature on race, crime, and violence have shown how the individual-level correlation between race and offending may be partly spurious and confounded with community- or macrolevel context (Jankowski, 1995; Rose & McClain, 1990; Sampson & Lauritsen, 1994, 1997; Sampson & Wilson, 1995). To date, however, individual and neighborhood effects have not been fully disentangled in research on race and crime. We propose that this task must be undertaken to begin to understand the causes of the ethnic and racial differences documented in this chapter.

Community-level explanations ask what it is about community structures and community-specific cultures that produce differential rates of crime across diverse, as well as similar, populations. This contrasts with many extant theories derived from individual-centered approaches that have tended to ask what attributes of individuals and the groups to which they belong lead to criminal involvement. Sampson and colleagues (Sampson & Lauritsen, 1994, 1997; Sampson & Wilson, 1995) and D. F. Hawkins (1995) have described how the work of Shaw and McKay (1969) is most insightful for understanding the relationship between race and crime. Shaw and McKay's contextual interpretation of the correlation between race and ethnicity and rates of juvenile delinquency was prompted by three important findings: (a) high rates of delinquency persisted in certain urban areas regardless of ethnic population composition; (b) rates of delinquency within race or ethnic subgroups varied across urban communities; and (c) rates of delinquency did not increase in lower crime areas as ethnic subgroups migrated to such communities. Because of these and other findings, Shaw and McKay rejected purely individual-level explanations and those that emphasized the importance of race or ethnic group cultural differences, focusing instead on the processes by which delinquent patterns of behavior were transmitted in areas of social disorganization and weak social controls.[9]

To demonstrate that the structural sources of variation in serious juvenile crime are not unique for black versus white youth, Sampson (1987) disaggregated 1980 rates of homicide and robbery by race for juveniles and adults in over 150 U.S. cities. Also disaggregated were explanatory variables of theoretical interest such as poverty, family disruption, joblessness, region, welfare benefits, and city size and density. The analyses showed that black male joblessness predicted variation in rates of black family disruption, which, in turn, was significantly and independently related to rates of black murder

and robbery, particularly by juveniles. Family disruption had a stronger influence on juvenile violence than adult violence, consistent with the idea that microlevel processes related to family structure within communities are related to macrolevel patterns of social control and guardianship, especially those regarding youth and their peers (Sampson & Groves, 1989). Sampson argues that these results indicate why unemployment and economic conditions have had weak or inconsistent direct effects on violence rates in past research—joblessness and poverty appear to exert much of their influence on family disruption, which, in turn, has a direct impact on juvenile violence rates.

The percentage of white and black families headed by a female had a significant relation to both white and black juvenile and adult violence, even though a higher level of family disruption was observed among blacks. In fact, black juvenile violence rates are affected by the same sociostructural factors as white juvenile violence rates. Thus, the causes of violence—whether by juveniles or adults—appear to be similar across race and rooted in the structural differences across communities and cities. Cultural influences are not necessarily dismissed by these findings; rather, such influences are likely to be prompted by the structural conditions of the community.

Because black and white variations in sociostructural context have similar impacts on serious juvenile violence, it becomes necessary to compare the community contexts within which black and white youth are raised. It is the case that in most U.S. cities whether an individual is black or white is confounded with whether one lives in a predominantly black or a predominantly white neighborhood. Consequently, multilevel studies across black, white, and other racial/ethnic groups, such as Hispanics and Asians, are needed to differentiate individual and neighborhood effects. Especially important in this regard would be before-and-after comparisons of individuals of different racial/ethnic characteristics who move to and from neighborhoods with different racial/ethnic compositions. Analyses conducted by numerous scholars (e.g., Massey, 1996; Sampson & Wilson, 1995; Wilson, Aponte, Kirschenman, & Wacquant, 1988), all have underscored the fact that blacks continue to live in communities strikingly different from those of whites. This reinforces our assertion that analysts of racial differences in rates of crime or violence must consider not only attributes of individuals but also the interaction between individual traits and neighborhood characteristics. Racial differences in levels of neighborhood poverty and family disruption are particularly pronounced. Whereas the majority of poor blacks live in communities characterized by high rates of family disruption, poor whites live in areas of relative family stability. According to Sampson and Wilson (1995; see also Sampson, 1987), racial differences in poverty and family disruption are so large that the most deprived urban areas in which whites reside usually are considerably better off than those in which blacks tend to reside.

Moreover, broader changes in the United States over the past three decades have produced increases in urbanization, inequality, and class segregation that have had a disproportionate impact on blacks (Massey, 1996). In 1970, approximately one of every five poor blacks lived in high-poverty areas. By 1980, this proportion had nearly doubled to two of five (Wilson et al., 1988), and by 1990 the percentage of blacks living in such poor areas continued to increase to slightly more than two out of five poor individuals (Kasarda, 1993). Comparably, in 1990 about 1 in 10 poor whites lived in very poor neighborhoods (Kasarda, 1993). These patterns illustrate the degree to which poverty and race

are concentrated, and thus confounded in U.S. cities (Land, McCall, & Cohen, 1990; Wilson, 1987).

The magnitude of the ecological differences under which black and white children are likely to be raised strongly suggests that the individual-level correlation between race and serious juvenile offending is a function of ecological conditions. If this is the case, then controlling for community context should eliminate the individual-level association. Research by Peeples and Loeber (1994) supports this interpretation. Using data from a longitudinal study of male juveniles in Pittsburgh, these authors found that when the "underclass" status of the juvenile's residential neighborhood was controlled, race/ethnic differences in delinquency disappeared. Moreover, the delinquency rates of black youth living in nonunderclass neighborhoods were essentially the same as those of white youth living in nonunderclass areas. These findings support the idea that the association between race and juvenile violence is primarily a function of community context. Similar conclusions have been reached in recent studies of violence among adults that report that racial differences in rates of violence may be largely a function of differences across races in levels of socioeconomic well-being (Centerwall, 1984, 1995; Lowry, Hassig, Gunn, & Mathison, 1988; Muscat, 1988)

These latter observations illustrate the extent to which our understanding of the relationship between race and violence has been limited by the minimal attention paid by researchers to exploring and documenting within-group differences. Black-white comparisons have dominated the literature at the expense of studies designed to study systematically the correlates and causes of differences *within* black, white, and other populations (Hawkins, 1983, in press). Analysts of racial differences have long noted that within-group differences are often as large and as etiologically interesting as differences between groups. For example, accompanying the increasing concentration and segregation of the black poor is the appearance of larger and more numerous black middle-class enclaves. Researchers have shown little interest in comparing rates of serious crime across socioeconomically and ecologically diverse black communities. A recent example of the value of such a comparison can be found in an epidemiological study by Fingerhut, Ingram, and Feldman (1992) of homicide victimization among 15- to 19-year-old U.S. males from 1979 to 1989. They reported that firearm death rates for black youth varied from 143.9 per 100,000 youth in the core areas of the nation's largest cities to 48.2 in small metropolitan areas and to 15.5 in non-metropolitan locations. Indeed, the firearm death rate for black youth in rural areas was lower than the rate for white youth living in the inner city. Racial differences in rates of offending across these areas are likely quite similar since offense rates among youth tend to mirror rates of victimization.

■ Reframing the Research and Policy Agenda on Race, Ethnicity, and Serious Offending

Although our contrasting of individual- and community-centered modes of explanation and research serves certain heuristic purposes, we do not mean to suggest that community-level approaches alone can adequately account for the variety of socioeconomic and psychosocial forces that lead to ethnic and racial differences in rates of serious crime. Rather, explanatory insights and empirical findings that result from community-level investigations highlight the need for researchers to move toward the use of multi-level research designs and theory that reflect

a variety of analytic methods. The use of this multilevel approach is nowhere more important than in the study of serious crime among adolescents, where life course and developmental concerns are paramount and economic and social stressors shape the lives of the most chronic offenders. Contemporary researchers who study crime and other problem conduct among economically disadvantaged children and youth have already begun to acknowledge the need to combine both individual-level and community-level theory and research. It is clear that an understanding of the pathways that lead to youthful involvement in serious crime must include studies of the individual as well as the myriad social and institutional forces that shape his or her life (e.g., Attar, Guerra, & Tolan, 1994). Less clear in many contemporary accounts of youth violence is the extent to which this combination of factors account for observed ethnic and racial differences.

Despite these caveats, we propose that our discussion of the interplay between community- and individual-level research offers several important policy-related insights. Our findings suggest that to be effective, public policies aimed at reducing both current levels of serious and violent juvenile offending and racial differences must be aimed at a transformation of the nation's urban communities. In this regard Sampson and Wilson (1995) and others have argued that the increasing concentration of poverty in urban neighborhoods produces a wide range of negative consequences, including decreased labor force attachment and involvement in quality schools, reduced access to jobs and job networks, and less exposure to conventional role models. They discuss how the concentration of poverty has been fueled by macrostructural economic changes related to deindustrialization. Furthermore, these broader processes and the increasing concentration of poor blacks in urban areas are not accidental; they have been influenced by policy decisions to isolate poor black families in public housing (Bickford & Massey, 1991; Massey & Denton, 1993).

Thus, the contextual approach to understanding the relationship between race/ethnicity and serious juvenile offending requires that theories of community social organization be linked with theories of political economy. Such a perspective focuses on how the sociostructural characteristics of urban neighborhoods affect a community's ability to regulate the behavior of its residents while recognizing that larger social and political processes shape local community structures and cultures.

This theoretical approach suggests that the macrosocial changes in black communities, particularly those in the late 1970s and 1980s, may be key to understanding recent increases in black juvenile violence. Carefully crafted historical studies would undoubtedly show that this same array of social forces (poverty, disorganization, etc.) has chronically affected large portions of the black community for the past century, thus accounting for the persistence of racial differences in rates of crime and violence. Research has shown that serious juvenile and adult offending is associated with an early onset and persistent delinquency (e.g., Moffitt, 1993; Patterson, Capaldi, & Bank, 1991; Sampson & Laub, 1993a). It is also known that family functioning processes influence early-onset delinquency, and that such functioning is in turn associated with life stress and economic hardships (e.g., Gorman-Smith, Tolan, Zelli, & Huesmann, 1996; Simons, Wu, Conger, & Lorenz, 1994). From this perspective, the roots of urban violence among today's adolescent cohorts (and race and ethnic differences across youth) may in part be attributable to childhood socialization experiences that occurred in the late 1970s and 1980s.

There is also evidence that psychosocial stressors associated with exposure to violence itself may also affect the likelihood of youth involvement in serious crime and violence in disadvantaged urban communities. A growing literature, stemming partly from the notion of an intergenerational "cycle of violence," suggests that the repeated witnessing by children of violent acts may itself lead to severe psychosocial stress and possibly higher rates of both violent victimization and offending among them (Jenkins & Bell, 1994; Maxfield & Widom, 1996; Osofsky, 1995; Widom, 1989).

We also note that in addition to the macrolevel, contextual forces described in community-based studies, a variety of less permanent, situational factors likely account for some of the ethnic and racial disparities seen in rates of serious crime (Clarke, 1983; Gabor, 1986; Harries, 1990; Monahan & Klassen, 1982). Many of these situations and circumstances stem from larger macrolevel forces. Others may reflect more fleeting and changeable social circumstances. Reiss and Roth (1993, pp. 17-19) noted that those circumstances and situations thought to be linked to violence include alcohol and drug use, drug trafficking, weapon displays, and threatening gestures. Neither individual-centered nor community-level theories fully account for the etiological impact of most situational factors, and research designs stemming from such theories are not likely to adequately measure them. Miethe and Meier (1994) also remind us that theories and research designs that focus exclusively on offenders may fail to account for the situational interplay between victims and offenders. Knowledge of the nature of this interplay may be of vital importance for the study of adolescents, among whom high levels of aggression are found among both potential (and actual) victims and offenders (Lauritsen, Sampson, & Laub, 1991). A focus on the situational and microcontextual correlates of serious crime may also have the benefit of helping to identify prevention and intervention protocols that may produce more immediate results than those aimed at macrolevel social forces.

The search for causes of ethnic and racial differences in youth crime will also benefit from the use of research methods not routinely used today, but which were quite common among youth gang researchers several decades ago. Studies by Anderson (1994), Jankowski (1995), and Sullivan (1989) provide persuasive arguments in support of the use of ethnographic methods for identifying and examining the effects of the situational linkages between inequality and crime in low-income neighborhoods. These ethnographic accounts suggest that there are limits to which arrest or self-report data alone and analyses and interpretations of them can be used to examine and explain group differences in rates of crime and violence.

As in other areas of criminological research, our explanations for group differences in rates of serious and chronic offending among youth will likely benefit from greater attentiveness to the effects of gender differences. Harris (1996) used a survey research design to assess the attitudes and aggressive behaviors of males and females. She concluded that aggressive behavior is influenced by individual, contextual, and cultural variables. She also noted that among her sample of Anglo, Hispanic, and African American respondents ethnicity sometimes interacted with gender to influence attitudes toward and involvement in aggressive behavior.

Finally, we note that research on the determinants of ethnic and racial differences in serious youth crime will not make significant progress without the use of more inclusive samples of offenders and victims. Our introductory remarks in this chapter and those of Hagan and Peterson (1995) provide some logic and justification for a focus on differences between blacks and whites. Both official record keeping practices and decisions regarding the choice of research sites have tended to foster black-white rather than other ethnic/racial comparisons. But it is clear that the increasing diversity of the U.S. population now means that this contrast alone is insufficient for the scientific study of group differences in rates of criminal behavior. For example, more careful analyses designed to explain the relatively high violence rates of some groups of Native Americans and Latinos, as well as the relatively low rates of some groups of Asian Americans, may help in our efforts to devise policies aimed at the reduction of the extremely high rates of violence found among African Americans.

Indeed, much evidence suggests that the failure of past researchers to disaggregate for the purposes of analysis the nation's black and white populations has also been problematic (Hawkins, in press). For example, in most analyses using national data sources, rates of crime are calculated for roughly 30 million African Americans and more than 200 million persons of European ancestry. This level of aggregation hardly allows for the kind of fine-tuned ethnic, racial, and social class comparisons that we have recommended in this chapter. Such analyses obviously ignore the considerable variation in rates of serious crime found within the black, white, and other populations (e.g., ethnic, regional, and class differences).

The scientific and policy relevance of these latter observations for the study and prevention of serious youth violence is increasingly clear. During the past two decades, the American population has grown more diverse ethnically and racially as large numbers of persons of Latin American, Middle Eastern, and Asian origins have immigrated here. The immigration of persons of African ancestry has also increased. These immigration trends have not only increased the size of nonwhite racial groups in the United States, they have also led to a greater ethnic mix within these groups. As measured by their ethnic and racial diversity, many American cities now look more like they did during the 1890s than during the 1960s. Some official data and anecdotal evidence suggest that these population changes may have already altered the ethnic/racial profiles of serious youthful offenders in some areas of the nation. In some cities, youth groupings and gangs of Eastern European, Asian, Latin American (other than Mexican), and Caribbean (other than Puerto Rican) ancestry are now found among those youth identified as serious and chronic offenders. Thus, broader theoretical integration and multilevel data (both quantitative and qualitative) drawn from more inclusive samples are necessary if we are to truly understand racial and ethnic differences in serious juvenile offending.

■ *Notes*

1. For a general overview of these data sources see O'Brien (1985), and for a detailed discussion of the complexity of measuring violent offending and victimization see Reiss and Roth (1993, especially Appendix B). For a recent review of trends in youth violence over the past 30 years, see Cook and Laub (in press).

2. Limited data on serious violent offenders can be found in juvenile and adult court statistics and, to a lesser extent, on youth incarcerated for violent crimes (see Snyder & Sickmund, 1995). However, acknowledging the potential for bias associated with the screening of cases/incidents of violence the further one moves into the juvenile justice, we do not examine court or correctional data in our effort to assess racial and ethnic patterns in serious violent offending among youth. Since the 1930s, commentators have recognized that the statistic closest to the criminal event was the most reliable and useful for the purposes of scientific research (Sellin, 1931).

3. Although the focus of this chapter is offending, we do note that there are racial and ethnic disparities in victimization. For example, blacks suffer much higher rates of homicide victimization than whites such that homicide is the leading cause of death among young black males and females (Rosenberg & Fenley, 1991). For a recent review of the available data on race-ethnicity and criminal victimization, see Sampson and Lauritsen (1997).

4. Because American Indians, Alaskan Natives, Asians, and Pacific Islanders make up such a small proportion of arrestees for serious violent offending, that is another reason why we restrict our attention in this chapter to white and black offenders.

5. Violent crime is also highly concentrated by sex. For example, in the 1995 UCR males under 18 comprised 86% of the arrests for violent crime. Unfortunately, published tables in the annual UCR and special reports by the FBI (1993) do not provide breakdowns of arrestees by age, race, and sex simultaneously. An examination of serious violent offending across age, race, and gender is beyond the scope of this chapter. However, for an analysis of serious crime by young black women using victimization survey data, see Laub and McDermott (1985).

6. The UCR publish arrest data for cities as well as for the nation as a whole. The racial distribution of arrestees for the crimes of interest here do not change dramatically looking at the data for cities. For analysis of serious offending, race, and urbanism, see Laub (1983).

7. The black and white rates for aggravated assault increased 116% and 94%, respectively, over the 1983-1992 time period. Interestingly, the annual black-white ratios for aggravated assault hovered around 4:1 over this 10-year period.

8. It should be pointed out that it is problematic to compare black:white ratios in prevalence and incidence (frequency) of offending. Prevalence ratios have a ceiling set by the prevalence of offending by whites. For example, a prevalence of 25% for whites sets a maximum black:white prevalence ratio of 4:1. There is no such limit for black:white incidence ratios. Therefore, it is possible that the black:white ratio in self-reports may be less than in official records because of the difference between prevalence and incidence ratios, not because of differences between self-reports and official records.

9. The work of Shaw and McKay has been criticized. For example, Jonassen (1949) pointed out the need to compare the delinquency rates of different racial/ethnic groups in the same area as well as the delinquency rates of the same racial/ethnic group in different areas (as Shaw and McKay did). For more details, see Jonassen's (1949) critique and Shaw and McKay's (1949) rejoinder. More recently, Bursik and Webb (1982) found that the relative rates of delinquency were not stable after 1950 and that neighborhood rates of delinquency were responsive to population changes in those neighborhoods. In fact, the greatest increases in delinquency rates of neighborhoods occurred when blacks moved from a minority to a majority. Nevertheless, social disorganization and accompanying weak informal social controls within the neighborhood still appear to be a viable explanation of these processes (Short, 1969).

CHAPTER 4

The Contemporaneous Co-Occurrence of Serious and Violent Juvenile Offending and Other Problem Behaviors

■ *David Huizinga & Cynthia Jakob-Chien*

This chapter examines the concurrent relationship of serious and violent juvenile (SVJ) offending to other problem behaviors during periods of active offending. The problems examined include drug use, school problems, psychopathology, and victimization. The overlap with other problem behaviors, such as involvement in various forms of delinquency and gang membership, is considered by Loeber, Farrington, and Waschbusch (Chapter 2, this volume) and by Le Blanc (Chapter 9, this volume).

With the exception of drug use, few studies focus on the overlap of SVJ offending with other problems and problem behavior, and those that do are frequently based on select samples, whose representativeness within the general serious offending popula-

tion is unknown. For this reason, findings from the Denver Youth Survey (Huizinga, Esbensen, & Weiher, 1991) are used to augment summaries from the literature. In the following, the overlap of drug use, school problems, psychopathology, and victimization with SVJ offending are each considered separately, and in a final section the overlap of various combinations of problems and delinquency is considered.

It is important to note that the descriptions in this chapter of the contemporaneous overlap of problem behaviors should not be construed to represent causal relationships between them. Rather, they serve to expand the description of the group of individuals identified as SVJ offenders and further indicate the nature and experiences of these individuals. Other chapters in this book examine these factors in correct temporal ordering to appropriately identify them as risk and causal factors related to serious and violent offending (see Chapter 5 by Tolan and Gorman-Smith, Chapter 6 by Lipsey and Derzon, and Chapter 7 by J. David Hawkins et al., this volume).

■ The Overlap of Serious and Violent Offending and Drug Use

There is a consistent finding across many empirical studies that as the seriousness of offending increases, so does the seriousness of drug use, both in terms of types of drugs used and in frequency of use. Thus, a greater proportion of serious and violent offenders use alcohol, marijuana, and other illicit drugs, and on average, they use these drugs with greater frequency than do other offenders or individuals. Reciprocally, many studies also report that a greater proportion of serious drug users, those using alcohol, marijuana, and/or other drugs, and those using these drugs with a higher frequency, are more serious delinquents. The findings are quite robust and are described in both national and local studies with a wide variety of sampling designs, including national and local probability samples of households, probability samples of school students, and select or targeted samples of offenders and drug user groups (Dembo et al., 1991; Elliott & Huizinga, 1984; Elliott, Huizinga, & Menard, 1989; Fagan, Weiss, & Cheng, 1990; Fergusson, Lynskey, & Horwood, 1996; Harrison & Gfroerer, 1992; Inciardi, Horowitz, & Pottieger, 1993; Johnson, Wish, Schmeidler, & Huizinga, 1991; Loeber, Van Kammen, Krohn, & Huizinga, 1991; Saner & Ellickson, 1996; Thornberry, Huizinga, & Loeber, 1995; White,

Pandina, & LaGrange, 1987; see also other reviews, e.g., Gandossy, Williams, Cohen, & Harwood, 1980; White, 1990).

There is variation across studies in the reported extent of overlap and strength of the relationship between alcohol, other illicit drug use, and serious delinquency, and there is variation in these relationships by age, drug, and temporal period. Nevertheless, the replication of the observed drug use-crime relationship across studies and across at least the past two and a half decades suggests a rather robust and enduring relationship.

To illustrate the relationship between drug use and serious and violent offending, data from the Office of Juvenile Justice and Delinquency Prevention's (OJJDP) Program of Research on the Causes and Correlates of Delinquency that includes similar longitudinal studies conducted in Denver, Pittsburgh, and Rochester are used (Thornberry et al., 1995). The prevalence of alcohol use and of a combined measure of marijuana and other drugs within "street," "other serious," "minor" and "nonoffender" groups for youths aged 13 to 17 is taken from Loeber et al. (1991) and given in Table 4.1. Street offenders are involved in serious violent and nonviolent offenses that are of concern to the general public (serious assaults, rapes, burglary, thefts over $100, drug sales, etc.). Serious offenders are involved in other serious offenses for which there is not as much concern (e.g., thefts under $50, joyriding, minor assault), and minor offenders include those who are involved only in status and public disorder offenses. The relationship between drug use and serious delinquency is illustrated by the observation that a greater proportion of the more serious street offenders are drug users than is any other delinquent type, and, in general, as seriousness of delinquency decreases, so does the percentage of that group that is in-

TABLE 4.1 Drug Use Among Types of Offenders: Denver, Pittsburgh, and Rochester, 1990 (in percentages)

Type of Offender in	*Marijuana and Other Drugs*[a]		*Alcohol Only*[b]	
	Offender Type Who Are Drug Users	Drug Users Who Are Offenders	Offender Type Who Are Alcohol Users	Alcohol Users Who Are Delinquent
Denver				
Street (21%)	37	51	29	26
Other serious (22%)	15	21	29	27
Minor (30%)	13	25	25	32
Nondelinquent (28%)	1	2	13	15
Pittsburgh				
Street (21%)	23	70	46	32
Other serious (29%)	5	23	31	30
Minor (11%)	1	2	33	13
Nondelinquent (39%)	1	5	20	25
Rochester				
Street (15%)	51	53	37	17
Other serious (23%)	17	28	42	30
Minor (14%)	10	10	56	23
Nondelinquent(49%)	3	9	20	30

a. Relationship between type of offender and drug use is statistically significant at the .001 level (chi-square, 3 *df*).
b. Relationship between type of offender and alcohol use is not statistically significant (chi-square, 3 *df*).

TABLE 4.2 Prevalence and Frequency of Drug Use Among Types of Offenders

Type of Offender	*Alcohol*		*Marijuana*		*Other Drugs*	
	%	Frequency	%	Frequency	%	Frequency
Serious violent (9%)	58	61	34	137	9	—[a]
Serious nonviolent (9%)	51	29	25	73	7	—
Minor (25%)	38	25	14	34	3	—
Nondelinquent (57%)	15	13	3	24	1	—
Females (*N* = 524)						
Serious violent (5%)	47	32	31	(164)	4	—
Serious nonviolent (5%)	56	32	36	(80)	4	—
Minor (26%)	45	31	16	37	5	—
Nondelinquent (64%)	15	13	3	7	1	—
Males (*N* = 580)						
Serious violent (14%)	61	69	35	129	11	—
Serious nonviolent (13%)	49	29	21	67	8	—
Minor (23%)	32	16	11	36	1	—
Nondelinquent (50%)	14	14	3	(33)	1	—

NOTE: Relationship between type of offender and prevalence of alcohol use, marijuana use, and drug use is statistically significant at the .001 level (chi-square, 3 *df*), with the exception of other drug use for females. Differences in prevalence between offender types are significant at the .001 level (ANOVA). Relationship between type of offender and user frequency of alcohol and marijuana use is statistically significant at the .01 level (chi-square, 3 *df*), with the exception of marijuana use for females. Differences in mean user frequency by offender type are significant at the .01 level for alcohol and for marijuana for the total sample.
a. Estimates based on insufficient number of cases (fewer than 20) are enclosed in parentheses and considered unreliable, and estimates with too few cases for analysis are indicated with a dash.

TABLE 4.3 Prevalence of Problem Use and Delinquency Type (in percentages)

Type of Offender	Problem Use, Alcohol			Problem Use, Marijuana			Problem Use, Other Drugs		
	Total	Male	Female	Total	Male	Female	Total	Male	Female
	Prevalence of problem use of drugs among types of offenders								
Serious violent	30	33	21	10	12	0	1	1	0
Serious nonviolent	22	19	31	9	9	12	2	2	4
Minor	10	10	10	4	2	5	0	0	1
Nondelinquent	12	2	2	1	1	1	0	0	0
	Prevalence of delinquency type within groups of problem users								
Serious violent	34	44	15	29	46	0	—[a]	—	—
Serious nonviolent	24	24	24	29	32	23	—	—	—
Minor	29	23	40	29	13	55	—	—	—
Nondelinquent	13	2	21	15	10	23	—	—	—

NOTE: Relationship between type of offender and problem use of alcohol, marijuana, and other drug use is statistically significant at the .001 level (chi-square, 3 df), with the exception of other drug use for males. Differences in prevalence rates between offender types are significant at the .001 level (ANOVA), except for other drug use for males.
a. Estimates based on insufficient number of cases for analysis are indicated with a dash.

volved in drug use. (Because drug sales are included in the street crimes measure, and drug use and sales are often correlated, additional analyses for a measure excluding drug sales have been conducted and confirm the general findings reported here.) Examining the relationship from the perspective of drug use indicates that roughly three quarters of the drug users are also serious street delinquents at each site.

Additional illustration of the drugs-serious delinquency overlap is given in data from the Denver Youth Survey (DYS). The DYS data used throughout this chapter are from 1990 when the respondents were 11, 13, 15, and 17 years old ($N = 1,184$). In these analyses, another delinquency typology is used. Serious violent offenders are those engaged in aggravated assault, robbery, rape, and gang fights. (Gang fights are included, because in a majority of reported fights individuals were left cut and bleeding and often unconscious or hospitalized, with injuries comparable or exceeding other aggravated assaults.) Serious nonviolent offenders are those not engaged in

serious violence but who are engaged in thefts over $50, burglary, auto theft, and so forth. Minor offenders are those engaged only in less serious minor property crimes, minor assaults, and public disorder crimes. Nondelinquents are those not involved in delinquency, with the exception of involvement in status crimes and a few trivial offenses.

The prevalence of drug use and annual frequency of use among users is given in Table 4.2 for different kinds of offenders. In general, serious offenders, both violent and nonviolent, had the highest prevalence of alcohol, marijuana, and other drug use. (Although for alcohol for girls, differences in prevalence between minor and serious offenders are small.) Similarly, the average frequency of use, among those using alcohol and marijuana, was generally higher among serious offenders than among other youth, and this was especially true for marijuana.

The prevalence of problem use is displayed in Table 4.3 for different types of offenders. Problem drug use was measured by individuals who reported that their alcohol or drug use resulted in problems with the police, at school, with their families, with their peers or others, or resulted in accidents. As seen in Table 4.3, a greater proportion of serious offenders of both genders that used alcohol reported problems related to their alcohol use than did minor or nonoffenders. For males, this rate was highest among serious violent offenders, whereas for females the rate was highest among the serious nonviolent offenders.

For males, similar patterns hold for marijuana. Serious offenders had the highest rate of problem use of marijuana, and they constituted a disproportionate share of marijuana users. For female users, the pattern is also similar. However, none of the female serious violent offenders reported using marijuana. Prevalence of problems associated with other drugs was quite small, although such problem use was restricted to delinquent groups.

It should be noted that within any offender type, the prevalence rate of problem use for any drug is only about one third or less, so that the serious offenders as a group cannot be characterized as problem users. On the other hand, as seen in the lower portion of Table 4.3, for males, serious offenders make up over two thirds of all problem users. For females, less than half of problem users are serious delinquents.

As these data and those of many other studies attest, there is a clear relationship between drug use and serious delinquent behavior. However, several comments about this relationship are in order. First, the exact levels of the relationship found in various studies vary by site, age, sex, and nature of sample. Although there is agreement about the general finding, there is no one magic figure that specifies the extent of overlap of drug use and serious delinquency. Even data from different years of longitudinal studies that have the same sample and site provide different results

(see, e.g., Elliott et al., 1989; Loeber, Van Kammen et al., 1991).

Second, although the relationship is robust, it would be incorrect to assume that all, or even most, serious delinquents are serious drug users. And, conversely, it would be wrong to assume that all serious drug users are SVJ offenders. This observation is important, because it calls into question the existence of a single problem behavior syndrome that lumps drug use, delinquency, and other problem behaviors into one problem behavior construct.

Third, it is now commonplace to note the existence of the drugs-crime relationship, and then to ponder whether this relationship reflects (a) that drugs cause crime, or (b) that crime leads to drug use, or (c) that the relationship is spurious and simply reflects the fact that both behaviors are dependent on other underlying social and personal factors. An attempt can then be made to test these propositions in empirical data using advanced statistical techniques. Unfortunately, the relationship is not monolithic or simplistic. It is possible for all three propositions to be true when applied to certain populations or groups of youth, and, as illustrated above, there are sizable numbers of serious delinquents who are not serious drug users, and sizable numbers of serious drug users who are not serious delinquents. For some youth, the desire for drugs may lead to various forms of delinquency, including serious delinquency, to obtain resources to buy drugs (see, e.g., Inciardi et al., 1993); for others, involvement in a delinquent peer group that uses drugs may lead to drug use (see, e.g., Akers, Krohn, Lanza-Kaduce, & Radosevich, 1979; Krohn, Lizotte, Thornberry, Smith, & McDowall, 1996); and others, who do not use drugs, may be involved in serious violence. In addition, there is a fourth hypothesis about the relationship of drugs and serious delinquency. That is, for some youth they may be reciprocally related, so that delinquency and drug use are mutually reinforcing (Thornberry, 1987).

Given these various observations about the relationship between drug use and serious offending, what meaning do they have for policy? Johnson et al. (1991) noted that in a national sample, the small group (less than 5%) of serious delinquents who are also serious drug users account for a disproportionate amount (well over half) of all serious crimes. Thus, identifying these individuals, who clearly exemplify the serious drug-serious crime connection, and providing successful interventions for them are of importance in reducing the overall volume of crime. A review of alternatives for intervention is provided by Inciardi et al. (1993), who emphasize the potential of therapeutic communities. Identifying these youth may not be easy, however, because a large proportion are not known to the justice system as serious offenders during a time of active offending (Huizinga et al., 1996). Early and effective prevention strategies that attempt to redirect or reduce future delinquency and drug use are also needed.

■ The Overlap of Serious and Violent Offending and Mental Health Problems

Criminal behavior, especially violence, committed by persons who are mentally ill is often of public fascination and concern, and mentally ill offenders are assumed to be especially dangerous and feared (Howells, McEwan, Jones, & Mathews, 1983; Marzuk, 1996). On the other hand, mental illness may be seen as an excusing condition for the commission of criminal behavior, and offenders are seen as less culpable or blameworthy for their criminal acts (Szasz & Alexander, 1968). Moreover, apprehended serious offenders with mental health problems may be in need of mental health services, but because screening and treatment options are often not available, these youth present special challenges to the juvenile justice system (Woolard, Gross, Mulvey, & Repucci, 1992).

Given the public and practical interest in the potential relationship between serious crime and mental health problems, it is surprising that there is very little empirical knowledge about the co-occurrence of serious and violent offending and mental health problems in juvenile populations, and most of that which does exist is based on unrepresentative captive or detained samples. There is a growing body of literature on adult offenders and mental illness (see, e.g., the entire June 1996 issue of the *Archives of General Psychiatry* for articles and references), but a focus on juvenile offenders, who commit a sizable proportion of serious and serious violent crimes, is not in evidence. Moreover, the few that include a juvenile focus often examine childhood and adolescent traits as predictors of future offending behavior, focus on conduct disorder or minor offending, or examine correlations or linear models between mental health problems and criminal behavior *variables*, none of which permit determination of the actual level of co-occurrence or overlap of serious offending and mental health problems.

How extensive is the overlap between serious violent and serious nonviolent offending and mental health problems? Given the paucity of information from general population studies, the answer is, we really don't know. To provide some illustration, however, data from the DYS are used. As described above, self-report delinquency measures were used to identify serious violent, serious nonviolent, and minor delinquents and non-delinquent individuals. Parent reports of their child's mental health problems were obtained using the Child Behavior Checklist (Achenbach & Edelbrock, 1983), and parents also reported on the use of mental health services by their child. In addition, measures of youth self-esteem and social isolation are used. The data for psychological problems are from the three oldest cohorts when they were 13, 15, and 17 years of age.

The prevalence of various mental health problems within the serious violent offender, serious nonviolent offender, minor offender, and nonoffender groups (defined above) is given in Table 4.4. For this purpose, individuals in the top quartile of the psychological problem measures were considered to display psychological problems. Included are measures of externalizing and internalizing symptoms, depression, uncommunicative, obsessive-compulsive, socially withdrawn, hyperactive, and aggressive problems. Significant group differences are indicated by a line separating the groups. Because statistical significance is dependent on sample sizes, some differences that appear to be substantively significant are not statistically different, especially for girls.

Not surprisingly, for the total sample and for males, serious violent offenders score significantly higher on externalizing symptoms and aggressive behavior. With these exceptions, however, differences in the prevalence of most other psychological problems lie between nondelinquents and delinquents. For most problems examined, both statistical and substantive differences between delinquency groups are small and nonsignificant, and delinquents of any kind have a higher prevalence of psychological problems than do nondelinquent youth.

It would thus appear that about half of the serious violent offenders display externaliz-ing and aggressive, "acting out" behaviors that are consistent with their violent offending. With this exception, however, for both genders, elevated levels of psychological problems are seen for all categories of delinquents and the lowest prevalence of mental health problems is found among the nondelinquents. Psychological problems do co-occur with serious and serious violent offending, but often at the same rate as for other, less serious delinquent groups. Also, it should be noted that with the exception of the externalizing and aggressive behaviors, very roughly about one third of the serious or serious violent offenders display high levels of each psychological problem. Although this is a sizable proportion, it would nevertheless be incorrect to characterize the group of serious or serious violent offenders as having psychological problems.

Given that a sizable proportion of serious and serious violent offenders do display psychological problems, it is interesting to see how many parents sought help for their child for these problems. The prevalence of mental health help seeking by parents of members of different delinquent groups is given in Table 4.5. As can be seen, a greater proportion of families of SVJ offenders sought help from a minister, rabbi, or priest than any other group, and this group also had the highest proportion seeking help from a mental health professional or agency. It is noteworthy that the rank ordering of the prevalence of seeking professional help matches that of the delinquent types. A greater proportion of the more serious offenders seek help. Similar findings are reported by Stouthamer-Loeber, Loeber, and Thomas (1992) from the Pittsburgh Youth Study. They found that greater proportions of the parents of moderately serious and serious seventh-grade male delinquents (42%-47%) sought help for mental health problems than did less serious delinquents (28%).

TABLE 4.4 Prevalence of Mental Health Problems Among Types of Offenders (in percentages)

Mental Health Problem and Type of Offender	Total	Male	Female
Externalizing problems			
Serious violent	<u>49</u>	<u>48</u>	53
Serious nonviolent	36	34	41
Minor	<u>27</u>	<u>30</u>	23
Nondelinquent	20	21	19
	**	**	ns
Internalizing			
Serious violent	35	3	<u>27</u>
Serious nonviolent	36	33	<u>42</u>
Minor	<u>29</u>	<u>29</u>	29
Nondelinquent	21	21	20
	*	*	*
Depression			
Serious violent	34	34	34
Serious nonviolent	37	38	36
Minor	<u>30</u>	<u>35</u>	26
Nondelinquent	23	24	22
	**	*	ns
Uncommunicative			
Serious violent	29	30	27
Serious nonviolent	37	35	41
Minor	29	28	29
Nondelinquent	21	21	21
	**	ns	ns
Obsessive-compulsive			
Serious violent	<u>43</u>	47	34
Serious nonviolent	34	<u>37</u>	25
Minor	<u>32</u>	25	37
Nondelinquent	24	25	24
	**	**	ns
Socially withdrawn			
Serious violent	37	36	41
Serious nonviolent	26	26	26
Minor	30	24	35
Nondelinquent	24	25	23
	ns	ns	ns
Hyperactive			
Serious violent	29	35	<u>7</u>
Serious nonviolent	37	38	36
Minor	30	34	27
Nondelinquent	24	27	21
	ns	ns	ns
Aggressive			
Serious violent	<u>49</u>	<u>48</u>	53
Serious nonviolent	33	32	41
Minor	<u>31</u>	<u>32</u>	<u>30</u>
Nondelinquent	19	19	20
	**	**	**

NOTE: General relationships between types of offenders and listed psychological problems are statistically significant at the .01 level (chi-square, 3 *df*), except for socially withdrawn and hyperactive. Level of statistical significance between offender type means indicated by * = less than .05, ** = less than .01, and *ns* = nonsignificant. Significant differences between groups are indicated by dividing lines.

TABLE 4.5 Prevalence of Mental Health Help Seeking Among Types of Offenders (in percentages)

Type of Offender	Friends/ Relatives	Minister/ Rabbi/Priest	School Personnel	Mental Health Professional/ Agency
Serious violent	17	11	7	22
Serious nonviolent	20	5	9	18
Minor	10	4	8	14
Nondelinquent	9	3	4	12
	**	**	ns	ns

NOTE: Level of statistical significance between offender type means indicated by * = less than .05, ** = less than .01, and ns = nonsignificant.

Two variables related to mental health, self-esteem and social isolation, have sometimes been described as being associated with delinquency. There is a rather traditional view that low self-esteem causes violence and that aggression or violence is one way of gaining prestige and esteem. This view has led to esteem-building activities in prevention and intervention programs. However, there is sufficient justification to question this view and to argue that it is high self-esteem and threats to high esteem that lead to violence (Baumeister, Smart, & Boden, 1996). Also, it is assumed that aggressive/violent individuals would be rejected by individuals around them and become socially isolated, and there is some evidence for this in childhood (Dishion, Patterson, Stoolmiller, & Skinner, 1991). However, whether this isolation extends into adolescence is questionable.

To address these questions, data from the DYS were used to examine differences between the offender types identified above in self-esteem and social isolation. This examination revealed no differences between the offender types on these variables. In fact, for both boys and girls, the statistical distributions were essentially identical. Given this, there clearly is a need for further examination of the causal relationship between these variables and serious delinquency, especially because affecting levels of these variables is a goal of some delinquency interventions.

■ *The Co-occurrence of Serious and Violent Offending and School Problems*

There is a widely held belief and considerable empirical evidence that school problems (poor academic performance, truancy, and dropout) are related to delinquent behavior. The relationship of school problems and delinquent behavior has been demonstrated in many studies and over a long historical period (see, e.g., Brier, 1995; Elliott et al., 1989; Elliott & Voss, 1974; Fagan & Pabon, 1990; Gold & Mann, 1984; Gottfredson, 1981; Maguin & Loeber, 1996; O'Donnell, Hawkins, Catalano, Abbott, & Day, 1995; Thornberry, Esbensen, & Van Kammen, 1991; Thornberry, Moore, & Christianson, 1985). Although the meaning of this relationship may not be completely understood, because arguments (a) that delinquency leads to school problems, (b) that school problems lead to delinquency, (c) that the relationship is reciprocal, and (d) that the relationship is spurious, with both being dependent on other causal variables, all have their advocates.

TABLE 4.6 Academic School Achievement, in Grades (in percentages)

Type of Offender	As and Bs			Cs			Ds and Fs		
	Total	Male	Female	Total	Male	Female	Total	Male	Female
	Grades achieved among types of offenders								
Serious violent	32	28	43	53	53	54	15	19	4
Serious nonviolent	49	49	54	42	44	36	8	7	10
Minor	51	39	62	42	50	34	8	11	4
Nondelinquent	64	60	68	31	34	27	5	5	5
	Types of offenders among youth with different grades								
Serious violent	5	8	3	14	17	8	21	29	4
Serious nonviolent	8	13	4	11	14	6	10	11	11
Minor	22	18	25	28	27	29	27	30	22
Nondelinquent	64	61	67	48	41	57	42	30	64

NOTE: Relationship between type of offender and school grades is statistically significant at the .001 level for total sample, males and females (chi-square, 3 *df*).

As with other co-occurring problems examined in this chapter, because most general population studies do not include a focus on serious delinquents and studies involving select samples of serious delinquents or individuals with school problems do not provide the information needed to assess co-occurrence issues, the co-occurrence of SVJ offending and school problems is not often examined. Moreover, many studies examine variable-oriented correlation or linear models that do not provide information about the actual level of co-occurrence. For this reason, data from the DYS are used to illustrate the extent of overlap of school problems and serious delinquency.

Academic School Achievement

The top half of Table 4.6 gives the percentage of each delinquent type that is getting As and Bs, Cs, and Ds and Fs. As can be seen, a greater percentage of nondelinquents received As and Bs. However, roughly one third of the serious violent offenders also received As and Bs, about one half received Cs, and

about one fifth received Ds and Fs. Similarly, roughly one half of the serious nonviolent offenders received As and Bs, 40% received Cs, and 10% received Ds and Fs. Thus, academic success and delinquency were correlated. Yet, in terms of co-occurrence, the largest proportion, over three quarters, of each delinquent group, including serious offender groups, received "satisfactory" grades of As, Bs, or Cs. Also, as illustrated in the bottom half of Table 4.6, the group of youth who had academic difficulty in school includes members of each delinquent type. In fact, the largest proportion of those getting Ds and Fs were nondelinquents.

As found in many other studies, there was a statistically significant relationship between academic troubles in school and delinquency and between academic troubles and serious delinquency. However, as these data illustrate, the extent of co-occurrence or overlap was not large. It would be wrong to characterize serious delinquents as individuals having academic trouble in school, and it would be wrong to characterize those having academic trouble in school as delinquent.

TABLE 4.7 Prevalence of Truancy Among Types of Offenders (in percentages)

Type of Offender	Truancy Among Offender Type			Offender Type Among Truants		
	Total	Male	Female	Total	Male	Female
Serious violent	68	69	64	20	29	9
Serious nonviolent	54	53	57	16	22	9
Minor	41	38	45	31	26	37
Nondelinquent	20	15	23	34	23	46

NOTE: Relationship between type of offender and truancy groups is statistically significant at the .001 level for total sample, males and females (chi-square, 3 *df*).

TABLE 4.8 Prevalence of School Suspension Among Types of Offenders (in percentages)

Type of Offender	Suspension Among Offender Type			Offender Type Among Those Suspended		
	Total	Male	Female	Total	Male	Female
Serious violent	55	59	42	21	26	12
Serious nonviolent	42	45	31	16	19	9
Minor	30	40	20	30	28	32
Nondelinquent	15	18	12	34	27	48

NOTE: Relationship between type of offender and school suspension is statistically significant at the .001 level for total sample, males and females (chi-square, 3 *df*).

Truancy and School Suspension

The relationship between truancy and delinquency is portrayed in Table 4.7. Truancy is defined as being gone from school for some portion of at least 3 school days. For both males and females, roughly two thirds of serious violent offenders and one half of serious nonviolent offenders were truant. This compares to about 40% for minor delinquents and 20% for nondelinquents. Thus, especially in comparison to others, a high proportion of serious offenders were truants. Examining the overlap from the perspective of the group of truants, it can be seen that, among males, serious offenders account for about one half of all the truants. However, this sizable overlap is not seen for females, where only 18% of truants were serious offenders.

Similar findings hold for school suspension (see Table 4.8). For males, slightly more than half of the serious violent offenders and slightly under half of the serious nonviolent offenders had been suspended from school, as compared to less than 20% of nondelinquents. Although the rates are lower, comparable findings hold for females. These two types of offenders were also disproportionately represented among all those who were suspended, accounting for 45% of those suspended among males and 21% among females.

These findings indicate a substantial overlap between truancy and serious delinquency and between suspension and serious delinquency. However, it should be noted that there was also a sizable proportion of serious offenders who were not truant and who had not been suspended from school. Once again, all serious delinquents cannot be characterized as truants or those suspended from school, and not all truants or those suspended are serious delinquents.

TABLE 4.9 Prevalence of School Dropout Among Types of Offenders (in percentages)

Type of Offender	Dropout Among Offender Type			Offender Type Among Dropouts		
	Total	Male	Female	Total	Male	Female
Serious violent	4	5	0	10	29	0
Serious nonviolent	4	4	5	10	20	5
Minor	3	1	5	25	13	31
Nondelinquent	3	2	5	55	38	64

NOTE: Relationship between type of offender and school dropout is *not* statistically significant for the total sample, males and females (chi-square, 3 *df*).

School Dropout

The relationship between dropping out of school and delinquency is displayed in Table 4.9. As can be seen, at least in this sample, dropout was not common. For males, dropout was slightly more prevalent among serious delinquents, but the difference among delinquent groups was not statistically significant. However, among the group of all male dropouts, 29% were serious violent offenders and 20% were serious nonviolent offenders. Thus, almost half of all male dropouts were serious offenders, and these serious offenders accounted for a very disproportionate share of dropouts.

In contrast, for females, the drop-out rate was constant across delinquency categories. Furthermore, within the group of all female dropouts, the proportion of dropouts accounted for by each delinquent type was proportional to the size of the delinquent group in the population. Thus, only a small proportion of serious offenders, 5% or less, were dropouts. For males, dropout is a potential contemporaneous identifying factor for serious delinquents (because about half of male dropouts were serious delinquents), but only a very small proportion of serious offenders can be identified in this way.

Somewhat comparable results have been found in other studies focusing on dropouts. For example, based on data from the National Longitudinal Survey of Youth, Jarjoura (1996) found that the prevalence of serious violent delinquency ran from 5% to 28% among dropouts, depending on social class and reasons for dropping out. He also found that the prevalence of serious theft among dropouts ranged from 14% to 41%. Chavez, Oetting, and Swaim (1994) report that prevalence of offending among dropouts varies by ethnic or cultural group. They found that among dropouts, prevalence rates ranged from 16% to 18% for cutting someone with a knife, from 17% to 23% for hitting someone with a club or chain, and from 21% to 26% for breaking into a house. The data presented by Chavez et al. also indicate that the prevalence of many offenses among dropouts was often twice or more than twice the prevalence among those still in school. This is similar to Denver findings in which 29% of dropouts were involved in serious violence compared with 14% of those still in school.

Any School Problem

It is also useful to examine the overlap of having any school problem and serious delinquency. For this purpose, the prevalence of those that had any school problem (academic problem, truancy, suspension, dropout) within delinquency type, and the prevalence of each delinquent type within the group who

TABLE 4.10 Prevalence of Any School Problems Among Types of Offenders (in percentages)

Type of Offender	Any School Problem Among Offender Type			Offender Type Among Those With Some School Problem		
	Total	*Male*	*Female*	*Total*	*Male*	*Female*
Serious violent	87	91	76	15	22	7
Serious nonviolent	79	80	76	14	18	7
Minor	65	67	63	29	26	33
Nondelinquent	41	40	42	42	34	52

NOTE: Relationship between type of offender and prevalence of any school problem is statistically significant at the .001 level for total sample, males and females (chi-square, 3 *df*).

had one or more school problems, are given in Table 4.10. As can be seen, the vast majority of serious violent offenders had some school problem, 91% for males and 81% for females. Large proportions of serious nonviolent offenders also had one or more school problems. And, in general, the seriousness of offending is rank ordered by the prevalence within the group of those with some school problem. On the other hand, as can be seen in the right-hand portion of Table 4.9, there are a large number of youth who had trouble at school who were not delinquent, and only a minority of these youth were serious delinquents. Thus, whereas some form of school problem may be considered characteristic of serious delinquents, the majority of those with school problems are not delinquent.

Summary. There is clear indication of overlap between school problems and serious delinquency. The greatest overlap of serious offending and school problems was found for truancy and school suspension, and substantially less overlap for school grades and for dropping out of school. There was sufficient overlap for most problems (dropout for males only) that school problems can be viewed as contemporaneous risk factors for delinquency, and may provide important targets for intervention programs. In addition, consideration of individuals having any one or more of the school problems indicated that the vast majority of serious offenders had some kind of school problem. The converse was not true, however. There are a large number of youth with one or more school problems who are not serious delinquents or even minor delinquents. Finally, it should be noted once again that contemporaneous co-occurrence does not imply causality. School problems and serious delinquency may both depend on other causal factors (Fagan & Pabon, 1990; Jarjoura, 1996; Krohn, Thornberry, Collins-Hall, & Lizotte, 1995; Maguin & Loeber, 1996) or school problems may lead to other proximal factors such as involvement with delinquent peers that in turn lead to serious delinquency (Chavez et al., 1994). The role of school problems as a factor in delinquency is a current issue of research and is further described in other chapters of this book.

■ *The Co-occurrence of Serious and Violent Offending and Victimization*

There is ample reason to suppose that those engaged in serious delinquency are also at risk for being victims of crime and thus that a substantial concurrent overlap may exist between victimization and delinquency.

TABLE 4.11 Prevalence of Victimization Among Types of Offenders (in percentages)

	Violent Victimization					
	Violent Victimization Among Offender Type			Offender Type Among Those Who Are Victims of Violence		
Type of Offender	Total	Male	Female	Total	Male	Female
Serious violent	42	49	22	20	28	7
Serious nonviolent	31	36	16	15	20	5
Minor	28	29	27	34	27	48
Nondelinquent	11	12	9	31	25	40

	Nonviolent Victimization					
	Nonviolent Victimization Among Offender Type			Offender Type Among Those Who Are Victims of Nonviolent Offenses		
	Total	Male	Female	Total	Male	Female
Serious violent	32	28	45	12	15	9
Serious nonviolent	37	37	38	14	19	8
Minor	27	32	21	26	28	24
Nondelinquent	21	20	22	47	38	59

NOTE: Relationship between type of offender and prevalence of violent and nonviolent victimization is statistically significant at the .001 level for total sample, males and females (chi-square, 3 df).

Those engaged in serious violence may also be injured by those defending themselves or in some form of retaliation at a later date. Those delinquents who live in environments that support serious delinquency may also have a greater chance of being victimized by that delinquency. For example, Thornberry and Figlio (1974) suggested that the juvenile years may be characterized by a general behavioral pattern involving both the commission of and victimization by various assaults and property offenses. Similar thoughts and empirical data to support the delinquency-victimization overlap have been given by Singer (1981, 1986), Jensen and Brownfield (1986), Sampson and Lauritsen (1990), and Esbensen and Huizinga (1991). In this section, the contemporaneous overlap of serious delinquency and victimization is illustrated using data from the DYS.

The co-occurrence of violent and nonviolent victimization with various forms of delinquency is presented in Table 4.11. For males, the rates of violent victimization were rank ordered, with serious violent offenders having the highest rate of violent victimization, followed by serious nonviolent offenders, followed in turn by minor offenders and nondelinquent individuals. For females, the nondelinquents had the lowest violent victimization rates, but the rates of violent victimization were highest for minor offenders, followed by serious violent offenders and then serious nonviolent offenders. Thus, for males, being a victim of violence was related to seriousness of delinquent offending and especially to violent offending, whereas for females being a victim of violence was more related simply to being delinquent. However, it should be noted that although delinquent status increases the probability of being a victim of violence, regardless of the delinquent group, less than half reported being a victim of violence.

Examination of the pool of individuals who report being victims of violence, in the top right portion of Table 4.11, indicates that, for males, approximately one fifth to one quarter of the victims came from each delinquent type. Thus, serious delinquents were overrepresented among the victims, because each type made up only about 9% of the population (see Table 4.2 for population prevalence of delinquency types). Male nonoffenders, however, made up roughly one quarter of the victims. Among female victims, the proportion of victims from each type was roughly proportional to that group's representation in the total population. Thus, although there was substantial overlap between being a victim of violence and being delinquent, there were also a large number of nondelinquents who were victims and a large number of delinquents, including serious delinquents, who were not victims of violence. Less than half of serious offenders were victims, and less than half of all victims were serious offenders. There is a clear overlap between violent victimization and delinquency, and violent victimization is a risk factor for concurrent violent offending. However, offenders, and violent offenders in particular, cannot as a group be characterized as victims of violence, nor can victims of violence as a group be characterized as serious or minor delinquents.

The relationship between nonviolent victimization and delinquency is illustrated in the bottom half of Table 4.11. For males, the prevalence of nonviolent victimization was lowest for nondelinquents, with higher and somewhat comparable rates for all the delinquency types. For females, both nondelinquent and minor delinquent groups had substantially lower victimization rates than did the serious offenders. Thus, as with violent victimization, there is a general relationship between nonviolent victimization and delinquency. For either sex, however, only a minority of each delinquent group had been a victim of nonviolent offenses. Also, as indicated in the lower right-hand portion of Table 4.11, for each gender, the representation of each delinquency group in the group of victims was roughly proportional to that group's representation in the population. The overlap of nonviolent victimization and delinquency or serious delinquency was thus not as great as for violent victimization.

In summary, these findings indicate a clear relationship or overlap of violent and nonviolent victimization with delinquency. The strongest such relationships were for males for violent victimization and violent offending, and for females, nonviolent victimization and serious offending. In general, although there was substantial overlap, the majority of delinquent and even serious delinquents did not report being victimized, a sizable proportion of victims were not delinquents, and a majority were not serious delinquents.

■ *Multiple-Problem Youth*

In this last section, we will examine the relationship between combinations of problems and serious delinquency. Included are the problems described individually above—school problems, drug use problems, mental health problems, and being victimized. There are very few studies that have examined all four of these issues simultaneously, so data from the DYS are once again used. For this purpose, individuals were classified as having school problems if they were receiving low academic grades (Ds or Fs), were truant, had been suspended, or had dropped out of school. Drug use problems were indicated by reports that drug use had resulted in a problem for the individual. Mental health problems were indicated by being in the top one quarter of the distribution of internalizing or

TABLE 4.12 Prevalence of Combined Problems Within Offender Types (in percentages)

School Problem	Victim	Mental Health	Drug Problem	Serious Violent T	M	F	Serious Nonviolent T	M	F	Minor Delinquent T	M	F	Nondelinquent T	M	F	Total T	M	F
No	No	No	No	2	3	0	9	9	9	11	8	14	33	34	22	22	20	25
No	No	No	Yes	0	0	0	0	0		1	1		1	1	0	0	1	0
No	No	Yes	No	0	0	0	3	1	7	5	5	5	11	11	10	7	7	8
No	No	Yes	Yes													0	0	0
No	Yes	No	No	5	1	10	7	1	8	14	3	14	11	5	12	11	9	12
No	Yes	No	Yes							0		1	0	0		0	0	0
No	Yes	Yes	No	4	3	5	3	5		4	4	4	4	5	4	4	4	4
No	Yes	Yes	Yes	1		5				0	1		0	0		0	0	0
Yes	No	No	No	18	16	25	17	18	13	18	17	20	20	19	21	19	18	20
Yes	No	No	Yes	6	7	4	4	3	8	5	4	6	1	1	1	3	3	0
Yes	No	Yes	No	9	9	9	11	10	14	13	15	11	8	7	9	10	10	10
Yes	No	Yes	Yes	5	5	5	3	3	4	2	2	2	0	0	1	0	2	0
Yes	Yes	No	No	18	19	15	21	23	15	14	16	12	7	8		11	13	8
Yes	Yes	No	Yes	9	10	8	8	8	7	1	1	1	0	0		2	3	1
Yes	Yes	Yes	No	13	13	17	6	8	0	9	11	8	4	4		6	7	5
Yes	Yes	Yes	Yes	10	13	0	10	8	16	2	1	3	1	0		3	3	2

NOTE: T = total sample; M = male; F = female. Percentages of 0 represent percentages greater that 0 but less than 0.5%. Table entries of "blank" represent true 0.

62

TABLE 4.13 Prevalence of Offender Types Within Combined Problem Types (in percentages)

School Problem	Victim	Mental Health	Drug Problem	Serious Violent			Serious Nonviolent			Minor Delinquent			Nondelinquent		
				T	M	F	T	M	F	T	M	F	T	M	F
No	No	No	No	1	2		4	6	2	12	9	15	83	83	84
No	No	No	Yes							30	39		70	61	
No	No	Yes	No				4	2	5	16	17	15	81	81	81
No	No	Yes	Yes												
No	Yes	No	No	5	5	4	6	9	3	32	34	31	57	52	62
No	Yes	No	Yes												
No	Yes	Yes	No	10	8	6	8	14		23	20	28	60	59	66
No	Yes	Yes	Yes	36	6	1				28	1	28	36	0	66
Yes	No	No	No	9	12	6	8	14	3	24	21	26	59	54	65
Yes	No	No	Yes	22	36	7	15	13	16	48	36	60	16	15	16
Yes	No	Yes	No	9	13	4	10	13	7	33	36	29	49	38	60
Yes	No	Yes	Yes	33	48	16	20	26	13	33	26	42	14		29
Yes	Yes	No	No	15	19	9	18	23	9	32	29	38	35	29	44
Yes	Yes	No	Yes	42	45	33	35	36	33	17	11	33	6	7	
Yes	Yes	Yes	No	19	23	16	9	14		38	35	40	35	28	44
Yes	Yes	Yes	Yes	34	54		34	31	38	20	10	35	13	5	27
Total				9	13	5	9	13	5	25	23	26	57	50	64

NOTE: T = total sample; M = male; F = female. Percentages of 0 represent percentages greater that 0 but less than 0.5%. Table entries of "blank" represent true 0.

63

TABLE 4.14 Offender Type and Number of Problems (in percentages)

No. of Problems	Serious Violent	Serious Nonviolent	Minor Delinquent	Nondelinquent
Percentage of group who are a specific offender type				
0	1	4	13	83
1	7	7	25	62
2	12	14	32	43
3	28	16	32	25
4	34	34	20	13
Total	9	9	25	56
Percentage of group who are a specific delinquency type, males				
0	2	5	10	83
1	9	10	24	57
2	16	19	30	36
3	32	21	27	20
4	54	31	10	5
Total	14	13	23	50
Percentage of group who are a specific delinquency type, females				
0	0	2	16	83
1	4	3	26	67
2	6	8	35	52
3	21	7	39	33
4	0	38	35	27
Total	5	5	27	64

NOTE: Relationship between type of offender and number of problems is statistically significant at the .001 level for total sample, males and females (chi-square, 3 df).

externalizing symptoms on the parent version of the Child Behavior Checklist, and victimization was indicated by being a victim of either a violent or nonviolent crime.

The relationship of multiple problems to serious offending is portrayed in Tables 4.12 through 4.15. Table 4.12 provides the prevalence of individuals with different combinations of problems within delinquency types, and Table 4.13 the prevalence of delinquency types within groups of individuals that have specific combinations of problems. Taken together, these two tables permit examination of the extent of overlap of multiple problems and serious delinquency. In Tables 4.14 and 4.15, the results are further summarized by the relationship between a simple count of the number of problems faced by individuals and their delinquent status.

Table 4.12 indicates that there is a clear relationship between combinations of problems and delinquent status. Serious violent and serious nonviolent offenders were underrepresented in the group of individuals with no problems. Most of these offenders display or experienced some other problems. However, with the exception of those who had school problems *and* who had been victimized, the prevalence of different patterns of problems among offender types was similar to the prevalence of that problem group in the population. The major exception to this generalization were those with both school *and* victimization problems. As can be seen by combining the

TABLE 4.15 Offender Type With Different Number of Problems (in percentages)

No. of Problems	Serious Violent	Serious Nonviolent	Minor Delinquent	Nondelinquent	Total
0	2	8	12	33	22
1	26	27	39	42	39
2	34	39	35	20	27
3	28	16	13	4	10
4	9	9	2	1	3
Percentage of delinquency type with different numbers of problems, males					
0	3	8	9	33	20
1	24	26	38	41	36
2	34	40	38	21	29
3	28	18	14	5	12
4	12	7	1	0	3
Percentage of delinquency type with different numbers of problems, females					
0	0	9	14	32	25
1	34	28	40	44	41
2	36	37	32	19	24
3	29	11	11	4	8
4	0	16	3	1	2

NOTE: Relationship between type of offender and number of problems is statistically significant at the .001 level for total sample, males and females (chi-square, 3 *df*).

last four rows in Table 4.12, these groups account for only 22% of the population, but account for 50% of serious violent offenders and 45% of serious nonviolent offenders. Similar patterns hold for both genders.

Examining co-occurrence in the other direction, that is, the percentage within each multiple-problem group that is a particular delinquency type (Table 4.13), reveals an even stronger relationship. For example, for the total population, among those who had school problems, who had been victimized, and who had a drug problem (row 14), 42% are serious violent and 35% were serious nonviolent offenders, so that 77% of these individuals were SVJ offenders. Similarly, 68% of those with all four problems (row 16) are SVJ offenders. This relationship is dependent largely on males, however. For males, 81% of those with school, victimization, and drug

problems and 85% of those with all four problems are SVJ offenders. For females, the relationship is much less in evidence, and a large proportion of most multiple-problem types were nondelinquent. It should also be noted that given the smaller proportion of females who are serious offenders, some of the prevalence estimates tabled are not particularly reliable.

The findings also suggest that school problems are, in a sense, a necessary condition for serious delinquency. The vast majority (89%) of serious violent delinquents and the vast majority (78%) of serious nonviolent delinquents had school problems (Table 4.12). Also, the influence of drug use among males can be seen in Table 4.13. As illustrated in this table, in general, matching for various combinations of school, victimization, and mental health problems, the addition of drug use problems more than doubles, and sometimes triples, the proportion within the group who are serious delinquents.

Examination of simple counts of the number of problems faced by different individuals reveals a similar picture. As can be seen in Table 4.14, in general, as the count of the number of problems increases, the proportion of that group that was delinquent and the proportion of that group that was seriously delinquent steadily increases. Alternatively stated, as the number of problems increased so did the probability of being a serious offender. Among the group of individuals with four problems, 68% were serious offenders, and for males this figure is 85%. However, it should be noted from Table 4.15 that only 9% of the serious violent and 9% of the serious nonviolent groups had all four problems. These findings hold for males and are not replicated for females. For females, among those with three or four problems, a large proportion were delinquent, but not necessarily serious delinquents.

In summary, it appears that a very large proportion of delinquents had additional problems. Of particular note is the proportion of serious delinquents who had school problems, especially when coupled with other problems, in particular, victimization. Multiple school, victimization, mental health, and drug use problems clearly are a risk factor for serious delinquency, and given the very large proportion of serious delinquents who had multiple problems, in some sense these offenders can be characterized as having combinations of other problems. On the other hand, there are sizable numbers of individuals with multiple problems who are not serious delinquents. The group of individuals with multiple problems cannot be characterized as being serious delinquents, nor can these multiple problems be used to identify the group of serious delinquents.

■ *Summary*

There is evidence of substantial co-occurrence or overlap between each of the problems considered in this chapter and serious violent and serious nonviolent offending, with some variation by gender and delinquency seriousness level. Included are drug use, problem drug use, mental health problems, school problems (poor academic achievement, truancy, suspension, and dropout), victimization, and different combinations of these problems.

There is a generalization about the extent of overlap of most of these problems with serious delinquency. Although this generalization necessarily ignores gender and some delinquent type differences and obscures some important distinctions noted in the chapter, it nevertheless serves as a reasonable summary of the findings. With the exception of multiple school problems and combinations of school and other problems, only about 50% or less of the serious delinquents were also contemporaneously involved or experiencing other specific problems. Also, although serious offenders were disproportionately represented among the group of youth who had a particular problem, they often made up less than half of all those experiencing a problem. Thus, although there is a clear relationship between serious offending and these other problems, it would be incorrect to characterize serious delinquents as having a particular problem, and it would be incorrect to characterize the group of youth having or experiencing a given problem as being made up of serious delinquents.

The obvious exception to this rule is for those having school problems. Eighty percent or more of the serious delinquent youth had one or more school problems. SVJ offenders might thus be characterized as a group as having school problems. It should be carefully observed, however, that the converse is not true. The largest proportion of youth having school problems are not serious delinquent.

As this generalization and other findings indicate, SVJ offenders were likely to have problems besides their involvement in delinquency. Over 90% had at least one other problem, and about 75% had two or more of the problems examined. In this sense, SVJ offenders can truly be considered multiple-problem youth.

■ *Some Recent Findings*

After completion of this chapter, exciting new information became available regarding one program that we had not had a chance to review earlier. The Children at Risk program (Harrell, 1996) was a randomized trial conducted in five sites that offered services to 11- to 13-year-olds. Children were referred to the program from various sources, based on either school risk, family risk, or personal risk factors. Some of the 761 youth received a comprehensive package of services, including educational, recreational, and family services; some children were enlisted as controls; and 203 youth in comparison neighborhoods were also followed. Although earlier reports (Sherman et al., 1997) highlighted the absence of positive effects, more recent analyses (A. Harrell, 1997, personal communication) have shown that participating children were significantly less likely to report current use of gateway drugs or recent participation in drug sales. The same youth also reported significant declines in risk factors in the peer and personal domains.

CHAPTER 5

Development of Serious and Violent Offending Careers

■ *Patrick H. Tolan & Deborah Gorman-Smith*

That serious and violent criminal behavior does not arise anew or serendipitously is among the core assumptions of most delinquency theories and is primary justification for early identification efforts and related prevention activities (Loeber, 1982, 1990; Moore, 1986). Whether the belief is that such behavior is the expression of an unfolding predisposition, training, or the culmination of neurological, psychological, and social damage to the child, there is an assumption that such behavior *develops* in some ordered fashion (Caspi, Elder, & Bem, 1987; Gottfredson & Hirschi, 1986; Moffitt, 1993). According to this view, understanding the course of such behavioral development can provide better understanding,

prediction, and prevention of serious and violent behavior than can occur from simply considering a given behavior at one point in time. Thus, whether a given child's behavior should be considered a harbinger of future crime; how it should be managed by the police, court, and social service systems; and what related policy formulations are optimal are thought to be better determined by understanding the common developmental trajectories of serious and violent behavior than by simply considering a given offense. This contention of orderly and differentiating development rests on three basic areas of scientific investigation: (a) identification of basic behavioral dimensions or parameters of development, (b) specification of the steps or sequences in developmental pathways toward violent and serious delinquency, and (c) identification of the predisposing and precipitating contributors to such development, including specification of their relative predictive power, accuracy, and utility (Blumstein, Cohen, Roth, & Visher, 1986; Loeber, 1982, 1988; Lorion, Tolan, & Wahler, 1987; Tolan & Guerra, 1994b; White et al., 1994). This chapter is concerned with the first two areas. The third area is addressed extensively in this volume in Chapter 6 by Lipsey and Derzon, Chapter 7 by J. David Hawkins et al., and Chapter 8 by Terence Thornberry.

Our evaluation is of the scientific and practical utility of behavioral aspects of the development of serious and violent offending. We first briefly identify, define, and review the empirical evidence of the role of the basic parameters of criminal activity/careers. This section includes a review of the theoretical issues and approaches within a developmental perspective on delinquency, highlighting issues of describing population trends versus predicting the behavior of individuals. The second section focuses on the relative utility of the current leading developmental model, including a test of the model's explanatory utility for explaining serious and violent offending among nationally representative and high-risk samples. The last section provides research and policy implications and recommendations.

A Methodological Note

In evaluating the pertinent scientific information for formulating policy and practices, the major interest is in the dependability and robustness of findings. Particular value should be attached to the extent to which developed schema can differentiate relative risk and can explain most delinquent behavior (Blumstein et al., 1986; Land, 1992). There

are three common features of much of the literature that impose limitations in drawing any conclusions and require qualifying interpretations. First, most studies have focused on population trends, or what is referred to as relations between variables, rather than on the patterns of behaviors over time within individuals or groups of individuals (see Le Blanc & Kaspy, in press, for an example of the latter type of analysis). However, it is transitional patterns within individuals that are most applicable for the decision making of the juvenile justice system.

Thus, much of the literature can illuminate overall trends and suggest likely patterns among the population, but are not able to directly indicate what transitions and outcomes are likely for what individuals with a given history exhibiting a given type of delinquent behavior (Gottfredson & Gottfredson, 1986). For example, we can demonstrate that for diverse populations, serious and violent behavior seems to be the final step in a developmental process of involvement, but the likelihood that a given individual will progress to the next step along that pathway and do so in a given order is harder to predict. Similarly, a critical finding spurring the developmental approach and the related interest in criminal careers is the strong stability coefficients for aggression across time (Farrington, 1991; Olweus, 1979). However, at the same time that there is substantial stability in relative aggression, particularly compared with most other behavioral tendencies, there is less strength in predicting who among those showing high aggression will go on to be involved in frequent and violent crime (Copas & Tarling, 1986; Patterson, 1982). Thus, the population patterns that indicate a general developmental understanding can be described. However, the application for probabilistic decision making is still quite limited (Land, 1992).

A major methodological reason such prediction is difficult is that the occurrence of serious and violent behavior is quite infrequent, even among the most substantially active criminals (Blumstein, Farrington, & Moitra, 1985). This makes the prediction of behavioral sequences statistically difficult enough that specification of pathway components and order can be impractical. The low base rates also impose strain on the power of correlational studies (Copas & Tarling, 1986).

This limited predictive power directly clashes with the judicial interest in prediction (see Moore, 1986; Mulvey & Phelps, 1988; Tolan & Gorman-Smith, 1997, for discussions of these tensions). Accurate identification of the uncommon but most serious offenders is of greatest interest. In most instances the desire is to minimize false positive identifications. Of particular interest is the minimization of stigmatizing and legal system intrusions without justification (Moore, 1986). This constraint means the literature must be interpreted with awareness that although reliable trends are evident, at this time the evidence may fall short of the levels of certainty required for legal decision making and policy formulation about serious and violent delinquent behavior.

A related qualification is that the understanding of developmental sequences and key behavioral dimensions requires frequent assessment of behavior over a long period of time. Few studies have had such features (the three studies constituting the Program on Research on Causes and Correlates of Delinquency are notable exceptions; Thornberry, Huizinga, & Loeber, 1995). Also, few analyses have focused on serious violent behavior as the predicted outcome. Thus, our ability to carefully evaluate and compare developmental approaches remains limited, especially as it applies to serious and violent offending. There is an acute need for analyses that can advance our knowledge of the specific trajectories.

A third limitation is the samples of the majority of studies available to date. Most studies have focused on males of Western European descent, whether in this country or others. There are substantial limitations in applying a knowledge base developed primarily with only one portion of an ethnically diverse society and with little inclusion of females. Fortunately, more diverse samples are being studied and culture and gender issues are included more in evaluating results. However, to date there has been very limited evaluation of how patterns and predictors that vary by social ecologies differ in opportunities, impediments, and other influences on development (Fagan, Piper, & Moore, 1986; Fagan & Wilkinson, in press; Tolan, Guerra, & Kendall, 1995). Much of what can be concluded here may only apply to males and a limited range of ethnic groups.

■ Basic Parameters of Antisocial Behavior Leading to Serious and Violent Delinquency Involvement

As has been the legal tradition for centuries, social scientists attempting to differentiate criminal behavior have focused not only on the specific acts but also on:

1. Frequency of offending over a given time period
2. Variety or number of types of crimes committed within a given time period
3. Seriousness of acts exhibited within a given time period

The basic assumption, which is supported by overwhelming evidence, is that those who are more frequently criminal, engage in more types of crime, or commit the more serious acts are at greater risk for future crime and for

TABLE 5.1 Arrest Probability Relation to Number of Prior Arrests

Study	*Probability of Another Arrest With*				
	1 Prior Arrest	*2 Prior Arrests*	*3 Prior Arrests*	*4-6 Prior Arrests*	*7 or More Prior Arrests*
Philadelphia cohort (Wolfgang, Figlio, & Sellin, 1972)	.35	.54	.65	.72	.80
Cambridge study (Farrington, 1983)	.33	.63	.73 (3-6)		.87
Marion County, Oregon (Polk et al., 1981)	.25	.47	.63 (3-5)		.74 (> 5)

SOURCE: Figures extracted from Blumstein, Farrington, and Moitra (1985) by Nagin and Farrington (1992b); used with permission.

committing more harmful acts (Cohen, 1986; Farrington, 1991; Loeber, 1982; Wolfgang, Figlio, & Sellin, 1972). This finding has been consistent across many studies (Elliott, Huizinga, & Ageton, 1985; Thornberry et al., 1995; Tolan & Lorion, 1988; West & Farrington, 1973; Wolfgang et al., 1972). It appears that frequent offending and serious offending are dependent on the same risk factors (Farrington, 1991). However, even though these dimensions tend to correlate highly, they are not interchangeable (Cohen, 1986; Loeber, 1982; Tolan & Lorion, 1988). There are frequent but not serious offenders and serious but not frequent offenders, and both of these variations can occur with a wide variety of crimes exhibited or with a few occurring (see Snyder, Appendix, this volume). Thus, all three are important parameters to consider in characterizing criminal careers.

Despite some variations in correspondence among a population, the general correlation of frequency, variety, and seriousness suggests they represent important dimensions of evaluating careers and identifying different developmental tracks that could differentiate propensity for extended involvement and exceptional harm to others (Blumstein, Cohen, & Farrington, 1988a). For example, Le Blanc and Kaspy (in press) identified four trajectories of delinquency involvement that differ in seriousness (whether

or not serious delinquency is exhibited), variety (e.g., presence of theft, violence), and frequency (total number of acts). This career approach de-emphasizes interest in a given act as revelatory about the criminal propensity and suggests that the needed focus is on the overall pattern of delinquent behaviors.

These considerations form the basis for a criminal career perspective, which, in turn, has led to research on how careers can be differentiated, to what leads to more serious and more frequent behavior, and to what are the common sequences of development of such behavior. For example, as summarized by Blumstein et al. (1986), several studies show (see Table 5.1) that the probability of another arrest increases with each subsequent arrest and the rates and pattern are quite consistent across samples. It appears that there is an increased probability of further offending of those with more previous offending compared with those with fewer instances. These patterns indicate the value in differentiating the many who have very limited involvement in delinquency from the few who show repeated offending. The findings also suggest that with increasing frequency of offending, the probability of individuals committing a violent offense or other serious offense increases (Tracy, Wolfgang, & Figlio, 1990). For example, Tracy et al. (1990) report that the probability of committing a violent offense increased from .26 following the first offense to .50 after the sixth offense for the 1958 cohort.[1]

The Serious and Violent Few

These arrest patterns led many to look at repeat offenders as a specific subgroup of offenders. Perhaps one of the most recurrent findings is that a small portion of the population commits a large portion of the crimes (see Loeber, Farrington, and Waschbusch, Chapter 2, this volume). In addition, it appears that these most active criminals also commit a larger portion of serious acts than of general crime, and are responsible for much of the violent crime (Moffitt, 1993; White, Moffitt, Earls, Robins, & Silva, 1990). Usually, the rates show that about 6%-8% of the general population of males commits about 50%-70% of the general crime, and 60%-85% of the serious (index) and violent crimes (see Loeber et al., Chapter 2; Gottfredson & Hirschi, 1986; Nagin & Farrington, 1992a; Tracy et al., 1990; Wolfgang et al., 1972).

If a distinct group of very active offenders followed definable trajectories of behavioral problems, this could be used for early identification and discrimination and for determining resource allocation. Subsequent studies suggested that this small group was different from other offenders and nonoffenders in not only the harm they imposed but also the age of initiation of criminal behavior, the likelihood of continuing involvement into adulthood, the likelihood of increasing seriousness of involvement, and the likelihood of showing differences on childhood and adolescent predictors (Farrington et al., 1990; Moffitt, 1993; Patterson, Capaldi, & Bank, 1991; Tolan, 1987). For example, Moffitt (1993) argued that a developmental taxonomy of antisocial behavior could be applied

that differentiated the most deviant over the life course from those likely to show temporary difficulties during adolescence. In part, the rationale was based on noting the consistency of the prevalence of antisocial behavior across the lifespan of males: The rate of conduct disorder during childhood is 4%-9%, the preadolescent first arrest rate is 6%, 3%-6% of young adult males are arrested for violent offenses, and 4% of male adolescents self-report sustained careers of serious violence (three or more per year for 5 years) (see Moffitt, 1993, for her sources).

However, there is substantial diversity among the serious offenders. In a reanalysis of the 1945 Philadelphia cohort data from Wolfgang et al.'s (1972) study, Weitekamp, Kerner, Schindler, and Schubert (1995) examined the career patterns within the 6% group identified by Wolfgang as chronic. They noted that of the 627 who fit this criteria for chronic, only one third were ever violent, and of those who were violent 88.5% had only one such instance. They also noted that 72.7% of aggravated assaults committed by this group were committed by 32 of the 627. In addition, 71.4% of the group's homicides (or 50% of all homicides from this cohort) were committed by 10 individuals. Thus, although it is clear that much crime is concentrated in a small portion of the population, much of the serious and violent offending is concentrated in a small portion of the repeat offending population (see Loeber et al., Chapter 2, this volume).

Age and Crime

The second finding that spurred interest in the distinction between delinquents based on likely offending trajectories is the age-crime curve (Blumstein et al., 1986; Farrington, 1986). Similar to the repeated finding that a small portion of youth commit much of the crime, it is repeatedly found that crime prevalence increases during early adolescence and peaks for most crimes in late adolescence (except drug sales, which peaks in early adulthood; Elliott, 1994). Related to this, most participants in adolescent delinquency desist from involvement by early adulthood, even those most involved during adolescence (Elliott, 1994; Loeber & Le Blanc, 1990). Thus, there is a need to recognize that delinquent behavior is most common during adolescence, but that the eventual outcome can vary substantially among those showing such behavior during adolescence (Moffitt, 1993).

■ The Relation of Early Aggression and Behavioral Problems to Later Serious and Violent Delinquency

The contention that there are different pathways of development for different groups of delinquents has been based on the recognition that relative aggression levels vary among children and that there is remarkable stability in aggression (Olweus, 1979). It is among the most stable characteristics, when measured for populations. As is frequently noted, Olweus (1979) conducted a careful review of longitudinal studies to that date and noted that with correction for attenuation, correlations averaged .63 over time, although diminishing as time between measurements increased. For example, in studies of 10- to 18-year spans, stability coefficients averaged .49. Subsequent analyses have attained lower correlations (usually about .25-.40 for males and lower for females), but still larger than the stability coefficients found for other human characteristics (Cairns, Cairns, Neckerman, Gest, & Gariepy, 1988; Coie &

Dodge, 1983). For example, Huesmann, Eron, Lefkowitz, and Walder (1984) reported that the correlation between aggression at age 8 and conviction was .24 for a crime by age 30, .21 for seriousness of crimes, and .25 for self-reported aggression among males (nonsignificant for females). Thus, aggression level seems an important precursor of risk for later serious and violent offending. In their review of predictors of delinquency, Stouthamer-Loeber and Loeber (1988) reported that childhood aggression level provided a 33% relative improvement over chance. This predictive level is surpassed only by family relations/parenting characteristics.

However, the correlations calculated include the high stability of the nonaggressive majority (nonaggressive throughout life course). For example, in the Huesmann et al. (1984) report, although the aggression levels are more stable for high-delinquency youth (.59) than exploratory delinquents (.37), the highest stability is for nondelinquents (.75). Whether these correlations would vary in the same way if childhood aggression was correlated with serious and/or violent offending only is unclear. There is evidence of some significant relations but not clarification of the extent to which the correlations vary substantially when the nonaggressive portion of the sample is removed (Farrington, 1989a; Magnusson, Stattin, & Dunér, 1983; Pulkkinen, 1983).

A second and perhaps more pertinent question is what proportion of highly aggressive children will commit criminal acts and, related to this volume's focus, the ability of such aggression to predict serious and frequent offending.[2] Patterson (1982b) reanalyzed the data used in the Eron, Walder, and Lefkowitz (1971) study and reported that 38.5% of those in the top 5% of aggression scores were in that same range 10 years later. Thus, only one out of three highly aggressive youths were not rated as such 10 years later. Huesmann et al. (1984) reported that of the highly aggressive youth, 23% of males and 6.3% of females had been convicted of a crime before age 30, versus 10% of low aggressive males and 0% of low aggressive females. Similarly, Pulkkinen (1983) found that peer-rated aggression at age 8 predicted the likelihood of multiple offending (including violence) 12 years later. Multiple offenders had ratings that were twice the score of others. However, the rate of this type of offending among the very aggressive youth was similar to that reported by Patterson (1982). This rate was also found by Osborn and West (1978), with 36.1% of boys rated as exceptionally troublesome at ages 8-10 becoming persistent recidivists. In this case, this rate was seven times that of those not rated troublesome. Similar elevations of risk seem present in the other samples, with one in three of the most aggressive boys likely to become serious criminals. Farrington (1991) reports from his London sample that 20.4% of the most aggressive males at age 8-10 were convicted of a violent offense by the age of 32, compared with 9.8% of the remainder of the sample. Estimates for females are less stable, but there is some suggestion of (a) a lower proportion of high aggression *but* (b) a higher proportion of serious criminal behavior among the more aggressive (Loeber & Hay, 1996).

These data suggest a consistent elevated risk for later violence and serious offending among the most aggressive children, but with rates of one in three or fewer, even among the most serious group. The likelihood of criminal behavior, particularly serious or frequent behavior, is low even for the most aggressive portions. The presence of high aggression may be predisposing but is not an inevitable precursor to criminal behavior, serious, violent, or otherwise.[3]

Disruptive Disorder Characteristics: Difficult to Discipline, Impulsivity, and Defiance

In addition to the utility of childhood aggression in discriminating risk for later serious and violent delinquency, two other childhood behavioral characteristics have been identified as potential precursors to later risk: impulsivity and oppositional behavior (Loeber & Schmaling, 1985). Richman, Stevenson, and Graham (1982) reported that 62% of 3-year-olds exhibiting discipline and impulsivity problems at age 3 showed them at age 8. Campbell and Ewing (1990) reported that 67% of those with such problems at age 6 also showed them at age 9.

Moffitt (1990a, 1993), among others, has argued that childhood hyperactivity and other inattention problems are behavioral precursors of delinquency, with common neuropsychological underpinnings. They point to the relation of early childhood motor problems and impulsivity ratings to later involvement in delinquency (White et al., 1994). However, others have found that it is the presence of aggression with attention problems that relates to later delinquency (Cadoret & Stewart, 1991; Loney & Milich, 1982). Furthermore, there is emerging evidence that it is inattention specifically rather than hyperactivity that relates to later risk (Loeber, 1988). There is also evidence that hyperactivity/inattention relates to the earlier onset of conduct problems and therefore influences risk (Loeber, Green, Lahey, Christ, & Frick, 1992). Moffitt (1990a) traced the involvement in delinquent behavior of children with attention deficit disorder (ADD) symptoms during childhood: 26.8% of the delinquent boys had such symptoms compared with 4.4% of nondelinquents. Of the 35 members of her sample with ADD, 54.3% were delinquent. She also noted that the ADD group seem to have more chronic and more serious involvement than the non-ADD group.In regard to serious and violent behavior, the closest link is from Farrington's (1991) analysis of his London cohort. Impulsivity at ages 8-10 was present in 37% of the nonviolent frequent offenders and 34% of the violent offenders versus 32% of the nonviolent offenders and 20% of the nonoffenders. Similar rates occur for poor concentration. Thus, there is a somewhat elevated rate, but this is general to delinquency.

Other early behavior problems have also shown links to later delinquency risk. The most specific study was by White et al. (1990), using children from Moffitt's New Zealand age cohort study at age 11 to compare those with no psychiatric disorder to those with disorders other than antisocial behavior problems (OD) and those with antisocial behavior problems (AD) to see how they differed on predictors taken at ages 3-5 and on later delinquency. The 57 boys with antisocial behavior disorder at age 11 (6% of participants included in these analyses) were differentiated from the other two groups on levels of motor activity and difficult behavior at ages 3-5 (and a few other indicators). Both the OD and AD groups were more likely to have police contact (32% of AD, 19% of OD, 10% of no-disorder groups). Recidivists were 3.5 times more likely to be among the AD than the OD or no-disorder groups (14% vs. 4% vs. 3%). Also, they committed 12% of the crime, even though they were only 5% of the sample. The OD group committed 8% of the crime, although they were 4% of the sample. Thus, these results suggest an elevated risk for later antisocial behavior if a childhood disorder is present, with the risk greatest (for an early) antisocial behavior disorder. In another analysis from the same study, Moffitt (1993) reported that those boys with repeated above-average ratings of antisocial behavior

between ages 5 and 15 were very likely to be delinquent at ages 13-15 (89%).

Behavior problems, particularly severe and ongoing problems during childhood, were linked to later criminal behavior by Robins and Price (1991). They used an epidemiological sample of adults drawn to identify rates of conduct disorders and other psychopathology among adults with antisocial personality disorder (the psychiatric disorder most similar to criminal behavior). Retrospective interviews indicate that about 4% of the sample reported symptoms equated with severe conduct disorder. Virtually all of the adult antisocial personality disorder cases reported conduct disorder earlier in their life. However, Robins (1986) found no significant difference in childhood conduct disorder of men with adult antisocial personality problems and other than antisocial personality and substance use disorders. Thus, it appears that conduct disorder may, like hyperactivity/inattention, portend adult antisocial behavior as well as mental health problems, but the extent to which conduct disorder is a precursor of later serious and violent offending has not been well documented as yet.

Overall, these analyses show a consistently elevated rate of criminal behavior among male children with hyperactivity/inattention (particularly if aggression is present) and of those showing other disruptive disorders. Also, there is consistency in findings of high, almost universal rates of such problems in the histories of more serious adolescent and adult offenders. At present, the evidence suggests the early problem behaviors elevate risk and their presence often is a requisite for sustained serious and violent offending. However, there is a need to carry out analyses that test these relations specifically to serious and violent juvenile offending versus as risk factors for general delinquent involvement.

Age of Onset

As noted above, initial investigations into variations in patterns of delinquency involvement suggested that age of onset might differentiate groups (see Farrington et al., 1990, for a review). In particular, Blumstein et al.'s (1986) analysis of first-arrest and later-arrest rates showed a nonlinear trend in the relation, with a substantial increase in number of arrests of those first arrested before age 14 than after. Similarly, Tolan (1987) noted that self-reported onset before age 12 related to higher levels of frequency and seriousness of crime. Tolan and Thomas (1995), in a longitudinal test of age of onset effects, found that among a nationally representative sample (the National Youth Survey data; Elliott et al., 1985), those with onset before age 12 were more likely to exhibit serious and chronic offending than those starting later. For example, late-onset offenders' rates of serious offending were one half to one third those of early-onset offenders in the 3 years following onset for males and one half to one seventh the rate per year for females. Moreover, only 2.5% of the late-onset group of males showed serious offending over 2 or more years, compared with 12.7% of the early-onset group. The prevalence of serious offending across 2 or more years for females was 3.8% for late-onset females versus 15.4% for early-onset females. However, in that study, early onset acted more as one of many predictors of involvement, seriousness, and chronicity rather than as a singularly influential determinant. In regression analyses, early versus late onset made the most substantial contribution to explaining chronic serious involvement of males, explaining about 6% of additional variance to the 31% attributable to prior levels of psychosocial predictors. However, age of onset added to but did not supplant psychosocial predictors, prior to or subsequent to onset, such as family characteristics, peer deviances, and deviant beliefs. Early onset contributed only 1% additional variance for females for this dependent variable.

Patterson et al. (1991) used the Oregon Youth Study boys to argue that there are two different pathways, differentiated or at least marked by age of onset. They suggest, as has Moffitt (1993), that the early starters' delinquency is a continuation of childhood aggression and an earlier form of adult criminality. They also suggest differential influence of family and peer risk factors. This study used a latent construct to assess delinquency and other antisocial behavior indicators so the meaning for serious and violent offending is somewhat obscured. However, by Grade 9, 51% of those in the top quartile of antisocial behavior at age 8 had been arrested (early starters) versus 7% of the low-risk group. They also had a rate of repeat offending three times the moderate risk group. They averaged an age of first offense of 10-11.

Tolan and Thomas (1995) found a dynamic relation between age of onset and predictors. Early-onset offenders not only looked like later offenders in many aspects of their delinquency but also on levels of predictors. Once delinquency started, there was no significant difference in subsequent predictor levels between early- and late-delinquency onset groups. Similar dynamic relations have been found by others (Le Blanc, McDuff, et al., 1991). Delinquent involvement seems to affect these predictors such that levels of predictors change post-onset from levels prior to onset.

The limitations of the utility of age of onset are shown in a study by Nagin and Farrington (1992a), who examined the extent to which prior arrest predicts later arrest in Farrington's London sample. In particular, this study was designed to test the extent to which stage dependence (offending at the prior data point) added to explaining later arrest beyond that attributable to early initiation (arrest).

The results indicated that the best overall fit was for a mixed model. However, in a subsequent, stricter testing, once initial differences in involvement were considered, subsequent delinquent involvement provided no additional explanation of probability of later arrest. A later study of Nagin, Farrington, and Moffitt (1995), however, suggested that serious offenders were convicted earlier and at higher rates in early adolescence than nonserious offenders, whether persistently involved or not. Also, some late-onset offenders persisted into adulthood. Nevertheless, there is evidence that earlier onset, particularly a pattern of earlier onset in increasingly serious offenses over time, seems to differentiate risk for serious offending. The specific relation to violent offending needs to be studied.

■ *Theories of Developmental Trajectories and Criminal Careers*

The issues of how many pathways (patterns of behavioral development or sequences of development in delinquency behavior over time), what distinguishes them, and the predictable sequences of development within each remain a matter of considerable debate (Blumstein et al., 1986; Gottfredson & Hirschi, 1986; Loeber & Hay, 1994; Loeber & Le Blanc, 1990; Nagin et al., 1995; Tolan & Loeber, 1993). In addition to the distinction of the frequent/serious and persistent group identified by many and described above, other distinctions have been suggested. For example, some data suggest that it may be useful to distinguish a subgroup of criminals who are primarily drug abusers and seem to be involved in different patterns and types of crime than others (Loeber, 1982; Tolan, Blitz, & Davis, 1992). Similarly, there have been suggestions that thievery is a specialty for some criminals

and that they are highly unlikely to be violent (Bursik, 1980). However, the general finding across most studies is that such specialization is not common or distinctive in regard to outcome and risk factors and therefore has only limited utility in organizing responses to delinquency (Van Kammen & Loeber, 1994). The limited utility demonstrated by these forays and the increasing evidence that aspects such as relative seriousness of early delinquency and age of onset are more discriminating have boosted a developmental approach focused on a few behavioral parameters to a central position in research and policy formulation (Huizinga, Esbensen, & Weiher, 1991; Loeber & Le Blanc, 1990).[4]

Two major developments have provided a base for a developmental perspective. First, attempts to factor and cluster analyze delinquent behavior, without regard to sequence or duration, have suggested that childhood aggression and delinquent behavior can both be divided into overt or defiant acts versus covert or sneaky acts. The former type of behaviors tends to be directly aggressive or rule-breaking defiance of authority, whereas the latter type involves acts such as stealing and lying (Loeber et al., 1993; Quay, 1986). More recent analyses have suggested that one can distinguish how overt/covert an act is on one dimension and how destructive or serious an act is on another (Frick et al., 1992; Loeber & Schmaling, 1985). Thus, there seems to be merit in evaluating how these types of antisocial and criminal behaviors develop and the relations between their development.

Second, as suggested by Loeber (1982) and examined in detail by Loeber and Le Blanc (1990), the study of the natural histories of antisocial behavior indicates that patterns of development over time can be differentiated in many ways. For example, they suggested that the timing of first aggressive and other criminal behaviors, other than those that appear normatively, might distinguish risk.

Similarly, the rate of involvement in increasingly serious delinquency (escalation) or the order of involvement would help distinguish risk. Finally, they suggest that a wider variety of involvement may suggest greater long-term risk; that some children may be developing a more versatile or varied set of delinquent behaviors, whereas others develop only a smaller set of usually less serious offenses (Loeber & Le Blanc, 1990; Tolan & Loeber, 1993).

Several theorists have suggested different pathways related to timing of onset (see, e.g., Elliott, Dunford, & Huizinga, 1987; Farrington, 1989a; Le Blanc, 1996; Loeber & Le Blanc, 1990; Moffitt, 1993; Patterson et al., 1991; Tolan, 1987) and/or by increasing levels of seriousness over time (Elliott et al., 1987; Moffitt, 1993). These pathways models focus on identifying an orderly series of behaviors marked by increasing seriousness that can culminate in serious and violent juvenile offending, and chronicity of involvement. For example, Elliott and colleagues (Elliott, 1994; Elliott et al., 1985; Elliott et al., 1987) have shown that rape and other sexual assault are almost invariably preceded by a sequence of increasing violent and harmful nonviolent acts. Thus, sexual violence represents a developmental end point or pinnacle of serious criminality that presumably serves as a marker of high probability of involvement in other acts and continued risk. These increasingly complex and sophisticated theoretical formulations have provided a strong consensus that a developmental pathways approach has much value for criminological research and great potential for practice. The most promising approach, to date, is to combine the distinction of overt and covert behavior with seriousness sequences (Loeber, 1988).[5]

Through tracing the normal patterns of onset and the relation of onsets of increasingly serious behaviors within the overt and covert domains, Loeber and his colleagues have demonstrated that a developmental pathways approach seems to explain the involvement of most delinquents over time (Loeber, DeLematre, Keenan, & Zhang, in press; Loeber et al., 1993). This model also extends a study of behavioral sequences down to elementary school ages by focusing on predelinquent behavior as well. Through several iterations, this approach has been theoretically developed and empirically evaluated. Thus, in analyzing the natural histories of aggression and the common clusters of aggressive, antisocial, and delinquent behavior in their longitudinal study, Loeber and colleagues have come to identify three pathways of development toward delinquency by splitting overt acts into those that represent aggression and those that represent authority defiance (Loeber, DeLematre, et al., in press; Loeber & Hay, 1994, 1996).

This pathways approach represented a shift toward understanding the developmental processes, represented by sequences of onsets of different behaviors as the preferred approach to identifying seriousness and long-term risk. This approach not only permitted evaluation of what are the likely precursors to later serious and violent delinquency, but it also permits testing of the orderliness and consistency of development across persons within groups (Loeber & Hay, 1996). In several tests with the Pittsburgh Youth Study (approximately 1,500 males, in three cohorts, ranging from age 7 to 13 at the first sampling, followed over 10 years, with 6-month intervals between assessments), Loeber and colleagues demonstrated that the three-pathway model can account for most of the delinquent behavior patterns. They also demonstrated that there is orderly average age of onsets for components in each pathway—with less serious problem behaviors and offenses starting

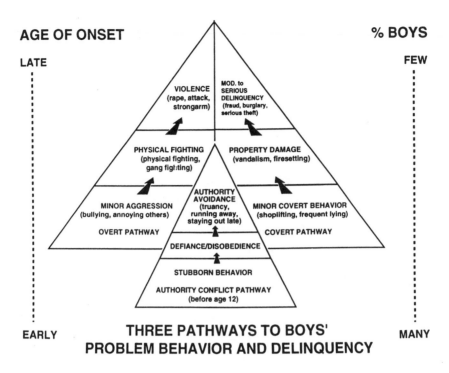

Figure 5.1. Three Pathways to Boys' Problem Behavior and Delinquency
SOURCE: Loeber and Hay (1994).

earlier—and that earlier onset is related to further progression in a given pathway and greater likelihood of involvement in all three pathways (Loeber, DeLematre, et al., in press; Loeber et al., 1993).

Figure 5.1 (from Loeber & Hay, 1994) represents the components of the three pathways and also illustrates a principle that as involvement in serious behaviors within a given pathway occurs, involvement in the other pathways is also more likely. In other words, there is a relation between involvement in more types of antisocial behavior and more serious offending. As can be seen there, the Overt Pathway begins with childhood aggression such as annoying and bullying others as the first step, followed by physical fighting, and then violent crime. The Covert Pathway begins with minor covert behaviors such as shoplifting and lying and then pro-

gresses to property damage such as vandalism and fire setting, and then to what Loeber labels "moderate to serious delinquency," acts such as fraud, burglary, and serious theft. The Authority Conflict Pathway progresses from stubborn behavior in childhood to acts of defiance and open disobedience, to more serious acts such as truancy, running away, and staying out late, and applies to juveniles below age 12 (Loeber & Hay, 1994).

These tests suggest that early identification may be plausible, based not on the presence of a specific behavior or behavioral tendency but on the involvement in a sequence of behaviors and an age-atypical involvement in these behaviors that is earlier than commonly seen. In addition, the more types of problems seen (e.g., overt, authority conflict, and aggression), the greater the likelihood of serious and long-standing delinquency.

■ A Test of Loeber's Developmental Pathways Model

Because there has not been a test of Loeber's theorized developmental pathways for predicting serious and violent behavior specifically, its utility for differentiating the group of interest in this volume needed to be ascertained. To do so we used two data sets. The first is the National Youth Survey (NYS), which was designed to be a nationally representative, general population sample of adolescents. Begun in 1976, this study employed a probabilistic sample of households in the continental United States. Youth were between ages 12 and 17 at the first sampling. Seventy-three percent of the solicited families agreed to participate. The data used for the present analyses were from the first five waves, which had 16% loss from the initial sampling, yielding 1,453 eligible participants. The demographic characteristics of the NYS sample have been described in detail many times elsewhere (see Elliott et al., 1985). This sample was used to test the applicability of Loeber's hypothesized pathway characteristics to a general sample.

To test the applicability to a high-risk sample, we used four waves of data from the Chicago Youth Development Study (CYDS; Tolan, Gorman-Smith, Huesmann, & Zelli, 1997). The boys who comprise the CYDS interview sample were drawn by screening 92% of all boys in fifth and seventh grade of 17 Chicago Public Schools serving the poorer and more crime-ridden neighborhoods ($n = 1,102$) to overrepresent high-risk youth (e.g., half the sample is high risk based on elevated aggression ratings). Of those contacted, 82% (399/486) agreed to be interviewed and interviews were conducted with 362 subjects (75%). Across the first four waves of data, 92% of participants were retained. The sample ($n = 238$) used here represents those with

no missing data for these variables across the four waves. The final sample was 56.8% African American and the rest were Latino. Sixty-two percent of the children lived in single-parent homes; 48% of the families had a total income below $10,000 and 74% below $20,000 per year.

We performed three sets of analyses using these two data sets, with the same analyses for each data set. First, we tested the applicability of the hypothesized developmental trajectories to the two samples, including testing the extent to which synergy (full progress across all three pathways) was notable. Second, we then separated out those in the samples meeting the definitional criteria for serious and for violent offending used in this volume and compared the proportions following the hypothesized developmental trajectories with the proportions from the overall samples. This permits some estimation of whether the models are useful for serious and violent offending in comparison to use for understanding more general delinquency. Finally, we examined whether age of onset for each stage was related to serious or violent offending by comparing age of onset for these two groups with the remaining delinquents from each sample.

Applicability of the Developmental Pathways Model to a Nationally Representative and a High-Risk Inner-City Sample

Because we had only four data points for the high-risk sample and five for the general sample, we focused on determining if there were substantial numbers of youth whose trajectories *did not* follow the hypothesized sequence. A test of exact following requires substantially more data points to be reliable; with 1-year intervals the actual sequence of

TABLE 5.2 Percentage of Loeber's Steps in Theorized Pathways

	National Youth Survey (representative)			Chicago Youth Development Study (high risk)		
Expected Prior Step	*Serious Offender*	*Violent Offender*	*Total Offender*	*Serious Offender*	*Violent Offender*	*Total Offender*
Defiant after stubborn	N/A	N/A	N/A	65	73	67
Avoidant after defiant	N/A	N/A	N/A	74	75	67
Property damage after minor covert	81	90	90	89	96	95
Moderately serious delinquency after property damage	66	68	73	60	67	68
Serious after moderately serious delinquency	65	65	82	66	75	83
Fighting after aggression	N/A	N/A	N/A	93	95	94
Violence after fighting	86	91	93	84	93	94
Full-steps authority conflict	75	92	86	74	89	81
Full-steps covert	76	75	79	79	85	94
Full-steps overt	95	96	97	89	97	100

involvement within the prior year is not determinable. We therefore calculated the proportion of youth in each sample whose exhibition of a later step in a sequence was at or after the earlier step. As can be seen in Table 5.2, for both samples, the vast majority of youth's development of antisocial behavior was congruent with the sequences hypothesized by Loeber and demonstrated with the Pittsburgh sample. This pattern is evident across the three pathways and regardless of how far in the given pathway a youth has progressed.

Similarly, when we calculated the proportion of the serious and violent offending groups following the sequence, the rates are high across pathways and regardless of stage in the sequence. In fact, a larger proportion of serious and violent offenders' developmental sequences follows the pathways than the general sample (see Table 5.3). The CYDS comparison is not significant because of the sample size.

We next evaluated the relation of age of onset to type of offending.[6] ANOVA analyses (Table 5.4 for the NYS) were computed comparing three groups of offenders: nonserious and nonviolent delinquents, serious but nonviolent delinquents, and violent delinquents. Because of the varying age of participants at

TABLE 5.3 Percentage of General Sample of Delinquents Whose Development Corresponded to the Developmental Pathways, Serious and Violent Delinquents

	National Youth Survey[a]			Chicago Youth Development Study[b]		
	General Delinquents	*Serious Delinquents*	*Violent Delinquents*	*General Delinquents*	*Serious Delinquents*	*Violent Delinquents*
Follow pathways	84	89	89	91	82	87
Do not follow pathways	16	11	11	9	18	13
Total	100	100	100	100	100	100

a. $\chi^2 = 8.026$, $p < .05$.
b. $\chi^2 = 3.977$, ns.

TABLE 5.4 Age of Onset of Pathways Steps as a Predictor of Different Delinquent Groups: National Youth Survey

	Group				
	Nonserious, Nonviolent Delinquents (adjusted mean)	*Serious Delinquents (adjusted mean)*	*Violent Delinquents (adjusted mean)*	*Group* F	p
Authority avoidance	.28	.10	−.19	7.291	.001
Minor covert	.06	.02	−.04	.619	
Property damage	.07	−.01	.00	.091	
Moderately serious delinquency	−.17	.16	−.21	5.949	.003
Serious delinquency	N/A	.20	−.26	14.777	.0001
Fighting	.06	.04	−.05	1.400	

NOTE: Means are standardized and adjusted for age as a covariate.

the initial sampling, for each sample we provide adjusted standardized means, with age entered as a covariate. As can be seen in Table 5.4, the trend among the NYS is for the violent group to have the lowest adjusted mean and the nonserious nonviolent offender group to have the highest (the exception is for moderately serious delinquency). Statistically significant differences were found in age of onset among the NYS sample for authority avoidance, moderately serious delinquency, and serious delinquency of the groups. As expected, the violent group had earlier onset of authority avoidance than the other two groups and earlier serious delinquency than the serious (but not violent) group.

When applied to the high-risk inner-city population, no significant differences were found and the trends did not suggest a generally earlier age of onset for the violent or serious offenders. These results suggest a less orderly development and differentiation by onset age in this population. This may be due to the sample being all young adolescents and overrepresentative of high-risk youth living in high-risk neighborhoods.

Thus, the analyses suggest that for general populations there is substantial cross-validation of the relation between age of onset and involvement in serious and violent offending. There are few differences between violent and serious offenders. For the high-risk inner-city sample, these characteristics are not demonstrated. This test differs from those applied previously to Loeber's Pittsburgh Youth Study sample in the emphasis on differentiating violent and serious offending from other delinquent careers. In addition, the CYDS is half Latino and half African American, whereas the Pittsburgh Youth Study is split between non-Hispanic Whites and African Americans. Also, the CYDS sample analyses are based on four data points. Those reported by Loeber and colleagues usually rely on more data points. Finally, the CYDS oversampled for high-risk youth, so the distinctions found for more general samples may not be found with this sample. However, the differences may also reflect a different social ecology of risk for inner-city youth than for others living in less harmful surroundings (see Hawkins, Laub, and Lauritsen, Chapter 3, this volume; Sampson & Laub, 1993a; Tolan, Henry, Guerra, VanAcker, Huesmann, & Eron, 1996; Tolan & Guerra, in press, for further discussion). The nature and reliability of these variations in findings merit exploration.

■ Conclusions and Recommendations

This review of the literature on behavioral parameters of the development of serious and violent behavior in adolescents suggests that there is an emerging perspective with substantial empirical support for explaining the general patterns of delinquency among general samples. This perspective suggests that the age of onset or the rate of escalation along three types of antisocial behavior helps explain relative risk for serious and violent offending. These three types have been labeled by Loeber and colleagues as *authority conflict, covert problem behavior,* and *overt problem behavior.* It also appears that the synergy or simultaneous involvement in all three relates to risk (Loeber & Hay, 1994).

However, the application of findings to date and the developmental models specified to individual risk and trajectories is less substantiated and remains speculative at this point. It is unclear what the determinants of moving from one level to another are or to what extent following versus not following the pathways relates to risk. Also, the available research has been developed almost exclusively on males, and until recently many studies underrepresented or excluded non-Anglos. The application to an inner-city Latino and African American sample, although all males, did not evidence the ties between relative age of onset and likelihood of violent or serious offending, seen in the Pittsburgh sample (which is about half African American, half non-Hispanic White) or the nationally representative NYS sample. Similarly, almost none of these findings have been tested for females.

It appears that violent and serious offenders can be differentiated from other offenders based on age of onset, presence of childhood behavior problems, and relative aggression level. At this point, these characteristics must be considered risk factors that correlate to greater probability of such behavior, not precursors or pathognomic markers. However, these outlines of relations between early and future behavior are quite valuable advances. For example, as we begin to understand the risk factors that differentiate violent offenders from other offenders, the likely differences in needed interventions can be considered (Gorman-Smith, Tolan, Zelli, & Huesmann, 1996; Tolan & Guerra, 1994b).

There seem to be two steps through research that can be taken that could efficiently provide substantial progress. These steps could advance the depth of our knowledge and the specificity of our understanding of the behavioral parameters related to later serious and violent offending. The first step is to reanalyze the major longitudinal data sets to identify the common developmental sequences of involvement in antisocial and delinquent behaviors and to compare how these sequences differ for serious and violent offenders compared with other offenders and nonoffenders. Through repeated cross-validation and/or meta-analyses, some ascertainment of the importance of the developmental model parameters should be plausible. For example, meta-analyses that examined how patterns varied as a function of demographic characteristics, community type, and individual and other risk characteristics could, perhaps, provide a level of reliable understanding that could permit translation of these promising theoretical contentions and overall trends into policy.

Second, these analyses should be focused on what natural patterns of involvement emerge from longitudinal samples (see Le Blanc & Kaspy, in press, for an example). For example, Tolan and Thomas (1995) found that a substantial portion of the NYS sample shows inconsistent involvement in crime over time. Loeber and Hay (1996) note the growing evidence that some late-starting delinquents persist and have serious involvement, including violence, whereas early starters do not inevitably show increasing seriousness and involvement over time (see also White et al., 1994). These studies suggest there is a need to enrich our findings about population trends with studies that show the relative rate and consistency of patterns of individuals' behavioral development across time within groups. In particular, it will be important to assess how consistent patterns found in one location, gender, or ethnic group are with those found in others (Laub & Lauritsen, 1993).

The results suggest it is premature to base policy on the assumption that there is a group of serious and violent offenders who can be readily identified prior to early adolescence and by their involvement in delinquent behavior. However, there is evidence that there can be methods of identifying relatively small sets of pathways. These pathways then can be used to type delinquents and at-risk groups by probable trajectory. The most promising distinction remains the relative age of onset and the frequency and seriousness of prior involvement over time (Elliott, 1994). However, much work needs to be done following promising tracts. These pathways can then provide the certainty that is needed for criminal justice system decisions (Moore, 1986).

■ Notes

1. These probabilities are greater in magnitude and difference than found with their 1945 cohort, suggesting secular increases in the absolute probability of violent offending as well as the relation to frequency of offending.

2. Another argument is that when one predicts rare events (such as violence) the strategy is to "break down" the sequence to violence on component steps, and predict from one step to the next. This provides better accuracy, but still has limitations for direct policy application.

3. Another critical question is the percentage of violent individuals with high aggression early in life. In analyses that follow that approach the rates are usually high; many violent individuals show early aggression.

4. There is considerable ongoing debate about whether serious and violent offending can be adequately accounted for by a single pathway, the same pathway, or require multiple pathways; that the key discrimination is of serious and violent offenders from other offenders or is to identify the multiple pathways that mark different patterns of serious and violent offending (see Loeber & Stouthamer-Loeber, in press; Patterson, 1982b; Robins & Ratcliff, 1979). Much of this debate remains theoretical at this time due to the difficulties in statistically determining, with confidence, whether a single-pathway or multiple-pathways approach is more valid or powerful. As has been demonstrated, one can fit different models to the same data and the preferability of one over the other re-

mains a matter of judgment, not a statistically verifiable difference (Loeber & Stouthamer-Loeber, in press; Patterson, 1982b). In addition, it may be that serious and violent offending have different models; one may be adequately explained by a single pathway, whereas the other may require multiple pathways. For example, it is rare to have serious offending without a preceding involvement over some time, whereas there are more frequent examples of singular violent acts. It seems likely that violent criminals are a more heterogeneous group. An important step in this area is to apply longitudinal latent class and cluster analytic techniques that can identify the most parsimonious but practically viable set of pathways for serious and for violent offending. Rasch or Guttman scaling could also be applied to determine if theorized sequences function as indicators of increasing risk and if so, for what portion of the population the scaling applies.

5. Criminology continues to struggle with issues of identifying heterogeneity versus universality among serious and violent offenders' behavior patterns. The overlap of serious and violent offending is substantial but not overwhelming (see Loeber et al., Chapter 2 in this volume, and Snyder, Appendix in this volume, for more detailed discussion of the relation of the patterns). Most longitudinal research on pathways to date has been limited in the extent of time over which individuals have been followed and/or the number of points of data over the se-

quence of time. Both characteristics limit the extent to which the critical components and discriminating characteristics of pathways can be identified as well as how well the number of pathways can be determined. Both prospective and retrospective studies have been able to show the sequence and functional relation of antisocial behaviors over time, but there is variation depending on when in the lifespan the measurement has occurred and whether there is retro-

spective examination of the common pathways of those exhibiting serious and/or violent behavior or if risk groups are followed prospectively (see Loeber & Stouthamer-Loeber, in press, for further discussion).

6. For the NYS and CYDS, age of onset is based on the first wave of evidence of offending; the exception is that retrospective inquiry at the first wave of the CYDS was also used.

CHAPTER 6

Predictors of Violent or Serious Delinquency in Adolescence and Early Adulthood

A Synthesis of Longitudinal Research

■ *Mark W. Lipsey & James H. Derzon*

In any birth cohort, the incidence and prevalence of violent and serious delinquency reach a peak during adolescence and early adulthood and are more frequent among males than females (Elliott, 1994; Farrington, 1986; Loeber, Van Kammen, & Fletcher, 1996; Moffitt, 1993). Moreover, a large proportion of the offenses during those peak years are committed by a relatively small number of offenders (Howell, Krisberg, & Jones, 1995; Wolfgang, Figlio, & Sellin, 1972). These circumstances make the concept of early intervention very attractive. Applied to the relatively small number of prospective serious offenders prior to the years of peak offending, effective intervention could potentially prevent some significant portion of the problem behavior and associated social damage that would otherwise appear during their adolescence and early adulthood.

Knowledge about the characteristics that distinguish those juveniles who are most likely to later develop serious delinquent behavior is critical to accomplishing this desirable result. These characteristics can be used to identify juveniles who are at risk for subsequent serious delinquency and, hence, are

AUTHORS' NOTE: The research reported in this chapter was supported in part by grants from the National Institute of Mental Health (MH51685) and the National Institute on Drug Abuse (DA09981).

candidates for preventive intervention. In addition, it is plausible that some of those risk variables are not only predictive of subsequent offending but are among the significant causes of that behavior. Thus, an intervention that favorably alters one or more of these variables should decrease the likelihood that serious offending will subsequently occur. In this regard, predictive risk variables are potentially useful for identifying not only juveniles at risk for subsequent serious offending but also the characteristics of those juveniles that preventive intervention might strive to change (Catalano & Hawkins, 1996; Farrington, 1996a; Lorion, Tolan, & Wahler, 1987; Lynam, 1996; Offord, 1990; Reid, 1993; Tolan, Guerra, & Kendall, 1995; Yoshikawa, 1995; Zigler, Taussig, & Black, 1992).

An essential first step in assessing the prospects for using risk variables diagnostically is to assess the nature and predictive strength of those variables that are presumed related to subsequent delinquency. To be suitable for identifying juveniles at risk, such variables should have sufficient predictive ability to distinguish youth with a relatively high probability of subsequent delinquency from those with a low probability. Moreover, if any of the most predictive variables are to be targets for intervention, they must be of such a nature that they can be favorably altered without insuperable difficulty (i.e., "dynamic" rather than "static"; Andrews & Bonta, 1994). Fortunately for this purpose, a substantial volume of research on the nature and predictive strength of risk variables for delinquency has already been generated (e.g., Elliott, Huizinga, & Ageton, 1985; Kazdin, 1987a; Loeber & Dishion, 1983, 1987; Loeber & Stouthamer-Loeber, 1986, 1987; Robins, 1966; Rutter & Garmezy, 1983; Werner & Smith, 1982; West & Farrington, 1973). Unfortunately for this purpose, it has not yielded a body of empirical findings that is easy to summarize. The volume of research is sufficiently large to be cumbersome; it presents such a diversity of methodological and procedural variations, sample characteristics, timing and intervals of measurement, and the like that findings from different studies cannot necessarily be assumed commensurable, and the particular issue of violent and serious delinquency is somewhat obscured by a range of outcome variables encompassing many less serious forms of antisocial and problem behavior.

The investigation reported in this chapter used the techniques of systematic research synthesis (meta-analysis) to sort out and summarize the complex research literature on the predictive risk factors for adolescent and early adult violent or serious delinquent behavior. A vigorous search was made for published and unpublished research reporting pertinent empirical findings. These were then coded into a database in the form of Pearson product-moment correlation coefficients indexing the strength of the relationship between predictor variables and the criterion variable (*effect sizes* for meta-analytic purposes). In addition, a wide range of descriptive information about the study methods, procedures, samples, and other such characteristics was coded into this database. With all this information systematically coded, it was then possible to use various statistical analysis procedures to examine the relative strength of different types of predictor variables measured at different ages while statistically controlling for between-study differences that would otherwise confound the comparison and aggregation of the relevant empirical findings. General meta-analysis procedures have been well described elsewhere (e.g., Cooper & Hedges, 1994; Lipsey & Wilson, 1996) and will not be detailed here.

These meta-analytic procedures were directed at two major questions: (a) What predictor (risk) variables observable prior to adolescence show the strongest empirical associations with subsequent violent or serious delinquency? (b) Are the largest of these empirical associations of sufficient magnitude to be useful for identifying juveniles at risk for serious or violent delinquency for the purpose of preventive intervention?

■ *Delinquency Risk Database*

The data for the current investigation were drawn from an ongoing meta-analysis of prospective longitudinal studies of the development of antisocial behavior (Derzon, 1996; Lipsey & Derzon, 1992). For the investigation reported here, effect sizes (correlations) for relationships between predictor variables and outcome measures representing serious criminal or violent behavior were first selected from this database. A rather restrictive definition was used for this purpose, emphasizing physical aggression or the threat of physical aggression against persons as the criterion for violent behavior, and index offenses or offenses of comparable seriousness on other scales of severity for delinquent and criminal offenses (Appendix A provides more detail regarding the nature of these outcome variables). After relevant effect sizes had been identified, a further screening revealed that measures of violent or serious delinquency were most frequent for the age 15-25 period when such behavior tends to peak. Measurement of predictor variables was found to be most frequent for two earlier age periods: mean age 6-11 and mean age 12-14. The analysis reported here, therefore, focuses on predictor variables measured either in the age 6-11 or 12-14 range and serious criminal or violent behavior in the same sample when their mean age was somewhere between 15 and 25.

This procedure identified 793 effect sizes from 66 reports of 34 independent studies (see Appendix C: Bibliography of Reports Contributing to the Database). With only 34 source studies, it is obvious that many of these effect sizes came from the same study sample and, hence, could not be considered statistically independent. Therefore, several steps were taken to reduce statistical dependencies in the analyses. First, the 793 effect sizes were sorted according to (a) the predictor construct (20 categories) and (b) the particular subject sample or subsample for which they were calculated. Next, cases with more than one effect size for a given sample or subsample and predictor construct category were identified, and those effect sizes were averaged together to yield one aggregate value (referred to as *aggregated effect size*). After removing two outlier effect sizes for all but descriptive analysis, the remaining 155 aggregated effect sizes were divided into those with the predictor variable measured when the sample was age 6-11 ($N = 68$) and those with the predictor measured at age 12-14 ($N = 87$).

■ *Profile of Effect Sizes in the Databases Used for Analysis*

Table 6.1 presents a summary of the major characteristics of the aggregated effect sizes that comprised the two databases used for analysis. The highlights of the profiles shown there are as follows:

1. The majority of the data came from studies conducted in the United States with a significant portion from Great Britain and Scandinavian countries.

2. The samples on which these effect sizes were based were most frequently drawn from the general population with smaller numbers representing persons in offender or treatment populations (the latter in treatment for something other than antisocial be-

havior per se). Most of these samples were white or ethnically mixed, primarily male, and working class.

3. The number of subjects in the typical sample was 200-500 with attrition less than 5% between predictor and outcome measurement. Predictor variables were generally measured in the 1960-1970 decade for the age 6-11 group and around 1975-1980 and 1985-1990 for the age 12-14 group. Outcome measurement occurred during the 1970-1980 decade for the largest number of studies, with the next largest group since 1985. Thus, the interval between measures was typically 5-10 years for the age 6-11 group and 1-5 years for the age 12-14 group.

4. There were relatively few aggregated effect sizes in each predictor construct category and many more outcome variables represented violence than serious offenses that were not necessarily violent. Predictor variables were somewhat more likely to be measured with surveys or interviews than with records or observations, whereas outcome variables were more likely to be obtained from records. Coders' ratings of the quality of the predictor and outcome measures were mostly *good* to *excellent* in terms of adequately representing the construct category into which they were coded and their general measurement characteristics.

■ Prediction From Age 6-11 Risk to Age 15-25 Violent or Serious Delinquency

The first analysis examined the predictive strength of variables measured during the elementary school years (age 6-11) for identifying those juveniles who engaged in violent or serious delinquent behavior during adolescence and early adulthood (age 15-25). Table 6.2 shows how the effect sizes were distributed according to the predictor constructs, the number of effect sizes from the original database that were averaged to produce the aggre-

gated effect sizes in each construct category, and the total number of subjects in the samples on which each set of aggregated effect sizes is based (Appendix B provides more detail about what was coded into each predictor construct category).

Table 6.2 indicates that available research provides only a limited number of independent estimates of the magnitude of the relationships of interest in this analysis, though each aggregated effect size often summarizes data from a large number of subjects. Table 6.2 also reports the weighted mean of the aggregated effect sizes in each construct category and the results of statistical tests on those effect sizes. Each mean effect size was significantly larger than zero despite the small number of effect sizes in most of the predictor categories. In addition, the Q-test for homogeneity reached significance for about half of the predictor categories, demonstrating that there was more variation among the aggregate effect sizes than would be expected from sampling error alone. To examine the extent to which the effect size variation was associated with differences among the studies in their methodological and procedural characteristics, a multiple regression analysis was conducted. In particular, each individual variable from a conceptually related cluster was added sequentially to a weighted hierarchical regression analysis and retained in the model if the Q-added (an analog to R^2 added) was statistically significant. The clusters of variables defined and sequenced for this procedure were, in order of entry: (a) sample demographics (gender mix, ethnic mix, average age, average socioeconomic status [SES]), (b) population type (dummy codes for general, treatment, and offender populations), (c) timing variables (mean ages at the time of predictor and outcome measurement, length of interval between predictor, and outcome measurement), and (d) method and procedure variables (e.g.,

TABLE 6.1 Characteristics of the Aggregated Effect Sizes Used in This Meta-Analysis: Age 6-11 and Age 12-14 Risk Variables Predicting to Age 15-25 Violent/Serious Delinquency

	Age 6-11 N^a (proportion)[b]	Age 12-14 N (proportion)		Age 6-11 N (proportion)	Age 12-14 N (proportion)
General			**Method features**		
Country in which study was conducted			Mean year predictor was measured		
United States	41 (.59)	62 (.72)	Before 1960	7 (.10)	11 (.13)
Great Britain	19 (.27)	15 (.17)	1960 to 1965	29 (.41)	6 (.07)
Scandinavia	10 (.14)	7 (.08)	1965.1 to 1970	29 (.41)	13 (.15)
Canada	0 (.00)	2 (.02)	1970.1 to 1975	5 (.07)	7 (.08)
			1975.1 to 1980		26 (.30)
Subject features			1980.1 to 1985		0 (.00)
Population sampled			1985.1 to 1990		24 (.28)
General	43 (.61)	48 (.55)			
General and treatment	7 (.10)	1 (.01)	Mean year outcome was measured		
General and offender	5 (.07)	8 (.09)	Before 1960	5 (.07)	9 (.10)
Treatment	12 (.17)	18 (.21)	1960 to 1965	0 (.00)	2 (.02)
Offender	3 (.04)	12 (.14)	1965.1 to 1970	2 (.03)	6 (.07)
Ethnicity			1970.1 to 1975	30 (.43)	12 (.14)
White	35 (.50)	16 (.18)	1975.1 to 1980	30 (.43)	29 (.33)
Minority	9 (.13)	0 (.00)	1980.1 to 1985	3 (.04)	3 (.03)
None dominant	26 (.37)	71 (.82)	1985.1 to 1990		26 (.30)
Gender			Mean interval between measures		
Male	39 (.56)	29 (.33)	One year or less	0 (.00)	21 (.24)
Female	4 (.06)	1 (.01)	1.1 to 5 years	6 (.09)	42 (.48)
None dominant	27 (.39)	57 (.66)	5.1 to 10 years	40 (.57)	21 (.24)
Estimated socioeconomic status			10.1 to 15 years	24 (.34)	3 (.03)
Low	0 (.00)	4 (.05)	Mean number of subjects		
Working	54 (.77)	75 (.86)	200 or fewer	17 (.24)	15 (.17)
Middle and above	16 (.23)	8 (.09)	201 to 500	31 (.44)	42 (.48)
Mean age when predictor was measured			501 to 1,000	7 (.10)	12 (.14)
(age 6-11 group)			More than 1,000	15 (.21)	18 (.21)
6.1 to 6.9	3 (.04)				
7.0 to 7.9	4 (.06)		**Study attrition**		
8.0 to 8.9	14 (.20)		0% to 5%	46 (.66)	65 (.75)
9.0 to 9.9	17 (.24)		5.1% to 20%	7 (.10)	17 (.20)
10.0 to 10.9	11 (.16)		20.1% to 50%	13 (.19)	3 (.03)
11.0 to 11.9	21 (.30)		Over 50%	4 (.06)	2 (.02)
Mean age when predictor was measured			**Measurement features**		
(age 12-14 group)			Predictor construct		
12.0 to 12.9		6 (.07)	Physical violence	0 (.00)	6 (.07)
13.0 to 13.9		6 (.07)	Aggression	8 (.11)	4 (.05)
14.0 to 14.9		46 (.53)	Person crime	0 (.00)	6 (.07)
15.0		29 (.33)	General offenses	2 (.03)	8 (.09)
			Problem behavior	3 (.04)	5 (.06)
			Substance use	2 (.03)	5 (.06)

sample size, attrition, nonresponse rates, data collection method, measurement quality).

The results of this regression procedure are presented in Table 6.3. The major findings were as follows:

1. Two variables in the cluster of subject characteristics attained significant Q values. The first was the proportion of the sample that

was white, with effect sizes lower when that proportion was higher; the second was the age range represented in the sample, with wider age ranges associated with larger effect sizes.

2. The population sampled showed a relationship to effect size with U.S. samples yielding lower effect sizes than those from other countries (primarily Great Britain and Scandinavia).

TABLE 6.1 *Continued*

	Age 6-11 N^a (proportion)[b]	Age 12-14 N (proportion)		Age 6-11 N (proportion)	Age 12-14 N (proportion)
Gender	4 (.06)	5 (.06)	Rated quality of predictor measures		
Ethnicity	2 (.03)	5 (.06)	Poor to fair	6 (.09)	3 (.03)
IQ	3 (.04)	1 (.01)	Good	23 (.33)	26 (.30)
Medical/physical	7 (.10)	0 (.00)	Very good	22 (.31)	39 (.45)
Psychological condition	9 (.13)	2 (.02)	Excellent	19 (.27)	19 (.22)
School attitude/ performance	3 (.04)	3 (.03)	Rated quality of outcome measures		
Antisocial parents	4 (.06)	2 (.02)	Poor to fair	2 (.03)	4 (.05)
Abusive parents	6 (.09)	4 (.05)	Good	30 (.43)	8 (.09)
Broken home	4 (.06)	4 (.05)	Very good	33 (.47)	50 (.57)
Parent-child relations	3 (.04)	5 (.06)	Excellent	5 (.07)	25 (.29)
Family SES	2 (.03)	10 (.12)	How predictor data were collected		
Other family characteristics	5 (.07)	7 (.08)	Survey or interview	39 (.56)	58 (.67)
Social ties	1 (.01)	1 (.01)	Records or observation	31 (.44)	29 (.33)
Antisocial peers	2 (.03)	4 (.05)	How outcome data were collected		
Outcome construct			Survey or interview	25 (.36)	34 (.39)
Violence	58 (.83)	59 (.68)	Records	45 (.64)	53 (.61)
Serious offense	12 (.17)	28 (.32)	Original effect size metric		
Whose status described by predictor			Correlation	11 (.16)	33 (.38)
Juvenile	44 (.63)	51 (.59)	Crosstab or breakout	59 (.84)	54 (.62)
Family or friends	26 (.37)	36 (.41)			

a. Number of aggregated effect sizes.
b. Proportion of aggregated effect sizes.

3. Longer intervals between predictor measurement and outcome measurement were associated with smaller effect sizes.

4. The only variable related to general method and procedure that made a significant contribution to the model was the coder-rated quality of the outcome variables. Composite measures that were diluted by items of limited relevance to violent or serious offending received lower quality scores. Higher quality scores were associated with larger effect sizes.

The regression model presented in Table 6.3 demonstrates that differences between studies in their procedures, samples, and the like accounted for more than 20% of the variation among the effect sizes in this database ($R^2 = .21$). Mean effect sizes would be more comparable across studies, and correspondingly, across predictor construct categories, if these irrelevant differences were partialled out of the effect size estimates. To accomplish this, we added each predictor construct category to the variables shown in Table 6.3 and refit the regression model to develop a set of prediction equations, one for each construct category. These were then used to estimate the mean aggregated effect size for each predictor construct category that would be expected under uniform average values of the variables shown in Table 6.3. The result was a set of "covariate adjusted" mean effect sizes in which the between-study differences on the most influential nuisance variables were statistically controlled. The results are shown in Table 6.4 as adjusted correlation coefficients along with the corresponding odds ratios.

Comparison of the adjusted estimates of the correlation coefficients in Table 6.4 for each predictor construct with the unadjusted estimates presented earlier in Table 6.2 reveals substantial similarity, but a few notable differences in which adjusting for irrelevant between-study differences has altered the relative magnitude of the aggregated mean

TABLE 6.2 Aggregated Effect Sizes by Predictor Construct for Prediction From Age 6-11 to Age 15-25 With Number of Original Effect Sizes and Sample Size

Predictor Construct	N^a	O^b	n^c	Mean Effect Size^d	Confidence Interval Lower	Upper	Q	p
Antisocial behavior								
Aggression	8	107	1,565	.21	.162	.262	4.66	.701
General offenses	2	2	321	.34	.258	.412	1.94	.163
Problem behavior	3	23	1,153	.16	.102	.217	8.89	.012
Substance use	2	2	677	.35	.274	.425	.27	.603
Personal characteristics								
Gender	4	11	2,974	.26	.227	.299	7.13	.068
Ethnicity	2	3	1,909	.18	.130	.220	31.58	.001
IQ	3	12	8,700	.11	.066	.146	8.40	.015
Medical/physical	7	12	3,998	.12	.085	.147	16.15	.013
Psychological condition	9	32	1,980	.22	.174	.258	44.78	.001
School attitude/ performance	2	6	7,958	.10	.058	.146	.03	.861
Family characteristics								
Antisocial parents	4	8	1,049	.27	.204	.325	5.00	.172
Abusive parents	6	7	4,973	.08	.049	.104	11.94	.036
Broken home	3	9	2,620	.06	.020	.103	6.00	.050
Parent-child relations	3	18	717	.16	.081	.228	7.80	.020
Family SES	2	9	4,726	.25	.207	.295	2.64	.105
Other family characteristics	5	12	1,138	.15	.096	.212	10.02	.040
Social factors								
Social ties	1	4	395	.16	.061	.259	.00	—
Antisocial peers	2	4	431	.12	.028	.217	4.35	.037
Total	68^e	281		.16	.149	.171	364.43	.001

NOTE: See Appendix B for descriptions of predictor constructs.

a. Number of aggregated effect sizes.

b. Number of original effect sizes that went into aggregated effect sizes for each construct category.

c. Total sample size represented by all aggregate effect sizes in each construct category.

d. Mean of the aggregated effect sizes in each predictor construct category weighted by the inverse variance.

e. Two outliers removed from original 70 aggregate effect sizes.

effect size. In such cases, the adjusted values should provide the more meaningful comparison across predictor construct categories. What Table 6.4 shows for the relative strength of different categories of risk variables measured at age 6-11 for predicting violent or serious delinquency at age 15-25 is as follows:

1. Many of the predictor constructs were found to have relatively high correlations for prediction of violent or serious delinquency, showing that some prediction is possible from observations made during the age 6-11 period to behavior at age 15-25.

2. The two largest correlations (general offenses and substance use) fell within the family of "antisocial behavior" predictors. Indeed, prior antisocial behavior was the best overall predictor of subsequent antisocial behavior.

3. Male gender, low family SES, and minority race were among the next strongest predictors.

4. Among the family characteristics, only family SES and antisocial parents showed correlations greater than .20.

TABLE 6.3 Weighted Hierarchical Multiple Regression Results for Aggregated Effect Sizes Regressed on Various Sample, Method, and Timing Variables (age 6-11 predictors)

	β^a	B^b	Q^c (df)	p
Juvenile characteristics				
Percentage white	−.4280	−.0017	38.52 (1)	.001
Age range	.4069	.0134	40.57 (1)	.001
Population sampled				
United States versus other countries	−.3703	−.0792	18.78 (1)	.001
Timing				
Predictor-outcome interval	−.3965	−.0154	31.92 (1)	.001
Method				
Measurement quality	.2014	.0298	10.35 (1)	.001
Regression constant		.3330		
Overall model			78.01 (5)	.001
Residual			286.42 (62)	.001
$R^2 =$	.21			

NOTE: Each effect size is weighted by inverse variance.

a. Standardized regression coefficient.

b. Unstandardized regression coefficient.

c. Homogeneity statistic indicating the amount of variance associated with each independent variable; Q is tested as chi-square at the indicated *df* to determine the statistical significance of the regression coefficient.

TABLE 6.4 Adjusted Effect Sizes Representing the Mean Correlation Coefficients and Odds Ratios Expected Under Uniform Conditions According to the Multiple Regression Results (age 6-11 predictors)

Predictor Construct	Estimated Correlation	Estimated Odds Ratio[a]	Predictor Construct	Estimated Correlation	Estimated Odds Ratio[a]
Antisocial behavior			**Family characteristics**		
Aggression	.21	4.40	Antisocial parents	.23[b]	5.04
General offenses	.38	16.68	Abusive parents	.07	1.72
Problem behavior	.13[b]	2.59	Broken home	.09	1.98
Substance use	.30	8.31	Parent-child relations	.15	2.96
			Family SES	.24	5.39
Personal characteristics			Other family		
Gender	.26	18.55[c]	characteristics	.12	2.42
Ethnicity	.20[b]	4.12			
IQ	.12[b]	2.42	**Social factors**		
Medical/physical	.13	2.59	Social ties	.15	2.96
Psychological condition	.15[b]	2.96	Antisocial peers	.04	1.38
School attitude/ performance	.13	2.59			

a. Odds ratio indicating relative odds of subsequent violent/serious delinquency for the 25% of the sample on the high-risk end of the predictor measure (except for gender) assuming 8% overall base rate for violent/serious delinquency.

b. There was significant heterogeneity in the residuals for the regression-estimated mean effect size for these predictor construct categories.

c. Odds ratio here based on relative odds for male 50% of sample.

TABLE 6.5 Aggregated Effect Sizes by Predictor Construct for Prediction From Age 12-14 to Age 15-25 With Number of Original Effect Sizes and Sample Size

Predictor Construct	N[a]	O[b]	n[c]	Mean Effect Size[d]	Confidence Interval		Q	p
					Lower	Upper		
Antisocial behavior								
Physical violence	6	29	7,142	.14	.107	.169	22.41	.001
Aggression	4	21	1,167	.27	.212	.326	10.61	.014
Person crimes	6	27	3,104	.13	.092	.164	14.12	.015
General offenses	8	45	5,841	.27	.240	.292	166.63	.001
Problem behavior	5	11	1,443	.09	.035	.138	11.33	.023
Substance use	5	67	1,599	.07	.024	.122	21.45	.001
Personal characteristics								
Gender	5	25	6,128	.17	.136	.194	25.13	.001
Ethnicity	5	57	3,143	.04	.001	.071	14.22	.007
IQ	1	6	406	.19	.093	.287	.00	—
Psychological condition	2	13	509	.28	.188	.362	.42	.519
School attitude/ performance	3	14	706	.28	.205	.352	3.89	.143
Family characteristics								
Antisocial parents	2	5	442	.25	.154	.340	1.31	.253
Abusive parents	4	34	1,224	.06	.008	.120	6.34	.096
Broken home	4	13	7,432	.10	.078	.127	14.18	.003
Parent-child relations	5	25	2,207	.22	.175	.258	6.79	.147
Family SES	10	61	7,065	.11	.082	.130	28.29	.001
Other family characteristics	7	30	7,173	.09	.061	.108	40.35	.001
Social factors								
Social ties	1	4	232	.47	.341	.599	.00	—
Antisocial peers	4	25	1,462	.43	.375	.478	10.39	.016
Total	87	512		.15	.139	.156	785.76	.001

NOTE: See Appendix B for descriptions of predictor constructs.

a. Number of aggregated effect sizes.

b. Number of original effect sizes that went into aggregated effect sizes for each construct category.

c. Total sample size represented by all aggregate effect sizes in each construct category.

d. Mean of the aggregated effect sizes in each predictor construct category weighted by the inverse variance.

5. Juveniles at risk on the stronger predictor variables were 5-20 times more likely than those not at risk to engage in subsequent violent or serious delinquency.

6. Despite the statistical control of some of the most influential of the irrelevant between-study differences, the residuals around some of these estimates were still heterogeneous, showing that there was significant variability among the aggregated effect sizes represented in the estimate (indicated by superscript *b* in Table 6.4). That is, different studies are generating significantly different estimates of the strength of the predictive relationship in these cases for reasons that are not controlled by the covariance adjustments applied in Table 6.4.

■ Predicting From Age 12-14 Risk to Age 15-25 Violent or Serious Delinquency

The second analysis investigated the predictive relationships of variables measured during the 12-14 age period with violent or serious delinquency measured in the sub-

TABLE 6.6 Weighted Hierarchical Multiple Regression Results for Aggregated Effect Sizes Regressed on Various Sample, Method, and Timing Variables (age 12-14 predictors)

	β^a	B^b	Q^c (df)	p
Population sampled				
Treatment population	−.2267	−.0840	28.45 (1)	.001
United States versus				
other countries	−.1062	−.0312	8.15 (1)	.004
Method				
Attrition	.1546	.0020	15.86 (1)	.001
Sample size	−.2021	−.0029	25.41 (1)	.001
Measurement quality	.2037	.0532	28.27 (1)	.001
Regression constant		−.0152		
Overall model			142.75 (5)	.001
Residual			643.01 (81)	.001
$R^2 =$	.18			

NOTE: Each effect size is weighted by inverse variance.
a. Standardized regression coefficient.
b. Unstandardized regression coefficient.
c. Homogeneity statistic indicating the amount of variance associated with each independent variable; Q is tested as chi-square at the indicated *df* to determine the statistical significance of the regression coefficient.

sequent age 15-25 interval. This analysis thus focuses on the period just preceding the age of peak delinquent activity and examines variables that may identify those juveniles who will be most seriously delinquent a few years later. Table 6.5 presents the distribution of the 87 aggregated effect sizes over the predictor constructs of interest.

Table 6.5 shows that, as in the earlier analysis, there were relatively few aggregated effect sizes representing each predictor construct, though they generally summarize information from a larger number of original effect sizes and a sizable subject sample. It also reveals that each mean aggregated effect size is statistically significant (the confidence intervals do not include zero) and that the effect sizes in 12 of the 19 predictor construct categories are heterogeneous (statistically significant Q values). As with the age 6-11 predictors, some of this heterogeneity was presumed to be associated with between-study differences in samples, methods, and the like. The effect size was, therefore, used as the dependent variable in a weighted hier-

archical multiple regression analysis that paralleled the one described earlier. The results are presented in Table 6.6 and include the following as the major findings:

1. The populations represented by the samples in these studies were important to effect size. Samples from treatment populations showed smaller effect sizes than those from other populations (mostly general population samples); similarly, effect sizes from U.S. samples were smaller than those from other countries.

2. A number of methodological variables were related to effect sizes. Greater attrition between predictor and outcome measurement was associated with larger effect sizes, and studies based on larger samples yielded smaller effect sizes. In addition, the coder-rated quality of the outcome variables was correlated with effect size. Larger effect sizes were associated with higher quality outcome measures, and composite measures diluted by items of limited relevance received lower quality scores.

As in the earlier analysis, the results of the multiple regression shown in Table 6.6 were

TABLE 6.7 Adjusted Effect Sizes Representing the Mean Values Expected Under Uniform Conditions According to the Multiple Regression Results (age 12-14 predictors)

Predictor Construct	Estimated Correlation	Estimated Odds Ratio[a]	Predictor Construct	Estimated Correlation	Estimated Odds Ratio[a]
Antisocial behavior			School attitude/ performance	.19	3.85
Physical violence	.18[b]	3.61			
Aggression	.19[b]	3.85	**Family characteristics**		
Person crimes	.14	2.77	Antisocial parents	.16	3.16
General offenses	.26[b]	6.20	Abusive parents	.09	1.98
Problem behavior	.12[b]	2.42	Broken home	.10[b]	2.12
Substance use	.06[b]	1.60	Parent-child relations	.19[b]	3.85
			Family SES	.10[b]	2.12
Personal characteristics			Other family characteristics	.08[b]	1.84
Gender	.19[b]	5.17[c]			
Ethnicity	.04[b]	1.38	**Social factors**		
IQ	.11	2.26	Social ties	.39	18.54
Psychological conditions	.19	3.85	Antisocial peers	.37[b]	15.09

a. Odds ratio indicating relative odds of subsequent violent/serious delinquency for the 25% of the sample on the high-risk end of the predictor measure (except for gender) assuming 8% overall base rate for violent/serious delinquency.
b. There was significant heterogeneity in the residuals for the regression-estimated mean effect size for these predictor construct categories.
c. Odds ratio here based on relative odds for male 50% of sample.

used to generate estimates of the various predictor-outcome correlations under uniform conditions. For this purpose, the regression model was used to estimate the mean aggregated effect size for each predictor construct in turn while controlling for the variables shown in Table 6.6. The results of this procedure are shown in Table 6.7 and can be summarized as follows:

1. Many of the predictor constructs showed relatively high correlations for prediction of violent or serious delinquency indicating that prediction is possible from observations made during the 12-14 age period for behavior at age 15-25.

2. Prior antisocial behavior is generally a good predictor of violent or serious delinquency outcomes. However, the best predictors from this age period have to do with juveniles' social relations, especially involvement with antisocial peers and lack of strong social ties.

3. Despite the adjustment to statistically control for nuisance variance from between-study differences in method and procedures,

the residuals remaining after estimation of the aggregated effect size showed significant heterogeneity for many of the predictors (indicated by superscript *b* in Table 6.7). This means that the variation among aggregated effect sizes was greater than could be expected from sampling error alone.

4. Transformations of the estimated aggregate correlational effect sizes into odds ratios revealed that juveniles at risk on the strongest predictors had 3-20 times the probability of engaging in subsequent violent or serious delinquency as juveniles not at risk on those predictors.

■ Comparison of Age 6-11 Predictors With Age 12-14 Predictors

Table 6.8 provides a rank-order listing of the predictors of violent or serious delinquency based on the regression-adjusted estimates shown in Tables 6.4 and 6.7. The various predictor constructs are organized into groups according to the boundaries of the

TABLE 6.8 Ranking of Age 6-11 and Age 12-14 Predictors of Violent or Serious Delinquency at Age 15-25

Age 6-11 Predictor (r)	*Age 12-14 Predictor* (r)
Rank 1 group	
General offenses (.38)	Social ties (.39)
Substance use (.30)	Antisocial peers (.37)
Rank 2 group	
Gender (male) (.26)	General offenses (.26)
Family SES (.24)	
Antisocial parents (.23)	
Rank 3 group	
Aggression (.21)	Aggression (.19)
Ethnicity (.20)	School attitude/performance (.19)
	Psychological condition (.19)
	Parent-child relations (.19)
	Gender (male) (.19)
	Physical violence (.18)
Rank 4 group	
Psychological condition (.15)	Antisocial parents (.16)
Parent-child relations (.15)	Person crimes (.14)
Social ties (.15)	Problem behavior (.12)
Problem behavior (.13)	IQ (.11)
School attitude/ performance (.13)	
Medical/physical (.13)	
IQ (.12)	
Other family characteristics (.12)	
Rank 5 group	
Broken home (.09)	Broken home (.10)
Abusive parents (.07)	Family SES (.10)
Antisocial peers (.04)	Abusive parents (.09)
	Other family characteristics (.08)
	Substance use (.06)
	Ethnicity (.04)

confidence intervals around the respective estimates. Within a group, the estimated aggregated effect sizes do not generally differ significantly from each other; between groups, most do differ. These tables give a clearer comparative picture of the relative strength of the various predictor constructs at the different ages. The most interesting aspects of the comparison in Table 6.8 are the following:

1. The best predictors were rather different for the early age period in comparison to the later period. Having a juvenile offense ("general offense") in the age 6-11 period is the strongest predictor of subsequent violent or serious delinquency even though this specific predictor category does not itself necessarily involve violence. For the 12-14 age period, it is also a strong predictor, but in the second rank rather than the first. Substance use, on the other hand, is also among the

best predictors for the age 6-11 period but one of the poorest for age 12-14. Thus, *early* substance use and delinquent offending are highly predictive, but the same behaviors are less predictive at a later age, especially in the case of substance abuse.

2. The two strongest predictors for the age 12-14 group both have to do with interpersonal relations, that is, lack of social ties and involvement with antisocial peers. By contrast, the analogous categories for the age 6-11 group are relatively weak predictors.

3. The second and third rank predictors are dominated by relatively fixed personal characteristics for the age 6-11 group (gender, family SES, ethnicity, antisocial parents), whereas those for the age 12-14 group have a heavier representation of behavioral characteristics (e.g., general offenses, aggression, school performance).

4. Broken homes and abusive parents are among the poorest predictors for both the age 6-11 and 12-14 groups. Antisocial peers and substance use show complete reversals, being among the weakest predictors for one age group despite being among the strongest predictors for the other.

■ Discussion and Conclusions

As a review of predictors of delinquent behavior, the investigation reported here has two distinctive features. One is the specific focus on violent or serious delinquency as the "outcome" of interest. The other is the use of meta-analysis techniques to make quantitative summaries of the empirical findings on this topic and provide analysis that attempts to control for between-study differences so that the relative strength of different predictors at different ages can be systematically compared. Unfortunately, the quantity of relevant research is limited and, as a result, the range and volume of available empirical findings are not sufficient to produce definitive results. Nonetheless, the topic is impor-

tant, and it is appropriate to glean what conclusions can be supported.

Perhaps the clearest conclusion of this meta-analysis is that the predictor variables most frequently studied in prospective longitudinal studies of antisocial behavior are statistically related to subsequent violent or serious delinquency. Despite the relatively small number of primary research studies investigating any one predictor construct, the mean aggregated effect sizes were statistically significant for all predictor categories at each period of observation examined in this meta-analysis. Statistical significance, of course, does not necessarily mean practical significance for the task of identifying juveniles who are at risk for subsequent violent or serious delinquency. For this task it is necessary that the risk variables identify juveniles with a relatively high probability of actually becoming violent/serious offenders and that those identified constitute a relatively large proportion of those who will become offenders without intervention. We turn now to a closer examination of the potential practical value of predictive relationships of the order of magnitude shown in Tables 6.4, 6.7, and 6.8.

An important aspect of prediction situations is the base rate of the behavior being predicted. We know that a relatively small proportion of the individuals in any birth cohort will engage in violent or serious delinquency during adolescence or early adulthood. The outcome of interest, therefore, has a rather low base rate and is consequently more difficult to predict. We estimated this base rate by pooling the general population samples from the studies in the meta-analysis. This procedure revealed that about 8% of the juveniles were typically classified as violent or seriously delinquent on the outcome measures taken during the age 15-25 period. Most of the predictor variables involved in these studies, on the other hand, had no natural "break points" between values that clearly constituted risk and those that did not. For purposes of simulating identification of at-risk juveniles, therefore, we assumed that the top 25% were selected. Though this is arbitrary, and other cut-off points could be used, it does approximate the practical reality of pre- ventive intervention that, to be cost-effective, must generally target some portion of the juvenile population that is not greatly larger than the base rate of the outcome it is attempting to prevent. With these values assumed, the prediction situation is essentially as follows:

	Will be delinquent	*Will not be delinquent*	
Identified as at risk	A	B	25%
Identified as not at risk	C	D	75%
	8%	92%	

Under these circumstances, the primary practical issue is whether correlation coefficients of the size found in this meta-analysis for the best predictors represent sufficient proportions in Cell A, relative to Cell B, to constitute useful identification of juveniles headed for violent or serious delinquency. Moreover, it would be desirable for the proportion in Cell C, relative to Cell D, to be small, indicating few false negatives. Table 6.9 presents the pertinent indicators for various criteria of predictive adequacy in this scenario for 2 × 2 prediction tables imputed from correlation coefficients in the .15-.40 range.

Looking first at the Positive Predicted Value column in Table 6.9, we see that selecting the top 25% of juveniles using predictor variables that correlate .15-.40 with subsequent offending will yield a group in which 15%-27% will become offenders. Furthermore, as the Sensitivity column shows, 47%-84% of those who will become offenders are included in this selection (with 16%-53%, therefore, being missed as "false negatives").

TABLE 6.9 Selected Correlation Values and the Associated Odds Ratios and Classification Probabilities Assuming a Predictor Selection Rate = .25 and Serious Offender Base Rate = .08

Correlation	Odds Ratio	Positive Predicted Value[a]	Sensitivity[b]	Negative Predicted Value[c]	Specificity[d]
.15	2.96	.15	.47	.94	.77
.20	4.12	.17	.54	.95	.78
.25	5.78	.20	.62	.96	.78
.30	8.31	.22	.69	.97	.79
.35	12.53	.24	.76	.97	.79
.40	20.73	.27	.84	.98	.80

a. Probability of positive outcome given positive predictor.
b. Probability of positive prediction given positive outcome.
c. Probability of negative outcome given negative predictor.
d. Probability of negative prediction given negative outcome.

Thus, using one of these predictors to select juveniles for preventive intervention will most likely treat the majority of the potential offenders but, for each juvenile who will later become an offender, the preventive intervention will also treat three to six juveniles who are identified as at risk but do not become offenders. The Negative Predicted Value column, on the other hand, shows that 94%-98% of those selected as not at risk in this scenario will indeed not become offenders. And the Specificity column reveals that 77%-80% of those who will not become offenders will not be selected as being at risk. Thus, whereas the overwhelming majority of the juveniles classified as not at risk will not become offenders, some 20%-23% of those who will not actually become offenders appear as false positives and are erroneously selected as at risk.

Whether these selection ratios provide the basis for a practical prevention program will depend on the success rate the program can be expected to have and the cost of treatment per juvenile. A program that prevented one subsequent offender for every four such offenders treated would need to treat some 15-30 at-risk cases to be sure of including 4 subsequent offenders. Given the number and seriousness of the offenses associated with one offender of the sort at issue, it is not unreasonable to think that the benefits of prevention might justify the cost of treatment for this many at-risk juveniles. From this perspective, therefore, the predictive strength of the risk variables identified in the meta-analysis with mean aggregated effect sizes of .20-.40 may well have practical significance.

The risk variables most predictive of subsequent serious or violent delinquency are also potential targets for intervention. For this strategy to be workable, of course, the targeted risk factors must be amenable to change. In this regard it is especially noteworthy that the strongest predictors from both the age 6-11 and 12-14 periods represent relatively malleable factors. For the younger age group, the two strongest predictors are committing general offenses and substance use (chiefly tobacco or alcohol). Both of these variables reflect behaviors that might be reduced by effective intervention, as is aggressive behavior, one of the predictors in the third-ranked category. The second rank of predictor variables for the age 6-11 group, however, is not so favorable for intervention. These variables include male gender, family SES, and antisocial parents. Although the antisocial behavior and SES of juveniles' parents may be amenable to change in theory, as a practical matter it is likely to be difficult. Moreover, their relationship to the juveniles' behavior may be cumulative from birth and, hence, a change in those variables when the youth are age 6-11 may not have much influence on their probability of later offending. Gender, of course, is not malleable, nor is ethnicity, the remaining predictor variable in the third-ranked category.

The strongest predictor variables for juveniles age 12-14 were lack of social ties, antisocial peers, and, in the second-ranked category, committing a general offense. All of these variables represent behavior and circumstances that intervention programs may be able to favorably affect. Similarly, the predictor variables in the third-ranked category are largely amenable to intervention. These include aggressive behavior, school attitudes and performance, various psychological conditions, parent-child relations, and physical violence. Only male gender in this predictor group is not a feasible target for preventive intervention. Thus, nearly all the strongest predictor variables from the age 12-14 period represent potentially malleable behaviors or conditions that can be addressed by intervention programs.

Although it would be comforting to have a larger number of studies to provide a greater depth of empirical support, the available evidence is encouraging. The best predictors from both the age 6-11 and 12-14 periods are capable of distinguishing juveniles whose risk for violent/serious offending during age 15-25 is high enough to warrant attention. Moreover, many of the strongest predictors are variables that are themselves malleable and may be appropriate targets for intervention. Especially striking is the prevalence of early antisocial behavior among the top-ranked predictors, for example, general of-fenses, substance use, aggression, and physical violence. Equally striking for older youth is the strength of predictors relating to problematic social and peer relations. These factors not only have diagnostic value for identification of high-risk juveniles, but they also suggest that disruption of early patterns of antisocial behavior and the peer support for such behavior may be an especially promising strategy for preventive intervention.

■ *Appendix A:*
Descriptive Summary of Outcome Variables Representing
Violent and Serious Delinquency

Categorized as Violent

Aggravated assault, atrocious assault, armed robbery

Arrests for murder, rape, robbery, assault

Consistent and overt aggression

Convicted of violent offense

Court/police contact for sexual or violent offense

Court appearance for sexual offense

Crime scale 4 = violence and rape

Crimes against persons

Delinquency: violent and sexual offenses

Delinquent type: serious violent offender

Felony assault

Felony assault, robbery

Fights a lot

Forced sexual behavior and attempts

Gang fight

Hit a teacher

Hurt someone badly

Injury offense

Mugging, assault

Offense in which victim sustains serious bodily injury

Offenses against persons: aggressive and sexual

Participated in serious acts of violence

Physically assaulted someone

Police contact for injury offense

Predatory crimes against persons

Rape

Rating: high fighters

Robbery

Sentenced for a serious violent offense

Serious violent offenders

Serious fight at school three or more times

Severity of physical aggression

Three or more serious violent offenses

Use of weapons

Used force to get money or valuables

Violent conduct problems

Violent offense or threat of violence

Violent felony arrest

Violent recidivism

Weapons in a fight

Categorized as Serious but Not Necessarily Violent

Arrest for serious offenses

Broke into building or car

Burglary

Felony property arrests

Felony theft

Felony conviction

General delinquency, mostly serious
    Grand larceny
    Heavy delinquents
    Index offenses
    Juvenile delinquent, serious crimes
    Police contact, felonies
    Predatory crimes against property
    Serious delinquent acts

Serious juvenile delinquency
Serious offenses
Seriousness of police contacts
Severity of criminal activity
Stole motor vehicle
Theft of more than $100
Warrants out for serious offense

■ *Appendix B:*
Descriptive Summary of Predictor Variables
in the Different Construct Groups

Antisocial Behavior
  Physical violence
    Violence, physical
    Violence, recidivism
  Aggression
    Aggressive and disruptive behavior
    Aggression, cannot tell
    Aggression toward objects
    Verbal aggression
  Person crimes
    Crimes against persons
    Sexual offenses
    Violence, mixed
  General offenses
    Crime, index/serious
    Crimes, mixed
    Property crimes
    Recidivism
    Status offenses
  Problem behavior
    Aggressively inclined
    Antiestablishment
    Antisocial behavior
    Poor behavior rating
    Problem behavior
    Temper tantrums
    Undesirable temperament
  Substance use
    Illicit drug use
    Alcohol use
    Tobacco use

Personal Characteristics
  Gender
    Male gender
  Ethnicity
    Minority race
  IQ
    Learning problems
    Low IQ
    Low IQ, nonverbal
    Low IQ, verbal
    Low language ability
  Medical/physical
    Developmental history
    Medical conditions
    Medical examinations
    Physical development
  School attitude/
  performance
    Dropped out from school
    Low interest in education
    Low school achievement
    Poor-quality school
    Truancy
  Psychological condition
    Behavior characteristics
    High activity level
    High daring
    Impulsiveness
    Poor eating habits
    Psychopathology
    Short attention span

Family Characteristics

Antisocial parents

Criminal parent

Parent psychopathology

Parent violent

Abusive parents

Child emotional abuse

Maltreated as child

Neglected as child

Physically abused as child

Sexually abused as child

Broken home

Broken home

Separated from parents

Parent-child relations

Discipline, mixed

Discipline, punitive

Low parent involvement

Low supervision

Low warmth

Negative attitude to child

Poor parent-child relations

Poor parental practices

Severity in child training

Socioeconomic status

Low SES, family

Low SES, juvenile

Low-quality neighborhood

Low-status job, parents

Not employed, juvenile

Other family characteristics

Parent background

High family stress

Large family size

Marital discord

Social

Social ties

Few social activities

Low popularity

Antisocial peers

Antisocial peers

Peer criminality

Peer normlessness

■ *APPENDIX C:*
Bibliography of Reports Contributing to the Database

Ageton, S. S. (1983). *Sexual assault among adolescents.* Lexington, MA: Lexington Books.

August, G. J., Stewart, M. A., & Holmes, C. S. (1983). A four year follow-up of hyperactive boys with and without conduct disorder. *British Journal of Psychiatry, 143,* 192-198.

Burgess, A., Hartman, C. R., & McCormac, A. (1987). Abused to abuser: Antecedents of socially deviant behavior. *American Journal of Psychiatry, 144,* 1432-1436.

Dembo, R., Williams, L., Getreu, A., Genung, L., et al., (1991). Recidivism among high-risk youths: Study of a cohort of juvenile detainees. *International Journal of the Addictions, 26,* 121-177.

Dembo, R., Williams, L., Getreu, A., Genung, L., Schmeidler, J., Berry, E., Wish, E. D., & La Voie, L. (1991). A longitudinal study of the relationships among marijuana/hashish use, cocaine use and delinquency in a cohort of high risk youths. *Journal of Drug Issues, 21,* 271-312.

Dembo, R., Williams, L., Schmeidler, J., Getreu, A., Berry, E., Genung, L., Wish, E. D., & Christensen, C.

(1991). Recidivism among high risk youths: A 2 ½-year follow-up of a cohort of juvenile detainees. *International Journal of the Addictions, 26,* 1197-221.

Dembo, R., Williams, L., Schmeidler, J., Wish, E. D., Getreu, A., & Berry, E. (1991). Juvenile crime and drug abuse: A prospective study of high risk youth. *Journal of Addictive Diseases, 11,* 5-31.

Dembo, R., Williams, L., Schmeidler, J., & Wothke, W. (1993). A longitudinal study of the predictors of the adverse effects of alcohol and marijuana/hashish use among a cohort of high risk youths. *International Journal of the Addictions, 28,* 1045-1083.

Elliott, D. S., & Ageton, S. S. (1980). Reconciling race and class differences in self-reported and official estimates of delinquency. *American Sociological Review, 45,* 95-110.

Elliott, D. S., Ageton, S. S., Huizinga, D., Knowles, B., & Canter, R. (1983). *The prevalence and incidence of delinquent behavior: 1976-1980* (Research Rep. No. 26, National Youth Survey). Boulder, CO: Behavioral Research Institute.

Elliott, D. S., & Huizinga, D. (1983). Social class and delinquent behavior in a National Youth Panel. *Criminology, 21,* 149-177.

Elliott, D. S., Huizinga, D., & Morse, B. (1986). Self-reported violent offending: A descriptive analysis of juvenile violent offenders and their offending careers. *Journal of Interpersonal Violence, 1,* 472-514. (The prediction and control of violent behavior: II [Special issue])

Elliott, D. S., & Voss, H. L. (1974). *Delinquency and dropout.* Lexington, MA: D. C. Heath.

Ensminger, M. E. (1990). Sexual activity and problem behaviors among black, urban adolescents. *Child Development, 61,* 2032-2046.

Farrington, D. P. (1973). Self reports of deviant behavior: Predictive and stable? *Journal of Criminal Law, Criminology and Policy Science, 64,* 99-110.

Farrington, D. P. (1978). The family background of aggressive youths. In L. A. Hersov, M. Berger, & D. Schaffer (Eds.), *Aggression and antisocial behavior in childhood and adolescence* (pp. 73-93). New York: Pergamon.

Farrington, D. P. (1989). Early predictors of adolescent aggression and adult violence. *Violence and Victims, 4,* 79-100.

Farrington, D. P. (1991). Childhood aggression and adult violence: Early precursors and later outcomes. In D. J. Pepler & K. H. Rubin (Eds.), *The development and treatment of childhood aggression* (pp. 5-29). Hillsdale, NJ: Lawrence Erlbaum.

Farrington, D. P., & Hawkins, J. D. (1991). Predicting participation, early onset and later persistence in officially recorded offending. *Criminal Behavior and Mental Health, 1,* 1-33.

Gittelman, R., Mannuzza, S., Shenker, R., & Bonagura, N. (1985). Hyperactive boys almost grown up: I. Psychiatric status. *Archives of General Psychiatry, 42,* 937-947.

Glueck, S., & Glueck, E. T. (1940). *Juvenile delinquents grown up.* New York: Commonwealth Fund.

Gunjonsson, G. H. (1982). Delinquent boys in Reykjavik: A follow-up study of boys sent to an institution. In J. Gunn & D. P. Farrington (Eds.), *Abnormal offenders, delinquency and the criminal justice system* (pp. 203-212). New York: John Wiley.

Hamparian, D. M., Shuster, R., Dinitz, S., & Conrad, J. (1978). *The violent few.* Lexington, MA: D. C. Heath.

Hogh, E., & Wolf, P. (1983). Violent crime in a birth cohort: Copenhagen 1953-1977. In K. T. Van Dusen & S. A. Mednick (Eds.), *Prospective studies in crime and delinquency* (pp. 249-267). Boston: Kluwer-Nijhoff.

Huizinga, D., & Elliott, D. S. (1987). Juvenile offenders: Prevalence, offender incidence and arrest rates by race. *Crime & Delinquency, 33,* 206-223.

Kagan, J., & Moss, H. A. (1962). *Birth to maturity: A study in psychological development.* New York: John Wiley.

Kaplan, H. B. (1978). Deviant behavior and self-enhancement in adolescence. *Journal of Youth and Adolescence, 7,* 253-277.

Kawaguchi, R., & Butler, E. W. (1982). Impairments and community adjustment of young adults: Alcohol use, drug abuse and arrest. *Chemical Dependency, 4,* 209-219.

Klinteberg, B., Andersson, T., Magnusson, D., & Stattin, H. (1993). Hyperactive behavior in childhood as related to subsequent alcohol problems and violent offending: A longitudinal study of male subjects. *Personality and Individual Differences, 15,* 381-388.

Kramer, J., & Loney, J. (1978, August). *Predicting adolescent antisocial behavior among hyperactive boys.* Paper presented at the meeting of the American Psychological Association, Toronto, Ontario.

Le Blanc, M., & Fréchette, M. (1989). *Male criminal activity from childhood through youth: Multilevel and development perspectives.* New York: Springer-Verlag.

Lewis, D. O., Lovely, R., Yeager, C., & Femina, D. D. (1989). Toward a theory of the genesis of violence: A follow-up study of delinquents. *Journal of the American Academy of Child and Adolescent Psychiatry, 28,* 431-436.

Loney, J., Kramer, J., & Milich, R. S. (1982). The hyperactive child grows up: Predictors of symptoms, delinquency, and achievement at follow-up. In K. D. Gadow & J. Loney (Eds.), *Psychosocial aspects of drug treatment for hyperactivity* (pp. 381-415). Boulder, CO: Westview.

Loney, J., Kramer, J., & Milich, R. S. (1982). The hyperactive child grows up: Predictors of symptoms, delinquency, and achievement at follow-up. In S. A. Mednick, M. Harway, & K. M. Finello (Eds.), *Handbook of longitudinal research: Vol. 1. Birth and childhood cohorts* (pp. 426-447). New York: Praeger.

Loney, J., Whaley-Klahn, M. A., Kosier, T., & Conboy, J. (1983). Hyperactive boys and their brothers at 21: Predictors of aggressive and antisocial outcomes. In K. T. Van Dusen & S. A. Mednick (Eds.), *Prospective studies of crime and delinquency* (pp. 181-207). Boston: Kluwer-Nijhoff.

Magnusson, D., Stattin, H., & Duner, A. (1983). Aggression and criminality in a longitudinal perspective. In K. T. Van Dusen & S. A. Mednick (Eds.), *Prospective studies in crime and delinquency* (pp. 277-301). Boston: Kluwer-Nijhoff.

Mannuzza, S., Gittelman-Klein, R., Konig, P. H., & Giampino, T. L. (1989). Hyperactive boys almost grown up: IV. Criminality and its relationship to psychiatric status. *Archives of General Psychiatry, 46,* 1073-1079.

Mannuzza, S., Klein, R. G., & Addalli, K. A. (1991). Young adult mental status of hyperactive boys and their brothers: A prospective follow-up study. *Journal of the American Academy of Child and Adolescent Psychiatry, 30,* 743-751.

McCord, J. (1990). Long-term perspectives on parental absence. In L. N. Robins & M. Rutter (Eds.), *Straight and devious pathways from childhood to adulthood* (pp. 116-134). New York: Cambridge University Press.

McCord, J. (1991). Family relationships, juvenile delinquency, and adult criminality. *Criminology, 29,* 397-417.

McCord, W., & McCord, J. (1959). *Origins of crime: A new evaluation of the Cambridge-Somerville Youth Study.* New York: Columbia University Press.

McCord, W., McCord, W., & Howard, A. (1961). Family interaction as antecedent to the direction of male aggressiveness. *Journal of Abnormal and Social Psychology, 66,* 239-242.

Mitchell, S., & Rosa, P. (1981). Boyhood behavior problems as precursors of criminality: A fifteen-year follow-up study. *Journal of Child Psychology and Psychiatry, 22,* 19-33.

Morse, B. J. (1987). Self-reported juvenile violent offenders and their offending careers: A descriptive analysis (Doctoral dissertation, University of Colorado, Boulder, 1987). *Dissertation Abstracts International, 47(9-A),* 3569-3570.

Moskowitz, D. A., Crawley, M. E., & Schwartzman, A. E. (1989, August). *Aggression, withdrawal, and academic achievement: A longitudinal study of criminal activity into early adulthood.* Paper presented at the meeting of the American Psychological Association, New Orleans, LA.

Nachshon, I., & Denno, D. (1987). Violent behavior and cerebral hemisphere function. In S. A. Mednick, T. E. Moffitt, & S. A. Stack (Eds.), *Causes of crime: New biological approaches* (pp. 185-217). New York: Cambridge University Press.

Piper, E. S. (1985). Violent recidivism and chronicity in the 1958 Philadelphia cohort. *Journal of Quantitative Criminology, 1,* 319-344.

Pulkkinen, L. (1983). Finland: The search for alternatives to aggression. In A. P. Goldstein & M. H. Segall (Eds.), *Aggression in global perspective* (pp. 104-144). New York: Pergamon.

Rivera, B., & Widom, C. S. (1990). Childhood victimization and violent offending. *Violence and Victims, 5,* 19-35.

Satterfield, J. H. (1987). Childhood diagnostic and neurophysiological predictors of teenage arrest rates: An 8-year prospective study. In S. A. Mednick, T. E. Moffitt, & S. A. Stack (Eds.), *Causes of crime: New biological approaches* (pp. 146-167). New York: Cambridge University Press.

Satterfield, J. H., Hoppe, C. M., & Schell, A. M. (1984). Childhood brain function differences in delinquent and non-delinquent hyperactive boys. *Electroencephalographic Clinical Neurophysiology, 57,* 199-207.

Schuster, T. L., & Butler, E. W. (1986). Labeling, mild mental retardation, and long-range social adjustment. *Sociological Perspectives, 29,* 461-483.

Spivack, G., & Cianci, N. (1989). High risk early behavior pattern and later delinquency. In J. D. Burchard & S. N. Burchard (Eds.), *Prevention of delinquent behavior* (pp. 44-74). Washington, DC: Government Printing Office.

Spivack, G., Marcus, J., & Swift, M. (1986). Early classroom behavior and later misconduct. *Developmental Psychology, 22,* 124-131.

Triplett, R. A. (1990). Labeling and differential association: The effects on delinquent behavior (Doctoral dissertation, University of Maryland, College Park, 1990). *Dissertation Abstracts International, 51,* 1784.

Verhulst, F. C., & Van der Ende, J. (1991). Four-year follow-up of teacher-reported problem behaviors. *Psychological Medicine, 21,* 965-977.

Wadsworth, M. E. J. (1976). Delinquency, pulse rates and early emotional deprivation. *British Journal of Criminology, 16,* 245-256.

Wadsworth, M. E. J. (1979). *Roots of delinquency: Infancy, adolescence, and crime.* New York: Barnes & Noble.

Wadsworth, M. E. J. (1980). Early life events and later behavioral outcomes in a British longitudinal study. In S. B. Sells, R. Crandell, M. Roff, J. S. Strauss, & W. Pollin (Eds.), *Human functioning in longitudinal perspective: Studies of normal and psychopathic populations* (pp. 168-180). Baltimore: Williams & Wilkins.

Wenk, E., Robinson, J., & Smith, G. (1972). Can violence be predicted? *Crime & Delinquency, 18,* 393-402.

Werner, E. E. (1990). Antecedents and consequences of deviant behavior. In K. Hurrelmann & F. Lösel (Eds.), *Health hazards in adolescence* (pp. 219-230). New York: Walter de Gruyter.

West, D. J. (1982). *Delinquency: Its roots, careers, and prospects.* Cambridge, MA: Harvard University Press.

West, D. J., & Farrington, D. P. (1977). *The delinquent way of life.* Third report of the Cambridge Study in Delinquent Development. London: Heinemann.

White, H. R. (1992). Early problem behavior and later drug problems. *Journal of Research in Crime and Delinquency, 29,* 412-499.

White, H. R., Pandina, R. J., & LaGrange, R. L. (1987). Longitudinal predictors of serious substance use and delinquency. *Criminology, 25,* 715-741.

Wolfgang, M. E., Figlio, R. M., & Sellin, T. (1972). *Delinquency in a birth cohort.* Chicago: University of Chicago Press.

CHAPTER 7

A Review of Predictors of Youth Violence

■ *J. David Hawkins, Todd Herrenkohl, David P. Farrington, Devon Brewer, Richard F. Catalano, & Tracy W. Harachi*

Lipsey and Derzon (Chapter 6, this volume) have conducted a synthesis of longitudinal research using techniques of meta-analysis to understand predictors of violent and serious crime among adolescents and young adults. They have developed a list of predictors of violence arranged in order of strength of association, measured in a sufficient number of studies to pass their criteria for meta-analysis (Lipsey and Derzon, Chapter 6, this volume). This is a major contribution to current knowledge, validating prior empirical work on predictors of delinquency, but extending it by focusing specifically on predictors of violent offending and allowing comparison of the relative strength of well-studied predictors of violence. Their study provides an important

summary of current knowledge of the relative strength of various predictors in contributing to violence and serious crime.

The current chapter also focuses on the predictors of violence. We are concerned here with malleable risk and protective factors for violence identified in longitudinal studies, even if these factors have been investigated in too few studies to be included in a meta-analysis. Relatively few high-quality multivariate longitudinal studies of predictors of violence have been completed. It is important to glean what can be learned from these studies about predictors of violence, even if they are few in number.

These studies provide important leads for policy and action seeking to prevent violence. We focus specifically on malleable risk and protective factors because they represent the precursors of violence that could be changed by preventive intervention. We provide a table describing results of specific studies and the strength and duration of longitudinal associations reported with respect to the developmental points at which they appear salient in prediction, so as to clarify implications for preventive intervention.

■ *Method*

Literature Search

To locate the studies to consider for inclusion in the review, we searched the bibliography constructed by Lipsey and Derzon (Chapter 6, this volume). We supplemented this bibliography with a literature search and research reports provided by the Office of Juvenile Justice and Delinquency Prevention Study Group members and analyses of the Seattle Social Development Project longitudinal data set.

Criteria for Inclusion

We included a result in our review if the following six criteria were met:

1. All subjects in the study were juveniles living in the community (i.e., not incarcerated) at the time of the first assessment.
2. The sample of subjects in the study was *not* defined on the basis of their having committed prior criminal or violent offenses.
3. The study included a measure of interpersonal physical violence. We defined interpersonal physical violence to be perpetration of acts resulting in physical injury or threat of physical injury to another person (including sexual violence). This definition

excludes suicidal behaviors. We included a study only if it was clear that it provided a measure of violent behavior serious enough to result in intervention by law enforcement authorities if they had been aware of it. We excluded studies that focused on relatively minor aggressive acts, such as pushing among elementary school-aged children, as outcomes. Studies that reported only general delinquency measures in which indicators of nonviolent delinquent behaviors (e.g., theft, burglary, and vandalism) or other constructs (e.g., attitudes toward violence) could not be separated from violent behavior were also excluded. A study was included if the measure of violence was based on self-report, report from another knowledgeable person (such as a parent or teacher), or official records (e.g., from police, courts, or other government agencies).

4. A predictor included in the study was a modifiable or malleable construct. Predictors that were conglomerations of multiple constructs were excluded, such as Raine, Brennan, Mednick, and Mednick's (1996) measure of biosocial risk that includes marital conflict, maternal rejection, family instability, parental crime, neurological problems, and slow motor development. Furthermore, because the relationships between gender and race and violent behavior have been discussed in Chapters 3 and 6 of this volume, we excluded from this review discussions of gender and race as predictors of violence.
5. The design of the study was longitudinal. In other words, the independent variable referred to a time period prior to the time period to which the dependent variable referred. Most results were based on prospective data, although we included results based on retrospective reviews of clinical or official records with clear time ordering of independent and dependent variables. Longitudinal studies based on retrospective searches of records are essentially equivalent, in methodological terms, to prospective studies because the information on independent variables was recorded before the information on violence.
6. Individual subjects were the unit of analysis for both the independent and dependent

variables. Thus, studies of influences on rates of violence in neighborhoods were excluded.

Procedures

Where possible, in Table 7.2, we report the measures of strength of association for the relationship between a particular factor and violence as expressed by Pearson's r and/or odds ratios. We present study findings in both ways to illustrate different estimates of the magnitude of the relationship between predictors and violence outcomes. Investigators from different methodological traditions have tended to report different measures of association. Although the correlation coefficient is essential for meta-analysis, the nonnormal distribution of violence in the population also suggests the utility of odds ratios for understanding the degree of increased risk for violence associated with the presence of different predictors in a sample or population. Both measures of association can help guide thinking regarding the selection of factors and subgroups for preventive intervention. Calculation of odds ratios requires dichotomization of samples into violent and nonviolent subgroups. The odds ratio is the odds of violence with a risk factor divided by the odds of violence without the risk factor. The odds ratio indicates the increased likelihood of violence associated with the presence of a particular predictor. An odds ratio of 2 indicates a doubling of risk in the presence of that factor. Where a report does not provide association measures directly (or they could not be calculated with the information provided), we describe the study results only in narrative terms.

In computing correlations from information in a report, we used the standard meta-analytic procedures detailed by Rosenthal (1991). When correlations between a particular predictor and an outcome were derived for two or more studies, we summarized these findings using a weighted mean correlation. For most studies, the effect sizes were reported clearly or could be easily calculated. However, in some cases, where several reports provided results from the same sample, we faced options for determining which results to report and how to carry out the computations. In these cases, we used the following steps to summarize the findings.

When it was clear that the samples in two or more reports overlapped (or were the same), then the results for the samples were considered to be from a single overall study. Thus, a study could contribute only one estimate of the effect size for a given independent variable at a specific developmental point, in accordance with standard practice (Rosenthal, 1991). When a study had multiple effect sizes for the relationship between an independent variable and violence (e.g., from assessments of the independent variable and/or dependent variable using multiple measures or partially overlapping samples from the same study), we computed the weighted (by degrees of freedom) mean r, using Fisher's z-transformed correlations (see Rosenthal, 1991, and Maguin & Loeber, 1996, for a discussion of similar procedures). The corresponding sample size for a study's weighted mean r was the mean sample size for the correlations from that study that were averaged. In cases where findings for subgroups differed notably, we reported separately the correlations for males and females and different racial groups. Studies with outcome measures of *juvenile and/or adult* violence were included, and results for officially recorded and self-reported violence were reported separately when these were available.

In some instances, when several studies provide effect sizes for a particular factor, we also include results of a brief meta-analysis that summarizes the central tendency and variation of the corresponding correlations. No more than five studies were included in any of our meta-analytic summaries. Therefore, we calculated only three statistics for each meta-analysis: the weighted (by degrees of freedom for each study) mean r, based on Fisher's z-transformations; the cumulative z-score that indexes the statistical significance of the combination of correlations; and the heterogeneity chi-square value that assesses the statistical significance of the variation among the correlations (Rosenthal, 1991). Unless otherwise noted, the variation among the correlations synthesized for a particular variable is *not* significant (i.e., $p > .05$ from the heterogeneity chi-square test).

■ Results

Samples and Designs of Studies Reviewed

Table 7.1 describes the samples and designs of the studies reviewed. When research designs differed substantially for reports based on the same sample or overlapping samples, these reports are listed separately even though they are derived from the same overall study.

Individual Factors

Characteristics of individuals interact with environmental influences and conditions to produce violent behavior (Reiss & Roth, 1993). Table 7.2 presents evidence regarding the predictive association of individual risk factors and violence. To the extent possible, we have organized this review of risk factors developmentally, beginning before birth.

Medical/Physical Conditions

Pregnancy and delivery complications. As shown in Table 7.2, prenatal trauma and pregnancy complications are somewhat predictive of later officially recorded violence, though findings vary with methods used to identify prenatal trauma and sample. Kandel and Mednick (1991) found that 80% of violent offenders scored in the high range of delivery complications compared with 30% of property offenders and 47% of nonoffenders (p. 523). There is evidence, however, that prenatal trauma is predictive of later violence only in children raised in unstable home environments (Mednick & Kandel, 1988), suggesting that a stable home environment may serve as a protective factor against prenatal trauma. Moreover, prenatal trauma also predicts increased risk for hyperactivity, itself a risk factor for later violence, suggesting several possible pathways from prenatal trauma to violent behavior. It is noteworthy that prenatal trauma and delivery complications are linked to later violence, but not to nonviolent criminal behavior (Mednick & Kandel, 1988), suggesting that they may result in damage to brain mechanisms that inhibit violent behavior specifically (Reiss & Roth, 1993).

It is noteworthy that Denno (1990) did not find that pregnancy and delivery complications predicted arrests for violence up to age 22 in a prospective study of African Americans born in Philadelphia in 1959-1962, nor did pregnancy and delivery complications predict violence in the Cambridge study (Farrington, 1997b).

Although the associations between pregnancy and delivery complications and violence are relatively weak and inconsistent across studies, they suggest that interventions that seek to provide greater prenatal care to mothers at risk for pregnancy and delivery complications should be evaluated for possible effects in preventing violent behavior of their children.

(text continued on p. 112)

TABLE 7.1 Samples and Designs of Studies Reviewed

Study	Sample	Design
Ageton (1983)	Subset of male youths from the National Youth Survey (probability sample of youth in the U.S. in the 1970s and 1980s); compared sexually assaultive youth with a stratified (by race and class) systematic sample of non-sexually assaultive youth	Prospective
Baker and Mednick (1984)	Persons born between September 1959 and December 1961 in the Rigshospitalet in Copenhagen, Denmark; Baker and Mednick (1994) examined a subsample	Retrospective
Raine, Brennan, and Mednick (1994) Denno (1990)	African Americans in Philadelphia whose mothers gave birth to them at Pennsylvania Hospital between 1959 and 1965 and participated in the Philadelphia Perinatal Project	Prospective
Elliott (1994) Tolan and Thomas (1995)	A national probability sample of youths in the U.S. who participated in the National Youth Survey (1970s-1980s)	Prospective
Farrington (1989a)	Men who attended one of six primary schools in a London working-class area in 1961-1962 (Cambridge Study in Delinquent Development)	Prospective
Farrington (in press)	Males who participated in the Cambridge Study in Delinquent Development and the Pittsburgh Youth Study	Prospective
Hechtman and Weiss (1986)	Persons diagnosed as hyperactive as children at the Child Psychiatry Clinic, Montreal Children's Hospital, and control subjects who were school classmates or work associates of the hyperactives with no history of hyperactivity	Prospective for hyperactives; controls identified retrospectively
Henry, Avshalom, Moffitt, and Silva (1996)	Males born in 1972-1973 who participated in the Dunedin Multidisciplinary Health and Development Study (New Zealand)	Prospective
Hogh and Wolf (1983)	Nearly all men born in 1953 in the Danish cities of Copenhagen, Frederiksberg, and Genofte, and the counties of Copenhagen, Roskilde, and Frederiksberg	Prospective
Kandel, Brennan, Mednick, and Michelson (1989) Kandel and Mednick (1991)	Subset of persons born between September 1959 and December 1961 in the Rigshospitalet in Copenhagen, Denmark	Prospective
Kawaguchi and Butler (1982)	Young adults originally included in a 10% random household survey of Riverside, California, in 1963	Prospective
Klinteberg, Andersson, Magnusson, and Stattin (1993)	All males who attended Grade 6 in a town (Orebro) in Sweden in 1968	Prospective
Loney, Kramer, and Milich (1983)	Persons diagnosed as hyperactive as children and treated at the University of Iowa Outpatient Psychiatry Clinic between 1967 and 1972	Retrospective
Loney, Whaley-Klahn, Kosier, and Conboy (1983)	Persons diagnosed as hyperactive and treated at the University of Iowa Outpatient Psychiatry Clinic between 1967 and 1972 and nonhyperactive controls who were the full brothers of the hyperactives	Prospective for hyperactives; controls identified retrospectively

TABLE 7.1 *Continued*

Study	Sample	Design
Maguin et al. (1995) Williams (1994)	Ethnically diverse youths who were fifth-grade students in 18 Seattle public elementary schools in high-crime neighborhoods in 1985 (Seattle Social Development Project); Williams (1994) included a subset of subjects from the overall study	Prospective
Mannuzza, Klein, Konig, and Giampino (1989)	White, English-speaking men who were diagnosed as hyperactive and treated at the Long Island Jewish-Hillside Medical Center, New York in the 1970s, and nonhyperactive controls who were seen in the medical center for physical exams/acute conditions or brothers of these patients	Prospective for hyperactives; controls identified retrospectively
McCord, McCord, and Zola (1959) McCord (1979)	Men who were judged at risk for delinquency and received intensive case management in the Boston area in the 1930s (Cambridge-Somerville Youth Study)	Prospective
McCord and Ensminger (1995)	African Americans who were first-grade students in Woodlawn, Illinois (a Chicago suburb) in 1966	Prospective
Mitchell and Rosa (1979)	Subset of a 10% random sample of students in schools in Buckinghamshire, England, in 1961	Prospective
Moffitt (1987)	Most of the males who were adopted by kin between birth and 18 months of age in Denmark between 1924 and 1947	Retrospective
Olweus (1977)	Boys who were in seven classes of four primary schools in central and eastern Stockholm, Sweden	Prospective
Olweus (1977)	Boys who were in 18 classes in six schools in Solna, Sweden (in Stockholm)	Prospective
Paschall (1996)	African American male youths in a small city in the southeastern U.S.	Prospective
Robins (1966)	Former psychiatric patients treated at the St. Louis Municipal Psychiatric Clinic during the 1920s and controls selected by year of birth, sex, and residential area.	Retrospective
Smith and Thornberry (1995)	A stratified random sample of adolescents in Rochester, New York, public schools in 1988; males and students from high-crime areas were oversampled (Rochester Youth Development Study)	Prospective
Stattin and Magnusson (1989)	A complete school grade cohort of students (age 10 in 1965) in a town (Orebro) in central Sweden	Prospective
Thornberry, Huizinga, and Loeber (1995)	Adolescents who attended Rochester (New York) public schools in 1988. At recruitment, students were in the seventh and eighth grades.	Prospective
Wadsworth (1976) Wadsworth (1978)	Members of a birth cohort sample of young men in England, Scotland, and Wales that was generally representative of all single legitimate live births between March 3 and 9, 1946 (National Survey of Health and Development)	Prospective
Wells and Rankin (1988)	A nationally representative sample of U.S. high school students in 1966-1967 (Youth in Transition Study)	Prospective
White (1992)	A representative sample of adolescents in New Jersey households with telephones in 1979-1981	Prospective

continued

TABLE 7.1 *Continued*

Study	Sample	Design
Widom (1989)	Children who were maltreated between 1967 and 1971 and identified from court records in a midwest U.S. metropolitan area, and nonmaltreated controls matched according to age, sex, race, hospital of birth, and school in childhood	Retrospective
Wikström (1985)	A birth cohort born in the greater Stockholm area in 1953 (the Project Metropolitan)	Prospective
Zingraff, Leiter, Myers, and Johnson (1993)	Children who were maltreated between 1983 and 1989 in Mecklenburg County and identified in a state registry of child abuse and neglect, nonmaltreated children in a random sample of students in county public schools in 1983-1989, and nonmaltreated children who were 9 years old in 1989 and whose families were involved with the Department of Social Services and generally poor	Retrospective

Low resting heart rate. A low pulse rate when at rest is also weakly predictive of violent crime (Farrington, in press; Wadsworth, 1976). Wadsworth (1976) reported that 81% of violent offenders and 67% of sexual offenders in the British National Survey of Health and Development had below-average heart rates (p. 249). It is thought that a low pulse rate is an indicator of a fearless temperament and/or underarousal that predisposes some individuals toward aggression and violence (Raine & Jones, 1987).

Clearly, at this point, the evidence is not sufficiently strong to allow the use of these medical/physical indicators of pregnancy and delivery complications or low resting heart rate to identify those at risk for future violence. More research on the link between biology and violent behavior is needed that capitalizes on advances in research on the brain, gene expression, and behavior.

Psychological Characteristics

Hyperactivity, attention deficit, impulsivity, and risk taking. As shown in Table 7. 2, research on a constellation of related psycho-logical characteristics including hyperactivity, attention or concentration deficits, impulsivity, and risk taking has revealed more consistent predictions of violence. The weighted mean correlation between hyperactivity and violence for the four studies reviewed in Table 7.2 is .13 (cumulative $Z = 3.94$; 1,059 subjects). Regardless of measurement methods used, there appears to be a consistent relationship between hyperactivity and later violent behavior.

For example, Loney, Whaley-Klahn, Kosier, and Conboy's (1983) research indicates that hyperactivity is an individual characteristic not shared with siblings. Boys diagnosed as hyperactive in their study were notably more violent than their male full siblings (weighted mean $r = .22$). The mechanisms linking hyperactivity to later violence are not well understood.

Teacher ratings of children's concentration problems also predicted later violence in both adolescence and adulthood among males. The weighted mean correlation between concentration problems and violence among males for the studies reviewed in Table 7.2 was .17 (cumulative $Z = 5.05$; 951 subjects). Concentration problems also predicted academic difficulties, which themselves predict later violence, again suggesting multivariate models for understanding violence.

Teacher ratings of restlessness, including difficulty sitting still, tendency to fidget, and frequent talkativeness, were positively related to later violence in males. The weighted mean correlation between restlessness and later violence for the studies reviewed is .20 (cumulative $Z = 6.18$; 951 subjects).

Farrington's (1989a) analysis of the Cambridge study of 411 London boys also found that impulsivity in childhood was somewhat predictive of both self-reported and officially recorded later violence.

Stronger relationships have been reported between risk taking or "daring" measured in late childhood and early adolescence and later violence. The weighted mean correlation between risk taking and violence for the two studies summarized in Table 7.2 is .25 (cumulative $Z = 8.32$; 1,147 subjects).

The evidence from these studies consistently reveals a positive relationship between hyperactivity, concentration or attention problems, impulsivity, and risk taking and later violent behavior. When combined, these factors appear particularly salient in predicting violence. In the Orebro longitudinal study in Sweden, for example, 15% of boys with both restlessness and concentration difficulties at age 13 were arrested for violence by age 26 compared with 3% of the remainder (Klinteberg, Andersson, Magnusson, & Stattin, 1993, p. 382). Hyperactive and restless boys, who have trouble concentrating in school and like to take risks, are at greater risk of future violence than boys without these characteristics.

Internalizing disorders: Nervousness/withdrawal, worrying, and anxiety. A second category of psychological characteristics investigated in relation to violent behavior is internalizing disorders including nervousness/withdrawal, worrying, and anxiety. Generally, these characteristics have been found to be slightly negatively correlated (Mitchell & Rosa, 1979) or unrelated to later violence (Farrington, 1989a). This suggests that nervousness/withdrawal is not strongly linked to violence in adolescence, though childhood nervousness/withdrawal may serve to protect, albeit weakly, against future violence.

Aggressiveness. Continuity in antisocial behavior from early aggression to violent crime has been noted by many researchers (Loeber, 1990, 1996; Loeber & Hay, 1996; Olweus, 1979). As shown in Table 7.2, aggressive behavior measured from age 6 through age 13 has been shown consistently to predict later violence among males across studies. Two thirds of the boys with high teacher-rated aggression scores at ages 10 and 13 in the Orebro, Sweden, study had criminal records for violent offenses by age 26 (Stattin & Magnusson, 1989, p. 714). In the Woodlawn, Chicago, sample of African American youths, nearly half of the boys rated as aggressive by their teachers at age 6 had been arrested for violent crimes by age 33, compared with a third of their nonaggressive counterparts (McCord & Ensminger, 1995, p. 10). McCord and Ensminger found similar results for females, but Stattin and Magnusson (1989) did not find a relationship between female aggression measured at age 10 and later officially recorded violent offenses.

These studies show a consistent relationship between aggressiveness in males measured from age 6 and later violent behavior. This relationship holds even in hyperactive samples (Loney, Kramer, & Milich, 1983). Although many boys who manifest aggressive behavior in childhood do not commit violent crimes, early and persistent aggressive behavior is an important malleable individual

(Text continued on page 132)

TABLE 7.2 Findings From Longitudinal Studies

Study	Predictor	Violence Measure	Strength of Association	Odds Ratio
		Individual Factors		
		Pregnancy and delivery complications		
Kandel and Mednick (1991)	Pregnancy complication identified at birth (males/females)	Official violent offenses by age 20-22	$n = 216, r = -.02$	9
	Multiple delivery complications identified at birth (males/females)		$n = 216, r = .18$	4.3
Raine, Brennan, and Mednick (1994)	Birth/delivery complications (males)	Official violent offenses by age 17-19	$n = 3,175, r = .15$	—
Kandel, Brennan, Mednick, and Michelson (1989)	Minor physical abnormalities at age 11-13 indicating first trimester pregnancy complications (males/females)	Official violent offenses by age 20-22	$n = 265, r = .15$	—
Farrington (in press)	Pregnancy complications measured at age 8-10 (males, London)	Official violent offenses between ages 10 and 21		.3
		Self-reported violence between ages 10 and 21		.9
	Delivery complications measured at age 8-10 (males, London)	Official violent offenses between ages 10 and 21		.5
		Self-reported violence between ages 10 and 21		1.2
Denno (1990)	Number of prenatal conditions measured at birth (males/females)	Official violent offenses at age 10-17	No association found	
	Number of birth complications measured at birth	Official violent offenses at age 10-17	No association found	
		Low resting heart rate		
Wadsworth (1976)	Low resting heart rate at age 11 (males)	Official violent offenses by age 21	$n = 1,813, r = -.04$	2.0
		Hyperactivity, attention deficit, impulsivity		
Hechtman and Weiss (1986)	Hyperactivity at age 6-12 (males/females)	Self-reported violence at age 21-33	$n = 61, r = .17$	.1/.0
Loney, Kramer, and Milich (1983)	Childhood hyperactivity (males)	Self-reported violence at age 21-23	$n = 44, r = .22$	2.34

TABLE 7.2 *Continued*

Study	Predictor	Violence Measure	Strength of Association	Odds Ratio
Hyperactivity, attention deficit, impulsivity (continued)				
Mannuzza, Klein, Konig, and Giampino (1989)	Childhood hyperactivity (males)	Official violent offenses by age 19-26 (assault)	$n = 189, r = .16$	4.3
		Official violent offenses by age 19-26 (robbery)	$n = 189, r = .08$	3.0
Maguin et al. (1995)	Hyperactivity/low attention at age 10 (males/females)	Self-reported violence at age 18	$n = 725, r = .13$	
	Hyperactivity/low attention at age 14 (males/females)		$n = 745, r = .16$	
	Hyperactivity/low attention at age 16 (males/females)		$n = 702, r = .08$	

Weighted mean correlation between hyperactivity and violence is .13 (cumulative Z = 3.94, 1,059 subjects)

Study	Predictor	Violence Measure	Strength of Association	Odds Ratio
Farrington (1989a)	Concentration problems at age 8-10 (males)	Self-reported violence at age 16-18	$n = 410, r = .06$	1.4
		Self-reported violence at age 32	$n = 410, r = .04$	1.2
		Violent crime convictions between ages 10 and 32	$n = 410, r = .11$	2.0
	Concentration problems at age 12-14 (males)	Self-reported violence at age 16-18	$n = 411, r = .14$	2.3
		Self-reported violence by age 32	$n = 411, r = .08$	1.6
		Violent crime convictions between ages 10 and 32	$n = 411, r = .17$	3.1
Klinteberg, Andersson, Magnusson, and Stattin (1993)	Concentration problems at age 13 (males)	Official violent offenses by age 26	$n = 540, r = .21$	5.0

Weighted mean correlation between concentration problems and violence is .17 (cumulative Z = 5.50, 951 subjects)

Study	Predictor	Violence Measure	Strength of Association	Odds Ratio
Klinteberg et al. (1993)	Restlessness at age 13 (males)	Official violent offenses by age 26	$n = 540, r = .20$	5.0
Farrington (1989a)	Restlessness at age 12-14 (males)	Self-reported violence at age 16-18	$n = 411, r = .18$	2.5
		Self-reported violence at age 32	$n = 411, r = .19$	2.6
		Violent crime convictions between ages 10 and 32	$n = 411, r = .20$	3.3

Weighted mean correlation between restlessness and violence = .20 (cumulative Z = 6.18, 951 subjects)

continued

TABLE 7.2 *Continued*

Study	Predictor	Violence Measure	Strength of Association	Odds Ratio
Hyperactivity, attention deficit, impulsivity (continued)				
Farrington (1989a)	Impulsivity at age 8-10 (males)	Self-reported violence at age 16-18	$n = 411, r = .09$	1.5
		Self-reported violence at age 32	$n = 411, r = .10$	1.5
		Violent crime convictions between ages 10 and 32	$n = 411, r = .07$	1.3
	Risk taking at age 8-10 (males)	Self-reported violence at age 16-18	$n = 408, r = .20$	2.5
		Self-reported violence at age 32	$n = 408, r = .21$	2.5
		Violent crime convictions between ages 10 and 32	$n = 408, r = .18$	3.0
	Risk taking at age 12-14 (males)	Self-reported violence at age 16-18	$n = 411, r = .15$	2.4
Farrington (1989a)	Risk taking at age 12-14 (males)	Self-reported violence at age 32	$n = 411, r = .18$	2.7
		Violent crime convictions between ages 10 and 32	$n = 411, r = .17$	3.3
Maguin et al. (1995)	Risk taking at age 14 (males/females)	Self-reported violence at age 18	$n = 700, r = .06$	
	Risk taking at age 16 (males/females)	Self-reported violence at age 18	$n = 698, r = .13$	
Weighted mean correlation between risk taking and violence is .25 (cumulative Z = 8.32, 1,147 subjects)				
Nervousness/withdrawal, worrying, anxiety				
Mitchell and Rosa (1979)	Worrying at age 5-15 (males)	Official violent offenses by age 20-30	$n = 321, r = -.09$	1.0
Farrington (1989a)	Nervousness/withdrawal at age 8-10 (males)	Self-reported violence at age 16-18	$n = 389, r = -.07$	.7
		Self-reported violence at age 32	$n = 389, r = -.05$	.8
		Violent crime convictions between ages 10 and 32	$n = 389, r = -.02$	.9
	Nervousness/withdrawal at age 14 (males)	Self-reported violence at age 16-18	$n = 385, r = -.01$	1.0
		Self-reported violence at age 32	$n = 385, r = -.03$	1.2

TABLE 7.2 *Continued*

Study	Predictor	Violence Measure	Strength of Association	Odds Ratio
	Nervousness/withdrawal, worrying, anxiety (continued)			
Farrington (1989a)	Nervousness/withdrawal at age 12-14 (males)	Violent crime convictions between ages 10 and 32	$n = 385, r = .02$	1.1
	Anxiety at age 12-14 (males)	Self-reported violence at age 16-18	$n = 411, r = .02$	1.1
		Self-reported violence at age 32	$n = 411, r = -.02$	.9
		Violent crime convictions between ages 10 and 32	$n = 411, r = .04$	1.5
	Aggressiveness			
Farrington (1989a)	High aggressiveness at age 12-14 (males)	Self-reported violence at age 16-18	$n = 411, r = .25$	3.1
		Self-reported violence at age 32	$n = 411, r = .15$	1.9
		Violent crime convictions between ages 10 and 32	$n = 411, r = .22$	3.6
McCord and Ensminger (1995)	Teacher-rated aggressiveness in first grade (males)	Official violent offenses by late 20s	$n = 455, r = .15$	1.7
	Teacher-rated aggressiveness in first grade (females)	Official violent offenses by late 20s	$n = 498, r = .15$	2.7
Loney, Whaley-Klahn, Kosier, and Conboy (1983)	Childhood aggression among hyperactive boys (males)	Self-reported violence at age 12-18	$n = 30, r = .20$	—
Olweus (1977)	Peer-rated aggression at age 13	Peer-rated aggression at age 14	$n = 85, r = .81$	—
Olweus (1977)	Peer-rated aggression at age 13	Peer-rated aggression at age 16	$n = 201, r = .65$	—
Stattin and Magnusson (1989)	Teacher-rated aggression at age 10 (males)	Official violent offenses by age 26	$n = 514, r = .22$	6.3
Stattin and Magnusson (1989)	Teacher-rated aggression at age 10 (females)	Official violent offenses by age 26	$n = 507, r = -.03$	0.0
	Teacher-rated aggression at age 13 (males)		$n = 538, r = .19$	4.7
	Teacher-rated aggression at age 13 (females)		$n = 547, r = .17$	.04/.00
	Early initiation of violence and delinquency			
Thornberry (1995)	Onset of violence by age 9	Self-reported violence at age 16	Positive association	

continued

TABLE 7.2 *Continued*

Study	Predictor	Violence Measure	Strength of Association	Odds Ratio

Study	Predictor	Violence Measure	Strength of Association	Odds Ratio
Early initiation of violence and delinquency (continued)				
Tolan and Thomas (1995)	Delinquent behavior before age 12 (male/female)	Official and self-reported violence during adolescence	Positive association	
White (1992)	Violent behavior at age 15 (males)	Self-reported violence at age 18	n = 205, r = .45	—
		Self-reported violence at age 21	n = 205, r = .21	—
	Violent behavior at age 15 (females)	Self-reported violence at age 18	n = 219, r = .28	—
		Self-reported violence at age 21	n = 219, r = −.02	—
Other antisocial behaviors				
Mitchell and Rosa (1979)	Parent reports of stealing at age 5-15 (males)	Official violent offenses by age 20-30	n = 321, r = .23	11.7
	Teacher reports of stealing at age 5-15 (males)		n = 321, r = .14	5.3
	Parent reports of destructive behavior at age 5-15 (males)		n = 321, r = .13	4.3
	Parent reports of disobedience at age 5-15 (males)		n = 321, r = .00	—
Robins (1966)	Antisocial behavior at age 6-17 (males)	Official violent offenses (robbery)	n = 329, r = .20	.19/.00
		Official violent offenses (rape)	n = 329, r = .06	.02/.00
		Official violent offenses (murder)	n = 329, r = .05	.01/.00
		Official violent offenses (sex crimes)	n = 329, r = .09	.04/.00
		Official violent offenses (robbery)	n = 112, r = .00	0.0
		Official violent offenses (rape)	n = 112, r = .00	0.0
		Official violent offenses (murder)	n = 112, r = .00	0.0
		Official violent offenses (sex crimes)	n = 112, r = .06	.01/.00
Farrington (1989a)	Self-reported delinquency at age 14 (males)	Self-reported violence at age 16-18	n = 405, r = .30	4.4
		Self-reported violence at age 32	n = 405, r = .15	2.1

TABLE 7.2 *Continued*

Study	Predictor	Violence Measure	Strength of Association	Odds Ratio
		Early initiation of violence and delinquency (continued)		
Farrington (1989a)	Self-reported delinquency at age 14 (males)	Violent crime convictions between ages 10 and 32	$n = 405, r = .26$	4.8
	Cigarette smoking before age 14 (males)	Self-reported violence at age 16-18	$n = 389, r = .13$	2.5
		Self-reported violence at age 32	$n = 389, r = .09$	1.6
		Violent crime convictions between ages 10 and 32	$n = 389, r = .13$	2.4
	Sexual intercourse by age 14 (males)	Self-reported violence at age 16-18	$n = 405, r = .27$	4.9
		Self-reported violence at age 32	$n = 405, r = .05$	1.3
		Violent crime convictions between ages 10 and 32	$n = 405, r = .22$	4.3
	Discipline problems at age 8-10 (males)	Self-reported violence at age 16-18	$n = 410, r = .13$	1.9
		Self-reported violence at age 32	$n = 410, r = .13$	1.9
		Violent crime convictions between ages 10 and 32	$n = 410, r = .14$	2.4
Maguin et al. (1995)	Drug selling at age 14 (males/females)	Self-reported violence at age 18	$n = 734, r = .18$	—
	Drug selling at age 16 (males/females)		$n = 735, r = .19$	—
		Attitudes and beliefs		
Williams (1994)	Self-reported antisocial beliefs at age 14 (African American) (males/females)	Self-reported violence at age 16	$n = 121, r = -.12$	—
	Self-reported antisocial beliefs at age 14 (European American) (males/females)		$n = 266, r = -.15$	—
	Self-reported antisocial beliefs at age 14 (females)		$n = 193, r = -.04$	—
	Self-reported antisocial beliefs at age 14 (males)	Self-reported violence at age 16	$n = 194, r = -.19$	—
Ageton (1983)	Deviant attitudes at age 11-17 (males)	Self-reported sexual assaults at age 13-19	$n = 66, r = -.28$	—

continued

TABLE 7.2 *Continued*

Study	Predictor	Violence Measure	Strength of Association	Odds Ratio
		Attitudes and beliefs (continued)		
Ageton (1983)	Deviant attitudes at age 12-18 (males)		$n = 66, r = -.16$	—
Elliott (1994)	Deviant attitudes at age 11-17	Self-reported violence during adolescence and adulthood	Positive association	—
Maguin et al. (1995)	Violent attitudes at age 14 (males/females)	Self-reported violence at age 18	$n = 732, r = .15$	—
Farrington (1989a)	Hostility to police at age 14-16 (males)	Self-reported violence at age 16-18	$n = 405, r = .20$	2.5
		Self-reported violence at age 32	$n = 405, r = .06$	1.3
		Violent crime convictions between ages 10 and 32	$n = 405, r = .23$	4.1
	Peer-rated dishonesty at age 10 (males)	Self-reported violence at age 16-18	$n = 353, r = .08$	1.5
		Self-reported violence at age 32	$n = 353, r = .15$	2.0
		Violent crime convictions between ages 10 and 32	$n = 321, r = .15$	9.0
Mitchell and Rosa (1979)	Dishonesty at age 5-15 (parent report) (males)	Official violent offenses by age 20-30	$n = 321, r = .13$	4.5
	Dishonesty at age 5-15 (teacher report) (males)		$n = 321, r = .16$	5.3
			$n = 321, r = .19$	

Weighted mean correlation between dishonesty and violence is .16 (cumulative Z = 4.14, 674 subjects)

Family Factors
Parental criminality

Study	Predictor	Violence Measure	Strength of Association	Odds Ratio
Baker and Mednick (1984)	Father's criminality (males/females)	Official violent offenses by age 18-23	$n = 188, r = .25$	3.8
Farrington (1989a)	Parents' criminal arrests before child was age 10 (males)	Self-reported violence at age 16-18	$n = 411, r = .16$	2.2
		Self-reported violence at age 32	$n = 411, r = .11$	1.7
		Violent crime convictions between ages 10 and 32	$n = 411, r = .18$	2.8

TABLE 7.2 *Continued*

Study	Predictor	Violence Measure	Strength of Association	Odds Ratio
\multicolumn{5}{c}{*Parental criminality* (continued)}				
Maguin et al. (1995)	Parents' criminality before child was 14 (males/females)	Self-reported violence at age 18	$n = 700, r = .06$	—
	Parents' criminality before child was 16 (males/females)		$n = 698, r = .13$	—
Moffitt (1987)	Parents' criminality (males)	Official violent offenses by age 29-52	$n = 5,024, r = .01$	1.0
McCord (1979)	Fathers' alcohol abuse and criminality (males)	Official violent offenses by adulthood	$n = 201, r = .00$	—
Moffitt (1987)	Parents' mental illness (psychosis) (males)	Official violent offenses by age 29-52	$n = 4,626, r = .01$	.03
	Parents' mental illness (social problem disorder) (males)	Official violent offenses by age 29-52	$n = 4,626, r = .02$	2.0
\multicolumn{5}{c}{*Child maltreatment*}				
Widom (1989)	Child sexual abuse (males/females)	Official violent offenses by adulthood	$n = 1,575, r = -.04$	.7
	Child physical abuse (males/females)		$n = 1,547, r = .02$	2.1
	Child neglect (males/females)		$n = 1,547, r = .06$	1.6
Zingraff, Leiter, Myers, and Johnson (1993)	Child abuse and neglect (total maltreatment) (males/females)	Official violent offenses	$n = 1,091, r = .06$	3.0
	Child physical abuse (males/females)		$n = 148, r = .01$	1.0
	Child neglect (males/females)		$n = 401, r = .07$	2.0
	Child sexual abuse (males/females)		$n = 84, r = -.02$	.3
	Frequency of abuse/neglect (males/females)		$n = 72, r = .05$	1.9
Smith and Thornberry (1995)	Child abuse and neglect prior to age 12 (males/females)	Self-reported violence at age 12-18	$n = 889, r = .09$	—

Weighted mean correlation between child maltreatment and violence is .06 (cumulative $Z = 3.84$, 3,555 subjects); sexual abuse and violence is $-.03$ (cumulative $Z = -1.59$, 2,666 subjects); physical abuse and violence is .02 (cumulative $Z = 0.79$, 2,666 subjects); neglect and violence is .07 (cumulative $Z = 3.62$, 2,666 subjects)

continued

TABLE 7.2 *Continued*

Study	Predictor	Violence Measure	Strength of Association	Odds Ratio
		Poor family management		
McCord, McCord, and Zola (1959)	Lax discipline by parents (males)	Official violent offenses by mid- to late 20s	$n = 250, r = .12$	8.0
	Punitive discipline by parents (males)		$n = 248, r = .13$	3.3
McCord (1979)	Aggressive discipline by parents (males)	Violent crime convictions by adulthood	$n = 201, r = .19$	—
Wells and Rankin (1988)	High parental strictness in Grade 10 (males)	Self-reported violence in adolescence	$n = 1,561$, eta[a] $= .10$	—
	Parental regulation/restriction in Grade 10 (males)		$n = 1,561, r = .00$	—
	Consistent discipline by parents in Grade 10 (males)		$n = 1,561, r = -.12$	—
	Parental punitiveness in Grade 10 (males)		$n = 1,561, r = .16$	—
Farrington (1989a)	Parent reports of poor child rearing at age 8 (males)	Self-reported violence at age 16-18	$n = 396, r = .07$	1.4
		Self-reported violence at age 32	$n = 396, r = .03$	1.2
		Violent crime convictions between ages 10 and 32	$n = 396, r = .13$	2.3
	Parent-reported authoritarian parenting style at age 10 (males)	Self-reported violence at age 16-18	$n = 299, r = .09$	1.5
		Self-reported violence at age 32	$n = 299, r = .08$	1.5
		Violent crime convictions between ages 10 and 32	$n = 299, r = .19$	3.1
	Parent-reported poor parental supervision at age 8 (males)	Self-reported violence at age 16-18	$n = 383, r = .18$	2.4
		Self-reported violence at age 32	$n = 383, r = .09$	1.6
		Violent crime convictions between ages 10 and 32	$n = 383, r = .17$	3.0
	Parent-reported harsh parental discipline at age 8 (males)	Self-reported violence at age 16-18	$n = 391, r = .12$	1.7
		Self-reported violence at age 32	$n = 391, r = .03$	1.2

TABLE 7.2 *Continued*

Study	Predictor	Violence Measure	Strength of Association	Odds Ratio
		Poor family management (continued)		
Farrington (1989a)	Parent-reported of poor child rearing at age 8 (males)	Violent crime convictions between ages 10 and 32	$n = 391, r = .17$	2.9
	Parent-reported cruel, passive, or neglecting parental attitude at age 14 (males)	Self-reported violence at age 16-18	$n = 384, r = .04$	1.2
		Self-reported violence at age 32	$n = 384, r = .10$	1.6
		Violent crime convictions between ages 10 and 32	$n = 384, r = .03$	1.3
	Parent-reported disagreements about child rearing at age 8 (males)	Self-reported violence at age 16-18	$n = 382, r = .01$	1.0
		Self-reported violence at age 32	$n = 382, r = .05$	1.2
		Violent crime convictions between ages 10 and 32	$n = 382, r = .15$	2.4
Maguin et al. (1995)	Poor family management at age 10 (males/females)	Self-reported violence at age 18	$n = 744, r = .07$	—
	Poor family management at age 14 (males/females)		$n = 734, r = .23$	—
	Poor family management at age 16 (males/females)		$n = 733, r = .22$	—
Williams (1994)	Proactive family management at age 14 (African American) (males/females)	Self-reported violence at age 16	$n = 121, r = -.13$	—
	Proactive family management at age 14 (European American) (males/females)		$n = 265, r = -.08$	—
	Proactive family management at age 14 (females)		$n = 193, r = -.05$	—
	Proactive family management at age 14 (males)		$n = 194, r = -.13$	—

Weighted mean correlation between poor family management and violence is .12 (cumulative Z = 6.10, 2,918 subjects)

		Parent-child involvement and interaction		
Williams (1994)	Family involvement/ communication at age 14 (African American) (males/females)	Self-reported violence at age 16	$n = 121, r = -.12$	—

continued

TABLE 7.2 *Continued*

Study	Predictor	Violence Measure	Strength of Association	Odds Ratio
Parent-child involvement and interaction (continued)				
Williams (1994)	Family involvement/ communication at age 14 (European American) (males/females)	Self-reported violence at age 16	$n = 266, r = -.15$	—
	Family involvement/ communication at age 14 (females)		$n = 193, r = -.04$	—
	Family involvement/ communication at age 14 (males)		$n = 194, r = -.19$	—
Farrington (1989a)	Fathers' involvement in leisure activities at age 12 (males)	Self-reported violence at age 16-18	$n = 299, r = .07$	1.4
		Self-reported violence at age 32	$n = 299, r = .19$	2.3
		Violent crime convictions between ages 10 and 32	$n = 299, r = .19$	3.3
	Parental involvement in education at age 8 (males)	Self-reported violence at age 16-18	$n = 381, r = .10$	1.8
		Self-reported violence at age 32	$n = 381, r = .10$	1.8
		Violent crime convictions between ages 10 and 32	$n = 381, r = .20$	3.7
Family bonding				
Williams (1994)	Family bonding at age 14 (African American) (males/females)	Self-reported violence at age 16	$n = 121, r = -.08$	—
	Family bonding at age 14 (European American) (males/females)		$n = 266, r = .03$	—
	Family bonding at age 14 (females)		$n = 193, r = -.03$	—
	Family bonding at age 14 (males)		$n = 194, r = -.01$	—
Elliott (1994)	Family bonding at age 11-17 (males/females)	Self-reported violence during adolescence and adulthood	No association found	—
Ageton (1983)	Negative family labeling at age 11-17 (males)	Self-reported sexual assaults at age 13-19	$n = 66, r = .10$	—
	Negative family labeling at age 12-18 (males)		$n = 66, r = .26$	—

TABLE 7.2 *Continued*

Study	Predictor	Violence Measure	Strength of Association	Odds Ratio
		Family and marital conflict		
Farrington (1989a)	Parental disharmony at age 14 (males)	Self-reported violence at age 16-18	$n = 326, r = .15$	2.2
		Self-reported violence at age 32	$n = 326, r = .12$	1.8
		Violent crime convictions between ages 10 and 32	$n = 326, r = .22$	4.1
McCord (1979)	Parents' marital conflict (males)	Violent crime convictions by adulthood	$n = 201, r = .19$	—
McCord, McCord, and Zola (1959)	Family conflict (males)	Official violent offenses during adolescence	$n = 253, r = .09$	2.3
Maguin et al. (1995)	Family conflict at age 10 (males/females)	Self-reported violence at age 18	$n = 718, r = -.01$	—
	Family conflict at age 14 (males/females)		$n = 734, r = .12$	—
	Family conflict at age 16 (males/females)		$n = 738, r = .18$	—

Weighted mean correlation between family/marital conflict and violence is .12 (cumulative $Z = 4.17$, *1,283 subjects)*

Elliott (1994)	Violence between parents at age 11-17 (males/females)	Self-reported violence during adolescence and adulthood	Positive association	—
		Parental attitudes favorable to violence		
Maguin et al. (1995)	Parents' attitudes favorable to violence at age 10 (males/females)	Self-reported violence at age 18	$n = 732, r = .15$	—
		Stressful family events		
Elliott (1994)	Family stress at age 11-17 (males/females)	Self-reported violence during adolescence and adulthood	No association found	—
		Residential mobility		
Maguin et al. (1995)	Changes in family residence at age 14 (males/females)	Self-reported violence at age 18	$n = 734, r = .06$	—
	Changes in family residence at age 16 (males/females)		$n = 743, r = .15$	—
		Separation from family and early home leaving		
Farrington (1989a)	Parent-child separation before age 10 (males)	Self-reported violence at age 16-18	$n = 411, r = .06$	1.3

continued

TABLE 7.2 *Continued*

Study	Predictor	Violence Measure	Strength of Association	Odds Ratio
Separation from family and early home leaving (continued)				
Farrington (1989a)	Parent-child separation before age 10 (males)	Self-reported violence at age 32	$n = 411$, $r = .10$	1.6
		Violent crime convictions between ages 10 and 32	$n = 411$, $r = .14$	2.5
Wadsworth (1978)	Family breakup before age 11	Official violent offenses by age 21		4.0
Henry, Avshalom, Moffitt, and Silva (1996)	Single-parent household at age 13 (males)	Violent crime convictions by age 18		3.3
McCord and Ensminger (1995)	Children's leaving home by age 16 (males)	Official violent offenses by adulthood	$n = 455$, $r = .11$	2.1
	Children's leaving home by age 16 (females)		$n = 498$, $r = .12$	3.0
School Factors				
Academic failure				
Denno (1990)	Academic achievement at age 7 (males)	Official violent offenses at age 10-17	$n = 487$, $r = -.09$	—
	Academic achievement at age 7 (females)		$n = 500$, $r = -.10$	—
	Academic achievement at age 13-14 (males)		$n = 487$, $r = -.14$	—
	Academic achievement at age 13-14 (females)		$n = 500$, $r = -.31$	—
Farrington (1989a)	Academic failure at age 11 (males)	Self-reported violence at age 16-18	$n = 386$, $r = .10$	1.5
		Self-reported violence at age 32	$n = 386$, $r = .06$	2.1
		Violent crime convictions between ages 10 and 32	$n = 386$, $r = .13$	3.2
	Low secondary allocation at age 11 (males)	Self-reported violence at age 16-18	$n = 411$, $r = .10$	1.5
		Self-reported violence at age 32	$n = 411$, $r = -.03$	.9
		Violent crime convictions between ages 10 and 32	$n = 411$, $r = .12$	2.0

TABLE 7.2 *Continued*

Study	Predictor	Violence Measure	Strength of Association	Odds Ratio
*Academic failure* (continued)				
Maguin et al. (1995)	Academic failure at age 10 (child report) (males/females)	Self-reported violence at age 18	$n = 718, r = .00$	—
	Academic failure at age 10 (parent report) (males/females)		$n = 536, r = .10$	—
	Academic failure at age 14 (child report) (males/females)		$n = 732, r = .11$	—
	Academic failure at age 14 (parent report) (males/females)		$n = 697, r = .20$	—
	Academic failure at age 16 (child report) (males/females)		$n = 714, r = .18$	—
*Low bonding to school (commitment/attachment)*				
Williams (1994)	Commitment/attachment to school at age 14 (African American) (males/females)	Self-reported violence at age 16	$n = 121, r = -.15$	—
	Commitment/attachment to school at age 14 (European American) (males/females)		$n = 266, r = -.04$	—
	Commitment/attachment to school at age 14 (females)		$n = 193, r = -.04$	—
	Commitment/attachment to school at age 14 (males)		$n = 103, r = -.14$	—
Maguin et al. (1995)	Low commitment to school at age 10 (males/females)	Self-reported violence at age 18	$n = 746, r = .03$	—
	Low commitment to school at age 14 (males/females)		$n = 730, r = .17$	
	Low commitment to school at age 16 (males/females)		$n = 726, r = .12$	—
Elliott (1994)	School bonding at age 11-17 (males/females)	Self-reported violence in adolescence and adulthood	No association found	—
Mitchell and Rosa (1979)	Commitment to school at age 5-15 (males)	Official violent offenses by age 20-30	$n = 321, r = .00$	—
Maguin et al. (1995)	Low educational aspirations at age 10 (males/females)	Self-reported violence at age 18	$n = 712, r = .03$	—
	Low educational aspirations at age 14 (males/females)		$n = 732, r = .10$	—
	Low educational aspirations at age 16 (males/females)		$n = 739, r = .09$	—

continued

TABLE 7.2 *Continued*

Study	Predictor	Violence Measure	Strength of Association	Odds Ratio
Truancy and early school leaving				
Farrington (1989a)	Truancy at age 12-14 (males)	Self-reported violence at age 16-18	$n = 411, r = .16$	2.3
		Self-reported violence at age 32	$n = 411, r = .17$	2.4
		Violent crime convictions between ages 10 and 32	$n = 411, r = .22$	3.8
	Leaving school before age 15 (males)	Self-reported violence at age 16-18	$n = 409, r = .25$	3.5
		Self-reported violence at age 32	$n = 409, r = .16$	2.0
		Self-reported violence between ages 10 and 32	$n = 409, r = .15$	2.7
School transitions				
Maguin et al. (1995)	School changes at age 14 (males/females)	Self-reported violence at age 18	$n = 740, r = .14$	—
	School changes at age 16 (males/females)		$n = 740, r = .18$	—
High delinquency rate school				
Farrington (1989a)	Attending high delinquency rate school at age 11 (males)	Self-reported violence at age 16-18	$n = 370, r = .01$	1.0
		Self-reported violence at age 10 and 32	$n = 370, r = .09$	1.6
		Violent crime convictions between ages 10 and 32	$n = 370, r = .03$	1.2
Occupational expectations				
Hogh and Wolf (1983)	Preferences for low-skill occupations at age 12 (males)	Official violent offenses between ages 15 and 22	$n = 7,917, r = -.06$	2.0
Peer Factors				
Sibling delinquency				
Maguin et al. (1995)	Sibling delinquency at age 10 (males/females)	Self-reported violence at age 18	$n = 592, r = .07$	—
	Sibling delinquency at age 14 (males/females)		$n = 718, r = .09$	—

TABLE 7.2 *Continued*

Study	Predictor	Violence Measure	Strength of Association	Odds Ratio
		Sibling delinquency (continued)		
Maguin et al. (1995)	Sibling delinquency at age 16 (males/females)	Self-reported violence at age 18	$n = 601, r = .23$	—
Williams (1994)	Sibling delinquency at age 14 (African American) (males/females)	Self-reported violence at age 16	$n = 121, r = .14$	—
	Sibling delinquency at age 14 (European American) (males/females)		$n = 266, r = .11$	—
	Sibling delinquency at age 14 (females)		$n = 193, r = .23$	—
	Sibling delinquency at age 14 (males)		$n = 194, r = .06$	—
Farrington (1989a)	Sibling crime involvement before age 10 (males)	Self-reported violence at age 16-18	$n = 411, r = .01$	1.1
		Self-reported violence at age 32	$n = 411, r = .05$	1.4
		Violent crime convictions between ages 10 and 32	$n = 411, r = .15$	2.9
	Sibling problem behavior by age 10 (males)	Self-reported violence at age 16-18	$n = 365, r = .09$	1.5
		Self-reported violence at age 32	$n = 365, r = .08$	1.5
		Violent crime convictions between ages 10 and 32	$n = 365, r = .14$	2.3
		Peer delinquency		
Maguin et al. (1995)	Association with delinquent peers at age 14 (males)	Self-reported violence at age 18	$n = 729, r = .27$	—
	Association with delinquent peers at age 16 (males)		$n = 720, r = .28$	—
Ageton (1983)	Exposure to delinquent peers at age 11-17 (males)	Self-reported sexual assaults at age 13-19	$n = 66, r = .16$	—
	Exposure to delinquent peers at age 12-18 (males)		$n = 66, r = .28$	—
Farrington (1989a)	Involvement with antisocial youths at age 14 (males)	Self-reported violence at age 16-18	$n = 405, r = .28$	3.7
		Self-reported violence at age 32	$n = 405, r = .13$	1.8
		Violent crime convictions between ages 10 and 32	$n = 405, r = .14$	2.6

continued

TABLE 7.2 *Continued*

Study	Predictor	Violence Measure	Strength of Association	Odds Ratio
		Peer delinquency (continued)		
Elliott (1994)	Exposure to delinquent peers at age 11-17 (males/females)	Self-reported violence during adolescence and adulthood	Positive association	—
Ageton (1983)	Commitment to delinquent peers at age 11-17 (males)	Self-reported sexual assaults at age 13-19	$n = 66, r = .28$	—
	Commitment to delinquent peers at age 12-18 (males)		$n = 66, r = -.14$	—
	Peer disapproval of delinquent behavior at age 11-17 (males)		$n = 66, r = -.25$	—
	Peer disapproval of delinquent behavior at age 12-18 (males)		$n = 66, r = -.28$	—
Elliott (1994)	Peer sanctions at age 11-17 (males/females)	Self-reported violence during adolescence and adulthood	Negative association	—
		Gang membership		
Maguin et al. (1995)	Gang membership at age 14 (males/females)	Self-reported violence at age 18	$n = 731, r = .18$	—
	Gang membership at age 16 (males/females)		$n = 730, r = .19$	—
		Community and Neighborhood Factors		
		Poverty		
Maguin et al. (1995)	Economic deprivation at age 10 (males/females)	Self-reported violence at age 18	$n = 504, r = .05$	—
	Economic deprivation at age 14 (males/females)		$n = 665, r = .03$	—
	Economic deprivation at age 16 (males/females)		$n = 678, r = .05$	—
Farrington (1989a)	Low family income at age 8	Self-reported violence at age 16-18	$n = 411, r = .15$	2.1
		Self-reported violence at age 32	$n = 411, r = .07$	1.4
		Violent crime convictions between ages 10 and 32	$n = 411, r = .19$	3.0
Farrington (in press-b)	Family on welfare at age 8-10 (males, London)	Self-reported violence between ages 10 and 21		2.0
		Official violent offenses between ages 10 and 21		7.5

TABLE 7.2 *Continued*

Study	Predictor	Violence Measure	Strength of Association	Odds Ratio
		Poverty (continued)		
Farrington (in press)	Poor housing at age 8-10 (males, London)	Self-reported violence between ages 10 and 21		1.6
		Official violent offenses between ages 10 and 21		2.1
	Family on welfare at age 10 (males, Pittsburgh)	Official violent offenses between ages 10 and 21		3.8
	Poor housing at age 8-10 (males, Pittsburgh)			1.2
Wikström (1985)	Low social class at birth (males/females)	Official violent crimes by age 25-26	$n = 14,539, r = -.08$	2.3
		Community disorganization and low neighborhood attachment		
Maguin et al. (1995)	Community disorganization at age 14 (males/females)	Self-reported violence at age 18	$n = 733, r = 20$	—
	Community disorganization at age 16 (males/females)		$n = 731, r = .27$	—
	Low neighborhood attachment at age 10 (males/females)		$n = 731, r = .09$	—
	Low neighborhood attachment at age 14 (males/females)		$n = 733, r = .02$	—
	Low neighborhood attachment at age 16 (males/females)		$n = 731, r = .11$	—
		Availability of drugs		
Maguin et al. (1995)	Availability of marijuana at age 10 (males/females)	Self-reported violence at age 18	$n = 732, r = .10$	—
	Availability of marijuana and cocaine at age 14 (males/females)		$n = 734, r = .21$	—
	Availability of marijuana and cocaine at age 16 (males/females)		$n = 739, r = .27$	—
		Neighborhood adults involved in crime		
Thornberry, Huizinga, and Loeber (1995)	Residence in a high-crime neighborhood at age 13-14	Self-reported violence at age 16		1.5
Maguin et al. (1995)	Adults involved in crime at age 14 (males/females)	Self-reported violence at age 18	$n = 732, r = .25$	—
	Adults involved in crime at age 16 (males/females)		$n = 737, r = .28$	—

continued

TABLE 7.2 *Continued*

Study	Predictor	Violence Measure	Strength of Association	Odds Ratio
		Exposure to violence in neighborhood		
Paschall (1996)	Exposure to violence at age 12-16 (males)	Self-reported violence at age 14-18		2.3
		Exposure to racial prejudice		
McCord and Ensminger (1995)	Racial discrimination/prejudice adulthood (males)	Official violent offenses by adulthood	$n = 455, r = .12$	1.9
	Racial discrimination/prejudice by adulthood (females)		$n = 498, r = .07$	1.8
		Community consequences for violence		
Maguin et al. (1995)	Likelihood of being apprehended by police at age 14 (males/females)	Self-reported violence at age 18	$n = 732, r = .06$	
	Likelihood of being apprehended by police at age 16 (males/females)		$n = 739, r = .08$	

a. Eta refers to a nonlinear relationship between variables.

characteristic predictive of later violence. Early aggressive behavior is a predictive risk factor but not an explanatory factor for violence, because both measure the same underlying construct.

Early initiation of violence and delinquency. Similarly, the early onset of violent behavior and delinquency predicts more chronic and serious violence (Farrington, 1991; Piper, 1985; Thornberry, Huizinga, & Loeber, 1995, p. 221; Tolan & Thomas, 1995), but it is not clear whether an early onset of offending predicts a higher rate or frequency of violent offending per year.

White (1992) assessed self-reported violence among 219 females and 205 males in the Rutgers Health and Human Development Project at ages 15, 18, and 21. As shown in Table 7.2, violence at age 15 predicted violence in later years for males, but less consistently and strongly for females.

There is a degree of continuity in violent behavior. Hamparian, Davis, Jacobson, and McGraw (1985, p. 16) found that 59% of violent juveniles were arrested as adults, and 42% of these adult offenders were charged with a violent offense. Farrington (1995, p. 14) found that half of the boys convicted for a violent offense between ages 10 and 16 were convicted of violence again by age 24, compared with only 8% of those not convicted of violence as juveniles. The nature of the relationship between early onset and violent careers requires greater exploration, but the evidence shows that early onset is associated with greater seriousness and chronicity of violence.

Other antisocial behaviors. More generally, involvement in a number of antisocial behaviors, including stealing, destruction of property, self-reported delinquency, smoking, early sexual intercourse, and drug selling, have been consistently linked to later violence among males, as shown in Table 7.2.

Mitchell and Rosa (1979) found that both stealing and destructive behavior at ages 5 to 15 predicted violent offenses in adulthood, but parent-rated disobedience was not predictive of later violence in their sample. Robins (1966) considered children's early deviant behavior and adult violence in her study of 524 former psychiatric patients. She found that men with histories of antisocial behavior from ages 6 to 17 were more often charged for robbery, rape, murder, and sex crimes as adults, but this pattern was not found for females, suggesting that there may be less consistency in antisocial behavior among females than among males. As shown in Table 7.2, in the Cambridge study, Farrington (1989a) found that discipline problems at ages 8 to 10, self-reported delinquency at age 14, regular cigarette smoking by age 14, and sexual intercourse by age 14 predicted later violence in males. Maguin et al. (1995) found that youths who reported selling drugs at ages 14 and 16 reported a greater variety of violent behaviors at age 18.

Consistent evidence suggests that involvement in virtually any form of antisocial behavior is associated with a greater risk of future violence among males. Because many of the predictors of violent behavior reviewed in this chapter are general precursors of substance use, delinquency, school dropout, and teen pregnancy (Dryfoos, 1991; Hawkins, Catalano, & Miller, 1992), preventive interventions seeking to change general precursors of antisocial behaviors may be specifically effective in preventing violence.

Attitudes and beliefs. Control theory asserts that beliefs or norms serve as internal controls against norm violating behaviors.

Several researchers have investigated individual attitudes and beliefs regarding violence as possible predictors of violence.

As shown in Table 7.2, dishonesty, antisocial beliefs and attitudes, attitudes favorable to violence, and hostility toward police have all been found to predict later violence among males. Where studied, these relationships appear less consistent among females (Williams, 1994). It may be that antisocial attitudes are symptoms of the same underlying construct as violence, and that this underlying construct persists throughout life.

The consistency of these findings regarding attitudes and behavior is not surprising but it is noteworthy (see also Zhang, Loeber, & Stouthamer-Loeber, 1997). The results suggest that a pattern of early attitudinal and behavioral defiance of basic rules of conduct such as honesty and truthfulness is associated with later violent behavior. Hence, preventive interventions that seek to help youths develop positive beliefs and standards for behavior that reject violence, cheating, and breaking rules and laws as well as positive attitudes toward law enforcement hold promise for reducing risks for violence. These findings underscore the importance of what some have called social and emotional literacy (Goleman, 1995), that is, the process of social development by which children learn to participate successfully in social life, by learning to take turns, wait in line, tell the truth, and so on.

Family Factors

Parental criminality. Baker and Mednick (1984) compared the violent crime arrest rates of Danish men with noncriminal fathers to those whose fathers had two or more recorded criminal offenses on the National Police Register of Denmark. Men aged 18-23 with criminal fathers were more likely to have committed violent criminal acts than those with noncriminal fathers. In the Cambridge study, Farrington (1989a) also found that parental arrest prior to boys' 10th birthday predicted respondents' self-reported and officially recorded violent crimes.

Moffitt (1987) investigated the possibility of a biological component in the influence of parental criminality on children's violent conduct. She studied the criminal records of 5,659 Danish male adoptees (whose adoptive parents had no criminal histories) and those of their biological parents and found that adult children (aged 29-52 at the time of assessment) with criminal parents were not much more likely to be registered for a violent offense than those with noncriminal parents. Her findings do not support a biological link between criminal parents and violent behavior of children, suggesting that violent norms and/or behaviors may be learned in criminal families. More research on the mechanisms by which criminal parents contribute to violence in children is needed.

Other studies have looked at related parental behavior problems as possible predictors of violence. Using a subsample of 201 boys from the Cambridge-Somerville Youth Study (McCord, McCord, & Zola, 1959), McCord (1979) assessed the relationship between paternal deviance, measured by whether the father was a known alcoholic, or was convicted for drunkenness or a serious crime, and officially recorded violent offenses of their sons. She did not find a link between the combined measure of fathers' alcoholism and criminal conduct and their sons' later violence in adolescence or adulthood. The relationship between parental mental illness and adolescent violence was investigated by Moffitt (1987) in her study of male adoptees. Parents' history of mental illness was assessed through a search of the Danish central register for psychiatric hospital admissions. She found very small and inconsistent relationships with violence in children.

Child maltreatment. Widom (1989) considered the criminal arrest rates for violent offenses, including murder, manslaughter, homicide, rape, and assault and battery, of adults who were abused or neglected as children as recorded in court records. As shown in Table 7.2, when compared with individuals with no prior abuse history, adults who were sexually abused were slightly less likely to commit a violent offense. Those who had been physically abused were slightly more likely to have been arrested for violence, whereas those who had been neglected were the most likely to commit violent crimes later in life. Zingraff, Leiter, Myers, and Johnson (1993) found similar results in an analysis of violent crime arrest rates for youths with a history of abuse or neglect and those with no record of maltreatment using North Carolina's central registry of child abuse and neglect. They also reported a positive association between the frequency of maltreatment and violence. In the Rochester study, Smith and Thornberry (1995) showed that adolescents with histories of abuse and neglect were more violent according to their own self-reports as adolescents. This relationship remained after controlling for gender, race, socioeconomic status, family structure, and family mobility.

The weighted mean correlation between child maltreatment and violence was .06 (cumulative $Z = 3.84$; 3,555 subjects). For sexual abuse and physical abuse independently, the weighted mean correlation with violence was negligible (sexual abuse: $-.03$, $Z = -1.59$; physical abuse: $.02$, $Z = 0.79$). The correlation for neglect and violence was stronger, $.07$, $Z = 3.62$, suggesting that neglect may be the form of child maltreatment most predictive of later violence.

Parent-child relations. Three separable dimensions of parent-child relations have been identified as predictors of crime in both theory and research: poor family management practices, involvement and interaction of the parent with the child, and bonding to the family. From the perspective of preventive intervention, it is important to consider each separately, because different interventions are required to change each of these factors. Furthermore, poor family management practices have typically been viewed as a risk factor for crime, whereas involvement and interaction of parents with their children and strong family bonding have typically been viewed as factors with the potential to protect children against the development of delinquent behavior (Catalano & Hawkins, 1996; Hirschi, 1969). The studies reviewed do not consistently allow determination of whether the latter two factors actually mediate or moderate the effects of risk exposure and, therefore, function as true protective factors (Farrington, 1993). Nevertheless, it is useful to identify them as possible protective factors for future analyses.

Poor family management practices. Research has consistently shown that parental failure to set clear expectations for children's behavior, poor parental monitoring and supervision of children, and excessively severe and inconsistent parental discipline of children represent a constellation of family management practices that predicts later delinquency and substance abuse (Capaldi & Patterson, 1996; Hawkins, Arthur, & Catalano, 1995). In fact, some have viewed child maltreatment as an extreme form of poor family management practices.

In the Cambridge-Somerville study, McCord et al. (1959) found that both lax and punitive parental discipline predicted convictions for violence among males through their late 20s. In a follow-up of the same sample, McCord (1979) found that poor parental supervision and the level of aggressiveness used by parents in disciplining children predicted convictions for personal crimes into the subjects' 40s.

Like the McCords, Wells and Rankin (1988) found a curvilinear relationship between parental strictness and self-reported violence in their sample of 10th-grade males. Boys with very strict parents reported the most violence. Boys with very permissive parents reported the second highest level of violence. And boys with parents who were neither very strict nor very lax reported the least violence. In their study, parental regulation/restriction (monitoring) was not predictive of later violence. However, boys whose parents punished them in a consistent manner were less likely to commit an offense against persons than boys whose parents punished them inconsistently. As in the McCord (1979) study, parental punitiveness in discipline was also predictive of later violence.

Farrington (1989a) found that poor child rearing, an authoritarian parenting style, poor parental supervision, harsh parental discipline, a cruel/passive/neglecting parenting attitude, and parental disagreement about child rearing each predicted later violence whether measured by self-reports or convictions for violent crimes.

In the Seattle Social Development Project, Maguin et al. (1995) assessed family management practices at ages 10, 14, and 16 using subjects' self-reports of their parents' childrearing practices (setting clear rules, monitoring, and using rewards and praise). Poor family management practices at ages 14 and 16 predicted self-reported violence at age 18, though children's reports of poor family management at age 10 were not significant predictors of violence at age 18. In an analysis of a subsample of the Seattle data set, Williams

(1994) found that proactive family management practices at age 14 negatively predicted self-reported violence at age 16 for African Americans and European Americans, males and females.

Parent-child involvement and interaction. Beyond the strategies parents use to manage their children, the degree to which parents interact with their children and are involved in their lives has also been hypothesized to predict crime and violence. Williams (1994) found that parent-child communication and involvement at age 14 was inversely related to self-reported violent behavior at age 16. As shown in Table 7.2, this relationship was relatively consistent for males, African Americans and European Americans, but was noticeably weaker for females. Similarly, Farrington (1989a) found that sons (age 12 at the time of assessment) whose fathers did not engage in leisure activities with them reported more violent behaviors as teenagers and adults and were more likely to be convicted for a violent offense. Low parental involvement in their sons' education at age 8 also predicted later violence. A lack of parental interaction and involvement in children's lives appears to contribute to a risk for future violence.

Family bonding. According to social control theory, bonding to the family inhibits crime and delinquency (Hirschi, 1969). However, few studies have looked specifically at the relationship between family bonding and violent behavior. Williams (1994) found that youths' self-reported bonding to their families at age 14 did not predict later self-reported violence. Elliott (1994) also reported a nonsignificant relationship between family bonding and violence in the National Youth Survey. In light of the relationship reported earlier between parental criminality and violence, studies addressing the link between family

bonding and later violent behavior may need to distinguish bonding to prosocial family members from bonding to antisocial or criminal family members to ascertain whether bonding to prosocial family members can inhibit later violence, as hypothesized by control theory. (See Foshee & Bauman, 1992, for a related discussion.)

Ageton (1983) assessed the link between a related variable called "negative family labeling" and sexual aggression in a sample of males from the National Youth Survey. Sexual aggression was measured by adolescents' self-reports of trying to have sex with someone against her or his will, pressuring a friend or date to engage in sexual acts, or physically hurting or threatening someone to have sex. A high degree of negative family labeling, measured a year and 2 years earlier, was positively associated with sexual aggression among 13- to 19-year-old boys.

Family and marital conflict. A few studies have investigated the relationship between family conflict, including discord and violence between adult partners, and the violent behavior of children. Farrington (1989a) found moderate correlations between parental disharmony and self-reported violence in adolescence and convictions for violent crimes. McCord (1979) also reported a link between marital conflict coded from case records and officially recorded violent crime in her sample of 201 boys, paralleling earlier findings from the Cambridge-Somerville Youth Study, which showed that boys raised in high-conflict families were more likely to be convicted of violent crime (McCord et al., 1959). In the Seattle Social Development study, Maguin et al. (1995) found that family conflict at age 10 was not associated with self-reported violence at age 18. However, high levels of family conflict at ages 14 and 16 were predictive of self-reported violent behavior at age 18. Elliott (1994) showed that individuals who were exposed to violent episodes between their parents were more violent as adults. These findings indicate that exposure to high levels of marital/family conflict increases the risk of violence.

Parental attitudes favorable to violence. There is evidence from studies of related health and behavior problems such as teen alcohol and drug use that parental attitudes predict adolescents' behaviors (Peterson, Hawkins, Abbott, & Catalano, 1994). However, this topic has been rarely investigated with regard to the effect of parental attitudes on the violent behavior of children. In the Seattle Social Development Project when children were aged 10, parents were asked a single question about the degree to which they approved of children's violent conduct. Children of parents who were more tolerant of violent behavior when they were 10 were more likely to self-report violent behavior at age 18 (Maguin et al., 1995). More study is needed on the relationship between parental attitudes toward adolescent violence and adolescent violence itself.

Stressful family events. Stressful life events have been linked to a broad range of psychiatric disorders. The influence of stressful family events on children's violent behavior was explored by Elliott when subjects in the National Youth Survey were between the ages of 11 and 17. He used a 15-item scale to assess family stresses resulting from serious illness, unemployment, divorce or separation, or a serious accident. Elliott (1994) found no relation between the number of stressful family events and children's later violence.

Residential mobility. Residential mobility has also been suggested as a predictor of violent behavior. Frequent moves may merely reflect a number of other factors such as poverty and family instability, or may inhibit the development of children's bonds in school and neighborhood and contribute to the risk of violence independently. Little research has focused on this question. In the Seattle data set, Maguin et al. (1995) found that the number of changes of residence in the past year assessed at age 16 predicted self-reported violent behavior at age 18, but residential mobility at age 14 did not significantly predict violence at age 18. These findings could indicate that residential moves have relatively short-term effects on behavior by disrupting bonds in school and neighborhood, and that these effects decrease with time as new bonds are formed in the new environment. Further research is needed to assess the contribution of residential mobility to violent behavior.

Separation from parents and early home leaving. There is evidence that disruptions of the parent-child relationship are predictive of later violent behavior of children. Farrington (1989a) found that parent-child separation before age 10 predicted self-reported violence among London boys in adolescence and adulthood as well as official convictions for violent crimes, confirming earlier findings from the British National Survey that showed that broken families before age 10 predicted convictions for violence up to age 21 (Wadsworth, 1978, p. 48). Similarly, a single-parent family at age 13 predicted convictions for violence by age 18 in the Dunedin study (Henry, Avshalom, Moffitt, & Silva, 1996, p. 618).

In a follow-up of the Woodlawn study of African American children, McCord and Ensminger (1995) investigated the relationship between children's leaving home at an early age and their later violence. Using retrospective accounts, the researchers determined whether study participants initially left their homes before age 16 or after reaching age 16. A search of Chicago court and

FBI records in 1993 provided data on officially recorded violent arrests. Early home leaving was associated with increased levels of violence for both men and women.

Again, parent-child separations may occur for many reasons that also predict violence suggesting the importance of theoretically guided multivariate studies of the relationships among family and other constructs in predicting violence.

School Factors

Measures of educational achievement and attainment, low interest in education, dropout, truancy, and poor-quality school are indicators of separable constructs related to schooling. Criminologists have hypothesized different mechanisms by which different aspects of school-related experiences affect criminal and violent behavior (Hawkins, Farrington, & Catalano, in press).

Academic failure. Poor academic achievement has consistently predicted later delinquent behavior (Maguin & Loeber, 1996). Denno (1990) found that academic achievement, assessed at age 7 and at age 13-14, was inversely related to violent offending across all subject areas for both males and females. In contrast to findings reported for other variables, the relationship between achievement and later violence was stronger for females than males, as shown in Table 7.2.

Farrington (1989a) found that low attainment in elementary school predicted convictions for violence. Twenty percent of those boys with teacher reports of low attainment in elementary school at age 11 were convicted of violence in adulthood, compared with less than 10% of the remainder of the sample. Allocation to a low academic track in secondary school by age 11 also nearly doubled the likelihood of adult convictions for violence

(Farrington, 1989a, pp. 85-85). Maguin et al. (1995) found that parental reports that their children had poor grades in school at ages 10, 14, and 16 predicted their children's self-reported violent behavior at age 18. Academic failure from the elementary grades is predictive of an increased risk of later violent behavior.

Low bonding to school. Theories of social control have emphasized the importance of a bond of commitment to schooling and attachment to school as an important protective factor against crime (Catalano & Hawkins, 1996; Hirschi, 1969). The available evidence generally supports the hypothesis that a low degree of bonding to school predicts later violent behavior, though it is somewhat mixed, varying in part, with the indicators of school commitment used.

In an analysis of a subsample of European Americans and African Americans from the Seattle Social Development Project, Williams (1994) found that bonding to school was more strongly linked to reduced violence among African American students and boys and less strongly linked with violence among European Americans and girls, as shown in Table 7.2.

Maguin et al. (1995) assessed the relationships between self-reports of low commitment to school at ages 10, 14, and 16 and self-reported violent behavior at age 18 in the Seattle data set. A low degree of commitment to school at age 10 did not predict later violence, but low commitment to school at ages 14 and 16 did. Similarly, low educational aspirations at age 10 did not predict later violence, but low educational aspirations at ages 14 and 16 did predict violent behavior at age 18, though less strongly than low commitment to school. In contrast, Elliott (1994) reported that school bonding was not a significant predictor of serious violent offending in the National Youth Survey, and Mitchell and

Rosa (1979) found no association between parents' early reports of their children's liking for school and their children's court-recorded violent crimes against persons between ages 20 and 30.

Truancy and dropping out of school. Truancy and dropping out of school may be behavioral indicators of a low degree of commitment to schooling, but there may be other reasons that children miss school or leave school early (Janosz, Le Blanc, Boulerice, & Tremblay, 1996). In the Cambridge study, those with high truancy rates at ages 12 to 14 were more likely to engage in violence in adolescence and adulthood and to be convicted of a violent offense (Farrington, 1989a). Similarly, leaving school prior to the age of 15 was predictive of later self-reported teenage violence, self-reported adult violence, and youth and adult violent convictions.

School transitions. In the Maguin et al. (1995) study, youths and parents in the Seattle Social Development Project were asked at ages 14 and 16 to indicate the number of times in the past year children had changed schools. Youths who had changed schools more often in the past year were more violent at age 18 than children who did not change schools. Again, it is important to understand how school transitions are related to other variables in predicting violence.

High delinquency rate school. Farrington (1989a) found that boys who attended schools with high rates of delinquency at age 11 reported slightly, but not significantly, more violent behavior than other youths.

Occupational aspirations/preferences. Hogh and Wolf (1983) considered the relationship between occupational aspirations/preferences and violence in a sample of 7,917 males, born in the Copenhagen area in 1953. A measure of occupational preferences was administered to study participants at the age of 12 and required that they rank 51 occupations according to their liking for them. Occupations were then categorized hierarchically according to their supposed professional status. The Denmark Central Policy Registry was used for collecting information on participants' subsequent violent crimes between the ages of 15 and 22. The researchers found that participants who indicated a preference for lower-status jobs were more likely to be registered for a violent offense between the ages of 15 and 22.

Peer-Related Factors

Delinquent siblings. Criminal parents predict a greater risk of violence. The effect of delinquent siblings on violent behavior has also been assessed. Farrington (1989a) found that delinquent siblings by age 10 predicted convictions for violence, but not self-reported violence in adolescence and adulthood. Twenty-six percent of boys in the Cambridge study with delinquent siblings by age 10 were convicted of violence compared with 10% of the remainder (Farrington, 1989a). Farrington also found a positive association between siblings' problem behaviors rated when subjects were age 10 and subjects' later convictions for violence.

Data from the Seattle study suggest that the relationship between sibling delinquency and subjects' violence is stronger when sibling delinquency is measured more proximately to violence and later in development (Maguin et al., 1995). This may reflect changes in the influences of siblings with development. Like delinquent peers, delinquent and antisocial siblings appear to have their strongest correlations with violent behavior during adolescence. Interestingly, Williams (1994) found that the influence of delinquent siblings was stronger for girls than for boys in the Seattle sample, as shown in Table 7.2.

Delinquent peers. As shown in Table 7.2, several studies have found consistent positive relationships between having delinquent or antisocial friends during adolescence and later violence. Delinquent peers may contribute to the spread of violence during adolescence, but they may be less relevant in predicting the violent behavior of life course persistent offenders who initiate their aggressive and violent behavior earlier in life (Moffitt, 1993).

Conversely, Ageton (1983) found that adolescents whose peers disapproved of delinquent behavior were less likely to report having committed sexually assaultive behavior later. Elliott (1994) reported similar results for all forms of violence in the National Youth Survey. Associating with peers who disapprove of delinquent behavior may inhibit later violence.

Gang membership. Recent research suggests gang membership contributes to delinquency over and above delinquent peers (Battin, Hill, Abbott, Catalano, & Hawkins, 1997). Research also suggests that gang membership is associated with serious and violent juvenile offending (see Thornberry, Chapter 8, this volume). As illustrated in the Seattle data, gang membership at ages 14 and 16 predicted violent behavior at age 18 (Maguin et al., 1995).

Community and Neighborhood Factors

Shaw and McKay (1942, 1969) identified three structural factors—poverty, ethnic heterogeneity, and residential mobility—that they hypothesized led to the disruption of local community social organization, and, in turn, to crime. Important research has been done on the characteristics of communities that are predictive of high rates of crime and violence (see Sampson & Lauritsen, 1994, for a review). As described by Hawkins, Laub, and Lauritsen in Chapter 3 of this volume, violent delinquency is more prevalent in inner-city areas characterized by poverty. Community-level analyses have also linked neighborhood poverty rates to violent crime (Beasley & Antunes, 1974; Block, 1979; Curry & Spergel, 1988; Messner & Tardiff, 1986; Mladenka & Hill, 1976).

Poverty. These results have been replicated in studies of individuals. Elliott found that the prevalence of self-reported felony assault and robbery in the National Youth Survey was higher among urban youths (Elliott, Huizinga, & Menard, 1989, p. 46), and about twice as high in youths from poverty as in middle-class youths (Elliott et al., 1989, p. 38). Farrington (1989a) found that low family income, measured when subjects were 8, predicted self-reported teen violence and convictions for violent offenses. Over 23% of boys from poverty compared with 8.8% of boys not from poverty were convicted of violent offenses (p. 85). Similar results have been reported from Stockholm (Wikström, 1985, p. 133), Copenhagen (Hogh & Wolf, 1983, p. 253), and New Zealand (Henry et al., 1996, p. 618). In a comparison of the London and Pittsburgh longitudinal data sets, Farrington (in press-b) found that family dependence on welfare significantly increased the odds of later violent behavior in both data sets.

Studies at the community level have raised questions about how poverty contributes to violence. For example, Smith and Jarjoura (1988) found that communities characterized by poverty and rapid population turnover had significantly higher violent crime rates than either stable poor areas or mobile areas that were more affluent (Sampson & Lauritsen,

1994). This has encouraged researchers to investigate other factors, beyond poverty, hypothesized by Shaw and McKay to predict crime and violence. Research has been conducted on the relationship between a number of characteristics of neighborhoods including mobility and community change, heterogeneity and racial composition, housing and population density, community social disorganization, and neighborhood rates of violent crime. Findings suggest that social disorganization and community change contributes to rates of violence in communities (Sampson & Lauritsen, 1994).

Low neighborhood attachment and community disorganization, availability of drugs, availability of firearms, exposure to violence in the neighborhood, exposure to racial prejudice, community laws and norms favorable toward violence, and media portrayals of violence all have been identified as community factors that may influence individual violence (Brewer, Hawkins, Catalano, & Neckerman, 1995). Few longitudinal studies have investigated the contribution of community or neighborhood characteristics other than poverty to violence at the individual level, though the Rochester Youth Development Study found that living in a high-crime neighborhood predicted self-reported violence (Thornberry et al., 1995, p. 227), and Sampson's current study of Chicago neighborhoods promises to provide important information on this topic.

Community disorganization and low neighborhood attachment. Maguin et al. (1995) investigated relationships between community disorganization, low neighborhood attachment, and violence in the multiethnic urban Seattle Social Development panel followed from age 10 through age 18. Community disorganization was assessed with a six-item self-report scale assessing respondents' perceptions of levels of crime, drug selling, gangs, and poor housing in their neighborhoods gathered at ages 14 and 16. A greater variety of violent acts at age 18 was reported by youths who grew up in disorganized neighborhoods.

In the same data set, a measure of neighborhood attachment was constructed from self-reports collected at age 10 using a three-item scale addressing children's perceptions of safety and affection for their neighborhood. The construct was assessed again at ages 14 and 16 using a nine-item self-report scale measuring respondents' perceptions of safety, affection for, and attachment to their neighborhoods. The degree of attachment to the neighborhood was less predictive of violence than was neighborhood disorganization, as shown in Table 7.2.

Availability of drugs. Maguin et al. (1995) also assessed the relationship between the availability of drugs and teenage violence. Drug availability was measured with a three-item self-report scale addressing students' access to marijuana at age 10 and to marijuana and cocaine at ages 14 and 16. Greater availability of drugs in childhood and adolescence predicted a greater variety of violent behaviors at age 18, as shown in Table 7.2.

Neighborhood adults involved in crime. Maguin et al. (1995) considered the relationship between the presence of neighborhood adults involved in crime and self-reported violence. Children who knew more adults in their neighborhoods who sold drugs or took part in other illegal activities were more likely to engage in violent behavior at age 18.

Exposure to violence. Paschall (1996) looked at the impact of children's exposure to violence on their violent conduct. A sample of 217 African American adolescents aged

12-16 were assessed using a self-report measure of exposure to violence. Exposure to violence generally, and in the home, was significantly related to violence among youths, after controlling for participants' age, socioeconomic status, and family structure. This significant relationship held when additional variables, such as fear of personal danger, hostility, and beliefs supporting aggression, were also controlled.

Exposure to racial prejudice. McCord and Ensminger (1995) found a relationship between retrospective accounts of racial discrimination/prejudice, including being denied a job and having problems finding housing, and self-reported violence among African American study participants in the Woodlawn study. Those who reported incidents involving racial discrimination were more violent as adults than those who reported no discrimination.

Community consequences for violence. In the Seattle project, children were asked at ages 14 and 16 about the likelihood of their being apprehended by the police if they were to commit a violent crime as an indicator of the degree to which community laws and norms were viewed as permissive toward violent behavior. Respondents' self-reports of the likelihood of being apprehended by the police were only weakly associated with later violence (Maguin et al., 1995), as shown in Table 7.2.

Community disorganization, neighborhoods in which drugs are readily available to adolescents, and neighborhoods in which adolescents are exposed to adults involved in crime, to violence, and to racial prejudice all may contribute to risk for violence. More research on the linkages between neighborhood characteristics and individual violent behavior is needed.

Situational Factors

Important research has focused on circumstances surrounding the violent event itself as possible predictors of violent behavior. Sampson and Lauritsen (1994) have defined situational-level factors as those factors, outside the individual, that influence the initiation, unfolding, or outcome of a violent event. Farrington (in press) has described these as factors that explain how an individual's potential for violence becomes the actuality in a given situation, that is, they explain why a person is more likely to commit violence in some situations than others.

The presence of a weapon, consumption of alcohol or other drugs, the role of bystanders, the motives of the offender in the situation, the relationship of the potential offender to the potential victim (stranger or nonstranger), and the behavior of the victim (resistance or nonresistance) have all been identified as possible situational predictors of violence (Farrington, in press-b; Sampson & Lauritsen, 1994). The work on situational predictors of violent behavior has underscored the importance of seeking to understanding the motives, interactions, and characteristics of the situation itself. However, as noted by Sampson and Lauritsen (1994), it is difficult to establish the independent contribution of situational factors to violent behavior because most currently available situational data contain only incidents in which violence occurred. Situations with similar characteristics in which violence did not occur are not often collected. "Thus, we are prevented from examining how variations across situations are causally related to the probability that violent events will occur" (Sampson & Lauritsen, 1994, p. 42). Immediate situational influences on violence are rarely measured in longitudinal studies, making it difficult to combine theories about the development of violence potential and theories about how the potential becomes the actuality of violent events. We recommend that longitudinal researchers inquire about situational triggers to violent acts in their studies. Questions could be included about the most recent act and/or the most serious act in the previous time period.

Multiple Predictors and Strength of Prediction

To further investigate the power of diverse factors to predict violent behavior, subjects in the Seattle Social Development Project were dichotomized into those who self-reported a violent offense in the past year at age 18 and the remainder. Predictors identified in this review and others available in the Seattle data set were dichotomized at ages 10, 14, and 16, following Farrington's convention of identifying those in the top 25% of the distribution as having the predictor and the remaining 75% as not having the predictor (unless the predictor was already in a categorical form, e.g., gang involvement). In keeping with the orientation of this chapter, we focus on the bivariate relationships involving predictors and the age 18 violence measure. Table 7.3 shows the results.

As shown in Table 7.3, individuals identified by their teachers or parents as characterized by hyperactivity/attention deficit at all three ages had twice the risk of violent behavior by age 18. Sensation seeking and involvement in selling drugs at ages 14 and 16 more than tripled the risk of later violence.

Parental attitudes favorable to violence when subjects were 10 more than doubled the risk that subjects would engage in violence by age 18, but poor family management practices and family conflict at age 10 were not significant predictors of later violence. In contrast, at age 14, poor family management predicted a doubled risk for later violence as did parental criminality (not assessed at age 10). At age 16, parental criminality, poor family management, family conflict, and residential mobility all were predictive of at least a doubling of the risk for violence at age 18.

With regard to school-related variables, low academic performance at all three ages predicted increased risk for violence at age 18. Behavior problems at school at age 10, as rated by teachers, also significantly predicted violence at age 18. By ages 14 and 16, low commitment to schooling, low educational aspirations, and multiple school transitions all were predictive of a significantly increased risk for violence at age 18.

At all three developmental points, having delinquent friends was predictive of an increased risk for later violence. Gang membership at age 14 more than tripled the risk of violence at age 18, and gang membership at age 16 more than quadrupled the risk of violence at age 18. With regard to community characteristics, community disorganization, availability of drugs, and adults in the neighborhood involved in criminal activities all are associated with large increases in risk for later violence.

Clearly, when considered in this way, a number of individual, family, school, peer, and community factors are associated with significant increases in risk for violent behavior. Over 17% of youths in the sample committed a violent act at age 18. Of these violent youths, four fifths (80.4%) were predicted to have done so using the significant age 10 predictors included in Table 7.3. Similarly, 84% of youths in the sample who committed a violent act at age 18 were predicted to have done so using the significant age 16 predictors included in Table 7.3. These "hit" rates need to be replicated in validation samples.

Finally, the probability of violence increases with the number of risk factors. For example, Figure 7.1 shows how the probability of

TABLE 7.3 Logistic Regression Results: Predictors at Ages 10, 14, and 16 With Violence at Age 18

Scale	Age 10 Predictors		Age 14 Predictors		Age 16 Predictors	
	B	Odds Ratio	B	Odds Ratio	B	Odds Ratio
Individual						
Sex (female = 0, male = 1)	0.84*** (n = 757)	2.31	—	—	—	—
Hyperactive (teacher rating)	0.78*** (n = 669)	2.17	0.68** (n = 637)	1.98	—	—
Hyperactive (parent rating)	—	—	0.75*** (n = 704)	2.11	0.67** (n = 703)	1.96
Risk taking	—	—	1.16*** (n = 735)	3.18	1.25*** (n = 740)	3.50
Drug selling	—	—	1.21*** (n = 735)	3.34	1.51*** (n = 738)	4.55
Early violence initiation (age 12-13)	—	—	1.31*** (n = 617)	3.71		
Child's proviolence attitudes	—	—	0.74** (n = 733)	2.09	—	—
Family						
Parental violence	—	—	0.61* (n = 689)	1.84	0.30 (n = 698)	1.35
Parental criminality	—	—	0.77** (n = 666)	2.16	0.71** (n = 699)	2.03
Poor family management	0.25 (n = 745)	1.29	0.75*** (n = 719)	2.11	0.97*** (n = 734)	2.63
Family conflict	0.04 (n = 719)	1.05	0.48* (n = 735)	1.61	0.77*** (n = 739)	2.16
Parents' proviolence attitude	0.84** (n = 695)	2.32	—	—	—	—
Residential mobility	—	—	0.27 (n = 735)	1.32	0.99*** (n = 739)	2.69
School						
Low academic performance	0.50* (n = 728)	1.65	0.72** (n = 736)	2.05	1.00*** (n = 717)	2.71
Low school commitment	0.09 (n = 747)	1.10	0.57** (n = 697)	1.76	0.59** (n = 726)	1.80
Low educational aspirations	0.18 (n = 713)	1.20	0.62** (n = 733)	1.86	0.47* (n = 740)	1.60
School transitions	—	—	0.60** (n = 731)	1.82	1.09*** (n = 737)	2.97
Antisocial behavior (teacher rating)	0.98*** (n = 670)	2.66	—	—	—	—
Peer						
Sibling delinquency	0.58 (n = 593)	1.79	0.34 (n = 701)	1.40	0.82*** (n = 601)	2.26
Peer delinquency	0.81*** (n = 648)	2.25	1.04*** (n = 730)	2.82	1.37*** (n = 721)	3.95
Gang membership	—	—	1.22*** (n = 732)	3.39	1.52*** (n = 731)	4.58

TABLE 7.3 *Continued*

Scale	Age 10 Predictors		Age 14 Predictors		Age 16 Predictors	
	B	Odds Ratio	B	Odds Ratio	B	Odds Ratio
Community						
Economic deprivation	0.47*	1.61	0.29	1.33	0.41*	1.51
	(*n* = 725)		(*n* = 735)		(*n* = 679)	
Community disorganization	—	—	0.78***	2.19	1.15***	3.16
			(*n* = 734)		(*n* = 732)	
Low neighborhood attachment	0.43*	1.54	0.00	1.00	0.53*	1.69
	(*n* = 732)		(*n* = 734)		(*n* = 732)	
Availability of drugs	0.57**	1.77	0.97***	2.63	1.13***	3.09
	(*n* = 703)		(*n* = 735)		(*n* = 740)	
Neighborhood adults involved in crime	—	—	1.15***	3.15	1.36***	3.90
			(*n* = 733)		(*n* = 738)	
Proviolence community norms	—	—	0.10	1.11	0.32	1.38
			(*n* = 733)		(*n* = 740)	
Percentage correctly classified as violent at age 18 given the set of significant univariate predictors at each age	80.4% correctly classified; 1.2% false positives 18.4% false negatives (*n* = 516)		84.3% correctly classified 1.5% false positives 14.2% false negatives (*n* = 536)		83.9% correctly classified 4.2% false positives 12.9% false negatives (*n* = 520)	

a conviction for juvenile violence between the ages of 10 and 20 varied with the vulnerability score at age 8-10 in the Cambridge Study in Delinquent Development (Farrington, in 1997b). The Cambridge study is a follow-up of 411 South London boys from age 8 to age 40. The vulnerability score was based on five risk factors: low family income at age 8, large family size (four or more biological siblings) up to the 10th birthday, low nonverbal IQ of the boy (90 or less on the Progressive Matrices test) at age 8-10, and poor parental childrearing behavior (a combined variable measuring harsh or erratic parental attitude or discipline and parental conflict) at age 8. Figure 7.1 shows that the percentage convicted for violence increased from only 3% of those with none of these risk factors to 31% of those with four or all five risk factors. Thus, the probability of convic-

tion for violence dramatically increases the higher the number of risk factors.

■ *Discussion*

A major problem in seeking to understand the predictors of adolescent violence is that few studies have focused specifically on violence as opposed to delinquency more generally. More studies are needed contrasting violent offenders with nonviolent offenders and nonoffenders.

Malleable or changeable individual predictors of violence identified in this review include pregnancy and delivery complications; hyperactivity, concentration problems, restlessness, and risk taking; aggressiveness; early initiation of violent behavior itself; in-

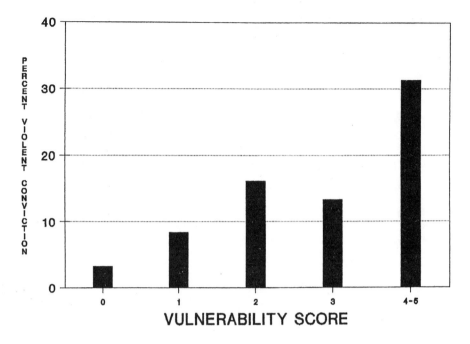

Figure 7.1. Percentage Convicted Versus Vulnerability
SOURCE: Farrington (1997b).

volvement in other forms of antisocial behavior; and beliefs and attitudes favorable to deviant or antisocial behavior including violence.

Within the family, living with a criminal parent or parents, harsh discipline, physical abuse and neglect, poor family management practices, low levels of parent involvement with the child, high levels of family conflict, parental attitudes favorable to violence, and separation from family have all been linked to later violence. Academic failure, low commitment to schooling, truancy and early school leaving, and frequent school transitions also predict violent behavior. Delinquent siblings, delinquent peers, and gang membership also predict violence, though the effects of these factors appear to be greatest in adolescence. Finally, poverty, community disorganization, availability of drugs, neighborhood adults involved in crime, and exposure to violence and racial prejudice in the community are linked to increased risk for later violence.

The evidence reviewed here indicates that violent behavior is a result of the interactions of contextual, individual, and situational factors. Multivariate models that include these factors in theoretically linked causal sequences need to be tested to guide the development of multicomponent violence prevention interventions that can significantly reduce risk for violent behavior. In addition, more research is needed to identify those factors that function truly in a protective fashion against risk exposure, serving to mediate or moderate the effects of risk.

CHAPTER 8

Membership in Youth Gangs and Involvement in Serious and Violent Offending

■ *Terence P. Thornberry*

Since the earliest days of gang research, such as Thrasher's (1927/1963) classic study of 1,313 gangs in Chicago, scholars have noted the tremendously disproportionate contribution that gang members make to the level of crime in society. Indeed, the observation that gang members are extensively involved in delinquency—especially serious and violent delinquency—is one of the most robust and consistent observations in criminological research.

This observation has been made across time, space, and methods of data collection.

Observational studies of gang behavior suggest that gang members are heavily involved in various forms of delinquent activities. This finding has been reported in the earlier research of Spergel (1964), Miller (1966), and Klein (1971), as well as many more recent observational studies such as those by J. W. Moore (1978), Hagedorn (1988), Vigil (1988), and Taylor (1990). Studies that rely on official data to compare gang and nongang members also have found a strong association between gang membership and delinquent activity (see Cohen, 1969; Huff, 1996a;

AUTHOR'S NOTE: This study was prepared under Grant 86-JN-CX-0007 (S-3) from the Office of Juvenile Justice and Delinquency Prevention, Office of Justice Programs, U.S. Department of Justice; Grant 5 R01 DA05512-02 from the National Institute on Drug Abuse; and Grant SES-8912274 from the National Science Foundation. I would like to thank Kim Tobin-Carambia for her assistance in developing this chapter. I would also like to thank Darnell F. Hawkins, James C. Howell, Malcolm W. Klein, Alan J. Lizotte, Walter B. Miller, and Carolyn A. Smith for helpful comments on earlier drafts.

147

Klein, Gordon, & Maxson, 1986; Klein & Maxson, 1989). Finally, several studies that rely on survey research techniques report higher rates of involvement in delinquency for gang members as compared to non-gang members. These include Short and Strodtbeck's (1965) classic study of Chicago gangs, Tracy (1979), Fagan, Piper, and Moore (1986), Fagan (1989, 1990a), and Huff (1996a). There is general agreement that the effect of gang membership is particularly pronounced for more serious offenses and for violent offenses. Thus, gang members are not only more extensively involved in delinquency, but they are more extensively involved in the types of delinquency that are the particular focus of this volume.

Not only are gang members more involved in delinquency than nonmembers, but in recent years there has also been a tremendous increase in the number of gangs and gang members in American society. Klein (1995) reports that between 1961 and 1970 there was a 74% increase in the number of gang-involved cities, an 83% increase from 1970 to 1980, and a phenomenal 345% increase from 1980 to 1992 (pp. 90-91). "Gangs are no longer a big-city problem" (Klein, 1995, p. 96); they have spread to cities of all sizes.

Curry, Ball, and Decker (1996a, 1996b) report quite similar results in surveys of law enforcement agencies conducted in 1991 and 1993. Based on "conservative estimates," Curry et al. (1996a) found that 57% of all American cities had a gang problem in 1993 but that 87% of the cities with a population of between 150,000 and 200,000 reported a gang problem and 89% of the cities with a population of over 200,000 reported a gang problem. According to Curry et al. (1996a), "The scope of the U.S. gang problem in 1993 was conservatively estimated at 735 (705-765) jurisdictions with 8,625 gangs [and] 378,087 gang members" (p. 3). These results represent a substantial increase over those

observed for 1991. Across just those 2 years, there was a 76.7% increase in the estimated number of gangs and a 51.9% increase in the estimated number of gang members.

The National Youth Gang Center (1997) surveyed over 4,000 law enforcement agencies at the end of 1995. Over half (58% of 2,007 respondents) of the responding agencies, covering all 50 states, reported youth gang problems during 1995. Overall, about 2,000 cities, towns, and counties reported the presence of more than 23,000 gangs with membership totaling nearly 665,000 in 1995 (National Youth Gang Center, 1997). Half of all cities and towns under 25,000 population reported gang problems.

All three of these studies are surveys of law enforcement agencies and, unfortunately, therefore, may share common sources of bias. For example, part of the increase in the number of cities with gangs may be due to a heightened awareness of gang problems in American society and an increased willingness to identify local problems as gang related. Nevertheless, the consistency of the results and the magnitude of the increase suggest there has been a substantial expansion of gang behavior in the recent past. This is alarming for several reasons. First is the sheer number of gangs and gang members in American society. Second is the percentage of cities that are currently experiencing gang problems; virtually all large cities, and well over half of all cities, report active gangs. Third is the tremendously rapid increase in the spread of gangs throughout urban America. In the space of about 10 years, gangs have spread from a relatively small number of cities to being a regular feature of the urban landscape.

Scope of This Review

Starting with the work of Thrasher in the 1920s, the research literature on gangs has expanded tremendously throughout the course of this century. Many of these studies are based on observational methods in which a researcher gains access to one or more gangs and spends a substantial period of time on the street corners with them, observing their behaviors and relationships. Other studies are comparative; researchers sample gang members and compare their behaviors and attitudes with those of nonmembers. Although our understanding of gangs and their contribution to crime and delinquency has been greatly enhanced by these studies, they have a curiously myopic quality to them. That is, both observational and comparative studies generally study gang members only during their period of active gang membership. These studies often contain little, if any, information on the lives of gang members before and after their active gang membership.[1] As a consequence, the general literature on street gangs often fails to take into account developmental and life course issues with respect to gang membership.

Several excellent reviews of the general literature on street gangs have been published recently. In particular, they include Klein's *The American Street Gang: Its Nature, Prevalence, and Control* (1995) and Spergel's *The Youth Gang Problem: A Community Approach* (1995). In addition, the second edition of Huff's book *Gangs in America* (1996b) contains an excellent set of contemporary essays on this topic. Rather than inadequately repeating the summaries presented by Klein, Spergel, and others, this chapter places gang membership in a developmental context by focusing on both the antecedents and consequences of gang membership. Unlike much of the previous literature that studies *gangs,* in this perspective individual *gang members* are the units of analysis. This approach certainly has its disadvantages; for example, it limits our ability to study group processes and to some extent it

decontextualizes the deviant behavior of gang members. Also, a developmental perspective requires longitudinal data, and virtually all longitudinal data sets that have measured gang membership have been conducted in newer or "emergent" gang cities. Thus, it is not clear whether the findings from these longitudinal studies are unique to emergent gang cities or whether longitudinal studies conducted in established gang cities (e.g., Los Angeles, Chicago) would produce similar results. It also has its advantages; it allows the study of gangs to be informed by developmental and life course perspectives and it addresses substantive issues that cannot easily be examined when the gang is the unit of analysis. This approach complements the very detailed understanding that prior research has presented about periods of active gang membership, and both types of studies are needed to fully understand the phenomenon of street gangs.

A developmental perspective is consistent with the transient character of gang membership for most gang members. Several recent longitudinal studies (described below) have shown that most gang members remain in the gang for less than 1 year and proportionately few remain members for multiple years. For example, in the Rochester Youth Development Study, 54% of the gang members were active for a year or less and only 21% were active for 3 or more years. The respective percentages in the Denver Youth Survey are 67% and 9% and in the Seattle Social Development Project, 69% and 14%. Given this distribution it is important to understand why adolescents join and leave gangs and how their period of active membership affects other life course trajectories. In examining this perspective here, we discuss the following specific topics concerning membership in street gangs. First, we will examine risk factors for individuals joining gangs. Second, we will examine the relative contribution that gang members make to the overall volume of crime in society. Third, we will examine the social processes by which membership in a street gang brings about an increased level of involvement in delinquency by gang members. And fourth, we will compare gangs and other law-violating groups to see if gangs are qualitatively different from those groups or simply an extension of a process by which association with delinquent peers increases involvement in delinquency.

■ Risk Factors for Gang Membership

Risk factors are "individual or environmental hazards that increase an individual's vulnerability to negative developmental outcomes" (Small & Luster, 1994, p. 182; see also Werner & Smith, 1982). A risk factor approach assumes that there are multiple, and often overlapping, risk factors in an individual's background that lead to adverse outcomes. Furthermore, it posits that it is the cumulation of risk in the life course that is most strongly related to adversity (B. C. Miller, 1995).

Identifying salient risk factors, especially those that occur early in the life course, has several advantages. Theoretically, identifying factors that increase risk suggests fruitful areas for exploration in more formal causal analyses. It can also help in isolating variables that mediate or translate increased vulnerability into actually experiencing the outcome. A risk factor approach also has practical advantages. Knowledge of risk factors helps structure the design of intervention programs by identifying at-risk youth for whom prevention and treatment efforts are most warranted. Also, the identification of salient risk factors suggests substantive areas or targets for intervention efforts. Despite these advantages, there have been surprisingly few

examinations of risk factors for gang membership.

This appears to be directly related to the limits of past research designs in the area of gang studies. A risk factor model examines *antecedent* conditions that increase risk for *later* outcomes and is best analyzed in longitudinal designs. Also, a risk factor model requires a general, representative sample that includes both those experiencing the outcome (i.e., gang membership) and those not experiencing it. Unfortunately, there are relatively few gang studies that combine both of these features and that follow gang members and comparison, non-gang members across time. Because of this, most prior studies are correlational studies that compare gang members and nonmembers in terms of attributes measured during periods of active gang membership. Proper temporal order is not established and it is therefore not clear whether the factors identified in these studies are actual risk factors for a later outcome. Thus, the results of prior studies suggest, rather than identify, potential risk factors for gang membership. In this section, we review the results of these studies; in the following section, we examine two current longitudinal research projects that in fact examine antecedent risk factors for later gang membership.

Prior Research

Consistent with the basic tenet of a risk factor approach that there are likely to be multiple rather than single pathways to adverse outcomes, prior research has examined risk for gang membership in a variety of domains. They include community, family, school, peer, individual characteristics, and prior problem behaviors.

Community risk factors. Living in socially disorganized areas is related to gang membership (Bowker & Klein, 1983; Curry & Spergel, 1992; J. W. Moore, 1978, 1991; Short, 1990). These findings are quite consistent with the general observation that gangs themselves tend to cluster in high-crime, socially disorganized neighborhoods (e.g., Fagan, 1996; Short & Strodtbeck, 1965; Vigil, 1988). It is not surprising, therefore, that youth who reside in those same neighborhoods are at increased risk for gang membership. These findings are also consistent with research results that suggest that the availability of drugs in the neighborhood (Curry & Spergel, 1992; Hill, Hawkins, Catalano, Maguin, & Kosterman, 1995) and the presence of gangs in the neighborhood (Curry & Spergel, 1992; Nirdorf, 1988) also increase the risk that an individual will become a gang member.

Although many studies find that community characteristics increase the risk of gang membership, several studies do not. For example, Bjerregaard and Smith (1993) did not find that social disorganization or neighborhood poverty is significantly related to the risk of gang membership. Fagan (1990a) also found no significant association between gang membership and social integration, neighborhood integration, and neighborhood violence. Similarly, Winfree, Backstrom, and Mays (1994) did not find that urban residence differentiates gang members from non-gang members.

Family risk factors. Several studies have examined family-based risk factors for gang membership. Some have found that low socioeconomic status or poverty is related to gang membership (Bowker & Klein, 1983; Moore, 1991; Schwartz, 1989). Structural characteristics of families have also been examined. Bowker and Klein (1983) and Vigil (1988) found that coming from single-parent families or from broken homes increases the risk of joining gangs, although Le Blanc and

Lanctot (in press), in a study comparing gang and non-gang members in a Quebec sample restricted to adjudicated boys, did not. Similarly, Bowker and Klein (1983) found that larger family size is related to gang membership.

In addition to concerns about family structure, many studies have examined family management style as a risk factor for gang involvement. In general, poor family management strategies increase the risk for gang membership by adolescents (Le Blanc & Lanctot, in press; Moore, 1991; Vigil, 1988). More specifically, low family involvement (Friedman, Mann, & Friedman, 1975; Le Blanc & Lanctot, in press), inappropriate parental discipline (Winfree et al., 1994), low parental control or monitoring (Bowker & Klein, 1983; Campbell, 1990; Le Blanc & Lanctot, in press; Moore, 1991), poor affective relationships between parent and child (Campbell, 1990; Moore, 1991), and parental conflict (Le Blanc & Lanctot, in press) put youth at risk for becoming gang members. These family-based risk factors are quite consistent with those generally observed as increasing risk for involvement in delinquency (see Hawkins, Catalano, & Miller, 1992; Loeber & Stouthamer-Loeber, 1986).

There are several, more specific family factors related to the phenomenon of gang membership. One of the most consistent risk factors for involvement in a gang is having relatives in a gang (Cohen, Williams, Bekelman, & Crosse, 1994; Curry & Spergel, 1992; Moore, 1991; Nirdorf, 1988). In addition, the absence of prosocial parental role models (Wang, 1994) and prodeviant norms on the part of the parents (Le Blanc & Lanctot, in press) increase risk for gang membership.

School risk factors. Educational variables have also been examined as risk factors for gang membership. Bowker and Klein (1983)

reported that students who have low educational expectations are at increased risk for gang membership, a finding also observed by Bjerregaard and Smith (1993) for females but not males. Gang membership is also more likely among adolescents whose parents have low educational expectations for them (Schwartz, 1989). Poor school performance and low commitment and involvement are also correlated with gang membership (Le Blanc & Lanctot, in press). In a related vein, gang membership is associated with educational frustration (Curry & Spergel, 1992) and stress (Le Blanc & Lanctot, in press).

Teachers also play a role in predicting the likelihood of gang membership. Gang members, as compared to nonmembers, are more likely to experience negative labeling by teachers (Esbensen, Huizinga, & Weiher, 1993) and are less likely to have a teacher as a positive role model (Schwartz, 1989; Wang, 1994), although Le Blanc and Lanctot (in press) did not find low attachment to teachers to be related to gang membership.

Low school self-esteem (Curry & Spergel, 1992; Schwartz, 1989) and educational marginality (Bjerregaard & Smith, 1993) also increase the risk for gang membership. Finally, having gang members as classmates (Curry & Spergel, 1992) and getting into trouble at school (Cohen et al., 1994) are risk factors for gang membership.

Peer risk factors. Having friends who are involved in delinquency is strongly related to being a gang member (Bjerregaard & Lizotte, 1995; Bjerregaard & Smith, 1993; Bowker & Klein, 1983; Curry & Spergel, 1992; Esbensen et al., 1993; Fagan, 1990a; Le Blanc & Lanctot, in press; Nirdorf, 1988; Winfree et al., 1994). The relationship between deviant peers and gang membership is perhaps the strongest one observed in this literature. That is not surprising, of course, because delinquent gangs are in many ways a specific version of associations with delinquent peers.

Curry and Spergel (1992) found that having drug-using peers is a significant risk factor for gang membership for African American youth but not for Hispanic youth. Associating with peers who carry guns and weapons also increases the likelihood of gang membership (Bjerregaard & Lizotte, 1995). Several researchers report that associating with peers who were themselves gang members also increases the risk of gang membership (Curry & Spergel, 1992; Nirdorf, 1988; Winfree et al., 1994). Finally, being approached to join a gang (Cohen et al., 1994) is related to gang membership.

Individual risk factors. Self-esteem is rather inconsistently related to the risk of becoming a gang member. On the one hand, Rice (1963), Schwartz (1989), Wang (1994), and Cartwright, Tomson, and Schwartz (1975) find that low self-esteem increases the likelihood of gang membership. On the other hand, Bjerregaard and Smith (1993), Bowker and Klein (1983), and Esbensen et al. (1993) have not found self-esteem to be related to gang membership.

The individual's attitudes also play a role in increasing the risk of gang membership. Winfree et al. (1994) found that progang attitudes are associated with gang membership, and Esbensen et al. (1993) found that gang members have a higher tolerance for deviance and higher levels of normlessness (see also Fagan, 1990a). Le Blanc and Lanctot (in press) reported that deviant beliefs and techniques of neutralization are related to gang membership.

The most systematic investigation of individual attributes as correlates of gang membership has been undertaken by Le Blanc and Lanctot (in press). In their comparison of adjudicated gang and non-gang members, they found that gang members had significantly poorer scores on 10 of their 13 personality scales. Gang members

> share attitudes and opinions of persons in lower socioeconomic classes such as the ethic of the tough and the premature adoption of adult behaviors (value orientation). In thinking and perceiving, they tend to distort reality according to their personal needs or desires (autism). Their alienation manifests itself by the presence of distrust and estrangement in their attitudes toward others, especially toward those representing authorities. They manifest awareness of unpleasant feelings, especially of anger and frustration, and react readily with these emotions. There is also obvious discomfort concerning the presence and control of these feelings (manifest aggression). They exclude conscious awareness of feelings and emotions that an individual normally experiences, in addition it reflects one's failure to label these emotions (repression). They are reluctant to acknowledge unpleasant events or conditions met in daily living (denial). They also score high on psychotisism, which indicates that they are cold, impersonal, lacking in sympathy, unfriendly, untruthful, odd, unemotional, unhelpful, antisocial, lacking in insight and strange, with paranoid ideas that people are against them. They show emotional instability (somatic and affective), they are not happy and they have a sense of being victimized (neurotism). Finally they are sociable, adventurous, sensation seekers and impulsive (extroversion). (Le Blanc & Lanctot, in press, p. 7)

Prior problem behaviors. Finally, several studies have found that adolescents who are already involved in deviant and problem behaviors are more likely to join gangs than are adolescents who are not involved in those behaviors. For example, gang membership has been shown to be related to sexual promiscuity (Bjerregaard & Smith, 1993; Le Blanc & Lanctot, in press), loitering or hanging out (Le Blanc & Lanctot, in press), alcohol and drug use (Bjerregaard & Smith, 1993; Cohen et al., 1994; Le Blanc & Lanctot, in press; Thornberry, Krohn, Lizotte, & Chard-Wierschem, 1993), violence (Friedman et al., 1975; Le Blanc & Lanctot, in press), being a gun owner (Bjerregaard & Lizotte, 1995), and general delinquency (Curry & Spergel, 1992; Esbensen & Huizinga, 1993; Le Blanc & Lanctot, in press; Nirdorf, 1988). In addition, official contact with the juvenile justice system has been shown to be related to gang membership (Cohen et al., 1994; Le Blanc & Lanctot, in press). Finally, victimization also appears to be a risk factor for gang membership (Fagan, 1990a).

Recent Findings

Because most prior studies examine correlates of gang membership rather than true risk factors, this section presents more detailed findings from two longitudinal studies, the Rochester Youth Development Study and the Seattle Social Development Project (Hill, Howell, & Hawkins, 1996). The Rochester study has followed a sample of 1,000 youth from the time they were middle school students until their early 20s; the Seattle study has followed 800 youth from the time they were elementary and middle school students until their early 20s. Both studies use a self-report measure of gang membership,[2] and both measure risk factors in a number of domains. The analysis is structured so that the risk factors are antecedent to the period of gang membership. In the case of the Rochester study, risk factors are measured during the Fall semester of 1988 and are used to predict the probability of joining a gang between 1989 and 1991. In the case of the Seattle project, risk factors are measured at Grades 5 or 6 and are used to predict the probability of joining a gang during Grades 7 through 12.

TABLE 8.1 Risk Factors for Gang Membership, Rochester Youth Development Study

	Logistic R for Joining a Gang Between Wave 3 and Wave 9	
Risk Factor at Wave 2	Males	Females
Community		
Neighborhood disorganization	.00	.13*
Neighborhood violence	.00	.08*
Neighborhood integration	−.06*	.18*
Family		
Living with both parents	−.04*	.00
Family below poverty level	.07*	.00
Parent attachment to child	−.11*	.00
Positive parenting	.00	.00
Child attachment to parent	.00	.00
Family violence	.00	.00
Parental involvement	.00	−.14*
Supervision	−.12*	.00
School		
Parent's expectations for school	−.14*	−.14*
Subject's expectations for school	−.05*	−.30*
Commitment to school	−.16*	−.11*
Attachment to teachers	−.14*	−.18*
Peer		
Association with delinquent peers	.16*	.00
Unsupervised time spent with friends	.10*	.00
Individual		
Perceived access to drugs	.14*	.09*
Positive values about drugs	.18*	.17*
Prosocial activities	.00	.00
Depression	.11*	.00
Negative life events	.24*	.00
Self-esteem	−.08*	.00
Problem behaviors		
General delinquency	.23*	.14*
Violent delinquency	.27*	.00
Drug use	.09*	.00

$*p < .05.$

Thus, the developmental period covered by the two studies is quite comparable. Because the dependent variable in these analyses is a dichotomy—gang members versus nonmembers—logistic regression models are used and the bivariate logistic R is presented in the tables.

Rochester study. Risk factors for members of the Rochester Youth Development Study are reported separately for males and females (Table 8.1). The risk factors are grouped into six domains, starting with more distal and moving to more proximal arenas. Because directional predictions can be made for these relationships, one-tailed tests are used in the Rochester analysis.

For males, in terms of community variables, growing up in neighborhoods in which there is a low level of neighborhood integration increases the risk of gang membership. Growing up in neighborhoods that are perceived by the parent respondents as disorganized or in which there is a high level of violence does not significantly increase the risk of gang membership, however.

Both structural and process variables in the area of the family are related to the probability of becoming a gang member. Growing up in families that are below the federally established standard for poverty or in families without both biological parents increases the risk of later gang membership. Of the family process variables, low parental attachment to the child and low parental supervision increase the probability of gang membership. The child's level of attachment to the parent, positive parenting, family violence, and involvement in family activities are not significantly related to gang membership.

School is a very potent arena for creating risk for later gang membership. Four school variables are analyzed and all are significant. Low expectations for success in school—measured both by the parent's expectations and the subject's expectations—increase the risk of gang membership. Students who have low commitment to school and who have low attachment to teachers are also at elevated risk for later involvement in gangs.

Peers have a very strong impact on later gang membership. Younger adolescent males who associate with delinquent peers and who spend more unsupervised time hanging around with friends are more apt to become gang members at some later point.

Several individual characteristics were also examined. Adolescents who perceive having easy access to drugs or who have positive values about drug use are more apt to become gang members than are their counterparts. Individuals with low self-esteem, who experience many negative life events, and who have depressive symptoms are more likely to join gangs later.

Finally, young adolescent males who use drugs and who are involved in delin-

quency, especially violent delinquency, are more apt to become gang members than are youth who are less involved in delinquency and drug use.

Somewhat different results are observed for the female participants. In general, there are fewer significant risk factors, which may be due to the smaller number of females in the Rochester study (75% of the sample are males and 25% are females).

Community variables have a larger impact on females than on males. Females who grow up in disorganized and violent neighborhoods are more likely to become gang members. Females who grow up in neighborhoods with high levels of social integration are also more apt to become gang members, a counterintuitive finding.

Few family factors are significant predictors of gang membership for females. In fact, only low parental involvement increases the risk of later gang membership. Family structure, family poverty, attachment, positive parenting, family violence, and supervision are not significantly related to gang membership.

School variables play a major role in accounting for the risk of gang membership for females, as they did for males. Low parental expectations and low student expectations for school success significantly increase the likelihood of gang membership. Similarly, low commitment to school and low attachment to teachers increase the likelihood of gang membership for females.

Peer effects are not significantly related to gang membership for females. Neither association with delinquent peers nor unsupervised time spent with peers is significantly related to the outcome variable.

In terms of individual characteristics, young females who perceive having easy access to drugs and who have pro-drug use values are significantly more likely to become gang members. On the other hand, prosocial activities, depressive symptoms, negative life events, and low self-esteem are not significantly related to gang membership.

Finally, of the delinquency measures only general delinquency is significantly related to the probability of later joining a gang for the females. Early involvement in violent offenses or in drug use is not statistically significant.

A brief comparison of risk factors for the males and females in the Rochester study indicates areas of both similarity and difference by gender. On the one hand, school variables, access to and values about drugs, and prior delinquency operate in generally similar ways for males and females. On the other hand, neighborhood characteristics appear to be much more important in increasing the likelihood of gang membership for the females than for the males. In contrast, family, peer, and psychological states (depression, stress, and self-esteem) are more potent predictors of gang membership for the males than the females.

Seattle study. In the Seattle study, Hill, Howell, and Hawkins (1996) conducted the risk factor analysis for male and female respondents combined (Table 8.2). One of two community risk factors is significantly related to the probability of joining a gang: Adolescents who come from neighborhoods where drugs are readily available are more apt to be gang members than are their counterparts.

Several family variables are related to the risk of gang membership. Family instability (indicated by the number of transitions in family structure) and low parental income increase the probability that adolescents will later join gangs. Low attachment to mother, family management problems, and parental proviolent attitudes all significantly increase the probability of later gang membership.

TABLE 8.2 Risk Factors for Gang Membership, Seattle Social Development Project

Risk Factor at Grades 5 and 6	Logistic R for Joining a Gang Between Grade 7 and Grade 12
Community	
Low neighborhood attachment	.00
Availability of drugs	.24*
Family	
Family instability	.11*
Extreme economic deprivation	.14*
Attachment to family	.00
Attachment to mother	−.07*
Attachment to father	.00
Family bonding	.00
Family management problems	.10*
Family conflict	−.03
Parent proviolent attitudes	.13*
Family involvement	.00
Parent respondent drinking	.00
Spouse drinking	.00
Both parents drinking	.00
Sibling antisocial behavior	.10*
School	
Low educational aspiration	.10*
Low school commitment	.14*
School attachment	−.10*
School antisocial behavior	.16*
Achievement test score	−.19*
Labeled learning disabled	.17*
Low grades	.13*
Peer	
"Bad" peers	.15*
"Good" peers	−.13*
Attachment to conventional peers	−.15*
Individual	
Conventional beliefs	−.16*
Achenbach externalizing	.23*
Achenbach internalizing	.03
Religious service attendance	.00
Hyperactivity	.15*
Social competence	−.18*
Gender (female)	−.18*
Asian	.00
African American	.17*
Other	.00
White	−.12*
Problem behaviors	
Respondent drinking	.09*
Age at first sex	−.32*

SOURCE: Hill, Hawkins, et al. (1996). Used with permission.
*$p < .05$.

Having siblings who are involved in antisocial behavior increases the risk of gang membership.

School variables are strongly related to the probability of joining gangs in Seattle. Low educational aspiration, low commitment to school, low school attachment, high levels of antisocial behavior in school, low achievement test scores, being labeled learning disabled, and receiving low grades are each related to gang membership in the expected direction.

Peers exert a fairly substantial influence on the probability of becoming a gang member. Associating with "bad" peers increases the likelihood of gang membership, whereas associating with "good" peers and being attached to conventional peers decrease that probability.

Individual factors were also examined. Of the demographic characteristics, white and female adolescents are less likely to be gang members and African American adolescents are more likely to be gang members. In terms of individual attributes, hyperactivity and externalizing behavior problems increase the probability of gang membership and holding conventional beliefs and social competencies decrease gang membership.

Finally, involvement in prior problem behaviors increases the likelihood of becoming a gang member. Young adolescents who report drinking and who are sexually precocious have a higher probability of joining a gang than do their counterparts.

Summary

Both the earlier correlational studies and the more recent longitudinal ones in Rochester and Seattle offer a rather consistent picture of risk factors for gang membership. In line with the basic assumption of a risk factor approach, there does not appear to be any single risk factor that leads adolescents to become members of street gangs. On the contrary, risk is generated in many life domains, including community, family, school, peer, and individual characteristics. Although the specific risk factors that are significant vary somewhat across studies, it seems reasonable to conclude that youth who grow up in more disorganized neighborhoods; who come from impoverished, distressed families; who do poorly in school and who have low attachment to school and teachers; who associate with delinquent peers; and who hold prodeviant belief systems and engage in various forms of problem behaviors are at increased risk for becoming gang members.

■ The Contribution of Gang Members to the Volume of Delinquency

Prior studies have demonstrated that gang members are significantly more involved in delinquency, especially serious delinquency, than are nonmembers. Despite the uniformity of this finding, we have surprisingly few estimates of the proportion of all delinquent or criminal acts for which gang members are responsible. That is, although we know that gang members have higher rates of offending than do nonmembers, we do not know how much of the total amount of crime is attributable to them. This is an important issue: If gang members are responsible for a very large proportion of all offenses, effective gang intervention may be a necessary ingredient in efforts to reduce the overall amount of crime in society.

The most straightforward way of addressing this analytic issue is to compare the proportion of gang members in the population with their proportionate share of the number of crimes reported. For example, if gang members represent 10% of the population we

TABLE 8.3 Percentage of Delinquent Acts Committed by Gang Members, Results From Four Projects

Three City Gang Study, Fagan (1990a)	%	*Denver Youth Survey, Huizinga (1997)*	%
Prevalence of gang membership (1 year)	23	**Cumulative prevalence of gang membership (Waves 1-5)**	14
Percentage of offenses		**Cumulative percentage of delinquent acts**	
Felony assault	67	Serious violence	79
Minor assault	66	Serious property	71
Robbery	66	Public disorder	44
Felony theft	72	Alcohol use	42
Minor theft	56	Marijuana use	53
Extortion	60	Drug sales	87
Property damage	61		
Weapons	53		
Illegal services	70		
Alcohol use	59		
Drug use	55		
Drug sales	71		

Rochester Youth Development Study, Thornberry (1996)	%	*Seattle Social Development Project, Battin, Hill, Hawkins, Catalano, and Abbott (1996)*	%
Cumulative prevalence of gang membership (Waves 1-9)	30	**Cumulative prevalence of gang membership (Grades 7-12)**	15
Cumulative percentage of delinquent acts		**Cumulative percentage of delinquent acts**	
General delinquency	65	Minor assault	51
Serious	86	Robbery	85
Moderate	67	Felony theft	54
Minor	59	Minor theft	53
Violent	68	Damaged property	59
Property	68	Drug selling	62
Street	64	General delinquency	58
Public disorder	60		
Alcohol use	63		
Drug use	61		
Drug sales	70		

would expect them to be responsible for approximately 10% of the crimes committed, if there were *no relationship* between gang membership and criminal involvement. To the extent that their proportionate share of crimes exceeds 10%, one can conclude that they are disproportionately contributing to the volume of crime in society. Results from four studies are presented in Table 8.3.

Fagan (1990a) analyzed a general adolescent sample by combining a cluster sample of high school students and a "snowball" sample of dropouts in San Diego, Los Angeles, and Chicago. He found the prevalence of gang membership to be 23% during the year

prior to the interview. Although only 23% of the population, gang members account for 67% of felony assaults, 66% of minor assaults, and 66% of robberies during that same time period. Fagan reported similar percentages for various forms of theft, ranging from 56% of minor thefts to 72% of felony thefts. Gang members are also disproportionately involved in weapons offenses, illegal services, drug use, and drug sales.

Thornberry (1996) examined cumulative measures of gang membership and self-reported delinquency in the Rochester Youth Development Study. Thirty percent of the Rochester sample reported being a member of a street gang prior to the end of high school. Although slightly less than one third of the population, gang members accounted for two thirds of the acts of general delinquency that were self-reported over a 4-year period, covering the junior high school and high school years. These gang members were also responsible for 86% of the serious acts of delinquency, 68% of the violent acts of delinquency, and 70% of the drug sales that were reported. Gang members, as compared to their share in the population, also had much higher rates of moderate and minor delinquency, property offenses, public disorder offenses, and alcohol and drug use.

Battin, Hill, Hawkins, Catalano, and Abbott (1996) report very similar patterns of results for gang members in the Seattle Social Development Project. Although gang members comprised only 15% of the total sample, they accounted for 85% of the robberies that were committed between Grades 7 and 12. They also accounted for at least 50% of all the other forms of delinquency measured in that project. These percentages ranged from 51% for minor assault to 62% for drug selling.

Using data from the Denver Youth Survey, Huizinga (1997) reported very similar results. Between 1988 and 1992, 14% of the Denver sample were gang members. They are responsible for 79% of the acts of serious violence, 71% of serious property offenses, and 87% of drug sales, however. They are also disproportionately involved in public disorder offenses, alcohol use, and marijuana use.[3]

The results of these studies confirm the finding of the many earlier studies that gang members have higher rates of involvement in delinquency than do non-gang members. They go beyond those results, however, to indicate that gang members, although representing a minority of the overall population, are responsible for the majority of the delinquent acts. These two findings are not duplicative. The first observation, that gang members are significantly more likely to be involved in delinquency than are non-gang members, can hold even if the second observation does not. That is, gang members could be responsible for only slightly more delinquent acts than their proportionate share in the population and still be significantly different from non-gang members. The results in these studies suggest, however, that this is not the case. Not only are gang members significantly different from non-gang members, they also account for the lion's share of all delinquent acts that are reported. Also, the proportionate contribution of gang members to delinquency is most pronounced for the more serious forms of delinquency. That is, gang members account for a very large proportion of felony offenses, serious offenses, violent offenses, and drug sales. Their contribution to more minor forms of delinquency, although still large, is somewhat muted.

■ *The Facilitation Effect of Gang Membership on Delinquency*

The previous sections have shown that gang members have higher rates of delinquency than non-gang members and also that gang members account for a disproportionate share of the crime problem relative to their share of the population. Those analyses, however, do not identify the processes by which this relationship is brought about.

Thornberry et al. (1993) have identified three models that could account for this relationship. The first is a social selection model. It suggests that gangs recruit or attract individuals who are already involved in delinquency and violence. If this is the case, then prior to periods of active gang membership, gang members should be more heavily involved in delinquency and violence than are non-gang members. The second model is a facilitation model. In this model, the norms and group processes of the gang are thought to facilitate involvement in delinquency and violence. If this model is accurate, then gang members would not be particularly different from nonmembers prior to or after their periods of active gang membership; during that period, however, they would be much more extensively involved in delinquency and violence. The third model is a mixed model. It suggests that both selection and facilitation effects are at work.

In their empirical analysis, limited to the male respondents in the Rochester Youth Development Study, Thornberry et al. (1993) report strong support for the facilitation model and virtually no support for the selection model:

> Perhaps the strongest support for the social facilitation model is found in the analysis of the type of behavior most often associated with gangs—crimes against the person. . . . Gang members have higher rates of person offenses only when they are active gang members. Of particular interest is the drop-off in the rate of person crimes once boys leave the gang. The means for crimes against the person for boys when they are active members of the gang are, by and large, at least twice as high as when they are not. Clearly, being in the gang is generative of violent behavior among these boys. (pp. 80-81)

A gang facilitation effect was also observed for general delinquency, drug sales, and to a somewhat lesser extent drug use. It was not, however, observed for property offenses.

Since the publication of these findings, several studies have replicated the facilitation effect that gang membership has on delinquency. Esbensen and Huizinga (1993) report that "prevalence rates for each type of [delinquent] behavior are highest during the gang member's year of actual gang membership" (p. 577). They also report some elevation in the prevalence of delinquency in the year

prior to joining a gang. Thus, the results from the Denver Youth Survey offer support for a mixed model, combining both selection and facilitation models.

Hill, Hawkins, et al. (1996) examined this issue in the Seattle Social Development Project. For violent delinquency their results are quite similar to those reported by Thornberry et al. (1993). Mean levels of violence are particularly elevated during the year of active gang membership. Violent delinquency is only slightly elevated in the year prior to joining a gang and reduces quite substantially in the years following active gang membership. With the exception of drug sales, similar findings are observed for other types of delinquency. During periods of active gang membership, involvement in drug sales is quite high (Hill, Hawkins, et al., 1996). Unlike other forms of delinquency, however, involvement in drug sales remains high after the individual leaves the gang. This finding has also been observed in more recent analyses of the Rochester Youth Development Study data (Bjerregaard & Lizotte, 1995; Lizotte, Howard, Krohn, & Thornberry, 1997).

The most recent investigation of this issue has been conducted in the Montreal longitudinal study by Tremblay (personal communication, November 1996). The Montreal study is based on 1,034 boys who attended kindergarten in 1984 in one of 53 low socioeconomic status schools in Montreal. The screening criteria "created a homogeneous low socioeconomic status, white, French-speaking sample" (Tremblay, Pihl, Vitaro, & Dobkin, 1994, p. 733). In replicating the study by Thornberry et al. (1993), Tremblay used self-reported data on gang membership and on delinquency and drug use for the 3-year period when the respondents were 14, 15, and 16 years of age.

The results for violent offenses are consistent with the facilitation model. Violent offending is higher during the year(s) of gang membership than either prior to or following active membership. Prior to joining the gang, gang members have somewhat higher rates of violent offending than do nonmembers, but the predominant change in behavior patterns occurs during periods of active gang membership. A similar pattern is observed for general delinquency and property crimes. As reported by Hill, Hawkins, et al. (1996) and Bjerregaard and Lizotte (1995), drug selling exhibits a somewhat different pattern. Involvement in drug sales increases during periods of gang membership, and it remains high after the youth leaves the gang.

The findings by Tremblay are important for several reasons. Prior studies of the facilitation effect were conducted in American cities and based on samples of gang members that were predominantly African American or Hispanic. Tremblay shows very similar effects in a large Canadian city with an exclusively white, French-speaking sample. The similarity of results suggests that gang processes may be quite similar in diverse settings.

Controlling for Risk Factors

Gang members have higher rates of delinquency, especially violent delinquency, when they are active gang members, and it appears that gang membership facilitates this increase. It is possible, however, that gang members have elevated rates of violence, not because of a gang facilitation effect but because of the accumulation of risk in their backgrounds. As we saw, gang members have substantial deficits in many social and psychological domains. As a result, it may not be gang membership that brings about the observed increase in violence; the increase may instead be caused by risk factors that are related both to gang membership and to violent behavior. Indeed, Le Blanc and Lanctot (in press) claim that Thornberry et al.'s (1993)

TABLE 8.4 Predicting the Incidence of Self-Reported Violence, Rochester Youth Development Study, Males Only (standardized OLS regression coefficients)

	Self-Reported Violence (logged)		
Risk Factor	Year 1[a]	Year 2[b]	Year 3[c]
Gang membership	.26***	.34***	.32***
Family poverty level	.04	−.06	.00
Parental supervision	−.10**	−.06	.01
Commitment to school	−.01	−.04	.02
Negative life events	.13***	.15***	.20***
Prior violence	.18***	.08*	.13**
Delinquent peers	.32***	.13**	.16***
R^2	.46	.31	.28
n	512	487	430

a. Year 1 violence combines data from Waves 2 and 3; risk factors are from Wave 2.
b. Year 2 violence combines data from Waves 4 and 5; risk factors are from Wave 3.
c. Year 3 violence combines data from Waves 6 and 7; risk factors are from Wave 5.
*$p < .05$. **$p < .01$. ***$p < .001$.

conclusion that there is a gang facilitation effect is premature: "We tend to favor the enhancement causal model. The delinquent with lower self and social control joins a gang, and the group activates its offending. . . . To thoroughly verify the nature of the causal role of the gang longitudinal data sets should be reanalyzed controlling self and social control characteristics of individuals" (p. 13).

To begin examining this possibility, we further examine data from the Rochester Youth Development Study.[4] Involvement in violent delinquency is grouped into the same three annual periods analyzed in Thornberry et al. (1993) and then regressed on a dummy variable indicating whether the subject was a gang member during that year and a variety of prior risk factors (Table 8.4). The inclusion of the dummy variable allows us to assess the facilitative effect of active gang membership on violent behavior net of the impact of antecedent variables. The antecedent variables are drawn from different domains and are among the strongest risk factors for gang membership (see Table 8.1) and for violence (see Chapters 6 and 7 in this volume). The specific risk factors that are included are family poverty level, parental supervision, commitment to school, experiencing negative life events, prior involvement in violence, and associating with delinquent peers. The risk factors are measured at the wave prior to the year of gang membership.[5] The analysis is limited to males because of the relatively small number of female gang members at later waves.

The results in Table 8.4 suggest that the relationship between gang membership and concurrent involvement in violent delinquency is not spurious. Even when family poverty level, parental supervision, commitment to school, experiencing negative life events, prior involvement in violence, and associating with delinquent peers are held constant, gang membership exerts a strong impact on the incidence of violent behavior at all 3 years.[6] In the equation for Year 1, for example, the standardized coefficient for gang membership is .26, approximately the same magnitude of coefficients observed for prior violence (.18) and for association with delinquent peers (.32), generally two of the strongest predictors of delinquent behavior (see Thornberry & Krohn, 1997). Indeed, across the years, gang membership has the largest impact on violent behavior.

Summary

Several recent longitudinal studies provide rather consistent support for the facilitation effect described by Thornberry et al. (1993). Rates of delinquency, especially violent delinquency and drug sales, are particularly high during periods of active gang membership. There is evidence of some selection effect in that gang members have somewhat higher rates of involvement in delinquency

prior to joining the gang, but this effect is less consistent and less powerful than the facilitation effect. Also, there tends to be a general drop-off in delinquency following the period of gang membership, with the notable exception of drug sales. In that case, the gangs appear both to facilitate entry into drug-selling markets and to facilitate continuation of involvement in those markets even after the individual leaves the gang. Finally, the impact of gang membership on concurrent involvement in violent delinquency was examined when major risk factors are held constant. Based on results from the Rochester Youth Development Study, the gang exerts a strong facilitative effect on violent behavior even when prior involvement in violence and several important risk factors are controlled. The pattern of results reported here, using a complementary methodology, is concordant with the portrait of gang behavior that is typically presented in the ethnographic literature (e.g., Hagedorn, 1988; Klein, 1995).

■ Gangs and Delinquent Peer Groups

One of the most consistent correlates of delinquency is association with delinquent peers (Thornberry & Krohn, 1997). Because youth gangs obviously constitute one form of a delinquent peer group, it is not clear whether the effects of gang membership described in this chapter are a function of gang membership or simply a function of association with delinquent peers.

Several gang researchers suggest that delinquent peer groups and gangs are qualitatively different. For example, Joan Moore (1991) has concluded that "gangs are no longer just at the rowdy end of the continuum of local adolescent groups—they are now really outside the continuum" (p. 132). Klein (1995) makes a similar point: "Street gangs

TABLE 8.5 Mean Logged Incidence of Self-Reported Violent Delinquency by Gang Membership and by Level of Delinquent Peer Group, Rochester Youth Development Study, Males Only

Interview Wave	Non-Gang Members				Gang Members
	Low Delinquent Peers	*Moderately Low Delinquent Peers*	*Moderately High Delinquent Peers*	*High Delinquent Peers*	
2	.11	.17	.38	.87	1.44*
3	.05	.13	.24	.58	1.73*
4	.05	.08	.25	.64	1.44*
5	.04	.09	.22	.50	1.29*
6	.04	.05	.15	.51	1.26*
7	.03	.09	.17	.38	1.11*
8	.01	.11	.22	.32	1.57*
9	.02	.03	.15	.27	1.05*

* $p < .05$ (one-tailed test) between the last two groups: non-gang members with high delinquent peers versus gang members.

are something special, something qualitatively different from other groups and from other categories of law breakers" (p. 197). Although these and other gang researchers view gangs as qualitatively different, there is virtually no quantitative research investigating this hypothesis. Because of that, several recent longitudinal studies have begun to investigate this issue.

In the Rochester Youth Development Study, we classified the male respondents into five groups at each interview wave.[7] One group consists of active gang members at that wave. Respondents who were not gang members were divided into quartiles based on their score on a scale measuring their association with delinquent peers, also at that wave. The most important comparison concerns the non-gang members in the highest quartile (those with the greatest number of delinquent peers) and the gang members. If Moore and Klein are correct, gang members will have substantially higher rates of delinquency than will the nongang members who associate with highly delinquent peer groups. If, on the other hand, gangs are simply another variant of highly delinquent peer groups, these two groups should not differ in terms of their delinquency.

Table 8.5 presents results for the logged incidence of violent delinquency. At all eight waves, gang members report committing violent offenses at significantly higher rates than do the nonmembers who associate with highly delinquent peer groups. For example, at Wave 2 the mean number of violent offenses for the gang members is 1.44 as compared to a mean of .87 for the nonmembers who associate with highly delinquent peers. There are even larger differences at the later waves: At Wave 9 the mean for the nonmembers who associate with highly delinquent peer groups is .27, whereas the mean for the gang members is 1.05. All of the differences between the nonmembers in the highly delinquent peer group and the gang members are statistically significant.[8]

Battin, Hill, Hawkins, et al. (1996) examined this issue with Seattle data. They created three groups: (a) those youth who were ever gang members from the 7th through the 12th grades, (b) those youth who were members of nongang law-violating youth groups, and (c) those who were neither. To establish the second group, they selected those youth who were never in a gang but for whom the majority of their three best friends had been arrested or who had done things to get them into trouble with the police. They then calculated the mean incidence of delinquency that each group reported committing between the 7th and 12th grades.

The results are quite similar to those in the Rochester study. Gang members reported substantially higher levels of involvement in all the offense types that were examined: minor assault, robbery, felony theft, minor theft, property damage, drug selling, and general delinquency. For minor assault, for example, the mean number of offenses reported by the gang members is 45.9 as compared to 14.1 for members of the law-violating youth groups. The mean number of robberies reported by gang members is 2.0, but it is only 0.2 for members of the nongang law-violating youth groups.

Finally, Huizinga (1996) examined this topic using data from the Denver Youth Survey, in which "youth aged 14-19 in 1991 were classified into four groups—those who had low, medium, and high involvement with delinquent friends, and those who were gang members" (p. 1). For both males and females, he observed higher levels of serious assaults and total assaults for the gang members as compared to the nonmembers who had highly delinquent peers. For example, among the males, 72% of the gang members reported involvement in serious assault, whereas only 20% of the nonmembers with highly delinquent peers did so. For the females, 72% of the gang members reported involvement in serious assault, and only 13% of the nonmembers with highly delinquent peers did so.

Battin, Hill, Hawkins, et al. (1996) tested this hypothesis from a causal modeling perspective. They used measures of association with delinquent peers and of gang membership to predict various forms of delinquent activity. Even when association with delinquent peers is included in the equation, the effect of gang membership is sizable and significant. This model was tested for a variety of outcomes—violence, theft, drug use, and drug selling, and for both self-reported and court-reported data—with similar results.

In line with the predictions by Klein and Moore, these three recent longitudinal studies find that gang membership appears to be qualitatively different from associating with delinquent peers in terms of its impact on delinquent behavior. Even when compared to nonmembers who associate with highly delinquent peer groups, gang members have substantially higher rates of delinquency.

■ Conclusion

This chapter examined a number of aspects of the relationship between membership in youth gangs and serious and violent delinquency. It focused specifically on developmental issues with respect to this relationship. Several conclusions appear warranted.

First, gang members are more extensively involved in delinquency, especially serious and violent delinquency, than are non-gang members. This is perhaps the oldest and most robust finding in the research literature on gangs.

Second, not only are gang members more heavily involved in delinquency than are nonmembers, but gang members are responsible for the lion's share of delinquent acts that are committed. Their disproportionate contribution to the overall volume of crime is particularly noteworthy for serious and violent offenses. Although gang members constitute a minority of the youth population, they are responsible for the majority of all delinquent acts that are committed.

Third, although gang members have higher rates of delinquency than do nonmembers, we have relatively little information about the causal processes that bring this about. It is possible that there are selection effects and that these youth would be extensively involved in violence and delinquency whether or not they joined gangs; this view is consistent with a social control perspective such as that advanced by Gottfredson and Hirschi (1990). It is also possible that the gang exerts a causal impact and that gang members, absent the deviant social environment provided by the gang, would not otherwise be particularly delinquent and violent; this view is consistent with a developmental or interactional perspective such as that advanced by Thornberry (1987).

Recent longitudinal studies in Rochester, Denver, Seattle, and Montreal indicate that there are major gang facilitation effects on involvement in delinquency, especially violent delinquency. During the periods when adolescents are actively involved in street gangs, their rates of violent delinquency increase tremendously. The rates are substantially lower prior to and following periods of gang membership. There are also indications of selection effects in that gang members report somewhat higher rates of delinquency in the year prior to joining the gang. Overall, though, the data are inconsistent with a pure selection model and are far more consistent with either a facilitation model or a mixed model that combines smaller selection effects with larger facilitation effects. Moreover, when major risk factors are held constant, gang membership continues to have a powerful effect on violent crime.

Fourth, consistent with the views of gang researchers such as Moore and Klein, it also appears that gangs differ substantially from simple delinquent peer groups. Even when compared to non-gang members who associate with highly delinquent peers, gang members are much more involved in delinquency, especially serious and violent delinquency.

Fifth, there does not appear to be a single pathway or risk factor that leads to gang membership. Both correlational studies and longitudinal, risk factor studies indicate that cumulative disadvantage, or adversity in many life domains, is associated with becoming a gang member. Adolescents who grow up in poor, disorganized neighborhoods; who come from poor, distressed families with poor management strategies; who do poorly in school and do not expect to continue in school; who associate with deviant peers; and who exhibit psychological distress, prodeviant attitudes, and earlier involvement in deviant behaviors are more apt to become gang members than are their counterparts. Although there are relatively few studies of risk factors for gang membership, the risk factors that have been identified are quite similar to those in the more general literature of risk factors for involvement in delinquency and violence. (See Chapters 6 and 7 in this volume.) That should not be surprising, of course, given the tremendous contribution that gang members make to those forms of behavior.

■ Discussion

The findings reported here, especially in the context of recent trend data, provide cause for great concern. Gang members are clearly major contributors to the level of serious and violent crime in American society—especially while they are active gang members. Moreover, Klein (1995), Curry et al. (1996a, 1996b), and the National Youth Gang Center (1997) report a massive expansion of gangs in recent years. As recently as the mid-1980s, gangs were found in relatively few, and generally very large, cities. By the mid-1990s, however, gangs have spread to virtually all large and middle-sized cities and to many smaller cities and towns. Given the facilitation effect that gangs appear to have on violent and serious delinquency, it is little wonder that the overall rate of these crimes for youth have increased so sharply during the past 10 years.

These findings highlight the importance of focusing on youth gangs as important targets for prevention and treatment programs. If gang members are indeed responsible for the majority of serious and violent delinquent acts, as suggested by all studies that have examined this topic, then it is unlikely that we will be successful in reducing the overall rate of serious delinquency unless we can bring gangs under control. That will not be an easy task, however.

Recent surveys to identify prevention programs that effectively reduce delinquency uniformly report that we have few, if any, truly effective gang prevention and suppression programs. In his masterful review of the scene, Klein (1995) has concluded that "the simple fact is that much of our local response and most of our state and federal responses to gang problems are way off base—conceptually misguided, poorly implemented, half heartedly pursued" (p. 19). The conclusions reached by Spergel (1995), Howell (1995;

Chapter 12, this volume), and others are hardly more encouraging. Effectively intervening in street gangs has proven remarkably difficult.

It seems, therefore, that one of the highest priorities that we can have in our effort to reduce the level of serious and violent delinquency in American society is to develop effective intervention programs for street gangs. This is, and will be, a most difficult challenge (see Howell, Chapter 12, this volume). It will not be done overnight and will require a carefully thought-out, long-term commitment to a "strategy of search" (see Thornberry, 1976). That is, potentially effective programs will have to be faithfully implemented and very carefully evaluated in a slow, iterative process that might eventually lead to the identification of effective programs. It is unlikely that any other approach will succeed. Yet the data reviewed in this chapter suggest the centrality of gangs to the production of serious and violent delinquency, and therefore the centrality of gang prevention to the reduction of serious and violent delinquency.

■ Notes

1. There are several exceptions to this general tendency, for example, studies by Hagedorn (1988), J. W. Moore (1978, 1991), Short and Strodtbeck (1965), Tracy (1979), and Vigil (1988).

2. Other longitudinal studies of gang members referred to in subsequent sections (i.e., Huizinga, 1996; R. E. Tremblay, personal communication, November 1996) also rely on a self-report measure of gang membership.

3. Because cumulative measures were used in the Rochester, Seattle, and Denver analyses, some of the offenses for which the gang members are responsible were committed either prior to or subsequent to periods of active gang membership. Because of the temporal patterning of membership and offending, however (see following section), it is likely that many of these offenses were committed while the gang members were actively involved in the gang.

4. I would like to thank David Farrington also for suggesting this line of analysis.

5. There is some overlap between risk factors and gang membership in the analysis for Year 1 because, with the exception of prior violence, the risk factors are measured at Wave 2 and gang membership combines data from Waves 2 and 3. This was unavoidable as not all risk factors were measured at Wave 1.

6. Equations also were estimated excluding association with delinquent peers because of the conceptual and empirical overlap between delinquent peers and gang membership. There were no substantive changes in the results when this was done.

7. These data are based only on males because of the relatively low base rate of female gang membership at later waves.

8. We also restricted the nonmembers to those in the top decile on the delinquent peer measure and to the top n respondents, where n is equal to the number of gang members at the particular wave. Differences between gang members and nonmembers are still large and statistically significant.

CHAPTER 9

Screening of Serious and Violent Juvenile Offenders

Identification, Classification, and Prediction

■ *Marc Le Blanc*

How can criminology help policy-makers and clinicians to select an appropriate screening strategy and to construct an accurate screening instrument for serious and violent juvenile (SVJ) offenders? The answer to this question is complex because there are many subquestions that have to be answered before discussing this main question. What does criminology know about screening? Why do policymakers and practitioners need to screen offenders? Who are the SVJ offenders? What are the available screening strategies? Can a screening instrument be accurate? What are the requirements of a sound predictive device? Should we screen on official delinquency or on self-reported delinquency? Do we need different screening instruments for different age groups, types of prevention programs, and decision points in the juvenile justice system? To answer these questions, this chapter is divided into three parts. First, the purposes of the identification of potential juvenile offenders and the classification of delinquents are discussed considering such a target as SVJ offenders. Second, a review of screening methods is undertaken to look for validated screening strategies and instruments. Third, several important legal, ethical, policy, and practical issues are discussed. The objective of this chapter is to guide the prevention researcher or the juvenile justice practitioner in selecting a screening strategy and constructing a screening instrument.

■ *Purposes of Screening*

In criminology, there are many categories of targets and within them many specific subtargets for which a prevention program can screen. In this chapter, we focus on SVJ offenders. As a consequence, our task is simplified but still not easy, because serious offenders are not necessarily violent offenders or chronic offenders and there are many chronic offenders that are not violent or serious offenders. As a consequence, there is a need to have a common understanding of these categories of offenders before discussing screening strategies and comparing screening instruments.

This question of the target for screening is fundamental, but there are two other equally important questions. First, on what criteria should prevention researchers and juvenile justice decision makers screen? They can discriminate on delinquent behavior using such criteria as number or nature of offenses, specialization, and so on, either using official records or using self-reports. They can screen SVJ offenders on personality characteristics such as antisocial personality, low self-control, psychopathy, and so forth. Alternatively, they can distinguish delinquents on social experiences such as a broken home, socioeconomic status, delinquent peers, school performance, and so on. Or they can use a combination of these three domains of variables. Second, is screening appropriate or necessary? A universal prevention program does not need a screening strategy or a screening instrument. At some points in the juvenile justice system, classification of SVJ offenders may not be pertinent or useful.

Besides these fundamental questions, the task of discriminating can be performed for two main purposes. First, screening can be a strategy to identify potential juvenile offenders to which some primary or secondary prevention program would be applied. Second, official juvenile offenders can be classified into homogeneous groups for treatment or security reasons, which can be called tertiary prevention. Whatever the type of prevention or juvenile justice decision, there is always an assessment of needs and risks in screening and there is necessarily a prediction about future offending behavior. It is essential to review these purposes and their consequences for the design and evaluation of screening strategies and instruments.

Target: SVJ Offenders

The adjectives *serious* and *violent* refer to many specific legal and research definitions. Legal definitions revolve around habitual offender laws. However, juvenile delinquency statutes generally do not provide habitual offender definitions. Because of the absence of common operational definitions among states, we cannot find in the legal definitions of seriousness, violence, and chronicity any clear advice for targeting these types of offenders for prevention or treatment.

Research definitions of SVJ offenders vary probably as much as legal definitions of these realities. However, these characteristics of offenders have been integrated into an overall theoretical paradigm, the criminal career view (Blumstein, Cohen, Roth, & Visher, 1986) or the developmental criminology perspective (Loeber & Le Blanc, 1990). In this paradigm, seriousness, chronicity, and violence are complementary descriptors of the nature of offending. The degree of involvement in a criminal career is assessed through the seriousness of the offenses, the frequency and continuity in offending, and the use of violence. In addition, from a measurement point of view, in this paradigm there is no equivalence between definitions of the same construct when researchers use official or self-reported data. Even if all operational definitions are arbitrary statistical decisions in particular universes, some definitions of these constructs are selected more often than others.

Concerning official data, the Wolfgang, Figlio, and Sellin (1972) definition of juvenile chronic offenders, those with five arrests or more, is widely referred to in studies of serious offenders. This operational definition of a chronic offender has been criticized because it does not take into account the exposure time of the offender (Blumstein et al., 1986). In addition, there have been very few systematic tests of this cut-off point as compared to others. And data from the 1958 cohort, compared with the 1945 cohort, indicate an increase in the proportion of chronic offenders from 6.3% to 7.5% and in the proportion of crimes they were responsible for, from 52% to 61% (Tracy, Wolfgang, & Figlio, 1990). The five or more cut-off point may also be an underestimation. Cohen's (1986) review estimates—irrespective of age and samples—that active violent offenders commit an average of two to four serious assaults a year, and active property offenders perpetrate an average of 5 to 10 crimes for each property crime for which they are arrested. In addition, Blumstein, Farrington, and Moitra (1985), in the only test of the Wolfgang et al. cut-off point, show that in four cohorts the best dividing point between chronics and other offenders is six arrests rather than five. Moving farther down in the juvenile justice system, Loeber, Farrington, and Waschbusch (Chapter 2, this volume) advocate three or more episodes of adjudication for criminal offenses as the definition of a chronic juvenile offender.

Self-reported studies, for their part, tend to use only one of the three constructs—seriousness, frequency, and variety—of serious or violent or chronic juvenile offenders. In general, they prefer a scale of variety of crimes or frequency of offenses, or sometimes subscales of violent or serious delinquency. As a consequence, the category of chronic juvenile offender is rarely present in the self-reported literature, whereas the constructs of violence and seriousness, when they are used, are operationalized as in the official data studies. However, from Elliott's (1994) report on serious violent offenders, we know that the cumulative "ever" prevalence to age 27 of serious violent offenders is 30%, 42% for males and 16% for females. By age 18, nearly 40% of the black males are serious violent offenders, compared with 30% of the white males. Most of them became serious violent offenders before age 16. This picture is quite different from the above description of serious violent offending with official data, even if Elliott (1994) was careful in retaining in his measures of aggravated assaults, robberies, and rapes that involved an injury or a weapon. However, this base rate of serious violent offenders is far from indicating the rate of SVJ offending.

There is a consensus between criminology and criminal justice on what constitutes of violent crimes. They are the assaults, rapes, robberies, and homicides of all kinds. These violent crimes are, and almost every researcher and juvenile justice official would agree, also the most serious crimes. Some other crimes are also defined as serious, such as burglary, arson, drug trafficking, motor vehicle theft, and theft worth more than $100. However, the sum of these crimes and the violent crimes, as listed by Loeber et al. in Chapter 2 in this volume, represent only around 40% of juvenile arrests if we look at crime statistics (Snyder, Sickmund, & Poe-Yamagata, 1996). Without a thorough review of the literature, we can estimate approximately the proportion of chronic juvenile offenders that are violent. On the basis of official data, SVJ delinquents, as defined by the commission of homicide, rape, assault, or robbery, represent between 53% (an estimate based on the Wolfgang et al. study) and 71% (Hamparian, Schuster, Dinitz, & Conrad, 1978) of the chronic delinquents.

As a consequence, we are faced with at least two categories of serious offenders, serious violent offenders and serious nonviolent offenders, for which the proportions vary certainly by sample, with the nature of the data, and the definition of seriousness/violence (see Snyder, Appendix, this volume). If we would accept these categories of juvenile offenders, we would have at least to retain three targets for screening in the context of this chapter. Is it feasible or necessary to retain these three categories of juvenile serious offenders? The feasibility and the necessity of these targets will be discussed throughout this chapter. This is a methodological question; among other criteria it depends on the base rate of these categories in the population or in the juvenile justice system. In addition, it may not be feasible to discriminate between categories of SVJ offenders in secondary prevention, but it may be possible to do so in tertiary prevention. The question of the necessity of distinguishing these targets is a substantive question. Do SVJ offenders display characteristics that distinguish them from serious or property offenders? Farrington's (1991) and Capaldi and Patterson's (1996) findings argue that it is not necessary to do so because predictors of violent and frequent offending appear the same. In contrast, research by Jessness and Haapanen (1982), Elliott, Dunford, and Huizinga (1987), and Fréchette and Le Blanc (1987) indicates that it is possible to discriminate between categories of chronic offenders.

The focus on SVJ offenders as opposed to other juvenile offenders may have important implications for the screening strategy, the choice of an instrument, and the content of the prevention programs that are to be applied. The screening strategy will probably need to be multistage because the potential offenders will have to be distinguished from the nonoffenders and then the SVJ offenders will have to be distinguished from the other offenders. Another consequence of our target will probably be that we will advocate secondary and tertiary prevention programs rather than primary prevention programs that are aimed at participation in offending.

Definition and Purpose of Screening

Screening occupies a central role in behavioral sciences, such as criminology, psychology, and social work. In criminology, screening has been a preoccupation since its early days with Lombroso's (1911) and Goring's (1913) classifications of offenders, which go back almost a century and have scientific and practical purposes. The identification of potential juvenile delinquents is also a long-standing object starting with the work by Binet and Simon (1907) in France. Finally, the prediction of future criminal behavior is of constant interest in criminal justice starting with the work of Burgess on parole decisions in 1928. The classification of offenders, the identification of potential delinquents, and the prediction of future offending are three components that are critical to theory development and ubiquitous in criminal justice. Screening, in the form of identification of potential delinquents, classification of known offenders, and prediction of future offending, is, then, basic to the effort to prevent crime.

The detection of potential delinquents for preventive intervention is prominent because of the resurgence of promising primary and secondary prevention programs and the recognition of the effectiveness of treatment programs (see Lipsey and Wilson, Chapter 13, this volume). Our object is individuals or groups at risk of SVJ offending. It is individuals selected from a population as displaying characteristics that are habitually found among SVJ offenders. It can also be social groups that are known to contain many SVJ offenders. For example, a prevention program may be proposed for all individuals in an underclass community or in some particular schools or gangs.

The identification of potential offenders not only involves a particular target, but it also requires a strategy and an instrument for the detection of a risk individual or group. As we will discuss what is available to juvenile justice practitioners and prevention researchers, strategies could be one-shot operations or multistage complex procedures. In addition, instruments can be of a variety of forms, from a scale with a few items to a multiple-settings and multiple-methods detection kit. These strategies and instruments may have to be specially constructed when SVJ offenders are targeted instead of offenders in general. They may also vary according to primary, secondary, or tertiary prevention; the age group; or the ethnic group receiving a prevention program.

In contrast, D. M. Gottfredson (1987) distinguished two different meanings of the term *classification* in criminology and criminal justice. First, a classification in criminology, is "the allocation of persons to initially undefined classes in such a way that the persons in a class are in some way similar or close to each other" (p. 1). Numerous classifications of juvenile offenders exist. Some are theoretical, other empirical. Some are developmental, others are not (see Loeber et al., Chapter 2, this volume). It is important from the statistical point of view to find a classification with the minimum number of classes minimizing within-group variance while maximizing between-group variance.

Gottfredson (1987) also identified a second meaning that is customary in criminal justice practice: "the process of choosing, for a new case, which of a number of already assigned classes should be selected for an allocation" (pp. 1-2). In the juvenile justice system, there are numerous decisions, such as arrest, prosecute, adjudicate, grant parole, and select a level of security or a treatment program. Some of these decision points regulate the flow, such as prosecution, whereas others involve programming decisions, such as correctional institutions, either for reasons of security or type of treatment. For most of the decision points, the factors that influence decisions are well documented in the literature (see, e.g., M. R. Gottfredson & D. M. Gottfredson, 1985). When intervention programming is in question, our knowledge of which program is most efficient for which type of offenders is insufficient (Palmer, 1992). It is important, in discussing classification, to stress the accuracy of the decision or the appropriateness of the treatment program or the security measure selected. When screening for prevention purposes, two meanings of the term classification are referred to. A classification of potential offender types must be developed first, then a method of allocation of the potential offenders must be designed. However, the particular target of potential SVJ offenders may impose certain constraints to the construction of a classification system and the allocation of potential delinquents in the various classes.

In addition, Gottfredson (1987) defined prediction as "an assessment of some expected future behavior by a person" (p. 2). Some criterion of future behavior must be chosen and validated. And the evaluation of the potential risk of the event or the state to be predicted "must be made independently of any steps used in arriving at the prediction" (p. 2). A target such as SVJ offenders may impose certain limitations to prediction. Particularly the question of the very low base rate of these offenders in the population in general and of their relatively low base rate at the entry point in the juvenile justice system will be discussed. What we must keep in mind is that the identification of potential offenders does not automatically imply the classification of individuals into potential or nonpotential offenders or the prediction of possible future offenses. This is an assessment of risks. On the contrary, a classification can be developed independently of any purpose of prediction. In summary, the purpose of screening is the identification of potential SVJ offenders. To attain that objective, there is a need to classify some population of individuals into at least two classes, potential SVJ offenders or others, and these classes must represent distinct probabilities of future frequent, serious, and violent offending.

■ Lessons From the Prediction Tradition

A reading of the Farrington and Tarling (1985) and Gottfredson and Tonry (1987) books clearly indicates that the field of prediction and classification has attained maturity. Because it is not immediately evident that the know-how of this literature is used in the prevention domain, it appears essential to list the methodological lessons that we should learn from this literature before we review existing and potential screening strategies and instruments. These lessons will serve as criteria for the evaluation of the proposed screening strategies and instruments.

Selecting a Criterion

Because the target is potential SVJ offenders, the screening instrument will have to be constructed using measures other than the common official delinquent/nondelinquent or recidivist/nonrecidivist dichotomies. Violence could be operationalized by a dichotomy, the presence or absence of violent index crimes, but it could also be a frequency measure. In the same way, seriousness can be operationalized by a dichotomy or a continuum, whatever its content, only the serious crimes against persons or the serious violent and property crimes. Instead of a dichotomy, chronicity is most often operationalized by a frequency measure. Such a frequency measure will introduce the difficult question of the selection of a cut-off point and its adaptation as time passes.

Researchers, using official data, tend to select the Wolfgang et al. (1972) measure of chronic offending. However, we need studies that test other cut-off points and, because violent offenses have increased over the past decades, the five arrests or more cut-off point may have to be revised. However, it is a practical question that can be solved partly with existing longitudinal data sets as did Blumstein et al. (1985). This question of the appropriate cut-off point for the outcome measure becomes much more difficult when self-reported measures of SVJ offending are used. It is a much more complex question because measures of delinquency vary enormously in their content from one study to another, such as the phrasing of comparable behaviors and in the number of behaviors in a scale. As a consequence, it is virtually impossible to replicate any test of various cut-off points on many existing data sets. Some researchers advocate the use of continuous variables (see Blumstein et al., 1986), because dichotomous variables are not sufficiently sensitive to the variations in the underlying continuous variable. However, the use of continuous variables will probably have to wait for appropriate statistical methods for the combination of predictors, because, as we will see, simpler additive methods are still more efficient. The selection of cut-off points is also complicated by the necessity of varying the cut-off point with the age of the juvenile. This may be useful because the frequency of criminal behavior (lambda) varies greatly with age (Blumstein et al., 1986; Le Blanc & Fréchette, 1989).

Cut-off points pose an enormous challenge to the base rate because they will vary alongside it and because, with the SVJ offender target, we are confronted with a relatively low base rate. The base rate is the relative frequency of SVJ offenders in a population. In criminology, it is expected to be around 6% in the general population of boys, 20% of the arrestees, and 45% of the population of adjudicated boys. Gottfredson (1987) stressed the well-known fact that prediction worsens the more the base rate differs from 0.5. In this context, the lower the base rate, the easier it is to predict that everybody in the sample will not become an SVJ offender; this prediction will be correct 94% of the time by chance alone.

Gottfredson (1987) identified two procedures to tackle the low base rate problem. He advocated either the use of a continuous criterion or a sequential prediction. In the first case, developers of prediction devices should look for a continuous criterion such as frequency of offending rather than the usual discrete criterion, such as delinquent or nondelinquent. In the second case, a homogeneous group is identified, for example, potential chronic offenders, then a subgroup is predicted among the first homogeneous group, for example, serious and violent offenders. As a consequence, the base rate is relatively large. However, for sequential prediction to work the overall sample size also has to be large.

Primary prevention concerns the use of universal programs to curb delinquency in general (e.g., the Perry Preschool Program; Berrueta-Clement, Schweinhart, Barnett, Epstein, & Weikart, 1984; see other examples in Chapter 10 by Wasserman and Miller, this volume). In this case, there is little use in developing a screening instrument for SVJ offenders because risk factors are of an epidemiological nature (e.g., low income, one-parent family) and the proportion of SVJ offenders is too low in the reference population. For tertiary prevention or treatment purposes, the base rate is sufficiently high at any point in the juvenile justice system to design a screening instrument, and there are numerous examples of promising risk and needs assessment devices (see Wiebush, Baird, Krisberg, & Onek, 1995). For secondary prevention, probably what we have to do concerning SVJ offenders is to respond to the following question: What is the population or the individual characteristic that will produce a base rate between 5% and 50%? In addition, we do not know what is the optimum base rate between these extremes.

The receiver operating characteristics (ROC) curve presented by Farrington, Loeber, Stouthamer-Loeber, Van Kammen, and Schmidt (1996) could help in choosing the optimal cut-off point. The ROC curve plots the probabilities of a "hit" (the percentage of delinquents identified at any selection criterion) versus the probability of a "false positive" (the percentage of nondelinquents identified at the same selection criterion). ROC provides a measure of strength of relationship unaffected by changes in sample size and row and column totals. Mossman (1994) used it to summarize the discriminating power of predictors in his meta-analysis, and Farrington et al. (1996) employed it in their validation of a multiple-informant delinquency seriousness scale.

Besides the cut-off point problem, there is the censoring problem. All predictions apply to a specific follow-up period that is not directly related to the nature of the outcome, and the probability of becoming a SVJ offender increases with time at risk. However, because we are concerned with juvenile offenders up to the age of 18, the censoring impact is limited. After 18, only a small group of offenders will become serious and violent offenders if they have not been before (see Farrington, 1989a, 1991). As a consequence, no adjustment for censoring is needed.

In summary, the nature of the target, SVJ offenders, imposes the choice of two of the three types of prevention. Because of the low base rate and, consequently, the weak predictive accuracy for SVJ offenders, primary prevention has to be ruled out in favor of secondary and tertiary prevention. Because of the lack of specificity in the types of risk factors involved in identifying SVJ offenders, primary prevention cannot target precisely these offenders. Primary prevention is not irrelevant or futile for the prevention of delinquency in general. It is inapplicable for targeting specifically SVJ potential offenders. Alternatively, a multistage screening strategy is probably the only appropriate solution for a low base rate phenomenon, such as SVJ offenders in the population. While adopting such a strategy, developers of screening devices should devote particular attention to the choice of a cut-off point for the outcome measure. A cut-off point may affect significantly the base rate, but it may also alter its relations with the predictors.

Selecting Predictors

In the field of prediction, the choice of predictors was traditionally determined by the availability of the information in case records and, as a consequence, only one source of information was used. Instead, Farrington and Tarling (1985) and Gottfredson (1987) concur in recommending the selection of predictors on theoretical grounds. There is another method of selection of predictors. This strategy involves the use of a meta-analysis to identify the most significant risk factors

found for SVJ delinquents, and Chapter 6 proposes a list of such potential predictors. There are many advantages and disadvantages to theoretical and meta-analysis strategies for the selection of predictors.

The meta-analysis method of selection has the advantage of standing on solid empirical grounds. However, research results may be contradictory for sampling or measurement reasons, and past research may represent an incomplete coverage of potential risk factors. In addition, the methodology of meta-analysis involves aggregating samples and measures of various natures, and we are well aware of the limits of aggregation in social sciences. The pure theoretical strategy is also difficult to apply because there is no general theory in criminology and even the most comprehensive theory, control theory (Gottfredson & Hirschi, 1990; Hirschi, 1969), does not receive total support from criminologists despite the fact that numerous replications are available (Kempf, 1993). An alternative method of selection of predictors would be to select those that have an empirical base and a theoretical significance; control theory and social learning predictors would probably be the only ones that would fit these criteria easily. Brennan (1987a) preferred theoretical clarity instead of the incoherence introduced by the adoption of the largest possible set of ad hoc variables. Brennan (1987a) also added that developers of instruments should be very sensitive to irrelevant, unreliable, and redundant variables that will introduce noise in the prediction device.

Independently of the adoption of either a strictly empirical strategy or a combined theoretical and empirical strategy, the question of the nature and the sources of information will have to be addressed. Risk studies, as shown by Lorion, Tolan, and Wahler (1987), are in two categories. First, there is the behavioral pattern strategy that focuses on aggressive and antisocial behavior patterns that precede delinquency. This research tradition identifies strong predictors such as early problem behavior and age of onset (see Lipsey and Derzon, Chapter 6, this volume). Second, there is the psychosocial strategy that seeks a large set of individual and social predictors (see Hawkins et al., Chapter 7, this volume). In this research tradition, there is no consensus as to the appropriate predictors because different studies have focused on specific sets of predictors rather than a comprehensive set. As for the sources of information, Farrington and Tarling (1985) cited studies indicating that the use of case record predictors is improved by home background data and personality tests. In the domain of the identification of potential offenders for prevention, studies from Loeber, Dishion, and Patterson (1984) to Charlebois, Le Blanc, Gagnon, and Larivée (1994) show that the use of multiple informants from multiple settings is a more efficient strategy than the selection of only one source of information.

Whatever the source of information or the strategy to select predictors, there will be a cut-off point problem for predictors, as it is for outcomes, because the simpler methods for the combination of predictors are more efficient than the more complex methods. Consequently, the cut-off point on each predictor will affect the selection ratio. The selection ratio, according to Loeber and Dishion (1983), is the marginal distribution on the predictor, whereas the base rate is the marginal distribution on the outcome. As for the outcome, cut-off points for the predictors may alter the number of valid positives and negatives. In addition, if the selection ratio is too low, 5%, 10%, or even 20%, a predictor may be discarded if the sample is small.

In summary, the selection of predictors should ideally involve multiple informants in multiple settings and it should rest on solid empirical evidence, as well as on theoretical significance. Whatever the nature of these predictors, structural variables, such as social status, discrete states, such as in or out of school, or variable states, such as social bonding or self-control measures, developers of screening instruments should be extremely cautious about cut-off points. They should systematically test various cut-off points before adopting one, and they should be critical of the use of available cut-off points in the literature because they could have been made empirically or based on theoretical choices.

Assuring Reliability of Predictors and Outcome

Reliability is the stability with which measurement may be made. Gottfredson (1987) stated that developers of prediction tables often improve or evaluate the reliability of the predictors but neglect the reliability of the outcome measures. The question of the reliability of the outcome variable becomes much more complex when researchers use self-reported measures of offending rather than official indicators of delinquency and when predictors are variable states, such as bonding and self-control variables, rather than discrete states, such as social status, sex, and age, or discrete change variables, such as being in school or in the workforce, being married or not. It is likely that in the future variable states and self-reported offending will more frequently be used in prediction and classification, either as predictors or outcomes.

Combining Predictors

When predictors and the criterion are appropriate and reliable, the next question is how to combine the predictors in a prediction equation to maximize predictive efficiency and to construct a prediction table to forecast who will become SVJ offenders. There are two basic methods for the combination of predictors. The first method is the simple additive method used by Burgess (1928) and the Gluecks (1950) in which a predictor gives an additional point and each point, or group of points, represents an increased probability of being an SVJ offender. In the second case, each predictor is weighted before the scores are added, and the weighting is arbitrary or it represents the strength of the relation between the predictor and the outcome. Farrington and Tarling (1985) cited studies showing that these two categories of the additive method are highly correlated and that they display quite similar predictive efficiency. The second method for the combination of predictors relies on multivariate statistical techniques such as multiple regression, hierarchical analyses, and log-linear and logistic techniques, which are more recent and about which there were high hopes that were not fulfilled.

Research wisdom would recommend additive methods over multiplicative methods. A recent review by Farrington and Tarling (1985) and empirical comparisons by Farrington (1985), S. D. Gottfredson and D. M. Gottfredson (1985), and Wilbanks (1985) indicate that the additive method is just as efficient as, or even more efficient than, the multiplicative method. In addition, the additive method of combining predictors has a practical advantage. The prediction score of an individual is very easy to calculate for a practitioner in juvenile justice or a field screener for a prevention program. They have to gather a small set of information and, with a simple table, they can obtain the prediction score applicable to an individual. It is true, however, that with the advent of microcomputers it is now easy to obtain a prediction score with any of the methods for the combination of the predictors.

Measuring Predictive Accuracy

Farrington and Tarling (1985) expressed that "it is unfortunate that there are no widely accepted methods of measuring predictive efficiency" (p. 20). Gottfredson (1987) reported that "none of the indices described can answer completely the question how accurate a prediction device is" (p. 31). There are two categories of measures of predictive accuracy, that is, the magnitude of the relation between the predictor and an outcome. First, there are the correlational measures, from phi to biserial correlations, that have to be chosen according to the nature of the data. Second, there are some indexes of predictive accuracy that estimate the proportional reduction in error. This offers an evaluation of predictive power above that afforded by the simple use of the chance or base rate. There are two well-known such indexes, the Mean Cost Rating (MCR) of Duncan, Ohlin, Reiss, and Stanton (1952), which compares false negatives to false positives, and Relative Improvement Over Chance (RIOC) of Loeber and Dishion (1983), which corrects this comparison by the selection ratio and the base rate. The advantage of RIOC over the MCR not only rests on the simultaneous consideration of the selection ratio and the base rate, it lies also in the fact that Copas and Loeber (1990) present methods to calculate confidence intervals, for testing the significance of individual values of RIOC, and for testing the difference between several values of RIOC from different studies. As we can see, methods for the estimation of predictive accuracy are well developed for dichotomous predictors and outcome. As a consequence, they can be applied readily to the additive procedures for the combination of the predictors. When multiplicative statistical procedures are preferred, the proportion of variance explained can replace the measures of predictive accuracy for discrete variables. However, there is no similar index to the RIOC for nondichotomous predictors, either continuous or categorical.

Whatever the measure of predictive accuracy, the question of the appropriate proportions of false positives and false negatives will remain. These proportions are embedded in the selection of cut-off points on the criterion and predictors that will produce particular base rate and specific selection ratios. Modifying the cut-off point on the criterion to increase the base rate, with the sensitivity of the predictive instrument held constant, will reduce the level of false positives, that is, identifying a potential offender as SVJ when actually he or she is not such a type of offender. In turn, the increase of the base rate will increase the likelihood of false negatives, that is, identifying a potential offender as only a delinquent when he or she is in fact an SVJ offender. This dilemma is resolved in two ways in the literature: the statistical and the social utility solutions.

The statistical solution consists of finding the optimum combination between cut-off points, the proportions of false positives and false negatives, and predictive accuracy to minimize errors while maximizing the predictive accuracy. Probably the best example of such an approach is presented by Blumstein et al. (1986) for the Greenwood five-factor scale. They concluded that no statistical solution provided a sufficient basis for defining the best classification rule that reflects all relevant statistical concerns. As a consequence, they favored the social utility solution, what they call the "civil-libertarian ratio" (Blumstein et al., 1985) to evaluate the relationship between the cut-off points, the

base rate, the proportions of errors, and the predictive accuracy.

Wilkins (1985) also concluded that the question of false positives and false negatives is not a statistical problem but a morality dilemma. He stated that even if the proportions of errors are as small as possible, there will always be a question of a tradeoff between them. There will be a need for a social consensus on what is more important, the risk to society, the potential SVJ offenders that will not be identified as such, or the risk to the individual, being the object of a preventive or a particular juvenile justice decision or treatment when he or she will not become an SVJ offender. In the case of false negatives, the costs are to the future victims of the crimes of these offenders and to society in terms of costs of incapacitation or treatment and other consequential social costs. In the case of false positives, the costs will be for the individual who will be part of a prevention program or a particular juvenile justice program, this without showing the requirements of this particular type of offending. It could be argued that in comparison to the prediction of delinquency in general, the errors of prediction for SVJ delinquency are less costly to society and the individual because SVJ offenders are a subgroup of delinquents. The false negatives and the false positives can be part of a general delinquency prevention program or they will be handled anyway by the juvenile justice system, consequently reducing the costs to society or the individual.

Validating the Screening Device

Validation is an empirical procedure used to obtain an estimate of the accuracy of predictions. Validation requires a representative sample and requires cross-validation; bootstrapping may increase the utility of prediction. Gottfredson (1987) referred to the importance of using groups of individuals who are representative of the population to which the prediction instrument is intended to be used. With such a representative sample, the base rate is appropriate and the shrinkage in the accuracy of predictions is limited. He argued that because no group is similar to any other, particularly concerning the relationship between predictors and the outcome, there is a danger of overestimating this. In this case, prediction about how members of another group will behave will be necessarily biased. As a consequence, we can argue that the use of Wolfgang et al.'s (1972) operational definition of a chronic offender born in Philadelphia in 1945 may not be representative of national or other city samples for later decades. The base rate, consequently, may vary even using the same operational definition of SVJ offending. In addition, we can expect that the relative importance of predictors may vary from sample to sample and over time (see also Farrington & Loeber, in press, which compares predictors in London in the 1960s and in Pittsburgh in the 1980s). Whatever the representativeness of the sample, Gottfredson (1987) reported that there is always shrinkage between predictive efficiency in the construction sample and the operational sample. Farrington and Tarling (1985) added that it is more of a problem with multivariate statistical techniques. This situation has consequences for the method of selection of predictors. Predictors chosen from a meta-analysis of many samples or from the theoretical and empirically based point of view may diminish shrinkage, but this hypothesis has to be tested empirically.

In addition, there is no other way than cross-validation to evaluate the accuracy of prediction. Cross-validation helps in distinguishing what part is peculiar to the characteristics of the sample and what part reflects the underlying relations between the predic-

tors and outcome. Cross-validation is accomplished by dividing the sample in two. The first subsample serves as the construction sample, and the second subsample is used in estimating predictive accuracy. In such a case, subsamples' predictive accuracy is expected to be normally distributed, and we then fall back on the representativeness problem. Gottfredson (1987) stated that there is no ideal answer to the cross-validation problem. A solution would appear to be a longitudinal validation that involves predicting who will become an SVJ offender in a sample and then waiting to the end of their adolescence to check who has become such an offender. When such a screening instrument will be validated, we will run into the representativeness problems that were outlined earlier.

Because the overlap between serious, violent, and chronic offending is far from perfect (see Loeber et al., Chapter 2, this volume), there are many categories of offenders that can be targeted. For example, there are the violent chronic offender and the property chronic offender. Then, to increase the validity and accuracy of the prediction equation, bootstrapping is promising. This procedure requires the identification of homogeneous subgroups, for example, those defined above, and the calculation of a prediction equation for each. These equations are then combined into an overall equation for the whole sample. Gottfredson (1987) recommends another type of bootstrapping, the combination of a statistical and a clinical prediction. The usefulness of this procedure may depend on the level of prevention. For primary prevention, we are working with a large population and epidemiological risk factors, where this kind of bootstrapping may be too costly and even unnecessary. For secondary prevention with potential SVJ offenders, we may rely on a different set of predictors, such as personality traits, and a clinical prediction may be envisaged. Finally, for tertiary prevention, when the allocation of SVJ offenders to an appropriate measure and a pertinent treatment program is in question, such bootstrapping may be very helpful.

In summary, the best solution to the problems of validation, as well as to the selection of predictors, may be the result of a meta-analysis that has enough studies with a similar SVJ offender outcome (see Lipsey and Derzon, Chapter 6, this volume). On such a data set, different combinations of predictors could be tested. The replication of the predictors from one study to the other may be the strongest form of validation that we could expect. Such replication, as advocated by Farrington, Ohlin, and Wilson (1986), should include different areas and times.

■ Review of Screening Strategies and Instruments

Screening for Prevention

The screening strategy. SVJ offenders are defined in various ways in different studies. In contrast, this book proposes a specific definition of SVJ offenders. It involves all violent index crimes and index property offenses and some non-index property offenses. Loeber et al.'s (Chapter 2, this volume) definition of SVJ offenders would imply a base rate higher than 5% of the population; however, it is difficult to specify this. With this definition in mind, we can conclude that to our knowledge no screening strategy has been proposed and validated for such a target population (see the reviews of the existing prevention programs targeting individuals or communities by Wasserman and Miller, Chapter 10, and Catalano et al., Chapter 11, this volume). However, the delin-

quency literature contains a variety of screening strategies. These strategies are elaborated according to one or more of the following four dimensions: the number of stages, the sources of information, the variable domains represented, and the methods of data gathering selected.

The first screening instrument, that of the Gluecks (1950), proceeded in a single stage and selected one source of information, the interviewer who visited the family, and one domain of variables, the family. Very rapidly, multiple-stage strategies were proposed (Kvaraceus, 1953), multiple domains of variables were tested to screen delinquents (personality and family; Briggs, Wirt, & Johnson, 1961), and multiple informants were used (teacher and subject; Le Blanc, Marineau, Fréchette, & Limoges, 1971). We had to wait for the 1980s for the proposition of multiple gating, a device with multiple stages involving multiple informants and multiple methods (Loeber et al., 1984) and later on for a multiple-stage strategy with multiple informants, multiple methods, and multiple settings (Charlebois et al., 1994). However, none of these procedures was developed for and validated with SVJ offenders.

Loeber et al. (1984) proposed a procedure consisting of three gates, which involved the teacher, the child, and the mother as informants, and three sets of data, that is, a teacher rating of 11 child behaviors; six short telephone calls on family organization, whereabouts of the child, and problem behavior; and measures of disobedience and monitoring (child and mother reports and interviewer impressions). The outcome was official delinquency, which was validated with self-reported offending. This procedure showed an increase of predictive accuracy (RIOC) from 37.6% for the first gate to 74.2% for the third gate and an increase of valid positives from 25.4% to 56.3%. This strategy required 3 hours 20 minutes of professional time and implied a cost of $185 per child compared with $445 if each child was evaluated with these instruments at the three gates. As recognized by the authors, this screening strategy has to be validated with a larger sample and in a different setting. In addition, this strategy was not concerned with SVJ offenders even if it identified six of the seven official recidivists in the sample. There are other validated examples of a similar multiple-gating strategy, such as the August, Realmuto, Crosby, and MacDonald (1995) procedure to screen children at risk for conduct disorder.

Charlebois et al. (1994; Charlebois, Le Blanc, Gagnon, Larivée, & Tremblay, 1993) targeted self-reported delinquency of 10-year-old boys. They proposed a three-stage procedure that involved multiple informants (teacher and mother) and multiple methods (ratings and observations) in multiple settings. They showed that predictive accuracy increased with the number of stages; with the nature of informants, from the teacher to the mother; and with the type of methods, from mother and teacher ratings to observation in single and multiple settings. The disadvantages of this strategy rest in the difficulties and costs in conducting observations in school, at home, and in the laboratory.

What is interesting about these two strategies is that they are school based and that they concern primary school children. In the delinquency prevention literature (Tolan & Guerra, 1994a), there are many promising programs for preschool children, for students in their first years of compulsory schooling, and then for the pupils at the middle or the end of elementary school. In the violence prevention literature (Guerra, Tolan, & Hammond, 1994), most of the programs are school based. There are many applications of the multiple-stage strategy, but they do not focus on the common outcome measures in criminology, that is, official and self-reported delinquency, or on SVJ offenders. For example, Wehby,

Dodge, and Valente (1991) proposed first a selection of an at-risk school, then teachers' ratings, then direct observations in structured and unstructured activities. The Walker et al. (1994) strategy is school based but it involves a rating of all students, then more in-depth evaluations of a small number of students by their teachers, and, finally, direct observations in class and on the playground.

These screening strategies are individually based; they seek at-risk individuals. There is another broad category of strategies that focus on at-risk groups by identifying community characteristics where SVJ offenders are most often found. For example, epidemiological characteristics of communities where SVJ offenders are numerous are targeted, such as communities where poverty is endemic, with numerous single-parent families, and so on. For example, some primary prevention programs for infants, such as the Yale Child Welfare Research Program (Provence & Naylor, 1983), and for preschoolers, the Perry Preschool Project (Berrueta-Clement et al., 1984), target more directly at-risk communities and families than individuals. Secondary prevention programs may target specific groups instead of communities, such as schools or gangs. For example, gangs are selected for secondary prevention through aggression replacement training (Goldstein & Glick, 1994).

The above strategies can be put in the context of primary, secondary, and tertiary prevention for potential SVJ offenders. Primary prevention seems contradictory to targeting SVJ offenders because it involves universal programs for the whole population in a community. Tertiary prevention implies the identification of potential SVJ offenders when they are processed by the juvenile justice system. The habitual single-gate and -informant strategy seems reasonable and it is certainly economic. However, many domains of predictors considered are limited to officially available data, and measures of the personality domain are often absent. The predictive accuracy of these instruments may be increased with self-reported criminal career data and even self-reported violence data. In addition, personality variables are probably useful according, for example, to Megargee and Bohn's (1979) classification, and to the results of Lipsey and Derzon's meta-analysis (Chapter 6, this volume). Personality is one of the best discriminators between types of chronic offenders (Jessness & Haapanen, 1982), and Lynam's (1996) review indicates that the children with hyperactivity, impulsivity, and attention problems and conduct problems, what he calls the "fledgling psychopath," can be identified early on and are at risk to become chronic offenders. In summary, even if the predictive accuracy of the risk assessment instruments, when available, is good, it might be improved by the inclusion of other predictor domains.

Secondary prevention requires the identification of individuals at risk for SVJ offending. Multiple gating seems, in this case, essential because of the low base rate problem. Multiple informants and multiple-variable domains seem preferable because of the complexity of the influences (see the predictors reviewed by Lipsey and Derzon, Chapter 6, this volume). Then, there are four practical questions. How many gates should be retained? At what age should we screen? Should we screen in school or elsewhere? What predictors should we select? The answers to these questions may depend on the context and on the nature of the prevention program. In some cases, we may have to screen communities or schools as a first step but not in other cases. School screening is the easiest but is not without practical problems (difficulties in access to school, absent students, etc.). The number of gates has never been tested, and as a consequence we do not know what is the most appropriate number

even if we know that three gates are efficient (Loeber et al., 1984).

The most arbitrary question is probably the age at which to screen. Some criminologists would propose preschool, whereas others would suggest school entry or after the onset of early delinquency, around 10 years of age. This choice is arbitrary because it refers to personal preferences that are grounded on a knowledge of the scientific literature. The literature does not propose a systematic comparison on a particular database of various screening ages. We can imagine that predictive accuracy will increase with age. Also, it will probably be higher during late childhood, because the average age of onset of delinquency of future SVJ offenders is between 8 and 14 (Le Blanc & Fréchette, 1989; Loeber et al., Chapter 2, this volume). Onset is also one of the most powerful predictors (Loeber & Stouthamer-Loeber, 1987) and is part of most risk assessment instruments (Wiebush et al., 1995). If predictive accuracy were to be selected as the main decision criterion, we would have to wait for late childhood before applying a screening strategy for secondary prevention. Then most of the SVJ offenders will have initiated delinquency, and self-reported data will also be available. Loeber et al.'s (1984) multiple-gating strategy could then be validated for SVJ offenders.

Many others will prefer an earlier point of screening, such as the entry into elementary school as suggested by the Gluecks. Some violence prevention programs have been implemented at that age (see Guerra et al., 1994), but none of them has reported a reduction in the number of SVJ offenders. The proponents of this screening age will argue for that period because they believe that the relationship between early conduct problems, such as aggression, and adolescent delinquency is sufficiently strong to permit an accurate screening. The relationship with official delinquency participation is not that strong (see Loeber & Stouthamer-Loeber, 1987). In addition, as Lipsey and Derzon showed (Chapter 6, this volume), aggression and problem behavior are not among the best predictors. Instead, the type of delinquent offense is the best predictor of later serious delinquency.

Why not select preschool children, between 3 and 5 years old? There are efficient prevention programs for delinquency participation at that age, but none of them has indicated an impact on the age of onset or on SVJ offending (Tolan & Guerra, 1994a). It may be possible to identify potential SVJ offenders at that age, and two stepping-stone strategies have been proposed. Kellam and Rebok (1992) suggested the use of universal prevention programs as the initial screening method. The children who do not profit from such programs and who display severe difficulties are then identified and referred to a secondary prevention program. Le Blanc (1995) proposed a strategy that involves the identification of potential delinquents for known efficient primary prevention programs, and then the selection of potential SVJ offenders according to clinical and research characteristics of SVJ offenders for which special components are added to the basic primary prevention programs. This strategy is similar to Gottfredson's (1987) proposition of statistical and clinical bootstrapping. Lynam (1996) advocated the last component that he calls the subtype strategy. He proposes the identification of children with hyperactivity, impulsivity, and attention problems and conduct problems because they are at the greatest risk for the development of adult antisocial personality.

In summary, whatever the age group retained for prevention or the nature of the program envisaged, multiple gates, multiple informants, multiple-variable domains, and multiple methods seem the best solution to the identification of potential SVJ offenders. Independently of this research wisdom, most prevention programs implemented since the beginning of the 1980s use only a single-step strategy and target directly individuals while using only one informant and a few variable domains in most cases (see Wasserman and Miller, Chapter 10, this volume). As a consequence, there is a large gap between research and practice. In the future, the strategy of using multiple gates, informants, variables, and methods should be considered more.

Screening instruments. Binet and Simon, in their 1907 book, were probably the first to screen for abnormal children in school who would become criminals later on. They suggested that the following criteria and tests should be used to identify children who should be sent to special classes: being delayed in their schooling, two teachers indicating that they display severe disobedience in class, and standardized achievement and IQ tests. Psychologists followed that tradition in the 1920s-1930s with tests designed, among other things, to screen delinquents. At least two of them were subjected to a validation study with delinquents, the Washburne Social-Adjustment Inventory by Washburne (1929) and the Personal Index by Riggs and Joyal (1938). However, it was not until after the Second World War that numerous psychometric instruments were proposed, some of them being the subject of various kinds of validation studies. Some of these screening instruments were general personality inventories that were shown to discriminate delinquents from nondelinquents, such as the MMPI (Hathaway & Monachesi, 1953) or the Maze test (Porteus, 1942). Some other screening instruments were social inventories that were validated: the Glueck Social Prediction Table (Glueck & Glueck, 1950), the Behavior Cards (Stodgill, 1950), the KD Proneness

Scale and Check List (Kvaraceus, 1953), and the Bristol Social Adjustment Scale (Stott, 1960).

The major innovation came from the Gluecks (1950). The prediction table used five family variables: the discipline of the boy by the father, the supervision of the boy by the mother, the affection of the father for the boy, the affection of the mother for the boy, and the cohesiveness of the family. The Gluecks obtained a remarkable discrimination between the delinquents and the nondelinquents, and they advocated that their prediction table should be used to identify potential delinquents at the time of school entrance. Farrington and Tarling (1985) made the following summary of the critics of this instrument. The main arguments against this scale were, first, that the delinquent and nondelinquents were extreme groups; second, that the equal proportion of delinquents and nondelinquents in the study made it easier to predict delinquency; third, that the relationships between the predictors and delinquency that were holding at 14-15 years of age may not stand for 6-year-olds; fourth, that there was no validation sample; and fifth, that the interviewers may have been biased by knowing who was delinquent or not. These deficiencies of the Glueck Social Prediction Table led to the discrediting of prediction in general. However, eight validation studies confirmed the predictive power of the combination of the five Gluecks' predictors (Craig & Glick, 1963; Dootjes, 1972; Feldhusen, Thurston, & Benning, 1973; Havighurst, Bowman, Liddle, Matthews, & Pierce, 1962; Hodge & Tait, 1963; Loftus, 1974; Trevvett, 1965; Veverka, 1971). After this controversial period there was little research on delinquency prediction (Feldhusen, Aversano, & Thurston, 1976; Wadsworth, 1978).

Even if potential instruments exist, today there is no device that is designed and validated for SVJ offenders. This conclusion is based on two observations. First, we did not locate a screening instrument that has a tested criterion and appropriate and reliable predictors, that has been validated, and that shows a high predictive accuracy for SVJ offending, and we identified only one candidate instrument for chronic offending. Even in the field of the prediction of violence, there are no recent satisfactory instruments because methodological concerns are still significant, according to Chaiken, Chaiken, and Rhodes's (1994) review.

Second, we reviewed the prevention programs that are surveyed by Wasserman and Miller, Chapter 10, and by Catalano et al., Chapter 11, this volume, and in most cases, no instrument was used and only a short list of criteria served as a screening device. For example, among the 41 prevention programs reviewed in Chapter 10, 25 (61%) used a list of criteria, generally less than five. These criteria are, for example, poverty, single mothers, referral to a particular service, and so on. Of the 16 secondary prevention programs that employed an instrument (nine programs) or a combination of criteria and an instrument (seven programs) to screen, 11 were conducted with elementary school-age children. The most common instrument was a measure of disruptive behavior as assessed by teachers. In this context, we can comment on a candidate screening instrument for chronic offenders while it is also possible to conceive an instrument based on the meta-analyses of the predictors of SVJ offending.

The candidate instrument could be called the Cambridge screening instrument because it is based on the Cambridge Study in Delinquent Development. According to Blumstein et al.'s (1985) analyses of the data, six characteristics, measured before 10 years of age, distinguish convicted offenders from nonconvicted persons, at the first conviction. These predictors of offending are (a) troublesomeness between ages 8 and 10, (b) a convicted parent at 10, (c) nervousness at 8, (d) poor elementary school attainment 10, (e) daring at 8, and (f) separation from a parent at 10. In addition, there are four characteristics that distinguish chronic offenders (six or more convictions) from other offenders. These predictors are (a) convicted at age 10-12, (b) convicted sibling at 10, (c) troublesomeness between 8 and 10, and (d) poor elementary school attainment at 10. These predictors could apply for secondary prevention programs from middle to late childhood and for screening in the juvenile justice system. The advantage of this instrument is threefold. First, the criterion, six offenses or more, has been tested on four data sets in the United States by Blumstein et al. (1985). Second, there are good indications that the predictors could be replicated for chronic offending on the Pittsburgh Youth Study data set. In a recent study, Farrington and Loeber (in press) show that several risk factors are similar in the Cambridge study in the 1960s and the Pittsburgh study in the 1980s. These predictors are hyperactivity and impulsivity, low school attainment, poor parental supervision, parental conflict, an antisocial parent, a young mother, large family size, low family income, and coming from a broken home. However, there were some predictors that were noncomparable from one study to the other. Considering the comparable results, it is probable that the analysis of Blumstein et al. (1985) for chronic offending could be replicated on the Pittsburgh data set. Third, this instrument could be used for violent offenders because Farrington (1991) and Capaldi and Patterson (1996) show that violent offenders display the same family and behavioral background characteristics as frequent but nonviolent offenders. However, it is essential to test that possibility before using the candidate instrument.

There is another alternative to developing a screening instrument for the prevention of SVJ offending. It uses the results of a meta-analysis such as the one reported by Lipsey and Derzon in Chapter 6 of this volume. According to Table 6.8 in that chapter, the age 6-11 predictors of physical aggression or threat of physical aggression against persons and index offenses at age 15-25 are very different from the age 12-14 predictors. For the age 6-11 prediction point, the predictors, in order, are for the Rank 1 group, general offense and substance use; for the Rank 2 group, gender, family SES, and antisocial parents; for the Rank 3 group, aggression and ethnicity; for the Rank 4 group, psychological condition, parent-child relations, social ties, problem behavior, school attitude/performance, medical/physical, IQ, and other family characteristics; and finally, for the Rank 5 group, broken home, abusive parents, and antisocial peers. For the age 12-14 prediction point, the predictors are, in turn, for the Rank 1 group, social ties and antisocial peers; for the Rank 2 group, general offenses; for the Rank 3 group, aggression, school attitude/performance, psychological condition, parent-child relations, gender, and physical violence; for the Rank 4 group, antisocial parents, person crimes, problem behavior, and IQ; and finally, for the Rank 5 group, broken home, family SES, abusive parents, other family characteristics, substance use, and ethnicity. From these two lists of predictors, we have to conclude that there are major changes in the importance of the predictors. For example, substance use is in the Rank 1 group for the age 6-11 predictors, whereas it is in the Rank 5 group for the age 12-14 predictors. Alternatively, the Rank 1 group predictors for age 12-14, social ties and antisocial peers, are part of the Rank 4 and Rank 5 groups for the age 6-11 predictors. As a consequence, these diverging results indicate that we will need a specific instrument for specific age groups and for various outcomes, such as juvenile and adult offending and serious, chronic, or violent offending.

A recently published meta-analysis of 131 studies and 1,141 effect sizes, by Gendreau, Little, and Goggin (1996), can also help in developing a screening instrument for SVJ offenders. This study used adult recidivism as the outcome variable and found that one category of variables displayed the highest effect size (identification/socialization with offenders) and that five categories of variables were a close second: adult criminal history, preadult antisocial behavior, antisocial personality, criminogenic attitudes, and race. However, risk scales are much better than these categories of variables in predicting adult recidivism; they obtained a 0.30 effect size in comparison to effect sizes in the range of 0.16 to 0.21 for categories of variables.

The results of the meta-analyses indicate the most important domains of variables that we have to consider, depending on the outcome and the prediction point. These variable domains are the careers of offending, antisocial peers, and antisocial personality. However, it is impossible to identify precisely the appropriate predictors within a domain because each of them includes many specific indicators that vary from study to study (see Appendix B of Chapter 6, this volume). For example, the predictor domain school attitude/performance is represented by five predictors: dropout from school, low interest in education, low school achievement, poor-quality school, and truancy. In addition, the potential lists of predictors, either from the Cambridge analyses or the meta-analysis, may contain intercorrelated items, and research has paid little attention to multicolinearity. As a consequence, these various lists of variables may indeed be good predictors in an additive scale. However, it is not likely that they are independent, and with additional research, they may reflect latent predictors that may be more efficient in identifying SVJ offenders than the variables composing them.

In summary, we have a candidate screening instrument for chronic offending and meta-analysis results that indicate what the predictor domains are that are best associated with a particular outcome. The Cambridge screening instrument can be applied only from late childhood on, and we would have to test if the statistical prediction model of chronic offending developed by Blumstein et al. (1985) applies to other data sets. The results of the meta-analysis by Lipsey and Derzon in Chapter 6, this volume, are not useful for chronic delinquency and they do not distinguish SVJ offending, but they indicate predictor domains for early, between 6 and 11, and late, between 12 and 14, secondary prevention. If we were to develop a screening instrument from meta-analysis results, we would need to find, first, what the predictors are at each prediction point and for specific outcomes, and second, which the best predictor is in a domain and what the best combination of predictors is with the best predictive efficiency. In the case of the candidate instrument, there is much to do before we can propose an instrument that has a tested criterion and appropriate and reliable predictors, that has been validated, and that shows a high predictive accuracy. Notwithstanding these difficulties, many longitudinal data sets are available to perform these tasks.

Screening in the Juvenile Justice System

Classifications of offenders have been developed and used in corrections since the middle of the 19th century (Barnes & Teeters, 1945), and they are routinely employed now (see Brennan, 1987a, 1987b; Glaser, 1987; Hoge & Andrews, 1996; Sechrest, 1987). Classifications of juvenile offenders were developed mainly after the Second World War, and most of the risk and needs assessment systems were constructed in the 1980s.

There are three main psychological classifications of juvenile offenders that have a theoretical rationale and some empirical base, at least for their construction but sometimes also for their validation. They are psychodynamic, developmental, and psychometric classifications. The psychodynamic point of view is represented by Hewitt and Jenkins's (1946) proposal of three categories of juvenile offenders—overinhibited, underinhibited, and pseudosocial—and by Quay's (Quay & Parsons, 1971) four types that extend Hewitt and Jenkins's classification based on a questionnaire and multivariate statistical analyses. The developmental perspective adopts the ego development paradigm and proposes the interpersonal maturity classification (Sullivan, Grant, & Grant, 1957), which is operationalized particularly by the Jessness Inventory (Jessness & Wedge, 1983). Finally, the psychometric perspective is the MMPI route with the Megargee and Bohn (1979) categorization of youthful offenders. There are many types in each of these major categories of classification that have similar characteristics (see Blackburn, 1993). However, because these researchers do not consider the nature of offending in the construction of their classification, they do not single out one or more categories of SVJ offenders.

Two multidimensional classifications relevant to serious/chronic offenders have been developed by Elliott (Dunford & Elliott, 1984; Elliott et al., 1987) and by Le Blanc (Fréchette & Le Blanc, 1987; Le Blanc & Fréchette, 1989; Le Blanc & Kaspy, in press). These classifications use self-reported offending as a starting point and propose a serious/chronic offender category. They draw, for each type of offender, a social profile, in Elliott's case, using a national sample of American adolescents, and a social and psychological profile, in Le Blanc's case, using a city sample and an adjudicated adolescent sample. In addition, they validate their typology using official delinquency. Le Blanc (1995) showed that the distribution of adolescents in the three main types of careers—common, temporary, and chronic delinquency—is similar across the studies.

Recent risk and needs assessment in juvenile correction has taken another direction. These instruments opted for a small set of predictors and an actuarial evaluation of outcome. In addition, instruments were developed for a particular decision point along the juvenile justice system. Authors such as Baird (1984), Clear (1988), Glaser (1987), and Wiebush et al. (1995) have characterized these practices as informal and discretionary. These screening devices have been applied by individuals with various levels of experience and training, with diverging ideologies about intervention, and with dissimilar criteria. These authors also concur in concluding that these practices resulted in decisions that were often erroneous, inconsistent, inequitable, and without justification. However, Wiebush et al. noted a tremendous effort to change that situation in collaboration with the National Council on Crime and Delinquency since the beginning of the 1990s. Concluding their evaluation of risk and needs assessment instruments, Wiebush et al. recommended, first, that instruments should be specific to the targeted decision point in the juvenile justice system. Second, they proposed that the assessment and classification process distinguish the risk of recidivism and the risk of future violence. Third and finally, they suggested that more research should be done on these instruments, particularly validation studies, and that no instrument should be adopted by a jurisdiction without a validation.

In the domain of risk assessment for juvenile justice purposes, the usual screening strategy is one stage, one source of information (the case record or the subject), and one method of data gathering (interview), but instruments are composed of variables from multiple domains (criminal behavior, drug use, school experience, family, etc.). In the future, these devices may be improved by coordinating them in a multiple-gate system for the whole juvenile justice system, by testing the use of multiple informants, by an increase of the variable domains considered, and by a test of the usefulness of multiple methods of data gathering.

The criterion for most existing instruments is the likelihood of recidivism. However, the definition of recidivism varies from device to device, either in the content of criminal activities or in the length of the follow-up period. In addition, existing risk assessment instruments do not use SVJ offending as their criterion, but are concerned with recidivism in general, according to Wiebush et al. (1995). As a consequence, they would have to be redesigned to fit the needs of that subgroup of juvenile offenders.

Concerning predictors, we have concluded that they should involve multiple informants in multiple settings and should rest on solid empirical evidence, as well as theoretical significance. Existing risk and needs assessment instruments are not grounded in any theory, but rely somewhat on the risk factors literature and on comparison of predictors. For example, Baird (1984) uses a large sample of probationers and parolees at five different sites to select the best predictors. However, this procedure is not standard in the field. Wiebush et al. (1995) reviewed eight risk assessment instruments and showed that they consider 16 categories of predictors. However, these predictors are not defined in the same manner in every instrument. First,

school problems is the only predictor that is present in every instrument. Second, age at first referral and drug/alcohol abuse are used in seven instruments. Third, number of prior offenses, peers, and family problems/parental control are employed in five or six instruments. Finally, prior assault, special education, mental health stability, runaway, victim of abuse/neglect, gender, and prior supervision adjustment are the least often used predictors. Risk assessment instruments for detention and placement decisions, according to Wiebush et al., incorporate more predictors about the seriousness of past and current offenses and the history of juvenile justice decisions and no predictors concerning school, parents, or peers.

Needs assessment instruments vary as much as risk assessment devices. In a national survey of juvenile needs assessment in 48 stages, Towberman (1992) used 10 categories of need. He reported the following percentages of states that consider these categories: 51% emotional/psychological; 43% educational deficits; 41% substance abuse; 33% physical problems, family dysfunction, and peer association; 31% vocational deficits; 27% sexual abuse deviance; and 22% violent behavior. According to Wiebush et al.'s (1995) more recent analysis of eight devices, there are 16 types of predictors and half of them are present in seven or eight of the instruments reviewed. The common types of needs assessment predictors are substance abuse, family relationship, mental health stability, intellectual ability/academic achievement, employment/vocational skills, school problems, peer relationship, and health/hygiene. Even if there are many common predictors in the needs assessment instruments, this does not imply that the operational definition of these predictors is standardized. The variation in the definitions of these needs assessment predictors is much larger than the variation in the definitions of the risk assessment predictors. This is because risk assessment relies more on official offending and past experiences with the juvenile justice system than on psychosocial experiences.

In summary, the needs predictors are from multiple settings (peers, school, individual, etc.) as are the risk predictors for intermediate sentences. This is not the case for the risk predictors for detention and placement decisions in which offending behavior is overrepresented, especially as the decision involves security. Our review of risk and needs predictors indicates that there is much research to be done before we can establish a common set of predictors of risk and need that are defined in the same way and that can be applied to arrest, detention, adjudication, and placement. Not only do we find a very large array of definitions of specific predictors, but the categories are sometimes arbitrary and are insufficiently documented in the manuals. For example, why is school attendance divided into three categories such as no problem, some truancy, and major truancy? How do we assess that our source of information is reliable? What is the distinction between some and major truancy? Such predictors may introduce unreliability between raters. Most instruments do not consider that difficulty. When the criterion and the predictors are appropriate, reliable, and valid, the question is how to combine the predictors. Risk and needs assessment devices are best used with the simple additive method with different weights for each predictor rather than the multivariate statistical procedure. The selection of the additive method follows on the results of the research literature. However, the weighting used in these assessment instruments seems arbitrary because there is no empirical comparison, for the same risk or need device, of the effectiveness of an equal weight for each predictor to a different weight for each.

Whatever the method for combining predictors, there are two fundamental lessons from the prediction tradition that are not always applied to decision-making instruments in the juvenile justice system. These lessons concern the necessity of validating the device and measuring its predictive accuracy. With the exception of the Baird (1991) validation of risk and needs assessment instruments for community corrections, there is very little validation of such devices currently in use. When a validation is undertaken in another jurisdiction, the results are disappointing (Ashford & LeCroy, 1990). In addition, a well-constructed instrument and classification such as the Dembo et al. (1995) classification of high-risk youths entering a juvenile assessment center does not have a validation sample. This situation brought Wiebush et al. (1995) to recommend to "conduct research necessary to validate any instrument adapted from another jurisdiction or one designed locally through consensus methods. Although such instruments may have face validity, there is no way of knowing how well they work until they are empirically tested" (p. 210). Validation is facilitated by the fact that in most jurisdictions the data from the use of this risk and needs assessment instruments are computerized. As a consequence, it is easy to analyze the appropriateness of the predictors, their weighting, and to test the instrument on another population, for example, with next year's offenders.

Baird (1991) presented a step-by-step procedure to construct a risk or a needs assessment instrument or reconstruct such a device for another jurisdiction or a subsequent period. His procedure was mainly limited to the discriminant validity of the predictors and the measurement scale, and the capacity to quantify different levels of risk and needs that predict different levels of behavior on a criterion. He did not use a validation sample. Even if there are no widely accepted methods of measuring predictive accuracy, it is an absolute necessity to calculate and report it. However, it is absent from the juvenile risk and needs assessment literature, even for the best developed instruments such as the one developed by Baird (1991). He used multiple regression to combine his predictors, but he does not report the proportion of explained variance that he placed between 8% and 15%. This is a low predictive accuracy when control causal models can attain 50% of explained variance (see Le Blanc, 1997).

One consequence of the development of a risk and needs classification instrument is the cross-tabulation of the risk and needs categories into a programming matrix that specifies a level of supervision for probation, a level of security for placement, or a type of program for treatment (see examples of such matrices in Wiebush et al., 1995). The risk and needs categories result from cut-off points that may be arbitrary because there was no test of various possibilities. In addition, the content of each cell in these matrices may have an ideological or organizational logic, but may not be constructed using measures of efficiency. Does this particular program display less recidivism in comparison to programs in cell x or y? Without an answer to such a question, these consensual matrices may be empirically wrong. Concerning risk and needs assessment in the juvenile justice system, the Office of Juvenile Justice and Delinquency Prevention (1995a) developed the concept of a community assessment center. Such a center should offer a single point of entry in the juvenile justice system, an immediate and comprehensive assessment in a community-based setting, a management information system, an integrated case management, and provision of input to the policymaker's process. A recent evaluation of the existing centers (Cronin, 1996) showed that in only three of the seven states a validated instrument was used, called the Problem-Oriented Screening

Instrument for Teenagers (POSIT: see Dembo et al., 1996, for validation in the juvenile justice system).

In summary, juvenile justice screening has come a long way from the times when juveniles were classified on their height, the small kids going to one unit and the big kids going to another unit. Principally, over the past decade, risk and needs assessment instruments have been developed for detention, probation, parole, and placements decisions. We could imagine the usefulness of such classification devices for arrests, court referrals, and transfers to adult court. We can imagine a day when screening instruments will be available for every decision in juvenile justice. Existing instruments display a sound face validity, but their reliability and empirical validity are controversial and rarely tested, either for use in a particular jurisdiction or for implementation in another juvenile justice system. To our knowledge only the Baird (1984, 1991) risk assessment instrument for community corrections has been validated. It is grounded in the risk factors literature, and its technical characteristics (method for combining predictors, reliability) are appropriate, but it has performed poorly in another jurisdiction (Ashford & LeCroy, 1990). However, this screening instrument cannot be used for identifying SVJ offenders because its criterion is recidivism in general.

■ Important Issues

We reviewed the methodological requirements of an adequate screening instrument for the identification of potential SVJ offenders and the classification of offenders in the juvenile justice system. We also concluded that no identification or classification instrument reasonably meets these requirements. However, the availability of a screening strategy, together with the knowledge of several predictors that are sufficiently replicable and valid, constitutes a first step toward the development of empirical screening instruments. This can best take place in the context of legal, ethical, policy, and practical restraints.

Legal and Constitutional Issues

Tonry (1987) comprehensively reviewed the legal and constitutional issues that are involved in the prediction and classification of offenders for juvenile justice decision making. Let us summarize these issues in the context of the screening of SVJ offenders.

First, predictors should not refer directly to race, ethnicity, political beliefs, or religion. For the identification of potential offenders, the meta-analysis of predictors of SVJ delinquency, Lipsey and Derzon in Chapter 6 of this volume showed that of these factors only ethnicity came out as a predictor. For the classification of offenders in the juvenile justice system, Wiebush et al.'s (1995) review of risk assessment instruments indicated that race is absent as well as ethnicity, political beliefs, and religion. Second, screening based on gender should be avoided. Gender has been used in only two of the eight jurisdictions that have risk assessment devices (Wiebush et al., 1995), and according to Chapter 6, gender (male) was not in the first group of predictors. The justification for the use of this predictor should be that very few females become SVJ offenders. Third, predictors that may indirectly favor or disfavor a racial or ethnic group are permitted if predictors such as socioeconomic status or a one-parent family are used with no intention of achieving some sort of discrimination.

These legal issues concern equally the identification of potential offenders and the classification of known offenders. There are some other issues that apply only to the classification of offenders in the juvenile justice

system. Here the principle is the respect of due process according to Tonry (1987). As a consequence prediction has to leave a margin of discretion; it should not be arbitrary and capricious; and it should not impose a cruel and unusual punishment. We are of the opinion that none of the classification devices reviewed by Wiebush et al. (1995) could be evaluated as having any of these characteristics.

Ethical Issues

It is not our intention to review possible ethical issues comprehensively and in depth. Some ethical issues are common to prevention and classification, whereas others are specific. The first of the common ethical issues is that relying on previous offenses to predict future offending may be empirically sound but unjust (see the Tonry, 1987, discussion about preventive sentencing; see also Moore, 1986). Screening may be unjust because the prevention and treatment programs will not be offered to the false negatives and they will be unnecessary for the false positives. From a just desert ideological position, no prevention program should be offered and no classification of offenders should be done, whereas for the utilitarian there are no problems with screening. There is no ethical solution to this dilemma. The practical solution is in reducing false positives and negatives. Measures of previous delinquent offenses are the most important predictors for the serious and violent delinquency outcomes identified by Lipsey and Derzon in Chapter 6 in this volume, and avoiding these predictors would reduce substantially the predictive accuracy of screening devices.

The second common ethical issue states that some predictors are inappropriate by their nature and should be avoided. Tonry (1987) lists three categories of such factors: those that are beyond the offender's control, such as sex; those that refer to status variables, such as socioeconomic status; and those that refer to self-reported offending. All of these categories of predictors make a significant contribution to the prediction of violent and serious delinquency whatever the age when the prediction is made (see Chapter 6, this volume). Accepting this ethical position would imply that only universal prevention programs could be offered in a community and that secondary and tertiary prevention programs would have to be avoided. Such an ideological position does not take into account the literature that shows that prevention (see Tremblay & Craig, 1995) and treatment (see Lipsey, 1992; Palmer, 1994) are efficient (see also Chapters 10 through 13, this volume).

The identification of potential SVJ offenders poses special ethical problems. The first concerns the proposal to participate in a program to the child and his or her parents and even the authorization to be part of a screening procedure. When the screening strategy is school based, there are certain standards that have to be met according to school board rulings. Whatever the screening procedure, the main ethical question is: Does the prevention researcher need to disclose the ultimate target, such as SVJ offending, or produce some intermediate ameliorative targets? We do not know of any research data addressing this question. And, as far as we know, advocates of prevention bypass, in most cases, the first part of the question. As a consequence, an intermediate target is publicly proposed and parents participate, in most cases without their child's explicit consent, to deal with their child's behavior problems.

The second ethical question is about the possible stigmatizing effect of secondary prevention programs. Primary prevention programs are universal by nature and, as a consequence, labeling is not an issue. For tertiary prevention, stigmatization cannot be avoided because of the intervention of the juvenile justice system. However, for secondary prevention it may be present because potential SVJ offenders are a clearly identified subgroup of potential delinquents. The impact of stigmatization of children as potential delinquents has been avoided by most prevention programs when they use intermediate and developmental objectives as official targets instead of delinquency. However, as indicated by Farrington and Tarling (1985), research is badly needed on this question.

A final ethical issue concerns evidence that some prevention programs may have undesirable effects. McCord (1978) documented such effects for the Cambridge-Somerville prevention program, particularly that the longer the participation in the prevention program and the more intense the intervention was, the more important were the negative effects for adult maladjustment. These kinds of effects are not specific to that program, because McCord (1988) cites other evaluations that report similar effects. However, these effects are not documented for more recent prevention programs. In addition, we do not know how frequently these undesirable effects occur, because there is no systematic review of the question and no meta-analysis documenting them.

Where the classification of known offenders is concerned, there are some special ethical issues that are discussed at length by Tonry (1987) and Blumstein et al. (1986). There is the possible injustice of being deprived of bail, parole, or of a particular treatment. There is the chance of the conviction of innocent people. There is the possibility of a breach of the principle of equal protection under the law. Finally, there is the blameworthiness of some offender characteristics such as use of drugs, being a juvenile, or being unemployed. In addition, the risk assessment instruments can foster self-fulfilling consequences, as mentioned by Gabor (1986), because predictions may produce action that validates them.

All of these ethical issues have no adequate solutions in the realm of ethics or in the domain of predictive accuracy. The solutions are avoiding identification, classification, and prediction from the just desert ideological position or implementing them, with a realistic view of efficiency, from the utilitarian viewpoint. The empiricist position is to increase the quality of screening instruments through a multiple-stage strategy and a better choice of predictors. The resolution of these ethical issues is part of the realm of policy.

Policy Issues

Policy issues about the identification of potential offenders and the classification of juvenile offenders revolve around the costs and benefits of false positives and false negatives. What are the costs and benefits of failing to identify a child as a true SVJ offender (the false negative problem) and of incorrectly labeling a child as an SVJ offender (the false positive problem)? The discussion of this policy issue can be approached from two perspectives, the technical and social utility views.

Most criminologists discuss their policy recommendations from a technical point of view. This perspective is reflected in some of the most authoritative texts in the field, for example, Monahan (1981), Farrington and Tarling (1985), Blumstein et al. (1986), and Gottfredson (1987). From this technical perspective, the levels of false positives and false negatives depend on the cut-off point on the outcome, the base rate. A low base rate would identify a few of the SVJ juvenile potential or official offenders, but would avoid incorrectly identifying too many delinquents as SVJ offenders. In contrast, a high base rate will capture more SVJ potential or official offenders, but also mislabel more delinquents as potential SVJ offenders. Advantages and

disadvantages of changes in the cut-off point depend on the nature of the outcome and the nature of the intended intervention.

What is most important, the cost of prediction errors to society or to the individuals? On the one hand, some criminologists will argue to increase the base rate when SVJ offending is the target because the cost of false negatives is substantially higher in this case because of the frequency of the potential crimes and the harm to persons caused by violent and serious crimes. On the other hand, some criminologists will argue to decrease the base rate of SVJ delinquency when the intended intervention is longer, more intensive, and more restrictive of liberty. In this case, criminologists would prefer not to impose a prevention program or a treatment on a child who is not a true SVJ offender. The technical solution to this dilemma is to find an optimum cut-off point as did Blumstein et al. (1985). If such an optimum cut-off point is not available, policymakers are left with their judgment to choose between these alternatives.

The other way of looking at policy issues is through an inventory of the personal, social, and financial costs and benefits of applying a prevention program or a treatment. Meta-analysis documents that treatment is efficient with delinquents (Lipsey, 1992; Lipsey and Wilson, Chapter 13, this volume) and that some prevention programs show positive results (Chapters 10 to 13). The social benefits are then evident even if the efficiency of these programs may not be as good for SVJ potential or official offenders. In addition, some empirical research supports the position that a prevention program can be beneficial for the individual and society. Farrington and West (1993) conclude that "because even the unconvicted vulnerable boys were leading relatively unsuccessful lives at 32, ameliorative intervention might have been justified for all vulnerable boys, thus avoiding the usual problem of false positives" (p. 521). The financial benefits of prevention have been insufficiently documented, but there are indications that they are considerable. For example, it has been calculated for the Perry Preschool Program that every $1 invested would save $7 later on (Schweinhart, Barnes, & Weikart, 1993).

Practical Issues

The practical issues for screening are the same as for any prevention program. They revolve around the transition from a small-scale prevention program to a large-scale routinely administered governmental program. In the transition, some of the results often vanish because the program is not implemented properly. Some other practical issues are more specific to screening. Gabor (1986) discussed three problems. First, he mentioned that in an effort to sell a screening strategy and instrument to policymakers, the researcher may be tempted to incorporate social utility rather than sheer accuracy. The researcher could overadjust for a factor, such as race, to rectify inequities in the juvenile justice system. Second, a policymaker may use a screening device to promote his or her position in an organization. Third, when applied by practitioners some biases could be inadvertently introduced; for example, a discretionary risk assessment instrument can become mechanically applied by some probation officers or used only by a small group of decision makers.

■ Conclusion

In this chapter, we reviewed the guidelines, from the criminological prediction tradition, that should be followed while developing a screening device for the identification of potential offenders and the classification of known offenders, particularly SVJ offenders. We were able to delineate an appropriate screening strategy for secondary and tertiary prevention while recognizing that validation studies need to be conducted. Secondary prevention of SVJ offending should rest on a multiple-stage, multiple-informant, multiple-method strategy and multiple-variable domains. In contrast, tertiary prevention could rely on only a single-stage screening with multiple-variable domains and multiple-informant strategy. It was not possible to identify a completely satisfactory instrument, either for prevention screening or for risk assessment in the juvenile justice system, because all have significant methodological deficiencies. Also, it was not possible to identify the best predictors for screening, although there is a large consensus about the variable domains that are most important. Finally, we observed that there is somewhat of a consensus in the research community concerning the construct of SVJ offenders, particularly its operational definition as an outcome measure.

In summary, much technical work still needs to be done before we can develop appropriate screening instruments for the identification of potential SVJ offenders or the classification of SVJ offenders. Some screening strategies and instruments are promising, but none can be recommended for immediate use to policymakers and practitioners. However, the research community can indicate how to develop good screening instruments. In addition, there are risk and needs instruments with excellent face validity, but their empirical validity remains to be proven in various juvenile jurisdictions.

PART II

Preventive Interventions and Graduated Sanctions

The Prevention of Serious and Violent Juvenile Offending

■ *Gail A. Wasserman & Laurie S. Miller*

It is well known that antisocial behavior is multiply determined, the result of the convergence of many risk factors. Hawkins et al. (Chapter 7, this volume) review a wide array of factors that operate at many levels to contribute to the development of antisocial behavior in youth. These include *distal contextual factors,* such as poverty, access to firearms or drugs, and neighborhood deterioration, and *proximal risk factors,* such as parent management practices, deviant peer groups, low child intelligence, and child social skills deficits. This chapter will review prevention programs that target proximal individual, family, and peer risk factors for violent offending.

The best predictor of adolescent antisocial behavior is early conduct problems. Although not all children who exhibit early aggressive behavior become antisocial adults, most serious violent offenders have a history characterized by earlier childhood misbehavior. The class of childhood behaviors that constitute early antisocial behaviors (i.e., physical aggression, disruptive behavior, covert behaviors, oppositional and defiant behaviors, conduct disorders) can be considered as either risk factors or early developmental precursors for later antisocial behavior.

If one considers these behaviors as early developmental precursors of later offending, then the specific risk factors for these behaviors are also of relevance to the prevention of violent offending. For example, if a prevention program designed to alter early parent-child attachment is effective in decreasing child oppositional behavior, such a program may in fact have a beneficial impact on later antisocial behavior. Similarly, if a diagnosis of *attention-deficit hyperactivity disorder* (ADHD) is a risk factor for later conduct disorder, then the amelioration of the symptoms of ADHD may decrease the chances of subsequent conduct disorder and violent offending.

Although this book focuses on serious and violent offending in youth, we have broadened the scope of this chapter to include prevention programs that not only target specific risk factors for serious and violent offending but also those programs that target risk factors for the precursors of serious and violent offending. First, we briefly review the different early developmental precursors of violent offending. Second, we provide an overview of different approaches to prevention. Third, we review the basic components of well-studied intervention programs and the limitations of single-focused intervention approaches for preventing antisocial behavior. Fourth, we provide examples of well-designed multisystemic preventive interventions that target proximal risk factors for early developmental precursors of later antisocial behavior as well as those that target proximal risk factors for violent offending. Examples of programs are provided by developmental periods; first, we describe programs designed for children prior to school entry (ages 0-5), followed by programs for school-aged children (ages 6-13), and then by programs for adolescents (ages 14-18). We conclude the chapter with a discussion of some of the key features of effective programs, issues regarding developmental periods to be targeted, and uncharted or understudied areas in the field.

■ Early Developmental Precursors

The youth considered throughout this volume are the concern of individuals from many diverse disciplines; many different terms have been used to describe them. Although terms may overlap, they differ in some important ways. *Juvenile delinquency* is a term used in the field of juvenile justice to describe minors who have committed actions that have been found in court to be illegal. Educators and mental health practitioners often refer to children who display these or related behaviors as *antisocial, aggressive, disruptive,* or *conduct disordered*; individuals manifesting a persistent and serious level of such behaviors are considered, according to the principal nosological system used by psychiatrists and psychologists (*DSM-IV*; American Psychiatric Association, 1994), to meet diagnostic criteria for *conduct disorder* (CD). Some symptoms of CD qualify as illegal activities (e.g., stealing, rape, and fire setting); others would not (e.g., lying). Many, although not all, of the criteria for CD involve physically aggressive or violent behavior. CD is one of a trio of related diagnoses that also includes ADHD and *oppositional defiant disorder* (ODD) that are known collectively as *disruptive behavior disorders*. In a significant proportion of cases, ADHD and/or ODD are developmental antecedents to CD. Similarly, a substantial portion of children with ADHD also have ODD or CD, currently or prospectively.

One result of the different perspectives employed by individuals in different disciplines to explain antisocial behavior is that treatments established in one discipline may not be widely reviewed or implemented by those working in another field. Although this means that, ultimately, treatments can be diverse and multilayered, it also leads to important gaps that become noticeable when we take a multidisciplinary perspective. One such gap concerns programs that target ADHD, a proximal risk factor for the development of serious antisocial behavior.

Given the overlap between ADHD and CD, and the likelihood that some youngsters with ADHD will develop serious antisocial behavior (e.g., Keller et al. 1992; Mannuzza, Klein, Bessler, Malloy, & LaPadula, 1993), one discipline's targeted treatment outcome is another's risk factor.

■ *Defining Approaches to Prevention*

Universal programs are applied to an entire population of children, such as a classroom, school, or neighborhood. Use of these programs is typically based on some community-level *risk factor* far removed from delinquency outcome, such as neighborhood poverty or local crime rates. Universal interventions are less likely to label children than are other interventions (Kellam & Rebok, 1992). They may also cost less per child than other interventions, although because they are directed to larger numbers of children, they are not necessarily more economical than targeted programs. *Selected* programs, in contrast, target high-risk children who may already show some level of antisocial behavior. Such programs might be directed toward all children in a school rated by their teachers as highly aggressive. *Indicated* programs treat children already showing clear signs of delinquent or antisocial behavior. This chapter includes programs of universal, selected, and indicated interventions for antisocial behavior.

The concepts of universal, selected, and indicated programs map onto levels of prevention. *Primary prevention* refers to preventing the occurrence of a disease or disorder, in this case, antisocial behavior. Efforts to prevent infants from being born at low birth weights by eliminating maternal smoking during pregnancy would be an example. *Secondary prevention* refers to early detection of a disorder, to cure it, slow its progression, or curtail its communicativeness; interventions for ADHD, aggression, or academic

underachievement would be good examples. When a disorder has already occurred and left damage, the goal is *tertiary prevention,* where we seek to limit disability or to ensure rehabilitation (Edelman & Mandle, 1986). This chapter focuses on programs of primary and secondary prevention.

■ *Components of Intervention*

Given the wide range of candidates for change, at the level of both proximal risk factors and early developmental precursors, the range of approaches to prevention is equally diverse. Careful evaluation research has documented the utility of a set of basic intervention components that deal with child and adolescent antisocial behavior. Each of these components has strengths and weaknesses. We review below those components of intervention that have demonstrated efficacy.

Family- and Parent-Focused Components

Parent management training. Parent management training (PMT) approaches attempt to alter children's deviant behaviors by promoting change in the proximal social environment (parenting). The value of targeting changes in parenting is supported by both social learning theory and observational studies that demonstrate increased rates of aversive interactions in families of children with behavior problems, as opposed to families of children without behavior problems (Patterson, 1979, 1982a). Parents of children with behavior problems, in general, tend to be more inconsistent and punitive in establishing and enforcing rules, and children with such problems use aversive behaviors to shape and manipulate their family environment (Patterson,

Reid, & Dishion, 1992; Wasserman, Miller, Pinner, & Jaramillo, 1996).

PMT attempts to change social contingencies in the family environment so that children are positively reinforced for their adaptive and prosocial behaviors, and child-aversive and antisocial behaviors are consistently ignored or punished. Therapeutic goals often include reduction of the use of physical punishment, in favor of more proactive forms of discipline, and developing clear standards for child behavior (Barkley, 1987; Eyberg & Boggs, 1989; Forehand & McMahon, 1981; Kazdin, 1987b; Patterson, 1982a; Patterson, Reid, Jones, & Conger, 1975; Webster-Stratton, 1984).

Individually or in groups, parents participate in interventions usually based in a clinic or a school setting. Parents learn social-learning principles and parenting strategies based on those principles; homework assignments are provided so that parents can practice application of new strategies at home. They are taught to (a) communicate clear expectations about positive and negative behavior to children, (b) identify positive and negative child behavior, (c) identify antecedents of problematic behavioral sequences, (d) provide positive consequences (praise, rewards, privileges) for children's positive behaviors, and (e) provide noncoercive negative consequences for inappropriate and noncompliant behavior (e.g., time-out, loss of privileges), rather than physical punishment. Importantly, parents are taught to anticipate problems so that they can prevent and manage future problems on their own. The homework assignments are given not only so that parents can practice these procedures at home but also to obtain feedback from the therapist. To increase the range and effectiveness of positive consequences, PMT programs also work on increasing positive, shared family activities (Barkley, 1987; Eyberg & Boggs, 1989; Forehand & McMahon, 1981; Hawkins,

Catalano, Morrison, et al., 1992; Webster-Stratton, 1984).

Systematic evaluations of PMT (see reviews by Dumas, 1989; Kazdin, 1987b; Miller, 1994a, 1994b; Webster-Stratton, 1991) demonstrate substantial changes in parent and child behavior. On the other hand, follow-up studies of families receiving PMT note that as many as 25%-40% of children continue to have clinically significant behavior problems at the conclusion of intervention (Forehand, Furey, & McMahon, 1984; Webster-Stratton, 1991). Families with limited economic and personal resources, parental psychopathology, low social support, and marital conflict are less likely to benefit from PMT (Forehand et al., 1984; Strain, Young, & Horowitz, 1981; Wahler, 1980; Wahler & Dumas, 1984). Additionally, focusing PMT solely within the home setting often fails to lead to generalization to other settings, such as the school environment.

Functional family therapy. Functional family therapy (FFT; Alexander, Barton, Schiavo, & Parsons, 1976; Alexander & Parsons, 1973; Barton, Alexander, Waldron, Turner, & Warburton, 1985; Klein, Alexander, & Parsons, 1977) uses behavioral techniques such as clear specification of rules and consequences, contingency contracting, use of social reinforcement, and token economy, as well as more cognitively based interventions (examining attributions and expectations) to increase communication and mutual problem-solving.

Variations on a token economy, for example, have been found effective in improving general management of oppositional adolescents (Stein & Smith, 1990). Primarily used with adolescents, this approach intervenes with the family as a whole. In well-controlled studies (Alexander et al., 1976; Alexander & Parsons, 1973; Klein et al., 1977), FFT is effective in improving family communication and in lowering recidivism of youth with a history of minor delinquency as well as those with more serious behavior problems.

Family preservation. Families of antisocial children very often have any number of related social problems pressing on them, such as unemployment, family conflict, and obtaining access to social services. These stressors may limit family adaptiveness. Modeled on Homebuilders, a program developed in Washington State (Akamine, O'Neill, & Haymond, 1980), several programs have used a multisystemic, crisis intervention model to deal with threat of immediate out-of-home placement resulting from abuse, neglect, or delinquency. Depending on the needs of a particular family, the range of offered services includes PMT, didactic training in life skills, home and budget management, assertiveness training, and coordination of existing community services. Family preservation services are usually short term (4-6 weeks) and intense (10-20 hours/week). The preservation staff member assigned to a family is available around the clock, 24 hours a day, 7 days per week. This entails low caseload size (usually fewer than five families per worker). The targeted outcome of these programs is reduction in out-of-home-placement, rather than a more direct mediator or precursor of youth violence. Family preservation is an increasingly common adjunct to programs aimed at reducing child behavioral problems (see Henggeler, below).

Recently, controlled trials in New Jersey (Feldman, 1991) and Michigan (G. H. Miller, 1995) have compared this program to regularly available services (Feldman, 1991) or to foster care placement (G. H. Miller, 1995). Both programs tracked program implementation comprehensively. In the New Jersey study, compared to families receiving usual services, preservation families failed to show more improvement, relative to baseline.

Nonetheless, the family preservation group had proportionally fewer children entering out-of-home placement, at each point from program termination through 9 months posttermination; beyond 9 months, the advantages of family preservation dissipated (Feldman, 1991). In Michigan, compared to families with children returning home following foster care placement, preservation families had significantly lower rates of further out-of-home placement through 30 months. This approach seems well suited to the diverse needs of the population targeted, so that the level of individualization offered is a clear advantage over programs that offer a predetermined package of services. On the other hand, the particular disadvantages of such a diverse approach include difficulties in tracking the reliability of program implementation. Finally, given recent well-publicized failures of social service agencies to prevent further abuse, or even death, in children remaining in the home, it is not at all clear that maintaining in-home placement, although cost-effective, is always of value.

Child-Focused Components

Social competence training. Aggressive children, relative to their peers, lack certain critical cognitive and social skills believed to be important for positive social interactions. Disruptive children may fail to attend to relevant social cues (Dodge, Bates, & Pettit, 1990), often see malign intent in others' actions (Dodge & Frame, 1982; Dodge, Murphy, & Buchsbaum, 1984; Lochman, 1987), and may believe that aggressive behavior is acceptable (Huesmann, Guerra, Miller, & Zelli, 1992). Compared to other children, they have poorer problem-solving abilities (Rubin & Krasnor, 1986) and are less empathic.

Social competence training (SCT) teaches children to increase the use of positive social behaviors (e.g., conversational skills, academic performance, and behavioral control strategies) and social-cognitive processes such as problem solving, self-control, and perspective taking. Most of these programs are school based and are not often applied to the treatment of serious conduct problems. For example, at the level of a universal intervention, the PATHS curriculum (Greenberg, Kusche, Cook, & Quamma, 1995) makes use of elementary school teachers to promote children's ability to understand and discuss emotions, to recognize emotions of importance for aggression in themselves and others, and to develop strategies to change emotional states.

The Interpersonal Cognitive Problem-Solving (ICPS) curriculum (Shure & Spivack, 1980; Spivack & Shure, 1989) aims to decrease impulsivity and inhibition. Daily lessons are provided in the form of games, with early lessons focusing on simple word concepts (*not* or *same*) and later lessons focusing on alternative solutions to interpersonal problems, consequential thinking, and recognition of and sensitivity to others' feelings. The program has been shown to significantly enhance behavioral adjustment. Compared to controls, children participating in the program were found to be less aggressive and socially inappropriate and to have better problem-solving skills (Shure & Spivack, 1980, 1982, 1988).

Kazdin's (Kazdin, Bass, Siegel, & Thomas, 1989) program for SCT is more effective for antisocial psychiatric inpatients (Kazdin, Esveldt-Dawson, French, & Unis, 1987b) and outpatients (Kazdin et al., 1989) in altering social skills than either relationship therapy or attention control conditions (Kazdin et al., 1987b), with therapeutic gains in both home and school settings that were long standing. On the other hand, despite clear gains, most children continued to be rated as exhibiting

deviant behavior within the clinical range following SCT.

The Brainpower program (Hudley, 1994) focuses on reduction of negative attributions (hostile attribution bias) in late-elementary-age children. Participants are "trained to search for, interpret and properly categorize the verbal, physical and behavioral cues from others in social situations" (Hudley, 1994, p. 317). The program has been tested among African American boys with high teacher/peer ratings of aggressiveness. Following random assignment to the intervention condition, or to either an attention control or no-treatment control condition, intervention students completed 12 weeks of a cognitive retraining program. At the close of intervention, relative to baseline, intervention boys offered fewer attributions of hostile intent to ambiguous scenarios, with corresponding declines in teacher-rated aggression. Long-term follow-up data are not yet available.

The PACT program (Hammond & Yung, 1991, 1992, 1993) a violence prevention curriculum specifically designed for African American youth (Brewer, Hawkins, Catalano, & Neckerman, 1995), is largely based on SCT. In twice-weekly sessions over the course of a semester, groups of middle school students are trained in giving positive feedback, giving and accepting feedback, resisting peer pressure, problem solving, and negotiation. Students watch sample videotaped vignettes and then practice role-playing the component skills. Students referred for behavior problems were assigned to either intervention or a no-treatment control; relative to baseline, intervention students improved in self- and teacher-rated behavior, whereas comparison students did not improve (Hammond & Yung, 1991). Intervention students' suspensions and expulsions decreased over time, whereas they increased for control students. Similar results are reported for follow-up and replications (Hammond & Yung, 1992, 1993), although, as noted by Brewer et al. (1995), intervention and control groups may not have been comparable at baseline; furthermore, teachers were not blind to assignment, and the authors do not present the statistical significance of their results.

Lochman's (1992; Lochman, Burch, Curry, & Lampron, 1984; Lochman & Curry, 1986) school-based program for aggressive and disruptive boys teaches (a) awareness of the level of their physiological arousal, especially when related to anger, and (b) use of self-talk and self-control strategies to cope with anger. Three years posttreatment, boys who received the intervention reported less substance use and improved self-esteem and social problem-solving skills compared to nonintervention controls, although neither the subsequent self-reported delinquency rate nor observed classroom behavior was different between groups. Lochman concluded that to have more long-lasting effects, intervention should include a parent training component (Lochman, 1992). This seems reasonable, given that the source of such cognitive deficits is often thought to be inconsistent or punitive parental discipline.

Brennan (1992, cited in Brewer et al., 1995) evaluated the Empowering Children to Survive and Succeed curriculum, for children in first and second grade. For 1 hour per week for 10 weeks, a specially trained group leader came into the classroom to implement a curriculum aimed at increasing self-control, listening, cooperation, and problem solving. The trainer modeled skills that were then practiced by children in small groups. In the comparison condition, children in other primary grades in other schools received 6 weeks of the same program. Over the school year, teacher and parent workshops were provided to further implement use of the curriculum. Before and after the intervention trial,

children were assessed orally to measure self-esteem, and attitudes toward learning and problem solving. Although in general, intervention students showed greater gains, there were numerous methodological problems that cloud interpretation (Brewer et al., 1995), including substantial pretest differences between intervention and comparison groups, and the global nature of the outcomes.

Most SCT programs have focused on the consequences of acts of *physical aggression or coercion,* and little or no attention has been paid to the social consequences of *covert* antisocial behavior, such as stealing or vandalism. Although covert acts are, by their nature, more difficult to observe independently, this is nonetheless an important omission, given that many acts of serious delinquency are covert.

Academic skills. The recent report of the American Psychological Association, Commission on Violence and Youth (1993), concluded that academic factors, such as poor school achievement, poor attendance, and suspensions, place youth at risk for antisocial behavior. Both theoretical models (e.g., Moffitt, 1990b) and comprehensive reviews of the literature (Maguin & Loeber, 1996) underscore the importance of academic difficulties in maintaining and worsening of antisocial behavior. Noncompletion of homework (De-Baryshe, Patterson, & Capaldi, 1993) and poor reading skills (Greenberg, 1974) are associated with aggressive behavior, and poorer cognitive functioning has been found to precede the appearance of serious antisocial behavior (Moffitt, 1993). Moreover, among antisocial youth, those whose offending is more serious or chronic had lower academic skills in childhood than did those showing less serious or less chronic antisocial activity achievement (Denno, 1990; Farrington, 1987), and lower academic skill predicts an escalation in delinquency across an 18-month period among elementary-age boys (Loeber, Stouthamer-Loeber, Van Kammen, & Farrington, 1991). These skills have been targeted by interventions seeking to reduce antisocial behavior (e.g., Kellam, Mayer, Rebok, & Hawkins, in press; Kellam & Rebok, 1992; Kellam, Rebok, Ialongo, & Mayer, 1994; Kellam et al., 1991). It would follow from this that programs aimed at improving academic skills might have a secondary impact on lessening conduct problems and delinquent behavior.

Bry (1982; Bry & George, 1980) describes a 2-year-long, behaviorally based group program in which seventh graders, referred because of academic or discipline problems, were randomly assigned to an intervention whereby they could earn points by positive teacher ratings and class attendance for extra school trips, or to a control condition. One year postintervention, in blind follow-up assessments, intervention youth were significantly less likely to have school-based academic and discipline problems, based on school records, and the intervention youth themselves reported fewer delinquent activities. Five years postintervention, significantly fewer of the intervention youth, compared to controls, had county court criminal records. Unfortunately, too little information is provided regarding measurement and attrition, so that we are unable to determine, for example, the difference in rates of discipline problems between intervention and control youth.

In reviewing well-designed programs that have considered both academic and behavioral outcomes in at-risk youth, Maguin and Loeber (1996) concluded that such programs, for the most part, have a positive impact on academic functioning, with effect sizes ranging from .20 to .35. Not all academically oriented programs were equally effective in reducing antisocial outcomes, however. Those

that did (Arbuthnot & Gordon, 1986; Gottfredson & Gottfredson, 1992) had smaller effect sizes, between .15 and .3, and made use of a law-related moral education program that educates youth about the role of law in society. Unfortunately, most programs using an academic approach toward improving both academic and behavior problem outcomes have been most commonly offered to elementary school-aged or high school students. By late elementary school, many children have already begun to manifest significant problems in both domains. Although programs providing reading instruction and tutoring may be less effective than law education with older children, basic skills programs might well be more effective with younger children (see Kellam et al., in press).

Medication. Psychostimulant medication (e.g., methylphenidate) is the most commonly used pharmacologic treatment for ADHD symptoms (Abikoff & Klein, 1992; Spencer et al., 1996). As noted previously, ADHD is a common risk factor and/or comorbid condition of CD. Hundreds of well-controlled studies document the positive impact of psychostimulant medications on reducing symptoms of inattentiveness, motor overactivity, and impulsiveness. Other studies have demonstrated the efficacy of psychostimulants on associated problems such as poor peer interactions (Gadow, Nolan, Sverd, Sprafkin, & Paolicelli, 1990; Pelham et al., 1993) and at least short-term improvement in academic functioning (Carlson, Pelham, Milich, & Dixon, 1992; Firestone, Kelly, Goodman, & Davey, 1981; Gittelman, 1982) in children with ADHD (see Greenhill, 1995, for a review).

Studies of the effectiveness of medication for treating CD in individuals free of ADHD have not been undertaken, primarily because of the considerable diagnostic overlap between ADHD and CD in children referred for these disorders. The subgroup of ADHD children who are also aggressive or show conduct symptoms are benefited by stimulant medication treatment as well (see Hinshaw, 1991; Spencer et al., 1996, for reviews). Specifically, when such children are treated with stimulant medications, reductions are noted in aggressivity (Gadow et al., 1990; Kaplan, Busner, Kupietz, Wassermann, & Segal, 1990) and in covert antisocial behavior such as stealing or vandalism (Hinshaw, Heller, & McHale, 1992), although, as with stimulant treatment in general, these alterations are not long term, once medication is terminated. Other medications less commonly used to treat ADHD include tricyclic antidepressants (e.g., desipramine), other antidepressants (e.g., fluoxetine), and antipsychotic medications, such as haloperidol (see Spencer et al., 1996, for a review).

Despite the benefits of stimulant medication, Abikoff and Klein (1992) note a number of limitations associated with stimulant treatment for ADHD symptoms when provided as the single intervention approach. Medication effects typically wear off by the end of the day, creating management problems at home. Furthermore, treatment gains associated with stimulant medication are short lived and improvements are not generally maintained when medication is discontinued. Additionally, not all children respond positively to medication. Finally, despite long-standing assurances of safety, some families are unwilling to institute a program of stimulant treatment.

Other interventions. Other single-focused, child-directed interventions for which there is little or no evidence to document clinically meaningful efficacy for antisocial children include *individual psychotherapy* and *behavioral anger control* programs (see Tolan & Guerra, 1994b, for a review).

Classroom Interventions

School-based interventions are also discussed in Chapter 11, this volume. Here we consider interventions that are classroom based, or those that are individually based but take place within the classroom. Catalano et al., in Chapter 11, consider programs that are schoolwide and are *not* classroom based.

Classroom contingency training. Behavioral classroom management strategies (e.g., Hawkins, Doueck, & Lishner, 1988) have been developed that adapt successful PMT techniques into the classroom. These techniques include establishing clear routines and expectations regarding attendance, student behavior, and classroom procedures; teachers are trained in the provision of targeted and contingent encouragement and praise. For example, Mayer (Mayer & Butterworth, 1979; Mayer, Butterworth, Nafpaktitis, & Sulzer-Azaroff, 1983; Sulzer-Azaroff & Mayer, 1994) provided guidelines for elementary and junior high school teachers for increasing praise for constructive classroom behavior by using group contingencies, clarifying classroom rules, and providing contingencies for compliance. After program completion, teacher and observer ratings (nonblind) of disruptive behavior were lower in program schools than in control schools. In intervention schools, yearly vandalism costs decreased, whereas costs in control schools actually increased. Hawkins et al. (1988) combined classroom contingency training (CCT) with academic skills enhancement in a program that included teacher training and supervision in proactive classroom discipline management, use of student learning partners, and a focus on clearly specified learning objectives. Seventh graders were randomly assigned to either CCT or control classrooms, with additional schools being designated as fully CCT or fully control. Outcome evaluation has focused on children with low achievement (in math). At the end of the academic year, those exposed to the intervention had more positive attitudes and expectations toward school. Relative to baseline ratings, at the end of the year, school disciplinary problems were lower in CCT than in control children, particularly among low-achieving children. There were no effects on delinquency.

In a program in Baltimore, children in Grades 7-9 with a history of multiple suspensions were assigned to a special classroom during their school day (Safer, 1996). Academic instruction took place in special small classes (10-15 students), and points for good behavior in class, via a token economy, could be applied to acquisition of various privileges, including a shortened school day. Attempts were made to develop comparable home-based token economies with parents. During the program's operation, compared to children in comparison schools, intervention youth had fewer expulsions/suspensions; there were no differences, however, in attendance or in standardized achievement scores. On the other hand, after program completion, intervention students were significantly more likely to enter high school, and to have higher attendance rates and better classroom behavior while there. There were no differences between groups in graduation rates. Unfortunately, behavior outside the classroom was not evaluated.

Peer-Based Interventions

Peer mediation. As summarized elsewhere (Hawkins, Catalano, & Brewer, 1995a), peer mediation programs have been offered in school settings for both children and adolescents. Mediators are trained in "active listening, communicating, taking command of adversarial situations, identifying points of

agreement, and maintaining confidentiality and a non-judgmental stance" (Brewer et al., 1995). Trained peer mediators assist students involved in a conflict to examine the problem and arrive at an agreed-on nonviolent solution. Most evaluations of the efficacy of peer mediation programs have failed to use a randomized control design and to use objective outcome measures; almost none has shown significant positive effects (Lam, 1989). One program (Tolson, McDonald, & Moriarty, 1992) that did use a randomized control in a middle-class suburban high school found that relative to the period prior to implementing the peer mediation program, intervention students, compared to those receiving traditional disciplinary actions, showed a decline in reported incidents of interpersonal conflict. However, intervention and control groups were not similar in that those assigned to mediation had more preintervention disciplinary referrals for interpersonal conflict, raising the possibility that these results may reflect statistical regression to the mean.

Conflict resolution. School-based programs to reduce interpersonal violence are a recent popular public health strategy, now widely used in many middle and high schools. These programs are generally psychoeducational and are aimed at increasing knowledge about the causes and consequences of violence, improving self-control, and augmenting social problem solving. Because conflict resolution programs are specifically oriented to reducing serious child and adolescent interpersonal violence, we include them here, despite their frequent lack of a multisystemic perspective. Unfortunately, though widely implemented, little evaluation data are available that would allow us to note which programs are most useful in reducing violence. In a recent review, Webster (1993) offers skepticism that such programs will prove to be effective, largely because, as universal programs, they presume that students are similar enough to benefit from a standardized program. Because adolescent groups include both "early starters" and "late starters" (Moffitt, 1993) on the path to antisocial behavior, individuals in one or the other of these trajectories are likely to differ greatly in the adequacy of their existing social skills. If conflict resolution programs are aimed at enhancing the interpersonal skills of adolescents, they are likely to intervene too late in the developmental career of the early starters, whose social skills deficits probably originate in childhood.

Webster argues further that there is little evidence that social skills deficits are at the root of interpersonal violence, so that improvements in social information processing may not be linked to changes in interpersonal violence. Finally, because of the multitude of contributory factors to youth violence, classroom-based social cognitive programs by themselves may be insufficient: "In the absence of other supporting interventions, classroom-based curricula generally have failed to produce sustainable behavior changes for other health and social problems among youth" (Webster, 1993, p. 127).

■ Limitations of Single-Focus Preventions

Several causal-modeling investigations demonstrate that children's antisocial behavior emerges from a context that includes risk factors at many levels (e.g., Elliott, Huizinga, & Ageton, 1985; Patterson et al., 1992; Simcha-Fagan & Schwartz, 1986). The theoretical framework for these conceptualizations is provided by Bronfenbrenner (1979), who notes that the child's environment consists of "nested ecological structures" having recursive influences on each other. In current mod-

els (see Tolan & Guerra, 1994a), these include, for example, the individual, his or her close interpersonal relations (family/peers), proximal social settings (school and neighborhood), and the social macrosystem (e.g., gun control policy).

For this reason, narrowly focused approaches to preventing or treating child antisocial behavior, however well conceptualized and well conducted, often fail to alter the course of antisocial behavior (e.g., Bank, Marlowe, Reid, Patterson, & Weinrott, 1991; Guerra & Slaby, 1990). Such programs are likely to have greater impact to the extent that they incorporate components directed at more than one type of risk factor (Coie & Jacobs, 1993; Dodge, 1993; Tremblay, Pagani-Kurtz, Vitaro, Mâsse, & Pihl, 1995). In fact, recent successful approaches to prevention incorporate multiple components with documented efficacy at the individual, family, and peer level.

Many factors influence the particular choice of components that intervenors might consider in designing preventive intervention programs. These include available institutional resources (Is the school setting able to implement the program?), the family environment (Can parents be engaged in the intervention process? Are there many correlated family problems that are likely to interfere with intervention success?), and the chronological age and developmental level of the targeted children.

Investigators have selected different combinations from the components described above, provided them in varying degrees of intensity and duration, in a range of settings, to children at different ages and stages, and to groups varying in level of risk factors. The manifestation of antisocial behavior varies with the child's developmental level, as does the relative impact of various risk factors. For example, school transitions, such as entry into primary school or middle school, may be points at which aggressive behavior is particularly amenable to intervention (Coie & Jacobs, 1993), perhaps because the peer group is reconstructed at such transitions.

These transitions may also bring into focus an array of new risk factors, such as changing peer and neighborhood influences. Below we consider examples of how investigators have offered and studied combinations of intervention components, at three developmental periods: prior to school entry, school age, and adolescence. In many cases, the age of the child influences the risk factors that are targeted, the setting in which the intervention is applied, and the intensity of the intervention. Where possible, we have tried to illustrate the effectiveness of various programs by noting effect sizes for intervention components, and by commenting on program implementation and attrition. Unfortunately, many reports provided insufficient documentation regarding sample size, statistical information, measures of process, or the degree of fidelity to program procedures.

■ Examples of Well-Designed Programs

In the review below, and in Tables 10.1 to 10.3, we have summarized information on a variety of interventions. The tables include information on the risk factors, the subjects, and the type of design used (e.g., randomized assignment, selected intervention). The tables also summarize the treatment components, the outcomes targeted for change (e.g., parenting), and the results of the prevention study. In general, the interventions outlined in the tables and further described below have been selected to illustrate the types of multicomponent programs that could have an influence on later antisocial behavior and that have been systematically evaluated. For programs oriented toward preschoolers, school-

aged children, and adolescents, we present those programs that target multiple systems, with child antisocial behavior or its precursors as an expected outcome. In contrast, we follow a different strategy for infant and toddler programs. For this early developmental period, a distinction between family and child components is developmentally unfeasible. Furthermore, we are aware of only one program for children younger than 2 years that followed children long enough to examine program impact on antisocial behavior (Olds, 1996). For this developmental period, then, we describe programs directed at parents and infants that are family focused and target either parenting behavior or child behavior. Although conflict resolution curricula are usually not multicomponent in nature, and many programs have yet to report outcome data, we have included them here because they are being widely promoted, and because they target directly the kinds of serious violent interpersonal behavior that is the focus of this book.

Prior to School Entry

Programs that target children prior to school entry are summarized in Table 10.1 and are described more fully below.

Rationale for this age range. As reviewed in Chapter 7 (Hawkins et al., this volume), a wide range of individual and familial risk factors could serve as potential targets for early intervention. Individual child factors that could be targeted include child physical health, cognitive development, academic achievement, and socioemotional development. Family factors that could be targeted for intervention include ecological factors (e.g., housing and neighborhood, financial resources, informal supports, access to formal supports), role configurations in the family (e.g., teenage pregnancy, single parent-hood, unemployment), and the nature of family interactions (e.g., marital interactions, parent-child interactions, parent-teacher interactions, teacher-child interactions and peer-peer interactions). See the review by Heinicke, Beckwith, and Thompson (1988).

Given this framework, any early intervention that targets change in one or more of these systems or processes could be viewed as a program aimed at preventing child antisocial or delinquent behavior. A review of programs aimed at this wide an array of risk factors is well beyond the scope of this chapter. On the other hand, to narrow our discussion to only those early interventions that follow young children long enough to allow for assessments of antisocial behavior or offending in adolescence would be too limited. The empirical demonstration that a program prevents delinquency, let alone serious and violent offending, is rare, not only because the task of prevention itself is very difficult, but also because the conduct of a longitudinal study designed to test such effects is highly costly and difficult. Therefore, we include programs that target risk factors for early developmental precursors of antisocial behavior. The few preventive intervention studies that begin prior to school entry and follow children into adolescence or young adulthood will be examined more carefully.

Universal interventions for infants and toddlers. Subjects in the Montreal Home Visitation Study (Larson, 1980) were 115 working-class Canadian women between 18 and 35 years old. Three types of interventions were provided: 10 home visits, from age 6 weeks to 15 months postpartum; one prenatal visit in the seventh month of pregnancy, one postpartum hospital visit, and nine postnatal home visits until the baby was 15 months old; and no intervention. Eighty mothers were randomly assigned to either the 10-home-

visit condition or to no intervention. Later, mothers entered the study receiving the prenatal and postnatal condition. Home visits focused on four areas: general caretaking, mother-infant interaction, mother's social support and social interactions, and child development. Findings revealed that the groups differed on the number of child injuries, with those receiving pre- and postnatal visits having the fewest injuries and those in the control group incurring the most injuries. Mothers receiving the more comprehensive intervention also received higher scores on the quality of the home environment compared to mothers from the other two groups.

Selected interventions for infants and toddlers. In a study of the University of Rochester Nurse Home Visitation Program (Olds, Henderson, Chamberlin, & Tatelbaum, 1986; Olds, Henderson, Tatelbaum, & Chamberlin, 1988), 400 pregnant and parenting low-income women in a small, semirural county in the Appalachian region of New York State were randomly assigned to treatment and control conditions. The region was characterized as having high rates of poverty and child abuse. Subjects were recruited if they met any of the following criteria: (a) younger than 19 years old, (b) unmarried, or (c) of low SES. The majority of subjects were Caucasian, and 23% were positive on all three risk factors. The goals of the program were to alter (a) pregnancy outcomes, (b) child health and development, and (c) parental life course. Early assessments of outcomes focused on birth weight, neurodevelopment, child abuse and neglect, childhood injuries (a marker of maltreatment or child impulsivity), number and spacing of pregnancies, and maternal labor force participation. Although these investigators did not initially conceive of this program as addressing risk factors for serious antisocial behavior, many of the program's targeted outcomes are indeed related to such risks.

TABLE 10.1 Interventions for Infants, Toddlers, and Preschoolers

Authors	Risk Factors	Subjects	Design	Rx Components	Targeted Outcomes	Findings
			Universal Interventions for Infants and Toddlers			
Olds, Henderson, Chamberlin, and Tatelbaum (1986); Olds, Henderson, Tatelbaum, and Chamberlin (1988): The Prenatal/ Early Infancy Project	Families from counties with higher rates of poverty and child abuse; mothers were either poor, young, or single	400 young (< 19 years) unmarried or low-SES mothers from a semirural county in the Appalachian region of New York State	Random assignment to I1 (90), I2 (94), I3 (100), and I4 (116)	I1: Developmental screening I2 = I1 plus free transportation to medical clinics I3 = I2 plus nine biweekly home visits during pregnancy by an RN I4 = I3 and home visit up to 2 years	Parenting, child development, maternal life course development	At 46 months, days on welfare and incidents of child abuse/neglect, I4 < I, = I2; for months employed, I4 < I, = I2: 43% fewer pregnancies, 82% more months employed, 4% abuse/neglect vs. 19% in I1/I2.
Larson (1980): Montreal Home Visitation Study	No more than high school education	115 Canadian working-class pregnant women in 7th month of pregnancy to 15 months	Random assignment to I1 (30), I2 (31), control (34)	Home visit by child psych undergrad I = information on development and parenting, emotional support C = no visits I1 = one visit during 7th month of pregnancy, and nine postnatal visits until the baby was 15 months I2 = 10 postnatal home visits from 6 weeks to 15 months	Parenting, child development, maternal life-course development	At 6, 12, and 18 months for HOME environment and parenting skill, I1 > I2 = C; for child injuries, I1 < I2 < C

Selected Interventions for Infants and Toddlers

Study	Risk	Sample	Design	Intervention	Outcomes	Results
Wasik, Ramey, Bryant, and Sparling (1990): Project CARE	Poverty, family disruptions, low education	62 infants (ages 0-5 months) at high risk because of low income, parental educational level, or family disruptions	Random assignment to Experimental Intervention 1 (15), Experimental Intervention 2 (24), control (23)	I1 = cognitively oriented day care and family education by home visit from teachers (biweekly for children 0-3 months, monthly for 4-5 months) I2 = family education through home visit by B.S. and professionals	Parenting, child academic functioning	For parenting, I = C through 54 months; for cognitive development between 12 and 30 months, I > C; for cognitive development between 31 and 54 months, I = C > I2
Lally, Mangione, and Honig (1988): Syracuse University Family Development Research Project	Poverty	Low-income mothers with less than high school education, 119 children 0 to 5 years	65 intervention and 54 matched controls (time lag recruitment of controls)	Home visits; informational (parenting, games, activities); emotional; educational (day care/preschool) for children 6 months to 5 years	Parenting, child academic functioning	At 3-year follow-up, for child cognitive and socioemotional ratings, I > C. At 10-year follow-up for delinquency convictions, I (6%) < C (22%); for chronic delinquency, I (25%) < C (42%). Effects primarily for boys
Seitz, Rosenbaum, and Apfel (1985, 1991); Seitz and Apfel (1994): Yale Child Welfare Project	Poverty	Low-income, primiparous mothers, of 30 children (20 boys and 10 girls), pregnancy to 30 months	Matched controls, time-lagged recruitment of control group	Home visit: (a) informational (parenting, job and educational counseling, emotional, referrals average of 28 home visit over 2.5 years); (b) medical: avg. 15 well-baby exams	Parenting, child social and emotional functioning	At immediate outcome, for child verbal ability, I > C. At 10-year follow-up, for receiving welfare I (13%) < C (46%); for delay in second pregnancy, I (9 year) > C (5 year); for years maternal education, I > C; for teacher-rated aggression, disobedience, lying, cheating, and special ed placement, I < C

(continued)

TABLE 10.1 *Continued*

Authors	Risk Factors	Subjects	Design	Rx Components	Targeted Outcomes	Findings
Selected Interventions for Infants and Toddlers *(continued)*						
Johnson and Walker (1987): Houston Parent Child Development Center	Poverty	Low-income Mexican American families with one child, 139 children (67 boys, 72 girls), 1 to 3 years	Randomized to intervention (51) and control (88)	2-year program: Y1 = 25 home visits by paraprofessionals: informational (development, parenting, family communication); Y2 = educational classes taught by paraprofessionals and teachers for parents on same topics, educational day care for children	Parenting, child academic functioning	At immediate outcome, for maternal positive affect and responsivity, I > C; for maternal punitiveness, I < C. At 1-year follow-up, for child cognitive scores, I > C. At 5- to 8-year follow-up, for teacher-rated fighting and disruptive, impulsive, and restless behavior, I < C
Selected Interventions for Preschoolers						
Berrueta-Clement, Schweinhart, Barnett, Epstein, and Weikart (1984); Schweinhart, Barnes, and Weikart (1993): High/Scope Perry Preschool	IQ between 60 and 90, poverty, at risk for school failure	Low-income African American families, 121 children (72 boys, 49 girls), 3 to 5 years; IQ 60-90	Randomized to intervention (58) and control (63)	Educational preschool for children, informational and emotional support for parents, weekly home visit by preschool teachers	Parenting, child academic functioning	At 2-year follow-up, for IQ I > C. At 14-year follow-up, I < C for chronic offending (7% vs. 17%), number of property/violent offenses (47 vs. 74), school dropout (20% fewer in I), teen pregnancy (50% fewer in I), and unemployment. Effects on delinquency primarily in boys

NOTE: I = intervention; C = control; RN = registered nurse; SES = socioeconomic status; Rx = treatment.

Currently, a 15-year follow-up study is under way (Olds, 1996). This long-term assessment focuses on the criminal histories of the mothers, and on school failure, CD, and other antisocial outcomes in the children (currently adolescents).

Four different levels of intervention were offered. Level One included information and support for child health and development. Level Two added free transportation to regular prenatal and well-child visits to the Level One services. Both these conditions were considered as controls. Level Three consisted of nursing home visits throughout pregnancy, and Level Four expanded this by continuing home visits through the child's second birthday. Thus, comparisons between Levels Three and Four allowed the investigators to contrast the timing of the intervention (prenatal vs. prenatal plus postnatal visits). Postnatal visits focused on three major activities: parent education regarding fetal and infant development, the involvement of family members and friends in child care and in support for the mother, and linkage of family members with other health and human services. The approach taken by the nurses was to focus on parental and family strengths.

Interim results showed that within the subgroup of mothers who smoked, treated mothers were more likely than controls to have babies who weighed more and were less likely to deliver preterm (there were 75% fewer preterm deliveries among intervention smokers). When children were 2 years old, treated mothers were seen in the emergency room fewer times and were less often seen by physicians for injuries and poisonings (a 56% reduction in emergency room visits). For the subgroup of unmarried teenagers, treated mothers were less likely than controls to abuse or neglect their children (assessed through incident reports). Home observations also revealed that treated mothers were less likely than control mothers to restrict and punish their children

and more likely to provide appropriate play materials.

Furthermore, treated mothers were more likely to return to school, to be employed, and to delay subsequent pregnancy. Importantly, for all these comparisons of early outcomes, Levels One and Two were significantly different from Level Four. In general, mothers receiving Level Three intervention (prenatal visits only) functioned at a level intermediate between the infancy nurse-visited and control conditions.

In a cost analysis up through age 4 years (Olds, Henderson, Phelps, Kitzman, & Hanks, 1993), the program was attributed with averting government spending of $1,772 per family (in 1980 dollars) for the sample as a whole and $3,498 for low-income families. Among low-income families, the distribution of government savings was as follows: 56% saved from Aid to Families With Dependent Children (AFDC), 3% saved from child protective services costs, 11% from Medicaid, 26% from food stamps, and 5% earned from families paying additional taxes. The authors concluded that the majority of early costs savings could be attributed to the program's positive effects on family size and on reliance on government programs because mothers were working. It is important to note that these figures are for government savings early on. They do not take into account long-term savings, such as those from reduced levels of delinquency, or savings from nongovernment sources.

Programs for preschoolers. In a review of early intervention studies initiated in the 1960s, Zigler, Taussig, and Black (1992) concluded that programs that combine early education and family support may be promising for the prevention of antisocial behavior. In general, these programs intervene with children through their broad environment rather than through a specific domain of risk. They attempt to influence the child's overall functioning by improving parents' interactions with social systems (school, child care services) and by helping parents support their child's physical, cognitive, and socioemotional development.

Several studies of early intervention programs include follow-up periods over 10 years. These studies began when children were 3 years old or younger and followed them past the period of risk for antisocial and delinquent behaviors. The four programs with long-term follow-up data, the High/Scope Perry Preschool Project, the Syracuse University Family Development Research Project, the Yale Child Welfare Project, and the Houston Parent Child Development Center, are reviewed below. None was specifically designed to prevent antisocial or criminal behavior. The children and families were considered at risk for poor outcome because of economic disadvantage.

In his review of early intervention programs, Yoshikawa (1995) reported effect sizes for these four programs of .42 for the Perry Preschool Project, .48 for the Houston Parent Child Development Center, .48 for the Syracuse program, and 1.13 for the Yale Child Welfare Project. Although the outcome of these studies is encouraging given the limited efficacy of treatment programs for antisocial behavior and delinquency, the possible mechanisms by which change occurred cannot be identified. Zigler et al. (1992) speculate that the reduction in delinquency in preschoolers may result, at least in part, from the emphasis on parent involvement. Parents are taught how to maintain the developmental gains, both social and emotional, that children achieve within the preschool.

These four programs shared a number of important features. They all provided child education (child care or preschool ranging from half-day summer sessions to full-day sessions 4 to 5 days/week) and family support (ranging from 25 to 60 sessions). The programs were all intensive (ranging from 2 to 5 years), and all included home visits. They all began early in development, with the Syracuse and Yale programs starting before birth, the Houston project at age 1, and the Perry Project at age 3. The four programs were all theoretically based with curricula thoroughly specified in treatment manuals. Staff-to-child/parent ratios were low, and training and supervision were extensive. Finally, all four programs included both child-focused and family-focused components. In contrast to the early intervention programs from the 1960s, the more recent program developed by Webster-Stratton, described below, was specifically designed to alter parenting practices to prevent the development of child conduct problems in low-income families.

Universal interventions for preschoolers. The Syracuse University Family Development Research Project (Lally, Mangione, & Honig, 1988) included educational, nutritional, health, safety, and human services resources to 109 low-income families (primarily African American). Program services were delivered to pregnant mothers and continued until the children reached elementary school. The program consisted of weekly home visits and quality child care. Child care was provided one-half day for 5 days a week for children 6 to 15 months, and full-day care was provided for children 15 to 60 months. The program was found to decrease the total number, severity, and chronicity of later involvement with the juvenile justice system. When the children were between 13 and 16 years old, 4 of 65 treated children identified at follow-up had probation records compared to 12 of the 54 controls.

The Yale Child Welfare Project (Provence & Naylor, 1983; Provence, Naylor, & Patterson, 1977; Rescarla, Provence, & Naylor, 1982; Seitz, Rosenbaum, & Apfel, 1985; Trickett, Apfel, Rosenbaum, & Zigler, 1982) targeted 17 impoverished, pregnant, African American women recruited between 1968 and 1970. Controls were 18 children who were recruited at the completion of the program (time-lag strategy). Groups were matched on sex, income level, number of parents in the home, and maternal ethnicity. The program began during pregnancy and continued until the children were 30 months old. Services included free pediatric care, developmental exams, social work, and psychological services as needed. Children received from 13 to 17 regular well-baby exams, and families received an average of 28 home visits. An average of 13 months of child care was also offered (ranging from 2 to 28 months). Services were provided by a pediatrician, a home visitor, a primary child care worker, and a developmental examiner. The primary focus was on the children's emotional and social development. At the end of the program, treated children showed advantages compared to controls on language development. Ten years after program completion, compared to controls, intervention mothers had more education, were more likely to be employed, had fewer children, and spaced their children further apart. Although no differences were observed on child IQ or academic achievement, treated children had better school attendance than controls and were less likely to require special school services. Importantly, treated children were rated by teachers as having lower antisocial behavior and better social adjustment compared to controls.

The Houston Parent Child Development Program (Johnson & Walker, 1987) provided home visits to low-income Mexican American families to promote children's social and intellectual competence. Services were of-fered over a 2-year period with families receiving approximately 550 hours, including 25 home visits during the first year of the child's life. The second year of the program included classes for mothers in child development, home management, and 4 half days/week of preschool for the children. In a 5- to 8-year follow-up, treated children were rated by their teachers as less obstinate, hostile, impulsive, disruptive, and aggressive compared to controls. Follow-up revealed no group differences on antisocial behavior; however, attrition was very high.

In a recently completed study of a universal preventive intervention, Webster-Stratton (1997) randomly assigned eight Head Start centers (25 classes) to experimental and control conditions. The experimental condition consisted of the PARTNERS program, designed by Webster-Stratton, and the control condition, comprising the regular center-based program. The PARTNERS intervention supplemented the Head Start program with (a) PMT, delivered by trained family service workers within the Head Start program, and (b) teacher training, which focused on supporting parental involvement in the classroom, promoting consistency from home to school, and strengthening teacher's use of behavioral contingencies within the classroom. The parenting program included 8 to 9 two-hour weekly parent group meetings, with 8-16 parents.

Two hundred ten Head Start parents and their 4-year-old children participated in the program, and 137 families participated in the intervention, attending an average of six sessions. Eighty-five percent of parents completed at least half of the parent training sessions. Assessments included teacher and parent reports of child behavior, and observations of parent and child behavior in the family's home. Outcomes were assessed in the following domains: parenting competence, parent involvement in school, child social competence and conduct problems at home, and child social competence and conduct problems at school. Compared to control parents, parents in the experimental condition made significantly fewer critical remarks; used less physically negative discipline; and were more positive, appropriate, and consistent in their discipline style. Seventy-one percent of experimental parents showed a decrease in critical statements, compared with 29% of control families. Furthermore, teachers reported that mothers who received the intervention were more involved in their children's education than control mothers.

According to observations of child behavior in the home, children in the experimental condition were more compliant, had more positive affect, displayed fewer negative behaviors, and were more prosocial than control children. In contrast, parent reports of child behavior did not significantly differ across groups. At school, experimental children were observed to display increased social skills with their peers, compared to controls. However, no significant differences were found on teachers' reports of externalizing behavior.

Importantly, most eligible parents signed up for the program, and consumer satisfaction with the 8-week program was high. Program response was not affected by parental educational level, minority status, level of depression, number of negative life events, or amount of support or prior involvement with abuse. The only factor that did predict outcome was parental substance abuse. This early preventive intervention program designed specifically for preventing conduct problems in poor children is not only feasible, but assessments indicated significant short-term improvements in parenting competence and child behavior in the experimental group compared to controls.

Selected interventions for preschoolers. The High/Scope Perry Preschool Project (Berrueta-Clement, Schweinhart, Barnett, Epstein, & Weikart, 1984) was aimed at preventing school failure in poor, African American 3- and 4-year-olds. Children were selected as at risk for school failure based on having IQ scores between 60 and 90. One hundred twenty-three children were randomly assigned to preschool or to no-preschool conditions. Home visits were provided by teachers to inform parents of the child's activities and to promote parental involvement in the child's educational experience. Parents also engaged in small monthly group meetings for support and information exchange. When reassessed at age 19 ($N = 121$), compared with control children, those who had received intervention performed better on measures of academic achievement (school grades and standardized tests) and were less likely to have repeated a grade or to have required special education services. They were more likely to have graduated from high school, more likely to be employed, and less likely to be on welfare. At ages 19 and 24, children in the preschool condition, compared to their untreated counterparts, were five times less likely to have been arrested (7% vs. 35%), and when they had been arrested, their crimes were less serious (for drug distribution and other drug-related offenses, 7% vs. 25%). The total number of lifetime arrests in the untreated group was twice as high as for the treated group (2.3 vs. 4.6 arrests). Compared to controls, significantly fewer program attenders were frequent offenders (arrested five or more times in their lifetimes) as juveniles (7% vs. 35%) or as adults (7% vs. 31%). In a cost analysis, the program was credited with reducing the costs associated with delinquency and criminal behavior by approximately $2,400 per child.

Programs for School-Aged Children

Programs targeting school-aged children are summarized in Table 10.2 and are described in detail below.

Rationale for this age range. Prior to elementary school entry, children and their families are not all equally easy to engage in prevention efforts: Not all children attend preschool, and those who do are likely to be from more well-functioning families than those who do not (Tolan & Guerra, 1994a) This sampling bias reduces the generalizability of findings of prevention studies in this age range. Because school attendance is mandatory, schools are common settings in which to implement universal programs.

Universal interventions for elementary-aged children. The Seattle Social Development Project (Hawkins, Catalano, Morrison, et al., 1992; Hawkins, Von Cleve, & Catalano, 1991; O'Donnell, Hawkins, Catalano, Abbott, & Day, 1995) incorporates elements of several intervention components, including PMT, SCT, CCT, and support for academic skills. By improving family management and academic success, this program aims to increase the child's attachment to school and family, to reduce involvement with antisocial peers, and ultimately, to reduce child aggressive behavior. First graders in six schools were randomly assigned to either intervention or control conditions. To control for "spillover effects," two additional schools were designated either as fully intervention or fully control. For the intervention, teachers were trained and supervised in the proactive management of classroom discipline and in the specification of clear learning objectives. Children's learning was enhanced by the use of student learning partners. Children were

provided with SCT via classroom-based curriculum offered in first and sixth grades by their teachers. Voluntary five- to seven-session PMT groups and parent academic support groups were offered in every elementary grade (except fourth) by professional staff. Second-grade outcome data were available on 458 children, and Grade 5 outcome was tested on 199 children who had participated in the intervention for at least one semester, compared to 709 who had not. Some analyses are presented for the subsample of Grade 5 low-income children (75 intervention and 102 controls), defined as those who were eligible to participate in the school lunch program. Grade 5 analyses are augmented by the inclusion of control children from other schools not originally participating in the randomization.

At Grade 2 (Hawkins, Von Cleve, & Catalano, 1991), intervention boys were rated significantly lower than controls on teacher-rated aggressive and externalizing behavior scales; the positive effect of intervention was confined to Caucasian boys only, with African American boys receiving scores comparable to the control Caucasian boys, regardless of group assignment. Intervention girls were rated by teachers as less self-destructive, but again this effect was confined to Caucasian, and not African American, girls. There was a trend for intervention Caucasian boys to be less likely to fall in the clinical range on externalizing behavior. At Grade 5, intervention students reported more family communication and involvement and more proactive family management by their parents than did controls (Hawkins, Catalano, Morrison, et al., 1992); intervention children were more committed to school and saw school as more rewarding than controls. At Grade 5, although there were no group differences in norms regarding drugs, intervention students generally reported significantly less

(text continued on page 224)

TABLE 10.2 Interventions for Elementary-Aged Children

Authors	Risk Factors	Subjects	Design	Rx Components	Targeted Outcomes	Findings
			Universal Interventions			
Hawkins, Von Cleve, and Catalano (1991); Hawkins, Catalano, Morrison, et al. (1992); Hawkins, Catalano, Kosterman, Abbott, and Hill (1997); O'Donnell, Hawkins, Catalano, Abbott, and Day (1995): Seattle Social Development Project	Urban children	First graders continuing through Grade 4. At Grade 2, intervention plus control n = 458. At Grade 5, intervention = 199, control = 709; at Grade 12/6-yr follow-up, total N = 598	Universal in eight Seattle schools; one designated as fully intervention (I), one as fully control (C), and six with both I and C classrooms; random assignment within school	Teacher training in CCT, use of SCT curriculum, and use of small groups with students as learning partners; PMT and workshops on how to increase children's academic skills on voluntary basis	Increased attachment to family and school, mediated by improvements in family management; increased endorsement of mainstream social values; academic skills; decreased involvement with antisocial peers	At Grade 2, for teacher-rated aggressive behavior in boys, I < C. By Grade 5, by self-report, for proactive family management, communication, and involvement, I > C; for school attachment and rates of alcohol and delinquency initiation, I < C. Mixed effects in girls. At Grade 12 for lifetime prevalence violent criminal behavior, heavy drinking, sexual intercourse, and pregnancy, I < C
Kellam et al. (1991); Kellam, Rebok, Ialongo, and Mayer (1994); Kellam, Mayer, Rebok, and Hawkins (in press); Kellam and Rebok (1992): Baltimore Prevention Study	Urban children	2,400 first graders, 66% African American, 32% Caucasian	Universal, randomized within school, in 19 Baltimore primary schools; certain schools were controls, others included one of two interventions plus control classrooms; follow-up through end of first grade and at sixth grade	2-year program; teachers implemented group-paced curriculum for enhancing reading (Mastery Learning: ML) and team-based behavioral management for teacher and peers (Good Behavior Game: GBG); no-treatment controls	Aggressive and shy behavior; reading achievement	At end of Grade 1, for teacher-rated shyness and aggressivity, GBG < C; for improved reading, ML > C. For boys, improved reading had indirect positive effect on Grade 1 aggression. For boys' Grade 6 aggression, GBG < C, only for children most aggressive at baseline

218

Selected Interventions

Study	Risk Factors	Sample	Design	Intervention	Outcomes	Results
Tremblay et al. (1991); Tremblay, Mâsse, et al. (1992); Tremblay, Vitaro, et al (1992); Tremblay, Pagani-Kurtz, Vitaro, Mâsse, and Pihl (1995); Vitaro and Tremblay (1994); McCord, Tremblay, Vitaro, and Desmarais-Gervais (1994): Montreal Longitudinal-Experimental Study	Poverty, gender, early disruptiveness	166 low-SES urban boys from 53 schools, rated high in disruptive behavior at the end of KG	Selected intervention, random assignment, yearly follow-up through age 15	I: 2 years of home-based PMT plus school-based SCT (n = 46); AC (attention control) (84); C (control) (42)	Parenting behavior, disruptive behavior, delinquency, academic adjustment	For grade-retentions through age 12 (3 years post-Rx), and for self-reported delinquency 1 to 6 years post-Rx, I < C. For teacher ratings of aggression in Ss and peer ratings of Ss' aggressiveness at age 12, I < C
Conduct Problems Prevention Research Group (1992, 1996): FAST Track	High levels of youth disruptiveness in neighborhood; disruptive behavior and poor peer relations at home and in school	448 I and 450 C children, screened in KG as being the top 10% on teacher-parent ratings of disruptiveness	Selected intervention; certain schools in four geographical areas randomly assigned as I or C; multistage screening of all KG children to select top 10% on disruptive behavior; intervention occurs in first and second grade	22 group sessions of PMT; biweekly home visiting with case management; in-school SCT; academic tutoring; behavioral classroom management	Lowered disruptive behavior at home and school; increased social competency; improved peer relations; gains in academic skills; improved family-school communication	Interim data for parenting skill and child problem-solving competence, I > C. For aggression and disruptive behavior, I < C
Guerra, Tolan, Huesmann, VanAcker, and Eron (1995); Guerra, Eron, Huesmann, Tolan, and VanAcker (1996); Tolan and McKay (1996): Metropolitan Area Child Study	Poverty, urban residence, teacher and peer ratings of aggressive behavior	Cohort 1: 1,935 children in 16 schools in Grades 2, 3, and 5 in 1995; 945 rated as aggressive; four subsequent cohorts	Universal for classroom component; selected intervention at two levels of intensity; three levels of timing of intervention; untreated controls	2-year program beginning at Grade 2/3, at Grade 5/6, or combining all 4 years. Universal: 2 (or 4 years) of classroom-based training in SCT plus other social-cognitive components. Selected: group sessions of SCT for 2 years with and without added group-based PMT in second year	Social cognitions: self- and interpersonal understanding, moral beliefs, sense of control, SCT; school environment, peer group, family context	Not yet available

(continued)

TABLE 10.2 Continued

Authors	Risk Factors	Subjects	Design	Rx Components	Targeted Outcomes	Findings
Selected Interventions (*continued*)						
Firestone, Kelly, Goodman, and Davey (1981)	Diagnosis of ADHD	43 outpatients, average age = 7	Selected intervention; random assignment to PMT alone (a); medication alone (b); PMT plus medication; pre-post	Stimulant medication; PMT: three individual and six group parent-training sessions over 3 months, plus two teacher consultations	Academic achievement, disruptive behavior	For parent and teacher ratings of disruptive behavior, all groups improved with Rx; only medication enhanced attention and impulse control; medication improved achievement more than PMT
Gittelman et al. (1980)	Diagnosis of ADHD	61 outpatients, average age = 8	Selected intervention; randomized assignment: individual PMT plus school consultation (a), medication (b), PMT, school consultation plus medication (c); pre-post	PMT: 8 weekly individual sessions with parent and teacher; stimulant medication or placebo control	Disruptive behavior	For teacher and observer ratings of acceptable behavior, c = b > a. Group c more likely to be rated as globally improved by teachers
Horn et al. (1991); Ialongo et al. (1993)	Diagnosis of ADHD	78, 7- to 11-year-olds completed treatment; 71 available for follow up 9 months later	Selected intervention; random assignment to placebo (a), low dose (b) or high dose (c) of medication alone or with (d, e, f) combination of PMT plus child group SCT	Stimulant medication; PMT/SCT: 12 weeks of group parent training plus (1x/wk) plus 12 weekly group sessions of SCT for children, plus three school consultations	Academic achievement, disruptive behavior, self-concept, attentiveness	In general, at the end of treatment, Groups b, c, e, and f outperformed a and d on teacher report of disruptive and inattentive behavior. Groups e and f were not better than b and c. Nine months after termination of medication, no lasting positive effects

Study	Diagnostic criteria	Sample	Design	Intervention	Outcome measures	Results
Pelham et al. (1993)	Diagnosis of ADHD	31 boys, 5-10 years old, attending special intensive summer program	Within-subject; selected intervention; three levels of medication (placebo, low/high dose) varied randomly across two counterbalanced levels of CCT: classroom alternated between behavioral management (BM) and no BM	8 weeks of intensive summer program; stimulant medication (placebo, low/high dose); CCT: intensive behavioral classroom procedures (token economy) vs. regular classroom condition	Observers' and teacher ratings of disruptive and social behavior; academic functioning	CCT improved rule following, peer relations, and disruptive behavior; medication improved all outcomes except classwork accuracy; medication improved efficacy of CCT for all measures; CCT failed to improve efficacy of medication for any measures
Carlson, Pelham, Milich, and Dixon (1992)	Diagnosis of ADHD	24 boys; boys, 6-12 years old, attending special intensive summer program	Within-subjects design; selected intervention; three levels of medication randomized within two counterbalanced levels of CCT	Stimulant medication (placebo, low/high dose); CCT: intensive behavioral classroom procedures (token economy) vs. regular classroom condition	Observations of off-task (a) and disruptive (b) behavior; academic skills (c)	Only medication lowered a and enhanced c; both medication and CCT reduced b; CCT improved efficacy of low-dose medication to that of high-dose medication alone
Abikoff and Hechtman (1996): New York/Montreal Study	Diagnosis of ADHD	7- to 9-year-old boys and girls in two cities (NY, Montreal) who meet criteria for ADHD	Selected; all children receive stimulant medication and in addition are randomly assigned to control (no other treatment), attention control (AC), or multimodal treatment (MMT) groups; groups balanced for race, gender, IQ, and rate of oppositional disorder	MMT: for children, 1 year of weekly group SCT, 8 months of tutoring, 3 months of weekly academic organizational skills group, 1 year of weekly individual therapy; for parents, 4 months of group PMT, 8 months of individual weekly parent counselling, crisis intervention. AC: activity and support groups for children and parents	Social, emotional, behavioral, and academic functioning	Not yet available

(continued)

TABLE 10.2 Continued

Authors	Risk Factors	Subjects	Design	Rx Components	Targeted Outcomes	Findings
			Selected Interventions (continued)			
Satterfield, Satterfield, and Schell (1987)	Diagnosis of ADHD	Drug treatment only (DTO): 116 Caucasian boys, 6 to 12 years old, consecutive referrals for services. Multimodality treatment: 70 similar boys, consecutive referrals seen 3 years later	Selected intervention: 81 DTO and 50 matched MMT children seen again approximately 10 years later	DTO: Stimulant drugs alone; MMT: stimulant medication plus intensive psychotherapy (components of BT, PT, FT, and educational Rx)	Delinquent behavior	For no. of felony arrests, institutionalizations, and likelihood of multiple felony arrests, DTO > MMT; findings not explained by differences in birth year
			Indicated Interventions			
Kazdin, Siegel, and Bass (1992)	Antisocial behavior	97 outpatients, screened for disruptive behavior, 7-13 years old	Selected intervention; random assignment to PMT ($n = 31$), to SCPS (29), or to combined intervention (37); post-Rx and 1-year follow-up assessments	PMT, SCPS, PMT, and SCPS	Antisocial behavior	Combined treatment improved parent and child report of antisocial behavior, and reported parental stress and depression
Kazdin, Esveldt-Dawson, French, and Unis (1987a)	Antisocial behavior	40 inpatients, screened for disruptive behavior, 7-12 years old	Selected intervention; random assignment to I or attention control; post-Rx assessment 1 month after Rx; follow-up 1 year postrelease	3 months of PT (parents) plus SCPS (children) begun in residence, continued as outpatients	Antisocial behavior	For parent- and teacher-reported child behavior problems, I < C at post-Rx and follow-up; for parent-reported social competence I > C at post-Rx and follow-up

Study		Sample	Design	Treatment	Measures	Results
Webster-Stratton and Hammond (1997)	Early-onset conduct problems	97 children with early-onset conduct problems, aged 4-8 years	Random assignment to PMT, child training (CT), PMT plus CT, or waiting-list control (C)	PMT = groups of 10-12 parents met weekly for 2 hours over a 22- to 24-week period CT = groups of 5-6 children met weekly for 22 two-hour sessions (both PMT and CT used videotaped modeling) PMT plus CT = combination of both C = 8-9 month wait list	Parenting, child conduct problems, child social competence (home and school)	At immediate outcome, CT and PMT + CT children showed improvements in problem-solving and conflict management skills compared with PMT and controls. PMT and PMT + CT parents and children had more positive interactions compared with CT and C. At 1-year follow-up, all significant changes were maintained. PMT + CT showed more improvements in child behavior than CT or PMT. Teacher reports of behavior problems in school showed increases in problem behavior in school for all three groups

NOTE: I = intervention; C = control; KG = kindergarten; SES = socioeconomic status; Rx = treatment; SCT = social cognitive training; CCT = classroom contingency training; PMT = parent management training; SCPS = social cognitive problem solving; Ss = subjects; ADHD = attention-deficit hyperactivity disorder.

initiation of delinquency and alcohol use than did controls, but these effects did not appear among the high-risk (low-income) subsample (O'Donnell et al., 1995).

For high-risk students, comparisons at Grade 6 were examined separately by sex. Unfortunately, for these analyses, numbers are small (approximately 60 girls and 50 boys) and comparisons are many: Of 70 possible comparisons, 13 were found to be significant at $p < .05$ (19%). Intervention girls, compared to control girls, reported significantly less smoking, fewer opportunities to obtain marijuana, more attachment and commitment to school, and more opportunities for cooperative and team learning methods in the classroom. Intervention boys, relative to controls, showed better social and school-work skills, obtained higher grades and standardized achievement scores, and had more of a commitment to school; teachers (but not the students themselves) reported that intervention boys had fewer antisocial peers than did controls. In the high-risk subsample, there was a trend for intervention boys to report less delinquency than did control boys; there was no effect for girls. It is not entirely clear why effects for boys and girls were not more consistent, although gender differences in program effectiveness are reported by others also (e.g., Farrell & Meyer, 1997). Overall, effect sizes were modest, ranging for the most part between .2 and .3. When analyses were examined separately by sex, effect sizes were stronger (approximately .6), although as noted above, findings were more spotty overall in the gender comparisons.

Because by Grade 5 many schools joined the program, the number of available control children increased. Comparisons between the additional controls and the original controls showed no differences on any outcome variables, except that added control girls had significantly higher achievement scores than did

the original control girls (Hawkins, Catalano, Morrison, et al., 1992). Comparisons between subjects available at Grade 6 in the Seattle Social Development Project and those not available (O'Donnell et al., 1995) indicated that retrieved subjects had been more likely, in Grade 5, to report attachments to nonantisocial peers and had fewer school suspensions than not-assessed subjects. There were no other differences in Grade 5.

Six years after program completion, when they would normally have been completing high school, 93% of the original consenting sample were successfully reinterviewed, and their official school and juvenile court records were reviewed (Hawkins, Catalano, Kosterman, Abbott, & Hill, 1997). Students exposed to the full intervention reported significantly less lifetime prevalence of violent criminal behavior, heavy drinking, sexual intercourse, and pregnancy. They reported better academic achievement, more commitment to school, and less school misbehavior. Official school and court records showed differences in the same direction, although generally not at statistically significant levels. Finally, the intervention had particular effectiveness for impoverished children in a number of areas: school attachment and achievement, school misbehavior, and driving while drinking. These results demonstrate the effectiveness of this approach into adolescence, a time of increased risk for many problem behaviors, 6 years *after* the completion of the program. Notably, this program is one of very few to report significant reductions, following intervention, in violent criminal behavior.

In the Baltimore Prevention Study, three schools in each of five areas were randomly designated as (a) academic intervention, (b) behavioral intervention, or (c) no intervention (Kellam et al., in press; Kellam & Rebok, 1992; Kellam et al., 1994; Kellam et al. 1991). Intervention took place over 2 years. Within each intervention school, children entering first grade were randomly assigned to either intervention or control classrooms. The ongoing study involves two cohorts of approximately 1,200 children each, 66% of whom are African American, and 32% of whom are Caucasian. The academic skills program, Mastery Learning (ML), systematically applied enrichment to the reading curriculum. The behavioral program, the Good Behavior Game (GBG), included teacher training in, and group-based application of, classroom behavioral contingency management (that we have otherwise referred to as CCT). GBG was implemented during game periods that increased in duration from three 10-minute sessions per week to 3 hours, three times per week. From the first cohort of 1,197 available children, 1,084 received baseline assessments. Of these, 693 participated in the same intervention or control condition for 2 years. Outcome evaluations have been conducted yearly and have been published for the end of first grade ($N = 864$) (Kellam et al., in press; Kellam & Rebok, 1992) and the end of sixth grade ($N = 590$) (Kellam et al., 1994). Comparisons of assessed and not-assessed children showed that those not reassessed were consistently more aggressive at baseline than those later assessed; reassessed and not reassessed children were found to differ in other baseline measures (shyness, depression, concentration, reading level) at some, but not all, later evaluations.

One year postintervention, controlling for baseline levels, teacher ratings of shyness and aggression were significantly lower in children participating in the GBG, relative to controls. Reading achievement was higher in children participating in ML, relative to controls. Effect sizes were approximately .4 for ML and substantially lower (.2) for GBG. At the end of Grade 1, improvements in behavioral control had no crossover effect on achievement, but for boys in the fall cohort, the reading improvements related to ML enhanced behavioral self-control. Oddly, there was no impact of the program on boys' aggression for the spring cohort.

The effects on behavior were not universally maintained once intervention ceased: At the end of Grade 6, the positive impact of GBG, relative to the control condition, was found only for boys and for those children who had been most aggressive at baseline. Effects for girls were more mixed, and varied as a function of achievement levels and timing (fall vs. spring) of the intervention (Kellam et al., in press).

Universal programs frequently make use of teachers both to implement the intervention and to evaluate change in children, leading to bias in ratings. Programs that make use of blind observation, or parent or child report (e.g., Hawkins, Catalano, Morrison, et al., 1992), are less prone to this sort of bias, but may be subject to other types of bias, such as social desirability. The best approach would be to make use of multiple informants across settings to note changes in targeted outcomes.

Selected interventions for elementary-aged children. To examine the impact of a 2-year preventive intervention on aggressive and prosocial behavior, Tremblay, Vitaro, McCord, and colleagues (McCord, Tremblay, Vitaro, & Desmarais-Gervais, 1994; Tremblay, Mâsse, et al., 1992; Tremblay et al., 1991; Tremblay et al., 1995; Tremblay, Vitaro, et al. 1992; Vitaro & Tremblay, 1994) randomly assigned boys from 53 schools in impoverished neighborhoods, rated by teachers at the end of kindergarten as highly disruptive, to (a) no-intervention no-contact control, (b) no-intervention attention control, or (c) intervention conditions. The 2-year-long intervention condition began in Grade 1 and combined PMT and child SCT. Over 80% of the sample in each group was reassessed yearly for 6 years postintervention; subjects lost through attrition did not differ from their counterparts in kindergarten ratings.

Through age 12 (3-year follow-up), treated boys were more likely than controls to be in age-appropriate regular classrooms and were less likely to be rated by their classmates and teachers as physically aggressive in school (with effect sizes ranging between .25 and .60). At each postintervention assessment, treated boys reported lower rates of delinquent acts. However, no differences were found for other important factors (e.g., hyperactivity, vandalism, prosocial behavior).

Several large-scale, multisystemic intervention trials aimed at preventing antisocial behavior are currently under way. Although initiated only recently, two studies (Conduct Problems Prevention Research Group, 1992; Guerra, Eron, Huesmann, Tolan, & VanAcker, 1996; Guerra, Tolan, Huesmann, VanAcker, & Eron, 1995; Tolan & McKay, 1996) illustrate the state of the art in prevention experiments informed by both longitudinal and treatment studies.

The FAST Track program (Conduct Problems Prevention Research Group, 1992) selects kindergarten children from varied environments (e.g., urban and rural) and ethnic groups who display high rates of disruptive behavior both at home and at school. Sets of schools within the four participating sites were randomly designated as intervention and control. Multistaged screening identified the top 10% of children based on teacher-parent scores for disruptive behavior. Altogether, 448 intervention and 450 control children were recruited. Currently, the oldest cohort is completing fifth grade, and the youngest, third grade. The program focuses on intensive interventions during the transitions at school entry and from elementary to middle school. Upon entrance into first grade, children in each of three successive cohorts who were assigned to the intervention receive a 1-year program, directed at key risk factors in multiple settings. Parents received 22 weeks of group PMT in the second grade, shifting to a monthly schedule for remaining years of the program. Weekly home visits help parents apply the skills learned during parent training in their natural environment. SCT targets children's peer relations and ability to solve problems and negotiate solutions. Children receive academic tutoring and teachers are trained in CCT (the PATHS curriculum). The universal component (CCT) continues through the fifth grade for each of the originally designated intervention schools. Short- and long-term intervention effects are being assessed through multimeasure assessments of family and child functioning. One important aspect of the FAST Track program is that it allows for integration across modality; for example, parents in the parenting group are schooled in how to support SCT components, which should promote generalization across settings. A recent early report (Conduct Problems Prevention Research Group, 1996) points to program impact in various outcomes following intervention. Observers noted more appropriate parenting in the intervention group; intervention children had more competent responses to social problem-solving tasks; on some, but not all, measures, teachers and observers noted less disruptive and aggressive behavior in intervention children; and intervention children were less disliked by their peers.

The Metropolitan Area Child Study (Guerra et al., 1996; Guerra et al., 1995; Tolan & McKay, 1996) seeks to modify the social cognitions that place children at risk for antisocial behavior as well as social environmental risk factors. This investigation combines components of psychoeducational, functional, and structural-strategic family therapy. The study provides less intensive intervention (e.g., classroom intervention) for all children and more intensive intervention (e.g., family intervention) for subsamples of at-risk children.

This strategy will allow for the dismantling of specific intervention components to inform the design of more parsimonious interventions. A graduated series of interventions is offered to groups of children at increasing levels of risk. A universal classroom-based SCT curriculum was offered all children in Grades 1-6 in 16 targeted schools in low-income, urban neighborhoods. The universal social-cognitive curriculum consists of 40 lessons taught by teachers over the 2 years of the intervention; the intervention addresses self- and interpersonal understanding, moral beliefs, sense of control, and SCT. The more intensive intervention spans 2 years, with some children receiving it early (Grades 2/3), some late (Grades 5/6), and some children receiving both early and late components. The first level of selected intervention includes 2 years (or 4 years in the combined group) of additional SCT in small groups for 28 weekly sessions; these sessions rehearse the issues raised in the universal classroom intervention. At the second level of selected intervention, the parents of half of these children also receive 22 group sessions in Year 2 of the intervention. Parent sessions offer training in PMT, improving family problem-solving skills, and family therapy (Alexander et al., 1976; Alexander & Parsons, 1973; Barton et al., 1985; Klein et al., 1977).

Although these two studies have different designs and intervention procedures, they share some important features. Both studies involve multiple-stage screening procedures in which all children in certain grades are assessed and high-risk children (based on ratings of disruptive behavior) are targeted for intervention. Randomized experimental designs are employed in both studies, and multiple measures and multiple informants are used to assess process and outcome variables. Intervention (based on detailed manuals) is multisystemic, targeting child and family factors in the school and home settings. Both programs are designed to foster positive relations within and between family and school systems and to be sensitive to the characteristics of the communities in which they are implemented (e.g., high-crime neighborhoods).

Selected interventions that include a medication component. As noted elsewhere (Hawkins et al., Chapter 7, this volume), a childhood diagnosis of ADHD (*DSM-IV*) carries considerable risk for subsequent antisocial behavior; comorbidity across disorders of ADHD and CD approach 90% in clinical populations (see Abikoff & Klein, 1992, for a review). Although studies that evaluate efficacy of treatments for ADHD might be considered *indicated* programs for that disorder, they can also be seen as *selected* programs for the prevention of CD.

Because studies that combine medication with other treatment components are not commonly reviewed in the literature directed specifically toward practitioners in the juvenile justice system, we will review them here. Earlier reviews have underscored the utility of stimulant medication and of behavioral strategies in treating ADHD (e.g., Hinshaw, Klein, & Abikoff, in press; Pfiffner & O'Leary, 1993). The benefits of psychostimulants, such as Ritalin, for treatment of the core symptoms of ADHD (inattentiveness, impulsivity, motor overactivity) have long been demonstrated (Klein, 1987). Even though cognitive-behavioral approaches alone (SCT) have been found ineffective with children with ADHD (see Abikoff, 1991; Hinshaw & Erhardt, 1991, for reviews), both PMT and CCT strategies have been used, alone and in combination with medication, to good effect. Because no single-treatment component can be considered universally useful, there is good reason to consider combining medication and behavioral components into a more comprehensive and, it is hoped, long-lasting treatment package.

In their review, Hinshaw et al. (in press) consider two types of behavioral programs: direct contingency management procedures (specialized, classroom-based intensive management strategies) and those they term "clinical behavior therapy" (usually involving PMT plus teacher consultation). They concluded that both direct contingency management and clinical behavior therapy procedures can produce significant short-term reductions in off-task and disruptive behavior. On the other hand, although behavioral approaches can be effective in combination with medication, medication alone is usually more effective than behavioral treatment alone in terms of (a) the amount of behavioral change, (b) the range of outcomes affected, and (c) the degree to which children can be considered as having moved into the nonclinical range for behavioral disturbance. On the other hand, Abikoff and Klein (Abikoff & Gittelman, 1984) reported that clinical behavior therapy was effective in normalizing observed aggression in children with ADHD.

Firestone et al. (1981) assigned 7-year-olds with a diagnosis of ADHD to either PMT alone, stimulant medication alone, or PMT plus medication groups. The PMT component consisted of a combination of individual and group sessions over 3 months' time, coupled with teacher consultation. Of 93 families meeting inclusion criteria, less than half (N = 43) followed the treatment and completed the posttests. Whereas children in all three groups improved, relative to baseline, in nonblind parent and teacher ratings of disruptive behavior, only medication enhanced attention and impulse control; medication improved

academic achievement more than PMT alone. Average effect sizes for disruptive behavior were somewhat larger for the medication groups (1.7 and 1.3 for medication alone and with parent training) than for the PMT alone group (1.1), whereas effect sizes for academic and attention measures clearly indicated the advantages of medication (.78, .58, and .32, respectively, for medication alone, medication plus PMT, and PMT alone conditions).

Gittelman, Abikoff, and their colleagues (Gittelman et al., 1980) randomly assigned 6- to 12-year-old children referred for ADHD to one of three treatment conditions. These were either a behavioral treatment combining individual PMT sessions with school consultation, stimulant medication, or medication plus the behavioral package. Treatment lasted 8 weeks, and 61 of 64 children completed therapy. Controlling for baseline levels, children in both medication groups were rated by blind observers as less disruptive. Posttreatment classroom observation showed that the group receiving combined treatment was indistinguishable from normal classmates, those receiving behavioral treatment alone were more disruptive than classmates, and the behavior of those receiving medication alone was somewhat, but not completely, "normalized." These findings were confirmed by teacher ratings: After treatment, teachers rated all of the "combined" group as improved, as compared to 76% of the medication-only group and 63% of the behavioral group. Effect sizes for medication with and without PMT on teachers' ratings ranged between 0.8 and 1.1. Mothers' ratings showed a less consistent pattern.

Horn and co-workers (Horn et al., 1991; Ialongo et al., 1993) randomly assigned 96 families of children meeting criteria for ADHD to one of six groups. Children received either placebo, or low or high dose of stimulant medication. Half of the families in each of the three medication groups also received group-administered SCT for children plus PMT groups for parents. Of the original 96 families, 78 completed treatment and 71 were available 9 months posttreatment. At the completion of treatment, teacher report of disruptive and inattentive behavior in groups receiving stimulant medication was lower than for those not receiving medication. There was no advantage of combined treatment relative to medication alone (Horn et al., 1991). Nine months after the termination of treatment (and of medication), treatment gains, even for "medication plus" groups, were not maintained (Ialongo et al., 1993).

Pelham and colleagues (Carlson et al., 1992; Pelham et al., 1993) have published a series of reports of combined stimulant and CCT treatment for boys with ADHD attending a special, intensive, therapeutic summer camp. In this context, CCT consists of a campwide strict behavioral regimen. In a within-subject design, level of stimulant medication (placebo, low dose, high dose) was varied randomly across counterbalanced levels of CCT. Although results differ somewhat across studies, in general, medication, with or without CCT, improved all behavioral and academic outcomes. CCT, with or without medication, enhanced behavioral outcomes. Importantly, in one study (Carlson et al., 1992), CCT enhanced the efficacy of low-dose medication, suggesting that children with ADHD who are receiving behavioral treatments may be able to be maintained on a lower dose of stimulants than those on medication alone. The average effect size for CCT was 1.24 without medication, but this increased to 2.94 and 2.73, respectively, at low and high doses of medication. Effect sizes for medication were comparable, whether or not the CCT component was included.

The longest trials of behavioral techniques (primarily PMT and CCT) used to date in comparative treatment studies for ADHD have lasted only a few months. Moreover, these comparative studies have only just begun to build on the use of other successful treatment components that are available. A series of promising reports from the early 1980s (Satterfield, Satterfield, & Schell, 1987) suggested that a comprehensive and long-term treatment package might be useful. The program combined methylphenidate treatment with components of individual, family, and educational therapy. Depending on the needs of children and their families, different components were provided for different families. In general, compared to those treated with medication alone, the 6- to 12-year-old children treated in this manner showed improvements in school and at home; academic skills increased and antisocial behavior decreased.

Although Hinshaw et al. (in press) note a number of design problems with these reports, including nonrandom assignment of families to treatment conditions and substantial attrition, they suggest that longer-term, multicomponent treatment packages might be efficacious in treating children with ADHD, including those with co-occurring antisocial behavior. Two ongoing studies examine the relative efficacy of medication versus more intensive and integrated psychosocial treatments. Although outcome data are not yet available from either study, it is reasonable to expect that these longer-term, multisystemic interventions will prove to be effective in reducing delinquent behavior.

The New York/Montreal Study (Abikoff & Hechtman, 1996) is a recently completed treatment study for children with ADHD being conducted in New York and Montreal. All children received stimulant medication and are randomly assigned to either no further treatment (stimulant medication only), to an attention control condition, or to multimodal therapy. Multimodal therapy provides for a combination of intensive and long-lasting interventions directed at both parents and children, including SCT, PMT, academic tutoring, and individual therapy.

The NIMH Multimodal Treatment Study of Children With Attention-Deficit Hyperactivity Disorder (MTA) is a multisite cooperative agreement sponsored by the National Institute of Mental Health (NIMH) and cosponsored by the U.S. Department of Education Office of Special Education Programs. It is the largest study of its kind. The aim of this project is to evaluate the long-term effectiveness of single-focused medication treatment versus behavioral treatment versus the combination of the two conditions, and to compare these intensive treatments with routine community care. The protocol consists of a parallel-groups design with 576 children (96 at each of six sites), age 7 to 9 with a diagnosis of ADHD. Children and families are thoroughly assessed and randomly assigned to one of four conditions: medication alone, psychosocial treatment alone, the combination of both, or community standard care. The 14-month-long psychosocial treatment integrates direct classroom contingency management (CCT) provided during the summer, along with weekly group and individual PMT sessions and teacher classroom consultation during the year.

Clinicians delivering care for the three active treatment conditions rely on decision algorithms and standardized treatment guidelines. Main outcome measures will test major study questions, including the hypothesis that those children randomized to the three intensive treatments will have better overall functioning at 14 and 24 months than those receiving community care.

It should be clear that although effect sizes in treatment studies are considerably higher than those for universal interventions, psychostimulant medication has a particularly powerful enhancing effect on the functioning of children with ADHD. Whether stimulant medication can be shown to have a long-term

impact in preventing antisocial behavior remains to be seen. On the other hand, to the degree that medication allows children to function better in school and at home, it permits acquisition of a set of adaptive, protective skills that enhance child functioning in the long run.

Indicated interventions for elementary-aged children. In an intervention conducted by Webster-Stratton and Hammond (1997), parents of 97 children with conduct problems were randomly assigned to one of four conditions: a PMT group, a child training group, a child and parent training group, or a waiting-list control group. Criteria for study entry were (a) child age 4 to 7 years old; (b) the child had no debilitating physical impairment, intellectual deficit, or history of psychosis and was not receiving any form of psychological treatment at the time of referral; (c) the primary referral problem was for child misconduct; (d) parents reported a significant number of child behavior problems; and (e) the child met *DSM-III-R* (American Psychiatric Association, 1987) criteria for ODD or CD.

Parents in the PMT groups met weekly with a therapist for 2-hour sessions, with approximately 10 other parents, for 22-24 weeks. The child training groups used a newly developed videotape program showing over 100 vignettes of children in a variety of social situations and settings. The program focuses on the following difficulties experienced by children with conduct problems: lack of social skills and conflict resolution skills, loneliness and negative attributions, inability to empathize or to understand another's perspective, and problems at school. Children attended group with 4 to 5 other children. Children viewed vignettes of child interactions and then participated in a discussion in which the child therapist elicited children's reactions, ideas, and questions about the material. Parent and child groups were led by master's- or doctoral-level clinicians with considerable experience with children with conduct problems. Clinicians received extensive training, and careful attention was paid to treatment integrity.

Families were assessed at baseline, 2 months after treatment, and 1 year later. Assessments included parent report, observations of parent and child interactions at home, and observations of peer interactions in the clinic playroom. Immediately postintervention, all three treatment conditions resulted in significant improvements compared to controls. The child group and the combined condition led to significant improvements in problem-solving as well as conflict management skills. Parents and children in the parent group and the combined group had significantly more positive interactions at home compared to children in the child-only and control conditions.

At the 1-year follow-up, all the gains made at the immediate postintervention assessment were maintained. Importantly, the combined group showed the most significant improvements in child behavior at follow-up. However, children in all three groups showed increases in conduct problems at follow-up as reported by their teachers.

Kazdin, Siegel, and Bass (1992) randomly assigned children (ages 7-13) who were inpatients at a child psychiatric hospital (Kazdin et al., 1987a) or who had been referred for antisocial behavior problems (Kazdin et al., 1992) to either PMT, SCT, or both. Of the 97 outpatient children beginning treatment (Kazdin et al., 1992), approximately 80% ($N = 76$) completed the program; dropouts were not distributed significantly differently across intervention conditions. Although children who dropped out of treatment had significantly lower IQ than completers, no other differences were found between completers and dropouts. Of the 40 inpatient children who began the study (Kazdin, Esveldt-Dawson, French, & Unis, 1987a), 36 completed treatment, and 1-year follow-up data were available from parents and teachers for approximately 80% of the subjects. One-year posttreatment, both inpatient and outpatient children and families who received the combined treatment made greater improvements in functioning than controls. For the combined treatment relative to controls, effect sizes were generally above .7 (Kazdin et al., 1987a). In addition, more children in the combined group moved into the nonclinical range of functioning compared to children receiving only a single mode of intervention, according to parent report but not teacher report (Kazdin et al., 1992). The mean level of problem behavior for the combined condition fell within the normal range according to both parent and teacher report. This relatively intensive combined treatment resulted in placing only 50% of the children in this condition into the normal range of behavior problems according to both parents and teachers.

Program implementation. Although a multicomponent program may be offered, not all families make equal use of the components in the condition to which they are assigned. Volunteer parent groups, in particular, are likely to have poor enrollment. For example, in the Metropolitan Area Child Study (Tolan & McKay, 1996), of the 387 families eligible for the parenting intervention, only 89% could be located; of those located, only 81% actually attended 3 or more of the intended 22 sessions, despite great effort from project staff. One of the few studies to systematically address issues of program implementation is the Seattle Social Development Project (Hawkins, Von Cleve, & Catalano, 1991). Even though use by the volunteer parent groups was very low, the number of parenting classes attended had essentially no relationship to subsequent teacher behavioral ratings. As for teachers' implementation of program, systematic classroom observations in the Seattle Social Development Project confirmed that intervention teachers were significantly more likely to make use of the experimental teaching techniques than were control teachers (Hawkins, Von Cleve, & Catalano, 1991).

Programs for Adolescents

Programs targeting adolescents are summarized in Table 10.3 and are described more fully below.

Rationale for this age range. By age 15, most individuals who will manifest serious antisocial behavior have already begun to do so. Interventions at this point are then often secondary prevention efforts to alter the course of such developmental trends. Although it is easier at this age to identify antisocial youth, behavior may have become so entrenched that it is increasingly resistant to change. Because of the increasing developmental importance of peers, most programs in this age range have included the peer group as either a target of change (when an individual is encouraged to abandon an antisocial group of friends) or a vehicle of change (when peers are used as counselors or mediators). Unfortunately, to a degree, this has meant that programs for this age range are less concerned with working with families than at other ages, although families still play an important role in the social control of adolescents.

Universal interventions for adolescents. Many programs aimed at violence reduction or conflict resolution among adolescents, especially early adolescents, have recently been developed (see Brewer et al., 1995; Hawkins, Catalano, & Brewer, 1995a, for additional re-

views). These offer didactic and group-based curricula to promote social skills and social problem solving.

Several of these programs are directed at African American youth (e.g., Hammond & Yung, 1991, 1992, 1993; Ringwalt, Graham, Pascall, Flewelling, & Browne, 1996) and have sought to make materials more culturally relevant, and to address particular strengths and weaknesses likely to be found in these populations, such as poverty or perceptions of ethnic pride. Unfortunately, studies of these programs frequently rely on self-report measures of behavioral or attitudinal change that are especially vulnerable to social desirability, or on nonblind teacher evaluations that are equally vulnerable to bias. Many programs also make use of anger control strategies, a component, as noted above, whose effectiveness has not been demonstrated (Tolan & Guerra, 1994b). Randomized assignment to intervention and control groups is rare, and many studies have made use of "matched" controls (from nonparticipating schools) with varying degrees of success. As with other school-based interventions, attrition is a substantial problem, because children from impoverished families show high rates of residential mobility, moving out of an intervention when they move out of a particular school district (see Brewer et al., 1995, for a review). As an added word of caution, certain programs have shown paradoxical effects, such that they may inadvertently lead to worsened outcomes for particular subgroups of children. However, given the small effect sizes of such programs, the large and varied populations intervened with, and the large number of statistical comparisons made in an effort to evaluate program efficacy, it is most likely that such paradoxically adverse outcomes are themselves unreliable, and effects may well be reversed with additional testing. Farrell and Meyer (1997), testing a social skills/social problem-solving curriculum designed primarily for African American sixth graders, noted that although both intervention and waiting-list control students reported more problem behaviors from the beginning to the end of the semester, the rate of increase in problems for boys in the intervention condition was significantly less than for control boys. Unfortunately, group differences were only assessed by youth self-report, rather than by other observers or by archival data, such as arrest data. The program also had *opposite* effects in one semester on boys and girls, so that intervention girls reported increased problem behavior relative to the rate of change in controls. The authors suggested that this may have been a consequence of the different forms of aggression seen in boys and girls, or may have been an inadvertent result of offering the program in mixed-sex groups and making use of only male group leaders, who may have supported and served as positive role models more for the boys in the groups than for the girls.

Orpinas, Parcel, McAlister, and Frankowski (1995) evaluated the effectiveness of the Second Step curriculum (Committee for Children, 1990) on sixth graders. Classrooms in two schools were assigned to either a control condition, one in which regular teachers taught a conflict resolution curriculum, or one in which the conflict resolution program was combined with trained peer mediators. Teachers taught the 15-lesson curriculum two-three times per week. Because peer mediators might have an impact on students not in their targeted classrooms, in two additional schools only the control and conflict resolution classrooms were designated. Unfortunately, analyses did not take advantage of this design feature to separately examine the conflict resolution condition alone in schools with and without a peer mediation component operating. Also, the choice of either school or classroom was not random: Principals nominated "good and interested" teachers to implement the curriculum, allowing the strong possibility that classes differed systematically in ways beyond the presence of the intervention. As with other similar studies, outcomes included only self-report measures. Overall, relative to baseline, the study reported no effect of the intervention on aggressive behavior, a marginal improvement in violence-related knowledge and social skills, and an improvement in attitudes toward violence only in the conflict resolution plus peer mediation condition.

Program implementation. Generally, these programs have problems with treatment fidelity, a likely result of lack of specification in a treatment manual. Student participation tends to be high, but many students do not complete assessments (e.g., Farrell & Meyer, 1997; Orpinas et al., 1995). Analyses have generally not examined the impact of program fidelity on outcome.

Selected interventions for adolescents. Gottfredson (1986) evaluated a well-designed multicomponent school-based program (Project PATHE) for impoverished 11- to 17-year-olds. Students in four high schools and four middle schools were selected for being in the top 10% of their schools for academic and behavior problems, and they were then randomly assigned to either a control condition or to a comprehensive, 3-year intervention. For comparison purposes, an additional high school and middle school were designated as controls. Intervention included vocational and behavioral counseling, tutoring, peer counseling, and use of a student leadership system. Teachers were provided with training and classroom consultation. Family intervention did not include a PMT component, but focused on enhanced communication with the family about academic and discipline problems. The program sought

(text continued on p. 238)

TABLE 10.3 Interventions for Adolescents

Authors	Risk Factors	Subjects	Design	Rx Components	Targeted Outcomes	Findings
			Universal interventions			
Gainer, Webster, and Champion (1993)	Residence in high-crime neighborhoods	I: two classes of fifth graders plus three classes of seventh graders (N = 135); C: same classes, following year (N = 115)	Matched cohort design, conducted in consecutive years	15, 50-minute classes, taught over 3 weeks, including SCT (7 sessions), changing proaggression beliefs, risks of weapon carrying, drug and alcohol avoidance (3 sessions)	Problem-solving skills, awareness of risks, endorsement of acceptability of aggressive behavior	For endorsement of acceptability of aggression, knowledge of risks for violence, I < C; for social problem-solving skills, findings mixed
Farrell and Meyer (1997)	Poverty	Sixth graders in six urban middle schools: 348 I and 350 C (a later program cohort)	"Waiting list" control: two staggered cohorts of classrooms began the program in either fall or spring; pre-post comparisons	18 sessions across one semester, conducted by "trained prevention specialists"; curriculum taught during health classes; didactic and group exercises, stressing social problem-solving skills and self-control	Self-report of (a) adjustment, (b) violent behavior, (c) illegal activities, (d) drug/alcohol use	Although for most children problem behavior increased with time, compared to baseline, I boys increased less in b, c, and d. I girls showed either no effect or worsened relative to controls
Orpinas, Parcel, McAlister, and Frankowski (1995)	Universal	223 sixth-grade students	In each of two schools, classrooms assigned to control (C), conflict resolution (CR), or conflict resolution plus peer mediation (CRP); in two other schools, classrooms assigned to C or CR; pre-post comparisons	Second Step: 15 classroom teacher-led lessons and role play, covering causes and consequences of violence, training in developing empathy and social problem-solving skills	Self-reported (a) aggressive behavior, (b) violence prevention knowledge and skills, (c) attitudes toward violence	Relative to baseline, compared to C, CR and CRP groups together showed no effect of the intervention on a, marginal impact on b, and significant impact on c only for the CRP groups

Study	Type	Sample	Design	Intervention	Measures	Results
Bosworth, Espelage, and DuBay (1997); Bosworth et al. (in press); Bosworth, Espelage, DuBay, Dahlberg, and Daytner (1996): SMART TALK	Universal	Pilot: 81 seventh graders in the same suburban middle school ($N = 404$). Randomized assignment by classroom, of sixth, seventh, and eighth graders assigned to I (403) or to C (429)	Pilot: pre-post comparisons. Randomized trial: pre-post comparisons	I: following training, 16 weeks of voluntary access to computer-based curriculum covering conflict resolution, anger control, and acquisition of prosocial skills	Self-report of (a) knowledge of triggers to conflict situations, (b) self-knowledge of how their behavior might escalate conflict, (c) self-reported prosocial behavior, (d) intent to use nonviolent strategies in the future, (e) frequency of "being in trouble" past 30 days	For pilot (404), relative to baseline, significant improvements in b, c, d, e. For randomized control (403, 429), for b and d: relative to baseline, I > C
Ringwalt, Graham, Pascall, Flewelling, and Browne (1996)	Poverty	Convenience sample of African American 14-year-old boys	Randomized comparison and waiting-list control, comparing controls (C: $N = 87$) with jobs plus Junior Achievement (JA) program (JJA: 85) and JJA plus rites of passage (ROP: 88)	ROP: 8 months of adult mentoring including 16 two-hour group sessions, focusing on conflict resolution, sexuality, and health and monthly parent meetings; 6-week paid summer job; 3-month JA program	Violent behavior, mediated by (a) beliefs supporting aggression, (b) conflict resolution skills, (c) hostility, and (d) ethnic identity	Not yet reported
Webster-Stratton (1997)	Poverty (Head Start participants)	210 Head Start mothers and their 4-year-old children from eight Head Start centers	Random assignment of centers to experimental and control conditions	I = PARTNERS program, included parent training and teacher training; C = regular center-based Head Start program	Parenting, child conduct problems, child social competence	I mothers were less critical, used less physically negative discipline and were more positive, appropriate, and consistent in discipline compared with C mothers. I mothers were more involved in child's education than C mothers. I children exhibited fewer negative behaviors were more compliant had more positive affect and more prosocial behaviors than C children

(continued)

TABLE 10.3 Continued

Authors	Risk Factors	Subjects	Design	Rx Components	Targeted Outcomes	Findings
			Selected interventions			
Gottfredson, D. C. (1986): Project PATHE	Poverty, academic and behavior problems	11- to 17-year-olds in four middle schools and four high schools, mostly African American and impoverished; top 10% on academic and behavior problems; also one high school and one middle school as controls; I: $n = 468$, C: $n = 401$	Selected intervention, random assignment as I or C within designated schools, 3 years of intervention; outcome assessed after 2 years; pre-post	Vocational and behavior counseling, tutoring, peer counseling, student leadership team, enhanced communication with family about attendance and disciplinary problems	Decrease academic failure, increase attachment to school, improve self-esteem, improve teachers' management skills, increase student-faculty communication	For promotion and graduation rates, I > C. For drug involvement, I > C. No other significant effects on delinquency
Gottfredson and Gottfredson (1992): Project STATUS	High-risk youth (not specified)	12- to 17-year-olds in one high school and one middle school; I: $n = 120$, C: $n = 127$	Selected intervention; random assignment to I or C; yearlong curriculum; pre-post	Law-related curriculum, covering school, family, interpersonal relations, justice system; field experiences and structured role play	Moral reasoning, endorsement of conventional social norms, increased school attachment	For self-report of delinquency and drug use, I < C. For grades, promotions, graduations, attachment to school, and self-esteem, I > C.
Gabriel (1996): Self-Enhancement, Inc. (SEI)	Teacher referrals, based on poor attendance, academic or behavioral problems.	I: 102 urban African American children, Grades 8-10, in three middle and one high school; C: 180 matched youth	I group matched to C group of students in same grade and school, on demographic, behavioral, and academic factors; pre-post comparisons	3 years, 14 hours/week, including (a) conflict resolution curriculum (anger management and mediation), (b) field trips to community organizations dealing with violence, (c) student participation in design of materials that communicate about violence to their communities	Risk behaviors: fighting, weapon carrying, alcohol or drug use; protective factors: personal and social competence, commitment to school, family and prosocial norms	After 1 year of the program, relative to baseline, I decreased in self-reported fighting, carrying a weapon; in general, C youth showed no changes in these over time. Both groups increased marijuana use. No changes in protective factors

Indicated interventions

Henggeler, Melton, and Smith (1992); Henggeler, Melton, Smith, Schoenwald, and Hanley (1993)	Delinquents at risk of imminent incarceration	84 delinquents (mean age = 15 years, mean number of prior arrests = 3.5) and their families	Randomized assignment of youth to MST (n = 43) or C: usual Rx (n = 41) by Division of Youth Services; post-Rx and 1-year follow-up (188); 2.5-year follow-up (369)	MST: 33 hours of family Rx, family preservation, plus problem-focused interventions with peers and at school, lasting 13 weeks	Lessening dysfunctional family relations, reducing criminal behavior and incarceration	At end of treatment, family cohesiveness increased in MST, decreased in C. After 1 year, for rearrests, days incarcerated and peer aggression, MST < C. After 2.5 years, for rearrest rate, MST < C
Borduin et al. (1995)	Delinquents with history of ≥ two arrests	140 delinquents and their families	Random assignment to MST or individual therapy, post-Rx and 4-year follow-up	MST (N = 77; duration = 24 hours): see above; IT (N = 63; duration = 29 hours): supportive, insight-oriented, focused on adolescent	Improved individual adjustment and family and peer relations; decreased rate and seriousness of criminal activity	After Rx, for father, mother, and adolescent adjustment, for family cohesion and adaptability, for observed family supportiveness: MST > IT; for family conflict: MST < IT. After 4 years, for number and seriousness of arrests, MST < IT
Mann, Borduin, Henggeler, and Blaske (1990)	Two or more prior arrests for delinquency	45 adolescents, 13-17 years old, from intact families; each had at least two prior arrests for delinquency and most recent arrest was for serious crime	Adolescents and their families were randomly assigned to MST (N = 27) or IT (N = 18); evaluated 1 week after completion of therapy	MST (mean duration = 21 hours) and IT (mean duration = 29 hours) (for description, see above)	MST: Help parents develop limit setting, resolve marital conflict, lessen parent-adolescent negativity, promote warmth and cohesion. IT: promote insight and expression of feelings, provide support for behavior change	Relative to baseline, for decreased symptoms in M, F, and adolescent MST > IT; for F/adolescent supportiveness and F/M verbal activity, MST > IT; for F/adolescent conflict and F/M conflict, MST < IT

NOTE: I = intervention; C = control; Rx = treatment; SCT = social cognitive training; MST = multisystemic therapy; IT = individual therapy; M = mothers; F = fathers.

to improve functioning on a wide range of targeted student outcomes, including attachment to school, academic failure, self-esteem, and student-faculty communication. After 1 year and at project completion, intervention students had higher promotion and graduation rates than did controls.

Effect sizes were in most cases quite small, never going above .25 (except for graduation rates, where effect size = .68). There was no effect of the program on antisocial behavior, except that at posttest, self-report of drug involvement was *higher* in intervention, than in control, youth. Provision of regular feedback about discipline to parents, rather than a parent component that included more proactive skill building, may account for the lack of impact on behavioral outcomes. And paradoxically, increased opportunity for student socializing, in the absence of more focused programs aimed at SCT or moral reasoning (see also Gottfredson & Gottfredson, 1992, below), may actually *increase* the dispersion of antisocial activities such as drug use.

In another carefully evaluated program, Gottfredson and Gottfredson (1992) conducted an evaluation of Project STATUS, for students between 12 and 17 years old in one high school and one middle school. Based on staff and self-report, students considered high risk for antisocial behavior were randomly assigned to either regular curriculum or a supplemental law-related and moral development curriculum that considered school, family, and interpersonal relations and how these integrate with broader societal norms as implemented by the justice system. Students were also exposed to a variety of field experiences and to structured role play about the operation of these systems. The curriculum had a positive effect on both academic and behavioral domains. Compared to control youngsters, at the close of the program, intervention students reported lower levels of delinquency and drug use and higher levels of self-esteem. Intervention students had higher grades and were more likely to be promoted and to graduate than controls.

Gabriel (1996) evaluated Self-Enhancement, Inc. (SEI), a violence prevention program designed for African American students in Grades 8-10, referred for a wide range of academic or behavioral problems. The 14 hours/week program combines a classroom-based curriculum and activities, field trips to agencies or organizations that deal with violence, and student-led antiviolence media campaigns. The classroom curriculum consisted of conflict resolution skills, such as anger control and mediation, taught through group role-playing exercises. Field trips to such locations as a battered women's shelter or the local penitentiary are followed by discussion and feedback about youth observations. Students participated in designing and implementing public information events regarding discussion of community violence and of ways to resolve conflicts peacefully. The program was intended to lower problem behavior by enhancing certain intermediary "protective factors," such as self-control, self-efficacy, social competence, and social bonding. Participating students were compared to matched controls at each grade level and within each participating school. The program had 28% attrition across the first year. The evaluation failed to detect any changes over time in mediating protective factors. However, after a year of program participation, compared to control students who showed no changes in problem behavior, intervention students reported decreased fighting and carrying of weapons. Both intervention and control groups increased marijuana use over time.

Indicated interventions for adolescents. In a series of reports, Henggeler and his colleagues have discussed the application of multisystemic therapy (MST) with juvenile offenders (Borduin et al., 1995; Henggeler & Blaske, 1990; Henggeler & Borduin, 1990; Henggeler, Cunningham, Pickrel, Schoenwald, & Brondino, 1996; Henggeler, Melton, & Smith, 1992).

Based on the understanding of the multiple determinants of youth antisocial behavior, MST integrates concepts from family therapy and PMT techniques designed for older children, such as use of contracting, as well as problem-focused interventions in the peer and school settings, in an intensive family preservation treatment program. The precise set of interventions used with any particular family varies depending on the family's needs, and averages between 25 and 30 hours per family.

Evaluations of MST are particularly important for the present review because it is one of the few interventions that actually addresses treatment of serious juvenile offenders (Borduin et al., 1995; Henggeler et al., 1996; Henggeler, Melton, Smith, Schoenwald, & Hanley, 1993). In a number of reports of efficacy, MST has been compared to the standard treatment offered by the South Carolina Department of Youth Services (Henggeler et al., 1992; Henggeler et al., 1993), and to individual, insight-oriented therapy (IT) (Borduin et al., 1995; Henggeler & Blaske, 1990). After treatment, families randomly assigned to MST increased in cohesiveness, relative to pretreatment baseline, whereas those in standard care actually decreased (Henggeler et al., 1992); families of serious juvenile offenders receiving MST showed greater adaptability and support (Borduin et al., 1995) and less father-mother and father-adolescent conflict (Henggeler & Blaske, 1990) than in those families in which the adolescent received individual therapy. Relative to standard care (Henggeler et al., 1992), and to individual therapy (Henggeler & Blaske, 1990), adjustment of the father, mother, and adolescent were all higher at the close of

treatment among MST families. Importantly, during the year after treatment ended, compared to Division of Youth Services care, MST adolescents were less likely to be rearrested and spent fewer days incarcerated (Henggeler et al., 1992); by 120 weeks postreferral, 61% of the MST group had been rearrested, compared to 80% of those in standard care. These advantages were maintained for serious offenders through a 4-year follow-up assessment (Borduin et al., 1995), when MST adolescents had had fewer and less serious subsequent arrests than those treated with individual therapy (Borduin et al., 1995). Treatment gains appear to be maintained: Compared to those serious offenders receiving standard treatment (Henggeler & Blaske, 1990), MST-treated adolescents took longer to be rearrested (56.2 weeks vs. 31.7 weeks for those receiving standard care). At the 4-year follow up, the overall recidivism rate for MST completers was 22.1%, for IT completers 71.4%, for IT dropouts 71.4%, for treatment refusers 87.5%, and for MST dropouts 46.6%. Effect sizes for dimensions of family functioning are encouraging: For supportiveness and conflict directed by either parent to the adolescent, effect sizes ranged between 0.34 and 1.06, with most between .70 and .90.

MST is generally better tolerated by families than is IT; in two separate reports, dropout rates from treatment were 10% and 15% versus 38% and 25% for MST and individual therapy, respectively (Borduin et al., 1995; Henggeler et al., 1992), although completers and noncompleters did not differ in any of the several comparisons tested (Borduin et al., 1995). With respect to program implementation, therapist records indicate that MST does indeed promote interventions across a range of systems; for 51% of cases assigned to MST, therapists reported interventions targeted at three or more systems (i.e., family, school, peers), whereas in 90% of those assigned to individual therapy, interventions targeted a single system (Borduin et al., 1995).

■ General Limitations to Prevention Strategies

Developmental Issues

In this review, we have attempted to illustrate the many different approaches to the prevention of antisocial behavior in youth from multiple disciplines and to discuss the available outcome literature. We reviewed the programs by developmental periods (preschool, school age, and adolescents) for a number of reasons. First, the developmental psychopathology literature suggests that risk factors may operate differently at different time periods. For example, parent-child attachment and parental responsivity to child behavior may be particularly salient during the preschool period. School success and peer relations may be more important later on in development. For these reasons, programs for children of different ages have generally targeted different risk factors.

Infants and toddlers. In general, programs for infants and toddlers have aimed to alter parent-child interactions by providing education and emotional and practical support to the primary caregiver. The majority of these programs target poor families during pregnancy or soon after birth. A number of them have employed relatively sophisticated designs, including random assignment to treatment alternatives. Programs for children up to age 2 tend to be delivered either in the hospital or in the family's home. In general, these intervention programs have not been stan-

dardized, or described in manuals, thus calling into question the reliability of program implementation and the ease of wide-scale dissemination. Although families tend to be the target of these interventions, no study includes a specific component in which parents are taught behavioral management techniques (PMT) as described previously, even though applications of behavioral techniques to infants and toddlers are possible. This is important to note, because the specific parenting behaviors that are the focus of PMT programs have been found, in longitudinal and intervention studies, to be related to antisocial outcomes for children and adolescents. Furthermore, although programs tend to be relatively long, follow-up on child functioning has been limited. Program outcomes have generally focused on parental attachment to the child, follow-through with the care of the child and child adjustment, primarily in terms of health, with less focus on child behavior. The 15-year follow-up currently being conducted by Olds (1996) should certainly add to our understanding of the long-term effects on antisocial behavior of a program initiated in the prenatal period.

Preschoolers. A number of studies for preschoolers have included random assignment to control or intervention conditions that include family support plus child education components. Again, most of these programs have not included the specific PMT described earlier, perhaps because they were initiated in the 1960s, prior to the establishment of a large literature implicating deviant parenting practices as important risk factors for later antisocial behavior.

Furthermore, although peer relations are an important predictor of outcome, preschool intervention has not generally included specific components targeted toward peer relations (a common focus, on the other hand, in programs for adolescents). Unlike the programs for infants and toddlers, at least four of these preschool programs have included long-term follow-up into the period of risk for serious violent offending. Impressively, all four programs reviewed in this chapter showed significant positive effects on antisocial behavior with effect sizes ranging from .42 to 1.13. It is important to note that none of these programs was specifically designed to influence delinquent outcomes in youth, so that the potential mechanisms by which antisocial behavior may have changed were not studied adequately. Thus, although early preventive interventions that combine family and child components appear to have positive effects on offending outcomes, the essential ingredients for change are not known, and therefore the programs cannot be easily or economically replicated. As noted by Yoshikawa (1995), because these programs were conducted over 20 years ago, "numerous demographic, social and economic changes have occurred since then which might affect the outcomes of early intervention," including higher rates of women's employment (that might reduce the practicality of delivering frequent home visits) and increased youth involvement in the drug trade and handguns. This "suggests that family-focused interventions alone, without broader efforts to attack these neighborhood-level causal factors, may not have their intended impact" (Yoshikawa, 1995, p. 70). It is likely that community-based prevention programs and early intervention programs need to be combined in a comprehensive approach. We need studies that include well-standardized interventions described in manuals with regular evaluations over time so that the specific elements for change can be documented and eventually replicated.

The preschool program recently developed by Webster-Stratton represents such an approach. This program, which includes a specified PMT component, is described in a treatment manual, and a variety of materials are available for parents, including videotapes for parent groups. Assessments of immediate and short-term outcomes are very positive. Thus, the available studies suggest that such an early intervention approach is feasible and effective in preventing early conduct problems and later delinquency.

School-age children. Programs for school-age children have generally been based in the school setting with additional components added. As noted previously, once children enter school, the school setting is an obvious choice for intervention. Unfortunately, in many cases, the family components of these interventions are given secondary status and are not well-used by families. Therefore, it is not always clear that the family component has been tested as well as the school-based component.

In this chapter, we have noted the high likelihood of ADHD in children at risk for CDs and for later offending. It is clear that, with the exception of programs specifically designed for ADHD children, preventive intervention programs for school-age children do not regularly assess for ADHD, nor do they refer out or provide for treatment of this disorder. School-age programs more commonly include components that address academic functioning, another clear need for children at risk for antisocial behavior. We hope that this chapter will raise for consideration the possibility of specifically targeting the symptoms of ADHD in preventive intervention programs.

Unlike the majority of studies of programs for preschool-aged children, a number of studies for school-age children have directly contrasted one intervention approach against another (with both contrasted against a no-treatment control). Such an approach is clearly necessary for drawing conclusions about essential program components as well as informing the field with regard to the development of antisocial behavior.

In general, classroom-level interventions that include control and intervention classrooms within the same school are subject to spillover effects, as the control classrooms may begin to adopt elements of the intervention curriculum. This has been minimized in certain designs (e.g., Hawkins, Catalano, Morrison, et al., 1992; Hawkins, Von Cleve, & Catalano, 1991; Kellam & Rebok, 1992; Kellam et al., 1991) by designating some schools as pure controls, some as purely intervention, and others as mixed with random assignment to control or intervention within the school.

Adolescence. In general, programs oriented toward adolescence concentrate heavily on educational approaches targeted toward the adolescent in isolation. One central omission is the relative lack of programs that include family components. As for younger children, the problems shown by adolescents carry over (or originate) in the home setting. Parenting and household management issues are surely relevant to the maintenance of antisocial behavior in adolescence, where insufficient monitoring, lack of consistent household rules, or excessive use of physical punishment may all contribute. We agree with Tolan and Guerra (1994a) that even in this age range, programs will be more successful to the extent that they "provide more opportunity for the students to be involved in prosocial activities at school and to establish a clear reward system that is closely tied to academic performance *and* is consistently implemented at home and among school personnel" (p. 263).

Decisions not to include a family component for adolescents may occur more commonly in universal programs, because of the practical difficulties of involving parents of nonreferred adolescents when the parents may not think they are in noticeable difficulty. It may be easier to include parents in selected or indicated programs, where the adolescent has already been identified as at risk or problematic. Despite such practical difficulties, however, we would strongly recommend creative initiatives to include a family component in programs aimed at adolescents, even if these are universal in design. The success of programs, such as Henggeler's (Borduin et al., 1995; Henggeler et al., 1992; Henggeler et al., 1993), that include a family management component in treating already seriously antisocial adolescents demonstrates the power of such an approach.

Treatment of the adolescent outside of the context of his or her family may be one factor behind the uneven results shown by conflict resolution programs. The uneven results of such programs include paradoxical effects (whereby the intervention group appears *worse,* relative to controls, after the intervention), minimal program effectiveness overall, or effects confined to subgroups (one school, one sex). Although such programs may teach adolescents (or others) in a school program how to negotiate, and how to use nonconfrontational dispute resolution strategies, if the home environment continues to model power-assertive approaches to disagreements, it is unlikely that the adolescent will internalize new learning and generalize it across settings.

The focus of adolescent programs on the adolescent alone also carries with it a unidimensional approach to assessment of outcomes and potential mediators. If the adolescent is the only individual available to the program developers, assessments are likely to rely exclusively on self-report and are thereby subject to informant bias. Programs that do not include independent records or raters who are blind to intervention assignment are quite limited in this regard. Such programs need to make an extra effort to obtain archival data, such as arrest information (Bry, 1982; Bry & George, 1980) or frequency of school vandalism incidents (Mayer et al., 1983; Mayer & Butterworth, 1979; Sulzer-Azaroff & Mayer, 1994). As suggested by Webster (1993), without these enhancements to their primarily psychoeducational approach, conflict resolution curricula are unlikely to have a substantive, sustained impact on youth violence.

General Problems in Defining and Measuring Outcomes

Defining targets. To be effective, programs should target outcomes that are either developmentally linked to later serious antisocial behavior (such as earlier aggressivity, serious disobedience, physical fighting, lying, and theft) or that are specific risk or protective factors (such as incompetent and inconsistent parenting, and overreliance on physical punishment). Unfortunately, a number of programs that focus on hypothesized risk factors, such as moral reasoning, do not measure behavioral outcomes. Changes in intermediary outcomes measured do not always correspond to a change in child behavior. For example, programs aimed at changes in moral reasoning may change children's cognitions, but if they do not also decrease antisocial behavior, then their utility is questionable.

Effectiveness. When risk factors, such as family process or early disruptive behavior, are targeted, effect sizes are generally small. Thus, for one of the better documented programs (Hawkins, Catalano, Morrison, et al., 1992), whereas targeted processes were influenced by the intervention, and differences were statistically significant, effect sizes

were in the range of .3, and odds ratios for lowered likelihood of later alcohol use or delinquent behavior remained close to 1.0. Medication studies of children with ADHD often show large effect sizes on the symptoms of inattention and disruptiveness. Findings from Kazdin's selected interventions (Kazdin et al., 1987a; Kazdin et al., 1992) are also exceptions, revealing substantial treatment gains (effect size > 1) a year after treatment completion.

Specificity. A further problem in defining outcomes is that although in the aggregate, antisocial children are likely to show certain intermediate deficits such as poor social skills, not all antisocial children show the same pattern of problems. Outcomes selected as the focus of treatment may not necessarily be deficient at baseline in certain subjects. Such children will be unlikely to show treatment gains, giving the false impression that the intervention has been only moderately effective when it has perhaps had a substantial impact on certain children and not others. This suggests that we need more research on which preventive approaches are most effective with certain subtypes of children, such as those with cognitive deficits or those with poor peer relations.

A neglected outcome. Moreover, as we have noted above, most interventions focus on reduction in overt aggressive behavior. Even though physical aggression is indeed an important precursor of subsequent serious and violent delinquency, and may be easy to observe, this has meant that not enough attention has been given to reducing covert antisocial acts. This is especially important, because the majority of later delinquent behaviors are covert in nature.

Length of follow-up. Because of the chronic and pervasive nature of child conduct problems, generalization across settings and long-term maintenance of treatment gains is important to demonstrate. Unfortunately, most studies fail to do so. There are very few reports of long-term follow-up, with follow-up of even a year a rarity (Kazdin, 1993).

Gender. Finally, we, among others, have argued elsewhere (Wasserman, 1996) that the manifestation and developmental sequencing of antisocial behavior may be very different for boys and girls. Overall, preventive interventions appear to have been designed with boys, and not girls, in mind; many programs have been applied only to boys; and in a number of cases, even when girls are included, there has been limited program effectiveness with girls (e.g., Farrell & Meyer, 1997; Kellam et al., in press). Newer conceptualizations of the nature of girls' antisocial behavior are currently being developed (Crick, Bigbee, & Howes, 1996; Crick & Grotpeter, 1995; Zoccolillo, 1993), and we look forward to a corresponding change in the design and effectiveness of prevention programs.

Mapping Selection Criteria and Targeted Outcomes Onto Risk Research

Conceptualizations of risk factors for problematic child outcomes, such as delinquency and violence, have included variables at numerous levels. For example, Hawkins and Catalano (1993), in defining risks for adolescent problem behaviors, include risks at the level of the community (such as media portrayals of violence), the family (such as family management problems), the school (such as early academic failure), and the individual/peer (such as exposure to deviant peers) as among the factors contributing to youth violence. Unfortunately, our ideas about risk factors do not map readily onto research into prevention. It is informative to contrast the risk factors for serious and violent offending with those that have been considered as risks, or as intermediate outcomes, in preventive interventions.

We must first distinguish between the degree to which factors such as those noted above have been targeted to *select* children at high risk or whether these factors have themselves been the *targets* of intervention. Individual or neighborhood poverty is very often a proxy for selecting children exposed to community risks, although it is very often not an accurate selection factor.

Interventions aimed at reduction of community risk factors, such as media portrayals of violence or residential mobility, reflect cultural concerns beyond the limits of what we generally view as preventive interventions. Community risk factors, then, are very often employed in selection criteria, but rarely targeted themselves for reduction. For family risk factors, however, the reverse seems to be the case. For example, children and families are rarely selected on the basis of observable family management problems, although these are quite typically the focus of intervention. Problems in family management, or family conflict, are *assumed* to be present in families selected on the basis of other risk factors, such as child aggressivity or family poverty.

Finally, for selected and indicated interventions, school and individual risk factors are often used as selection criteria for the inclusion of children already showing problem behavior. They are also very commonly the focus of intervention. In a number of instances, targeted outcomes designated by prevention efforts include those not identified by descriptive/predictive risk studies as being linked to serious violent offending or to offending at all. These targeted outcomes include "social competency," "improved peer relations," "sense of self-control," "self-concept," "adjustment," "prosocial behavior," "violence prevention knowledge," "ethnic identity," and "student-faculty communication." Some of these, such as improved peer relations, adjustment, or self-concept, are just too general to be considered useful targets for intervention. For example, although exposure to deviant/antisocial peers *is* a documented risk, there is little evidence that global deficits in peer relations are contributory to the development of antisocial behavior. For the most part, items in this list are positive qualities, behaviors, and skills, although this does not mean that they are protective factors whose growth might lessen risk for antisocial behavior. For certain targeted outcomes, such as ethnic identity or violence prevention knowledge, there is little information one way or the other to indicate that their absence would, in fact, operate as risks. In this light, we should reemphasize, *protective factors* are not simply the opposite end of measures of *risk factors*.

Beyond this, there are some known risk factors that are not commonly examined in prevention research. For example, family history of problem behavior, although obviously not a suitable candidate for intervention, is an excellent selection criterion, because children whose family members (including siblings) have shown antisocial behavior are at risk themselves (Cadoret, 1991; Patterson, 1984; Rowe & Gulley, 1992; Wasserman et al., 1996). Programs aimed, for example, at preventing offending in the younger siblings of identified delinquents, for example, reflect an underused strategy. Furthermore, as we have noted elsewhere in this chapter, constitutional risks (such as comorbid psychiatric conditions, including ADHD) are important both as selection criteria and as intervention targets, although programs aimed at prevention of serious and violent offending have not included components for either referral or treatment of such children. These are important gaps for future research to consider.

Practical Issues

Feasibility of recruiting and maintaining participants. As mentioned earlier, one reason that school-based programs have increased in popularity is that the children and adolescents provide a relatively "captive audience." That is, the program is brought to the school instead of asking the participants to come to the program. Although it is clear that family involvement is a necessary aspect of intervention at all ages, the practical difficulties in involving families are quite complex. The rate of failed appointments in general outpatient child psychiatry clinics is very high, especially in families with antisocial youth. Given the fact that parents who are seeking treatment fail to cooperate, one might anticipate that parents who are not seeking help for current problems would be even more unlikely to be motivated to attend sessions after initial interest in the prevention program. The retention of control families in prevention studies is also a major challenge.

Investigators have used many techniques to maximize cooperation and minimize dropouts in family-focused studies. For example, Miller and Klein (1996) conducted a pilot randomized clinical trial with 30 families of children at high risk for the development of antisocial behavior. Subjects were 30 preschoolers (ages 2 to 4 years) who had older siblings with documented histories of antisocial behavior. The majority of families were recruited through court records. Subjects were primarily poor, minority, single-parent families from New York City. The intervention was family focused, provided in a hospital setting and in the family's home. The intervention offered 60 sessions over 1 year, and required approximately 5 hours of participation a week. Families attended hospital-based parent and child groups twice weekly and received home visits twice each month.

A number of procedures were instituted specifically designed to maintain parent participation. Families were paid for assessments and for costs associated with clinic visits; food was provided; initial contact assessments were conducted in the home; cards were sent to families for holidays, birthdays, and so on; families were tracked on a regular basis; names, telephone numbers, and addresses of two family members or friends who could be contacted were obtained; and referrals for appropriate services for family members were provided during the study for both control and intervention families. In addition, although groups were conducted in English, 50% of the intervenors were bilingual so that home visits could be conducted in Spanish.

The attrition rate (dropouts) and rate of attendance are the best indexes of the efficacy of the procedures. Only two families dropped out of the control group (not able to locate), and one dropped from the active intervention, representing an attrition rate of 10%. Attendance at the clinic-based groups was excellent, averaging 70%. Intervention parents completed a Consumer Satisfaction Questionnaire (Webster-Stratton, 1989). Satisfaction with the program was very high. All parents (100%) indicated that the material covered in the program was "very" to "extremely" useful and "easy" to implement. All (100%) endorsed that they would recommend the program to a friend. Given the low attrition rate, high program attendance and high satisfaction, it appears that an intensive, lengthy intervention can be implemented with high-risk families, given sufficient incentives for participation and attention to the needs and strengths of the families. A randomized clinical trial with 100 families is under way (Miller & Klein, 1996).

Identifying salient components. Each of the components discussed in this chapter has shown efficacy in preventing serious violent delinquency, or its precursors, at least in the short run. As we have noted throughout, long-term effectiveness has rarely been shown, especially for those programs that begin after school entry. Current theories concerning the development of chronic aggression suggest that intervention in any single domain is unlikely to be very effective. What seems to be most promising are multifaceted interventions that are directed toward the major domains of behavioral development and that last for many years, covering all the developmental periods considered here. Because antisocial behavior is often acquired and maintained in the home and peer settings, components oriented toward PMT and peer relations are strongly recommended. Further academic failure and other forms of child psychopathology that commonly appear along with antisocial behavior interfere with the acquisition of prosocial skills and alternatives to aggression; programs that enhance academic success, and those that include procedures for identification and referral for other treatable comorbid conditions, such as ADHD, are also strongly recommended. Additionally, because aggression appears early in development and is increasingly difficult to alter as the child gets older, preventive interventions should be focused early in development and during important developmental transitions, such as school entry or the transition to middle school. Finally, multicomponent programs should ensure that they integrate treatment across domains (family, school, peers), so that skills acquired in one setting will generalize across settings.

Conclusions

Child antisocial behavior emerges from the convergence of multiple risk factors; designating any single factor as a target for change is unlikely to be a successful intervention strategy. Clearly, programs that ignore the family in strict reliance on school-based interventions, or those that fail to consider and refer for treatment children with other psychopathology, are unlikely to show powerful effects.

Finally, interventions that work very well with problematic (selected, indicated) samples may not transfer well to application in a universal setting, where not all children will be showing similar levels of problem behavior. Interventions must be theory driven and well described, taking into account both developmental and contextual factors, regardless of the specific age or risk group targeted.

CHAPTER 11

Comprehensive Community- and School-Based Interventions to Prevent Antisocial Behavior

■ *Richard F. Catalano, Michael W. Arthur, J. David Hawkins, Lisa Berglund, & Jeffrey J. Olson*

The knowledge base for developing effective interventions to prevent antisocial behavior among children and adolescents has expanded dramatically in recent years (e.g., Hawkins, Arthur, & Catalano, 1995; Howell, Krisberg, Hawkins, & Wilson, 1995; Institute of Medicine [IOM], 1994; Jessor, 1993; Pepler & Rubin, 1991). Longitudinal research has revealed a consistent set of predictors of the development of antisocial behavior (Farrington, 1996a; Loeber, 1990). Risk factors that predict increased likelihood of antisocial behavior have been identified at the individual, family, school, peer group, and community levels (see chapters by J. David Hawkins and colleagues, Chapter 7, this volume, and Lipsey and Derzon, Chapter 6, this volume). The research also indicates that the likelihood of serious antisocial behavior is substantially greater among those exposed to multiple risk factors (Bry, McKeon, & Pandina, 1982; Howell, 1995; IOM, 1994; Newcomb, Maddahian, & Bentler, 1986). Moreover, many of the same risk fac-

AUTHORS' NOTE: We gratefully acknowledge support from the Office of Juvenile Justice and Delinquency Prevention, U.S. Department of Justice, Center for Substance Abuse Prevention, Substance Abuse and Mental Health Services Administration, and the Assistant Secretary for Planning and Evaluation/Department of Health and Human Services in the preparation of this chapter.

248

tors predict adolescent delinquency, violence, and substance abuse, and also predict dropping out of school, early sexual involvement, and teen pregnancy (Cairns, Cairns, & Neckerman, 1989; Coie et al., 1993; Dryfoos, 1990; J. D. Hawkins, 1995; Yoshikawa, 1994).

Studies have revealed, however, that many children avoid serious involvement in antisocial behavior despite exposure to multiple risk factors (e.g., Garmezy, 1985; Rutter, 1985; Werner & Smith, 1992). These studies have explored protective factors that appear to buffer against or mitigate the negative effects of risk exposure. Protective factors have been identified within individuals and within the social environment. Individual protective factors against antisocial behavior include female gender, high IQ, a resilient temperament, and a positive social orientation (Garmezy, 1985; Rutter, 1985). Social protective factors include warm, supportive relationships and social bonding to adults (Rutter, 1979; Werner & Smith, 1992); recognition for involvement in positive extracurricular activities (Rae-Grant, Thomas, Offord, & Boyle, 1989); and social institutions such as peer groups, schools, and communities that emphasize positive social norms, prosocial behavior, and educational success (Brewer, Hawkins, Catalano, & Neckerman, 1995; Rutter, Maughan, Mortimore, Ouston, & Smith, 1979). Preventive interventions should focus on enhancing protective factors while reducing risk factors.

The research suggests that interventions that reduce risk factors while enhancing protective factors in family, school, peer, and community environments over the course of infant, child, and adolescent development hold promise for preventing multiple adolescent health and behavior problems (Howell et al., 1995; Yoshikawa, 1994). A current challenge is to apply this knowledge base to reducing the prevalence of adolescent antisocial behavior (Biglan, 1995; Hawkins, Catalano, & Associates, 1992; Howell, 1995). Comprehensive interventions that support enduring community-level reductions in risk factors and increases in protective factors are required to achieve sustained reductions in the prevalence of antisocial behavior (Flay et al., 1989; Hawkins, Arthur, & Catalano, 1995; IOM, 1994).

The most promising comprehensive prevention models have been adapted from the field of public health (Hawkins, Arthur, & Olson, 1997; IOM, 1994; Moore, 1995). Comprehensive programs focused on reducing risk factors for heart and lung disease have demonstrated that community-level risk reduction is a viable prevention strategy (e.g., Farquhar, Fortmann, & Flora, 1990; Lefebvre, Lasater, Carleton, & Peterson, 1987; Perry, Kelder, Murray, & Klepp, 1992; Puska et al., 1989; Vartiainen, Pallonen, McAlister, & Puska, 1990). Given the success of these comprehensive interventions in reducing risk factors for heart disease, comprehensive interventions designed to reduce risk factors for violence, delinquency, and drug abuse are currently being implemented (Hawkins, Catalano, & Associates, 1992; Howell, 1995). The challenges presented by this approach include (a) using theories that are comprehensive and include both individual and environmental causes of problem behavior; (b) creating local ownership of the prevention efforts; and (c) providing community members with the skills needed to design a strategically selected, coordinated package of interventions that include effective risk reduction and protective factor enhancement strategies, to implement the selected interventions broadly with fidelity, and to monitor the effects of the community's efforts and adjust them appropriately.

This chapter reviews comprehensive school and community interventions to reduce risks and enhance protection to prevent adolescent antisocial behavior. Although few of these programs have examined their impact on serious and violent juvenile (SVJ) offending, these types of programs that address multiple risk factors in multiple domains may be the most effective approaches for preventing such problems from developing. Suggestions and promising leads for research and intervention with SVJ offenders will be addressed. Antisocial behavior includes conduct problems, violence, delinquency, and substance abuse in recognition of the interrelationships among these problems and the risk and protective factors that predict them. In this chapter, *comprehensive interventions* are defined as "interventions designed to change the social conditions and institutions (e.g., families, peers, social norms, clubs, [schools and other organizations]) that influence offending in residential communities" (Farrington, 1995). Because both schools and the broader community have been the setting for comprehensive preventive interventions, the chapter is divided into two sections; one on comprehensive school-based interventions and one on comprehensive community-based interventions.

To place this review of current interventions in perspective, the recent history of comprehensive approaches to reduce antisocial behavior in America is reviewed first. Interventions that have shown promising results in studies employing experimental or quasi-experimental designs are reviewed next. Then, methodological limitations of current research in studying and evaluating comprehensive interventions are discussed. Finally, conclusions about the state of the field and directions for further research and intervention are discussed.

The Chicago Area Project of the 1930s played a vital role in broadening delinquency prevention efforts to include social-ecological factors (Shaw & McKay, 1969). The Chicago Area Project was founded on the observation that a large proportion of delinquents in Chicago resided in poor, inner-city neighborhoods characterized by rapid residential turnover, high unemployment, and a lack of citizen involvement. Sociologist Clifford Shaw hypothesized that the high rates of delinquency in these neighborhoods were caused by a breakdown in the communities' abilities to supervise and transmit prosocial values to youths. To address these problems, the project focused on mobilizing adults in the neighborhoods to increase their daily involvement with youths to restore the supervision and socializing structures missing in the neighborhoods. To motivate local adults to participate, project staff recruited community members to share in decision making and lead the intervention efforts.

This landmark effort stood in sharp contrast to the child guidance clinics that were popular at that time, in that the Chicago Area Project attempted to prevent antisocial behavior by changing the social environment rather than changing the behavior of individual youths. It was the first large-scale, planned community intervention to prevent antisocial behavior (Krisberg & Austin, 1978).

In the late 1950s and early 1960s, a second major attempt to mobilize community members to address neighborhood poverty and other risks for delinquency was mounted in New York City as the Mobilization for Youth project. Although this attempt met with resistance from some local officials threatened by the efforts to give residents a voice in defining their problems and desired solutions, it laid the groundwork for subsequent efforts to mobilize communities to prevent antisocial behavior (Krisberg & Austin, 1978). The Mobilization for Youth project marked the first time the federal government invested large sums of money (about $2 million per year) in attempting to prevent antisocial behavior. These efforts were supported by the emergence of sociological theories, such as Cloward and Ohlin's (1960) strain theory, that shifted the causal emphasis from individual factors to social structural factors such as the inequality of opportunities to achieve aspirations and attain goals through legitimate means.

The 1960s brought the war on poverty and a broad array of interventions to address poverty, including efforts to prevent school failure through programs such as Head Start (Zigler & Valentine, 1979). Youth service bureaus were created to bring together local residents and social service agency staff to develop necessary services within the community for local youths and families (Krisberg & Austin, 1978). The youth service bureaus emphasized diversion of youths from the juvenile justice system, but efforts were limited by lack of adequate funding and conflict between community residents and agency staff over program goals. Despite these community-based efforts to reduce antisocial behavior, the country's primary response to juvenile antisocial behavior remained the juvenile justice system.

In the 1980s and 1990s, the community's responsibility for preventing juvenile delinquency and drug abuse has become firmly entrenched in current policies and practice (Howell, 1995). For instance, Title V of the Juvenile Justice and Delinquency Prevention Amendments of 1992; the Office of Juvenile Justice and Delinquency Prevention's (OJJDP) Comprehensive Strategy for Serious, Violent, and Chronic Offenders; the Weed and Seed program of the Bureau of Justice Assistance; the Center for Substance Abuse Prevention's Community Partnership Demonstration Program; and the Robert Wood Johnson Foundation's Fighting Back and Healthy Nations initiatives all emphasize community involvement in planning comprehensive strategies to prevent antisocial behavior, and they represent significant investment in community prevention efforts. A recent survey of community drug prevention activities in America identified over 1,250 coalitions representing communities in every state (Join Together, 1992). The increase in community prevention programming since the late 1980s has created demand for information about effective intervention models and strategies.

Efforts to prevent antisocial behavior through comprehensive school and community interventions have shown positive results on reducing risk while enhancing protection and, in studies with long-term follow-up, on reducing juvenile crime and substance use. These studies are reviewed briefly in the next two sections. Where the data reported in the original documents allow it, significant changes in key outcomes are described in quantitative terms, either as percentages or as effect sizes (ESs). ESs are calculated as follows: $ES = (mean_{post} - mean_{pre} / SD_{pre})$. Although limited by the many methodological challenges confronting the evaluation of comprehensive interventions, these studies provide evidence that comprehensive interventions have the potential to reduce the prevalence of antisocial behavior within communities.

■ Schoolwide Interventions to Improve School Bonding and Academic Achievement and to Reduce Antisocial Behavior

One important locus for prevention programming is the school. Schools provide universal access and are settings where critical developmental tasks are completed (Dryfoos, 1990). Weissberg and Greenberg (1997) point out that high-quality instruction and learning environments that foster the acquisition of basic skills are important objectives of school-based interventions. Moreover, as demonstrated in a meta-analysis by Maguin and Loeber (1996), academic failure is related to the prevalence and onset of delinquency, as well as the escalation in the frequency and seriousness of offending, and interventions that improve academic performance have been shown to reduce delinquency. As compulsory institutions that permit sustained contact with most young people during the formative years of development (Rutter et al., 1979), schools may be ideal sites for comprehensive prevention and positive youth development programming (Bond & Compas, 1989; Dryfoos, 1994, 1995; Durlak, 1995; Zigler & Finn-Stevenson, 1997; Zins & Forman, 1988).

Preventive interventions have been used in schools to improve both behavior and achievement. Five different kinds of schoolwide, non-classroom-based interventions have been evaluated: structured playground activities; behavioral consultation; behavioral monitoring and reinforcement of attendance, academic progress, and school behavior; metal detectors in schools; and schoolwide organizational changes. These school-based interventions can address the protective factors of bonding to school, opportunities for active involvement, social and cognitive competencies, recognition of positive behavior, and positive norms regarding behavior, and several risk factors including transitions, academic failure, alienation and rebelliousness, low commitment to school, norms favorable to antisocial behavior, association with violent and delinquent peers, and early and persistent aggressive behavior.

Structured Playground Activities

Murphy, Hutchison, and Bailey (1983) evaluated a playground program at an elementary school in Tallahassee, Florida, to reduce aggressive behavior among 344 kindergarten through second-grade boys and girls. The program consisted of organized games (jump rope and running races) for the children who arrived on the playground during the 40 minutes before school started. Three aides supervised these activities and used a time-out procedure for students who committed particularly unruly behaviors. Observers recorded students' disruptive behavior including aggression, property abuse such as taking someone else's books, and violations of school rules. Most of the disruptive incidents involved aggression. The mean number of disruptive incidents per observation period during the experimental periods was significantly less (53%) than during the baseline periods.

Behavioral Consultation

Mayer and Butterworth (1979) evaluated a program in which graduate student consultants trained in applied behavioral analysis and behavioral consultation worked with elementary school teams to develop classroom and schoolwide antivandalism programs. The behavioral interventions and training focused on (a) matching academic materials to students' skill levels, (b) increasing positive reinforcement for appropriate classroom behavior and academic progress, (c) reducing the use of punishment, (d) applying various learning and behavioral management principles, and (e) educating school counselors/psychologists in behavioral consultation methods.

The evaluators used a true experimental design to assess program impact. Nineteen elementary schools in Los Angeles County participated in the study, with 10 randomly assigned to the program and 9 randomly assigned to the control group. In most study schools, students were predominantly from low-income African American or Latino families.

Vandalism costs decreased by 57% for experimental schools but increased by 320% for control schools. However, the statistical significance of these findings was not reported, and it should be noted that vandalism costs are highly sensitive to single, very expensive incidents. During the program year, observer-rated disruptive behavior significantly decreased (ES = −.66) for experimental students relative to control students, and experimental students' on-task classroom behavior (as rated by observers) increased significantly (ES = .48) in comparison to controls.

Mayer, Butterworth, Nafpaktitis, and Sulzer-Azaroff (1983) evaluated essentially the same type of program as the one described by Mayer and Butterworth (1979). The evaluators used a delayed-intervention control group design. Eighteen elementary and junior high schools from 12 school districts in Los Angeles County participated in the study, with 9 schools randomly assigned to the experimental group (Group I) and 9 schools randomly assigned to the control group (Group II). Group I schools received the program for 3 continuous years and Group II schools received the program for the second and third years.

Following initiation of the program, significantly more experimental (6/9) than control schools (1/9) reduced their vandalism costs in the first project year. A similar decrease appeared when the program began for Group II schools in the second project year. In comparison to baseline levels, vandalism costs (adjusted for school size) decreased in project schools by 79% on average during the years the program was in place. Relative to controls in Group II schools, experimental students in Group I schools significantly decreased their disruptive and off-task behavior after the program was in place. Program ef-

fects on student behavior were maintained in following years of the project.

Behavioral Monitoring and Reinforcement of Attendance, Academic Progress, and School Behavior

Bry (1982) evaluated a 2-year behavioral intervention focused on low-achieving, disruptive seventh-grade students who had low bonding to their families. Program staff interviewed participants' teachers weekly about participants' tardiness, class preparedness, class performance, and behavior. Program staff then met with participants in weekly small group sessions to review their behavior at school. Participants earned points for positive ratings from the teacher interviews, for attendance, and for lack of disciplinary referrals, as well as for lack of inappropriate behavior during the weekly meetings. Participants could use the points they accumulated during the school year for an extra school trip of their own choosing. Program staff contacted participants' parents periodically to inform them of their child's progress. During the year after the 2-year intervention period, program staff conducted teacher interviews biweekly and offered small group "booster" review sessions biweekly.

The evaluation used a true experimental design. Twenty-two male and 11 female pairs of identified at-risk students from the same classrooms were matched on academic achievement and school attendance, and one student in each pair was randomly assigned to the experimental group and the other to the control group. Approximately half of the study youths were from an urban school system and the other half were from a suburban school system. Forty-two percent of the study youths were African American and the rest were white.

At the end of the program, experimental youths had significantly better school grades and attendance than controls (Bry & George, 1979, 1980), and program impacts were uniform across race, sex, socioeconomic, and achievement motivation groups. In the year after the main program intervention, experimental youths displayed significantly fewer problem behaviors at school (i.e., suspensions, academic failure, poor attendance, and tardiness as determined from school records) than controls. In the 1½ years after the main program period, experimental youths self-reported significantly less abuse of illegal drugs (3% vs. 16%) and less criminal behavior (11 instances vs. 45 instances for control youths) (Bry, 1982). These significant program impacts on delinquency were long term: 5 years after the main program period ended, experimental youths were 66% less likely than control youths to have a juvenile record with the county probation office (Bry, 1982). Although the sample was somewhat small, the study had a very strong design and very little attrition of study participants.

Metal Detectors in Schools

Another type of schoolwide intervention to reduce violence in the schools involves the use of metal detectors. Metal detector programs usually entail security personnel or school staff searching some or all students for metal weapons, such as guns and knives, with metal detectors. In schools with this program, a team of security officers scans randomly selected students with handheld metal detectors as they enter the school building. These programs are targeted at reducing the availability of firearms within the school building. Ginsberg and Loffredo (1993) conducted a survey of a representative sample of all New York City high school students, stratified by schools with and without metal detector pro-

grams. Sixty-seven percent of students in 3 schools with a metal detector program and in 12 schools without a metal detector program participated in the survey.

The students in schools with and without metal detector programs were virtually identical in terms of their self-reports of being threatened or involved in fights at school or away from school. Students in the two groups also were equally likely to have reported carrying a gun, knife, and/or another kind of weapon somewhere in the previous 30 days. However, self-reported weapon carrying at school was significantly less prevalent in schools with a metal detector program than in those without. Students in schools with a metal detector program were approximately half as likely to carry a gun, knife, and/or other weapon inside, to, or from school as were students in schools without a metal detector program. Although schools were not randomly assigned to receive a metal detector program, students in schools with and without a program were very similar in their overall experience with interpersonal violence and weapon carrying. The results from this survey imply that metal detector programs may have a site-specific impact on weapon availability, an important risk factor for serious and violent delinquency, which might decrease the escalation and lethality of interpersonal conflicts at such sites. However, the effects of this situational prevention strategy do not appear to influence weapon-carrying behavior in other settings.

School Organization

A fifth category of schoolwide interventions focuses on changing the organizational structure of schools. School organization approaches can involve a wide variety of interventions, including changes in school ecology; parent involvement; development and communication of school policies; and teams of school administrators, teachers, and parents that plan and implement school policies and programs.

Cauce, Comer, and Schwartz (1987) and Comer (1988) evaluated a comprehensive school organization intervention that included four primary program components: (a) a social calendar that integrated arts and athletic programs into school activities; (b) a parent program in support of school academic and extracurricular activities, which fostered interaction among parents, teachers, and other school staff; (c) a multidisciplinary mental health team that provided consultation, especially for school staff, in managing student behavior problems; and (d) a representative governance and management team composed of school administrators, teachers, support staff, and parents that oversaw the implementation of the other three program components. This team identified and assessed problems and opportunities in the school, developed and allocated resources, created programs to address problems and opportunities, evaluated program outcomes, and modified such programs as necessary. The intervention was implemented in two inner-city public elementary schools in New Haven, Connecticut. Ninety-nine percent of students at these schools were African American and the overwhelming majority came from low-income families. Before the program, these schools were characterized by poor attendance, low achievement, discipline problems, and high teacher turnover.

The researchers used a nonequivalent comparison group design in evaluating program effects. Study youths were seventh-grade students in the same division of a middle school. Experimental students had attended the program elementary school, whereas comparison students had attended some other elementary school. Comparison students were matched with experimental

students on age and sex. The outcomes showed that experimental students had significantly higher middle school grades, academic achievement test scores, and self-perceived social competence than comparison students. These results, however, are limited by the small sample size and questions about whether the study groups were comparable in terms of characteristics other than sex and age.

Another comprehensive, schoolwide approach to prevent violence, in this case bullying, was evaluated by Olweus (1991). Bullying has been defined as repeated negative actions by one person to one or more others who are younger or weaker (Olweus, 1991). Bullying is a prevalent aggressive behavior among children and youth, especially in elementary school. To reduce bullying, a large-scale anti-bullying program was conducted in Norway. The five components of the program were (a) a booklet for school personnel distributed to all Norwegian comprehensive schools (Grades 1 to 9), which described bully/victim problems, provided suggestions about what teachers and the school could do to counteract and prevent such problems, and dispelled myths about the nature and causes of bullying; (b) an information and advice packet about bullying distributed to all families in Norway with school-age children; (c) a videocassette depicting episodes from the daily lives of two early-adolescent bullying victims available for purchase or rental at a highly subsidized price; (d) a brief anonymous questionnaire about bullying problems administered to students in all comprehensive schools and used to inform school and family interventions; and (e) a meeting between project staff and school staff in Bergen, Norway, held 15 months after the program was first offered to schools, to provide feedback on the program and emphasize main program principles and components.

The evaluation used a quasi-experimental design employing time-lagged contrasts between age-equivalent groups. The program was implemented nationwide at the same time, so the design involved comparisons among successive cohorts of children for particular grade levels. Data were collected from approximately 2,500 students originally belonging to Grades 4 to 7 in 42 Bergen schools. Time 1 measurements were made 4 months before the program began, and Time 2 and 3 measurements were made 1 and 2 years after Time 1, respectively.

Significantly fewer students (approximately 50% less in most comparisons) reported being victims and bullies at 8 and 20 months after the program began (Olweus, 1991). There were corresponding decreases in students' estimates of the number of classmates who were bullies and victims. Students also reported significantly decreased delinquent behavior (vandalism, theft, truancy) at 8 and 20 months after the program began, although the magnitude of these changes is hard to interpret from the scale scores reported. In sum, the intervention appeared to reduce both aggressive and general delinquency. Because bullying often involves repeated assaults, this program appears to have directly reduced the risk factor "early and persistent antisocial behavior" as well as violent, assaultive behavior itself.

Gottfredson (1986) evaluated Project PATHE (Positive Action Through Holistic Education), a comprehensive school organization intervention for secondary schools. PATHE's six main components were (a) teams composed of teachers, other school staff, students, parents, and community members who designed, planned, and implemented school improvement programs, with the assistance of two full-time project staff; (b) curriculum and discipline policy review and revision, including student participation in the development of school and classroom rules and ongoing in-service training for teachers in instructional and classroom management

practices; (c) schoolwide academic innovations, including study skills programs and cooperative learning techniques; (d) schoolwide climate innovations, including expanded extracurricular activities, peer counseling, and a school pride campaign intended to improve the overall image of the school; (e) career-oriented innovations, including a job-seeking skills program and a career exploration program; and (f) special academic and counseling services for low-achieving and disruptive students.

The evaluation used a nonequivalent comparison group design involving four middle schools and four high schools in low-income, predominantly African American urban and rural areas in Charleston County, South Carolina. One school at each level was designated as a comparison school. In addition, in experimental schools a selective preventive component was experimentally tested. Students experiencing academic and behavioral problems were randomly assigned to an experimental group, which received the special academic and counseling services, or a control group, which did not.

Gottfredson (1986) reported changes in outcomes over time for experimental and comparison schools separately, but did not directly compare the outcomes for experimental and comparison schools, making interpretation of results difficult. Over the course of the program, students in experimental high schools reported significant decreases in delinquency (ES = −.12) and drug involvement (ES = −.10), and significantly fewer school suspensions (ES = −.23) and punishments (ES = −.14). Students in experimental middle schools reported significant declines in suspensions (ES = −.11) only. Students in comparison schools did not show the same reductions in these outcomes.

The students in experimental schools who received special academic and counseling services reported significantly higher grades

(ES = .09) and were less likely to repeat a grade (ES = –.15) than control group students in the experimental school. Seniors who received these services were significantly more likely to graduate (76%) than seniors in the control group (42%). However, there were no significant differences between those students who received the special services and their respective controls on self-reported delinquency or court contacts.

D. C. Gottfredson (1987) also evaluated Project CARE, a 2-year school organization intervention for secondary schools. Within the context of an organizational development activity (program development evaluation), a team of teachers, administrators, and other school staff planned and implemented school improvement programs. The two major components implemented were classroom management techniques (assertive discipline and reality therapy) and cooperative learning. Several additional components were partially implemented, including a parent volunteer program, a community support and advocacy program, and other programs used by Project PATHE (Gottfredson, 1986). The evaluation used a nonequivalent comparison group design involving two junior high schools in low-income, predominantly African American areas in Baltimore, Maryland. One school was designated the experimental school and the other was designated the comparison school. In the experimental school, the program was primarily implemented in only one of three physically separate units of the school. A cohort of students from other units in the school was used for comparison with the students in the experimental unit.

D. C. Gottfredson (1987) did not report direct comparisons between experimental and control schools in terms of outcomes. Over the course of the program, students' self-reports of delinquency decreased significantly in the experimental school (ES = –.20) but increased significantly in the comparison school (ES = .11). Comparison school students reported a significant increase in rebellious behavior (ES = .15), whereas students in the experimental school did not change. Experimental school teachers reported a significant increase in classroom orderliness (ES = .50) over the program period, compared to no change in the comparison school.

Within the experimental school, students in the experimental unit reported significantly more office referrals (perhaps as a result of the classroom management strategies) but significantly fewer suspensions than comparison cohort students (2% vs. 5%). The lack of direct comparisons between experimental and comparison schools again hampers the assessment of program effects. Furthermore, the control school may not have been adequately comparable to the experimental school given the control school staff's resistance to the program.

Gottfredson, Karweit, and Gottfredson (1989) evaluated another multicomponent school organization intervention for middle schools. The four main program components were (a) a school discipline policy review and revision to develop school rules (including provisions for systematically rewarding positive student behavior) that were clear, specific, administered fairly, and coordinated with individual classroom policies; (b) a behavior tracking system for recording individual students' positive and negative referrals to the office and disciplinary actions, which was used for notifying parents of their child's school behavior; (c) classroom organization and management, which focused on clear and effectively communicated rules and procedures, monitoring, clear instruction, activity transitions, fair grading, and frequent and systematic feedback on student academic progress; and (d) behavioral modification techniques in which teachers reinforced positive behavior and consistently responded to misbehavior according to the communicated rules and consequences. These components were implemented in the context of an organizational development activity (program development evaluation) intended to increase school staff commitment to and ownership of the program and equip them with the skills and information needed to manage program implementation effectively.

The evaluators used a nonequivalent comparison group design. This intervention included eight study schools in Charleston County, South Carolina, selected for their high levels of student punishment. Six of these schools were assigned to the program and two were designated as comparison schools. Comparison schools were roughly similar to experimental schools in terms of school size and unspecified demographic factors. The experimental program ran for 3 years. Over the project period, students in experimental schools perceived significant increases in classroom order (ES = .35), classroom organization (ES = .31), and rule clarity (ES = .40). In contrast, students in comparison schools reported similar, though mostly nonsignificant, changes in these variables. The evaluators did not report any direct comparisons between experimental and control schools and did not report program effects on students' behavior.

However, Gottfredson, Gottfredson, and Hybl (1993) examined the same program's impact on classroom environment and students' behavior, comparing the three schools that fully implemented the intervention (high implementation), the three experimental schools that experienced visible implementation problems or low levels of administrative support (medium intervention), and the two control schools (low implementation). They found that the program's positive effects on classroom order and organization appeared only for the high-implementation schools, and the increases in rule clarity appeared in both the high- and medium-implementation schools. They also found that teacher ratings of students' on-task behavior increased significantly (ES = .09) in the high-implementation schools, but did not change significantly in the medium- or low-implementation schools. Moreover, teacher ratings of students' disruptive behavior decreased significantly (ES = −.12) in the high-implementation schools, increased significantly (ES = .12) in the medium-implementation schools, and did not change in the low-implementation schools (Gottfredson et al., 1993).

The Multimodal School-Based Prevention Demonstration was a school-based multicomponent prevention program operating in a middle school in Charleston, South Carolina. The program's major objective was reduction of problem behaviors, and program components included interventions aimed at academic achievement, social competency development, and social bonding (Gottfredson, Gottfredson, & Skroban, 1996). Academic achievement was addressed through instructional improvement interventions such as cooperative learning techniques, a Career and Educational Decision Skills program, and one-on-one tutoring. Social bonding was addressed through social support interventions including prosocial adult models who taught appropriate skills and behaviors, and a mentoring program. Social competence promotion was addressed through a Life Skills Training course for all sixth graders, augmented by a 29-session cognitive self-management course for seventh graders. A cognitive self-instruction course for all students and a 21-lesson violence prevention curriculum were also included to increase self-regulation skills. Organization development strategies including frequent feedback regarding the quality and quantity of program implementation, and "forcefield analysis" to identify obstacles to implementation and resources that would help promote it were used to strengthen the integrity of implementation.

Although still below the intended level of implementation, the third year of the program was judged by the authors as ready for outcome evaluation. Outcome measures were taken from surveys, teacher checklists, and school archives. Gottfredson et al. (1996) caution that the control and experimental schools were not equivalent, particularly by the end of the measurement period, due to factors such as highly transient populations. The evaluation results to date indicate a positive effect of the program on grade point average (ES = .33) and a decrease in peer drug influence for high-risk program students compared with high-risk comparison students.

Another group of studies funded by the Centers for Disease Control and Prevention (CDCP) has just gotten under way and provides examples of current directions for comprehensive school-based interventions to prevent violence. CDCP is currently supporting 15 evaluation projects in 12 cities to promote reduction of youth violence. Evaluations are designed as 2-year assessments. Of the total 15, 3 have comprehensive school components and are briefly described here because no follow-up data are yet available.

The Students for Peace project is a violence prevention program for urban middle school students in Texas (Kelder et al., 1996). The Students for Peace intervention included four components: modification of the school environment, a violence prevention curriculum, peer leadership, and parent education. It is using a nested cross-sectional and cohort design in which schools were randomized to intervention and control conditions, and are the unit of design, allocation and analysis. The project includes eight schools, four intervention and four control.

The Self-Enhancement program in Albina, Oregon, focuses on "building relationships and

resilience" to prevent youth violence through classroom and community activities designed to enhance protective factors (Gabriel, Hopson, Haskins, & Powell, 1996). The program components include mentoring, proactive education, classroom exposure to agencies that deal with the causes and consequences of violence in the community, and social competence promotion including anger management, conflict resolution, and problem solving.

The Resolving Conflict Creatively Program (RCCP) is a comprehensive, school-based program in conflict resolution and "intercultural understanding" (Aber, Brown, Chaudry, Jones, & Samples, 1996; Fetzer Institute, 1994). The study involves 9,600 children, 5-12 years old, in 15 schools. The components include teacher training; classroom instruction and staff development; and training for administrators, parents, and peer mediators. Primary outcome objectives of RCCP were to achieve a long-term reduction in violence and violence-related behavior; to promote caring and cooperative behavior among children, adolescents, and adults in and out of school; and to promote intergroup understanding and positive intergroup relations.

Summary of Schoolwide Interventions

These comprehensive school-based preventive interventions vary in their degree of demonstrated effectiveness. Monitored, structured activities outside of the classroom, such as on the playground, may reduce antisocial behavior, particularly aggression, in these contexts. In addition, behavioral consultation in elementary and secondary schools may have the potential to improve students' school behavior and reduce school vandalism. Behavioral monitoring and reinforcement of attendance, academic progress, and school behavior is effective in improving attendance, school behavior, and academic achievement for both elementary and secondary school children. Also, metal detectors in schools appear to reduce weapon carrying within and around the schools themselves, but do not appear to influence weapon carrying or violence in other contexts.

School organization interventions are noteworthy for their comprehensiveness and system-oriented prevention approach. In several evaluations, various school organization interventions appeared to reduce risk factors and increase protective factors including reductions in academic failure, dropout, and rebelliousness, and increases in commitment to school and attendance. Two of the Gottfredsons' studies showed significant decreases in delinquency. Olweus's (1991) evaluation of a multicomponent antibullying program presented evidence of significant reductions in violent and delinquent behavior. However, none of these evaluations used a true experimental design, and several evaluations did not report a complete analysis of the outcome data, which hinders a clear interpretation of evaluation results. Although school organization interventions are potentially promising, future evaluations of such programs should use more rigorous designs and include thorough data analysis. Interestingly, a recent meta-analysis of alternative education programs (Cox, Davidson, & Bynum, 1995) found no impact of these programs on delinquency.

Although none of the programs examined effects specifically on serious or violent delinquency, two programs were selective interventions working with students at risk for developing serious delinquent behavior. In one program, regular behavioral monitoring and reinforcement of appropriate school behavior and performance promoted positive outcomes, including less officially reported delinquency, for adolescents at risk by virtue of academic failure, persistent behavior problems, and low bonding to family (Bry, 1982).

Also, Olweus (1991) found significant reductions in both aggressive and general antisocial behavior following a comprehensive effort to reduce bullying in Norwegian schools.

■ Community Interventions to Reduce Risks and Enhance Protection Against Antisocial Behavior

Current community interventions to prevent antisocial behavior have been heavily influenced by public health efforts to prevent cardiovascular disease. These strategies have often been based on social learning, community development, and innovation diffusion theories of behavior change emphasizing social norm changes and citizen participation in the change efforts (Hyndman et al., 1992; Perry, Klepp, & Sillers, 1989). Communitywide health education, policy change, policing, and media interventions have been designed to change community and personal norms to promote healthy lifestyles over health risk behaviors. Community mobilization strategies have been employed to encourage community ownership of the change efforts, thus increasing adoption and diffusion of behavior change messages. Mentoring and afterschool recreational programs have also been employed in community settings to encourage increased opportunities for positive involvement and bonding.

Studies reviewed here include a range of antisocial behaviors because specific evaluative information on the impact of these approaches on SVJ offending is often not examined. The studies provide valuable information about both the potential and the difficulties of this approach. Community mobilization, situational prevention, comprehensive community intervention, mentoring, afterschool recreation, policing strategies, policy change, and mass media interventions have shown promise as community-wide prevention strategies that can influence risk and protective factors at multiple levels.

Community Mobilization

Community mobilization strategies encompass a diversity of programs that seek to prevent crime and violence by organizing citizens for grassroots efforts. Community mobilization approaches may address the risk factors of low community attachment and community disorganization, availability of drugs and firearms, and laws and norms favorable to crime and violence. Protective factors addressed can include opportunities for involvement in the community, bonding to community, skills to monitor and positively influence neighborhoods, and healthy beliefs and clear standards for behavior. To date only two kinds of community mobilization approaches to crime and violence prevention have been evaluated: neighborhood block watch and citizen patrol.

Neighborhood block watch. These programs are based on the rationale that residents are in the best position to monitor suspicious activities and individuals in their neighborhood. Social connections among residents made as a result of block watch meetings also might facilitate neighborhood monitoring and communication about suspicious events.

Lindsay and McGillis (1986) evaluated the effectiveness of a neighborhood block watch program in Seattle, Washington. Professional community organizers affiliated with the city police department initiated the formation of block watch groups by recruiting interested residents. After the recruitment phase, block watch groups held organizing meetings during which the community organizer discussed neighborhood burglary

problems and burglary prevention techniques, informational materials about home security were distributed, residents elected a block watch captain and exchanged telephone numbers, and appointments were made to use a property engraver. Organizers also visited participating residents' homes to perform brief home security inspections. Project organizers also produced a newsletter, which was given to block watch captains to distribute to neighbors, and organized follow-up meetings.

The evaluation used a nonequivalent comparison group design. A few census tracts in Seattle with high burglary rates were targeted to receive the intervention. Two tracts were designated as comparison areas that were adjacent and similar in burglary rates to some of the experimental tracts. Residents in experimental areas who participated in the program reported significant reductions in burglary to their residences. There was a 33% reduction in burglary victimization overall in experimental tracts compared with a 5% reduction in adjacent comparison tracts, although neither of these reductions was statistically significant. The authors did not directly compare the experimental and comparison areas for changes in victimization over time.

Rosenbaum, Lewis, and Grant (1986) tested a similar block watch program implemented in middle- and lower-middle-class neighborhoods in Chicago, Illinois. The intervention lasted 1 year and consisted of block watch meetings every month or few months. In their evaluation, the researchers used a quasi-experimental design with five experimental areas selected on the basis of having well-established volunteer community organizations, interest in a block watch program, and resources/support to be able to carry out such a program. One set of comparison neighborhoods included areas that met only the first criterion. Another set of citywide comparison areas was selected for each program area, including three census tracts with similar demographic characteristics (ethnicity, age, home value, and rental rate) chosen randomly from a set of tracts throughout the city sharing these characteristics.

The intervention did not produce any consistent changes in residents' crime prevention activities or neighborhood social cohesion. Overall, there were no program effects on victimization or perceived disorder. Residents in experimental areas did report significant increases in perceived crime and fear of crime, and displayed significant decreases in attachment to their neighborhoods relative to residents in comparison areas.

Another neighborhood mobilization intervention similar to block watch programs was the police-initiated community organization in Houston (Wycoff, Skogan, Pate, & Sherman, 1985b). Program staff, including four police officers and an urban planner, helped organize 13 small neighborhood meetings, which were attended by 6 to 18 residents and two to three officers over an 8-month period. The program also mailed newsletters, which discussed neighborhood crime problems, to approximately 8% of area households. Approximately 20 residents from the neighborhood meetings agreed to form a neighborhood task force that worked without program staff's direct involvement. This neighborhood task force held a drug information seminar, designated 30 "safe houses" where children could go for assistance, organized a 1-month trash and junk clean-up effort in the neighborhood, and promoted property marking and resident ride-alongs with police officers.

Survey results showed that residents in the experimental area perceived significantly decreased crime and social disorder and significantly increased police service in comparison to comparison area residents. However, there were no decreases in victimization or increases in satisfaction with the area associated with the program. The authors discussed several difficulties in implementing the program, including no permanent organization location/office, only moderate levels of perceived crime in the experimental area, no previously existing neighborhood organizations, and program staff's lack of familiarity with the area.

Citizen patrol. Another community mobilization strategy is the active patrolling of neighborhoods by citizens who are not sworn law enforcement officers. One controlled study has evaluated the impact of the Guardian Angels, a nonprofessional foot patrol organization (Pennell, Curtis, Henderson, & Tayman, 1989). The Guardian Angels consists of unarmed, racially diverse youths who wear red berets and patrol the streets. The organization specifically seeks to prevent or deter crimes that involve force or personal injury. Using a quasi-experimental design, Pennell et al. (1989) compared an experimental area where Guardian Angels patrolled with an area not patrolled by the Guardian Angels in San Diego, California. Details on the study areas were not provided by the authors. The researchers obtained data on the reported crimes for a baseline period 6 months prior to the onset of the Guardian Angels' patrol and for 3 years of Guardian Angels' patrol. The level of patrol over the 3-year period was less than that recommended in the Guardian Angels' guidelines. Outcomes indicated a 22% decline in major violent offenses in the experimental area, but a 42% decline in the comparison area. For property crimes, there was a 25% decline in the experimental area and a 15% reduction in the comparison area. Statistical significance was not reported for any of these results.

Summary of Community Mobilization

The three controlled evaluations of block watch programs did not produce evidence of significant effects on crime in experimental neighborhoods. The only available evaluation of a citizen patrol also failed to demonstrate a significant preventive effect on crime. Clearly, more evaluations with more rigorous, randomized research designs are required to determine the preventive effects of these community mobilization approaches. Furthermore, other types of community organizing such as strategies that involve community leaders and grassroots citizens in comprehensive crime risk assessment and risk reduction planning and action strategies should be evaluated for their potential.

Situational Prevention

Police agencies and communities have also explored methods to control crime and reduce antisocial behavior by focusing on techniques that increase the risk and difficulty of offending through reducing the opportunities for criminal or antisocial activities. Such control methods were originally developed through the strategies of target hardening, and more recently they have been integrated within the broader theoretical framework called situational prevention (Clarke, 1995). Whereas the primary aim of situational prevention is to reduce criminal opportunities, it also aims to affect criminal decision making by changing contributing factors, such as the perceived difficulty of committing the act or the perceived risk of being caught (Farrington, 1995). Target hardening was once a strategy primarily associated with law enforcement, but it has become one of a number of techniques embraced within the newer police-community collaboration models.

Clarke (1995) reviews the effectiveness of situational prevention techniques, describing a total of 12 techniques, including target hardening, that represent well-delineated methods of situational prevention. The other techniques of situational prevention include access control, deflecting offenders, controlling facilitators, entry/exit screening, formal surveillance, surveillance by employees, natural surveillance, target removal, property identification, the removal of inducement, and rule setting. Target hardening reduces opportunity through the implementation of physical barriers. An example of its effectiveness has been demonstrated in studies in West Germany, in which the introduction of steering locks into the country produced a substantial decline in the country's rate of car theft from 1963 to 1994 (Webb, 1994; Webb & Laycock, 1992). Similarly, access control is a central component of the concept of defensible space and incorporates recent developments in sophisticated technology, such as using electronic personal identification numbers for access to computerized systems. Poyner and Webb (1987) reported significant reductions in vandalism and theft through combining access controls for a London public housing project, including entry phones, strategic fencing, and electronic garage access.

Strategies for deflecting offenders focus on channeling people's behavior in socially appropriate directions to minimize the potential for antisocial actions. An example is separating rival soccer fans into different enclosures at a sports stadium (Clarke, 1983). As another example, effective crowd management at Disney World has been shown to reduce the potential for antisocial behavior in this recreational setting. Control methods include the use of pavement markings, signs, physical barriers, and instructions from Disney employees (Shearing & Stenning, 1986). The technique of controlling facilitators operates on the principle that certain materials facilitate criminal or antisocial activity, and their control will produce corresponding harm reduction. Applications have ranged from exchanging glass beer mugs for plastic to prevent their use as weapons (Scottish Council on Crime, 1975) to restricting alcohol, automobiles, checks and credit cards, and telephones (Clarke, 1995).

Entry/exit screening is distinct from access control in that the purpose is less to exclude potential offenders than to increase the likelihood of detecting those who are not in conformity with entry/exit requirements. Developments in electronics permit widespread use of this situational technique in retailing, reflected in merchandise tagging, bar coding, and electronic point-of-sales systems (Hope, 1991). The implementation of surveillance techniques now includes its formal application, as with police and security forces; its use with employees who perform roles within specified business settings; and natural surveillance, in which the physical environment is manipulated to capitalize on observations provided by people going about their everyday business. Surveillance methodology has broader applications across a number of settings, as with improved street lighting (Ramsay, 1991). An apartment watch program that combined natural surveillance with target hardening showed a reduction of 82% in reported burglaries in four apartment blocks in Ottawa (Meredith & Paquette, 1992).

Target removal has been successful as a technique in crime prevention programs such as the introduction of safes with locks in Australian betting shops, which substantially reduced robberies (Clarke & McGrath, 1990). Identifying property has proven effective in auto theft reduction, as when Illinois became one of the last states to require vehicle registration and thefts dropped from 28,000 to 13,000 in 1 year (Hall, 1952). Prevention through removing inducements has been proven with graffiti control, as in the New York Transit Authority's effective policy of immediate cleansing of its subway cars (Sloan-Howitt & Kelling, 1990). Rule setting has been applied

to events such as the Australian Motorcycle Grand Prix, which offered motorcyclists the opportunity to set their own rules for conduct in advance of the event, and thus contributed to a trouble-free event for that year (Veno & Veno, 1993).

Summary of Situational Prevention

There is now an extensive review literature indicating possible relationships between crime and the physical environment (Clarke, 1995). However, the field of situational prevention has a number of ongoing issues and challenges. First, much of the research has been correlational and suffers from a variety of confounding possibilities that have been inadequately addressed (Taylor & Gottfredson, 1986). The failure to test the linkages in the model—that is, that environmental design promotes natural surveillance and that natural surveillance deters crime (Hope, 1995)—has hindered the further development of the model. Moreover, the multidimensional nature of most programs has made it difficult to isolate the dynamics of the components effects.

The challenge for research is to help practitioners avoid potential pitfalls by providing a sounder base of knowledge on which to act. What is currently known is that some measures work well in certain conditions, but as Tilley (1993) points out, what is needed ideally is to know which measures work best, in which combination, deployed against what kinds of crime, and under what conditions (Poyner, 1993). Farrington (1995) suggests that situational prevention may need to focus more on identifying risk and protective factors. Wikström (1995a) said that situational prevention is unlikely to be very useful for people with high self-control, who basically will not offend no matter what the temptation or risk, or for people with low self-control, who basically will offend in spite of any opportunity-reducing measures used. Wikström suggests that situational prevention was most likely to be effective for people with medium self-control. Furthermore, Farrington (1995) warns that the effects of changing situational factors may wear off as committed offenders work out how to overcome other impediments. As Taylor and Gottfredson conclude, "Simple effects of physical environment on crime range from small to moderate. It appears that alteration of physical environment features cannot have stand-alone crime prevention effectiveness. Resident dynamics are the key mediators of the environment-crime linkage" (quoted in Bottoms & Wiles, 1988, p. 86).

Comprehensive Community Interventions

Another approach to community-wide prevention of antisocial behavior involves mounting a coordinated set of mutually reinforcing preventive interventions throughout the community. For example, the Midwestern Prevention Project (Pentz, MacKinnon, et al., 1989) was a multilevel community intervention to prevent substance abuse. The project was initiated in 1984 in 42 public middle/junior high schools in 15 school districts in the Kansas City area, using a quasi-experimental design. Project components included (a) mass media programming, (b) school-based educational curricula, (c) parent education and organization, (d) community organization, and (e) health policy. These components were introduced sequentially into communities over 4 years, starting with the mass media, school curricula, and parent interventions delivered during the middle/junior high school years (Pentz, Brannon, et al., 1989).

After the first year of mass media and school-based intervention, prevalence rates for monthly use of cigarettes (17% vs. 24%),

alcohol (11% vs. 16%), and marijuana (7% vs. 10%) were significantly lower for the intervention schools than for schools in the control condition that received the media intervention only. Over the 1-year period, the net increase in drug use prevalence within intervention schools was half that within delayed-intervention (control) schools (Pentz, Dwyer, et al., 1989). In subsequent analyses examining only the eight schools randomly assigned to the study condition 3 years following initiation of the interventions, significant differences between conditions were found for cigarette and marijuana use, but not alcohol use. Similar reductions in use were observed for youth with different levels of 11 risk factors measured at baseline (Johnson et al., 1990). The results indicated that the comprehensive community-based approach was more effective than the media intervention alone at preventing the onset of substance abuse among both high-risk and general populations of students.

A second series of studies of comprehensive community interventions to prevent adolescent smoking and alcohol use has been implemented in Minnesota by Perry and her colleagues (Perry et al., 1992; Perry et al., 1993; Perry et al., 1996; Williams et al., in press). The Class of 1989 study was part of the Minnesota Heart Health Program (MHHP), a research and demonstration project designed to reduce cardiovascular disease in three communities from 1980 to 1993 (Luepker et al., 1994; Perry et al., 1992). The Class of 1989 study was designed to evaluate the combined impact of a classroom-based social influence smoking prevention curriculum delivered to the class of 1989 during their sixth, seventh, and eighth grades and the community-wide cardiovascular health promotion activities of the MHHP. Community-wide activities included seven strategies: (a) cardiovascular risk factor screening for adults,

(b) grocery and restaurant point-of-purchase food labeling for health education, (c) community mobilization and task forces to create annual risk factor education campaigns, (d) continuing education of health professionals to promote community awareness of cardiovascular disease risk factors and prevention, (e) mass media education campaigns, (f) adult education, and (g) youth education. Using a quasi-experimental design, a single intervention community was matched with a reference community.

Seven annual surveys were conducted from 1983 to 1989, following the cohort of students who were in sixth grade in 1983. All students in both the intervention and comparison communities were eligible to be surveyed each year. Identifying information was collected at each survey administration, allowing the data to be analyzed as a longitudinal cohort design for the students present at multiple years, or as repeated cross-sectional designs including all students present at each time point. Analyses of both the cohort and cross-sectional data revealed significant differences in smoking prevalence between the intervention and comparison communities. At the end of the 7-year period when the students were seniors in high school, 14.6% of the cohort in the intervention community smoked compared to 24.1% of the cohort in the reference community (Perry et al., 1992). The findings suggest that the combined school and community interventions produced a significant reduction in smoking prevalence among middle and high school youths. However, the findings are limited by the study design, which matched a single pair of communities and relied on data analysis at the individual rather than community level.

A second study, Project Northland, is using a similar combination of community-based and classroom interventions, along with a parent intervention component, to prevent alcohol use among adolescents in several small communities from six counties in northeastern Minnesota with a high prevalence of alcohol-related problems (Perry et al., 1993). The multilevel, multiyear intervention recruited 20 school districts and their surrounding communities to participate. The 20 districts were blocked by size and randomized to treatment and delayed-treatment control conditions (Perry et al., 1993; Perry et al., 1996).

The 3-year, multicomponent intervention program was initiated in 1991 with sixth-grade students. It consisted of (a) social behavioral curricula in schools, (b) peer leadership, (c) parental involvement/education, and (d) community-wide task force activities. All students in the grade cohort were surveyed at baseline in the fall of 1991, and then in the spring of 1992, 1993, and 1994. The data were analyzed using mixed-model ANCOVA, with combined school district specified as a nested, random effect (e.g., Koepsell et al., 1991; Murray & Wolfinger, 1994).

After 3 years of intervention, students in the intervention school districts reported significantly lower scores on a Tendency to Use Alcohol scale, and significantly lower prevalence of monthly (23.6% vs. 29.2%) and weekly (10.5% vs. 14.8%) alcohol use (Perry et al., 1996). Significant differences in the hypothesized direction were also observed for survey scales measuring peer influences to use alcohol, perceived norms regarding teen alcohol use, parents' communicating sanctions for their child's alcohol use, and reasons for teens not to use alcohol (Perry et al., 1996). These effects on alcohol-related attitudes and behaviors are noteworthy, given the wide prevalence of alcohol use among adolescents. Differences between the intervention and comparison groups in cigarette use, smokeless tobacco use, marijuana use, perceived self-efficacy, and perceived access to alcohol were not significant.

Summary of Comprehensive Community Interventions

Three tests of comprehensive community-wide interventions have been conducted. These preventive interventions have targeted norms against substance use and social influences to use. The interventions have comprehensively addressed these risk factors in multiple domains including the community, school, parents, the media, and peers. By taking this comprehensive approach, they have generally affected the outcomes they targeted. These preventive interventions have primarily affected cigarette use, with two studies showing effects on alcohol use, and one on marijuana use. Effects of these interventions on delinquency or violence were not examined. Similar interventions targeting delinquency and violence by addressing multiple risk factors across multiple domains may hold promise, but have yet to be evaluated.

Mentoring

Mentoring programs typically involve nonprofessional volunteers spending time with individual youths in a supportive, nonjudgmental manner while acting as role models. Mentoring interventions may address several risk factors, including alienation, academic failure, low commitment to school, and association with delinquent and violent peers, as well as the protective factors of opportunities for prosocial involvement, skills for and recognition of prosocial involvement, bonding to prosocial adults, and healthy beliefs and clear standards for behavior.

Evidence from 10 evaluations consistently indicates that noncontingent, supportive mentoring relationships do not have desired effects on such outcomes as academic achievement, school attendance, dropout, various aspects of child behavior including misconduct, or employment (Dicken, Bryson, & Cass, 1977; Goodman, 1972; Green, 1980; McPartland & Nettles, 1991; Poorkaj & Bockelman, 1973; Rowland, 1992; Slicker & Palmer, 1993; Stanwyck & Anson, 1989). This lack of demonstrated effects has occurred whether mentors were paid or unpaid and whether mentors were college undergraduates, community volunteers, members of the business community, or school personnel.

However, when mentors used behavior management techniques in one small, short-term study, students' school attendance improved. Fo and O'Donnell (1975) evaluated the Buddy System mentoring program designed for multiethnic youths aged 11-17 with behavior management problems. Mentors included men and women ranging in age from 17 to 65 who were diverse in terms of ethnicity and socioeconomic status. The program paid mentors up to $144 per month for making weekly contact with their participants; submitting weekly behavioral data on and completing weekly assignments with their participants; submitting weekly log sheets, and attending biweekly sessions. Mentors received 18 hours of training before the program began and biweekly training sessions on behavior management throughout the program.

In two Hawaiian cities, youths were referred to the program from the schools, police, courts, social welfare agencies, community residents, and parents for behavior problems such as truancy. The researchers used a true experimental design in which youths were randomly assigned to one of three experimental groups or a no-treatment control group. In the three experimental groups, mentors were given $10 to spend on each participant each month. The three experimental groups were (a) relationship only, where mentors established warm and positive relationships and spent the $10 per month on the participant in a way not contingent on the participant's behavior; (b) social approval, where mentors responded to the participants warmly and positively contingent on appropriate and desired behavior, but spent the $10 monthly allotment for the participant in a noncontingent manner; and (c) social and material reinforcement, where mentors provided social approval and the $10 monthly allotment contingent on appropriate and desired behavior. Study youths' school attendance rates were monitored for three consecutive 6-week periods: baseline, first intervention period (where experimental youths received one of the three mentor interventions), and second intervention period (where all experimental youths received the social and material reinforcement mentoring intervention).

Truancy decreased significantly from baseline to the first intervention period for the social approval and social and material reinforcement experimental groups, but increased nonsignificantly for the control group. During the first intervention period, the social approval and social and material reinforcement experimental groups had significantly lower truancy rates than the relationship-only and control groups. Truancy decreased significantly for the relationship-only group from the first intervention period to the second intervention period, when mentors in this group began to use the social and material reinforcement intervention. There were no significant differences among experimental groups for truancy in the second intervention period, but each experimental group had significantly lower truancy rates than the control group. Thus, truancy was reduced when mentoring relationships included reinforcement contingent on appropriate behavior, but not when mentoring relationships did not include contingent reinforcement. This evaluation was limited by the short intervention periods, a very small sample (26 youths participated in the whole study), and no information on implementation. More evaluations with randomized designs are needed to test conclusions about mentoring.

Afterschool Recreation Programs

Afterschool recreation programs for youths can address the risk factors of alienation and associating with delinquent and violent peers. Protective factors addressed may include opportunities for involvement with prosocial youths and adults, skills for leisure activities, and bonding to prosocial others.

Jones and Offord (1989) evaluated the effects of an afterschool recreation program that targeted low-income children ages 5 to 15 residing in a public housing project in Ottawa, Ontario. Program staff actively recruited all children in the housing development to participate in structured afterschool courses for improving skills in sports, music, dance, scouting, and other nonsport areas. After children reached a certain skill level, they were encouraged to participate in ongoing leagues or other competitive activities in the surrounding community. The 32-month-long program was evaluated with a nonequivalent comparison group design. The experimental housing project was matched with another public housing project that had only minimal city-provided recreational services.

The number of arrests for juveniles residing in the experimental complex during the program declined significantly from the 2 years before the intervention, whereas the number of arrests for youths residing in the comparison project increased over the same time period (there was a 75% decrease in the experimental project but a 67% increase in the comparison project). There were no such differences in the number of arrests for adults, lending credence to the effect of the program. In addition, the number of security reports due to juveniles at the experimental complex declined significantly after the intervention began in comparison to the control. Sixteen months after the program had ended, these positive changes had diminished significantly. The reductions in antisocial behavior in the experimental complex did not carry over to home and school. Parent- and teacher-rated social behavior of youths in the experimental complex did not change significantly over the course of the intervention. The authors also show that the financial benefits of the program far exceeded the program costs.

From these results, it seems likely that the program impact was due to the program providing prosocial opportunities for youths in the afterschool hours where these opportunities had not previously existed. Providing these opportunities appears to have reduced youths' involvement in delinquent behavior in the community. Afterschool recreation programs that aggressively recruit youths and maintain high participation rates may be a promising intervention for preventing delinquency and violence, but should be evaluated further with research designs employing random assignment to study groups.

Policing Strategies

In recent decades, various innovations in policing practices have been used in attempts to reduce crime. Three of these policing strategies have been evaluated and are reviewed here: intensified motorized patrol, field interrogation, and community policing, including foot patrol, neighborhood storefront police stations, and citizen contact patrols. These strategies may address the risk factors of community disorganization and low neighborhood attachment, and norms tolerant of crime and violence. Protective factors addressed may include healthy beliefs and clear standards for behavior, opportunity for citizens' involvement with police, and citizens' bonding to police.

Intensified motorized patrol. Four controlled evaluations of intensified motorized patrol have been conducted. The Kansas City, Missouri, Preventive Patrol Experiment was a well-documented, quasi-experimental evaluation of different levels of motorized patrol (Kelling, Pate, Dieckman, & Brown, 1974). The three patrol conditions were normal (one car per beat), reactive (police responded only to service calls, with no regular car on the beat except for one patrolling a beat's perimeter), and intensive (two to three cars per beat). In all conditions, police cars were marked. There were five sets of three beats, and one beat in each set was assigned to a different patrol condition. All beats in a set were matched for level of crime, number of calls for service, ethnic composition, income, and transiency of population. Overall, the beats were diverse in terms of residents' income level and ethnicity. The intervention lasted 12 months.

There were no significant differences between conditions in rates of victimization, officially reported crime, arrests for an array of offenses including serious and violent crimes, or traffic accidents. There also were no significant differences across conditions in citizen and business perceptions of the police, quality of their interactions with police, or police response time to service calls.

Schnelle, Kirchner, McNees, and Lawler (1975) evaluated the effectiveness of an intensified motorized home-burglary patrol in Nashville, Tennessee. Over a period of 5 weeks, plainclothes officers patrolled experimental zones in unmarked cars at levels four to eight times greater than normal during the 8:00 a.m. and 4:00 p.m. shifts. Patrolling officers also were provided with information on suspects frequenting the patrol areas. Time-series analyses were conducted on officially recorded home burglaries for three experimental zones during the saturation patrol shift and during other shifts, and for three randomly chosen comparison zones in the city. There were no significant changes in officially recorded burglaries associated with the intervention in the experimental zones or in comparison zones. Burglary arrests increased significantly after the saturation patrols began in the experimental zones and increased nonsignificantly in the comparison zones.

Schnelle, Kirchner, Casey, Uselton, and McNees (1977) investigated another intensified motorized patrol intervention in Nashville, Tennessee. In this intervention, four additional marked patrol cars were assigned to patrol zones that normally had one patrolling car. Officers in these preventive saturation patrol cars were instructed not to respond to ordinary service calls, except for emergencies and crimes in progress. Saturation patrol cars were to patrol areas at sustained slow speeds. The saturation patrol was tested in four patrol zones that had consistently high rates of serious crime. Two patrol zones were randomly assigned to day saturation patrol (from 9 a.m. to 5 p.m.), and the other two zones were assigned to night saturation patrol (from 7 p.m. to 3 a.m.). The saturation patrols lasted for 10 days in each zone.

Reported serious crimes decreased significantly during night saturation patrols in comparison to the baseline and postsaturation patrol periods. There were no significant increases in crime in zones adjacent to zones with night saturation patrol, so it is unlikely that this decrease in crime represented displacement of crime to other neighborhoods. However, there were no significant changes in reported serious crimes for day saturation

patrols. Furthermore, the number of arrests did not change significantly in any of the patrol zones over the course of the experiment.

Sherman (1990) (cited in Sherman, 1992) conducted a randomized trial of targeting patrol at very specific high-crime locations or "hot spots" in Minneapolis, Minnesota. These hot spots were characterized by high frequencies of reported crimes over a period of 2 years. The hot spots were no larger than one half block in each direction from an intersection and no hot spot was visible from any other. Intensive hot spot patrols were to provide 3 hours of intermittent patrol presence between 11 a.m. and 3 a.m. Officers left the location to answer service calls, but returned to the hot spot at unpredictable intervals to write reports, talk with pedestrians, and generally maintain a presence. The intervention lasted 1 year. The researchers used a true experimental design to evaluate the program. Observational data showed that crime or disorder was reduced from 4% to 2% of addresses. Although crime-related calls to the police increased, the increase was lower for the extra patrol group, 5% versus 17% growth (Sherman & Weisburd, 1992). This evaluation did not assess the possibility that crime was displaced to other areas.

Field interrogation. Boydstun (1975) evaluated the effects of field interrogation (FI) in San Diego, California. FI involved officers stopping persons who were suspicious in the officer's opinion, questioning them about their activities, and sometimes searching them and/or their vehicles. If the person's explanations were satisfactory to the officer, no record of the contact was made, but if reasonable cause existed, the officer could arrest the person. If an officer did not have reasonable cause for an arrest but still found the person suspicious, the officer filed a FI report that recorded the contact. FI was a regular part of motorized patrol officers' activities in San Diego in the early 1970s.

The evaluators used a quasi-experimental design involving three comparison areas to assess program impacts. In one comparison area, FI was maintained as usual, in another comparison area FI was maintained but patrolling officers were given supplementary training in how to reduce friction between FI subjects and officers, and in a third area FI was discontinued entirely for 9 months. The three areas were noncontiguous patrol beats that were matched in terms of demographic, physical, and crime history characteristics. The evaluators collected data on reported crime rates and total arrests in the three areas for 7 months prior to and 5 months after the 9-month intervention period. The evaluators also conducted separate probability sample surveys on residents' victimization and attitudes toward police before and after intervention.

The researchers observed a significant increase (from 75/month to 104/month) during the intervention period in reported "suppressible" crimes in the area where FI was discontinued in comparison to the areas were FI was maintained. When FI was reinstituted in the area where it had been discontinued, reported crime decreased significantly (from 104/month to 81/month). Arrest rates did not vary significantly as a result of the FI program. Experience with crime (as a witness or victim) and perceptions of the level of crime increased significantly in the FI-discontinued area and, counter to expectation, in one area where FI was maintained. Fear of crime also increased over time in the neighborhood where FI was discontinued. FI was not related to any changes in residents' attitudes toward police. Although the tactics of FI can be controversial and have been described as unconstitutional (Skolnick & Bayley, 1988), this evaluation provides evidence that the tactics can be carried out in a respectful manner. However, these techniques require close managerial oversight.

Community policing. Three community policing evaluations examined physical and social disorder and satisfaction with the area (Pate, Skogan, Wycoff, & Sherman, 1985; Skogan & Wykoff, 1986; Wycoff, Skogan, Pate, & Sherman, 1985a), and all three studies documented reductions in physical and social disorder, whereas two studies reported positive effects on resident satisfaction with the area. Only one of the four community policing evaluations with victimization data showed reductions in victimization rates. The main component of this program (Wycoff et al., 1985a) was a citizen contact patrol in which police officers visited residents at their homes to inquire about crime problems. Given the current popularity of community policing, it is imperative that rigorous evaluations of this strategy be undertaken.

Summary of Policing Strategies

Of the various policing strategies reviewed, intensified motorized patrol by marked cars during high-crime times in high-crime, densely populated areas appears to be effective in preventing various types of serious crime. The related practice of field interrogation also may be a potentially promising crime prevention tactic. These results suggest that increased police presence must be judiciously directed at high-risk times, areas, and people to deter crime. Simply increasing the number of police is not likely to prevent crime (Wycoff, 1982). In general, community policing interventions were associated with decreases in residents' perceived crime and fear of crime and, in many cases, improved evaluations of the police. Finally, it should be pointed out that although crime reductions are based on reported crime, the portion due to juveniles is unknown.

Policy Change Interventions

Changing policies and laws governing the availability, sale, and use of alcohol, cigarettes, and firearms have shown some evidence of effectiveness at preventing antisocial behavior. Social norms are codified to some degree in policies and laws that influence behavior.

Regulation of the use of alcohol and cigarettes. Changes in state policies regarding liquor taxes (Cook & Tauchen, 1982; Grossman, Coate, & Arluck, 1987; Levy & Sheflin, 1985), liquor sales outlets (Holder & Blose, 1987; Wagenaar & Holder, 1991), and the legal drinking age (Hingson, Heeren, Howland, & Winter, 1983; Saffer & Grossman, 1987; Williams & Lillis, 1986) have been shown to influence rates of alcohol consumption and alcohol-related traffic accidents (George, Crowe, Abwender, & Skinner, 1989; O'Malley & Wagenaar, 1991).

For example, O'Malley and Wagenaar (1991) examined annual data for the years 1976-1987 from the Monitoring the Future national surveys of high school seniors and found a significantly higher prevalence of self-reported alcohol use in states with a minimum drinking age of 18 compared to states with a minimum drinking age of 21. Moreover, these differences disappeared and prevalence rates declined after the early 1980s when all states raised their minimum drinking age to 21 (O'Malley & Wagenaar, 1991). They also found that archival rates of single-vehicle nighttime crashes, a proxy measure for alcohol-related car crashes, showed declines similar to the declines in self-reported alcohol use following the law changes in states that raised the minimum drinking

age. Studies of alcohol taxation and alcohol outlets also indicate that policies that reduce alcohol availability are associated with reduced consumption and problems associated with alcohol use (Gruenewald, Ponicki, & Holder, 1993; Wagenaar & Holder, 1991; Watts & Rabow, 1983). Given the correlational nature of these studies, it is impossible to infer causality, yet the consistency of the observed relationships suggests that policy interventions to reduce availability and communicate norms against teen alcohol use can be an effective prevention strategy.

Regulations on the purchase and sale of firearms. Some studies of the impact of firearm regulations have also revealed positive results (Brewer et al., 1995). Sloan et al. (1988) compared rates of violent crime in Seattle, Washington and Vancouver, British Columbia between 1980 and 1986, and suggested that laws restricting the sale and purchase of handguns prevented violent, gun-related crime. This conclusion is supported by Loftin, McDowall, Wiersema, and Cottey (1991), who evaluated a 1977 Washington, D.C., ordinance that set prohibitions against the purchase, sale, transfer, and possession of handguns by civilians unless they already owned a handgun. Sixty days after the law was passed, new purchases of handguns became illegal for all but military and police personnel. A multiple time-series design was used to examine monthly frequencies of firearm homicides in Washington, D.C., and in adjacent metropolitan areas in Virginia and Maryland from 1968 to 1987. The analysis revealed that homicides in Washington, D.C. decreased by 25% immediately after institution of the law, and the reduction was maintained through 1987.

In contrast, McDowall, Lizotte, and Wiersema (1991) did not find an impact on rates of assault with or without firearms following passage of a 1981 Morton Grove, Illinois law that banned the sale of handguns as well as their possession by private citizens. A time-series design was conducted, beginning 5 years before and ending 5 years after passage of the law. The authors reported no change in assault rates, but did find that reported burglaries decreased significantly. They cited minimal enforcement of the law in interpreting the lack of impact on assaults. Jung and Jason (1988) used a time-series design (30 months) to examine a similar change in the law in Evanston, Illinois. They compared prevalence of firearm assaults and firearm robberies in Evanston and Rock Island, a city that did not change its laws. Firearm assaults in Evanston decreased significantly during the preintervention period, attributed to intensive media coverage of the new law, but showed no change in the postintervention period. Firearm assaults did not change significantly in Rock Island, but the evaluation did not include direct comparisons between pre- and postintervention periods for either city. The lack of consistent findings regarding the impact of laws regulating handgun purchases and ownership may reflect weak enforcement of the laws in some areas (Brewer et al., 1995).

Regulations on the place and manner of carrying firearms. Regulations on the place and manner of carrying firearms have been enacted by state and local governments in efforts to reduce the number of persons who carry and use firearms in public. O'Carroll et al. (1991) evaluated a 1986 Detroit ordinance implemented at the beginning of 1987 that imposed a mandatory 30- to 90-day jail sentence and $100-$500 fine for anyone convicted of carrying a concealed, loaded pistol on one's person or carrying a loaded firearm in a car. The researchers performed an interrupted time-series analysis of monthly homicide frequencies in Detroit from 1980 through 1987. Two time-series analyses were conducted: One compared inside (private) to outside (public) homicides, and the other compared gun homicides to non-gun homicides. When the ordinance went into effect, homicides were increasing in Detroit. Although the ordinance did not reverse the increasing trend in homicides, it was related to a lower rate of increase for outside homicides (10% increase, $p = .418$) than for inside homicides (22% increase, $p = .006$). In addition, non-gun homicides increased slightly and nonsignificantly (16% increase) as did gun homicides (13% increase). Although 1,020 persons were charged under the ordinance in 1989, only 22 defendants were sentenced to jail.

Jung and Jason (1988) evaluated the impact of an East St. Louis, Illinois, law that required a mandatory $500 fine and possible 6-month jail term for persons found carrying a firearm on the street. The researchers used a time-series design to examine intervention effects on firearm assaults and firearm robberies in East St. Louis and Rock Island, a city which had a level of reported crime similar to East St. Louis. In East St. Louis, firearm assaults declined significantly approximately 1 year before the law went into effect, and then increased significantly approximately 5 months after the law went into effect. Changes in East St. Louis firearm robberies over time paralleled those for firearm assaults. The evaluators also mentioned that there were no significant substitution effects (i.e., replacing firearms with other weapons) for assaults and robberies in East St. Louis. Jung and Jason (1988) suggested that the preintervention decline might be attributable to media coverage of the proposed law, although they did not report how much this coverage coincided with the decrease in gun-related crime. In Rock Island, there was no significant variation in firearm assaults and firearm robberies in either the pre- or postintervention periods. This evaluation, however, did not include direct comparisons between pre- and postintervention periods for either city.

Mandatory sentencing laws for felonies involving firearms. At both the federal and state levels, mandatory sentencing laws have been enacted that impose more stringent sentences for offenders who use or carry a firearm during the commission of a felony. Fife and Abrams (1989) evaluated the effects of New Jersey's 1981 Graves Amendment, which mandated a minimum prison sentence for any person convicted of one of several serious crimes who was in possession of a firearm or used a firearm during the commission of the crime. The evaluators examined annual percentages of homicides that involved a firearm from 1974 to 1986 for New Jersey and the United States as a whole. The proportion of New Jersey homicides that involved firearms increased nonsignificantly from 1974 to 1980, but decreased significantly from 1980 to 1986. The difference between these rates of increase and decrease was significant. For the United States as a whole, the proportion of homicides that involved firearms decreased significantly in the preintervention period and decreased at a slightly lower (but nonsignificant) rate for the postintervention period. The difference between the pre- and postintervention decreases for the whole United States was not significant. However, the evaluators did not examine the patterns of firearm homicide rates over time and compare them with the corresponding patterns of non-firearm homicides. Additionally, the time-series included few (13) observations.

McDowall, Loftin, and Wiersema (1992) and Loftin, McDowall, and Wiersema (1993) performed a meta-analysis of their evaluations of mandatory sentencing laws that imposed strict, mandatory sentences for felonies committed while in possession of a firearm (Loftin, Heumann, & McDowall,

1983; Loftin & McDowall, 1984). The researchers combined the time-series results of intervention impacts on homicide, aggravated assault, and robbery in six cities (Detroit, Jacksonville, Tampa, Miami, Philadelphia, and Allegheny County). Gun homicides decreased in all six cities after mandatory enhancement sentencing laws were enacted, and the overall effect across studies was substantial and significant (mean ES = −.69). Non-gun homicides decreased only in two cities after mandatory sentencing laws were passed, and the overall effect across evaluations was virtually nonexistent (mean ES = −.03). The effects of the sentencing laws on aggravated assault and robbery were estimated by cumulating results from Detroit, Jacksonville, Miami, Tampa, and the state of Pennsylvania. After the laws were adopted, gun assaults declined in four of the five jurisdictions, but the overall intervention effect was modest and nonsignificant (mean ES = −.36). Other types of assaults decreased in only two of the five jurisdictions and did not change appreciably after the laws were passed (mean ES = −.06). Armed robberies decreased in two of the five jurisdictions, and the combined effect was essentially null (mean ES = .08). Unarmed robberies increased in all five jurisdictions, and the aggregated effect was moderate but nonsignificant (mean ES = .68). For each of these six subtypes of crimes, there was significant variation in the magnitude of intervention effects among the cities.

Although the aggregate effects of the sentencing laws on aggravated gun assaults and armed robberies were not significant or large, they were more in the preventive direction than the aggregate effects for other assaults and unarmed robberies. As McDowall et al. (1992) noted, the homicide data are probably more completely and accurately reported than the assault or robbery data. Greater inaccuracies in the assault and robbery data might have masked the impact of the sentencing laws on these crimes. Furthermore, in these evaluations armed robbery did not specifically refer to robberies committed with a gun (except for the Pennsylvania data), and this additional imprecision in coding could further mask intervention effects.

Summary of Policy Change Interventions

There is evidence that community policy change interventions can prevent juvenile antisocial behavior. For example, changing policies regulating the availability and legal use of tobacco and alcohol appears to have some impact on juvenile use of these substances, although most studies in this area are correlational rather than experimental and none of the studies reviewed looked at impact on SVJ offending. There are mixed findings from studies of regulations on the purchase and sale of firearms, suggesting that local community support and enforcement of these laws may mediate their effects. Similar results are found concerning regulations on the place and manner of carrying firearms, suggesting again that community norms and local enforcement of these regulations influence their effectiveness.

In contrast, mandatory sentencing laws for crimes involving firearms appear to prevent homicides involving firearms. Such laws also may prevent other types of violent crime involving firearms, but the available evaluations do not yet permit this conclusion. As McDowall et al. (1992) urged, more research on the impact of sentencing laws with probability samples of jurisdictions is needed to identify the key mechanisms of the laws, their publicity, and/or their enforcement that bring about the preventive impact. Unfortunately, these studies do not allow differentiation between juvenile-perpetrated crime and adult-perpetrated crime. In each of these areas, more research is needed to determine the impact of local norms and enforcement on the effectiveness of these policy change interventions.

Media Interventions

An eighth community-level prevention strategy that has shown positive effects is use of the media to change public attitudes, educate community residents, and support other community interventions. Although none of these interventions was aimed at changing attitudes or behaviors related to serious juvenile offending, they illustrate a promising direction for future research related to changing community antiviolence norms and behaviors. The media and advertising industries have cooperated in a national project, Partnership for a Drug Free America, to encourage negative attitudes toward the use of illegal drugs through the use of antidrug advertising (e.g., "This is your brain on drugs"). Results of mall intercept surveys indicate that saturation advertising in 10 markets was accompanied by significant changes in norms and by attitudes less favorable to marijuana and cocaine when compared with other markets over a 1-year period (Black, 1989). However, others have questioned the motives and effectiveness of such attempts to change individuals' health behavior through advertisements emphasizing individual, rather than social and environmental factors (Dorfman & Wallack, 1993). Although media campaigns have shown limited effectiveness as isolated strategies (Schilling & McAlister, 1990), they have been found to enhance the effects of related school- and community-based prevention programs (Flynn et al., 1992; Goodstadt, 1989; Pentz, Brannon, et al., 1989; Perry et al., 1992; Vartiainen, Pallonen, McAlister, Koskela, & Puska, 1986; Vartiainen et al., 1990) and to increase participation and exposure to parent training programs

(Didier, 1990; Hawkins, Catalano, & Kent, 1991).

Flynn et al. (1992; Flynn, Worden, Secker-Walker, Badger, & Geller, 1995) evaluated the effectiveness of a combined school and mass media intervention to prevent cigarette smoking among adolescents in four widely separated communities. Over the course of 4 years, beginning with Grades 5, 6, and 7, students in two communities received both interventions while students in two other matched communities received only the school intervention. The school intervention consisted of grade-specific, four-session curricula delivered in Grades 5 through 10. The sequence of units covered smoking and health knowledge, decision-making skills, social influence and stress management skills, smoking cessation skills, and social support for nonsmokers. The media program consisted of 30- and 60-second radio and television messages addressing the same objectives as the classroom curricula and designed to appeal to six target age and gender groups using a variety of formats (e.g., comedy, music videos, cartoons, testimonials, and drama). An average of 190 television, 350 cable, and 350 radio broadcasts were purchased in each of the 4 intervention years in each of the two program condition media markets.

The results indicated that significantly fewer students in the combined media and school intervention condition than the school-intervention-only condition initiated smoking by the end of the intervention (Grades 8-10) (Flynn et al., 1992) and by the 2-year follow-up (Grades 10-12) (Flynn et al., 1995). Moreover, students in the combined intervention condition reported less favorable norms and attitudes toward smoking than students in the school-intervention-only condition. The findings suggest that targeted media messages can enhance the effectiveness of school prevention curricula.

Media intervention can also be used to influence community attitudes regarding other prevention initiatives. Casswell and her colleagues (Casswell, Gilmore, Maguire, & Ransom, 1989) evaluated an intervention in New Zealand designed to educate community members about alcohol-related problems and the need for regulation of alcohol sales and advertising. Two sets of three matched communities were assigned to receive a media campaign, a media campaign plus a full-time paid community organizer, or a no-treatment comparison group. The study found that residents in the four communities that received the media or media plus community organizing intervention maintained supportive attitudes toward stricter regulations on alcohol sales, price, and advertising, whereas attitudes among residents of the two comparison communities and the broader country shifted in favor of greater access to alcohol (Casswell et al., 1989).

Summary of Media Interventions

Media interventions have primarily been used alone or in combination to affect cigarette and alcohol use. Evaluations conducted to date have found that media interventions can be effective in reducing favorable norms regarding smoking and alcohol use, and in combination with classroom curricula have been found to reduce smoking initiation. To date, no quasi-experimental evaluations of media interventions that target delinquency or violence have been conducted.

Summary: Characteristics of Effective Community Prevention Programs

Experimental and quasi-experimental studies of community interventions to reduce risk and enhance protection against antisocial behavior have demonstrated positive effects of community mobilization, situational, comprehensive, mentoring, afterschool recreation, policing, policy change, and media interventions. Generally, these interventions have targeted risk factors including easy availability of firearms and drugs, community disorganization, and favorable community norms and attitudes toward antisocial behavior. They have also targeted protective factors of social bonding and clear norms against antisocial behavior. These studies suggest that multiple prevention strategies crossing multiple domains that are mutually reinforcing and that are maintained for several years produce the greatest impact. If comprehensive community interventions are to reduce SVJ offending, mutually reinforcing messages against violence would need to be included: messages such as it isn't healthy to hit in families, and that solving problems nonaggressively and alternatives to physical fighting are preferred. Although not studied directly, intensive media campaigns related to changes in firearm laws appear to play some role in reducing firearm-related offenses as seen in time-series analyses indicating decreases in offenses prior to law enactment and after the media campaign concluded (Jung & Jason, 1988).

■ *Limitation of Current Research on Comprehensive Interventions to Prevent SVJ Offending*

Mobilization and Readiness for Prevention

Comprehensive intervention strategies frequently involve mobilizing community members to participate actively in planning and widely implementing prevention activi-

ties (e.g., Fawcett, Paine, Francisco, & Vliet, 1993; Giesbrecht & Ferris, 1993; Hawkins, Catalano, & Associates, 1992). Thus, local "ownership" is a vital component of successful comprehensive prevention interventions (Haglund, Weisbrod, & Bracht, 1990; Watt & Rodmell, 1988). Mobilization is believed to increase the impact of preventive interventions by reducing social disorganization, promoting strong community norms against antisocial behavior, and creating community ownership and investment in prevention activities.

Yet there are gaps in the theoretical and empirical knowledge base regarding community mobilization approaches to prevention. We know that community members who feel they can influence how their community's problems are defined and how these problems are addressed are more likely to support such efforts (Hyndman et al., 1992) and that women, longer-term residents, homeowners, and those who perceived greater problems on the block, a greater sense of community, and greater political efficacy are more likely to participate in block organizations (Perkins, Florin, Rich, Wandersman, & Chavis, 1990; Wandersman, Florin, Freidmann, & Meier, 1987). Yet we know little about strategies to promote these feelings of efficacy, empowerment, need, or community attachment to create an environment that embraces mobilization. Although prevention planners and researchers have recognized that readiness for change is an important determinant of successful community interventions (Haglund et al., 1990; Oetting et al., 1995; Price & Lorion, 1989), less research has been conducted to examine factors that influence a community's readiness to implement such initiatives (Arthur et al., 1996; Oetting et al., 1995). Little research has been done to develop a systematic framework for understanding, measuring, and addressing readiness for prevention at the community level (Fortmann, Flora, & Winkleby, 1995; Oetting et al., 1995). Research on readiness for change is more advanced in the areas of individual and organizational development (Bandura, 1986; Prochaska, DiClemente, & Norcross, 1992; Rogers, 1995).

Theoretical and practical approaches to mobilization and readiness for change have been developed; however, empirical evaluation of these approaches is in early stages (Bracht & Kingsbury, 1990; Fawcett et al., 1993; Rothman & Tropman, 1987; Thompson & Kinne, 1990). Two important principles emerge from the literature regarding readiness for change. First, communities can be described as complex, open systems with multiple interrelated subsystems. Thus, prevention can be conceptualized as systems change. Second, both attitudinal characteristics and structural characteristics are consistently reported to be important influences on communities' abilities to change. Further study of factors related to citizen participation and community readiness is needed to develop the knowledge and theory base for comprehensive prevention initiatives (Biglan, 1995).

Methodological Issues

Knowledge of the effectiveness of community interventions has been limited by a number of methodological concerns (Connell, Kubisch, Schorr, & Weiss, 1995). Community intervention research involves study designs that must address threats posed by measurement constraints, mixed units of analysis, and implementation integrity as well as the interpretive challenge presented by heterogeneous effects across populations and along the developmental life course. Each of these issues and potential methods for addressing them are discussed in the following sections.

Measurement issues. Focusing on the individual as the unit of measurement is appropriate for intervention and research designs that focus on creating and documenting changes in individuals and/or their perceptions of their environments. However, for interventions and research that emphasize changes in social environments and community systems, community-level measures are needed to assess such changes adequately. Recently, efforts have been made to develop and validate community-level indicators of important independent and dependent measures (Cairns et al., 1990; Coulton, 1995; McAuliffe et al., 1993; Six State Consortium for Prevention Needs Assessment Studies [SSC], 1994).

For example, for the past 3 years the authors have been collaborating with a consortium of six states to identify, collect, and validate standardized survey and archival indicators of risk and protective factors, drug abuse, crime, and violence, with funding from the Center for Substance Abuse Prevention (Arthur, Hawkins, Catalano, Pollard, & Howze, 1997; Pollard, Catalano, Hawkins, & Arthur, 1997; SSC, 1994). This effort reflects a triangulation approach using household and student surveys and archival records to comprehensively measure risk and protective factors and antisocial behavior at the community and individual levels to support coordinated prevention strategies. It represents one potential solution to obtaining multilevel, multi-informant measurements that match the multilevel constructs of interest. However, although valid and reliable measures of multiple risk and protective factors and antisocial behavior now exist, they have not yet been used in comprehensive prevention experiments.

Mixed units of analysis. Studies of comprehensive prevention initiatives operate simultaneously at multiple ecological levels. In many published studies of comprehensive prevention programs, a basic premise of experimental design—that the unit randomized to experimental condition is the unit of analysis—is violated. Communities, schools, or classrooms are often the unit of random assignment to experimental or control condition, but analyses of the impact of the intervention are often assessed using the individual as the unit of analysis. Community, school, or classroom differences are thus confounded with program effects on individuals (Biglan & Ary, 1985). Some studies have addressed this problem by assigning multiple communities, schools, or classrooms to each condition, then analyzing at the same level at which randomization occurs (Biglan et al., 1987; Botvin, Baker, Renick, Filazzola, & Botvin, 1984; Hansen, Johnson, Flay, Graham, & Sobel, 1988; Pentz, MacKinnon, et al., 1989; Perry et al., 1993). Careful assessment of the power of the research design is an important step in studies using small numbers of randomized communities (Koepsell et al., 1991; Murray & Hannan, 1990).

When scarce resources impose limits on the number of units that can be randomly assigned, some alternative solutions have been suggested, including matching communities prior to randomization on variables related to the outcomes of interest (Peterson, Hawkins, & Catalano, 1992), randomized block and factorial designs to stratify communities by factors known to affect key outcomes (McKinlay, Stone, & Zucker, 1989), mixed-model analyses of variance (Koepsell et al., 1991), hierarchical linear modeling (Bryk & Raudenbush, 1992), and generalized estimating equations (Liang & Zeger, 1986) to estimate both the individual- and group-level components of variation. Alternatively, to account for variability attributable to the community, multiple investigators conducting similar studies with different populations in comparable or contrasting community settings could build a collective case for the general effectiveness of a given approach (Coie et al., 1993; Conduct Problems Prevention Research Group, 1992). Clear specification of the settings and careful attention to implementation integrity are included. Although methods and strategies have been developed, they have been infrequently applied.

Heterogeneity of effect across different populations. Some prevention studies have shown differential effectiveness with different demographic, gender, class, and racial/ethnic groups. Such differences can mask the effects of community-level interventions delivered to diverse populations. When sample sizes are sufficiently large, researchers can investigate directly the differential effects of preventive interventions on different groups. When subgroups are not large enough for such analysis, Dwyer et al. (1989) have proposed statistical methods using combined logistic and multiple regression models to estimate interaction effects between intervention condition and baseline risk levels. Oversampling of smaller demographic groups can also be used to generate large enough samples to investigate differential program impact. Ultimately, replication studies are needed to confirm the utility of specific prevention strategies with different populations. Again, these analytic strategies have been infrequently applied to the evaluation of comprehensive preventive interventions.

Systematic attrition, accretion, and ecological validity. Problems of attrition are acute in community- and school-based studies that are designed to follow longitudinal cohorts including those who make frequent residential changes and truants. Many published studies of community-based prevention interventions have not addressed attrition, reporting results only for youths remaining in experimental and comparison conditions. The external validity of results from many school- and community-based preventive interventions has been compromised by systematic attrition of those at highest risk for antisocial behavior. This is especially true in neighborhoods with high rates of alcohol and other drug use, crime, and violence.

Where attrition has been investigated, studies have consistently shown that subjects with higher baseline levels of antisocial behavior are most likely to be lost at follow-up (Ary et al., 1990; Biglan et al., 1987; Hansen et al., 1988; Tebes, Snow, & Arthur, 1992), raising questions as to the generalizability of reported results to those at greatest risk. Several solutions to this problem have been proposed though they have not yet been used extensively. McKinlay et al. (1989) recommend the "intention-to-treat" approach, in which all subjects in the original cohort are assessed and retained for the analysis, even if they have left the community or opted out of the intervention, to avoid the bias of differential attrition and preserve the integrity of the randomization. Alternatively, direct observation of the effects of missing data due to attrition may be obtained by including a dummy-coded variable for subjects lost to the study in the analysis (Raymond, 1987). Estimates of attrition effects on external validity can also be derived from analyses of accretion samples (i.e., subjects that are added to the setting and data collection after baseline data collection, randomization, or intervention), because accretion and attrition samples typically have similar characteristics (Tebes, Snow, Ayers, & Arthur, 1996). Recent advances in statistical methods for imputing missing data (e.g., Graham & Donaldson,

1993; McArdle & Hamagami, 1991) provide another alternative for adjusting estimates of program impact that are threatened by participant attrition and accretion.

Intervention implementation integrity and intensity. Prevention studies should also investigate the effects of differential intervention implementation integrity and intensity (IOM, 1994; McKinlay et al., 1989; Peterson et al., 1992). Given the multiple factors likely to influence comprehensive prevention program implementation, this issue is particularly important for community prevention studies. By randomly and independently selecting samples of residents in intervention communities at each measurement point, factors hypothesized to influence the impact of the intervention may be examined (e.g., length of exposure, level of teacher training, variety of media employed). In our own prevention studies, we have proposed and used three steps in examining implementation: (a) collection of data to assess degree of implementation, (b) reporting of data on implementation for each dimension of the intervention, and (c) inclusion of implementation data in the tests of efficacy (Hawkins, Abbott, Catalano, & Gillmore, 1991; Hawkins & Lam, 1987).

■ *Current Directions and Implications for Future Work*

Although limited by the difficulties inherent in evaluating comprehensive interventions, the research suggests that comprehensive schoolwide and community interventions can reduce risk factors, enhance protective factors, and prevent adolescent antisocial behavior (Wasserman and Miller, Chapter 10, this volume). Moreover, these interventions appear to have the greatest impact when multiple strategies are employed simultaneously in a coordinated fashion. The current challenge for prevention is to develop theoretical and implementation models that can guide community members in the design, implementation, and evaluation of comprehensive, coordinated, multicomponent prevention strategies.

If communities are to prevent SVJ offending, they must use the entire knowledge base to take an approach that targets the most virulent risk factors or weakest protective factors in communities where children are exposed to multiple risk factors. After this targeting, communities must use preventive interventions with demonstrated effects on targeted risk and protective factors. To date, only one approach has used this knowledge base comprehensively in communities: Communities That Care.

Our research team has developed a model, called Communities That Care (CTC) (Hawkins, Catalano, & Associates, 1992), for comprehensive community intervention to reduce risk and enhance protection based on the social development model (Catalano & Hawkins, 1996; Hawkins & Weis, 1985). The social development model organizes identified risk and protective factors into a theoretical model of antisocial behavior that specifies four submodels for different developmental periods from birth through adolescence.

The CTC strategy consists of three phases. In the first phase, key community leaders including the mayor, superintendent of schools, chief law enforcement officer, judges, and business and other community leaders are provided a half-day orientation to the project. If they commit to implementing it, they decide as a group to become the oversight body for the project and to appoint a prevention board of diverse members of their community. During the second phase, the community prevention board is constituted and trained to conduct a community risk and re-

source assessment. Over a 6-month period, the board gathers archival and survey data on indicators of the risk and protective factors for adolescent health and behavior problems in the community. Based on these data, the board prioritizes risk and protective factors for preventive action. The board then designs its prevention strategy to address targeted risk factors and enhance protective factors, selecting preventive interventions from a menu of programs and strategies that have shown positive effects in adequately controlled studies. In the third phase, the board implements and evaluates the combined effects of the selected preventive strategies, using task forces composed of community members with a stake in the outcome and expertise in the particular intervention component. Baseline risk assessment data serve as the benchmark against which to judge community progress in risk reduction in subsequent years.

With funding from the U.S. Department of Education, we field tested an early version of the strategy in Washington State (Harachi Manger, Hawkins, Haggerty, & Catalano, 1992). We demonstrated that key community leaders (i.e., mayors, police chiefs, school superintendents, business leaders) could be successfully involved in creating community boards (29 of 32 participating communities formed community boards). We also showed that the community boards would use the risk reduction and protective factor enhancement approach to prevention and the social development model as tools for assessing and reducing risks and enhancing protective factors and processes in the community.

From this demonstration, we learned important lessons regarding communities' organizational and technical assistance needs. First, it became clear that risk assessments should be solidly grounded in empirical epidemiological evidence and not dependent on personal judgments of board members.

Hence, we developed an archival data-based risk and resource assessment process for use in communities implementing the strategy. These data allow for an empirically grounded prioritization of risk and protective factor indicators to be targeted for strategic preventive intervention.

In this first demonstration, communities also requested assistance in identifying empirically tested preventive interventions to address the risk factors they had prioritized. The investigative team's reviews of risk reduction interventions led to the identification of a set of effective interventions for risk reduction that simultaneously enhance protective factors (see Brewer et al., 1995; Developmental Research and Programs, 1996; Hawkins, Arthur, & Catalano, 1995; Hawkins, Catalano, & Associates, 1992; Hawkins, Catalano, & Brewer, 1995b; Hawkins, Catalano, & Miller, 1992). These approaches have been included in CTC to enable communities to select effective preventive interventions for inclusion in their comprehensive risk reduction and protective factor enhancement strategies.

We extensively revised the training and technical assistance package to address issues emerging from the Washington pilot (Harachi Manger, 1991; Harachi Manger et al., 1992) and field tested it in Oregon under a demonstration grant from the Center for Substance Abuse Prevention. Forty communities were invited to send key leaders to an orientation in 1990, and 37 of those communities formed 36 community boards (one pair of communities decided to form a joint board). Thirty-five community boards attended both of the project's board trainings, 34 communities developed action plans identifying prevention programs to reduce specified risk factors, and 21 (60%) had implemented effective risk reduction programs within 1 year after receiving the training, even though they had not been provided funding to implement pro-

grams (Arthur, Ayers, Graham, & Hawkins, 1997). Moreover, 31 boards were still active in their communities 4 years later, monitoring community risks and resources and implementing risk reduction prevention programs (Harachi, Ayers, Hawkins, Catalano, & Cushing, 1995). By comparison, in a similar project in Washington State using a different community risk reduction strategy, only 13 (23%) of 56 community teams that received training, technical assistance, and funding for programs had implemented at least one promising risk reduction strategy by the 1-year follow-up (Arthur, Ayers, et al., 1997).

Our experience with these projects has revealed the importance of ongoing training and proactive technical assistance during the first few years of the community mobilization process to ensure the institutionalization of risk- and protection-focused prevention. It also has indicated the importance of developing epidemiological methods for assessing risk and protective factors in the community to guide the prioritization of targets for preventive intervention. Currently, through the Six State Consortium project (funded by the Center for Substance Abuse Prevention), we have developed and validated a standardized risk and protective factor assessment system that incorporates and integrates archival, student, and household survey data on risk and protective factors and prevalence of antisocial behavior (Arthur, Hawkins, et al., 1997; Pollard et al., 1997). These standardized data allow local communities to plot their own unique profiles and trends in risk and protective factors relative to state and national averages and in relation to other communities.

This experience suggests the utility of the approach, which combines community mobilization and epidemiologically based social planning approaches with preventive interventions with evidence of effectiveness. This strategy empowers communities to develop theory-based, empirically grounded prevention systems that coordinate multiple prevention strategies and that address the specific epidemiological risk and protective factor profiles of each community. Based on this field experience and the empirical and theoretical basis of the risk and protective factors and effective prevention programs, the OJJDP chose CTC training for community coalitions as a way of assisting these coalitions to plan for spending Title V delinquency prevention block grants. A report by the General Accounting Office (GAO) reported early results from this effort. GAO (1996) found that communities targeted a variety of risk and protective factors, used strategies with demonstrated effectiveness, and that the federal dollars leveraged close to an equal amount of community resources. In addition, CTC has been chosen as the prevention component of OJJDP's Comprehensive Strategy to reduce SVJ offenders (Wilson & Howell, 1993). Although controlled studies have yet

to be conducted, the Rowntree Foundation in Great Britain has approved funding for a test of the CTC process.

For communities to become protective environments for healthy development, community members will ultimately have to take responsibility for identifying, prioritizing, and addressing risk and protective factors in the community as well as for implementing strategies with demonstrated effectiveness to reduce salient risks and enhance salient protective factors. Recent advances in prevention science and health epidemiology are providing knowledge communities can use to plan and implement strategic, outcome-focused plans for reducing the prevalence of serious, violent antisocial behavior among adolescents and young adults. The interventions reviewed in this chapter provide evidence that risk factors can be reduced and protective factors enhanced by comprehensive school and community interventions.

CHAPTER 12

Promising Programs for Youth Gang Violence Prevention and Intervention

■ *James C. Howell*

The United States has seen rapid growth of youth gangs[1] since 1980. During this period, the number of youth gang problem cities has increased from an estimated 286 with over 2,000 gangs and nearly 100,000 members (Miller, 1982) to about 2,000 cities, towns, and counties with more than 23,000 gangs and membership totaling nearly 665,000 in 1995 (National Youth Gang Center, 1997). The 1995 National Youth Gang Survey covered over 4,000 law enforcement agencies in the United States, 58% of which reported gang youth problems in their jurisdiction, using their own definition (National Youth Gang Center, 1997).

Preventing and controlling youth gangs is important because recent studies show that gang members, who represent a minority of adolescent samples, account for the majority of all self-reported offenses among urban juveniles in gang problem cities, and from about half to over two thirds of all serious and violent offenses committed by adolescents in Denver (Esbensen & Huizinga, 1993), Rochester (Thornberry, Chapter 8, this volume), and Seattle (Battin, Hill, Abbott, Catalano, &

AUTHOR'S NOTE: Preparation of this chapter was supported in part by an Office of Juvenile Justice and Delinquency Prevention award (#95-JD-MU-K001) to the National Youth Gang Center, Institute for Intergovernmental Research (IIR). I am grateful to Rolf Loeber, David Farrington, David Altschuler, Jim Short, Walter Miller, John Moore, Bruce Buckley, Joan Moore, Cheryl Maxson, David Curry, and Rebecca Block for helpful comments on earlier drafts.

Hawkins, in press). Moreover, studies in all three of these sites show an increase in the incidence of serious and violent offending while adolescents are active gang members (Esbensen & Huizinga, 1993; Hill, Hawkins, Catalano, Kosterman, Abbott, & Edwards, 1996; Thornberry, Krohn, Lizotte, & Chard-Wierschem, 1993). In Rochester, nearly two thirds of chronic violent offenders self-reported gang membership at some point in their adolescent years (Thornberry, Huizinga, & Loeber, 1995).

Can the youth gang problem be solved? Miller (1974) suggests:

> It happens that great nations engage in national wars for almost identical reasons [that gangs do] . . . personal honor, prestige, and defense against perceived threats to one's homeland. . . . When a solution to this problem [of fighting nations has been found], we will at the same time have solved the problem of violent crimes in city gangs. (p. 112)

Is there basis for more optimism than Miller expresses?

The history of efforts to solve the youth gang problem in the United States is largely filled with frustration and failure. Early in our nation's history, youth gang work emphasized prevention. These programs were followed by interventions designed to reintegrate particular gangs into conventional society. Then a major shift occurred as programs, led by the police, aimed to suppress youth gangs. Currently, a mixture of approaches is being tried across the nation, predominantly police suppression programs (Spergel & Curry, 1993). None of these approaches has been demonstrated conclusively through rigorous research to be effective. Two factors appear to account for this: the difficulties associated with gang intervention work and the complexity of program evaluation in this area.

Youth gang intervention is a very formidable enterprise. Because we lack a clear understanding of why and how youth gangs form, preventing their formation is problematic. Gang interventions rarely are based on theoretical assumptions. This lack of knowledge impedes efforts to disrupt existing gangs and divert youth from them. Gangs dissolve and disappear for reasons that are poorly understood. In some cities, youths who join gangs leave them within about 1 year. Yet we do not understand why. Future youth gang research must address the formation of gangs, disruptive forces, and factors that account for diversion of youths from gangs.

Evaluation of youth gang interventions is an equally complex undertaking. Not only must gang formation, dissolution, and diversion be shown but also delinquency prevention or reduction. Because each youth gang is unique and each community is different in some respects, obtaining comparable comparison groups or communities is difficult. Measurement problems abound. There is no commonly accepted definition of a youth gang; therefore, comparing study results is problematic. Most important, very few rigorous evaluations of youth gang programs have been undertaken.

With these caveats in mind, we review the existing literature. Evaluations of youth gang programs and new approaches for preventing and reducing youth gang problems are reviewed. A youth gang prevention and intervention program strategy is recommended based on this review. The general questions guiding this review are: What can we learn from what has been tried? What has failed? What looks promising? In the next section, we review gang program evaluations. That section is followed by recommended approaches our review suggests. Three strategies are recommended: targeting gang problems directly; targeting gang problems within a comprehensive strategy for dealing with serious, violent, and chronic juvenile delinquency; and targeting gang-related (and gang-motivated) homicides. Our third program recommendation is based in part on the Epidemiology of Youth Gang Homicides at the end of this chapter (Table 12.2).

■ A Review of Gang Program Evaluations

Space limitations here preclude a detailed review of all gang program evaluations. See Table 12.1 for summary information on selected evaluations.

Prevention and Intervention Programs

Prevention. The early history of gang programming in the United States emphasized preventing both gang emergence and joining, based on the gang and delinquency research conducted by Shaw (1930), with his colleague, McKay (Shaw & McKay, 1931), and Thrasher (1927/1963). The Chicago Area Project (CAP), created in 1934 by Clifford Shaw, was designed to implement the community organization theory he and his colleagues developed on "social disorganization," proffering the notion that community organization could be a major tool for reducing crime and gang problems. CAP was designed to involve local community groups, that is, indigenous community organizations, in improving neighborhood conditions that Shaw believed permitted the formation of youth gangs. "Tying informal community structures to formal agencies—schools, enforcement, welfare—would provide the social structure for healthy socialization and vitiate the need for gangs and other forms of deviance" (Klein, 1995, p. 139). CAP invented "detached workers" (agency representatives

detached from their offices and assigned to communities). CAP also originated the community gang worker role. "Indeed, the concept of 'detached workers' or 'gang workers' . . . became the more narrow essence of major gang projects for decades to come" (Klein, 1995, p. 140).

CAP was a massive program. Because its influence and program activities extended throughout Chicago, one must wonder if it could be evaluated except in comparison with another similar city. Nevertheless, Kobrin's (1959) 25-year retrospective assessment concluded that the project had been successful, on "logical and analytical" grounds (see Alinsky, 1946; Klein, 1995, pp. 139-140). Claims of the success of the CAP program continue to be publicized (Sorrentino, 1959; Sorrentino & Whittaker, 1994) despite the absence of rigorous evaluation results. The program is still operating, which says something about views of its value among Chicago officials.

More important, CAP created a legacy in gang programming in its emphasis on the role of the community and its private organizations. As Witmer (quoted in Klein, 1995) put it, CAP demonstrated:

Local residents can organize themselves with effective mechanisms for dealing with youth problems. Such organizations can endure over long periods of time. Local talent can be discovered and enlisted in the battle. One need not be dependent on existing bureaucratic entities. (p. 141)

Literally hundreds of community committees were formed, which emphasized different community concerns (Klein, 1995, p. 140). Local workers became the staff of community programs. Local programs sponsored recreation opportunities, community self-renewal, mediation, and advocacy before government agencies, especially school, probation, and parole officials (Schlossman & Sedlak, 1983a, 1983b). Most of these efforts were directed at community improvements, securing services for residents, and organizing direct intervention in delinquency and gang activity (Klein, 1995, p. 140).

Another community-based gang program that, like CAP, relied on indigenous community organizations was established much later. The House of Umoja began operating in Philadelphia during the 1970s (Spergel, 1995). It consists of a residential and nonresidential program for gang and other delinquent youths, providing a sanctuary for them from street life while assisting target youths through a comprehensive program that included educational development, career development, employment assistance, and individual counseling. The House of Umoja is a unique grassroots program initiated by community residents (David and Falaka Fattah). Based on the extended family concept and a "new concept of peace," the program organized a gang summit, resulting in a gang warfare truce (Spergel, 1995; Woodson, 1981, 1986). Woodson's (1981) assessment concluded that the truce and other House of Umoja activities were instrumental in reducing the number of gang deaths in the city from an average of 39 per year in 1973, to 6 in 1976, and to only 1 in 1977. Although other programs claimed credit for part of this reduction in gang homicides, there is no doubt that House of Umoja played a key role. The 1974 gang summit leading to the truce drew 500 members from 75% of the city's gangs (Fattah, 1987). No gang members died during the 60-day truce that resulted.

Only one program designed to prevent youths from joining gangs has been evaluated rigorously and shown to have promise. It was a component of Project Broader Urban Involvement and Leadership Development (BUILD) (Brewer, Hawkins, Catalano, & Neckerman, 1995; Ribisl & Davidson, 1993). The prevention component consisted of a gang prevention curriculum and an after-school program. The school gang prevention curriculum consisted of 12 classroom sessions conducted over 12 weeks that focused on background information on gangs, gang violence, and substance abuse in gangs; gang recruitment strategies and methods of resisting gang recruitment; consequences of gang membership; and values clarification. Most classroom sessions were led by project staff; others were led by a prosecuting attorney and by ethnic minority guest speakers who held various positions in the community. The curriculum was taught to eighth-grade students in Chicago middle schools located in lower- and lower-middle-class areas with high levels of gang activity. Following completion of the curriculum component, youths from the classrooms considered to be at high risk for joining a gang were invited to participate in an afterschool program. It provided recreational activities, job skills training workshops, educational assistance programs, and social activities. At-risk youth were identified by teachers and project staff (using gang rosters compiled by detached street gang workers on the basis of interviews with gang members). The selected youth were not already gang members, to the best knowledge of project staff and teachers.

Thompson and Jason's (1988) evaluation of the program incorporated a "nonequivalent comparison group" design, in which three pairs of public middle schools were matched on the basis that the same gang actively recruited members from both schools in a pair. One school in each pair was randomly assigned to be an experimental school, and the other was designated as a comparison school. The researchers assessed gang membership again at the end of the school year using the same method as was used to select at-risk youth. All of the at-risk youth received the school curriculum, and 51% of them participated in at least one of the several afterschool activities. Results showed that experimental

TABLE 12.1 Selected Gang Program Evaluations: 1936-1997

Program	Study	Design	Type of Intervention	Results
New York City Boys Club	Thrasher (1936)	Descriptive and case study	Prevention—general delinquency	Negligible impact
Community Area Project	Kobrin (1959); Schlossman and Sedlak (1983a, 1983b)	Descriptive and case study	Prevention—community organization	Indeterminable
Total Community Delinquency Control Project (Midcity Project)	Miller (1962)	Field observation and quasi-experimental	Prevention—community organization, family services, and detached worker	Negligible impact
Chicago Youth Development Project	Caplan, Deshaies, Suttles, and Mattick (1967); Gold and Mattick (1974); Mattick and Caplan (1962)	Quasi-experimental community comparison	Prevention—detached worker and community organization	No differential impact
Chicago YMCA Program for Detached Workers	Short (1963); Short and Strodtbeck (1965)	Field observation and quasi-experimental observation	Prevention—detached worker	Early results encouraging; no final results: evaluation suspended
Group Guidance Program	Klein (1969, 1971)	Quasi-experimental	Prevention—detached worker	Significant increase in gang delinquency
Ladino Hills Project	Klein (1968)	Quasi-experimental	Prevention—detached worker	Significant reduction in gang delinquency
Community Action Program (Woodlawn Organization)	Spergel, Turner, Pleas, and Brown (1969); Spergel (1972)	Descriptive statistical trends	Social intervention	Ineffective
Wincroft Youth Project (United Kingdom)	Smith, Farrant, and Marchant (1972)	Quasi-experimental	Prevention—detached worker	No differential impact
Gang Violence Reduction Program	Torres (1981, 1985)	Quasi-experimental	Suppression and crisis intervention	Declines in gang homicides and intergang violence
House of Umoja	Woodson (1981, 1986)	Descriptive, case study, statistical trends	Prevention, crisis intervention, and social intervention	Effected truce among warring gangs; reduced homicides; sanctuary
Operation Hardcore	Dahmann (1981)	Quasi-experimental (process)	Suppression (vertical prosecution)	Successful gang prosecution process

TABLE 12.1 *Continued*

Program	Study	Design	Type of Intervention	Results
San Diego Street Youth Program	Pennell (1983)	Quasi-experimental community comparison	Prevention— detached worker	Indeterminable
Crisis Intervention Services Project	Spergel (1986)	Quasi-experimental community comparison	Crisis intervention and suppression	Some reduction in serious and violent crimes
Gang prevention curriculum	Thompson and Jason (1988)	Quasi-experimental school comparison	Prevention— discouraging adolescents from joining gangs	Marginal reduction
Youth Gang Drug Prevention Program (ACYF)	Cohen, Williams, Bekelman, and Crosse (1994)	Quasi-experimental treatment and control comparison	Prevention— discouraging adolescents from joining gangs; community mobility	Little/no effects on gang involvement; some delinquency reduction
Aggression Replacement Training	Goldstein and Glick (1994)	Quasi-experimental treatment and control comparison	Skill streaming, anger control, and moral education	Preliminary results with members of 10 gangs positive
General Reporting Evaluation and Tracking (GREAT) system	Kent and Smith (1995)	Quasi-experimental (process)	Suppression— targeting gang members for prosecution and supervision	Successful targeting process
Gang Violence Reduction Program	Spergel and Grossman (1995, 1996, 1997)	Quasi-experimental community comparison	Prevention, social intervention, and suppression	Preliminary results positive; best results with combined approach
Youth Gang Drug Intervention and Prevention Program for Female Adolescents	Curry, Williams, and Koenemann (1996, 1997)	Quasi-experimental (in Pueblo, Colorado; Boston; Seattle)	Prevention and social intervention	Pueblo program showed positive results with culture-based program for Mexican American females
Gang Resistance Education and Training (G.R.E.A.T.) program	Esbensen and Osgood (1997)	Quasi-experimental treatment and control comparison	Prevention— discouraging adolescents from joining gangs	Preliminary results are positive

youth were less likely to join a gang than comparison youth, but the difference was only marginally statistically significant. The evaluation was limited by the short-term follow-up period and the relatively small sample size (74 experimental youth and 43 comparison youth), given the low prevalence of gang membership (4 of the 43 comparison youth had joined gangs by the end of the school year and only 1 of the 74 experimental youth had). This kind of intervention appears to hold promise for preventing adolescents from joining gangs. A more recent evaluation of a gang prevention curriculum produced a stronger basis for curricular approaches.

Evaluation of the Bureau of Alcohol, Tobacco, and Firearms' Gang Resistance Education and Training (G.R.E.A.T.) program, initiated in 1991 by Phoenix law enforcement agencies, has shown positive preliminary results (Esbensen & Osgood, 1997). The G.R.E.A.T. program is a school-based intervention gang program in which uniformed law enforcement officers teach a 9-week curriculum to middle school students. These weekly sessions consist of nine lessons:

1. Introduction—acquainting students with the G.R.E.A.T. program and the presenting officer
2. Crime/victims and your rights—students learn about crimes, their victims, and their impact on the school and neighborhood
3. Cultural sensitivity/prejudice—teaching students how cultural differences affect their school and neighborhood
4. and 5. Conflict resolution (two lessons)—students learn how to create an atmosphere of understanding that would enable all parties to better address interpersonal problems and work together on solutions
6. Meeting basic needs—teaching students how to satisfy their basic social needs without joining a gang
7. Drugs/neighborhoods—students learn how drugs affect their school and neighborhood
8. Responsibility—students learn about the diverse responsibilities of people in their school and neighborhood
9. Goal setting—teaching students the need for personal goal setting and how to establish short- and long-term goals

Police instructors are trained in the G.R.E.A.T. curriculum in a management training session. They are taught how to use role-playing techniques and group exercises. This teacher training includes learning how to prepare students to present a lesson in the G.R.E.A.T. program, preparing them for later teaching in their own classrooms. The G.R.E.A.T. curriculum concludes with a graduation ceremony.

Evaluation of the G.R.E.A.T. program incorporated a quasi-experimental research design (Esbensen & Osgood, 1997). A cross-sectional survey of nearly 6,000 students in 315 classrooms in 42 different schools was conducted in 11 geographically and population-representative sites after the G.R.E.A.T. curriculum was administered. Because the G.R.E.A.T. program was taught in the seventh grade, eighth-grade students were surveyed to allow for a 1-year follow up, while guaranteeing that none of the sample was currently enrolled in the program. Two ex post facto comparison groups were created to allow for evaluation of program effects. Because preventing adolescents from joining gangs and engaging in criminal activity were the major goals of the program, a self-reported measure of gang joining and involvement in illegal activity was included in the cross-sectional survey.

Creation of the two comparison groups of students in the 42 schools (one group that received the G.R.E.A.T. curriculum and another that did not receive it) resulted in nonequivalent comparison groups. Comparison of sex, race, age, family status, and family education background characteristics of students in the two samples revealed that they differed on race and family socioeconomic status. Therefore, analyses controlled for between-school differences. Schools also were found to vary substantially in terms of the number of students who completed the G.R.E.A.T. program. Therefore, all analyses were replicated, limiting the total sample to a restricted sample of 28 schools in which there were at least 15 participants and nonparticipants. This procedure tended to strengthen the magnitude of the programmatic effect.

Students who completed the G.R.E.A.T. program reported lower levels of gang affiliation and self-reported delinquency, including drug use, minor offending, property crimes, and crimes against persons. Compared to the control group, the treatment group reported more positive attitudes to the police, more negative attitudes about gangs, having more friends involved in prosocial behavior, higher levels of perceived guilt at committing deviant acts, more commitment to school, higher levels of attachment to both mothers and fathers, more communication with parents about their activities, fewer friends involved in delinquent activity, less likelihood of acting impulsively, lower likelihood of engaging in risky behavior, and lower levels of perceived blockages to academic success.

The study authors caution that these results are preliminary and need to be viewed with caution. First, significant differences existed between the two groups. Second, a quasi-experimental design has been implemented in the longitudinal phase of the evaluation, in a prospective panel design at six representative sites. Both pre- and posttest measures have been obtained. Adding strength to this design, postprogram measures will be obtained in a planned 3-year follow-up.

Interventions using detached workers. A significant shift in youth gang program approaches, from prevention through community organization to interventions relying almost exclusively on detached workers, occurred in the late 1940s with the establishment of the New York City Youth Board (1960). Created to combat the city's growing number of fighting gangs, this city-run program relied on detached workers to transform street gangs, most of which was to be done in the streets, where gangs met, played, and

hung out. Worker activities included going fishing with gang members, securing health care, employment counseling, advocacy work with the police and court, and most any other action that might transform gangs or woo juveniles away from them (Geis, 1965). The Youth Board's gang program "lost the community focus [of the Chicago CAP] and developed instead a rather narrowly focused worker program which, nonetheless, became the model for future street work programs" (Klein, 1995, p. 142). Although the program was never evaluated, it served as a forerunner of detached worker programs.

The Boston detached worker program was evaluated (Miller, 1962), in perhaps the most rigorous gang program evaluation ever conducted. For 3 years, project staff in the Midcity Project (established in Roxbury, Boston in 1954) worked with 400 members of 21 corner gangs, providing intensive services to 7 gangs. This "total community" project consisted of three major program components: community organization, family service, and gang work. The project aimed to open channels of access to legitimate opportunities, especially in the education and employment areas. The project plan was comprehensive and unusually well implemented. However, Miller's (1962) evaluation proved the project to be ineffective. All of his measures of delinquency—disapproved actions, illegal behavior, during-project court appearances, before-during-after court appearances, and control group court appearances—provided consistent support for a finding of "negligible impact" (p. 187). The results were very disappointing to the field because of the quality of the program.

Evaluation of a California detached worker program brought into even more serious question the value of this approach. The Group Guidance Program of the Los Angeles Probation Department was evaluated by Klein (1969, 1971, 1995). The program, begun in

1961, was designed to employ "group guidance" by street workers in an attempt to intervene in the emergence of Black gangs in South-Central Los Angeles. Group activities, including weekly club meetings, sports activities, tutoring, individual counseling, and advocacy with community agencies and organizations, were designed to "de-isolate" gang members from their community institutions. Klein found that officially recorded arrests of gang members increased during the project period. He concluded that "increased group programming leads to increased cohesiveness (both gang growth and gang 'tightness'), and increased cohesiveness leads to increased gang crime" (Klein, 1995, p. 145).

The Ladino Hills Project, created in South-Central Los Angeles in 1961, was an experiment Klein (1968, 1971, 1995) designed to test his gang cohesiveness hypothesis, that if gang cohesiveness could be reduced through nongroup interventions, then gang delinquency would be reduced. Project staff, working with a gang that had the highest rate of commitments to correctional facilities of any gang in Los Angeles County, were to work individually with gang members. Interventions included helping gang members get jobs, tutoring, recreation in established agencies, and individual therapy. Program implementation was relatively successful. Klein's (1968) evaluation showed that gang cohesiveness was reduced by about 40%. Although individual arrest rates remained relatively constant, an overall reduction of 35% in gang member arrests was observed (attributed mainly to fewer members). However, several years later, the gang reassumed its preproject, gang-ridden character. Klein (1995) concluded that "we had affected the [gang members] but not their community. The lesson is both obvious and important. Gangs are by-products of their communities: They cannot long be controlled by attacks on

symptoms alone; community structure and capacity must also be targeted" (p. 147). Because of the success of his experiment, Klein has repeatedly warned practitioners against any activities that might contribute to gang cohesion, because these might increase gang delinquency. However, his findings have been challenged (J. W. Moore, 1978). Several other detached worker programs have been evaluated, generally with negative results (see Table 12.1).

Although there is disagreement concerning the effectiveness of detached worker programs (see Bursik & Grasmick, 1993; Goldstein & Glick, 1994), we must conclude that this program model, in its original concept, has not produced positive results. Indeed, evaluation of a Chicago detached worker program (Caplan, Deshaies, Suttles, & Mattick, 1967; Gold & Mattick, 1974; Mattick & Caplan, 1962) and another one in Los Angles (Klein, 1969) showed that they may have increased delinquency. Numerous reasons have been offered to account for the ineffectiveness of this strategy. Klein (1971; see also Spergel, 1966) suggests that it was unclear whether these programs were designed to control gangs, treat gang member personality problems, provide access to social and cultural opportunities, transform values, or prevent delinquency. Conflicting program objectives made evaluation difficult.

Spergel (1995) contends that a detached worker strategy by itself is inadequate to deal with complex problems such as remedial education, job preparation and development, and community issues. Perhaps this is why the detached worker concept has been expanded over the past 30 years to incorporate other interventions (Fox, 1985), including temporary shelters for low-income youths, mentoring programs, activity centers, postsentencing social services, drug treatment programs, and intergang mediation (Spergel & Curry, 1990).

Detached worker programs with these augmentations have not been evaluated, although one modified approach (gang transformation within a comprehensive youth services program) has shown positive results (Goldstein & Glick, 1994) in an initial trial. The authors believe the positive results they observed are attributable to the combination of skill streaming (a broad array of interpersonal and daily living skills), anger control, and moral reasoning. However, important details of the evaluation are not presented, such as how the treatment and control samples were selected and their comparability. The significance of the results is also dampened by small samples.

Crisis Intervention

In the next era of youth gang programming, detached workers were put in vehicles and sent to "hot spots" of gang activity. Philadelphia's Crisis Intervention Network (CIN), established in 1974, pioneered the new approach assigning gang workers to areas, not gangs. They were to patrol hot spots in radio-dispatched cars, attempting to defuse potentially violent situations. Although the CIN was not evaluated, it was acclaimed to be successful, though this conclusion has been challenged (Klein, 1995; Needle & Stapleton, 1983; Spergel, 1995).

Spergel (1986) evaluated the Crisis Intervention Services Project (CRISP) (see Ribisl & Davidson, 1993), which operated in a gang-ridden section of Chicago. Spergel (1995) described the program as a "mixed social intervention or crisis intervention approach, with strong deterrent and community involvement characteristics." Staff patrolled areas where gang violence was likely to erupt during evening and late-night hours, attempting to mediate conflicts. Secondary compo-

nents of the program included intensive counseling for gang youth and their families referred from juvenile court, mobilization of local neighborhood groups, and establishment of a neighborhood advisory group that oversaw the project. The program focused on several target areas in four police precincts characterized by high levels of gang activity.

The evaluation (Spergel, 1986) compared the number and type of gang incidents in the target area with a matched set of nontarget areas. Offenses were categorized as Type I, serious violent crimes (homicide, robbery) and Type II, less serious violent crimes (simple assault, intimidation, gang recruitment). Spergel's evaluation showed that gang crimes and overall crime increased in both the target and comparison areas. However, he found a significant reduction in the rate of increase in Type I offenses in the project areas compared to the control areas, comparing the preproject period with the project period. Little difference in Type II offenses was found between the experimental and control areas. Comparisons within the target areas suggested that the positive effects of the program were greater in the areas where program implementation closely followed the original design. The program appeared to be more effective for juveniles than for young adults, but it appeared to have little effect on nongang crime. Nevertheless, these were the most encouraging gang intervention results to date.

Gang Suppression Programs

The use of gang suppression techniques originated in the Philadelphia CIN program, with its deployment of mobile units to gang crisis areas. California criminal justice officials soon expanded the concept (Klein, 1995) in prosecution and police programs.

Operation Hardcore, a prosecutorial gang suppression program, was created by the Los Angeles District Attorney's Office in 1979 and is still operational today (Genelin, 1993). It was the first prosecution program to target serious, violent, juvenile gang-related offenses (Klein, Maxson, & Miller, 1995). Modeled after "major crime units" established in other cities' district attorney's offices, its distinctive features include vertical prosecution, reduced caseloads, additional investigative support, and resources for assisting victims.

An independent evaluation of the program (Dahmann, 1981) compared handling of defendants and cases by Operation Hardcore with other cases in Los Angeles handled by nonprogram attorneys both before and during program operations. It showed that Operation Hardcore had more convictions, fewer dismissals, more convictions to the most serious charge, and a higher rate of state prison commitments than the normal prosecutorial process. Dahmann concluded that "these results suggest that selective prosecution has been an effective strategy in Los Angeles and that the Operation Hardcore program has obtained demonstrable improvements in the criminal justice handling of gang defendants and their cases" (p. 303). Operation Hardcore remains a highly regarded program. Evaluation of the program has not examined its impact on gang crimes (Klein, 1995).

Police gang suppression programs (see Klein, 1995) drew impetus from the apparent growth of youth gang problems in the Southwest in the early 1980s. Gang Units (see Jackson & McBride, 1985) were created in law enforcement departments, carrying out gang intelligence, investigation, suppression, and prevention functions (Klein, 1995). Deliberate suppression tactics employed by the Los Angeles Police Department's CRASH (Community Resources Against Street Hood-

lums) operations took the form of "gang sweeps," "hot spot targeting," and "intensified patrol" to apply "excruciating pressure" on gangs. Other terms used to characterize police "crackdowns" include saturation, special surveillance, zero tolerance, and caravanning (cruising neighborhoods in a caravan of patrol cars) (Klein, 1995).

In contrast, law enforcement suppression activities can be incorporated in a balanced approach, such as in the activities of the Los Angeles Sheriff Department's Operation Safe Streets (OSS). Based on gang crime statistics, it appears that the OSS has done a more effective job in combating gang violence than CRASH (Klein, 1995). This could be expected, given that police crackdowns have shown limited effectiveness, generally short term (Sherman, 1990). In contrast, OSS employs "street-level intelligence, carefully nurtured" (Klein, 1995). OSS officers employ tactics attuned to the nature of gangs. They often work in the same community many years, know the gangs and their members very well, and thus are better able to diffuse volatile situations (see Jackson & McBride, 1985).

Operation Hammer, perhaps the worst example of a police suppression program, is described by Klein (1995). It was a Los Angeles Police Department CRASH antigang street sweep, launched in the South-Central section of the city in 1988. It consisted of a force of 1,000 police officers who swept through the area on a Friday night and again on Saturday, arresting likely gang members on a wide variety of offenses, including already existing warrants, new traffic citations, gang-related behaviors, and observed criminal activities. A total of 1,453 arrests resulted. All those arrested were taken to a mobile booking operation adjacent to the Memorial Coliseum. Most of the arrested youths were released without charges. Almost half were not gang members. There were only 60 felony arrests, and charges were filed in only 32 instances (Spergel, 1995). "This remarkably inefficient process was repeated many times, although with smaller forces—more typically one hundred or two hundred officers" (Klein, 1995, p. 162).

The newest gang suppression strategy is gun control. The Boston Gun Project (Kennedy, Piehl, & Braga, 1996) consists of a coordinated strategy based on analysis of the city's youth violence problem and illicit gun market. Research on Boston's youth violence problem has centered on youth gangs and their use of firearms. Mapping of gang territories and homicides revealed the central role gangs play in the city's youth gun problem. The Gun Project working group developed use-reduction and gun market disruption schemes that are being implemented and evaluated. Coerced use-reduction targeting gang members is the main strategy.

In sum, suppression programs have not been rigorously evaluated; therefore, their effectiveness is unknown. Following his review of the basic tenets of deterrence theory and tests of its viability, Klein (1993) concluded:

> It is not so much that suppression does or does not "work": evidence one way or another is sorely lacking. There are logical, as well as experiential, reasons to believe that suppression programs can have deterrent effects and thus, by our reasoning, can contribute substantially to gang and drug activity prevention. (p. 100)

Several researchers have noted that youth gang problems have not decreased in the areas where suppression programs have been implemented (Klein, 1995; J. W. Moore, 1978, 1991; Spergel, 1995). However, as Jackson and McBride (1985) note, gangs accept punishment when it is justified.

Legislative Approaches

A recent summary by the National Conference of State Legislatures (NCSL, 1995; see also Hunzeker, 1993) indicates that enforcement suppression has been a predominant theme in new legislation over the past few years (see also Johnson, Webster, & Connors, 1995). States including California, Nevada, Florida, Georgia, Illinois, and Louisiana have enhanced penalties for crimes carried out in participation with or at the direction of gangs. The California Street Terrorism Enforcement (STEP) Act of 1988 (California Penal Code, sec. 186.22) has served as a model for emulation by Florida, Georgia, Illinois, and Louisiana. A unique notification process is used to inform persons that they can be prosecuted under the STEP Act (Klein, 1995): Police and/or prosecutors gather evidence that a targeted gang fits the act's definition. This information is presented to the court, resulting in an enabling judicial order. Known gang members are then notified in writing that they are members of such a group. Following such notice, the act can then be applied to these members, enhancing penalties for subsequent offenses.

A number of states have enacted new youth gang prevention measures (NCSL, 1995). Florida created gang prevention councils in 1990 through which judicial circuits develop strategies to reduce gang activities. The state of Washington enacted a Youth Gang Reduction Act in 1991 that targets elementary and secondary students. Oregon enacted a statute in 1995 that provides tax credits for employers who hire gang-involved or gang-affected youth. A 1995 Texas law provides for the establishment of a gang information system. Hawaii also established legislatively a comprehensive program in 1991 that includes a statewide law enforcement task force on youth gangs, prosecution efforts that target career gang criminals, school-based prevention programs, and parks and recreation programs. A two-pronged strategy is embodied in the Hawaii Youth Gang Response System: prosecution of hard-core gang criminals, and reducing the growth of gangs through prevention and education focused on younger kids. Although preliminary results of a process evaluation of Hawaii's program are encouraging, outcome results are yet preliminary (Chesney-Lind et al., 1995a, 1995b; Chesney-Lind, Marker, Stern, Song, et al., 1992; Chesney-Lind, Marker, Stern, Yap, et al., 1992). These statutory changes show some states' interest in a combination of prevention and intervention approaches, although most of the recent legislation favors suppression tactics. Gang suppression legislation has not been evaluated.

National Assessment of Youth Gang Programs

Only one national survey of youth gang programs has been conducted. Spergel and his colleagues (Spergel, 1991; Spergel & Curry, 1993) conducted a nationwide assessment of youth gang prevention, intervention, and suppression programs under Office of Juvenile Justice and Delinquency Prevention (OJJDP) support. The assessment (conducted in 1988) included a survey of 254 respondents in 45 communities and 6 special program sites regarding strategies they employed and their perception of the most effective strategies they used. All surveyed sites were jurisdictions that had a youth gang problem and an organized response to the problem. Responses were categorized into the major program types that Spergel (1991) identified in his literature review of gang programs: community organization, social intervention, opportunities provision, and suppression. A fifth response category was added

by the survey team: organizational change and development.

Suppression was the most frequently employed strategy in the 51 jurisdictions (44%), followed by social intervention (31%), organizational change and development (11%), community organization (9%), and opportunities provision (5%). "Chronic gang problem" cities tended to combine suppression, social intervention, and community organization strategies, whereas "emerging gang problem cities" favored singular approaches, either community organization, organizational development, or suppression (Spergel, Curry, et al., 1994). Respondents were also asked to assess the effectiveness of the approaches they had tried. Provision of social opportunities was perceived to be most effective in chronic gang problem cities. Community organization (mobilization) was also believed to be an effective strategy, but only when social opportunities were also provided. In contrast, respondents in emerging gang problem cities saw community organization (mobilization) as the most effective strategy. Overall, respondents were not confident that their antigang efforts were particularly productive. Only 23% of the police and 10% of all other respondents believed their community's gang situation improved between 1980 and 1987.

Spergel and Curry (1993) conducted a validity check on respondents' perceived effectiveness of program interventions by comparing responses to actual changes in five empirical indicators—numbers of gangs, gang members, gang-related homicides, gang-related assaults, and gang-related narcotics incidents—in a random sample of 21 cities in the survey. Their analysis of the data (which were reasonably complete for most of the variables) showed that perceptions correlated perfectly with the empirical indicators, whether there was improvement or deterioration in the gang situation.

In another component of the national assessment, in seven of the study sites, Curry (1990) surveyed a sample of current and former gang members who were identified through service agency contacts with them. According to client reports, the most commonly received services were recreation and sports. These services, together with job placement, were viewed as most helpful in curtailing gang activity. Service recipients were mainly males under age 21. Although Hispanic youth reported receiving fewer services than other youths, they rated the services they received as more helpful than black or white recipients toward achieving their employment goals.

As a result of the national assessment, Spergel and his colleagues developed the Comprehensive Community-Wide Approach to Gang Prevention, Intervention, and Suppression Program that consists of 12 program models for police, prosecutors, judges, probation, parole, corrections, schools, youth employment, community-based youth agencies, and a range of grassroots organizations (Spergel, Chance, et al., 1994). Two of the models, general community design and community mobilization, are cross-cutting systemwide models that encompass planning and coordination efforts. Each of the 12 models identifies program rationales, policies, procedures, and leadership roles appropriate for implementing each of them. Spergel and his colleagues also recommended that communities create a community-based youth agency to provide a continuum of services to gang and gang-prone youth.

Because gang migration is an important aspect of the youth gang problem, law enforcement views of programs that might work are valuable. In the course of their national gang migration study, Maxson, Woods, and Klein (1996) conducted interviews with law enforcement representatives in 211 cities that have experienced street gang migration,

and community representatives in about one fourth of these cities. Respondents were asked to assess the use and effectiveness of several gang policies and practices. Most respondents said operational coordination with local, state, and federal law enforcement agencies was relatively common. However, few law enforcement officers viewed this as effective in reducing gang migration or illegal activities. Selective law violations (e.g., narcotics laws) were targeted in three fourths of the surveyed departments, but only 42% of them viewed this strategy as effective. Enforcement of specific gang laws (e.g., STEP) was not viewed as a particularly effective response. About 40% of the surveyed law enforcement agencies used gang sweeps and other suppression strategies, which were believed to be effective by a majority of officers. Almost two thirds of the 211 street gang migration cities employed community collaboration strategies, and over half believed these to be effective.

In sum, the only strategies perceived to be effective by a majority of law enforcement respondents were community collaboration (54%), crime prevention activities (56%), and street sweeps (62%) or other suppression tactics (63%). Interviews with community respondents did not identify any innovative or promising strategies to address gang migration. Most respondents cited collaborative approaches that targeted overall gang activity or youth crime in general as holding promise.

Klein (1995) cites five reasons for the current tendency to embrace suppression as the favored approach to youth gangs: (a) the lack of demonstrated success of the community organization and detached worker programs, (b) the proliferation of gangs in more and more cities, (c) the perceived increase in gang violence and victimization of innocent bystanders, (d) the crack cocaine epidemic and the purported involvement of gangs in drug trafficking, and (e) the swing of the sociopolitical pendulum to more conservative philosophies. Yet Klein has noted the resurfacing of community organization approaches that target weaknesses in community structures including employment, schools, social services, health programs, and the like. He believes that improvements in these areas hold much more promise than suppression because "street gangs are byproducts of partially incapacitated communities. Until we dedicate the state and federal resources necessary to alter these community structures, gangs will continue to emerge despite value transformation, suppression, or other community efforts" (Klein, 1995, p. 153).

Klein contends that much of the interest in community-centered approaches that seek improvements in social and economic systems is emanating from the law enforcement community. For example, he cites Los Angeles Sheriff Sherman Block, who said: "As long as gang cultures exist, we are chasing our tails. Law enforcement cannot break the cycle, only social improvements can break it" (quoted in Sahagun, 1990, cited in Klein, 1995, p. 152) and Los Angeles Undersheriff Robert Edmunds: "Our experience is ill-suited to preventing the emergence of new gangs or the increased membership of existing gangs. . . . Obviously, we miscalculated the solution. . . . What is needed are partnerships involving all segments of our society" (quoted in Sahagun, 1990, cited in Klein, 1995, p. 152).

There is considerable disagreement over the issue of whether social improvements through community organization can be achieved, although the importance of social conditions to gang organization and violence is not disputed. Short (1990) reminds us that, like individuals, "communities, too, have careers in delinquency" (p. 224). In addition to community factors, Short's (1990, 1995a, 1995b, 1996) analysis of the critical features

of the youth gang problem specifies individual characteristics and group processes that must be taken into account in developing gang prevention and intervention programs. Short contends that community factors that contribute to gang delinquency and violence consist of both macro- and microlevel influences. Macrolevel forces that produce youth gangs include the spread of gang culture, youth culture, and a growing underclass (Short, 1995b, 1996).

> More than ever before in history, young people, targeted for commercial exploitation and isolated from mainstream adult roles and institutions, confront economic conditions beyond their control. Economic decline, severe unemployment, and the unavailability of "good jobs," are associated not only with street gangs, but with their transformation into "economic gangs" (including drug gangs), and with ethnic, racial, and class-related antagonisms that lead to other types of collective violence. These same forces alter both intergang relationships and relationships between gangs and their communities. (Short, 1995b, p. 19)

Quantifying these forces and connecting them to gang problems is difficult. Group processes operate at the microlevel (individual, peer group), influenced by the macrolevel (community) forces, and interact to produce gang violence (Short, 1990, 1995b, 1996). Thus, Short urges development of comprehensive programs targeting both levels (such as the CAP) and multifaceted early-intervention programs such as the Beethoven Project in the Chicago Robert Taylor Homes, a public housing community (Center for Successful Child Development, 1993).

Miller (1993) argues that the primary target of change should be the behavior of individuals rather than institutions, organizations, or structural features of the larger society, such as the employment situation, income distribution, health delivery systems, and the like. Not that these social system features are less important; changes in them should be supported, but are outside the scope of his specific proposal. Second, efforts to alter the balance between procrime and anticrime incentives should be directed not at the general category of criminal behavior, but at specific offenses such as theft, armed robbery, and assault. Third, incentives to commit crimes derive from the community subculture. He argues that a substantial reduction in criminal behavior could be achieved by interrupting the intergenerational transmission of subcultural features in the lower class. If this intergenerational transmission (of criminal culture) could be interrupted or modified, the incentive balance could shift toward strengthening anticrime incentives.

Miller (1993) proposes a four-component program focused on the strategy of weakening procrime incentives and strengthening anticrime incentives: (a) reducing procrime incentives at the community subcultural level, (b) increasing anticrime incentives at the community level, (c) reducing procrime incentives at the national level, and (d) increasing anticrime incentives at the national level. He contends that "incentives that appear to be clearly related to motivation for crime appear to be amenable to change, and can be feasibly acted on become the high priority targets for change" (p. 14). Miller suggests that this strategy could be implemented and tested most easily in small or medium-size cities, in high-gang neighborhoods. The first-priority target group would be preschool children (aged 1-5), then preadolescent (6-11), and adolescents (12-19). He suggests that program interventions could be added to or made part of programs already involving the target groups, such as Boys and Girls Clubs, afterschool programs, Head Start, and so on. Because there is some evidence that the provision of incentives to high-risk youth can enhance academic success (see, e.g., Greenwood, Model, Rydell, & Chiesa, 1996; Taggart, 1995), Miller's proposed approach merits testing.

We have reviewed in this section the results of the only national survey of youth gang programs and a national survey of law enforcement agencies. To these results, we added the perspectives of several experienced gang researchers. None of these information sources prescribes interventions for particular types of gangs (e.g., violent, nonviolent) or specific gang crimes (e.g., drug sales, assault, robbery). The state of the art of gang programming has not been advanced to the level of linking program interventions to specific gang types and criminal patterns. In the next section, we recommend three gang intervention strategies that the literature reviewed in this section suggests might work in combating gang problems in general.

■ Recommended Strategies and Programs

No single program has been demonstrated through rigorous evaluation to be effective in preventing or reducing gang violence. There are several reasons for this. Like many other social problems, youth gang problems remain unsolved (Miller, 1990). The complexity of gang problems makes prevention and intervention difficult. Finally, as we saw in the last section, few rigorous evaluations of gang interventions have been conducted.

Nevertheless, our literature review suggests that youth gang problems can be ameliorated, that is, reduced in prevalence and severity (Miller, 1990). Three promising gang program strategies are recommended based on this review. The first one targets gang problems directly. The second one targets gang problems within a comprehensive strategy for dealing with serious, violent, and chronic juvenile delinquency. The third approach targets gang-related (and gang-motivated) homicides.

Comprehensive Community-Wide Approach to Gang Prevention, Intervention, and Suppression Program

This program model (see earlier discussion) was designed specifically to target youth gang problems, as the product of a nationwide assessment of youth gang prevention, intervention, and suppression programs in the late 1980s (Spergel, 1991, 1995; Spergel & Curry, 1993; Spergel, Curry, et al., 1994). As already mentioned, 12 program components developed by Spergel and his colleagues (Spergel, Chance, et al., 1994) are available for the design and mobilization of community efforts by police, prosecutors, judges, probation and parole officers, corrections officers, schools, employers, community-based agencies, and a range of grassroots organizations (Spergel, Chance, Ehrensaft, Regulus, Kane, & Alexander, 1992). Technical assistance manuals are available to support local program development (Spergel, Chance, Ehrensaft, Regulus, Kane, & Laseter, 1992). Variations of these models are currently being implemented and tested in Bloomington, Illinois; Mesa, Arizona; Tucson, Arizona; Riverside, California; and San Antonio, Texas. An independent evaluation is being conducted by the University of Chicago.

The most promising gang violence prevention and intervention program is being conducted in the Little Village area of Chicago, a low-income and working-class community of about 90% Mexican Americans (Spergel & Grossman, 1994, 1995, 1996). Called the Gang Violence Reduction Program, it is administered by the Research and Program Development Division of the Chicago Police Department. The program targeted over 200 of the "shooters," "influentials," or gang leaders (aged 17-24) of two of the city's most violent Latino gangs. These two gangs account for almost 70% of the gang homicides and other violent gang crimes in the community.

The Gang Violence Reduction Program consists of two coordinated strategies: (a) targeted control of violent or potentially hardcore violent youth gang offenders, in the form of increased probation department and police supervision and suppression, and (b) provision of a wide range of social services and opportunities for targeted youth, to encourage their transition to conventional legitimate behaviors through education, jobs, job training, family support, and brief counseling. Managed by the Neighborhood Relations Unit of the Chicago Police Department, the project is staffed by tactical police officers, probation officers, community youth workers (from the University of Chicago), and workers in Neighbors Against Gang Violence, a new community organization established to support the project. The program incorporates a complement of prevention, intervention, and suppression strategies, based on a comprehensive model Spergel and his colleagues developed (Spergel, Chance, et al., 1994). These multiple strategies are "employed interactively" (Spergel & Grossman, 1995, p. 3).

Preliminary evaluation results (after 4 years of program operations) are positive (Spergel & Grossman, 1996). Program interventions "have been associated with a decline, or at least a reduction in the rate of increase, in gang violence" (p. 24). Overall, gang-motivated violence arrests increased by 32% in Little Village, compared to an increase of 77% in the control area (p. 28). Compared to nontargeted gangs, the two gangs targeted in the program were still responsible for the preponderance of serious and violent gang crimes in the area, but generally experienced a smaller combined rate of increase in number of offenders involved in gang homicides and other violent crimes. Examination of arrests among program clients in both gangs showed an increase in the average number of arrests over a 3-year period (Spergel & Grossman, 1997). However, reductions were observed for gang members over 19 years of age. Thus, by this measure, the project was much more successful with older gang members.

Self-reported measures among program subjects showed significant reductions in both violent and property-related crimes between the first time interval and the last one. Among program clients, reductions in total crime and violence were almost twice as great for those who received services or contacts from both police and gang workers compared to youth who did not receive such coordinated contacts. The reduction in drug selling was more than eight times greater for youth receiving combined services from police and gang workers, compared to program youth receiving noncoordinated or alternate forms of services (Spergel & Grossman, 1996).

In sum, the Little Village Gang Violence Reduction Program appears to have been successful in reducing gang crime, during a period in which gang violence was increasing significantly in the Little Village area. The success of the program is much more evident by self-reported measures than by arrest data. However, Spergel and Grossman (1996) note that arrest increases may partially be accounted for by a change in police data collection practices instituted in 1993, and by organizational policy changes in police practices resulting in more emphasis on suppression activities.

OJJDP's Comprehensive Strategy for Serious, Violent, and Chronic Juvenile Offenders

Targeting gang problems within a community's comprehensive strategy for dealing with serious, violent, and chronic juvenile offenders is the second recommended approach. OJJDP's Comprehensive Strategy for Serious, Violent, and Chronic Juvenile Offenders (Wilson & Howell, 1993) provides a framework for strategic community planning and program development. OJJDP's *Guide for Implementing the Comprehensive Strategy for Serious, Violent, and Chronic Juvenile Offenders* (Howell, 1995) is a resource for carrying out the OJJDP Comprehensive Strategy. It contains numerous promising and effective program models that will help prevent and reduce gang problems while targeting serious, violent, and chronic juvenile offenders.

The theoretical foundation of the Comprehensive Strategy is the "social development model" (Catalano & Hawkins, 1996; Hawkins & Weis, 1985), a risk-focused approach to delinquency that identifies risk factors contributing to delinquency, prioritizes them, and specifies ways to buffer and reduce those risks. The Comprehensive Strategy consists of prevention and graduated sanctions components, encompassing the entire juvenile justice and human service fields. The graduated sanctions component uses structured decision-making tools (risk and needs assessments) to achieve the best match between public safety risks and offenders' present and treatment needs in a continuum of sanctions and program options.

Because separate causal pathways to gang participation versus nongang serious and violent offending have not been identified, programs found to be effective or promising for preventing and reducing serious and violent delinquency in general may hold promise in combating gang delinquency and violence. Promising programs that might be included in a comprehensive youth gang program follow. These address known risk factors for gang participation.

Prevention component. The prevention component of the Comprehensive Strategy incorporates a risk- and protective-factor approach for systematically assessing community risk factors, identifying and prioritizing the most prevalent risk factors, then selecting from promising and effective interventions those that best target the priority risk factors and strengthen protective factors. Communities That Care (Hawkins & Catalano, 1992) is a structured process for analysis of risk factors and the development of approaches that reduce them and buffer their negative effects by increasing protective factors. The major risk factors for gang involvement are found in the individual, family, school, peer group, and community domains (see Thornberry, Chapter 8, this volume). Promising programs that seek to reduce these risk factors are noted below.

A public education campaign is needed to educate national, state, and local leaders, parents, children, and adolescents about the risks associated with gang participation. This educational campaign should be based on the elevated risk of homicide among gang members— 60 times the risk of homicide among the general population (Morales, 1992)—and focus particularly on inner cities and low-income areas.

Discouraging children and young adolescents from joining gangs is the most cost-effective approach to reducing serious gang crime (National Drug Intelligence Center, 1994). As we saw earlier, two gang prevention curricula (Project BUILD and G.R.E.A.T.) have showed positive results (Esbensen & Osgood, 1997; Thompson & Jason, 1988).

A number of promising *family-based* early-intervention programs have been identified (see Hawkins, Catalano, & Brewer, 1995b, pp. 52-60; Horne, 1993), including: pre- and perinatal medical care, intensive health education for the mother, child immunizations, parent training, child cognitive development activities, home visitation (Olds, Henderson, Tatelbaum, & Chamberlin, 1988), and home-based parent training and skills training for juveniles (Tremblay, Vitaro, et al., 1992). These aim mainly to strengthen family management and can reduce the likelihood that offspring will join gangs (see Yoshikawa, 1995).

Promising *school* programs include the Perry Preschool Project (Schweinhart, Barnes, & Weikart, 1993); the Syracuse University Family Development Research Program (Lally, Mangione, & Honig, 1988); a variety of classroom organization, management, and instructional interventions, including school-based behavioral interventions (for a review and summary, see Brewer et al., 1995); graduation incentives for high-risk youths (Taggart, 1995; see also Greenwood et al., 1996); and an antibullying program (Olweus, 1992).

Promising *peer group* and *individual-focused* programs include manhood development (Watts, 1991); employment training, education, and counseling (Corsica, 1993); conflict resolution and peer mediation in tandem (Hawkins, Farrington, & Catalano, in press); alternatives to gang participation (Klein, 1995); equipping peers to help one another (Goldstein & Glick, 1994); and techniques for separating youths from gangs (Hunsaker, 1981; Kohn & Shelly, 1991).

Community programs must increase social and economic alternatives to gang involvement. Promising programs include community reconstruction (Eisenhower Foundation, 1990), Empowerment Zones (revitalization of communities through economic and social services), and Enterprise Communities (promoting physical and human development). Empowerment Zones and Enterprise Communities are large-scale programs supported through the federal Department of Housing and Urban Development (see OJJDP, 1995c) that aim to reconstruct selected inner-city areas. Other programs are needed that help improve social and economic conditions in impoverished communities, providing "social capital" for young people (Short, 1995b), enabling them to reach turning points such as gainful employment in pathways to success outside gangs (Sampson & Laub, 1993a). Community norms supporting gang crime and violence must also be changed. Strengthening anticrime incentives and weakening procrime incentives may work (Miller, 1993).

Promising programs designed to prevent gang problems in particularly low-income areas and public housing projects include the Beethoven Project in Chicago's Robert Taylor Homes (Center for Successful Child Development, 1993); Neutral Zone (Thurman, Giacomazzi, Reisig, & Mueller, 1996); Community Outreach Program (Kodluboy & Evenrud, 1993); and Boys and Girls Clubs: Targeted Outreach (Feyerherm, Pope, & Lovell, 1992).

Community policing is an essential component of a comprehensive gang prevention program. Several community policing programs appear to have realized some success in dealing with youth crime problems (see

Cronin, 1994, for three promising models). One of these is the Norfolk Police Assisted Community Enforcement (PACE) program, focused in low-income housing areas. Although the PACE program has not been evaluated, crime has decreased by an estimated 29% in the targeted neighborhoods (Cronin, 1994). Police report fewer service calls and a significant drop in on-street drug trafficking and gunfire in the targeted areas. One key to the apparent success of the PACE program is the formation of partnerships between police and neighborhood organizations, empowering neighborhoods through community mobilization to develop in concert with the police and other city agencies solutions to gang and other crime problems. These solutions include social and human service needs.

Another community policing model that specifically targets youth gangs is the Reno, Nevada, program (Weston, 1995). Through the formation of the Community Action Team (CAT), the Reno Police Department involves minority neighborhoods, community service agencies, and political leaders in a community solution to the city's serious youth gang problem. The CAT program, developed in response to gang problems, had two strategies: (a) creation of a highly specialized team of officers to target the top 5% of violent gang members in a repeat offender program, and (b) a prevention and early intervention program that targeted the city's estimated 80% of local gang members who were not involved in criminal activity and not considered to be hard core. Neighborhood advisory groups provide feedback from community residents, and an interagency group coordinates prevention and intervention resources. Although the program has not been independently evaluated, Weston (1995) reports that "it would appear that limited violence and limited growth in gang membership is related to the many success stories resulting from intervention efforts" (p. 300). Neighborhood block watch also appears to be a useful community crime prevention technique (Lindsay & McGillis, 1986; Rosenbaum, Lewis, & Grant, 1986).

Successful prevention of gang problems cannot be accomplished without involving community leaders and neighborhood organizations, because of the integral relationship between gangs and community conditions and dynamics (Spergel, Chance, et al., 1994). Thus, community mobilization is a key component of a comprehensive gang prevention program. It is a process of consciousness raising, objective identification of gang problem dimensions, and developing a community commitment to take action. "The essence of the community mobilization process is to reinvigorate or reorganize community structures so that community energies and resources are developed to address the youth gang problem, and these resources are integrated and targeted on the gang problem" (Spergel, Chance, et al., 1994, p. 6).

It is also critical that gang prevention program developers solicit input from gang members. Gang leaders have identified program strategies they believe would be most valuable in their communities. These included gutting and burning abandoned structures, building counseling centers and recreation areas, beautification of the neighborhood, renovation of educational facilities, tutoring programs, health care facilities, replacement of welfare programs with state-sponsored employment, economic development programs, and an increased role for residents in law enforcement activities (Bursik & Grasmick, 1993, p. 178).

Graduated sanctions component. The graduated sanctions component should consist of structured sanctions, including priority arrest, adjudication, intensive probation, incarceration, and aftercare for juvenile offenders (see Krisberg & Howell, Chapter 14, this volume). Vertical prosecution of older, chronic, serious and violent gang offenders should be pursued in the criminal justice system (Genelin, 1993; Weston, 1995). A continuum of juvenile corrections treatment options should be provided in an intensive supervision program (Krisberg, Neuenfeldt, Wiebush, & Rodriguez, 1994).

Interpersonal skills training appears to hold promise for improving social skills, reducing anger, and possibly violence reduction among street gang youth and with institutionalized populations, some of which have included gang members (Goldstein, 1993; Goldstein & Glick, 1994). In a recent experiment, Aggression Replacement Training (ART) was tested as a gang intervention program with 10 aggressive juvenile gangs in New York City. Goldstein and Glick (1994) report a reduction in arrest rates, as well as other evaluation results, supporting the effectiveness of a 2-year project using the ART intervention approach. In an 8-month follow-up, 13% of the ART group were rearrested, compared to 52% of the control group. On other measures, compared to the control group, the ART group showed significant improvements in community functioning, and slightly better improvements in interpersonal skills and anger control. The ART model teaches gang members anger control and other skills, and it attempts to turn their real-world reference group, the gang, from an antisocial group into a prosocial one (Goldstein & Glick, 1994).

The multisystemic therapy (MST) program appears to be a promising treatment and rehabilitation program for gang members even though it has not specifically targeted them. MST has been found to be effective in treating multiple problems of serious and violent juvenile offenders in different settings (Henggeler, Melton, & Smith, 1992; Henggeler, Melton, Smith, Schoenwald, & Hanley,

1993). A Columbia, Missouri program (Borduin et al., 1995) targeted chronic serious juvenile offenders referred to the project by juvenile court personnel. Two hundred families were randomly assigned to the treatment program or to the control group. Therapeutic interventions were based on the multisystemic approach to the prevention and treatment of childhood and adolescent behavioral problems (Henggeler & Borduin, 1990). The follow-up (4 years later) showed that 22% of MST youth were rearrested, compared to 72% of youths who received individual counseling and 87% of youths who refused either treatment (Borduin et al., 1995).

MST incorporates a socioecological view in which antisocial behavior in youth is seen as linked to multiple systems in which the youth is embedded, that is, the key characteristics of youth and the family, peer, school, and neighborhood systems. MST uses interventions that are present focused and action oriented, directly addressing intrapersonal (i.e., cognitive) and systemic (i.e., family, peer, school) factors known to be related to adolescent antisocial behavior. Empowering parents with the skills and resources to independently address the difficulties of rearing adolescents is an overriding treatment goal. Although multiple systems may be involved, MST involves a single therapist for each client, providing brief (about 4 months) but intensive treatment, generally in the home or in community locations (e.g., school or recreation center) (Borduin et al., 1995).

MST appears to have applicability as a juvenile justice system rehabilitation approach for youth gang members. Treatment groups in various MST experiments have included gang members. This discovery provided the basis for fielding an experiment specifically targeting gang members. Thus, the MST model is currently being tested in Galveston, Texas in the Second Chance program, which targets gang-involved youth (Thomas, 1996).

The "8% Solution" program (also known as the 8% Early Intervention Program) in Orange County, California, implements the graduated sanctions component of the Comprehensive Strategy. The program is based on an analysis of court referrals showing that 8% of referred adolescents account for more than half of all repeat offenses in the county (Kurz & Moore, 1994). Risk assessment and analysis of the characteristics of the 8% group (who had four or more court referrals in the following 3 years) showed that four factors correctly classified 70% of the chronic recidivists who were under 16 years of age: (a) school performance, (b) family problems, (c) substance abuse, and (d) antisocial behavior (stealing, running away, gang affiliation). Thus, the 8% Solution program targets initial court referrals under age 16 with these characteristics because they are at risk of becoming chronic juvenile offenders (and adult offenders as well, 53% in a 6-year follow-up). Potential 8% cases are initially identified during probation intake and verified through a comprehensive assessment process.

Once youths are admitted to the 8% Solution program, the initial goal is to bring their behavior under control and in compliance with probation terms and conditions while working to achieve stability in the adolescent's home (Orange County Probation Department, 1995). From that point a broad range of sanctions options (from day reporting to community confinement) are used in conjunction with a continuum of program options for the juvenile and family members to achieve habilitation goals while providing intensive case supervision. These options include individual incentives, family problem assessment and intervention services, family preservation and support services (including home-based intervention, respite care, and parent aids), individualized treatment for particular problem behaviors (e.g., mental health, drug and alcohol abuse), and a wide range of community service opportunities for the project clients.

A preliminary evaluation comparing a pilot group of program clients with the original study group shows about a 50% reduction in new offenses, court petitions, probation violations, and subsequent correctional commitments among the 8% program group in a 12-month follow-up (Orange County Probation Department, 1996). An independent assessment of the 8% program (Greenwood et al., 1996) concluded that it is cost-effective. Greenwood and his colleagues estimate (p. 38) that the program costs about $14,000 per serious crime prevented (about 70 serious crimes per million dollars). The California legislature recently appropriated funds for replication and testing of the program in six other counties within the state.

The gang component of the 8% Solution program targets gang leadership and the most chronic recidivists through a coordinated program of gang interdiction, apprehension, and prosecution (Capizzi, Cook, & Schumacher, 1995). These three strategies are integrated and coordinated by TARGET (Tri-Agency Resource Gang Enforcement Team), consisting of the Westminster Police Department, the Orange County District Attorney, and the County Probation Department. The Gang Incident Tracking System (GITS) identifies and tracks gang members, providing the information base for the TARGET program, which supports gang interdiction, apprehension, and prosecution. TARGET uses intelligence gathering and information sharing to identify and select appropriate gang members and gangs for intervention. Civil abatement procedures are used to suppress the criminal activities of entire gangs.

During its first 2 years of operation, the TARGET program (a) identified and verified 647 individual gang members; (b) targeted 77 verified gang members for intensive investi-gation, probation supervision, and prosecution, 69% of whom were placed in custody; (c) prosecuted 145 cases involving 168 gang member defendants and achieved a 99% conviction rate; (d) supervised an average caseload of 52 probationers regarded as hardcore gang members; and (e) documented a 62% decrease in serious gang-related crime (Kent & Smith, 1995). Begun in Westminster, TARGET is being replicated in six other cities within Orange County. Klein et al. (1995) suggest that "focused efforts of this type can produce positive effects in smaller gang cities."

Effective police and agency interventions can be enhanced by sound, current gang information. The Chicago Early Warning System (Block & Block, 1991) is a model for this purpose, and it can be replicated in other jurisdictions. This system, stimulated by earlier research in Chicago (see Curry & Spergel, 1988) is based on a statistical model that consolidates spatial information and uses automated "hot spot area" identification and other geographic statistics to predict potential crisis areas. The Early Warning System is used in the Chicago Police Department's Police Area Four project, in which the police identify problem areas, then target prevention efforts in those areas. Up-to-the-minute information is necessary for targeting specific neighborhoods, because of knowledge that gang violence changes over time, following a pattern of escalation, retaliation, and revenge that often occurs across a spatial border that also changes over time (Block & Block, 1993). Information provided by the Early Warning System is used to inform police and community agency interventions to head off the cycle of retaliation and retribution, if possible, through the use of mediation and crisis intervention. The Chicago Early Warning System effectively supports the Little Village project (discussed above) by providing timely information on criminal gang activity (see Spergel & Grossman, 1997).

The main target crime in the Police Area Four project is gang-related homicides. Although conventional wisdom suggests that homicide cannot be prevented, the Blocks disagree (Block & Block, 1991). They contend that homicides can be prevented by targeting efforts on (a) the "specific Homicide Syndromes [e.g., expressive] that are the most dangerous and have the highest chance of successful prevention, (b) specific neighborhoods in which the risk of being murdered is especially high, and (c) specific groups who are at the highest risk of victimization" (p. 57).

These conclusions are supported by extensive gang homicide research the Blocks have conducted in Chicago, principal findings of which Block and Block (1993) summarized as follows:

First, most of Chicago's street gang crime can be identified with the city's four largest gangs. From 1987 to 1990, they accounted for 69% of all street gang-motivated crimes and for 56% of all street gang-motivated homicides, although they represent only about 10% of the "major" Chicago youth gangs and 51% of the estimated number of street gang members.

Second, gangs varied in the types of criminal activities in which they engaged. Some specialized in instrumental crimes. Most gang violence was emotional defense of one's identity as a gang member, defense of the gang and gang members, defense and glorification of the reputation of the gang, gang member recruitment, and territorial expansion. Except for the Vice Lords, a majority of street gang offenses for all other gangs in the city were turf related.

Third, "the connection between street gangs, drugs, and homicide was weak and could not explain the rapid increase in homicide in the late 1980s" (p. 4). Only 3% of gang-motivated homicides between 1987 and 1990 were related to drugs.

Fourth, the most lethal areas were along disputed boundaries between small street gangs. These were mainly Latino gangs fighting among themselves over limited turfs.

Fifth, neighborhood characteristics were associated with specific types of gang crime. "Street gangs specializing in instrumental violence were strongest in disrupted and declining neighborhoods. Street gangs specializing in expressive violence were strongest and most violent in relatively prospering neighborhoods with expanding populations" (p. 8).

Sixth, the most lethal violence (and highest level) occurred in neighborhoods where turf battles occurred, not in those where street gang activity focused on drug offenses.

Seventh, although street gang assaults did not increase during the period, and gang-related homicides did, the increase in deaths was attributed to an increase in the lethality of weapons, mostly high-caliber, automatic or semiautomatic weapons.

Eighth, many areas that had high levels of gang-related homicides had low levels of other types of homicide.

Ninth, the predominant type of street gang activity in neighborhoods often changed from year to year, or even month to month, and tended to occur sporadically.

Gun access and use reduction is an essential component of a comprehensive strategy. Recent studies have shown the proliferation and use of firearms among youth gangs (Block & Block, 1993; Maxson, Gordon, & Klein, 1985). Gang members are significantly more likely than nonmembers to own a gun illegally (Bjerregaard & Lizotte, 1995). Adolescents who own guns for protection are more likely to be involved in gangs and to commit serious crimes (Lizotte, Tesoriero, Thornberry, & Krohn, 1994). Therefore, limiting gun access and use is an important means of reducing lethal gang violence.

Numerous proposals for firearms reduction have been made that merit testing (Cook, 1981a, 1981b, 1991; Cook & Nagin, 1979; Newton & Zimring, 1969; Zimring, 1985, 1993, 1996; Zimring & Hawkins, 1987). Several approaches suggested recently have particular applicability to the youth gang firearm problem. Police seizures of illegally carried guns in hot spot areas have been found to reduce gun crimes, homicides and drive-by shootings, though not significantly (Sherman, Shaw, & Rogan, 1995). "Coerced use reduction" may be effective (Kennedy, Peihl, & Braga, 1996). Undercover purchases of firearms from adolescents, control of the supply channels, creation of ammunition scarcity, bilateral buy-back agreements, and nonuse treaties with financial compliance incentives hold promise (Zimring, 1996). Interdicting supply channels may be more feasible than commonly assumed because of the newness of guns used in gang homicides and their purchase within the state (Kennedy et al., 1996; Zimring, 1976). Equally important, research is needed on the relationship between firearms and violent street gang activity, on the extent of youth gun ownership and use, and patterns of acquisition of guns by minors in the gang gun inventory environment (Zimring, 1993, 1995).

Multiagency coordination of investigations, prosecutions, and sanctioning criminal gang members is important for effective and efficient law enforcement. One model, JUDGE (Jurisdictions United for Drug Gang Enforcement), targets drug-involved gang members in San Diego. The multiagency task force enforces conditions of probation and drug laws and provides vertical prosecution for probation violations and new offenses involving targeted offenders. Evaluation of JUDGE showed vertical prosecution to be a cornerstone for successful implementation and the advantages of a multiagency approach (Office of Justice Programs, 1996).

The gang program model that holds the most promise is likely to contain multiple components, incorporating prevention, social intervention, treatment, suppression, and community mobilization approaches. Involvement of all sectors of the community is essential (Bursik & Grasmick, 1993). To work, gang program components must be integrated in a collaborative approach, supported by a management information system.

A Strategy to Prevent and Reduce Youth Gang-Related (or Gang-Motivated) Homicides

Because of recent increases in gang homicides (see Howell, 1997), a third gang program strategy for targeting them is recommended. Of course, reducing youth gang-related (or gang-motivated) homicides should be a priority wherever they occur. But studies in Chicago and Los Angeles indicate that these two cities disproportionately account for gang-related homicides[2] in the United States. In Chicago, the number of street gang-motivated homicides increased almost fivefold between 1987 and 1994, from 51 to 240 (Block, Christakos, Jacob, & Przybylski, 1996). Gang-related homicides in Los Angeles County more than doubled from 1987 to 1992, from 387 to 803 (Klein, 1995). Chicago and Los Angeles alone accounted for nearly 1,000 gang homicides in 1992. Hutson, Anglin, Kyriacou, Hart, and Spears (1995) concluded that "gang-related homicides in Los Angeles County have reached epidemic proportions and are a major health problem" (p. 1031).

The Epidemiology of Youth Gang Homicides (Table 12.2) summarizes demographic information and research on risk factors for gang homicides. The major risk factors are community conditions (weapon availability/lethality, social disorganization, racial and class discrimination, immigrant adjustment, changing economic situation, drug market conditions), communities where gangs and gang violence are most prevalent, and where gangs are involved in turf disputes in closely concentrated geographical areas within specific years and specific age groups. Consideration of these risk factors with available knowledge of promising and effective programs suggests a strategy that may work to prevent and reduce youth gang-related homicides. They are preventable (Block & Block, 1993; Hutson, Anglin, & Mallon, 1992).

Chicago's Gang Violence Reduction Program appears to be a promising program model for targeting gang-motivated violence and homicides (Spergel & Grossman, 1995, 1996, 1997). It should be replicated and tested in other Chicago communities, in specific Los Angeles communities, and in other cities experiencing significant levels of gang homicides. One key to its success is the Early Warning System Geoarchive of the Illinois Criminal Justice Information Authority, which provides up-to-date information on hot spots of gang violence for targeted intervention efforts by the police and other agencies.

This literature review has identified other promising interventions that should be considered in designing a comprehensive gang homicide prevention and reduction program: a hospital emergency room intervention program for injured victims that could be established by adding a gang specialist to the Suspected Child Abuse and Neglect Team— SCAN—now found in many hospitals (Morales, 1992), serving to initiate entry into programs to break the cycle of gang violence (Hutson et al., 1995), and counseling for victims of drive-by shootings to reduce the traumatic effects of victimization and discourage retaliation (Groves, Zuckerman,

Marans, & Cohen, 1993; Hutson, Anglin, & Pratts, 1994; Pynoos & Nader, 1988).

Access to firearms by violent street gangs should be reduced by legislation, regulation, and community education and by removing illegal guns from the possession of gang members. A number of promising strategies have been recommended (Block & Block, 1993; Cook, 1981a, 1981b, 1991; Cook & Nagin, 1979; Hutson et al., 1995; Kennedy et al., 1996; Sheley & Wright, 1993; Sherman et al., 1995; Wright, 1995; Zimring, 1976, 1993, 1996; Zimring & Hawkins, 1987). A firearm wounding and fatality reporting system should be established to determine sources of weapons and assist interdiction efforts (Teret, Wintemute, & Beilenson, 1992; see also American Academy of Pediatrics, 1992; Cristoffel, 1991; Kellerman, Lee, Mercy, & Banton, 1991).

Effective program strategies must be built on continuously updated information, because of the frequently changing patterns (Block & Block, 1993). Short-term successes can be realized by targeting the causes of acute escalation in violence levels (Block & Block, 1993). As the Blocks have shown, programs must take into account the instrumental and expressive characteristics of gang violence. "For example, a program to reduce gang involvement in drugs in a community in which gang members are most concerned with defense of turf has little chance" (Block & Block, 1993, p. 9). Because juveniles tend to shoot others of their own ethnic group (Hutson, Anglin, & Eckstein, 1996), prevention programs must be culture specific (Soriano, 1993) and age appropriate (Block & Christakos, 1995; Centers for Disease Control, 1990; Hutson et al., 1994; Hutson et al., 1995; Klein & Maxson, 1989).

Several studies have refuted the supposed strong correlation between gang-related homicides and drug trafficking. Analyses of arrests in Boston (Miller, 1994), Chicago

TABLE 12.2 Epidemiology of Youth Gang Homicides

I. The United States is one of the most violent countries in the world, 5th among 41 countries.[a]
    Has the highest homicide rate in the world.[b]

A. Prevalence	Gang members are 60 times more likely to die of homicide than are members of the general population (600 per 100,000 gang members).[c]
	Gang homicide rate in St. Louis is 1,000 times higher than U.S. rate.[d]
	In 1989-1993, 33% of L.A. gang-related homicides were drive-bys.[e]
	In 1985-1994, 7% of Chicago gang-motivated homicides were drive-bys.[f]
B. Incidence	Chicago had 240 street gang-motivated homicides in 1994.[f]
	Los Angeles County had just under 800 gang-related homicides in 1994.[g]
C. Victim/offender	75% of Chicago gang-related homicides are intergang; 14%, nongang victims, and 11%, intragang.[f]
	Peak age of homicide offenders is 18.[f]
	64% of Chicago gang-related homicide victims are age 15-19.[f]
	82% of juvenile gang homicides in L.A. are intraracial.[b]
	63% of gang homicides in L.A. result from intergang interactions.[b]
	23% of L.A. drive-by shooting victims are innocent bystanders.[e]
	64% of gang homicide victims are gang members.[b]
D. Weapons	Firearms are used in 95% of gang-related homicides[b]; use of fully automatic or semiautomatic weapons increased 13-fold in Chicago from 1987 to 1994.[f]

II. Risk factors: In addition to the risk factors for gang membership, fatalities are mainly related to:
    Turf disputes in closely concentrated geographical areas within specific years and specific age groups.[h]
    Expressive violence in relatively prospering neighborhoods with expanding populations, acts of instrumental violence (e.g., drug disputes) in disrupted/declining neighborhoods.[i]
    Racial and class discrimination, immigrant adjustment, changing economic situation, drug market conditions.[i]
    Setting and participant characteristics.[j]
    Weapon availability/lethality, more gangs and gang violence.[k]
    Social disorganization (immigrant resettling).[l]
    Drug trafficking is not strongly correlated with youth gang homicides.[m]

a. Rosenberg and Mercy (1986).
b. Hutson, Anglin, Kyriacou, Hart, and Spears (1995).
c. Morales (1992).
d. Decker and Van Winkle (1996).
e. Hutson, Anglin, and Eckstein (1996).
f. Block, Christakos, Jacob, and Przybylski (1996).
g. Maxson, in press
h. Block (1993).
i. Block and Block (1993).
j. Maxson, Gordon, and Klein (1985).
k. Block and Block (1993); Hutson et al. (1995); Miller (1982).
l. Curry and Spergel (1988).
m. Block (1993); Block and Block (1993); Hutson et al. (1994, 1995); Kennedy et al., 1996; Klein, Maxson, and Cunningham (1991); Hutson et al. (1994); Meehan and O'Carroll (1992); Miller (1994).

(Block & Block, 1993; Block et al., 1996), Miami (Dade County Grand Jury, 1985, 1988; Inciardi, 1990), and Los Angeles (Hutson et al., 1995; Klein, Maxson, & Cunningham, 1991; Maxson, 1995; Meehan & O'Carroll, 1992) have consistently shown a low correlation between gang-related homicides and drug trafficking (see Howell, 1997, for a detailed review). Therefore, gang homicides and narcotics trafficking involving adolescents and young adults should be addressed as separate risk factors for homicide rather than as interrelated cofactors (Meehan & O'Carroll, 1992).

■ *Summary*

This review of the gang program literature suggests that comprehensive gang programs can be structured in two ways. One method involves gearing them specifically toward gang problems; the other one aims to reduce gang delinquency within a broader strategy aimed at serious, violent, and chronic juvenile offenders. The program model that proves to be most effective is likely to contain multiple components, incorporating prevention, social intervention, treatment, suppression, and community mobilization approaches. Gang program components must be integrated in a collaborative approach with full interagency coordination, supported by a management information system and rigorous program evaluation.

The Comprehensive Community-Wide Approach to Gang Prevention, Intervention, and Suppression Program developed by Spergel and his colleagues targets gang problems. It emphasizes community change as its main theoretical approach. The original model contains 12 program components for the design and mobilization of community efforts by police, prosecutors, judges, probation and parole officers, corrections officers, schools, employers, community-based agencies, and a range of grassroots organizations. Technical assistance manuals are available to support local program development. Variations of these models are currently being implemented and tested in five sites under OJJDP support. Another version of this comprehensive model, the Gang Violence Reduction Program, has been implemented in Chicago and is showing very promising results.

The second approach, reducing gang delinquency by targeting serious, violent, and chronic delinquency, is accomplished by implementing the OJJDP Comprehensive Strategy for Serious, Violent, and Chronic Juvenile Offenders. A number of program options are suggested, based on this literature review. This chapter organized these options under the prevention and graduated sanctions components of the Comprehensive Strategy. Its theoretical underpinnings are grounded in the social development model, a risk- and protection-factor approach, fashioned after the public health model. The graduated sanctions component uses risk and needs assessments as management tools to place offenders in a continuum of graduated sanctions and treatment options.

The 8% Solution program implements the graduated sanctions component of the OJJDP Comprehensive Strategy for Serious, Violent, and Chronic Juvenile Offenders. Assessment of gang involvement is included in the criteria for early-intervention services. The gang component of the 8% Solution program targets gang leadership and the most chronic recidivists. The program uses intelligence gathering and information sharing to identify and select appropriate gang members and gangs for intervention.

Finally, a strategy to prevent and reduce youth gang-related (or gang-motivated) homicides is recommended. It incorporates program strategies that look promising for preventing and reducing gang homicides. The central program intervention is the Chicago Gang Violence Reduction Program. To be effective, it must be supported by up-to-date information on hot spots of gang violence for targeted intervention efforts by the police and other agencies. Replication of the Early Warning System Geoarchive of the Illinois Criminal Justice Information Authority is recommended for this purpose. It is recommended that the proposed homicide reduction strategy be implemented in specific Chicago and Los Angeles communities, where gang homicides have reached epidemic proportions.

■ Some Recent Findings

Boston's anti-gang strategy (see Kennedy et al., 1996) has received a great deal of national attention. Although evaluation results are not yet available, a reduction in juvenile homicides of some 80% from 1990 to 1995 in the city has been reported (DOJ, 1997), and none has been recorded for 1996 or through September 1997 (Harden, 1997). Other official data indicate lower juvenile arrest rates for aggravated assault and battery with a firearm (1993-1995) and fewer violent crimes in public schools from 1995 to 1996 (DOJ, 1996).

■ Notes

1. The term *youth gang* is commonly used interchangeably with *street gang*, referring to neighborhood or street-based youth groups. Motorcycle gangs, prison gangs, racial supremists, and other hate groups are excluded. Our operational definition for this review coincides closely with Miller's (1982) definition: "A youth gang is a self-formed association of peers, united by mutual interests, with identifiable leadership and internal organization, who act collectively or as individuals to achieve specific purposes, including the conduct of illegal activity and control of a particular territory, facility, or enterprise" (p. 21).

2. Law enforcement agencies in Los Angeles and Chicago define *gang homicides* differently (see Maxson & Klein, 1990). In Los Angeles, the basic element is evidence of gang membership on the side of either the suspect or the victim. Maxson and Klein call this a "gang member" definition (p. 77). In Chicago, a homicide is considered gang related only if the preponderance of evidence indicates that the incident grew out of a street gang function, that is, gang-motivated (Block et al., 1996).

CHAPTER 13

Effective Intervention for Serious Juvenile Offenders

A Synthesis of Research

■ *Mark W. Lipsey & David B. Wilson*

lthough not all juvenile offenders recidivate, the proportions are sufficient to warrant concern (Snyder, 1988). Effective intervention with such offenders as an integral part of the dispositions and sanctions applied by the juvenile justice system, or as an adjunct to that process, is therefore an important tactic in any strategy to diminish the incidence of delinquency. This is especially true for juveniles whose offenses have been of a serious nature. These juveniles have already demonstrated a capability to engage in harmful behavior, have the potential for long criminal careers, and, even when apprehended and incarcer-

ated for a serious offense, are likely to be on the streets again while still within the age period of peak offending.

What, however, constitutes effective intervention with serious juvenile offenders? Indeed, is there any effective intervention for such delinquents? The recent generation of research reviews has affirmed the ability of some intervention programs to lower recidivism with youthful offenders (Andrews et al., 1990; Cullen & Gilbert, 1982; Garrett, 1985; Gendreau & Ross, 1987; Lipsey, 1992; Palmer, 1994). But these reviews have typically been oriented to the question of whether intervention is, or can be, *generally* effective in

AUTHORS' NOTE: The research reported in this chapter was supported in part by grants from the National Institute of Mental Health (MH42694 and MH39958) and the Russell Sage Foundation.

reducing the rate of subsequent offending among offenders and preoffenders. This is hardly surprising, given the history of doubt about this matter (Lipton, Martinson, & Wilks, 1975; Martinson, 1974). The result, however, is that little systematic attention has been given to reviewing the evidence for effectiveness with distinctive types of offenders, especially those most serious offenders who might be presumed among the most resistant to treatment. A further problem is that relatively little intervention research has been conducted specifically with serious offenders. Even when research samples are selected in such a way as to include serious offenders, they are often mixed in with less serious cases and not separately identified and analyzed.

Nonetheless, the issue of whether intervention of a feasible sort is able to decrease recidivism for the most serious delinquents is an important one. The purpose of this chapter is to review what pertinent intervention research is available to address that issue. It focuses on two basic questions: (a) Does the evidence indicate that intervention programs generally are capable of reducing the reoffending rates for serious delinquents? and (b) if so, what types of programs are most effective? These are questions that are answered most convincingly by experimental or quasi-experimental studies in which the subsequent offending rate of juveniles given treatment is contrasted with that of an otherwise comparable control group not given treatment. Such research yields statistical findings that represent the magnitude of the treatment effect observed in each study. In essence, the questions for this review, then, are whether the average size of the effects of intervention with serious offenders is positive and, if so, for which types of interventions it is largest.

One very direct way of addressing questions of this sort is through *meta-analysis,* the systematic synthesis of quantitative research

results. In meta-analysis, the statistical findings of each research study are coded as *effect sizes* along with other pertinent descriptive information, for example, the nature of the intervention studied and the characteristics of the subject sample to which it was applied. This information is compiled in a database that can itself be statistically analyzed to examine mean effect size, the relationship between effect size and the type of intervention, and so forth. The review reported in this chapter used techniques of meta-analysis to synthesize experimental and quasi-experimental research on the effectiveness of intervention for serious juvenile offenders. Two different circumstances of intervention were examined: (a) programs for offenders in the community, though possibly on probation or parole, and (b) programs for institutionalized juvenile offenders.

■ Procedures

This review updated the data collection from a more extensive meta-analysis of the effects of intervention on delinquency (Lipsey, 1992, 1995) and analyzed a subset of research studies selected for relevance to serious juvenile offenders. Because few studies in the intervention research literature deal exclusively with serious offenders, the approach taken here was to identify those studies from the meta-analytic database that involved the high end of the severity continuum as it appears in the delinquency intervention research. That is, although few studies have focused specifically on the effects of intervention on serious offenders, many studies have included such offenders within a more diverse sample of delinquents. In particular, studies were selected with the following characteristics:

1. The great majority, or all, of the juveniles were reported to be adjudicated delinquents. In addition, most, or all, of the juveniles had a record of prior offenses and those offenses involved person or property crimes, or an aggregate of all offenses, but not primarily substance abuse, status offenses, or traffic offenses.

2. The referral to the intervention program was made by a juvenile justice source (not schools, parents, etc.) or the juveniles were recruited directly by the researcher.

3. If not otherwise selected by the above criteria, studies were added for which coding showed an aggressive history for "most" or "all" of the juveniles or that the thrust of the intervention under study was to attempt to change aggressive behavior.

This selection resulted in 200 experimental or quasi-experimental studies of intervention with samples that involved serious juvenile offenders to some degree. Although more stringent criteria might have produced a set of studies with a still denser concentration of serious cases, the smaller number selected under such criteria would not have supported meta-analysis as well and, moreover, would narrow the range of situations and interventions represented. A bibliography of these studies appears as an appendix in this chapter.

■ Analysis and Results

Profile of Studies in the Database

Table 13.1 presents a summary of the characteristics of the 200 studies that comprised the database for this meta-analysis. The more general features of this pool of studies are as follows:

1. The majority of the studies was conducted in the United States by psychologists, criminologists, or sociologists and published since 1970 as journal articles, book chapters, or technical reports.

2. The juvenile samples were largely male, mostly Anglo or of mixed ethnicity, and with an average age of 14 to 17 years old. Most or all of the juveniles had prior offenses, usually reported as an aggregate of mixed offenses or as predominantly property crimes. For two thirds of the samples, there were indications that some or all of the juveniles had a prior history of aggressive behavior.

3. In most studies, the intervention under investigation was mandated and the juveniles were under the authority of the juvenile justice system at the time of treatment, usually probation or institutionalization. Treatment was administered by juvenile justice personnel for more than one third of the groups, by public or private agency mental health personnel for about one fifth, and by other counselors, laypersons, or researchers.

4. The predominant types of intervention studied with noninstitutionalized juveniles were counseling, skill-oriented programs (tutoring, social skills, vocational skills, drug abstinence), and multiple services. For institutionalized juveniles, they were counseling, skill-oriented programs, and community residential programs. The typical treatment program lasted from 1 to 30 weeks and involved either continuous (institutional) contact or sessions ranging from daily to 1-2 per week for 0.5 to 10 hours total weekly contact time.

5. Nearly half of the studies used random assignment to experimental conditions with most of the remainder employing some form of matching. Control groups typically received "treatment as usual," for example, regular probation or institutional programs without the enhancement that constituted the experimental treatment. The recidivism outcome variables measured most frequently were police contact/arrest, court contact, or parole violations. Treatment group sample sizes generally ranged from 10 to 100 (though a few were quite large), and control group samples were similar.

TABLE 13.1 Characteristics of the 200 Studies Used in the Meta-Analysis

Variable	Number	Proportion	Variable	Number	Proportion
General study characteristics			**Predominant ethnicity of juveniles**		
Publication year			Anglo	77	.39
1950-1959	4	.02	Black	28	.14
1960-1969	28	.14	Hispanic	3	.02
1970-1979	81	.41	Mixed	44	.22
1980-1989	62	.31	Missing	48	.24
1990-1995	19	.10	**How many juveniles with prior offenses**		
Missing	6	.03	None	1	.01
			Most	43	.22
Type of publication			All	155	.77
Book	16	.08	Missing	1	.01
Journal/book chapter	79	.40			
Dissertation/thesis	21	.11	**Predominant type of prior offense**		
Technical report	83	.41	No priors	1	.01
Conference paper	1	.01	Mixed	116	.58
			Person crimes	7	.04
Discipline of senior author			Property crimes	71	.35
Psychology	58	.29	Missing	5	.03
Criminology	38	.19			
Sociology	17	.08	**Juveniles with indications of aggressive history**		
Education	15	.07	None	38	.19
Psychiatry/medicine	7	.04	Some	110	.55
Political science	5	.03	Most or all	21	.11
Social work	3	.02	Missing	31	.16
Other	1	.01	*Treatment characteristics*		
Missing	56	.28			
Country in which the study was conducted			**Source of juveniles treated**		
United States	180	.90	Criminal justice referral,		
Canada	8	.04	voluntary	69	.35
Britain	10	.05	Criminal justice referral,		
Other	2	.01	mandatory	123	.62
Juveniles in treatment			Solicited by researcher	8	.04
			Juveniles under juvenile justice		
Gender mix among juveniles			**authority at time of treatment**		
No males	7	.04	Yes	126	.63
Some males	3	.02	No	74	.37
Mostly males	67	.34			
All males	107	.53	**Personnel who administer treatment**		
Missing	16	.08	Juvenile justice	74	.37
			School	3	.02
Mean age of juveniles at time of treatment			Mental health, public	20	.10
10.0-12.9	4	.02	Mental health, private	26	.13
13.0-13.9	11	.06	Non-mental health counselors	22	.11
14.0-14.9	34	.17	Laypersons	33	.16
15.0-15.9	47	.23	Researcher	8	.04
16.0-16.9	46	.23	Other	7	.04
17.0-17.9	14	.07	Missing	7	.04
18.0-18.9	10	.05			
19.0-19.9	12	.06	**Type of treatment—noninstitutionalized juveniles**		
20.0-20.9	3	.02	Reduced caseload,		
21.0-21.9	2	.01	probation/parole	12	.10
Missing	17	.09	Restitution, probation/parole	10	.09

TABLE 13.1 *Continued*

Variable	Number	Proportion	Variable	Number	Proportion
Deterrence programs,			20.1-40.0	9	.05
shock incarceration	6	.05	40.1-60.0	5	.03
Counseling, all types	31	.26	Continuous	57	.28
Behavioral programs,			Missing	41	.21
all types	7	.06			
Skill-oriented programs,			**Methods and procedures**		
all types	20	.17	**Procedures for assignment**		
Multiple services	17	.15	**to experimental conditions**		
All other	14	.12	Random	89	.45
			Regression discontinuity	2	.01
Type of treatment—			Waiting list control	4	.02
institutionalized juveniles			Matching participants	48	.24
Counseling, all types	17	.20	Equated groupwise	10	.05
Skill-oriented treatment,			Other nonrandom	47	.24
all types	15	.18			
Behavioral treatment,			**What the control group receives**		
all types	2	.02	Nothing, wait list, or		
Community residential	14	.17	minimal contact	19	.10
Guided group,			Placebo	14	.07
milieu therapy	10	.12	Treatment as usual, probation	43	.22
Multiple services	6	.07	Treatment as usual,		
All other	19	.23	institutional	72	.36
			Treatment as usual, other	52	.26
Weeks from first to last treatment event					
1-10	39	.19	**Recidivism outcome:**		
11-20	46	.23	**Type of delinquency**		
21-30	34	.17	Unofficial delinquency	12	.06
31-40	15	.08	Police contacts/arrests	86	.43
41-50	12	.06	Probation contact	10	.05
51-100	39	.19	Court contact	41	.21
Missing	15	.08	Parole contact	23	.12
			Institutional infraction	8	.04
Frequency of treatment contact			Institutionalization	18	.09
Continuous	54	.27	Other	2	.01
Daily	24	.12			
2-4 per week	20	.10	**Treatment group sample size**		
1-2 per week	62	.31	4-49	91	.45
Less than weekly	14	.07	50-99	57	.29
Missing	26	.13	100-199	28	.14
			≥ 200	24	.12
Mean hours per week of treatment contact					
≤ 1.0	38	.19	**Control group sample size**		
1.1-2.0	18	.09	4-49	97	.48
2.1-4.0	12	.06	50-99	51	.26
4.1-10.0	14	.07	100-199	33	.17
10.1-20.0	6	.03	≥ 200	19	.10

Recidivism Effect Size

To avoid problems of statistical dependency, only one recidivism outcome measure was selected from each study in the database.

Police contact/arrest recidivism was selected if available (because this was the most common outcome measure) and, if not, the outcome most comparable to police arrest was used, for example, officially recorded contact with juvenile court, offense-based probation violations, or the like.

The effect size index used to represent the outcome for each study was the difference between the treatment and control group means on the selected recidivism measure, standardized by the pooled standard deviation. This *standardized mean difference* effect size is commonly used for representing the results of experimental comparisons (Cooper & Hedges, 1994) and takes the following form:

$$d = (\overline{X}_t - \overline{X}_c) / \sigma_p$$

Hedges's (1981) small sample correction was applied to each effect size, and all computations with effect sizes were weighted by a term representing the sampling error associated with the estimate to reflect the greater stability of estimates based on larger samples (Hedges & Olkin, 1985; Shadish & Haddock, 1994). For the 200 effect sizes representing intervention effects on recidivism for the entire set of studies, the following summary statistics were obtained:

Weighted mean effect size: .12
95% confidence interval: .10 to .15
Heterogeneity (Q): 679.66 ($p < .001$ by chi-square test)

The overall mean recidivism value for treated juveniles was thus .12 standard deviation units less than that for the control group, and this effect was statistically significant. To put this value in perspective, a mean effect size of .12 is equivalent to the difference between a 44% recidivism rate for treated juveniles and a 50% rate for the untreated control group. This 6-percentage-point difference represents a 12% decrease in recidivism (6/50), which does not seem trivial, but is not especially impressive either.

This overall result gives a simple answer to the question of whether intervention, gen-

erally, can reduce recidivism rates for serious juvenile offenders. The grand mean effect size was positive, statistically significant, and large enough to be meaningful even if not enormous. The most important finding of this analysis, however, was the large variability (heterogeneity) of the effect sizes around the grand mean. Thus, some of the studies reported effects much larger than the overall mean, and others reported much smaller effects. The remainder of this chapter explores the nature of that variability in observed effects and attempts to identify the characteristics of the interventions that have the largest effects on recidivism.

Variation in Study Methods and Procedures

The first, but least interesting, source of effect size variability that must be addressed stems from differences among studies in method and procedure. Some studies may generate larger effects than others because of their methodological characteristics rather than the effectiveness of the interventions they investigate. To the extent that this happens, comparison of effect sizes across studies can be very misleading if differences are taken as indications that one intervention is more effective than another. To obtain a clearer view of actual intervention effects, therefore, it is desirable to first identify the variability in effect sizes attributable to differences between study method and then statistically control that variability in the effect size analysis. This was done using multiple regression to "predict" effect size solely from the methodological and procedural features of the studies, then subtracting the predicted value from each effect size. The resulting regression model included five variables that accounted for about 12% of the variance in effect sizes. It showed that the effect sizes were at least partially a function of the following features of study method (see Table 13.1 for breakdowns on the variables referred to here):

1. *The nature of the assignment to experimental groups.* Studies with random assignment to conditions produced smaller effect sizes than those using matching or other quasi-experimental comparisons.

2. *Attrition.* Studies with more subject attrition between the time of assignment to experimental conditions and the time of outcome measurement reported lower effect sizes.

3. *Type of delinquency outcome measure.* Studies that measured recidivism using police contact or arrest information showed larger effect sizes than those that measured recidivism with some other indicator, for example, court contact or parole violation.

4. *Sample size.* Studies that used larger samples tended to yield smaller effect sizes.

5. *Statistical power.* Studies rated by coders as having high statistical power, based on sample size *and* application of variance control techniques (e.g., use of analysis of covariance), exhibited smaller effect sizes.

Using the regression equation resulting from this analysis (not shown), it was possible to estimate what the mean effect size over the 200 studies would be if all the studies were uniform with regard to the methodological variables represented in that equation. For this purpose, we assumed a situation in which participants were assigned randomly to experimental conditions, there was no attrition between the time of that assignment and outcome measurement, recidivism outcomes were measured using police contact/arrest records, the total sample size was 130 (the median for the 200 studies), and statistical power was rated at the mean for all studies ("moderate"). Entering the respective values for these circumstances into the regression equation resulted in an estimate of the mean effect size as .18, somewhat larger than the observed mean of .12. This indicates that most of the departures from the method profile assumed for this estimate act to degrade the observed effect size. If the estimate of the mean effect size under uniform study methods is added to the residual value for each effect size, we have estimates of the effect sizes that would be observed if the studies did not vary on the method variables used in the regression model. These *method-adjusted effect sizes* were then analyzed in relation to various treatment variables to determine which were associated with larger effects.

Intervention for Noninstitutionalized Juveniles

The characteristics associated with effective intervention may be different for programs provided to juvenile offenders in institutional custody than for noninstitutional programs. Not only are the circumstances of treatment different, but the nature and response of the juveniles who receive the treatment may differ as well. The database, therefore, was divided into studies of intervention with noninstitutionalized juveniles ($N = 117$) and studies of intervention with institutionalized juveniles ($N = 83$). This section reports the analysis of the effects of noninstitutional treatment using the method-adjusted effect size values described above and exploring four categories of variables in relationship to effect size: (a) the characteristics of the juvenile offenders, for example, the proportion with prior offense records, the proportion with indications of prior aggressive behavior, gender mix, mean age, and ethnic mix; (b) general program characteristics, for example, the age of the program, who provides treatment (criminal justice, mental health, or other personnel), and whether the juveniles are under juvenile justice authority while in the program; (c) treatment type, for example, restitution, counseling, behavioral programs, and multiple services; and (d) the amount of treatment, for example, average number of weeks from first to last treatment event, frequency of treatment, and coders' rating of integrity of treatment implementation.

The task of identifying the characteristics associated with intervention programs that showed large effects on recidivism was approached initially by determining the relative magnitude of the relationship between each of the above clusters of variables and effect size. The procedure for accomplishing this was hierarchical weighted multiple regression with the items in the clusters listed above stepped in groupwise as predictor variables and the method-adjusted effect size as the dependent variable. The regression model resulting from this procedures is summarized in Table 13.2. It is very informative with regard to the general factors that are related to differences among studies in the magnitude of the treatment effects they report, as follows:

1. More than half of the variation among method-adjusted effect sizes across studies is related to variables in the four clusters. Given that the remaining variance includes sampling error and unreliability in the measures represented in the effect sizes, this model provides a good account of between-study differences in effect size and indicates that they should be largely understandable in terms of the study characteristics represented in the four clusters.

2. Each of the four clusters of predictor variables added significantly to the Q value of the model (Q-added, the analog of R^2 added). Thus, none of these four broad domains of intervention characteristics appears to be redundant or irrelevant in accounting for differences among studies in the size of the intervention effects reported.

3. The largest proportion of the effect size variance was associated with the characteristics of the juveniles who received treatment.

Further analysis, reported below, sheds additional light on the characteristics of the juveniles responding more and less favorably to intervention.

4. The cluster of variables identifying specific types of treatment showed the next largest relationship to effect size, followed closely by the cluster representing the amount of treatment delivered. This finding justifies an attempt to determine which modes and doses of treatment generally reduce recidivism the most. This too was examined in further analysis reported below.

5. The cluster of general program characteristics was stepped into the model last on the hypothesis that, once treatment type and amount and the characteristics of the recipients were accounted for, these more general features of the program would not add anything else. Though the proportion of effect size variance associated with this cluster was the smallest of the four, it was nonetheless not negligible. Various aspects of the way in which a program is organized, staffed, and administered, then, appear to have some independent influence on intervention effects.

Although the analysis shown in Table 13.2 gave some insight into which global categories of program characteristics had the most influence on the effects, it did not provide a very exact identification of the specific factors that most sharply discriminate effective from ineffective intervention. For that purpose, a "reduced" model was developed that included only the most important predictors. This was done by first dropping any variable that had a very small (< .05) zero-order correlation with effect size and then successively dropping any of the remaining variables in each cluster that did not make a significant individual contribution to predicting effect size. The reduced model resulting from this procedure involved only six variables and is shown in Table 13.3. Assessed in terms of the strength and independence of their empirical relationships, these variables represent the

TABLE 13.2 Hierarchical Weighted Multiple Regression Results for Predicting Method-Adjusted Effect Sizes for Intervention With Noninstitutionalized Offenders

Variable Cluster	Q-Added for Each Cluster	df	p	Proportion of Total Q for Model
Characteristics of juveniles[a]	77.79	7	< .001	.40
Amount of treatment[b]	37.70	8	< .001	.20
Treatment type[c]	49.60	14	< .001	.26
General program characteristics[d]	28.19	9	< .001	.15
Overall model	193.28	38	< .001	1.00
Residual	156.01	73[e]	< .001	
$R^2 =$	.55			

NOTE: Q is the homogeneity statistic indicating the amount of variance associated with each predictor variable; Q is tested as chi-square at the indicated *df* to determine the statistical significance of the regression coefficient.

a. Proportion with prior offenses, type of prior offenses, extent of aggressive history, proportion of males, mean age, ethnic mix, and heterogeneity rating.

b. Total weeks of treatment, frequency of treatment, mean hours/week, mean hours total contact, rated amount meaningful contact, rated intensity of treatment event, integrity of treatment implementation, and difficulties in treatment delivery.

c. Reduced caseload—probation/parole, restitution—probation/parole, academic programs, early release—probation/parole, employment related, deterrence programs, vocational programs, individual counseling, interpersonal skills, group counseling, drug abstinence, family counseling, wilderness/challenge, advocacy/social casework, multiple services, and behavioral programs.

d. Program age, demonstration program, criminal justice agency program, criminal justice facility, criminal justice treatment personnel, mental health treatment personnel, juvenile justice authority, voluntary vs. mandatory, and researcher's role.

e. For chi-square test, 5 degrees of freedom were subtracted to account for methods model fit previously.

characteristics of intervention most closely connected with its effectiveness in reducing the recidivism of noninstitutionalized serious juvenile offenders. What Table 13.3 indicates about this situation is as follows:

1. Among juvenile characteristics, two variables related to prior offense history showed strong, independent relationships to effect size. The strongest of these was "type of prior offenses," a dichotomy that differentiated juvenile samples with prior offense records that consisted almost exclusively of property crimes from those for which only mixed or total offenses of all types were reported. In most cases, the latter included some proportion of "person offenses," which are generally more violent and/or serious than property offenses. Treatment effects were *larger* for juvenile samples with mixed priors than those with mostly property priors. Similarly, when "all" the juveniles in the treatment sample were reported to have priors, treatment effects were *larger* than when only "most" were so described. To the extent that there was a relationship

between offender severity and treatment effectiveness, therefore, the effects seemed to be larger for more serious offenders than for the less serious.

2. Regarding amount of treatment, three variables showed strong, independent, but somewhat contradictory relationships with effect size. Duration of treatment ("total weeks," median = 23) was positively associated with effect size, whereas the mean number of hours per week of treatment (median = 5-10 hours) was negatively correlated; that is, *fewer* contact hours were associated with larger effects. Reported difficulties in treatment delivery (information in the research report indicating that some juveniles may not have received the intended treatment protocol) were associated with smaller effects, as would be expected.

3. The only variable from among general program characteristics to make a significant, independent contribution to effect size in the reduced model was the researcher's role in the treatment (four categories: delivered, planned and supervised, influential but did not design or supervise, independent). The

TABLE 13.3 Weighted Multiple Regression "Reduced" Model for Predicting Method-Adjusted Effect Sizes for Intervention With Noninstitutionalized Offenders

Variable	β	B	Q (df)	p
Proportion with prior offenses	.1252	.0755	4.80 (1)	.029
Type of prior offenses	−.2446	−.1441	18.58 (1)	.001
Total weeks of treatment	.1565	.0014	7.96 (1)	.005
Mean hours/week contact	−.2142	−.0456	10.90 (1)	.001
Difficulties in treatment delivery	.1678	.0622	9.08 (1)	.003
Researcher's role	−.2187	−.0639	12.37 (1)	.001
Regression constant		.5450		
Overall model			87.06 (6)	.001
Residual			262.22 (105[a])	.001
$R^2 =$	.25			

NOTE: β = standardized regression coefficient; B = unstandardized regression coefficient; Q is the homogeneity statistic indicating the amount of variance associated with each predictor variable; Q is tested as chi-square at the indicated *df* to determine the statistical significance of the regression coefficient.

a. For chi-square test, 5 degrees of freedom were subtracted to account for methods model fit previously.

less involved the researcher was in the design, planning, and delivery of treatment, the smaller the effect size. This variable appears to distinguish those projects carefully constructed by the researcher for demonstration or research purposes from ongoing, real-world programs with which the researcher is involved primarily as an evaluator.

Type of Treatment and Effects on Recidivism

The regression model shown in Table 13.3 allows the mean effect size to be predicted on the basis of the juvenile and program characteristics most strongly associated with effect size. It reflects the method adjustments that were made earlier to statistically control for method and procedural variation among the studies, and it accounts for the differences in intervention effects expected on the basis of different juvenile characteristics, amount of treatment, and the role of the researcher in the program. Because this reduced model was designed to represent the most important and robust variables related to treatment effects, and because it "levels the playing field" by

adjusting for between-study differences that make direct comparison of observed effect sizes ambiguous, it will be the primary basis for drawing conclusions about the most effective types of treatment for noninstitutionalized serious juvenile offenders.

To compare different treatments using the regression model of Table 13.3, the dummy code for each treatment type was added to the variables already in the model and the regression equation was refit. This resulted in separate regression equations for each treatment type in which all the variables were the same except for treatment type itself. From these, the mean effect size associated with each treatment type could be estimated for conditions in which the values on all the other variables were the same simply by plugging in the across-study means on those variables. We can thus compare the mean effect expected for individual counseling with that for, say, behavioral programs when both are assumed to be provided for the same number of weeks, same number of hours per week, to juveniles with the same prior offense histories, and so forth for all the variables in Table 13.3. We will call these estimates the *equated effect sizes.* This meta-analysis also generated two other forms of effect size estimates that could be broken down by type of treatment. One is simply the original effect size computed from the statistics presented in each study, that is, the *observed effect sizes.* The other is the *method-adjusted effect sizes* used as the dependent variable for the regression analyses shown in Table 13.3 and which attempted to control for between-study differences in method and procedure.

Each of these different estimates has advantages and disadvantages. The observed effect sizes are most descriptive of the findings reported in the original research studies, but comparisons between types of treatments on this index may be distorted by other differences between studies that also influence the effects. The method-adjusted effect sizes simulate a situation in which uniform methods and procedures were used in each study and thus give the best comparison of the effects produced by the different types of treatment as those that were actually delivered in the various studies. As such, however, they do not separate differences in effectiveness associated with the specific types of treatment and those associated with differences in the characteristics of the juveniles receiving treatment, different amounts of treatment, and the like. The equated effect sizes, in turn, simulate a situation in which method and procedure were similar across studies *and* juvenile characteristics, amount of treatment, and so on were uniform as well. They thus give the best indication of the differential effects of specific types of treatment, but may represent unrealistic scenarios with regard to the characteristics of the juveniles to whom those treatments are likely to be given, the customary amounts, and so forth.

The approach taken here is to use all three of these estimates to examine the different treatment types in relation to three considerations. The first consideration is the magnitude of the mean effect for each treatment type according to each estimate, assessed in part by statistical significance testing. The second is the variance around each of those means for the respective effect estimates from the individual studies. Homogeneity tests (Q test) can be applied for this purpose; they indicate whether the effects estimated from different studies differ by more than expected on the basis of sampling error. The third consideration is the extent of agreement across the three different effect size estimates. Agreement indicates that the different statistical controls associated with the different estimates have not made much difference and, hence, the effect size findings are relatively robust to between-study differences on other characteristics. Disagreement means that such between-study differences are confounded with treatment effects and create ambiguity about the actual size of the treatment effect.

The mean effect size for each treatment type for each effect size estimation procedure is shown in Table 13.4. This table first presents the number of studies for each type of treatment as a reminder that they are few—most of these treatments have not often been studied in application to noninstitutionalized serious juvenile offenders. The different types of treatment are then grouped according to the pattern of findings across the effect size estimates. The top group consists of those treatment types that show consistent positive treatment effects. All the means for all the estimates are statistically significant (indicated with an asterisk) and notably larger than the means across all the treatment types together (at the bottom of the array). Moreover, the effect sizes averaged into each of these means are homogeneous (indicated with a dagger), showing no significant variance across studies around that mean. These are the treatment types with the strongest evidence of effectiveness in reducing the recidivism of nonin-

TABLE 13.4 Mean Effect Sizes for Different Treatment Types for Observed and Statistically Adjusted Effect Size Estimates (noninstitutionalized juvenile offenders)

Treatment Type	N	Observed Effect Size	Method-Adjusted Effect Size	Equated Effect Size
Interpersonal skills	3	.46*†	.38*†	.49*†
Individual counseling	8	.52*†	.43*†	.40*†
Behavioral programs	7	.49*†	.43*†	.35*†
Multiple services	17	.26*	.32*	.25*†
Restitution, probation/parole	10	.16*†	.17*†	.13*
All other	14	.08	.25*	.37*
Employment related	4	.13	.14	.30*†
Academic programs	2	.10	.19	.29*†
Advocacy/social casework	6	.11	.15*†	.27*†
Group counseling	9	.02	.04	.18*
Family counseling	8	.24*	.27*	.11
Reduced caseload, probation/parole	12	−.09*	.00	.02
Wilderness/challenge	4	.13†	.07†	.17†
Early release, probation/parole	2	.10†	.11†	−.05†
Deterrence programs	6	−.03†	−.02†	−.10†
Vocational programs	4	−.17†	−.20*†	−.16†
Overall	117	.14*	.18*	.18*

*$p < .05$ (statistical significance). †$Q > .05$ (homogeneity).

stitutionalized serious juvenile offenders. Ranked according to the mean equated effect size, this top group was composed of interpersonal skills training (with only three studies), individual counseling, and behavioral programs.

Close behind this top group was a second tier of treatment types for which the evidence was also rather convincing. Each showed statistically significant mean effects on all of the effect size estimates. Not all these mean effect sizes were based on homogeneous sets of individual effect sizes, however. Though this is in part due to the larger number of studies in these categories, giving the Q test more statistical power for rejecting the hypothesis of homogeneity, it does raise some question because not all the studies represented in these groups agreed on the size of the effect. The two treatment types in this tier are multiple services (e.g., service brokerage, multi-

modal service) and restitution programs for juveniles on probation or parole.

The bottom group in Table 13.4 consists of those treatment types with means based on homogeneous effect size estimates, but not significantly different from zero (except one case that is significantly negative). These treatment types show the strongest and most consistent evidence that they were not effective in reducing the recidivism of noninstitutionalized serious juvenile offenders. This group included wilderness/challenge programs, early release from probation or parole (only two studies), deterrence programs (mostly shock incarceration), and vocational programs. We should note that vocational programs are distinct from employment-related programs in this categorization. Programs that provided vocational training, career counseling, job search and interview skills, and the like were classified as vocational. Only those that actually involved paid employment were classified as employment.

The second tier from the bottom in the groupings includes only one treatment type, reduced caseload programs for juveniles on probation or parole. The different effect size estimates agreed in finding no significant positive mean effects for these programs (but one significant negative effect). However, the individual effect sizes averaged into these means were not homogeneous, indicating that some of the studies showed significantly larger effects than others.

In the middle of Table 13.4 is a group of treatment types that presented mixed or ambiguous evidence. Although some of their effect size means were statistically significant and some were homogeneous, especially for the equated effect size estimates, there was inconsistency across the various estimation procedures. This indicates that the statistical adjustments being applied by the different effect size estimation procedures are relatively large, and therefore, differences among these treatment types are confounded with differences in study method or other characteristics of the intervention, such as amount of treatment or characteristics of the juvenile recipients. On the positive side, the equated effect size estimate is the one designed to smooth out these differences as much as possible, and it showed results that were generally favorable for the treatment types in this group. However, without a better accounting of the source of the differences in the various estimates of mean effect sizes, it is uncertain whether the mean effects shown for treatment types in this group represent actual treatment effects or artifacts.

In the concluding section of this chapter, we return to the issue of which interventions are most effective for serious juvenile offenders. More detail is given there about the nature of the interventions that generated the largest effect sizes in Table 13.4. First, however, we review the findings regarding intervention with institutionalized offenders.

Intervention for Institutionalized Juveniles

Of the 200 studies investigating intervention with serious juvenile offenders, 83 dealt with programs for institutionalized youth. Of those, 74 studied programs in juvenile justice institutions and 9 involved residential facilities under private or mental health administration. The typical study of intervention with institutionalized juveniles compared a control group receiving the usual institutional program with an experimental group receiving that plus some additional service that was the treatment of interest in the research.

The same analysis procedures were followed for these studies as are described above for studies involving noninstitutionalized juvenile offenders. The first step was to construct a hierarchical weighted multiple regression model that included all the variables describing characteristics of the juvenile clients and the treatment and program circumstances that had been identified in preliminary screening as potentially important on either conceptual or empirical grounds. These variables were added to the regression analysis stepwise as full clusters to determine if each successive cluster added a significant, independent increment to the model's account of between study variation in the method-adjusted effect sizes. The results of this omnibus regression analysis are shown in Table 13.5. The major findings presented there regarding the relative contribution of each of these clusters of predictor variables are as follows:

1. As with the corresponding analysis earlier, a large proportion of the variation among

TABLE 13.5 Hierarchical Weighted Multiple Regression Results for Predicting Method-Adjusted Effect Sizes for Intervention With Institutionalized Offenders

Variable Cluster	Q-Added for Each Cluster	df	p	Proportion of Total Q for Model
Characteristics of juveniles[a]	13.08	7	.070	.10
Amount of treatment[b]	34.22	8	< .001	.27
Treatment type[c]	32.50	12	.001	.26
General program characteristics[d]	45.26	9	< .001	.36
Overall model	125.05	36	< .001	1.00
Residual	119.01	38[e]	< .001	
$R^2 =$	.51			

NOTE: Q is the homogeneity statistic indicating the amount of variance associated with each predictor variable; Q is tested as chi-square at the indicated *df* to determine the statistical significance of the regression coefficient.

a. Proportion with prior offenses, type of prior offenses, extent of aggressive history, proportion of males, mean age, ethnic mix, and heterogeneity rating.

b. Total weeks of treatment, frequency of treatment, mean hours/week, mean hours total contact, rated amount meaningful contact, rated intensity of treatment event, integrity of treatment implementation, and difficulties in treatment delivery.

c. Guided group, milieu therapy, teaching family home, community residential, individual counseling, group counseling, behavioral programs, employment related, interpersonal skills, drug abstinence, wilderness/challenge, and multiple service.

d. Program age, demonstration program, criminal justice agency program, criminal justice facility, criminal justice treatment personnel, mental health treatment personnel, juvenile justice authority, voluntary vs. mandatory, and researcher's role.

e. For chi-square test, 5 degrees of freedom were subtracted to account for methods model fit previously.

method-adjusted effect sizes across studies was systematically related to variables in the four clusters. The overall R^2 for the full regression model was .51, indicating that about half the variance was associated with the predictor variables in this model.

2. Each of the four clusters of predictor variables except the first added significantly to the Q value of the model (Q-added). The first cluster, characteristics of juveniles, was only marginally significant ($p = .07$).

3. The smallest proportion of the effect size variance accounted for in the model was associated with the characteristics of the juveniles who received the intervention programs. This was in marked contrast to the results for intervention with noninstitutionalized juveniles (Table 13.2), where this cluster made the largest contribution. It may well be that there is much less variation among samples of institutionalized juveniles than among noninstitutionalized ones and, therefore, less scope for their differences to be related to effect sizes. In any event, this finding indicates that treatment effects are much the same for a given program whatever the sample characteristics.

4. The cluster of general program characteristics showed the strongest global relationship with effect size. Again, this stands in sharp contrast with the results shown in Table 13.2 for intervention with noninstitutionalized juveniles, where this cluster was the weakest. For intervention with institutionalized juveniles, therefore, certain aspects of the way in which a program is organized, staffed, and administered are importantly related to the size of the recidivism effects above and beyond that accounted for by the specific type of treatment and the amount of that treatment delivered.

5. The cluster of variables identifying specific types of treatment was in the middle with regard to its relationship to effect size and was very similar in magnitude to that found for intervention with noninstitutionalized juveniles. The cluster representing the amount of treatment delivered showed a similar middling relationship.

The analysis shown in Table 13.5 demonstrates the overall contribution of the different clusters of variables and sheds some light

TABLE 13.6 Weighted Multiple Regression "Reduced" Model for Predicting Method-Adjusted Effect Sizes for Intervention With Institutionalized Offenders

Variable	β	B	Q (df)	p
Total weeks of treatment	.2041	.0025	9.61 (1)	.002
Integrity of treatment implementation	.2589	.0965	14.40 (1)	.001
Program age	.2568	.1390	13.87 (1)	.001
Mental health treatment personnel	.2581	.1643	15.05 (1)	.001
Regression constant		−.2985		
Overall model			48.09 (4)	.001
Residual			195.97 (73[a])	.001
R^2 =	.20			

NOTE: β = standardized regression coefficient; B = unstandardized regression coefficient; Q is the homogeneity statistic indicating the amount of variance associated with each predictor variable; Q is tested as chi-square at the indicated *df* to determine the statistical significance of the regression coefficient.

a. For chi-square test, 5 degrees of freedom were subtracted to account for methods model fit previously.

on their relative importance. As in the application to noninstitutional juveniles earlier, however, this model included too many incidental variables to provide a good summary representation of the data and a basis for properly estimating the treatment effects to be expected under different circumstances. A "reduced" model was therefore developed following the same procedure described earlier, that is, individual variables with trivial zero-order correlations were dropped, the weakest predictors in each cluster individually were pruned, then all remaining variables were entered together in the prediction model and any nonsignificant in this competition were also omitted. The final regression model resulting from this procedure is shown in Table 13.6. It gave a good accounting of the between-study variation in method-adjusted effect sizes with only four predictor variables, all having to do with amount of treatment and general program characteristics. What it revealed about the variables with the most important, independent relationship to the size of the intervention effects is the following:

1. None of the variables describing the characteristics of the juveniles made sufficiently large contributions to be included in this model, despite a procedure that gave them equal opportunity with variables in the other clusters. The most important implication of this finding is that the conclusions this model yields about treatment effects need not be differentiated according to such characteristics of the juveniles treated as age, gender, ethnic mix, and history of prior offenses within the range of typical variation found among serious institutionalized offenders.

2. Two of the variables related to amount of treatment proved important in this model. The strongest was the integrity of the treatment implementation, that is, the extent to which there was monitoring to ensure that all juveniles received the intended treatment. Studies in which there was indication of high monitoring yielded larger effects than those in which implementation integrity was rated as low. The duration of treatment in number of weeks was also related to the size of the treatment effect, with greater duration associated with larger effects. The median length of treatment for the studies in this sample was 25 weeks, and the frequency and hours of weekly contact were mostly rated as "continuous," indicating that treatment was spread over or integrated into the institutional regimen.

3. Among general program characteristics, the largest treatment effects were found for programs that were relatively well established

TABLE 13.7 Mean Effect Sizes for Different Treatment Types for Observed and Statistically Adjusted Effect Size Estimates (institutionalized juvenile offenders)

Treatment Type	N	Observed Effect Size	Method-Adjusted Effect Size	Equated Effect Size
Interpersonal skills	3	.40*†	.36*†	.42*†
Teaching family home	6	.41*†	.32*†	.26*†
Multiple services	6	.11*	.19*	.29*
Community residential	8	.24*	.32*	.24*
All other	19	.10*	.16*	.23*
Behavioral program	2	.21†	.34†	.44*†
Individual counseling	8	.09†	.21*	.19*
Group counseling	9	−.01	.08	.10*
Guided group	7	.13*	.15*	.03
Drug abstinence	5	.02	.11	.14
Wilderness/challenge	5	.04	.12	−.01
Employment related	2	.18†	.11	.13
Milieu therapy	3	.02†	.12†	.13†
Overall	83	.10*	.17*	.17*

*$p < .05$ (statistical significance). †$Q > .05$ (homogeneity).

(2 years or older). The variable that was most strongly related to effect size, among all those in the model, however, was administration of the treatment by mental health personnel (in contrast, primarily, to juvenile justice personnel). This latter finding is quite striking considering that most of these juveniles were being treated in juvenile justice institutional settings. It may be that justice personnel, as the authorities in these institutional settings, are in a role that makes effective treatment more difficult.

Type of Treatment and Effects on Recidivism

As in the earlier application, the reduced regression model can generate estimates of the treatment effect sizes that would be expected for each type of treatment under uniform treatment conditions (e.g., type of juvenile recipient, amount of treatment) studied with uniform methodology (because the method-adjusted effect sizes were used in this model). To make estimates of expected effect sizes

with the regression model reported in Table 13.6, the predictor variables were set to the mean values across the 83 studies of intervention with institutionalized juveniles, and the regression equation was used to calculate the expected effect size for that situation. The mean treatment effect sizes that result are shown in Table 13.7 along with those from the two other estimation procedures described earlier.

As in the version of this table for noninstitutionalized juveniles (Table 13.4), the different types of treatment were grouped according to the magnitude of the mean effect sizes *and* the consistency of the estimates within and between those averaged values. It is worth emphasizing once again the small number of studies on which many of these estimates were based. Although it is useful to draw what insights we can from these empirical findings, many more studies of intervention with institutionalized serious offenders will be needed before strong conclusions can be reached.

The top group of treatment types in Table 13.7 showed relatively large, statistically significant mean effect sizes across all the estimation procedures that were based on homogeneous sets of individual effect sizes. The two types of treatment in this group were interpersonal skills programs and the teaching family home program. Interpersonal skills training, recall, was also one of the stronger treatments for noninstitutionalized juveniles (Table 13.4). In the next tier were treatment types with consistently significant mean effects for all the estimation procedures, but some had significant heterogeneity among the individual effect sizes that were averaged into the mean. Although these, too, represent very favorable results, the heterogeneity across studies indicates that different studies of this treatment type found significantly different results, some larger and some smaller than the mean values shown. The types of treatment in this grouping were multiple service programs, community residential programs (mostly non-juvenile justice), and the miscellaneous category for "other" treatments that could not be classified elsewhere.

At the bottom of Table 13.7 is one treatment type that showed consistent null effects (milieu therapy) and, in the tier above, three types of treatment that did not show statistically significant mean effects, but with means that were based on heterogeneous distributions. Thus, some studies of these types of treatments found effects significantly larger than the mean values shown, whereas others found significantly smaller effects. This grouping includes drug abstinence programs, wilderness/challenge programs, and employment-related programs (which showed larger effects for the noninstitutionalized offenders).

The middle tiers of treatment types in Table 13.7 showed mixed evidence. Some mean effect sizes were statistically significant, some were averaged over homogeneous findings from the different studies, and some were consistent across the three estimation procedures. None, however, met all of these criteria. Therefore, the evidence was ambiguous for these groups of treatment types. In the case of behavioral programs, the problem may simply be too few studies (two) because, other than the failure of the relatively high effect size means to reach statistical significance in two instances, the positive evidence was generally consistent. For the three counseling varieties (individual, group, and guided group), however, the effect size estimates were quite inconsistent. Some were positive and statistically significant, some near zero; none was consistent across the estimation procedures; and only one was based on a homogeneous set of individual effect sizes. Observed effects in the studies in these groups appear to be confounded with other study characteristics so that it is difficult to disentangle the actual treatment effects.

■ *Summary and Discussion*

The meta-analysis reported in this chapter reviewed the statistical findings of 200 experimental or quasi-experimental studies of the effects of intervention with serious juvenile offenders and attempted to answer two questions: (a) Can intervention programs reduce the reoffending rates of serious delinquents? and (b) if so, what programs are most effective?

The first of these questions can be answered rather easily and convincingly, even though the answer is not very informative. The studies examined in this meta-analysis represented a large portion, if not virtually all, of the interventions with serious delinquents that have been studied with methods that yield some assessment of their impact on recidivism. The average intervention effect for these studies was positive, statistically significant, and equivalent to a recidivism reduction of about 6 percentage points, for example, from 50% to 44% (mean effect size = .12). The variation around this overall mean, however, was considerable. Some studies and groups of studies reported effects much larger than this, and others reported effects very much smaller. The average effect, therefore, does not provide a good summary of what can be expected from intervention with this juvenile population. The interesting question, then, is the second one above: Given a range of results from very bad to very good, what types of programs are the best for reducing recidivism?

That question was much more difficult to answer. Although 200 research studies might appear quite sufficient for the purpose, in fact, it is not an altogether satisfactory number. The range and diversity of intervention programs represented in these studies, the differences among the samples of juveniles, and the assortment of methods and procedures used to study the results all interact to produce a bewildering variety of combinations and permutations. As a result, there were relatively few studies of any one type of intervention, and those generally differed appreciably among themselves with regard to the juvenile samples represented and the research methods applied. This circumstance must be kept firmly in mind as the findings of this meta-analysis are interpreted because it makes virtually all of the principal conclusions tentative. It might be said, therefore, that the first finding of this meta-analysis is that sufficient research has not yet been conducted on the effects of intervention with serious juvenile offenders.

With this caveat in mind, we turn to those findings of the meta-analysis that address the issue of *which* intervention programs are most effective for reducing the recidivism of serious juvenile offenders. The first finding

has to do with the differentiation of those intervention programs administered to offenders who were institutionalized and those administered to offenders in the community, that is, those not institutionalized. The former were primarily incarcerated in juvenile justice facilities, and the latter were mostly on probation or parole. The circumstances of intervention were so different for these two situations that they were analyzed separately. The mean effect sizes were similar, however: .14 for noninstitutional intervention and .10 for institutional intervention. Even though the latter is smaller in magnitude, the difference was not statistically significant.

The contrast between these two situations became most apparent in the omnibus analyses examining the relationship of the intervention effect sizes to four clusters of variables that generally provided a profile of (a) the characteristics of the juveniles in the treatment samples, (b) the amount of treatment, (c) the type of treatment, and (d) the general program characteristics. For noninstitutional intervention, effects were most strongly related to the characteristics of the juveniles, especially their prior offense histories. The influence of treatment type and amount was intermediate, and general program characteristics were only weakly related to effect size. For intervention with institutionalized juveniles, however, this ordering was reversed. General program characteristics showed the strongest relationship to the size of the intervention effects, especially the age of the program and whether service was administered by mental health or juvenile justice personnel. The type and amount of treatment displayed moderate relationships to the size of the intervention effects, and the characteristics of the juveniles were not especially important.

More detail will be provided shortly about the characteristics associated with effective intervention in each of these situations. What is important to note here is that the program characteristics most closely connected with success in reducing the reoffense rates of serious offenders were quite different for institutional programs with incarcerated offenders than for noninstitutional programs for offenders on probation and parole in the community. Furthermore, those characteristics were not fully embedded in the nature of the intervention, for example, counseling, restitution, or drug abstinence, but were part of the administrative context for the intervention or related to the makeup of the juveniles to whom that intervention was applied. Effective intervention, therefore, requires more than a "magic bullet" program concept—it also depends on a good match between program concept, host organization, and the clientele targeted.

Intervention With Noninstitutionalized Offenders

Whereas institutionalized offenders, almost by definition, represented relatively serious cases, there is some question about whether the noninstitutionalized offenders in the 117 studies selected for this meta-analysis can be characterized as serious offenders. Few intervention studies deal exclusively with serious offenders, especially outside of institutional settings. Thus, to give some representation to the range of relevant intervention programs, the selection criteria for the studies in this analysis were not highly restrictive. With only a few exceptions, all that was required was that the intervention sample be at least "predominantly" adjudicated delinquents, that "most" or "all" have prior offenses involving person or property crimes, and that the referral for services be made by a juvenile justice source, for example, law enforcement. Even though these criteria excluded very lightweight cases, for example, first offenders, they nonetheless selected studies involving juvenile samples that varied considerably in the severity of their offense records.

For those interventions that were found in this meta-analysis to be effective in reducing the recidivism of these juveniles, therefore, a question arises as to whether they would be equally effective if applied only to the most serious offenders. Given the limited volume of research addressing that issue directly, we have no assurance that the answer is necessarily yes. However, the analysis of the effect size data provided some important indications that the interventions identified as most effective overall for the noninstitutionalized juveniles were also effective for the subset of serious offenders. In particular, the regression analyses reported in Tables 13.2 and 13.3 examined the extent to which the magnitude of treatment effects across studies was associated with the characteristics of the samples of juveniles to which the treatment was applied. If there were significant differential effects for more versus less serious offenders, we would expect to see some substantial correlations between effect size and the sample characteristics related to offense severity. However, most of the sample characteristics were not significantly related to effect size in these regression analyses, including extent of aggressive history and the gender, age, and ethnic mix represented.

The most telling results were those involving the prior offense records of the juveniles in the samples. The variables relating to this issue were "proportion with prior offenses" and "type of prior offenses," each indicating that a sample had a greater or lesser concentration of serious offenders. These two critical variables, in fact, did show significant, independent correlations with intervention effect size in the regression analyses. However, the direction of that correlation was

TABLE 13.8 Summary of Most and Least Effective Types of Treatment and Size of the Effects They Are Estimated to Produce on Recidivism Rates

Noninstitutionalized Offenders			Institutionalized Offenders		
Treatment Type	Midpoint of Estimated Effect Sizes	Equivalent Treatment/ Control Recidivism Contrast[a]	Treatment Type	Midpoint of Estimated Effect Sizes	Equivalent Treatment/ Control Recidivism Contrast[a]
Positive effects, consistent evidence					
Individual counseling	.46	.28/.50	Interpersonal skills	.39	.31/.50
Interpersonal skills	.44	.29/.50	Teaching family home	.34	.33/.50
Behavioral programs	.42	.30/.50			
Positive effects, less consistent evidence					
Multiple services	.29	.36/.50	Behavioral programs	.33	.34/.50
Restitution, probation/parole	.15	.43/.50	Community residential	.28	.36/.50
			Multiple services	.20	.40/.50
Mixed but generally positive effects, inconsistent evidence					
Employment related	.22	.39/.50	Individual counseling	.15	.43/.50
Academic programs	.20	.40/.50	Guided group	.09	.45/.50
Advocacy/casework	.19	.41/.50	Group counseling	.05	.47/.50
Family counseling	.19	.41/.50			
Group counseling	.10	.45/.50			
Weak or no effects, inconsistent evidence					
Reduced caseload, probation/parole	−.04	.52/.50	Employment related	.15	.43/.50
			Drug abstinence	.08	.46/.50
			Wilderness/challenge	.07	.46/.50
Weak or no effects, consistent evidence					
Wilderness/challenge	.12	.44/.50	Milieu therapy	.08	.46/.50
Early release, probation/parole	.03	.48/.50			
Deterrence programs	−.06	.53/.50			
Vocational programs	−.18	.59/.50			

a. Recidivism of treatment group in comparison to assumed control group recidivism of .50.

such that intervention effects were *larger* for the samples with greater concentrations of serious offenders. If anything, then, it would appear that the typical intervention in these studies was *more* effective with serious offenders than with less serious offenders. Combined with the fact that little differentiation was found with respect to other characteristics of the juvenile samples (i.e., extent of aggressive history; gender, age, and ethnic mix), these results indicate that the effects of the interventions studied in this meta-analysis were much the same for different juvenile samples except that those effects tended to be larger for samples of more serious offenders. Therefore, despite the fact that not every intervention found effective for noninstitutionalized delinquents in this meta-analysis dealt with the most severe offenders, there is good reason to believe that they would be at least equally effective if applied exclusively to such a population.

Effectiveness of Different Treatment Types With Noninstitutionalized Offenders

Table 13.8 presents a summary of the various groupings of treatment type that were developed in this meta-analysis and a summary of the average size of their effects on recidivism. For intervention with noninstitutionalized offenders, the treatments in the top two groupings showed the most impressive effects overall. This list looks much like the ranking generated in earlier meta-analysis work on the effects of intervention for general delinquency (Lipsey, 1992). What works for delinquents in general, therefore, also seems to work for noninstitutionalized serious offenders. Correspondingly, what does not work for general delinquents also does not work for these more serious offenders. The one rather striking departure from this generalization has to do with the effects of individual counseling. Among studies of general delinquency, this treatment was not found to have especially large effects. Curiously, for these noninstitutionalized serious offenders it seems to be much more effective—indeed, it emerged as one of the most effective treatments. This apparent discrepancy warrants further examination, but that goes beyond the scope of the present review.

Given an identification of the treatment types and circumstances that appear to produce the largest effects on the reoffense rates of noninstitutionalized serious offenders, it is relevant to ask just how large those effects are in practical terms. As Table 13.8 summarizes, the standardized mean difference effect size index that was the statistical indicator of effect size used in this meta-analysis was found to have mean values of around .40 for the most effective types of treatment. These values are more readily interpretable if they are transformed into equivalent recidivism rate values. For this purpose, we assumed that the untreated control groups in these studies had a police contact/arrest reoffense rate of .50 during the first year after intervention. In fact, the actual value was very near this for the subset of studies reporting police contact/arrest as proportions. With this baseline, the reoffense rate of the treatment group could be determined as the proportion that, when contrasted with .50, yields the mean effect size value actually found for the treatment of interest. Cohen (1988) provides arcsine tables that make this procedure straightforward. This conversion was made for each summary effect size mean displayed in Table 13.8.

As is evident, the magnitude of the effects on recidivism for the best treatments was appreciable when viewed in terms of relative reoffense rates. The most effective treatment types had an impact on recidivism that was equivalent to reducing a .50 control group baseline to around .30. In other words, we estimated that without treatment the recidivism rate for these juveniles would have been 50%. If they received the most effective of the treatments reviewed in this meta-analysis, their recidivism would drop to about 30%. Clearly, this is a rather substantial drop; indeed, the rate is nearly cut in half. If we proportion the 20-percentage-point decrease against the 50% baseline (20/50), we find that these treatments reduced recidivism by about 40%. Given that the juveniles involved were on the upper end of the severity continuum, this is a rather impressive effect.

To show more detail about the nature of the intervention programs represented in the top group in Table 13.8, we have pulled a selection of the contributing research reports from our files and summarized the authors' description of the treatment. These are provided below, with the bibliographic citations, for the treatment types that produced the largest mean effects.

Individual Counseling

1. *A program for juvenile probationers that used citizen volunteers in conjunction with regular probationary supervision to counsel offenders on a one-to-one basis.* The volunteers were screened and matched with offenders based on sex, ethnicity, educational background, intellectual level, vocational aspirations, and recreational interests (Moore, 1987).

2. *Reality therapy counseling was given in weekly hour-long sessions for 12 weeks by two female graduate students enrolled in post-master's-level counseling courses.* The reality therapy involved recycling eight steps until clients learned to take charge of their lives in a constructive manner: involvement/ goal setting, behavior assessment, behavior evaluation, concrete plans of action, commitment to action plans, no excuses, no punishments, and no giving up with resistant clients (Bean, 1988).

3. *Juvenile sexual offenders were treated under multisystemic therapy.* Each youth or family received 21 to 49 hours of therapy in which doctoral students in clinical psychology attempted to ameliorate deficits in the adolescents' cognitive processes (denial, empathy, distortions), family relations (family cohesion, parental supervision), peer relations, and school performance (Borduin, Henggeler, Blaske, & Stein, 1990).

Interpersonal Skills

1. *An experimental training program used drama and the making of video films as vehicles for helping delinquent juveniles see themselves from the perspective of others and as remedial training in deficient role-taking skills.* There were 10 training sessions occur-

ring once a week for 3 hours each at a neighborhood storefront. Sessions were run by three graduate students who facilitated the efforts of the participants while enforcing certain ground rules: (a) The skits must be about real situations involving people of the participants' ages, (b) everyone gets a part, (c) everyone gets a chance to play every role, and (d) the video recordings are viewed to see how they could be improved (Chandler, 1973).

2. *An intensive 10-day course in a large group camp or church retreat facility for juveniles.* The course included lecture and discussion, group demonstrations and learning processes, daily exercise, challenging outdoor activities, discussion of responsible behavior in the context of the group setting, opportunities for voluntary group service, and leadership. The follow-up phase involved a commitment to one or more personal and community projects. For a 12-month period, the youth participated in monthly meetings, personal counseling, tutoring, sponsored social events, job skills training, involvement in production of future courses, and special workshops (Delinquency Research Group, 1986).

Behavioral Programs

1. *Adjudicated delinquents were court-ordered to the Family Counseling Program as a condition of probation.* The therapy program was divided into three phases: the assessment phase, in which problem behavior within the family was identified through interview and observation; the therapy phase, in which family members' intentions were relabeled to render them benign or positive; and the education phase, in which parenting skills and family living skills were taught in a structured manner (Gordon, Graves, & Arbuthnot, 1987).

2. *Probationers were included in a contingency contracting program as a method of behavior therapy.* The average treatment was based on an agreement worked out between the parole officer and the juvenile to modify specific problem behaviors. Contracts usually provided some sort of monetary reward for exhibiting desired behavior or refraining from unwanted behavior. When applicable, parents and teachers were included in deciding on and carrying out the terms of the contact (Jessness, Allison, McCormic, Wedge, & Young, 1975).

Multiple Services

1. *A probation program offered 24 different treatment techniques with no juvenile receiving more than 12 or fewer than 4.* The core procedure, used with almost 50% of the youths, trained responsible citizens from the community to act as unofficial counselors, friends, and role models. Other treatments included group counseling, work crews, alcohol awareness, and vocational training (Morris, 1970).

2. *Project New Pride provided 3 months of intensive services to probationed youth, followed by approximately 9 months of follow-up services.* The primary services included educational testing and remediation, disability testing and remediation, employment counseling, pre-vocational training, job development and placement, personal counseling, cultural education, recreation, and client advocacy (Browne, 1975).

3. *Youth were placed under intensive case management and received an array of services to meet their particular needs.* Some categories of treatment were recreation, after-school programs, inpatient therapy, outpatient child therapy, outpatient family therapy,

supervised group and independent living services, and vocational placement (Weisz, Walter, Weiss, Fernandez, & Mikow, 1990).

Intervention With Institutionalized Offenders

The 83 studies of the effects of intervention with institutionalized offenders examined in this meta-analysis included 74 that involved juveniles in the custody of juvenile justice institutions and 9 that involved residential institutions administered by mental health or private agencies. Although the juveniles within such institutions varied with regard to the severity of their offense histories and, especially, the extent of their violent behavior, all, of course, had committed offenses sufficiently serious to convince the authorities that they must be either confined or closely supervised in an institutional facility.

Effectiveness of different treatment types with institutionalized offenders. Table 13.8 (introduced earlier) presented the various groupings of treatment type that were developed in this meta-analysis and a summary of the average size of their effects on recidivism. The treatment types in the top three groupings showed the largest mean effects overall, but the results were somewhat inconsistent for all but the top group. Once again, the relatively small number of studies in each category when the full set was subdivided by treatment type made it difficult to draw any firm conclusions about the relative effectiveness of different treatment types for institutionalized offenders.

Table 13.8 also summarizes the results for each treatment type on the standardized mean difference effect size index used in this meta-analysis. This was found to have mean values of .35-.40 for the most effective types of treatment, a notch lower than for the corresponding category of intervention with noninstitutionalized offenders. Viewed in terms of the equivalent recidivism rate differentials, the most effective treatment types had an impact on recidivism that was equivalent to reducing a .50 control group baseline to around .30-.35. That is, if we assume that the recidivism rate for these juveniles would have been 50% without treatment, the most effective of the treatments reduced it to 30%-35%. This is a considerable decrease, especially in light of the fact that it applies to institutionalized offenders, who can be assumed to be relatively serious delinquents.

To furnish additional details about the nature of the intervention programs represented in the top groups in Table 13.8 for institutionalized offenders, the authors' description of the treatment has been summarized below for a selection of the research reports represented in the five treatment types in the two highest groups.

Interpersonal Skills

1. *Adolescent boys living in a community home school participated in 12 one-hour sessions of social skills training over a 6-week period.* Training was carried out in groups of four and involved the use of instructions, discussion, modeling, role-played practice, videotaped feedback, social reinforcement, and homework tasks (Spence & Marzillier, 1981).

2. *Adolescent boys at the Youth Center participated in aggression replacement training, a multimodal, psychoeducational intervention.* The intervention was made up of three components: structured learning training, anger control training, and moral education. There were 30 sessions over a 10-week period (Glick & Goldstein, 1987).

3. *The Social Interactional Skills Program was a structured didactic program that encouraged youth to recall past experiences that were problematic and identify the aversive social stimulus that impinged on their social interaction.* This was followed by systematic desensitization using imagery techniques and cognitive reappraisal. They were then taught to enhance their behavior repertoire by experimenting with new behaviors (Shivrattan, 1988).

Teaching Family Home

1. *Achievement Place was a community-based, family style, behavior modification, group home for six to eight delinquents.* This program was administered by a couple, referred to as "teaching parents," who develop positive teaching relationships with the youths to impart needed behavioral skills, assume responsibility for the youths, and act as advocates for them in the community. Youths were able to return to their own homes on the weekend and remain in their local schools (Kirigin, Braukmann, Atwater, & Worl, 1982).

2. *Adjudicated delinquents went to a community-based, family style, behavior modification group home where "teaching parents" used a token economy.* The teaching parents also closely monitored the youths' progress in school and worked individually to counsel the youths on difficulties they have in their lives (Wolf, Phillips, & Fixson, 1974).

Behavioral Programs

1. *Incarcerated male and female adolescents participated in a 12-week cognitive mediation training program involving small discussion groups ranging in size from 10 to 14 youth.* The program focused on remediating

those social problem-solving skill deficits and modifying those beliefs that supported the use of aggression through instruction and structured discussion (Guerra & Slaby, 1990).

2. *Institutionalized male delinquents participated in a stress inoculation training program that included defining anger, analyzing recent anger episodes, reviewing self-monitoring data, and constructing an individualized 6-item anger hierarchy.* Specific coping skills taught were self-instructions, relaxation, backward counting, pleasant imagery, assertive responding, and self-reinforcement. Role playing and modeling were also used (Schlicter & Horan, 1981).

3. *Girls in a correctional institution were trained in reinforcement therapy principles and acted as peer counselors for newer, incoming wards.* As the newer girls progressed, they were exposed to the techniques through their peer counselors and by the staff, eventually achieving the role of peer counselor themselves (Ross & McKay, 1976).

Community Residential Programs

1. *The treatment center was a community-based, all-girls group home.* Residents were provided advocacy, counseling, educational support, and vocational support (Minnesota Governor's Commission on Crime Prevention and Control, 1973).

2. *Institutionalized youths were placed in a 32-bed therapeutic community setting in an inner-city neighborhood.* Here they received individual and group counseling, remedial education services, vocational assessment and training, and other needed services (Auerbach, 1978).

3. *A community-based residential treatment center for adjudicated youths used extensive group discussion as a therapeutic community and emphasized progressive assumption of self-responsibility* (Allen-Hagen, 1975).

Multiple Services

1. *Camp Fenner was an experimental program of the Probation Department.* Its distinctive aspects were the provision of supportive services, including vocational training, skill-oriented education, and job placement by a private contractor; cottage living; and enriched probation department staffing (Kawaguchi, 1975).

2. *Institutionalized boys were treated in a multifaceted program to overcome academic, vocational, and psychological deficits.* Various therapeutic methods were available to meet their particular needs, as well as education, training, work opportunities, and supervision from a community volunteer upon release (Thambidurai, 1980).

3. *The Planned Re-Entry Program was a short-term, 52-bed living unit that included cottage living, counseling, education, and recreation activities.* The counseling component consisted of individual and small group counseling. The educational component taught everyday survival skills such as basic reading and math, consumer education, problem solving, and job getting and keeping. The recreational program was designed to enhance the youths' use of leisure time. The program emphasized time management, interpersonal relationships, personal responsibility, and rule conformity (Seckel & Turner, 1985).

The Challenge of Effective Intervention With Serious Juvenile Offenders

Andrews et al. (1990) described the "risk principle" as one of the elements of effective therapeutic intervention with juvenile delinquents. According to the risk principle, treatment for delinquent behavior is most effective when the juveniles to whom that treatment is administered have appreciable risk of actually reoffending. This principle reflects, in part, the truism that there must be potential for bad behavior before bad behavior can be inhibited. The contrary view is often expressed—that it is the more serious, "hardened" cases that will be least amenable to treatment. The 200 studies of intervention with serious offenders in this meta-analysis supported the risk principle over the view that serious delinquents cannot be helped to reduce their offending. For both institutionalized and noninstitutionalized offenders, the "average" intervention program represented in the research literature produced positive, statistically significant effects equivalent to about a 12% reduction in subsequent reoffense rates. The effects of the average program, however, were not representative of the impact achieved by the best programs. These were capable of reducing recidivism rates by as much as 40%, an accomplishment of considerable practical value in terms of the expense and social damage associated with the delinquent behavior of these juveniles. On the other hand, the "below average" programs generally had negligible effect on recidivism, indicating that success is not ensured in this domain. This chapter has attempted to quantify and summarize the evidence that intervention can reduce the recidivism of serious offenders and to identify the characteristics of effective intervention in a way that can aid the design and implementation of useful programs.

■ APPENDIX:
Juvenile Delinquency Meta-Analysis Bibliography

Part 1: Intervention With
Noninstitutionalized Offenders

Allen, R. F., Dubin, H. N., Pilnick, S., & Youtz, A. C. (1970). *Collegefields: From delinquency to freedom.* Seattle, WA: Special Child Publications.

Andrews, D. A., Kiessling, J. J., Robinson, D., & Mickus, S. (1986). The risk principle of case classification: An outcome evaluation with young adult probationers. *Canadian Journal of Criminology, 28,* 377-396.

Bank, L., Marlowe, J. H., Reid, J. B., Patterson, G. R., & Weinrott, M. R. (1991). A comparative evaluation of parent-training interventions for families of chronic delinquents. *Journal of Abnormal Child Psychology, 19*(1), 15-33.

Barton, C., Alexander, J. F., Waldron, M., Turner, C. W., & Warburton, J. (1985). Generalizing treatment effects of functional family therapy: Three replications. *American Journal of Family Therapy, 13*(3), 16-26.

Barton, W. H., & Butts, J. A. (1990). Viable options: Intensive supervision programs for juvenile delinquents. *Crime & Delinquency, 36,* 238-256.

Bauer, M., Bordeaux, G., Cole, J., Davidson, W. S., Martinez, A., Mitchell, C., & Singleton, D. (1980). A diversion program for juvenile offenders: The experience of Ingham County, Michigan. *Juvenile and Family Court Journal, 31,* 53-62.

Bean, J. S. (1988). The effect of individualized reality therapy on the recidivism rates and locus of control orientation of male juvenile offenders (Doctoral dissertation, University of Mississippi, 1988). *Dissertation Abstracts International, 49*(06), 2370B. (University Microfilms No. 88-18138)

Berger, R. J., & Gold, M. (1978). An evaluation of a juvenile court volunteer program. *Journal of Community Psychology, 6,* 328-333.

Bishop, D. M., Frazier, C. E., Lanza-Kaduce, L., & Winner, L. (1996). The transfer of juveniles to criminal court: Does it make a difference. *Crime & Delinquency, 42,* 171-191.

Boisvert, M. J., Kenney, H. J., & Kvaraceus, W. C. (1976). Massachusetts deinstitutionalization—Data on one community-based answer. *Juvenile Justice, 27,* 35-40.

Borduin, C. M., Mann, B. J., Cone, L. T., Henggeler, S. W., Fucci, B. R., Blaske, D. M., & Williams, R. A. (1995). Multisystemic treatment of serious juvenile offenders: Long-term prevention of criminality and violence. Special Section: Prediction and prevention of child and adolescent antisocial behavior. *Journal of Consulting and Clinical Psychology, 63,* 569-578.

Browne, S. F. (1975). *Denver high impact anti-crime program: Evaluation report.* Denver, CO: Denver Manpower Administration.

Byles, J. A., & Maurice, A. (1979). The juvenile services project: An experiment in delinquency control. *Canadian Journal of Criminology, 21,* 257-262.

Carter-Hosac, K. L. (1992). An evaluation of intensive and regular probation supervision for serious, habitual juvenile offenders (intensive supervision, juvenile offenders) (Doctoral dissertation, University of Idaho). *Dissertation Abstracts International, 53*(06), 1764A. (University Microfilms No. 92-30112)

Castellano, T. C., & Soderstrom, I. R. (1992). Therapeutic wilderness programs and juvenile recidivism: A program evaluation. *Journal of Offender Rehabilitation, 17,* 19-46.

Chandler, M. J. (1973). Egocentrism and antisocial behavior: The assessment and training of social perspective-taking skills. *Developmental Psychology, 9,* 326-333.

Compass Management Group, Inc. (1978). *Program evaluation of the youth community service project: Final report.* Everett, WA: Snohomish County Superior Court, Juvenile Court Division.

Criminal Justice Coordinating Council and Vera Institute of Justice. (1972). *The Manhattan Court Employment Project.* New York: Vera Institute of Justice.

Cross-Drew, C. (1984). *Project Jericho evaluation report: Final report.* Sacramento: California Youth Authority.

Crotty, J., & Meier, R. D. (1980). *Evaluation of juvenile restitution program Project Detour: Final report.* East Lyme, CT: Behavioral Systems Associates, Inc. (NCJRS Document No. NCJ87942)

Davidson, W. S., Redner, R., Blakely, C. H., Mitchell, C. M., & Emshoff, J. G. (1987). Diversion of juvenile offenders: An experimental comparison. *Journal of Consulting and Clinical Psychology, 55,* 68-75.

Davidson, W. S., Seidman, E., Rappaport, J., Berck, P. L., Rapp, N. A., Rhodes, W., & Herring, J. (1977). Diversion program for juvenile offenders. *Social Work Research and Abstracts, 13*(2), 40-49.

Delinquency Research Group. (1986). *An evaluation of the delinquency of participants in the Youth at Risk program.* Claremont, CA: Claremont Graduate School, Center for Applied Social Research.

Dennison, D., & Prevet, T. (1980). Improving alcohol-related disruptive behaviors through health instruction. *Journal of School Health, 50,* 206-208.

Dunivant, N. (1982). *Improving academic skills and preventing delinquency of learning-disabled juvenile delinquents: Evaluation of the ACLD remediation program.* Williamsburg, VA: National Center for State Courts.

Empey, L. T., & Erickson, M. L. (1972). *The Provo experiment: Evaluating community control of delinquency.* Lexington, MA: Lexington.

Erdman, P. M. (1978). Can education effectively reduce crime and delinquency? Fresno County's youth and law class. *Crime Prevention Review, 5,* 1-6.

Evaluation Unit of the Governor's Commission on Crime Prevention and Control. (1976). *Residential community corrections programs in Minnesota: An evaluation report.* Minneapolis, MN: Author.

Florida Division of Youth Services. (1977). *Evaluation of Florida's Intensive Counseling Program.* Tallahassee, FL: Department of Health and Rehabilitative Services.

Goldberg, R. T., & Johnson, B. D. (1972). *Vocational and social rehabilitation of juvenile delinquents: Final report.* Boston: Massachusetts Rehabilitation Commission.

Gordon, D. A., Graves, K., & Arbuthnot, J. (1987). *Prevention of adult criminal behavior using family therapy for disadvantaged juvenile delinquents.* Unpublished manuscript, Ohio University, Athens, OH.

Greater Egypt Regional Planning and Development Commission. (1979). *Menard Correctional Center Juvenile Tours Impact Study.* Carbondale, IL: Author.

Greenwood, P. W., Deschenes, E. P., & Adams, J. (1993). *Chronic juvenile offenders: Final results from the Skillman Aftercare Experiment.* Santa Monica, CA: RAND.

Henggeler, S. W., Melton, G. B., & Smith, L. A. (1992). Family preservation using multisystemic therapy: An effective alternative to incarcerating serious juvenile offenders. *Journal of Consulting and Clinical Psychology, 60,* 953-961.

Higgins, P. S. (1974). Evaluation of the Minnesota youth-advocate/delinquency-rehabilitation program (Doctoral dissertation, University of Minnesota, 1974). *Dissertation Abstracts International, 35*(02), 1021B. (University Microfilms No. 74-17251)

Higgins, P. S. (1974). *The Minnesota Youth Advocacy Corps: A project evaluation.* St. Paul, MN: Governor's Commission on Crime Prevention and Control, Project Evaluation Unit.

Homant, R. J. (1981). The demise of JOLT: The politics of being "scared straight" in Michigan. *Criminal Justice Review, 6,* 14-18.

Howitt, P. S., & Moore, E. A. (1991). Efficacy of intensive early intervention: An evaluation of the Oakland County Probate Court Early Offender Program. *Juvenile & Family Court Journal, 42*, 25-34.

Hunter, E. F. (1968). *Reduction of delinquency through expansion of opportunity (RODEO): A preliminary analysis* (Research Rep. No. 33). Los Angeles: County of Los Angeles Probation Department.

Jessness, C. F., Allison, F. S., McCormic, P. M., Wedge, R. F., & Young, M. L. (1975). *Evaluation of the effectiveness of contingency contracting with delinquents.* Sacramento: California Youth Authority.

Johns, D., & Bottcher, J. (1980). *AB 3121 impact evaluation: Final report.* Sacramento: California Youth Authority.

Johnson, B. D., & Goldberg, R. T. (1983). Vocational and social rehabilitation of delinquents: A study of experimentals and controls. *Journal of Offending Counseling Services and Rehabilitation, 6*, 43-60.

Kantrowitz, R. E. (1980). Training nonprofessionals to work with delinquents: Differential impact of varying training/supervision/intervention strategies (Doctoral dissertation, Michigan State University, 1980). *Dissertation Abstracts International, 40*(10), 5007B. (University Microfilms No. 80-06139)

Kelley, T. M., Schulman, J. L., & Lynch, K. (1976). Decentralized intake and diversion: The juvenile court's link to the youth service bureau. *Juvenile Justice, 27*, 3-11.

Kemp, M., & Lee, R. (1975). *Project Crest: A third year experimental study.* Gainesville, FL: Project Crest.

Kijewski, K. J. (1983). The effect of the decision to charge upon subsequent delinquent behaviour. *Canadian Journal of Criminology, 25*, 201-207.

Kloss, J. D. (1978). The impact of comprehensive community treatment: An assessment of the complex offender project. *Offender Rehabilitation, 3*, 81-108.

Koch, J. R. (1986). Community service and outright release as alternatives to juvenile court: An experimental evaluation (Doctoral dissertation, Michigan State University, 1985). *Dissertation Abstracts International, 46*(07), 2081A. (University Microfilms No. 85-20537)

Kraus, J. (1974). The deterrent effect of fines and probation on male juvenile offenders. *Australian and New Zealand Journal of Criminology, 7*, 231-240.

Lamplin, A. C., & Taylor, G. G. (1973). *Santa Clara County day care treatment center for delinquents: Second year evaluation report.* San Jose, CA: American Justice Institute. (NCJRS Document No. NCJ16327)

Langer, S. (1978). *The Rahway state prison lifer's group: A critical analysis.* Union, NJ: Kean College.

Lee, R., & Haynes, N. M. (1978). Counseling delinquents: Dual treatment revisited. *Rehabilitation Counseling Bulletin, 22*, 130-133.

Lee, R., & Haynes, N. M. (1978). Counseling juvenile offenders: An experimental evaluation of Project Crest. *Community Mental Health Journal, 14*, 267-271.

Lee, R., & Olejnik, S. (1981). Professional outreach counseling can help the juvenile probationer: A two-year follow-up study. *Personnel and Guidance Journal, 59*, 445-449.

Lewis, R. V. (1981). *The Squires of San Quentin: An evaluation of a juvenile awareness program.* Sacramento: California Youth Authority.

Lewis, R. V. (1983). Scared straight—California style: Evaluation of the San Quentin Squires program. *Criminal Justice and Behavior, 10*, 209-226.

Lichtman, C. M., & Smock, S. M. (1981). The effects of social services on probationer recidivism: A field experiment. *Journal of Research in Crime and Delinquency, 18*, 81-100.

Lincoln, S. B. (1976). Juvenile referral and recidivism. In R. M. Carter & M. W. Klein (Eds.), *Back on the street: The diversion of juvenile offenders* (pp. 321-328). Englewood Cliffs, NJ: Prentice-Hall.

Lipsey, M. W., Cordray, D. S., & Berger, D. E. (1981). Evaluation of a juvenile diversion program: Using multiple lines of evidence. *Evaluation Review, 5*, 283-306.

Mann, C. M., & Pratt, M. D. (1980). *Building Bridges, Inc.: An evaluation of a work therapy program designed for juvenile probationers.* Dayton, OH: Montgomery County Juvenile Court.

Marlowe, H., Reid, J. B., Patterson, G. R., & Weinrott, M. R. (1986). *Treating adolescent multiple offenders: A comparison and follow-up of parent training for families of chronic delinquents.* Eugene, OR: University of Oregon, Oregon Social Learning Center.

McPherson, S. J. (1981). Family counseling for youthful offenders in the juvenile court setting: A therapy outcome study (Doctoral dissertation, University of Oregon, 1980). *Dissertation Abstracts International, 42*(01), 382B. (University Microfilms No. 81-09550)

McPherson, S. J., McDonald, L. E., & Ryer, C. W. (1983). Intensive counseling with families of juvenile offenders. *Juvenile and Family Court Journal, 34*, 27-33.

Miller, D. (1964). *Growth to freedom: The psychosocial treatment of delinquent youth.* Bloomington, IN: University Press.

Miller, M. O., & Gold, M. (1984). Iatrogenesis in the juvenile justice system. *Youth & Society, 16*, 83-111.

Moore, R. H. (1987). Effectiveness of citizen volunteers functioning as counselors for high-risk young male offenders. *Psychological Reports, 61*, 823-830.

Moore, R. H., & Levine, D. (1974). *Evaluation research of a community-based probation program.* Lincoln: University of Nebraska at Lincoln, Department of Psychology.

Morris, J. A. (1970). *First Offender: A volunteer program for youth in trouble with the law.* New York: Funk & Wagnalls.

Noble, J. H., Jr. (1967). Evaluation of the Weekend Rangers Program: An action demonstration program designed to reduce the volume and seriousness of delinquent behavior among lower class male youth (Doctoral dissertation, Brandeis University, 1966). *Dissertation Abstracts International, 27*(12), 4365A. (University Microfilms No. 66-13653)

O'Brien, W. J. (1964). An experimental use of modified group therapy in a public school setting with delinquent adolescent males (Doctoral dissertation, University of California, Berkeley, 1963). *Dissertation Abstracts International, 24*(12), 5203. (University Microfilms No. 64-05330)

O'Connor, G. (1980). *Evaluation of the community and state diagnostic services project.* Olympia, WA: Department of Social and Health Services.

Odell, B. N. (1974). Accelerating entry into the opportunity structure: A sociologically-based treatment for delinquent youth. *Sociology and Social Research, 58,* 312-317.

Orchowsky, S., & Taylor, K. (1981). *Insiders juvenile crime prevention program: An assessment of a juvenile awareness program* (Rep. No. 79111). Richmond: Virginia Department of Corrections, Division of Program Development and Evaluation, Research and Reporting Unit. (NCJRS Document No. NCJ079768)

Ostrom, T. M., Steele, C. M., Rosenblood, L. K., & Mirels, H. L. (1971). Modification of delinquent behavior. *Journal of Applied Social Psychology, 1,* 118-136.

Palmer, T. (1970). *California's Community Treatment Project—The Phase I, II, and III experiments: Developments and progress* (Research Rep. No. 10). Sacramento: California Youth Authority.

Palmer, T. (1973). The Community Treatment Project in perspective: 1961-1973. *California Youth Authority Quarterly, 26,* 29-43.

Palmer, T. (1979). Juvenile diversion: When and for whom? *Youth Authority Quarterly, 32*(3), 14-20.

Palmer, T. B. (1971). California's Community Treatment program for delinquent adolescents. *Journal of Research in Crime and Delinquency, 8,* 74-92.

Palmer, T. B., Neto, V. V., Johns, D. A., Turner, J. K., & Pearson, J. W. (1968). *Community Treatment Project: An evaluation of community treatment for delinquents* (Research Rep. No. 9, Parts 1, 2, & 3). Sacramento: California Youth Authority.

Palmer, T., & Lewis, R. V. (1980). *An evaluation of juvenile diversion.* Cambridge, MA: Oelgeschlager, Gunn & Hain.

Performance Resources, Inc. (1979). *Evaluation of the CETA restitution work experience projects.* Olympia: Washington State Employment Security Department.

Piercy, F., & Lee, R. (1976). Effects of a dual treatment approach on the rehabilitation of habitual juvenile delinquents. *Rehabilitation Counseling Bulletin, 19,* 482-492.

Pond, E. M. (1983). The Monrovia Experiment: Evaluating program goals and correctional effectiveness (Doctoral dissertation, University of Southern California, 1983). *Dissertation Abstracts International, 43*(12), 4051A.

The prevention of delinquency: An empirical evaluation of the Youth Service Program. (1975, April). Paper presented at the meeting of the Western Psychological Association, Sacramento, CA.

Ramirez, M. V. (1976). *Evaluation of the San Diego County Probation Department program—Operation Summit: Final report.* San Diego, CA: San Diego County Probation Department, Program Evaluation Unit.

Reid, J. B. (1983). *Home-based treatment for multiple-offending delinquents.* Eugene, OR: Evaluation Research Groups.

Roberts, C. F., & Switzer, A. (1976). *Community-centered drug program: First sample findings* (Research Rep. No. 6). Sacramento: California Youth Authority.

Rosen, L., & Fenwick, C. (1975). *Philadelphia Court of Common Pleas—Pre-hearing Intensive Supervision Program—Evaluation and final progress report, 1974-1975.* Harrisburg: Pennsylvania Department of Justice, Pennsylvania Governor's Justice Commission.

Roundtree, G. A., & Faily, A. (1980). An intervention model for the resocialization of a group of adjudicated delinquents. *Journal of Offender Counseling, 4,* 331-336.

Roundtree, G. A., Parker, J. B., & Jones, A. (1979). Behavioral management in the resocialization of a group of adjudicated delinquents. *Corrective and Social Psychiatry and Journal of Behavior Technology, 25,* 15-17.

Scarpitti, F. R., & Stephenson, R. M. (1968). A study of probation effectiveness. *Journal of Criminal Law, 59,* 301-309.

Schneider, A. L. (1986). Restitution and recidivism rates of juvenile offenders: Results from four experimental studies. *Criminology, 24,* 533-552.

Schneider, A. L., & Schneider, P. R. (1985). The impact of restitution on recidivism of juvenile offenders: An experiment in Clayton County, Georgia. *Criminal Justice Review, 10,* 1-10.

Schwitzgebel, R. K., & Baer, D. J. (1967). Intensive supervision by parole officers as a factor in recidivism reduction of male delinquents. *Journal of Psychology, 67,* 75-82.

Schwitzgebel, R., & Kolb, D. A. (1964). Inducing behaviour change in adolescent delinquents. *Behavior Research and Therapy, 1,* 297-304.

Seidman, E., Rappaport, J., & Davidson, W. S., II. (1980). Adolescents in legal jeopardy: Initial success and replication of an alternative to the criminal justice system. In R. R. Ross & P. Gendreau (Eds.), *Effective correctional treatment* (pp. 103-123). Toronto, Canada: Butterworth.

Severy, L. J., & Morton, O. S. (1981). *Memphis Metro Youth Diversion Project: Local evaluation* [Final report]. Washington, DC: U.S. Department of Justice, Law Enforcement Administration, Office of Juvenile Justice and Delinquency Prevention.

Severy, L. J., & Whitaker, J. M. (1982). Juvenile diversion: An experimental analysis of effectiveness. *Evaluation Review, 6,* 753-774.

Shichor, D., & Binder, A. (1982). Community restitution for juveniles: An approach and preliminary evaluation. *Criminal Justice Review, 7,* 46-50.

Shorts, I. D. (1986). Delinquency by association? Outcome of joint participation by at-risk and convicted youths in a community-based programme. *British Journal of Criminology, 26,* 156-163.

Sontheimer, H., Goodstein, L., & Kovacevic, M. (1990). *Philadelphia intensive aftercare probation evaluation project.* Philadelphia: Shippensburg University of Pennsylvania.

State of California, Department of Youth Authority. (1977). *An evaluation of seven selected probation subsidy programs.* Sacramento: Author.

Stephenson, R. M., & Scarpitti, F. R. (1969). Essexfields: A non-residential experiment in group centered rehabilitation of delinquents. *American Journal of Correction, 31,* 12-18.

Stephenson, R. M., & Scarpitti, F. R. (1974). *Group interaction as therapy: The use of the small group on corrections.* Westport, CT: Greenwood.

True, D. A. (1974). Evaluative research in a police juvenile diversion program (Doctoral dissertation, University of Oregon, 1973). *Dissertation Abstracts International, 34*(09), 4679B. (University Microfilms No. 74-06909)

Vera Institute of Justice. (1972). *Pre-trial intervention: The Manhattan Court Employment Project.* New York: Author.

Vreeland, A. D. (1982). Evaluation of Face-to-Face: A juvenile aversion program (Doctoral dissertation, University of Texas Health Science Center at Dallas, 1981). *Dissertation Abstracts International, 42*(10), 4597A.

Walter, T. L., & Mills, C. M. (1980). A behavioral-employment intervention program for reducing juvenile delinquency. In R. R. Ross & P. Gendreau (Eds.), *Effective correctional treatment* (pp. 187-206). Toronto, Canada: Butterworth.

Wax, M. L. (1977). The effects of symbolic restitution of presence of victim on delinquent shoplifters (Doctoral dissertation, Washington State University, 1977). *Dissertation Abstracts International, 38*(03), 1313A. (University Microfilms No. 77-20123)

Weeks, S. Z. (1986). The effects of Sierra II, an adventure probation program, upon selected behavioral variables of adolescent juvenile delinquents (Doctoral dissertation, University of Virginia, 1985). *Dissertation Abstracts International, 46*(12), 3607A. (University Microfilms No. 85-26895)

Weisz, J. R., Walter, B. R., Weiss, B., Fernandez, G. A., & Mikow, V. A. (1990). Arrests among emotionally disturbed violent and assaultive individuals following minimal versus lengthy intervention through North Carolina's Willie M Program. *Journal of Consulting and Clinical Psychology, 58,* 720-728.

Wiebush, R. G. (1993). Juvenile intensive supervision: The impact on felony offenders diverted from institutional placement. *Crime & Delinquency, 39,* 68-89.

Willman, M. T., & Snortum, J. R. (1982). A police program for employment of youth gang members. *International Journal of Offender Therapy and Comparative Criminology, 26,* 207-214.

Winterdyk, J., & Roesch, R. (1982). A wilderness experiential program as an alternative for probationers: An evaluation. *Canadian Journal of Criminology, 24,* 39-49.

Wooldredge, J., Hartman, J., Latessa, E., & Holmes, S. (1994). Effectiveness of culturally specific community treatment for African American juvenile felons. *Crime & Delinquency, 40,* 589-598.

Yarborough, J. C. (1979). *Evaluation of Jolt: A deterrence program.* Lansing: Michigan Department of Corrections, Program Bureau.

Part 2: Intervention With Institutionalized Offenders

Adams, S. (1959). *Assessment of the Psychiatric Treatment Program: Second interim report* (Research Rep. No. 15). Sacramento: California Youth Authority.

Adams, S. (1959). *Effectiveness of the Youth Authority Special Treatment Program: First interim report* (Research Rep. No. 5). Sacramento: California Youth Authority.

Adams, S. (1961). *Assessment of the Psychiatric Treatment Program, Phase 1: Third interim report* (Research Rep. No. 21). Sacramento: California Youth Authority.

Adams, S. (1961). *Effectiveness of interview therapy with older youth authority wards: An interim evaluation of the PICO Project* (Research Rep. No. 20). Sacramento: California Youth Authority.

Adams, S. (1962). The PICO Project. In L. Savitz & M. Wolfgang (Eds.), *The sociology of punishment and correction* (2nd ed., pp. 548-561). New York: John Wiley.

Allen-Hagen, B. (1975). *Youth crime control project: A final report on an experimental alternative to incarceration of young adult offenders* (Research Rep. No. 75-1). Washington, DC: D.C. Department of Corrections.

Andrews, D. A., & Young, J. G. (1974). Short-term structured group counseling and prison adjustment. *Canadian Journal of Criminology and Corrections, 4,* 5-13.

Auerbach, A. W. (1978). The role of the therapeutic community "Street Prison" in the rehabilitation of youthful offenders (Doctoral dissertation, George Washington University, 1977). *Dissertation Abstracts International, 38*(09), 4532B. (University Microfilms No. 78-01086)

Birkenmayer, A. C., & Polonoski, M. (1976). *The community adjustment of male training school recidivists: Part II, The D.A.R.E.* Ontario, Canada: Ministry of Correctional Services, Planning and Support Services Division.

Borduin, C. M., Henggeler, S. W., Blaske, D. M., & Stein, R. J. (1990). Multisystemic treatment of adolescent sexual offenders. *International Journal of Offender Therapy & Comparative Criminology, 34*(2), 105-113.

Bottcher, J. (1985). *The Athena program: An evaluation of a girl's treatment program at the Fresno County Probation Department's juvenile hall.* Sacramento: California Youth Authority.

Bottoms, A. E., & McClintock, F. N. (1973). *Criminals coming of age: A study of institutional adaptation in the treatment of adolescent offenders.* London: Heinemann.

Chiles, A. M. (1985). Antecedents and outcomes of male delinquents referred to the Utah State Youth Development Center or survival training (Doctoral dissertation, Brigham Young University, 1984). *Dissertation Abstracts International, 45*(09), 2997A. (University Microfilms No. 84-25296)

Cornish, D. B., & Clarke, R. V. G. (1975). *Residential treatment and its effects on delinquency* (Research Rep. No. 32). London: Home Office Research Study, HMSO. (NCJRS Document No. 034165)

Cosby, J. W. (1980). Combining the use of guided group interaction and Innovative Sciences, Inc.: A learning system in an institutional setting to modify the behavior of juvenile through the courts as delinquents (Doctoral dissertation, Rutgers University, 1979). *Dissertation Abstracts International, 40*(10), 5595A. (University Microfilms No. 80-08868)

Cowden, J. E., & Monson, L. (1970). An analysis of some relationships between personality adjustment, placement, and post-release adjustment of delinquent boys. *Journal of Research in Crime and Delinquency, 6,* 63-70.

Cox, G. B., Carmichael, S. J., & Dightman, C. (1977). An evaluation of a community based diagnostic program for juvenile offenders. *Juvenile Justice, 28,* 33-41.

Craft, M., Stephenson, G., & Granger, C. (1964). A controlled trial of authoritarian and self-governing regimes with adolescent psychopaths. *American Journal of Orthopsychiatry, 34*(03), 543-554.

Empey, L. T., & Erickson, M. L. (1972). *The Provo experiment: Evaluating community control of delinquency.* Lexington, MA: Lexington.

Empey, L. T., & Lubeck, S. G. (1971). *The Silverlake experiment: Testing delinquency theory and community intervention.* Chicago: Aldine.

Ford, V. B., (1975). An investigation of the selection process and drug treatment of explosively aggressive adolescent females (Doctoral dissertation, University of Maryland, 1974). *Dissertation Abstracts International, 36*(03), 1387A. (University Microfilms No. 75-18096)

Friedman, A. S., & Friedman, C. J. (1970). *Comparison of three treatment models in delinquency: Research and demonstration project, July 1, 1966 to October 31, 1970* [Final report]. Washington, DC: Department of Health, Education and Welfare.

Glick, B., & Goldstein, A. P. (1987). Aggression replacement training. *Journal of Counseling and Development, 65,* 356-362.

Gottfredson, D. C., & Barton, W. H. (1993). Deinstitutionalization of juvenile offenders. *Criminology, 31,* 591-611.

Gottman, G. S. (1963). *Effects of short term psychiatric treatment* (Research Rep. No. 36). Sacramento: California Youth Authority.

Greenwood, P. W., & Turner, S. (1987). *The VisionQuest Program: An evaluation.* Santa Monica, CA: RAND.

Greenwood, P. W., & Turner, S. (1993). Evaluation of the Paint Creek Youth Center: A residential program for serious delinquents. *Criminology, 31,* 263-279.

Grunhut, M. (1955). Juvenile delinquents under punitive detention: A study of the first hundred Campsfield House boys. *British Journal of Delinquency, 5,* 191-209.

Guerra, N. G., & Slaby, R. G. (1990). Cognitive mediators of aggression in adolescent offenders: 2. Intervention. *Developmental Psychology, 26,* 269-277.

Hartstone, E., & Cocozza, J. (1983). Violent youth: The impact of mental health treatment. *International Journal of Law and Psychiatry, 6,* 207-224.

Hollin, C. R., & Courtney, S. A. (1983). A skills training approach to the reduction of institutional offending. *Personality and Individual Differences, 4,* 257-264.

Ingram, G. L., Gerard, R. E., Quay, H. C., & Levinson, R. B. (1970). An experimental program for the psychopathic delinquent: Looking in the "correctional wastebasket." *Journal of Research in Crime and Delinquency, 7,* 24-30.

Jessness, C. F. (1965). *The Fricot Ranch Study: Outcomes with small versus large living groups in the rehabilitation of delinquents* (Research Rep. No. 47). Sacramento: California Youth Authority.

Jessness, C. F. (1971). The Preston Typology Study: An experiment with differential treatment in an institution. *Journal of Research in Crime and Delinquency, 8,* 38-52.

Kawaguchi, R. M. (1975). *Camp Fenner Canyon evaluation: Final report.* Los Angeles: Los Angeles County Probation Department. (NCJRS Document No. NCJ036121)

Kirigin, K. A., Braukmann, C. J., Atwater, J. D., & Worl, M. M. (1982). An evaluation of teaching-family (Achievement Place) group homes for juvenile offenders. *Journal of Applied Behavior Analysis, 15*(1), 1-16.

Knight, D. (1969). *The Marshall program: Assessment of a short-term institutional treatment program: Part I. Parole outcome and background characteristics* (Research Rep. No. 56). Sacramento: California Youth Authority.

Knight, D. (1970). *The Marshall program: Assessment of a short-term institutional treatment program* (Research Rep. No. 59). Sacramento: California Youth Authority.

Lefkowitz, M. M. (1969). Effects of diphenylhydantoin on disruptive behavior: Study of male delinquents. *Archives of General Psychiatry, 20,* 643-651.

Levitt, J. J., Young, T. M., & Pappenfort, D. M. (1981). *Achievement Place: The teaching-family treatment model in a group-home setting.* Washington, DC: U.S. Department of Justice.

Markland, F. J. (1979). *Periodic detention: A comparison of residential and non-residential centers* (Study Series No. 4). Wellington, New Zealand: Department of Justice, Planning and Development Division.

McMurran, M., & Boyle, M. (1990). Evaluation of self-help manual for young offenders who drink: A pilot study. *British Journal of Clinical Psychology, 29,* 117-119.

Minnesota Governor's Commission on Crime Prevention and Control. (1973). *An evaluation of the Group Residence Program for juvenile girls—June 1972 through April 1973.* St. Paul: Minnesota Department of Corrections.

Molling, P. A., Lockner, A. W., Jr., Sauls, R. J., & Eisenberg, L. (1962). Committed delinquent boys: The impact of perphenazine and of placebo. *Archives of General Psychiatry, 7,* 70-76.

Molof, M. J. (1967). *Forestry camp study: Comparison of recidivism rates of camp-eligible boys randomly assigned to camp and to institutional programs.* Sacramento: California Youth Authority.

Monson, L., & Cowden, J. E. (1968). How effective is aftercare? *Crime & Delinquency, 14,* 360-366.

Moore, C. B. (1978). Ego strength and behavior: A study of a residential treatment program for delinquent girls (Doctoral dissertation, California School of Professional Psychology, 1977). *Dissertation Abstracts International, 38*(10), 5033B. (University Microfilms No. 78-02837)

Person, R. W. (1966). Psychological and behavioral change in delinquents following psychotherapy. *Journal of Clinical Psychology, 22,* 337-340.

Peters, M., Albright, K., Gimbel, C., Thomas, D., Laxton, G., Opanga, M., & Afflerbach, M. (1996). *Evaluation of the impact of boot camps for juvenile offenders: Denver interim report.* Washington, DC: Office of Juvenile Justice and Delinquency Prevention. (NCJRS Document No. 160927)

Peters, M., Bullman, S., Gimbel, C., Thomas, D., Laxton, G., Opanga, M., Afflerbach, M., & Croan, G. (1996). *Evaluation of the impact of boot camps for juvenile offenders: Mobile interim report.* Washington, DC:

Office of Juvenile Justice and Delinquency Prevention. (NCJRS Document No. 160926)

Pond, E. M. (1970). *The Los Angeles Community Delinquency Control Project: An experiment in the rehabilitation of delinquents in an urban community.* Sacramento: California Youth Authority.

Randall, L. E. (1973). The effects of a vocational education program in rehabilitating youthful public offenders (Doctoral dissertation, University of Connecticut, 1973). *Dissertation Abstracts International, 34*(04), 1786A. (University Microfilms No. 73-24428)

Roberts, C. F., Switzer, H. L., & Vitt, P. (1976). *Community-centered drug program: First sample findings* (Research Rep. No. 6). Sacramento: California Youth Authority. (NCJRS Document No. NCJ32580)

Robinson, S. C. (1994). Implementation of the cognitive model of offender rehabilitation and delinquency prevention (cognitive skills training) (Doctoral dissertation, University of Utah). *Dissertation Abstracts International, 55*(08), 2582A. (University Microfilms No. 95-02199)

Ross, R. R., & McKay, B. (1976). A study of institutional treatment programs. *International Journal of Offender Therapy and Comparative Criminology: An Interdisciplinary Journal, 20*(2), 167-173.

Schlicter, K. J., & Horan, J. J. (1981). Effects of stress inoculation on the anger and aggression management skills of institutionalized juvenile delinquents. *Cognitive Therapy and Research, 5,* 359-365.

Schoenthaler, S. J. (1983). The Alabama Diet-Behavior Program: An empirical evaluation at the Coosa Valley Regional Detention Center. *International Journal of Biosocial Research, 5,* 79-87.

Seckel, J. P. (1965). *Experiments in group counseling at two youth authority institutions* (Research Rep. No. 46). Sacramento: California Youth Authority.

Seckel, J. P. (1967). *The Fremont experiment: Assessment of residential treatment at a youth authority reception center* (Research Rep. No. 50). Sacramento: California Youth Authority.

Seckel, J. P. (1975). *Assessment of Preston Family Drug Treatment Project.* Sacramento: California Youth Authority.

Seckel, J. P., & Turner, J. K. (1985). *Assessment of Planned Re-Entry Programs (PREP).* Sacramento: California Youth Authority.

Sheard, M. H., Marini, J. L., Bridges, C. I., & Wagner, E. (1976). The effect of lithium on impulsive aggressive behavior in man. *American Journal of Psychiatry, 133,* 1409-1413.

Shivrattan, J. L. (1988). Social interactional training and incarcerated juvenile delinquents. *Canadian Journal of Criminology, 30,* 145-163.

Silberman, M. (1975). *Pennsylvania Governor's Justice Commission—Central Region—Three residential treatment programs.* Harrisburg: Pennsylvania Department of Justice, Pennsylvania Governor's Justice Commission.

Smith, W. R., Horwitz, A. V., & Toby, J. (1983). *Contextual effects of juvenile correctional facilities intra-institutional change and post-release outcome: Final report.* New Brunswick, NJ: Rutgers University, Institute for Criminological Research, Department of Sociology.

Spence, S. H., & Marzillier, J. S. (1981). Social skills training with adolescent male offenders: II. Short-term, long-term and generalized effects. *Behavior Research & Therapy, 19,* 349-368.

Thambidurai, G. A. (1980). A comparative outcome study of a contract parole program for individuals committed to the youth correctional complex in the state of New Jersey (Doctoral dissertation, Rutgers University, State University of New Jersey, 1980). *Dissertation Abstracts International, 41*(01), 371B. (University Microfilms No. 80-16503)

Thomas, D., Peters, M., Gimbel, C., Laxton, G., Opanga, M., Afflerbach, M., & Croan, G. (1996). *Evaluation of the impact of boot camps for juvenile offenders: Cleveland interim report.* Washington, DC: Office of Juvenile Justice and Delinquency Prevention. (NCJRS Document No. 160928)

Truxaw, K. O. (1974). Recidivism differences among delinquent teacher aides (Doctoral dissertation, University of Southern California, 1973). *Dissertation Abstracts International, 34*(11), 7058A. (University Microfilms No. 74-11713)

Tupker, H. E., & Pointer, J. C. (1975). *The Iowa differential classification and treatment project.* Eldora: Iowa Training School for Boys.

Weeks, H. A. (1953). Preliminary evaluation of the Highfields Project. *American Sociological Review, 18,* 280-287.

Weeks, H. A. (1958). *Youthful offenders at Highfields: An evaluation of the effects of the short-term treatment of delinquent boys.* Ann Arbor: University of Michigan Press.

Williams, M. (1970). *A study of some aspects of Borstal allocation.* London: Great Britain Home Office Prison Department.

Wolf, M. M., Phillips, E. L., Fixson, D. L. (1974). *Achievement Place: Phase II* (Vol. 1). Rockville, MD: National Institute of Mental Health, Center for Studies of Crime and Delinquency.

CHAPTER 14

The Impact of the Juvenile Justice System and Prospects for Graduated Sanctions in a Comprehensive Strategy

■ *Barry Krisberg & James C. Howell*

This chapter examines the effectiveness of the juvenile justice system in handling serious, violent, and chronic juvenile offenders. This review focuses on traditional juvenile corrections and recent policy and procedural changes in traditional features of the juvenile justice system, consisting of targeted arrest and prosecution, and transferring juveniles to the criminal justice system.

After addressing these areas, we provide an overview of programs that jurisdictions might consider in implementing the graduated sanctions component of the Comprehensive Strategy for Serious, Violent, and Chronic Juvenile Offenders (Howell, 1995; Wilson & Howell, 1993). We include promising and effective programs not covered in Altschuler's (Chapter 15, this volume) review of "intermediate sanctions," and highlight some of the most effective programs in Lipsey and Wilson's (Chapter 13, this volume) review that illustrate how the Comprehensive Strategy can be implemented. We conclude with some suggestions for a research agenda on juvenile justice system handling of serious, violent, and chronic juvenile offenders.

AUTHORS' NOTE: We would like to thank Darlene Grant, Carolyn Haynes, and Kelly Dedel for editorial comments and research assistance that helped improve this chapter.

■ *The Impact of Juvenile Corrections*

Conceptualizing the impact of juvenile corrections on serious and violent juvenile (SVJ) offenders is no simple task. Juvenile corrections consists of a range of facilities that vary widely with respect to their size, location, security levels, and staffing patterns. Juvenile corrections encompasses 15-bed secure facilities in Massachusetts and individual California Youth Authority institutions that hold over 1,000 youthful offenders. There are training schools, detention centers, camps, ranches, wagon trains, environmental institutes, group homes, boot camps, residential programs for emotionally disturbed youths, chemical dependency programs, correctional sailing ships, and independent living arrangements. Although most juvenile facilities are run by government agencies, an increasing share of the residential "market" is held by nonprofit and for-profit organizations. Most SVJ offenders are confined in facilities operated by state juvenile corrections agencies, but the current trend is creation of special institutions for SVJ offenders and others for older juveniles and young adults that are operated by adult departments of corrections (Torbet et al., 1996).

States vary widely in their juvenile correctional policies (Krisberg, Litsky, & Schwartz, 1984). For instance, the ages defining the jurisdiction of juvenile corrections vary tremendously—and laws setting these age ranges are changing rapidly. States differ on the mix of correctional programs operated by state versus county government. States such as Ohio, Pennsylvania, and California operate many correctional programs at the local level, whereas state agencies in Georgia, Florida, Massachusetts, Louisiana, and Tennessee control virtually all juvenile corrections programs in their jurisdictions. In Maryland, most juvenile corrections facilities

are operated by private agencies. Massachusetts contracts out about half of its secure beds and all of its community-based programs to nonprofit groups, whereas California and Missouri use few, if any, private providers. States also differ on the extent to which they provide aftercare or postrelease services. As noted earlier, there is substantial variability in the size of facilities, the security of these programs, and the quality and quantity of educational and treatment resources.

The general status of juvenile corrections is not very good. A national study of the conditions of confinement revealed that many juvenile correctional facilities were not meeting minimal professional standards (Parent, Leiter, Livens, Wentworth, & Stephen, 1994). Other data suggest that juvenile corrections facilities are becoming more crowded, especially the larger urban facilities. In the competition for tax dollars, juvenile corrections has lost out to prisons and jails. There has been little new construction or renovation of juvenile facilities, increasing the number of youthful inmates housed in unsafe and deteriorated institutions. Reports of institutional violence and escapes, which have plagued juvenile corrections from its inception, continue to the present day (Krisberg, 1996).

Whether juvenile confinement halts or accelerates, juvenile criminal behavior has been debated since the mid-19th century. Advocates of alternatives to incarceration from Charles Loring Brace to Jane Addams to Jerome Miller have argued that institutionalization breeds crime (Krisberg & Austin, 1993). Defenders of juvenile corrections have claimed that confinement, even in terrible conditions, exerts a deterrent effect (DiIulio, 1995; Murray & Cox, 1979). Defenders of juvenile corrections have asserted that institutional treatment is a useful response to youth crime (Rhine, 1996). This policy debate has rarely been informed by empirical data.

Presumably, reoffending rates would be instructive in calculating the impact of juvenile corrections on SVJ offenders, but there is no agreement among practitioners on how to measure recidivism or the crime control effects of incapacitation for serious and chronic offenders. Studies examining the success of juvenile corrections have employed a number of different indicators to gauge subsequent criminality. The most frequently employed measures include (a) the proportion of youths who are crime free during a specified follow-up period, (b) the incidence or frequency of reoffending before and after correctional interventions, and (c) the severity of the crimes committed before and after intervention. Other researchers have examined "survival rates," which measure the distribution of time until the next criminal event. The vast majority of studies employ official data to measure recidivism and are subject to the known limitations of these data. In particular, official data are as much indicative of justice system policies and practices as they are descriptive of individual behavior (Lerman, 1975). Few researchers have employed self-report data to measure postprogram performance (Austin, Joe, Krisberg, & Steele, 1990; Barton & Butts, 1988; Gottfredson & Barton, 1992). However, the interpretation of self-report delinquency data when used in program evaluations raises many additional methodological concerns. For instance, offenders subject to intensive community supervision are not likely to reveal all of their current lawbreaking behavior to researchers (Austin et al., 1990). Due to the well-known problems of virtually all recidivism measures, it is generally advisable to use multiple indicators, although this advice has rarely been followed (Maltz, 1984).

The main empirical findings on the impact of juvenile corrections derive from follow-up studies on cohorts of youths released in a given year. Although each of these studies has limitations, especially weak research designs, they offer some important insights.

Tollett (1987) examined recidivism among a cohort of 1,664 youths released from a variety of Florida juvenile correction programs in 1984. Recidivism was defined as having been placed on probation or confined in an adult or juvenile facility within 1 year of the date of exit from the original juvenile corrections placement. During this period, 44% of the sample were convicted (or had sustained delinquency petitions) for new charges. The study does not indicate how many others were arrested and whether these charges resulted in convictions. However, only 26% of the group were recommitted to a correctional facility in the 1-year period. Tollett also found that two nonresidential programs had the lowest failure rates and that the worst results were recorded for youths released from Florida's most secure juvenile facilities. These findings must be viewed cautiously because the research did not control for the differing risk levels of youths in different programs.

The Pennsylvania Juvenile Court Judges Association sponsored a study of 10 residential placement programs (Goodstein & Sontheimer, 1987). The measure of recidivism was rearrest and reconviction within the first 12 to 18 months after release. The study consisted of random samples of youths released from 10 programs. The final sample contained approximately one third of all those released from these programs in 1984. By the end of the follow-up period, 55% of the sample had been arrested; 48% were arrested during the first 12 months. Nearly one third of the study sample were convicted of a new offense during the follow-up period. Juveniles with the most extensive prior arrest records were much more likely to be arrested, convicted, or incarcerated during the follow-up period. The same finding held true for youths with more extensive histories of residential placements. The younger the age of first arrest, the higher the failure rates. Poor school performance and difficulties in adjusting to institutional placements were predictive of higher recidivism rates. Race was not predictive of differential failure rates. Goodstein and Sontheimer (1987) did not find statistically significant differences among the 10 programs in terms of recidivism data, although the small sample sizes from each program would have permitted them to detect only large differences among the programs. The study authors note that interprogram differences may be masked because judges actually have a very narrow range of options for individual cases. They suggest that "future research should direct itself to performing 'head to head' comparisons of placements which pose themselves as *real* choices for judges to make" (p. 58).

Many other studies have confirmed the finding of very high rates of failure for graduates of the secure juvenile corrections programs. The National Council on Crime and Delinquency (NCCD) examined the postrelease behavior of 2,200 youths from the California Youth Authority between 1981 and 1982. The California Youth Authority wards had experienced an average of 14 months of confinement in large training schools. Within 12 months of their release, 70% of this group were arrested (Baird, 1987). Another NCCD study found that 79% of those released from Utah's secure juvenile facilities were arrested in the subsequent 12 months (Austin et al., 1990). A study of youths released from the Massachusetts training schools, before they were closed by Jerome Miller's reforms, revealed rates of subsequent arraignments of 66% (Coates, Miller, & Ohlin, 1978). This same Harvard University study revealed that the failure rate of youths placed in the early

community-based programs was 74%. However, later research involving a cohort of Massachusetts youths released from the community-based programs in the mid-1980s reported a rearraignment rate of 51% (Austin, Elms, Krisberg, & Steele, 1991).

More recent data from the Office of Juvenile Justice and Delinquency Prevention's (OJJDP) Juveniles Taken Into Custody (JTIC) research program expands the coverage of states reporting recidivism data (Krisberg, DeComo, Wordes, & Del Rosario, 1996). This project tracks individual data on youths entering and exiting juvenile corrections in 35 states. By examining those states that report comparable data each year, it is possible to calculate the proportion of youths who exited a youth corrections system and who were readmitted to that same system within 1 year of their release dates. This is a very conservative measure of failure. It is limited to those juveniles whose new crimes result in commitments to state juvenile institutions and does not cover youngsters who are transferred to the adult system or who "age out" of the jurisdiction of the juvenile court; notwithstanding these limitations, the JTIC database shows a robust rate of juvenile recidivism.

Twenty states in the JTIC reported programs that share age 18 as the upper age of juvenile jurisdiction, permitting readmission rates to be calculated over a reasonable time period. Of the 8,057 youths released in 1992 (who were younger than 17 years and thus had at least 1 more year's eligibility to be sent back to the juvenile corrections system), 27% were readmitted within 1 year of their release. Male readmission rates were much higher than for females (28% and 16%, respectively). Property and drug offenders had the highest failure rates. There was a strong relationship between the number of prior correctional commitments and readmission rates.

Analyses of similar data from seven states whose upper age of juvenile court jurisdiction was age 17 showed similar results. There were two exceptions in these states: (a) the overall readmission rates were higher, and (b) failure rates for these younger juveniles charged with violent offenses were as high as for property offenders.

A somewhat different picture is observed if one looks at the incidence of recidivism rather than its prevalence. Put simply, the prevalence measures reviewed above examine the issue of absolute desistance from justice system contacts during a specific period. Thus, they do not measure declines in the incidence of reoffending (the rate of crimes per time period), as well as changes that might occur in the severity of the offenses being committed. Corrections policy might well be posed as a problem in managing chronic illnesses (i.e., if we cannot cure the disease, can we at least lessen the frequency and severity of relapse?). Murray and Cox (1979) were among the first to popularize this measure, calling it "the suppression effect." They reported substantial reductions in the frequency of offending (67.5%) of Illinois youths when comparing their arrest patterns 1 year before and 1 year after correctional interventions. This suppression effect held up for youths placed in secure training schools and other intensive residential placements. Youngsters placed on probation also showed suppression effects, but these were of much smaller magnitude than the incarcerated juveniles.

Murray and Cox's (1979) work set off a professional firestorm, in part because much of the book is a polemic on behalf of deterrence strategies. Liberals, who had always argued that incarceration made troubled youngsters become more hardened criminals, did not like the idea that locking up youths might exert positive influences. Researchers, most notably Michael Maltz (1984), attempted to illustrate

that the suppression effect was a statistical artifact (produced by regression to the mean) or was produced by maturation (in theory, rates of offending slow down with aging). The methodological debate was inconclusive.

In a replication of the Illinois research, the NCCD conducted a study of all youths adjudicated in the Salt Lake City, Utah, Juvenile Court (Austin et al., 1990). The results were remarkably similar to those reported by Murray and Cox (1979). Probation showed small suppression effects, compared to the much larger declines in the rate of offending for youths placed in residential programs. Similar to the Illinois research, large suppression effects were seen for youths who had short-term residential stays, as well as longer periods of institutionalization. The NCCD research also indicated that minimal supervision produced the same crime reductions as intensive forms of probation supervision and services. The Salt Lake City data suggested that maturation and regression to the mean explained some, but not all, of the reduced frequency of offending for juveniles committed to state correctional programs. Interestingly, Utah correctional programs tended to involve smaller facilities and were more community based than the Illinois correctional programs.

NCCD's study of the Massachusetts Department of Youth Services (DYS) replicated the findings of the Utah and Illinois studies. Youths showed sharp reductions in the frequency and severity of their offending after leaving the DYS program, compared to the past 12 months prior to incarceration (Austin et al., 1991). Compared to the preprogram period, the number of offenses declined by more than half in the first 12 months that they were in the community after DYS placement. The number of offenses committed by these youths remained at the lower level for the next 2 years. Whereas regression to the mean and maturation exerted some impact on these

Massachusetts recidivism data, these two explanations were insufficient to explain the observed results.

An extensive follow-up study was completed by Haapanen (1990) based on samples of youths released from the California Youth Authority in the 1960s. He found that over 96% of the sample continued to be arrested into their adult years. Haapanen examined the entire juvenile court histories of his study group and compiled arrest records on them for approximately 15 years after their release from the Youth Authority. Thus, his research maps the criminal careers of a large cohort of serious juvenile offenders.

Long-term crime patterns differed among the racial groups in Haapanen's (1990) sample, with African Americans having the highest proportion of violent offending. Offending rates declined steadily over time, and a strong maturation effect was evident in the data. Criminal careers exhibited a high degree of instability over time, making it very difficult to predict which offenders would be high-rate offenders in the future. In general, the frequency of offending increased rapidly in the years immediately before commitment to the Youth Authority and dropped off just as rapidly in the years immediately following release from correctional facilities.

Haapanen (1990) concluded that the observed decline in the frequency of offending was partly due to maturation and regression to the mean, but that strong correctional interventions did appear to suppress some criminal behavior. But the sharp decline in offending rates and the general instability of crime rates did not support the idea that longer sentences would produce further crime reductions. Haapanen estimates that adding more years to the incapacitation of these youths would be a very expensive policy that would produce 1% to 3% reductions in the crime rate. The study also raised serious questions

as to whether selective incapacitation programs would enhance the crime control potential of the Youth Authority. Haapanen (1990) notes:

> Under these conditions, it would be difficult (if not impossible) to identify high-rate offenders for differential sentencing. It would also be difficult to take seriously models that forecast the effects of lengthening prison sentences for various offenders, since their behavior cannot be counted on to stay the same. (p. 147)

The Haapanen study lends considerable support to similar findings in the Illinois, Utah, and Massachusetts studies. His study illustrates that most serious and high-rate offenders slow down their rate of offending after correctional interventions. Although there is some instability or lack of predictability in offending rates, the best prediction one could make is that over time serious offenders continue to offend, albeit at lower frequency rates and with less serious offenses.

Tracy and Kempf-Leonard's (1996) follow-up study of the 1958 Philadelphia birth cohort, in which they tracked delinquents up to age 26, found that the timing of probation makes a very significant difference in curbing juvenile delinquent careers into adulthood. Compared to delinquents who received late-career probation, delinquents who received informal court adjustment, early probation, or midcareer probation had significantly lower odds of continuing their recidivism and becoming adult offenders. The study authors also examined the effects of incarceration on offender career progression, using a parallel measure for the timing of commitments. Committing male delinquents to a correctional facility did not appear to be an effective disposition in reducing the likelihood of adult crime. Juvenile males who were never committed to a correctional facility had significantly lower odds of adult crime compared to delinquents who were sent to a correctional facility either early, at midpoint, or late in their delinquent careers.

This research review raises as many questions as it resolves. Overall, we note that large percentages of serious juvenile offenders continue to commit crimes and come back into the juvenile justice system. Furthermore, there is some evidence that intensive correctional interventions do not stop criminal careers, although these interventions may slow the rate and severity of offending. Finally, the juvenile court appears to be most effective in curtailing the criminal careers of serious, violent, and chronic juvenile offenders.

Studies of released offenders can offer only a very incomplete view of how correctional experiences mold future behavior. We need to open the corrections "black box" and describe the experience of confinement in juvenile facilities. Is it the benign treatment world portrayed by many administrators, or is it a world of violence, sexual exploitation, and cruelty, as described by current and former inmates and youth advocates? What are we really measuring when we attempt to gauge the impact of the corrections experience on young people? Far more detailed descriptive as well as evaluative data on educational, vocational, drug treatment, counseling, and family reunification services provided by juvenile corrections agencies are needed. The lack of data on these specific components of juvenile corrections makes it quite difficult to defend current practices, particularly against those who argue that juveniles should be placed in adult prisons and jails.

■ Targeted Arrest and Prosecution

Studies of programs designed to target arrest and prosecution of serious, violent, and chronic juvenile offenders have not produced impressive results. Research conducted by Cronin, Bourque, Gragg, Mell, and McGrady (1988) examined the Habitual Serious and Violent Juvenile Offender Program (HSVJOP) funded by the OJJDP. This project examined targeted prosecution models in several cities. The study found that targeted prosecution programs were able to overcome the initial resistance of the juvenile justice system and became institutionalized components of the local justice systems. There have been subsequent iterations of the HSVJOP approach known as SHO/DI (Serious Habitual Offender Drug Involved Program) and SHO/CAP (Serious Habitual Offender Comprehensive Action Program) that have been less well researched but have yielded similar results.

Cronin and her colleagues (1988) found that the key ingredients to the success of these programs were more experienced prosecutors, more case preparation resources, greater interaction with victims and witnesses, and greater continuity in case handling. In some locations this led to speedier prosecution of habitual, serious juvenile offenders and contributed to increases in conviction rates, as well as increases in the numbers of youths transferred to criminal courts. However, it was less clear whether the program increased sentences in the juvenile justice system. Furthermore, OJJDP had hoped that comprehensive treatment responses would complement the prosecution efforts; these did not materialize. Cronin and her colleagues suggested that case screening and identification criteria were overly broad and produced more cases than the project's resources could handle.

The evaluation of the HSVJOP could not answer a number of crucial policy concerns. The projects were able to select high-rate offenders (those who had committed a large number of offenses). However, it is less clear whether the screening criteria are the best predictors of criminal involvement in the future. Other selection criteria might have been employed, such as violent offenders with no prior convictions, or offenders with long histories of misdemeanors but no serious offenses. Cronin et al. (1988) could not predict the consequences of focusing on different offender groups. The study also could not answer questions about the consequences, intended and unintended, of holding youths in juvenile facilities for longer periods of time or placing them in adult facilities. Ultimately, the HSVJOP research could not determine if targeted prosecution programs actually deter youths from continued criminal behavior. The core questions that must be resolved are whether traditional juvenile correctional interventions or adult style punishments exert positive, neutral, or negative impacts of youthful criminal careers. For example, if correctional interventions are criminogenic, as some advocates have asserted, then getting more youngsters into "schools for crime" for longer stays seems self-defeating. But if one can demonstrate crime suppression effects of correctional interventions, then successful and speedy prosecutions may make a difference.

Other researchers have raised similar concerns about prioritized prosecution programs. Chaiken and Chaiken (1987) studied programs aimed at career criminals in Los Angeles and in Middlesex, Massachusetts. They found that information contained in case files was not very helpful in discriminating between high-rate and lower-rate offenders. The Chaikens were better able to identify the much smaller group of high-rate offenders that committed the most serious crimes (see also Weiner, 1996). The best predictors of future violence were the frequency and severity of violence in the youth's recent past.

A recent exploratory study by Rasmussen and Yu (1996) appears to lend some support to the claim that timely intervention for high-risk youths and increased incarceration of ju-

venile habitual offenders can have large public safety benefits. The authors use economic modeling techniques to conclude that the efforts of Florida's Duval County State's Attorney's Office and the Sheriffs Department led to preventing over 7,200 robberies, burglaries, and motor vehicle thefts by incarcerating habitual juvenile offenders between 1992 and 1995. The researchers arrived at these estimates by comparing the experience in Duval County with two other Florida counties that did not have a similar program. Rasmussen and Yu admit that their analysis is more suggestive than conclusive. They were unable to control for a broad range of other community factors that may have produced the observed reductions in youth crime. Furthermore, the juvenile justice system in Duval County simultaneously introduced a number of innovations, making it impossible to attribute the results to only one aspect of this multifaceted program. It should also be noted that the incarceration program in Duval County contained extensive educational and mentoring services. Moreover, Duval County youths sent to this program may have spent less time in custody in the local Sheriffs Department facility than if they had been placed in the custody of the Florida Department of Juvenile Justice. In addition, youths exited the Duval County program with the record of this conviction expunged. Reducing the effects of a punitive criminal conviction may have played some role in the positive results.

Not surprisingly, policies of targeting the dangerous few have generated intense support among law enforcement officials and politicians. Unfortunately, the ample investments in these programs have not been matched with adequate research designs. We know little more today about the efficacy of targeted enforcement and suppression programs than we did two decades ago (see Klein, 1995, for a review of youth gang suppression programs). One of the problems is that few SVJ offenders are arrested specifically for this type of offense (only 6% in the Denver Youth Survey; see Huizinga, Esbensen, & Weiher, 1996). Among juveniles who injured someone in this Denver sample, 74% were arrested at some point. But about one fourth were arrested before they committed a serious violent offense, about one fourth were arrested during the same year, and about one fourth were arrested after initiating their serious and violent offending.

Prosecutor-run programs need to be evaluated because the current trend is to mount more and more of them. The Duval County program is an innovative one that combines early intervention and diversion programs with criminal court prosecution of juveniles, followed by supervision and aftercare in conjunction with probation and parole (Shorstein, 1995). It needs more rigorous evaluation. "Community prosecution" is also a new concept that is being tried in Portland, Manhattan, Boston, and Indianapolis (Boland, 1996). These need to be evaluated.

Innovative local law enforcement and community policing programs are also being implemented (OJJDP, 1996b). Several are curfew centers, which are being evaluated. Others that are receiving considerable attention include Boston's Operation Night Light, a cooperative effort between the city's Police Youth Violence Strike Force and the Probation Department, and the New Haven program of delinquency prevention through child-centered community policing. These, too, need rigorous evaluation.

■ Transfer of Juveniles to the Criminal Justice System

Few juvenile justice policies have received more political and media attention in recent years than the idea of shifting juveniles to the adult system. Yet no one knows for sure how many juveniles are transferred to the adult court system, and very little about the consequences. Current estimates are no better than the first national studies of transfers (Hamparian et al., 1982) because data are kept only on judicial waivers. Data are not available on legislative exclusion of juvenile court jurisdiction or on prosecutor direct files. Snyder and Sickmund (1995, p. 155) estimate that as many as 176,000 youths below the age of 18 were tried in adult courts in 1991 in states that set the upper age of juvenile court jurisdiction at ages 16 or 17. (Others are transferred because legislatures exclude certain juvenile offenses from juvenile court jurisdiction.) In comparison, in 1991 juvenile court judges waived just 9,700 cases to criminal courts. In 1994, 12,300 cases waived from juvenile courts to the adult system (Butts, Snyder, Finnegan, Aughenbaugh, & Poole, 1996), an increase of 27% in the 3-year period. In Florida there were 7,000 prosecutor direct files in 1993 (Snyder & Sickmund, 1995, p. 156). In 1993, slightly over 5,200 adolescents age 17 or younger were confined in adult prisons, about twice as many as in 1982 (National Institute of Corrections, 1995).

A recent review of studies of the three transfer mechanisms noted above (Howell, 1996) found that, of 50 studies reported to date, 36 examined judicial waiver, 3 assessed legislative exclusion, and 5 studies examined prosecutorial direct file. Only a handful of studies have compared juvenile and criminal justice handling. Only judicial waiver has been definitively examined.

Howell (1996) concluded that studies to date suggest that judges appear to be more adept than prosecutors or state legislatures in selecting serious, violent, and chronic offenders for transfer. Recidivism rates are much higher among juveniles judicially waived to criminal court than among those retained in the juvenile justice system. The few comparative studies suggest that waived juveniles are more likely to reoffend, more quickly, at a higher rate, and perhaps with more serious offenses than juveniles retained in the juvenile court. Thus, the short-term public safety benefits of waiver and incarceration is offset by higher recidivism rates. Although SVJ offenders retained in the juvenile justice system are less likely to be incarcerated, some type of sanction is more likely to be imposed, more quickly, and recidivism rates are lower than in the criminal system. However, this does not necessarily show that adult court is less effective. An evaluation of the effectiveness of the adult court for SVJ offenders is inherently complicated because certain types of offenders and not others are selected and processed by this type court.

The higher success rate with SVJ offenders in the juvenile justice system may be partly because of judges' use of graduated sanctions. In finding that, compared to juveniles who are retained in juvenile court, juvenile offenders transferred to criminal court in Minnesota had significantly higher recidivism rates, Podkopacz and Feld (1995, p. 170) offered three possible explanations: (a) by emphasizing prior records, juvenile courts may succeed in identifying the most chronic offenders for transfer; (b) the greater effectiveness of treatment in the juvenile justice system; or (c) the failure of criminal justice system punishment to deter juveniles from committing future offenses.

Studies suggest that legislation that excludes certain offenses from juvenile court jurisdiction has the least chance of success (Howell, 1996). The main reason is that these statutes generally target a single violent offense for transfer, and the current offense is the worst predictor of a subsequent violent offense. Snyder (Appendix, this volume) found that among juveniles referred to the Phoenix juvenile court over a 16-year period, only 17% were referred for a second violent

offense. Few state legislatures incorporate chronicity into excluded offense criteria (Fritsch & Hemmens, 1995).

Although it is the least researched transfer method, prosecutorial direct file has not yet demonstrated the ability to select the most serious, violent, and chronic juvenile offenders for transfer. The lack of success may result from prosecutors' lack of familiarity with the offending history, provision of and response to treatment, and the importance of weighing a variety of key factors in making these decisions. However, studies of prosecutorial direct file have been conducted only in Florida. The most recent of these studies (Bishop, Frazier, Lanza-Kaduce, & Winner, 1996) found that the transferred group had higher rates of recidivism, committed more serious subsequent offenses, and experienced a shorter time to failure than the matched sample of nontransfer youths. Bishop et al. (1996) concluded that Florida's transfer policy had little deterrent value. They noted that the short-term benefits of incapacitating juvenile offenders in the adult system were negated quickly as the transferred youths returned to the community and committed many more crimes than their juvenile justice system counterparts. Subsequent analyses over a longer follow-up period (6 years) by Winner and his colleagues (Winner, Lanza-Kaduce, Bishop, & Frazier, 1997) indicate that the differences between the two groups' recidivism prevalence rates disappeared after 4 years beyond release. This result could be anticipated, because of the long-term effects of returning parolees to their original criminogenic communities. The long-term follow-up confirmed the original study results with respect to individual recidivism rates: Transferred youths reoffended more quickly and with a higher frequency of rearrest.

Data on the comparative outcomes of those transferred to the criminal court system versus those handled in the juvenile court system are rare. An early study by White (1985) compared juveniles charged with very serious crimes in the juvenile justice system with similar cases involving young adults in criminal courts. White found that criminal courts were slightly more likely to convict and incarcerate young defendants than juvenile courts. The young adults served considerably more time in prison than the juveniles in state training schools. The young adult offenders had a recidivism rate that was much higher than that of the juveniles. In another study, Fagan (1995) contrasted the handling of SVJ offenders in New York and New Jersey. He looked at almost 1,200 felony offenders who were ages 15-16, arrested for robbery or burglary, in matched counties. Because of state laws, the New Yorkers would be more likely to be handled in the adult system, and the New Jersey youths were mostly processed by the juvenile justice system. In fact, Fagan discovered that the sanctions were more certain and more severe for the New Jersey sample, compared with the New York sample. However, the New York youths had higher recidivism rates, committed more new offenses, and were crime free for a shorter time period than the New Jersey offenders (Fagan, 1995). Although these results are intriguing, the findings are clouded by the inability to truly match offenders from the same jurisdiction. It is difficult to interpret the results: Were they produced by the lesser penalties of the New York system, the adverse consequences of adult correctional interventions, or other differences between the New York and New Jersey youths?

There are also unintended consequences of juvenile incarceration in adult prisons that have not yet been fully researched. Forst and his colleagues (Forst, Fagan, & Vivone, 1989) interviewed nontransferred youths subsequently incarcerated in juvenile training schools and youths transferred to criminal court who were later imprisoned. Juveniles were far more likely to be violently victimized in adult prisons than in juvenile correctional facilities (Forst et al., 1989). Although property crime victimization rates were about the same for the two groups, 37% of the juveniles in training schools versus 47% of juvenile prison inmates suffered violent victimization, including violence at the hands of staff. Sexual assault was five times more likely in prison, beatings by staff nearly twice as likely, and attacks with weapons almost 50% more common.

In sum, there is remarkably little empirical evidence that transferring juveniles to the criminal justice system produces any positive benefits. More evaluation of criminal court sanctions is needed, particularly of the prosecutorial direct file method, and of innovative methods of transfer that are currently being developed. Current research in Florida is evaluating the effectiveness of the state's "blended sentencing" approach to treatment of transferred juveniles (see Thomas & Bilchik, 1985, for a description), "through a three-tiered approach that gives prosecutors expanded discretionary power in making jurisdictional decisions as the age of defendants and the severity of offenses increases" (OJJDP, 1996a, p. 27). Minnesota enacted a blended sentence law in 1995 that creates a new offender category called "extended sentence jurisdiction juveniles" for serious chronic offenders over age 14. Once convicted of a crime, this offender category receives both a juvenile disposition and a suspended criminal sentence. If they do not successfully meet the conditions of the juvenile disposition, offenders can be incarcerated under the criminal sentence. Juvenile court jurisdiction is extended to age 21 (OJJDP, 1996a, p. 27).

■ A Comprehensive Strategy

The above review and other chapters in this volume suggest that the OJJDP Comprehensive Strategy for Serious, Violent, and

Chronic Juvenile Offenders (Wilson & Howell, 1993) holds considerable promise for dealing with the subjects of this volume. The Comprehensive Strategy incorporates two principal components: (a) preventing youths from becoming delinquent by focusing prevention programs on at-risk youths, and (b) improving the juvenile justice system response to delinquent offenders through a system of graduated sanctions and a continuum of treatment alternatives that include immediate intervention, intermediate sanctions, and community-based corrections sanctions, incorporating restitution and community service when appropriate.

The initial target population for prevention programs is juveniles at risk of involvement in delinquent activity. Although primary delinquency prevention programs provide services to all youths wishing to participate, maximum impact on future delinquent conduct can be achieved by seeking to identify and involve in prevention programs youths at greatest risk of involvement in delinquent activity. The next target population is youths, both male and female, who have committed delinquent (criminal) acts, including juvenile offenders who evidence a high likelihood of becoming, or who already are, serious, violent, or chronic offenders.

Prevention and Early Intervention

Catalano and his colleagues (Chapter 11, this volume) illustrate how the prevention component of the Comprehensive Strategy can be implemented using the Communities That Care model (Hawkins, Catalano, & Associates, 1992). The Communities That Care strategy elevates prevention to a science while empowering each community to assess its own profile of risk and protection and to identify effective actions to address that profile in outcome-driven prevention. Their chapter also reviews prevention programs,

identifying effective ones that communities can select to address identified risk factors and increase protective factors in comprehensive delinquency prevention programming.

Early intervention is the bridge between prevention and juvenile justice system graduated sanctions. The Children's Research Center (CRC, 1993) model is an innovative method of identifying families at high risk for continued abuse or neglect among those that already have a substantiated abuse or neglect referral. Using child protective services case records, CRC applies risk assessment instruments to classify cases according to risk levels. These instruments are based on the statistical relationship between family characteristics and case outcomes, using large samples of previously substantiated cases. The risk level is used to set a service level for opened cases, and in some states, as a key criterion in case-opening decisions. The risk assessment instruments have distinguished significant differences in the risk potential of the client population. Families classified as high risk had a recidivism rate 10 times higher than low-risk families (Wiebush, Baird, Krisberg, & Onek, 1995). The results of these risk assessments can be linked with criminal justice system data to identify problem families for early intervention through family strengthening programming.

Graduated Sanctions

The efficacy of graduated sanctions is substantiated in a wide array of studies. Many of these are referenced in Lipsey and Wilson's (Chapter 13, this volume) review of institutional and noninstitutional programs. Indeed, several of the examples of programs their meta-analysis showed to be most effective incorporate graduated sanctions. These include the contingency contracting program (Jessness, Allison, McCormic, Wedge, & Young, 1975), Achievement Place (Kirigin, Braukmann, Atwater, & Worl, 1982), teaching parents (Wolf, Philips, & Fixson, 1974), and the Planned Re-Entry Program (Seckel & Turner, 1985). Several other reviews and evaluations of juvenile justice system programs show the effectiveness of graduated sanctions (Altschuler & Armstrong, 1994a; Hamparian, 1984; Mahoney, 1987; Pennell, Curtis, & Scheck, 1990). However, there is one important exception. Schneider (1990) found a differential response to graduated sanctions in restitution programs, depending on the self-image of the juvenile. Detention may have damaged youths' self-image, leaving incarceration with about the same results as less coercive policies such as restitution and probation. Graduated sanctions may not work for all adolescents; moreover, the effects of the most severe sanctions, detention and incarceration, are not well understood.

Perhaps the best example of an effective juvenile justice system program of graduated sanctions is the Illinois Unified Delinquency Intervention Services (UDIS) program for chronic inner-city juvenile offenders, studied by Murray and Cox (1979). Their evaluation compared three levels of graduated sanctions. Level I sanctions consisted of less drastic interventions, such as arrest and release. Level II comprised the UDIS program of community-based services for those who recidivated in Level I. Level III, to which those who failed in Level II were transferred, consisted of placement in the Illinois Department of Corrections. Murray and Cox's analysis showed that more crimes were "suppressed" at each subsequent level of sanctions.

The Comprehensive Strategy's graduated sanctions component consists of the following levels of interventions: immediate intervention, intermediate sanctions, secure care, and aftercare. These gradations (and sublevels within them) are viewed as forming a continuum of intervention options (or graduated sanctions) that needs to be paralleled by a continuum of treatment options. As offenders progress in the graduated sanctions system, treatments must become more structured and intensive to effectively deal with the more intractable problems that more difficult and dangerous offenders present.

A key premise of the Comprehensive Strategy is that a combination of interventions can achieve a larger measure of overall juvenile crime reduction than is possible by means of a single intervention. A recent cost-benefits study of juvenile delinquency prevention and treatment programs illustrates the cumulative benefits of multiple-program approaches. RAND researchers (Greenwood, Model, Rydell, & Chiesa, 1996) found that a combination of only four delinquency prevention and treatment programs achieve the same level of serious crime (violent crimes plus burglary) reduction as California's "three strikes" law—at less than one fifth the cost. The successful interventions Greenwood and his colleagues identified are home visits and day care, parent training (see Wasserman and Miller, Chapter 10, this volume, for reviews of these two interventions), school graduation incentives (Taggart, 1995), and delinquent supervision (the 8% Early Intervention Program, also called the 8% Solution, reviewed below).

To achieve a high level of effectiveness, a continuum of program options must be combined with graduated sanctions in a comprehensive framework. Placement of offenders in a system of graduated sanctions is determined by state juvenile codes that prescribe sanctions for specific offenses, risk assessment instruments, and assessments of treatment needs. Risk assessment instruments sort offenders into groups with differing probabilities of reoffending (Wiebush et al., 1995), using a predetermined set of scale items known to have a statistical relationship with recidivism. These instruments are designed to estimate the likelihood of reoffending within a given time period (say, 18-24 months) and are based on the statistical relationship between youth characteristics and recidivism rates (see Wiebush et al., 1995, pp. 181-183, for a discussion of the essential properties of assessment and classification systems). Wiebush and his colleagues illustrated the use of risk and needs assessment instruments in a Model Case Management System developed by the NCCD (Baird, 1984). We next discuss a system of graduated sanctions with several of the most promising and effective programs that are appropriate at the various levels. Aftercare programs are not discussed here (see Altschuler, Chapter 15, this volume).

Immediate intervention. The target group for immediate intervention is first-time delinquent offenders (misdemeanors and nonviolent felonies) and nonserious repeat offenders (generally misdemeanor repeat offenses).

Immediate intervention with early-onset delinquents is illustrated in the "8% Solution" in Orange County, California, Probation Department. This program is based on an analysis of court referrals showing that 8% of referred adolescents account for more than half of all repeat offenses among probationers (Kurz & Moore, 1994). Potential 8% cases are identified during probation intake and verified through a comprehensive assessment process using a risk assessment instrument based on an analysis of characteristics of the 8% group.

A broad range of sanctions (from day reporting to community confinement) is used in conjunction with a continuum of program options for the juvenile and family members to achieve habilitation goals while providing intensive case supervision. These options include individual incentives, family problem assessment and intervention services, family preservation and support services (including home-based intervention, respite care, and parent aids), individualized treatment for particular problem behaviors (e.g., mental health, and drug and alcohol abuse), and a wide range of community service opportunities for the 8% minors. A preliminary evaluation comparing a pilot group of program clients with the original study group shows about a 50% reduction in new offenses, court petitions, probation violations, and subsequent correctional commitments among the 8% program group in a 12-month follow-up (Orange County Probation Department, 1996).

Some jurisdictions, such as Florida cities, are using Juvenile Assessment Centers (JACs; Dembo & Rivers, 1996) to perform a complete psychosocial assessment on youths apprehended by the police, to ensure that their service needs are addressed in dispositional recommendations, to refer at-risk youths and their families to needed services, and to track outcomes of these problem identification and program linking activities. Juveniles who are in early stages of pathways to delinquency (e.g., truants) are specifically targeted for alternative services. In the Florida JACs, a wide range of services is made available including substance abuse treatment, mental health services, mental retardation services, literacy training, and other educational services. Youths referred for services are tracked for the purpose of assessing services and program development. It is important that mechanisms like the Florida JACs be established at the entry level of immediate sanctions to integrate the juvenile justice, mental health, social services, child welfare, and education systems because they often have the same clients, even simultaneously—both the children and their families—yet may be working at cross-purposes or duplicating services.

Intermediate sanctions. Offenders who are inappropriate for immediate intervention (first-time serious or violent offenders) or who fail to respond successfully to immediate intervention as evidenced by reoffending (such as repeat property offenders or drug-involved juveniles) would begin with or be subject to intermediate sanctions.

The San Diego County Probation Department (1996) operates a Juvenile Correctional Intervention Program (JCIP) that incorporates five levels of sanction and treatment options for such offenders, beginning at the point of delinquency adjudication. In the first level, the probationer is enrolled in a community program, REFLECTIONS (intensive in-home parent development and family support services). Home detention is required in the second level, along with a stayed commitment to a correctional facility. In the third level, offenders with a stayed commitment are placed in secure detention for a maximum of 30 days, then released to home confinement. The fourth level carries a commitment to a minimum-security facility (for boys) or a local correctional facility (for girls), followed by admission to an aftercare transition program. In the fifth level, the probationer is committed to either a boys or girls minimum-security facility. An assessment team recommends a specific option level and a treatment plan, based on risk-needs assessments. The Probation Department's graduated sanctions plan also specifies intensity of supervision in each sanction level. Offenders are moved up the sanction levels when behavior does not improve; they are moved down the levels commensurate with behavioral improvements.

For more serious and violent juvenile offenders, multisystemic therapy (MST; see Wasserman and Miller, Chapter 10, this volume) is one of the effective programs identified by Lipsey and Wilson (Chapter 13, this volume). Consistent with family preservation models, MST directly addresses intrapersonal (e.g., cognitive) and systemic (i.e., family, peer, school) factors that are known to be associated with adolescent antisocial behavior. It has been found to be effective in a number of clinical trials in treating multiple problems of SVJ offenders in different settings (Family Services Research Center, 1995), including violent offenders (Borduin et al., 1995). MST has also been shown to be much more cost-effective than incarceration. Its cost per client is about $3,500 compared to nearly $18,000 for institutional placements (Henggeler, Melton, & Smith, 1992), thus the efficacy of this model as an alternative to incarceration has been demonstrated.

A substantial body of research indicates that many incarcerated adolescents can be managed in well-structured community-based programs. Table 14.1 summarizes the results of perhaps the most referenced studies in this area. These studies, often making a direct comparison with juvenile justice system incarceration (or restrictive supervision), led researchers to conclude that alternatives to secure confinement for serious and chronic juveniles are *at least as effective* in suppressing recidivism as incarceration, but are considerably less costly to operate. These include studies in Illinois (Murray & Cox, 1979), Massachusetts (Austin et al., 1991; Coates et al., 1978), Utah (Austin et al., 1990), and Michigan (Barton & Butts, 1988). Only a few studies, such as Gottfredson and Barton's (1992), have found that institutionalized youths in Maryland performed better than those in community-based programs. But their results may be a function of a very sudden move to deinstitutionalization in Maryland and the less-than-ideal implementation of the community alternatives. Early studies of the Massachusetts reforms showed similar results (Coates et al., 1978). Lipsey and Wilson (Chapter, 13, this volume) report that programs over 2 years of age produce larger positive effects than newer programs.

More important, Lipsey and Wilson's review shows that among programs producing consistent evidence of positive effects for

TABLE 14.1 Major Research on Alternatives to Institutionalization for Serious Juvenile Offenders

Study	Intervention	Setting	Participants	Outcome Measures	Results
Palmer (1971)[a]	Intensive, long-term counseling, group homes in lieu of state institutions	Four northern California communities	13-19 years old	Prevalence or recidivism, attitudinal changes, parole behavior, school adjustment, employment	Program clients performed better on all measures, except employment, than institutionalized youths. Both groups were equivalent on employment measures.
Empey and Lubeck (1971)[a]	Community-based group home in lieu of traditional training school	Los Angeles, California	10-17 years old	Incidence and prevalence of delinquency	Large and equivalent drops in the incidence of reoffending in both groups; comparable results in both groups on prevalence measure.
Empey and Erickson (1972)[a]	Intensive supervision plus daily counseling vs. traditional treatment	Provo, Utah	10-17 years old	Incidence and prevalence of recidivism	Intensive group performed better on all measures compared to traditional probation supervision with a matched group of youths.
Coates, Miller, and Ohlin (1978)	A range of community-based sanctions begun after closure of training schools	Massachusetts statewide	7-17 years old	Prevalence of recidivism, attitudes toward conformity	Recidivism rates of training school releases were lower than those of new community programs; community program youths showed better attitudinal improvements than institutionalized youths.
Murray and Cox (1979)	A range of sanctions for juvenile offenders	Illinois statewide	10-17 years old	Incidence of recidivism	Large reductions in incidence of recidivism; the most intensive community programs produced equivalent suppression effects to institutionalization.
Greenwood and Turner (1987)	Wilderness program in lieu of county correctional facility	San Diego, California	10-17 years old	Prevalence of recidivism	VisionQuest clients performed better than comparison group.
Austin, Krisberg, Joe, and Steele (1990)	A range of community-based and small secure programs	Utah statewide	7-17 years old	Incidence and prevalence of recidivism	Large declines in the incidence of recidivism after correctional intervention.
Barton and Butts (1988)	Three versions of intensive supervision in lieu of commitment to state facilities	Wayne County, Michigan	10-17 years old	Incidence of recidivism, self-reported delinquency	Experimentals performed comparably to controls on official recidivism measures; the intensive supervision group performed better on self-report delinquency measures.
Austin, Elms, Krisberg, and Steele (1991)	Community-based small secure program	Massachusetts statewide	7-17 years old	Incidence and prevalence of recidivism	Youths in Department of Youth Services programs showed sustained declines in incidence of recidivism; prevalence rates were lower than other states studied.

a. Studies involved random assignment to experimental and control groups; other studies used posttest only or nonrandom companion groups.

SVJ offenders, noninstitutional programs produced greater reductions in recidivism than institution-based programs. Compared to control groups, the better institutional programs reduced recidivism by 34% to 38%; in contrast, the better noninstitutional programs reduced recidivism by 40% to 44%. More rigorous research on both institutional and noninstitutional programs is needed, even though it is clear that community-based interventions for serious and chronic offenders can be safely expanded, and produce enormous cost savings. For example, a South Carolina study (Rivers & Trotti, 1995) found that if the state could reduce graduation of juveniles from juvenile probation into the criminal justice system just 5 percentage points, from 33% to 28%, the state could save $37 million in adult prison and probation costs over a 10-year period.

It will be important to evaluate if the effectiveness of correctional interventions can be further enhanced through improved aftercare and community reentry services (Altschuler, Chapter 15, this volume; Armstrong & Altschuler, 1994; Greenwood, Deschenes, & Adams, 1993). Miller and Ohlin (1985) summarize this view as follows:

> Delinquency is a community problem. In the final analysis the means for its prevention and control must be built into the fabric of community life. This can only happen if the community accepts its share of responsibility for having generated and perpetuated paths of socialization that lead to sporadic criminal episodes for some youths and careers in crime for others. (p. 1)

Secure care. The criminal behavior of many serious, violent, and chronic juvenile offenders requires the application of secure sanctions to hold these offenders accountable for their delinquent acts and to provide a structured treatment environment. As we noted earlier, large congregate-care juvenile facilities (training schools, camps, and ranches) have not proven to be particularly effective in rehabilitating juvenile offenders. Although some continued use of these types of facilities will remain a necessary alternative for those juveniles who require enhanced security to protect the public, the establishment of small community-based facilities to provide intensive services in a secure environment offers the best hope for successful treatment of those juveniles who require a structured setting. Secure sanctions are most effective in changing future conduct when they are coupled with comprehensive treatment and rehabilitation services.

Application of risk assessment instruments to correctional populations in 14 states (Krisberg, Onek, Jones, & Schwartz, 1993) revealed that an average of 31% of juveniles housed in these facilities were at low risk for subsequent offending and thus could be placed in less secure settings at much less cost. An excellent example of such a facility is the Thomas O'Farrell Youth Center. It is a 38-bed, unlocked, staff-secure residential program for male youths committed to the Maryland Department of Juvenile Services. The typical O'Farrell juvenile has numerous prior court referrals, generally for property crimes and drug offenses. Graduated sanctions are built into the O'Farrell treatment program. The program begins with an orientation phase of about 1 month. In Phase I, about 60 days, youths acquire more knowledge about O'Farrell and its normative system. To move to Phase II, residents must demonstrate consistent and positive behavior in all aspects of O'Farrell life, including school attendance, work details, group meetings, and so forth. In Phase II, youths must demonstrate high levels of success in on-campus jobs and are encouraged to find part-time employment in the community. Aftercare (Phase III) lasts for 6 months and includes assistance in reentering school, vocational counseling, crisis intervention, family counseling, transportation, and mentoring.

Even confined violent juvenile offenders can be effectively controlled and rehabilitated in a secure correctional confinement. One secure treatment model is the OJJDP Violent Juvenile Offender (VJO) program that provided treatment for violent and property felony offenders, beginning with small secure facilities, followed by gradual reintegration into the community through community-based residential programs, then intensive neighborhood supervision. Evaluation of the program (Fagan, 1990b) showed that in the two sites that best implemented the program design, VJO youths had significantly lower recidivism rates, for less serious offenses, and less quickly than the control group.

The Florida Environmental Institute (FEI), also known as the "Last Chance Ranch," serves some of the state's most serious and violent juvenile offenders, most of whom are referred back from the adult system for treatment under a special provision in Florida's law. Almost two thirds of FEI youths are committed for violent crimes; the remainder, for chronic property or drug offenses (Krisberg, DeComo, Rudenstine, & Del Rosario, 1995). FEI, an environmentally secure program (located in a swamp in a remote area of the state), provides a highly structured program with a low staff-to-student ratio consisting of several phases. After about a year of therapeutic hard work, educational and vocational training, restitution, and reintegration programming, clients are assisted with community living in an extensive aftercare phase. Evaluation of the program has shown quite promising results (dampened only by small sample sizes and lack of an experimental design in the research). FEI has produced much lower recidivism rates than other Florida programs. The state of Florida is convinced of its effectiveness and is replicating it in other parts of the state.

Benefits of the Comprehensive Strategy

The graduated sanctions component of the Comprehensive Strategy is premised on a firm belief that the juvenile justice system can effectively handle delinquent juvenile behavior through the judicious application of a range of graduated sanctions and a full continuum of treatment and rehabilitation services. Expected benefits of this approach include (Wilson & Howell, 1993):

1. *Increased juvenile justice system responsiveness.* This program will provide additional referral and dispositional resources for law enforcement, juvenile courts, and juvenile corrections. It will also require these system components to increase their ability to identify, process, evaluate, refer, and track juvenile offenders.

2. *Increased juvenile accountability.* Juvenile offenders will be held accountable for their behavior, decreasing the likelihood of their development into serious, violent, or chronic offenders and tomorrow's adult criminals. The juvenile justice system will be held accountable for controlling chronic and serious delinquency while also protecting society. Communities will be held accountable for providing community-based prevention and treatment resources for juveniles.

3. *Decreased costs of juvenile corrections.* Applying the appropriate graduated sanctions and developing the required community-based resources should reduce significantly the need for high-cost beds in training schools. Savings from the high costs of operating these facilities could be used to provide treatment in community-based programs and facilities.

4. *Increased responsibility of the juvenile justice system.* Many juvenile offenders currently waived or transferred to the criminal justice system could be provided opportuni-

ties for intensive services in secure community-based settings or in long-term treatment in juvenile training schools, camps, and ranches.

5. *Increased program effectiveness.* This volume adds considerable information to knowledge of the characteristics of chronic, serious, and violent offenders, and effective programs for their treatment and rehabilitation. However, more must be learned about what works best for whom under what circumstances to intervene successfully in the criminal careers of serious, violent, and chronic juvenile offenders. Follow-up research and rigorous evaluation of programs implemented as part of this strategy should produce valuable information to inform future interventions.

The combined effects of delinquency prevention and increased juvenile justice system effectiveness in intervening immediately and effectively in the lives of potential chronic offenders should result in measurable decreases in delinquency in sites where the above concepts are demonstrated. In addition, long-term reduction in crime should result from fewer serious, violent, and chronic delinquents becoming adult criminal offenders.

■ Concluding Observations

This review summarizes the state of our knowledge about the effects of the juvenile justice system on SVJ offenders. Although there is some evidence that strong justice system sanctions reduce the rate of subsequent criminal offending, there is not much support for the thesis that traditional sanctioning policies reduce the likelihood of subsequent offending or recommitments. Given the enormous fiscal and human consequences of various sanctioning approaches, it is tragic that our research base is so slender. In particular, juvenile corrections policies and

practices, and the movement to transfer more youths to adult prisons, are informed by anecdotes, flawed research, and media-popularized fads. Juvenile and criminal justice policies freely and quickly move from "scared straight" to "tough love," from boot camps to chain gangs.

The research agenda to remedy the present knowledge gap must be bold and ambitious. The largely unexplored world of the juvenile justice system needs to be opened up for research. Despite the increase in humanistic rhetoric about the value of funding more prevention, the justice system will continue to expend the lion's share of state and local tax dollars in the near term. It is in our communal interest to attempt to minimize the damage done by some justice system operations (e.g., discriminatory practices toward minorities, violent victimization of adolescents in facilities, unhealthy conditions of confinement) and to promote those interventions that genuinely advance public safety.

Researchers should develop models to help policymakers forecast the likely impacts of policy changes (e.g., mandatory waiver laws, new truancy and curfew laws, or school expulsion policies) on various components of the justice and social service systems. Work should be commenced to measure the relative cost-effectiveness of new expenditures in law enforcement, incarceration, treatment, or prevention programs. The work of Greenwood and his colleagues (1996) is a very important first step in this direction.

Experimental studies are essential for developing knowledge of "what works" with youthful offenders. Three issues deserve priority attention: (a) determining the most cost-effective length of stay in correctional facilities, (b) measuring the utility of earlier or more immediate responses to juvenile lawbreaking, and (c) the appropriate mix of residential and home-based services for different types of offenders. It is likely that states and communities will continue to devote substantial funding in these areas without much guidance from research. Experimental studies should also be launched to refine offender classification and risk assessment systems to better identify the fit of treatment responses to different types of offenders.

In particular, future programs should incorporate randomized designs to test whether special handling of selected offenders produces any measurable deterrent effects. Moreover, researchers need to examine critically the current decision-making processes used by these programs, especially the relationship of these criteria to predicting future criminal behavior. Whether the addition of comprehensive treatment components improves the productivity of these programs remains to be determined. The additive effects of aftercare services should also be examined. Studies that cover much longer follow-up periods in offender careers are needed. Furthermore, cohort studies in the future should collect detailed data on the extent of various correctional interventions among the general youth population and among high-risk youths. These studies have implicitly assumed that criminal misconduct is somehow independent from the social response to that behavior (but see Lemert, 1951).

Investments that have already been made in specifying the causes and correlates of criminal behavior must be expanded to include data collection on the impact of societal interventions on criminal careers. Previous longitudinal research has delivered important, albeit largely ignored, insights on effective prevention strategies. This situation can be remedied by enhancing the existing longitudinal research to gather data on the experiences of participants in these studies in the child welfare system, child protective services, mental health, and other social programs.

Improvements in the design and methods of studies need to be made. There is an obvious need to use stronger experimental designs to assess the relative effectiveness of different institutional correctional programs for different types of youths. Another pressing research priority is more sophisticated use of self-report data in correctional evaluations. Data on desistance and continuity in criminal behavior are woefully inadequate. Not surprisingly, Sampson and Laub (1993a) needed to use Sheldon and Eleanor Glueck's *data from the 1930s* to examine the transition from juvenile crime to adult criminal careers. Studies are needed that examine the effects of criminogenic environments to which youths return to upon their release from custody. Existing longitudinal studies in Denver, Rochester, Pittsburgh, and Seattle should be enhanced to follow youths into adulthood to examine the impact of confinement on criminal careers.

More fundamentally, the policy and practitioner communities need to work with researchers to establish standard measures of success and failure. Justice system administrators and researchers also need to work together to develop standards to assess the performance of a wide range of interventions. Good public policy choices cannot be made if misleading, and often meaningless, data are offered as proof that one or another program is "working." Objective evaluations must be routinized in the operations of justice system agencies. The necessary information and data systems should be integrated in correctional programs to permit accurate comparisons of different programs and policies.

Current work by OJJDP in the area of performance-based standards for juvenile corrections is an excellent start toward improving measurement of successful programming. Ideally, these performance-based standards would be derived from rigorous research and would be tested to determine the levels of compliance that improve longer-term outcomes for youths passing through correctional programs. These studies should inform policy on areas of needed cost savings and streamlining, as well as programmatic areas in which higher levels of service should be delivered. Future research should answer questions about the best mix of services for different offender populations and should provide guidance on the optimum timing, duration, and intensity of justice system interventions.

It is important to remember that several studies document the successes of small-scale programs aimed at SVJ offenders. Research indicates that intensive community-based sanctions are more effective in reducing recidivism than are more restrictive and expensive policies of long-term confinement. Indeed, the effective programs Lipsey and Wilson (Chapter 13, this volume) identify are add-ons to traditional institutional (correctional) and noninstitutional (probation and parole) juvenile justice system components. In addition to numerous programs Lip-

sey and Wilson identify, more of the promising approaches for serious, violent, and chronic juvenile offenders are identified in Howell, Krisberg, Hawkins, and Wilson (1995) and Montgomery et al. (1994).

OJJDP is presently helping a large number of communities apply best practices in local and state juvenile justice systems by implementing the Comprehensive Strategy. The progress of these field tests needs to be carefully monitored and evaluated. It remains to be seen whether the juvenile justice system, particularly juvenile corrections, can improve fundamentally practices that lack precision (e.g., risk assessment) and put to good use available knowledge summarized in this volume. The latter challenge means achieving a much better match between offender risks and needs and effective programs. Although this volume moves the field a step closer to specifying what works best for whom under which conditions, much remains to be learned.

CHAPTER 15

Intermediate Sanctions and Community Treatment for Serious and Violent Juvenile Offenders

■ *David M. Altschuler*

This chapter reviews intermediate sanctions and different forms of community treatment for serious and violent juvenile (SVJ) offenders. Various intermediate sanctions such as electronic monitoring, house arrest, home detention, drug and alcohol testing, community tracking, intensive supervision, boot camps, split sentences, day treatment/reporting centers, community service, and restitution are increasingly being used across the country with juvenile offenders as alternatives to (a) institutionalization, (b) routine probation, and (c) routine parole or aftercare. Used as an alternative to institutionalization, intermediate sanctions are typically (though not exclusively) intended for nonviolent, as well as

chronic but still relatively less serious, delinquents who are considered "incarceration bound." For the institution-bound class of offenders, the intent is generally to reserve limited and expensive bed space for others deemed more appropriate, and thus the strategy is one largely designed to address institutional crowding and save money: This is the classic intermediate sanctions as an institutional population control mechanism.

By contrast, intermediate sanctions in juvenile corrections are also used as an alternative to routine probation, where they are conceived as the means to provide greater accountability (punishment if you like), control (through more monitoring) and public safety (achieved through deterrence, treatment, or both). For the probation-bound class of offenders, the fundamental intent of intermediate sanctions is to get at least serious, if not tougher, with juvenile probationers than would ordinarily be possible through routine probation. In a similar vein, the very same intermediate sanctions are increasingly being used as an alternative to traditional juvenile parole and aftercare (the terms *parole* and *aftercare* are used interchangeably), when it is believed it is necessary to offer more accountability, control, and public safety than that routinely available through standard parole.

Juvenile repeat offenders who have committed serious and even violent offenses as well as those at risk of committing such offenses are, in fact, represented to various degrees among those who receive intermediate type sanctions. Juveniles on probation, incarcerated, and on parole display wide variation in terms of the extent and nature of both their criminal record and their risk of recidivism. This chapter is intended to clarify how and in what ways intermediate sanctions can be used with SVJ offenders in each of the three populations, who should be included, and what are some of the major issues that must be addressed from the standpoint of program design, management, cost, implementation, and evaluation.

■ *Background and Context*

It is important to emphasize at the outset that so-called intermediate sanctions are not entirely new to either juvenile or adult corrections. Although some of the sanctions such as electronic monitoring (Baumer & Mendelsohn, 1992; Vaughn, 1991) and boot camps—also known as shock incarceration—(MacKenzie & Parent, 1992) came on board in the mid-1980s and are of relatively recent vintage, intensive supervision programs (ISPs) for adult

offenders actually go back to the 1960s (Armstrong, 1991; Clear & Hardyman, 1990; Lurigio & Petersilia, 1992; Morris & Tonry, 1990). Intensive probation supervision programs for adult and juvenile offenders have been around the longest and are one of the most popular intermediate sanctions, though no one has to be reminded that correctional boot camps have caught on like wildfire in both the juvenile and adult corrections systems (Cowles & Castellano, 1995; MacKenzie & Hebert, 1996; Thomas et al., 1996). It should also be noted that various intermediate sanctions are often combined in practice so, for example, intensive supervision may use some electronic monitoring and community service. Community tracking programs may incorporate drug and alcohol testing. Moreover, individual programs can include both institution-bound juvenile offenders and those who are candidates for routine probation.

The net effect of mixing different intermediate sanctions and classes of offenders is that intermediate sanction programs not only vary considerably from one to another, but individual programs frequently combine goals that can operate at significant cross-purposes. Intermediate sanction programs designed principally as an institutional population reduction mechanism would obviously want to target for diversion the *likely* institution-bound offenders, not customary probation cases. This is because of the intent of intermediate sanctions to alleviate institutional crowding. By contrast, intermediate sanction programs designed principally as enhancements to probation would want to target those customary probation cases exhibiting the highest risk potential for public safety, but not institution-bound offenders. This is because of the intent to provide more public safety than does traditional probation. To the extent that intermediate sanction programs attempt to achieve both aims, it can be much more difficult to accomplish either one optimally. For example, intermediate sanctions emphasizing electronic monitoring, drug testing, and intensive supervision—some of the staples of surveillance-oriented intermediate sanctions—constitute a terrible waste of resources when applied to lower-risk offenders. Yet many of the intermediate sanction programs are being used for the "easier, less risky, or safe" type offenders (Austin & Krisberg, 1982; Clear & Byrne, 1992; Erwin, 1987; Pearson, 1988). The problem, however, is when low-risk offenders on enhanced probation end up incarcerated only on the basis of technical violations, and as a result, institutional crowding problems are exacerbated. Clear and Byrne (1992) suggest that a plausible solution involves disentangling each intermediate sanction with respect to the aims it can best serve.

There is no doubt that both juvenile and adult corrections are witnessing an enormous expansion in both the numbers of offenders under their jurisdiction and the use of intermediate sanctions. These two developments are obviously not unrelated as correction systems increasingly scramble to somehow meet the population onslaught. Perhaps less obvious is that at least some of the approaches being used may well be contributing to the population explosion itself. For example, when intensive probation supervision is the intermediate sanction used as the means to alleviate institutional crowding, it obviously places a greater burden on the probation system itself. Bulging offender populations, of which institutional crowding is one symptom, has not skipped probation. The number of juvenile cases placed on probation, both formal and informal, increased 21%, from 428,500 in 1989 to 520,600 in 1993 (Torbet, 1996).

According to Torbet (1996), beyond providing probation to these half-million cases, probation departments also screened most of the nearly 1.5 million delinquency cases handled by juvenile courts in 1993, made detention decisions on some, prepared investigation reports on most, and delivered aftercare services to many of the juveniles released from institutions. Probation has and continues to be the overwhelming sanction of choice for the nation's juvenile courts, where 56% of all cases adjudicated for a delinquency offense received probation, 28% were placed in some type of residential facility, and 12% received some other disposition (e.g., restitution). Whereas most cases (54%) placed on formal probation in 1993 involved juveniles adjudicated for property offenses, probation officers are finding more violent youth on their caseloads. Indeed, it is among cases involving person offenses (homicide, rape, robbery, assault, kidnaping, etc.) that reflect the largest percentage increase (45%) since 1989. It is likely that the push to alleviate institutional crowding along with increases in the amount and type of juvenile crime coming to the juvenile court is resulting in the sentencing of more serious offenders to probation. As probation receives more cases overall and more serious cases in particular, the obvious question is its capability and capacity to provide in addition to traditional probation supervision and its other duties, intermediate sanctions that serve both as alternatives to institutional confinement and enhanced probation.

In many respects, intermediate sanctions pose similar challenges and opportunities for juvenile aftercare as they do for probation. In fact, innovation and experimentation in intensive aftercare—though still in its infancy—has substantially drawn from the earlier experiences and lessons of intermediate sanctions used with adults and juvenile probationers (Altschuler & Armstrong, 1991; Armstrong, 1991). There are some notable organizational and structural differences, however (Hurst & Torbet, 1993). Whereas probation is administered at the county level or a combination[1] of the counties and state government in 40 states, predominantly under the judiciary, juvenile aftercare services are predominantly provided by the same state executive department that oversees the state juvenile correctional facilities. The authority for the administration of state institutions for juveniles rests with the executive branch of state government in all 50 states, mostly within a social service agency (22 states and the District of Columbia) followed by a corrections department or a separate youth services department (11 states).

Because the authority over state juvenile correctional facilities and aftercare predominantly rests with state government (in contrast to probation), discussions regarding the use of intermediate sanctions as an alternative to routine parole (i.e., intensive aftercare) most always broach concerns over how to handle the transition from a state-run correctional facility back to the home community. The transition issues can become quite complex because frequently authority over the case can simultaneously involve parole, the local judiciary, state corrections, and sometimes additional review boards. Not infrequently, fundamental disagreements erupt over what constitutes the appropriate balance between accountability, rehabilitation/treatment, and public safety. Although it is easy in the abstract to call for a balanced approach (Maloney, Romig, & Armstrong, 1988), it is quite another matter in actual practice to provide an acceptable balance among all goals.

Intermediate sanctions involving probation, whether at its front end as an alternative to routine probation or its back end as an alternative to institutionalization, are certainly not immune to the conflict over the use of intermediate sanctions as punishment versus intermediate sanctions as intensified treatment, service provision, and support. Quite to the contrary, this issue has permeated the whole debate over the proper use of intermediate sanctions overall and its implications

for what types of offenders, services, staff, workload, policies, and procedures are required (Armstrong, 1991; Byrne & Pattavina, 1992; Clear, 1991; Lurigio & Petersilia, 1992; Petersilia, 1987; Petersilia, Lurigio, & Byrne, 1992).

■ Research Findings on Intermediate Sanctions

Byrne and Pattavina (1992) reviewed the basic findings about recidivism, cost-effectiveness, and diversionary impact from 18 evaluations of intermediate sanction programs for adult offenders as of 1989. They found that the majority of the evaluations did not show intensive supervision significantly reducing the risk of offender recidivism. Speculating on why, Byrne and Pattavina suggested that the day-to-day emphasis of the programs was more on offender surveillance and control (e.g., drug and alcohol testing, electronic monitoring, curfew checks, strict revocation policies) and less on treatment and services related to substance abuse, employment, and family problems. That intensive supervision did not generally reduce recidivism in their review of 18 studies as well as most other studies (see, e.g., Banks, Porter, Rardin, Silver, & Unger, 1977; Byrne & Kelly, 1989; Byrne, Lurigio, & Baird, 1989; Neithercutt & Gottfredson, 1973; Petersilia, 1987; Petersilia & Turner, 1990; Petersilia, Turner, & Deschenes, 1992) prompts Byrne and Pattavina to suggest that perhaps surveillance and control *accompanied* by treatment might make the difference.

The call for intensified treatment to accompany intensive supervision has many proponents, but it remains abundantly clear that in practice most intermediate sanction programs—even those for juveniles—are first and foremost, surveillance and control oriented. Even juvenile intensive probation programs, which at least in theory, emerge from a model in which counseling and rehabilitation are at least on an equal footing with control and punishment, succumb to surveillance-oriented intermediate sanctions (Armstrong, 1991). In a 1986 survey of 157 juvenile probation departments throughout the United States, more than one third reported providing a juvenile intensive probation supervision (JIPS) component, and of those with JIPS, 78% stated their primary goal was intensifying the level of surveillance (Armstrong, 1988). This is hardly surprising and is consistent with Byrne et al.'s (1989) observation that intensive probation supervision "is quite compatible with broad changes in correctional policies that emphasize community protection over offender rehabilitation" (p. 8). Lurigio and Petersilia (1992, pp. 9-10) sum it up by acknowledging that most intensive probation supervision models advocate control and that "in essence, [intensive probation supervision] has become a way for probation administration to combat long-standing negative perceptions, to restore public and judicial confidence in probation as a meaningful and 'tough' sentence, and to 'revitalize probation, establishing it again as a powerful cog in the machinery of justice' " (Clear & Hardyman, 1990, p. 47).

As noted above, introducing intermediate sanctions into a juvenile aftercare context takes the form of using intensive aftercare as an alternative to routine aftercare. One substantial difference with probation is that only a minority of probationers are returning directly from a correctional facility, whereas all parolees have been incarcerated and thus parole has the added responsibility and formidable challenge of bridging the gap between the institution and the community, as well as easing the transition. Integrating and coordinating institutional and parole services directly affects how two very distinct parts of the juvenile justice system operate (i.e, institutions and parole), neither of which has been particularly open to change (Altschuler & Armstrong, 1995). Even when institutions and parole are lodged within the same agency, the culture and orientation of each are often fundamentally at odds. In short, intensive aftercare has as many major implications for the way institutions operate and function as it does for parole. Institutional and community corrections can literally be worlds apart, a formidable challenge for intensive aftercare.

As earlier chapters (Lipsey and Derzon, Chapter 6; Hawkins et al., Chapter 7, this volume) make clear, risk and protective factors associated with SVJ offenders include much more than criminal history characteristics (e.g., early age of onset, number of prior referrals to juvenile services, number of prior commitments to juvenile facilities) alone. Rather, it is the combination of justice system contact factors and particular problem/need factors—so-called criminogenic (Andrews & Bonta, 1994) or instability (Krisberg, Rodriguez, Bakke, Neuenfeldt, & Steele, 1989) factors—that cumulatively place a juvenile into a high-risk category. It is not the presence of one factor but the potent combination of several that seems to make the difference. Among the several risk/need factors that are commonly included in the potent combination are those involving family functioning, participation in school and/or work, nature of peer group, and drugs. Consequently, it seems logical to pose one central question: To what extent and how do intermediate type sanctions address the *combination of factors* (i.e., risk and protective) commonly found to predict SVJ offending?

First, it is obvious that punishment and surveillance alone are not intended to address, at least directly, the risk/need factors. Rather, the aim is "that [intensive probation supervision]—its case monitoring, coupled with threats of detection and subsequent incarceration—will influence the crime-related choices by individuals participating in the program" (Lurigio & Petersilia, 1992, p. 9). But the research to date on intermediate supervision strongly suggests that the predominantly surveillance-oriented intermediate sanctions that have been employed are, on the whole, not producing lower recidivism. This finding is certainly consistent with the view that when intermediate sanctions reflect the classic deterrence strategy, they are largely not succeeding. To be sure, as Lurigio and Petersilia (1992) remind us, the close supervision, increased probability of detection, and swift revocation are regarded by some as an incentive for participants to be employed, go to school, attend counseling, and perhaps be rehabilitated, but intensive probation supervision is not counting on rehabilitation and treatment to ensure public safety, and as already suggested, the surveillance orientation has generally edged out concerns over treatment and rehabilitation.

Byrne and Pattavina (1992) have speculated that it is the combination of treatment, surveillance, and control that can produce lower recidivism. As evidence for this, they point to the evaluation of the Massachusetts Intensive Probation Supervision program (Byrne & Kelly, 1989), where surveillance (i.e., contacts) and more intensive treatment provision (i.e., changes in employment, substance abuse, and marital/family problems) best predicted success. But the questions remain: Is it possible, in practice, to combine punishment with treatment and how might this be accomplished? On a practical basis, is it even possible to differentiate clearly between intermediate sanctions that serve punishment purposes and those that are predominantly treatment oriented? Clear (1991) proposes an interesting test to differentiate intermediate sanctions on the basis of their punishment and treatment orientation:

Even if we knew beforehand that restitution (or community service, for that matter) would not change a particular juvenile's attitude, we would still impose the intervention. The reasoning would be something like this: "Just because the kid's attitude is bad doesn't mean that he can avoid paying back the victim or the community. He has to pay that price because his actions deserve it." The underlying rationale is clearly punitive, although we are pleased that in many instances the imposition of such punishment seems to have a remarkably ameliorative effect on juvenile attitudes. *Yet even without the ameliorative effect, we would feel justified in imposing these sanctions because they demonstrate the unacceptableness of the behavior.* (p. 39, emphasis added)

In contrast, it is hard to imagine that treatment and various rehabilitation components, such as family therapy, job placement, educational remediation, drug counseling, anger management, conflict resolution, and social skills training, would be imposed only because some delinquent action warranted it; rather, a positive rehabilitative outcome is quite explicitly being sought.

The point is that punitive interventions and sanctions *need not* demonstrate an ameliorative effect to justify their use, but treatment and rehabilitation *are expected* to demonstrate success to justify their use. The result is that it is common for punishment to be accepted for punishment's sake and it requires neither further justification nor an independent demonstration of success, whereas treatment is held to an entirely different standard. But what about the feasibility of an intermediate sanction system in which punishment through intensive surveillance coexists with enhanced treatment provision: Can it be implemented, and what outcomes are possible? After all, punishment and treatment goals have been traditionally pitted against each other and viewed as thoroughly inconsistent and incompatible. But if, as some claim, intermediate sanctions provide in concept a means by which punishment—expressed through intensive surveillance and control—can be reasonably balanced and reconciled with treatment and rehabilitation, the question remains as to whether it is possible, in practice, to implement such a balance.

Intensive Aftercare

A number of recent studies specifically on intensive aftercare are instructive. RAND conducted a 4-year evaluation of two experimental intensive aftercare programs, one in Michigan and the other in Pennsylvania (Greenwood, Deschenes, & Adams, 1993). In one of the programs, the average age at first arrest was 14.4 and the participants averaged 2.5 prior arrests. Over half of the participants were known to be drug dealers, nearly half had a drug use problem, and the current offense of just over half was a crime against persons. In the other program, the average age of first arrest was 14 and the participants averaged 4.6 prior arrests and 3.7 adjudications. Their current offense was most frequently a property crime. The study found no difference between experimental and control groups in the proportion of youth arrested, self-reporting offenses, or drug use during a 12-month follow-up period. Equally important, compared to the controls, youth in the experimental programs did not participate any more frequently in educational or work activities. Also, most of the families viewed delinquency as the youth's problem to deal with and were not interested in making major changes, and in neither of the two sites did the aftercare program have a significant effect on the youth's associations with delinquent peers. In the one program that did not use early release, there were no apparent cost savings in residential placement costs, and the aftercare program resulted in an overall

increase in cost per placement. In the other program, the reduced time in residential placement produced a slight reduction in total placement costs.

It could well be argued that because there was not an impact on participation in school and work, family involvement, and delinquent peer associations, there is in fact very little reason to expect lowered recidivism. Greenwood et al. (1993) concluded that a number of factors could explain what happened: (a) Aftercare workers provided only general support and assistance, rather than targeting specific problems that were contributing to risk; (b) aftercare workers devoted less attention to programming that addressed risk factors more directly related to delinquent behavior, such as substance abuse treatment and anger management; (c) inappropriateness of a surveillance/casework model, particularly when faced with the kind of problems and temptations encountered by the youth in their home communities; and (d) the need for more formal methods of ongoing needs and progress assessments, including drug testing, reports by third parties, or tests of specific skills.

In another experimental design study, Sontheimer and Goodstein (1993) found that compared to traditional aftercare in Philadelphia, intensive aftercare reduced the average number of rearrests, but not the percentage of persons rearrested. They concluded that although the program did not turn youths away from their propensity to commit crime, it appears to have prevented youths in the community from incurring multiple arrests. The mean number of annualized rearrests was less for the experimental group (1.65 vs. 2.79), as was the mean number of felony arrests (0.41 vs. 0.76). To be eligible for the program, the incarcerated juveniles had to have at least one prior adjudication for aggravated assault, rape, involuntary deviate sexual intercourse, arson, robbery, or a felony-level narcotics offense, or at least two prior adjudications for burglary.

Sontheimer and Goodstein (1993) propose two models or mechanisms through which recidivistic behavior might be reduced by intensive aftercare. There is the "aftercare effect" model, whereby close surveillance deters crime commission and rehabilitation prompts behavioral change. Collectively, according to Sontheimer and Goodstein, specific deterrence and rehabilitation would produce an actual change in the propensity to commit crime, and this aftercare effect would be apparent in a lower percentage of persons rearrested. In contrast, the "system response effect" model does not assume reduced propensity to criminality, but rather an officer's quick response (e.g., house arrest, court review) to a violation or relapse would serve to reduce the number of offenses a juvenile would have the opportunity to commit.

Although study data support a system response effect using the researchers' own decision rules, Sontheimer and Goodstein (1993) reject the idea that intensive aftercare officers merely revoke all intensive aftercare offenders after the first arrest subsequent to release and do away with service delivery. They believe that the reduced number of offenses committed by the experimental group can be attributed to both the increased knowledge of each case gained by the supervising officer and the officers' ability to devote considerable attention to each case. The question remains, however, why the program—much like the two programs studied by RAND—did not reduce the propensity to reoffend.

One possibility can be gleaned from the finding that the average number of reported *contacts completed* fell substantially short of the minimum number mandated, leading the researchers to comment that this situation raised serious questions about program implementation. In fact, the reason for the low contact rates was that during a 2-month period

the six-person intensive aftercare team experienced complete turnover, and as a result, many of the participants had no supervising officers for extended periods. Moreover, this astounding turnover problem and the difficulties likely to have both preceded and followed it must have created enormous programmatic turmoil and confusion, including questionable commitment from staff, and at best, uneven staff training and accountability. In fact, aftercare staff reportedly received few guidelines about the philosophy or mission of the program (Sontheimer & Goodstein, 1993):

> The program was not defined, for example, as emphasizing a social control or rehabilitative perspective. No effort was made to articulate whether the emphasis of the program would be on enhancing family ties and prosocial relationships, on facilitating educational or vocational growth, on increasing probationers' perceptions of accountability through surveillance, or on some other combination of principles assumed to reduce criminality. (p. 204)

Supervising officers were simply given the contact requirements and they followed a fairly traditional casework approach. Indeed, it is hard to imagine how the program could not have faltered under such circumstances.

The experience in Philadelphia draws particular attention to the philosophical and programmatic thrust of the program; the type of services provided; and the allegiance, commitment, and orientation of staff. It is no wonder that recidivism has been so difficult to affect. Part of the problem is the tendency for ISPs to function much more as surveillance enhancement than treatment enhancement. It has also been shown that the traditional probation/parole casework model is not oriented toward the direct immersion into the family, peer group, daily routine, and neighborhood spanning weekends and all hours.

It has, unfortunately, not been uncommon for programs that have attempted to transition juvenile offenders from various forms of residential placement into community aftercare to encounter difficulties in providing the very treatment services in the community that are deemed so critical in breaking the cycle of recidivism. It is this fact that is often cited to explain why gains made in various residential programs tend to dissipate. For example, a RAND study (Deschenes, Greenwood, & Marshall, 1996) of a Michigan program designed to test the impact of 3 months of wilderness challenge followed by 9 months of intensive community-based aftercare found that alternative program participants received formal substance abuse treatment only during the residential phase. Deschenes et al. also found that compared to juveniles in traditional residential placements, apparently less family counseling took place in the alternative program. Over time, moreover, families of youths in both the experimental and comparison groups showed a general decline in family functioning.

There also was a substantial problem encountered by the alternative program in successfully retaining participants during the first 12 months (including residential and community phases). A staggering 60% of youth in the alternative program were either transferred or placed in another custodial program during the first year, and an additional 10% were rearrested during the second 12 months of the total 24-month study period. By contrast, the traditional residential program participants that comprised the comparison group exhibited a 16% unsuccessful completion rate (where length of stay averaged 15.5 months) and a 14% rearrest rate during the remaining months in the 24-month study period. The RAND analysis suggests that the main weakness in the alternative program was related to the community phase, which of course, is the ultimate test of any sanction or disposition. During that phase, the traditional residential program participants were rearrested at about the same rate. The researchers concluded that regardless of the intervention, youths who were released back into the same environment faced the same difficulties with readjusting to the community setting without relapse. They recommend strengthening the community phase, particularly with reference to substance abuse treatment, family functioning, and targeting younger juveniles.

As has been shown, issues regarding the inadequacy of the service model and orientation of the program along with the quality and fidelity of the implementation are never far removed from evaluations attempting to explain the "no difference on recidivism" finding. The reason is that many of the individual evaluations of alternative programs have not consistently found that recidivism is less when compared to some traditional or routine sanction. The research response has taken several distinct directions. More and more research is looking at the extent, nature, and quality of the implementation, as well as the conceptual logic linking a program's orientation with the desired outcome (Fagan, 1990b). Some research is sorting out which type of offender is succeeding and under what circumstances in individual programs (Palmer, 1992). Other researchers are using meta-analysis to see if patterns may be detected from looking at groups of studies that meet certain criteria and standards (see Lipsey and Wilson, this volume). Still others are employing cost-benefit analysis to understand more fully how one approach or method compares to another on a variety of possible impacts including multiple measures of recidivism; behavioral, psychological, and cognitive changes; institutional population projections and crowding; and the public's perceptions about crime, safety, and justice (Greenwood, Model, Rydell, & Chiesa, 1996).

Alternatives to Commitment

Barton and Butts (1990) evaluated three in-home ISPs that served as alternatives to state commitment for adjudicated delinquents in Wayne County (Detroit) Michigan. Over two thirds of the youths in the study sample had been on regular probation prior to the evaluation, averaging 3.2 prior delinquency charges, with nearly one fourth having five or more priors. Although the emphasis, range, and intensity of services varied among the three programs, on all counts they exceeded what would be expected from routine probation. However, comparing the randomly assigned in-home program youth with others committed to the state, the researchers found no substantial differences in terms of official and self-reported recidivism (controlling both for seriousness of the offense and amount of time in the community over the 2-year study period), family relationships, school participation, attachment and performance, conventional and deviant values, self-concept, and aspirations. Concluding that after 2 years it seemed to make little difference whether commitment-bound youths were diverted into community-based programs or were committed and incarcerated as intended, Barton and Butts argue that at about one third the cost, the in-home programs were able to achieve case outcomes at least no worse than those of commitment. At the same time, they acknowledge that the primary cost is a marginal loss of incapacitation, in which despite the equivalence of recidivism, the in-home program youth have more opportunity to commit new offenses immediately following their assignment to the programs. Barton and Butts concluded that the bottom-line policy question is how effective

intermediate sanctions have to be for cost advantages and rehabilitative potential to outweigh the short-term public safety benefit of taking some young offenders off the streets for a time.

The question remains, however, as to whether the lack of differential outcome may be a consequence of poorly conceptualized program designs, inadequate client targeting, incompetent management, or flawed implementation. Little is reported about these aspects of the three programs, and unfortunately, all the outcome data are reported for participants in all three programs combined. Combining outcome data is problematic because the three programs differed in service emphasis. One focused primarily on monitoring school attendance and court-ordered counseling, another emphasized job training and preparedness as well as educational and recreational activities, and the third adopted a therapeutic approach stressing youth and family counseling. Is it possible that the program might have produced superior results if more of an effort had been made to match up juveniles whose risks and needs corresponded most directly with the orientation of each of the programs? Is it also possible that more flexible service provision in the programs might have made a difference?

One study that attempted to sort out the effects of implementation integrity on outcome was an experimental evaluation of the federally funded Violent Juvenile Offender (VJO) program (Fagan, 1990b). Eligible youth were assigned randomly to experimental programs, which were initially small secure facilities followed by transitional residential programs and intensive supervision in the community. Participants were selected after adjudication for a Part I offense felony *and* had a prior adjudication for at least one other designated "major" felony. The intervention model incorporated case management procedures, multiphased programming, and community reintegration strategies. Four sites were involved in the study, and each was ranked on the extent to which it adhered to the intervention model. The well-implemented programs (two of the four sites) demonstrated significant reductions in the number and severity of arrests for experimental youths, as well as in significantly greater time until rearrest. The researchers report that it was complications in establishing the program elements that produced the weak implementation in the two other sites.

What is becoming more and more evident is that reducing the number of clients on a caseload, increasing the frequency of contact, and expanding the surveillance, monitoring arsenal is not likely to produce superior results unless and until the traditional, "business as usual" probation/parole casework model is reformed within both a corrections system and community context. Although evidence on intermediate sanctions points to the potential for cost savings without increasing the risk to public safety, it still must be asked what it would take to achieve superior results through various intermediate sanctions. What would probation/parole reform within a corrections system and community context look like? What changes would be needed, and are they possible?

Boot Camps

Here again existing research is instructive, though by no means definitive. Based on an eight-state evaluation of adult shock incarceration programs funded by the National Institute of Justice, MacKenzie and Souryal (1994) speculate that devoting a considerable amount of time to rehabilitation and treatment-oriented programming (e.g., education, employment, substance abuse, problem-solving/decision-making skills) followed up by intensive supervision and continued educa-

tional, employment, and treatment opportunities may explain why participants in particular programs did better than comparison cases on at least some measures of recidivism. Although other factors might influence effectiveness, including the length of the program, whether or not participation is voluntary, and the extent of boot camp dropouts and washouts, MacKenzie and Souryal (1994) concluded that "if success is measured in terms of recidivism alone, there is little evidence that the in-prison phase of boot camp programs have been successful" (p. 30). Unfortunately, however, because individual-level data were not available on supervision intensity in several of the sites and the comparison groups were not intensively supervised, it was not possible for the study to disentangle the effects of intensive community supervision from the in-prison boot camp phase. Still, the researchers point out, if the boot camp phase alone had an impact on participants, one would anticipate that they would have lower recidivism rates than their comparison groups, but this did not occur. In fact, in several of the sites the boot camp graduates did worse (i.e., had more technical revocations) than prison parolees.

In an Office of Juvenile Justice and Delinquency Prevention-funded demonstration initiative, three juvenile boot camps were developed, implemented, and evaluated using an experimental design (Peters, Albright, et al., 1996; Peters, Bulman, et al., 1996; Peterson, 1996; Thomas et al., 1996). The boot camps were located in Cleveland, Ohio; Denver, Colorado; and Mobile, Alabama, and focused on adjudicated, nonviolent offenders under the age of 18. The programs were designed as highly structured, 3-month residential programs followed by 6 to 9 months of community aftercare. All three programs experienced considerable difficulty in their aftercare component, both in terms of the transition into aftercare from the boot camp and the linkage between aftercare operations and the local community. In none of the boot camps did graduates exhibit less recidivism than the control group, and in one site boot camp graduates did worse. The evaluation points to a number of implications for future boot camp projects, notable among them that more attention be paid *at the outset* to developing the aftercare and transition strategy and to anticipating likely problems and challenges related to procuring critically needed, high-quality support services involving education, employment, and counseling.

As shown, the question concerning the role of treatment and attempts to address various criminogenic factors is commonly addressed in research on intermediate sanctions. It appears that treatment frequently plays a very subsidiary role relative to surveillance and control, and it has been pursued both halfheartedly and unevenly. This is certainly not surprising given the fact that the funding for treatment services is thin, the communities themselves lack adequate resources to deliver essential treatment services, existing treatment programs in communities are minimal, and the capacity of community corrections agencies is low.

Treatment and Intensive Supervision

The dominance of surveillance in adult intensive supervision and parole and, ironically, the potential benefit related to treatment, when available and delivered, were documented in a national demonstration project sponsored by the Bureau of Justice Assistance and evaluated for the National Institute of Justice by RAND using an experimental design (Petersilia & Turner, 1993). The demonstration involved 14 programs in nine states, ran from 1986 to 1991, and involved about 2,000 adult offenders. The study revealed that participation in treatment compo-

nents, although not high in the experimental ISPs (e.g., less than half of the ISP offenders received some counseling during the follow-up period), exceeded that involving the control participants. RAND conducted an analysis of the programs in California and Texas, which indicated a relationship between treatment participation and recidivism. The analysis revealed that higher levels of treatment *participation,* not just referral, were associated with a 10%-20% reduction in recidivism. Importantly, however, it was not possible to determine whether the lower recidivism was attributable to the treatment or the type of offender in treatment, because offenders were not randomly assigned to receive treatment. Still, as Petersilia and Turner point out, the results are consistent with literature indicating the positive outcomes of treatment.

The RAND study of ISP certainly raises the question of whether more resources devoted to treatment and rehabilitation would prompt higher levels of participation in treatment and, equally important, whether high levels of participation in rehabilitation services would produce even better outcomes. As already shown, resource-strapped communities and traditional casework-oriented community corrections have produced intermediate sanction programs in which the level and type of treatment actually provided has fallen considerably short of what many would expect from intermediate sanctions *in a community treatment context.* Because in general there has been more surveillance than treatment in intermediate sanctions to date and the outcomes have generally not shown that predominantly surveillance-oriented intermediate sanctions are producing superior results, it seems reasonable to ask two questions: (a) What is known about the extent and type of treatment that could be more fully incorporated into intermediate sanctions? and (b) what policy and operational changes would be needed to ensure that such treatment would be available and actually delivered in the community?

■ *Treatment and Service Provision in a Risk-Based Context*

Earlier chapters (Lipsey and Derzon, Chapter 6; Hawkins et al., Chapter 7, this volume) have shown that SVJ offenders, as a group, tend to exhibit a variety of risk factors that when accumulated over time, produced an increased likelihood for antisocial and offending behavior. The four domains that seem to consistently emerge include family, peers, school, and community. Although it is obviously critical to know the domains that require attention and intervention, more specific information is still required to understand what kind of strategy and programs are most likely to reduce individual offending and protect the public. The Lipsey and Wilson analysis (Chapter 13, this volume) is instructive in this regard because it points to certain types of treatment that show promise in lowering recidivism *when compared* to customary or more traditional and routine forms of sanctioning. Most notable among those types of interventions for *noninstitutionalized* juveniles that produced the greatest reduction in recidivism was the grouping of evaluated programs that included interpersonal skill training (Chandler, 1973; Delinquency Research Group, 1986), behavioral contracting (Barton, Alexander, Waldron, Turner, & Warburton, 1985; Gordon, Graves, & Arbuthnot, 1987; Jessness, Allison, McCormic, Wedge, & Young, 1975; Kantrowitz, 1980; Schwitzgebel & Kolb, 1964), and individualized counseling that is cognitive-behavioral oriented (Bean, 1988; Borduin, Henggeler, Blaske, & Stein, 1990; Kemp & Lee, 1975; Lee & Haynes, 1978a, 1978b; Lee & Olejnik, 1981; Moore, 1987; Moore & Levine, 1974;

Piercy & Lee, 1976). It is the noninstitutional community treatment settings where enhanced probation, intensive aftercare, and institution diversion cases are likely to be placed, and thus it is Lipsey and Wilson's noninstitutional category that initially seems most relevant for providing guidance on an appropriate intermediate sanctioning strategy.

Common to the types of treatment that displayed the most positive results was their highly structured and focused emphasis around the development of basic social skills; behavior-specific management through contingency contracting; and individual counseling in which conduct, attitudes, and perceptions are confronted and addressed in an ongoing way. The treatments mostly involved highly trained staff (including some volunteers) who largely maintained a sharp focus on skills, conduct, and attitudes relating to a variety of settings and influences, such as family, peers, school, work, and community. It should be noted that the evaluated programs included in the meta-analysis represent only those programmatic efforts that meet certain methodological standards, and consequently the programs have likely been developed and implemented under relatively optimal circumstances with better than average treatment integrity. In fact, among the noninstitutional programs, the more successful programs were those that involved the researcher in the design, planning, and delivery of the treatment. These more successful programs can thus be contrasted with many operational programs in which the researcher is only involved in the evaluation. One implication is that the quality and integrity of program implementation, as well as the competence and quality of the staff, are necessary ingredients in effective programming. This should serve as a caution in thinking that *any* program claiming to provide the identified treatments can expect success.

Lipsey and Wilson (Chapter 13, this volume) also subjected to meta-analysis a variety of institutional programs, but of course, these would not be directly applicable to intermediate sanctions related to enhanced probation and institutional diversion. Enhanced and intensive parole/aftercare is a distinct case, however, because the transition from the institution and the connection of institutional services and culture to aftercare services and supervision are all potentially important aspects of institutional life that may affect success in the community. Several of the more successful programs included in Lipsey and Wilson's institutional meta-analysis focused to varying degrees on community reentry. Moreover, and quite interesting, was the fact that among those types of treatments in institutional settings that produced the greatest reduction in recidivism was the grouping of evaluated programs that included interpersonal skill training (Glick & Goldstein, 1987; Shivrattan, 1988; Spence & Marzillier, 1981), teaching family homes programs (Kirigin, Braukmann, Atwater, & Worl, 1982; Wolf, Phillips, & Fixson, 1974), and cognitive-behavioral approaches (Guerra & Slaby, 1990; Schlicter & Horan, 1981). As already noted, two of these types of treatment were also among those included in the most successful noninstitutional programs. Also included among the most successful type of institutional programs were multimodal approaches (Grunhut, 1955; Kawaguchi, 1975; C. B. Moore, 1978; Seckel & Turner, 1985; Thambidurai, 1980), which were among the treatments offered by the second most effective group of noninstitutional programs.

In short, the overlap of effective treatment types between the institutional and noninstitutional programs would suggest the potential for stronger and more lasting recidivism reduction if effective institutional programs were followed up with quality (noninstitutional) aftercare programs. The overlap of treatment types also suggests that from a treatment modality and programmatic standpoint, aftercare programs and their staff have a sound basis for their being integrated into the institutional setting. The goal would be to establish direct continuity and reinforcement across the institutional and noninstitutional settings. The outstanding research question that must be asked, however, is whether the types of treatment among those found most effective in either institutional or noninstitutional programs could be even more effective and enduring when linked in a full-fledged reintegrative-oriented intervention. It is research that answers this question that will directly address the value of transition and aftercare over and above what has been gained during confinement.

■ Critical Issues in System Reform, Program Design, and Implementation

The research and program literature and the experience of decades of correctional practice have highlighted a number of implications absolutely crucial to the development of sound and workable intermediate sanction policy and day-to-day operations. The implications can be grouped into five basic areas: (a) jurisdictional authority and control, organizational turf, and interagency collaboration; (b) targeted population, assessment, and classification; (c) managing technical violators and devising guidelines on both graduated consequences and incentives; (d) differentiating surveillance and monitoring from treatment provision and service delivery within an overall accountability framework; and (e) staff roles and responsibilities, training, workload, and caseload.

Politics, Bureaucracy, and Structure

Whether the intermediate sanctions are a form of enhanced probation, prison diversion, enhanced parole, or some combination, the complexity and fragmentation of the justice system tend to work against the collaboration and continuity necessary to achieve a multifaceted intensive sanctioning system. If the intent is to develop and fully implement intermediate sanctions, not merely intensive surveillance, then it is likely to require alliances and partnership among departments, organizations, and interests not ordinarily accustomed to cooperating with one another.

As the existing system is presently structured in most states, however, administering and managing juvenile justice poses particularly tough challenges. The division of authority and responsibility is dispersed among state and local levels of government, conflicting bureaucratic and organizational interests, as well as divergent professional orientations. Depending on the state, the key decision makers involved with juvenile justice include judges, prosecutors, state youth corrections agencies, institution staff, parole authorities and community review boards, county government and court service staff, plus other public and private service providers. The sheer size and organizational complexity of the juvenile justice "system" make it exceedingly difficult to achieve basic communication, much less collaboration. Furthermore, the forces that support leaving institutional corrections to function as it always has are well organized, entrenched, and formidable (Miller, 1991).

Pressures and directives affecting juvenile corrections emanate from still other sources, including the public, judiciary, public defenders and private defense attorneys, governors, legislatures and state agencies, career civil servants, unions, private sector contractors and service providers, victims groups, child advocates, and the media. They represent an almost overwhelming collection of vying interests and countervailing forces, many of which by their very nature are adversarial. The net effect is a kind of inherent organizational fragmentation that, if not very consciously, carefully, and properly treated and soothed, can result in chaos, fingerpointing, and scapegoating. Public accountability is often lacking.

It will take strong commitment from the top, policy-making levels of the system along with buy-in and support at both the midlevel manager and line staff levels to offset the long-standing and deep-seated differences among the various stakeholders and interests involved in different parts of the system. One strategy is to establish special interagency teams representing all the parties with decision-making authority and jurisdiction over targeted offenders from the point of first contact with the system all the way to official termination. Vesting such teams with authority and flexible resources to cover the full range of needed services, both surveillance and treatment, can create a powerful incentive for cooperation, mutual support, and a collective interest in seeing that success lies with promoting community protection through offender change. In short, a successful development and implementation effort will likely require strong leadership within the program, coupled with the involvement of key stakeholders both in and outside the program and ties to the wider political and bureaucratic structure within which the program operates.

Target Population and Classification

Explicit criteria specifying the type of offenders eligible to participate in an intermediate sanctions program should be directly related to the ultimate purpose and goals of the program. In the event of multiple goals, understanding how each criterion relates to every goal is important in clarifying any potential inconsistencies or conflicts. Common goals associated with intermediate sanctions include relieving institutional crowding, creating alternatives to incarceration, lowering correctional costs, strengthening or toughening probation/parole, and reducing recidivism. Intermediate sanction programs vary on their eligibility criteria, having accepted a wide range of offenders including those who are violent and nonviolent, serious and minor, chronic and first-timers, probation and parole violators, high and low risk, and high and low need.

Eligibility criteria are relevant to the attainment or displacement of particular goals in several different ways. An example of one of the most obvious ways is where an intermediate sanction program designed principally to relieve institutional crowding draws from an offender pool that is, in fact, prison bound. An example of a less obvious way that eligibility criteria can impede goal attainment is the situation where a relatively low-risk offender is placed into an intermediate sanction as a form of enhanced probation and ends up revocated on the basis of a technical violation. If the enhanced probation is more costly than routine probation and if the revocation results in even lengthier supervision or some form of incarceration for the violator, the intermediate sanction may neither be saving money, reducing the use of more restrictive sanctions, nor promoting public safety.

Assessment and classification *for risk* is only one aspect of eligibility, but its overall significance in the use and abuse of intermediate sanctions looms large for SVJ offenders. Because juveniles who have committed certain felonies are included in the serious offense category (see Loeber and Farrington, Chapter 2, this volume), such juveniles might well be considered eligible for intermediate sanctions, but research suggests that it is by no means clear that these serious type offenders represent a high risk for committing future crimes. Moreover, it is also an open question as to whether such serious type offenders typically are incarcerated and whether they should be. Consequently, the eligibility of such offenders for intermediate sanctions depends on the specific goals and purposes chosen.

Probation/Parole Conditions, Technical Violations, and Graduated Consequences

It is precisely because of the finding that intermediate sanctions are likely to produce a high rate of technical violators (and violations) that it becomes imperative to build into intermediate sanction correctional policy and program design a structured system of both graduated consequences for technical violators and incentives to prevent technical violations from occurring in the first place. It is commonplace for juvenile offenders on probation or parole to be given a variety of conditions, violation of which can result in a revocation of the probation or parole status and a period of incarceration. It is equally commonplace that the conditions are the same for everyone and that it is left to the discretion of the probation officer (PO) to decide on the extent and nature of enforcement.

The problem, as many POs know, is that some of the conditions are unrealistic, largely unenforceable, or highly unlikely to be met (Altschuler & Armstrong, 1994a; Krisberg et al., 1989) and that frequently the violations have no bearing on the likelihood of offenders actually committing additional crimes (Lurigio & Petersilia, 1992; Petersilia & Turner, 1991; Turner & Petersilia, 1992). Classic examples of the problem include violations on the basis of a positive drug test when no drug treatment was made available, and not attending school when the school environment is clearly unsuitable for the youngster and unresponsive to specific educational needs. The result is that with some notable exceptions, POs are left either to ignore some violations or to respond disproportionately to the violation. Either response is obviously counterproductive. It is also important to note that, as rare as graduated sanctions are, recognition of achievement is more so.

Intermediate sanction programs need policy-driven guidelines that specifically address the following: the establishment of realistic and enforceable individualized conditions, a hierarchy of violations that incorporate the risks posed to public safety, a continuum of graduated responses, and a range of incentives used routinely to acknowledge and reward positive behavior. Efforts that begin to go in this direction for adult corrections have been under way for some time by the National Institute of Corrections (Burke, 1997) and are part of the intensive juvenile aftercare demonstration initiative (Altschuler & Armstrong, 1994b).

The Surveillance, Control, and Treatment Nexus

The reviewed research makes clear that there is a fundamental distinction between surveillance and monitoring, on the one hand, and treatment provision and service delivery, on the other. Punishment and immediate risk control form one important part of the justice sanctioning system, but so too does treatment and service delivery focused on the specific risk factors associated with a case. It seems clear that intermediate sanctions that are predominantly punishment and surveillance are insufficient in general in producing lower recidivism, though there is some evidence that as an alternative to incarceration it is possible—under the right circumstances—to real-

ize some cost savings. As discussed, however, the research suggests that when treatment is provided, additional benefits in the form of reduced recidivism may accrue. Although further research is needed, the signs are encouraging and certainly sufficient to justify a large-scale, rigorously tested demonstration initiative. It should be pointed out that general PO contacts, drug and alcohol testing, curfews, electronic monitoring, and at least according to some, community service and restitution are largely punishment and control strategies. This is not to say that they do not have a rehabilitative impact or that they cannot be part of a broad-based sanctioning strategy in which treatment, surveillance, and control were all firmly in place.

Staffing and Workload

Finally, staff roles and responsibilities, training requirements, workload, and caseload size must be given the utmost consideration and attention. The debate on the role of probation and parole agents as case manager versus direct service provider, police officer versus counselor, and tracker/community outreach worker versus traditional, office-based, standard-hours worker is not new, but assumes particularly critical importance for intermediate sanction kinds of programs. The various roles assumed by staff must be carefully and thoughtfully delineated. Intermediate sanctions that are interagency oriented, cross-disciplinary, and multifaceted require openness, creativity, and flexibility. Consequently, job descriptions that carefully specify day-to-day responsibilities and role expectations should be used to establish the criteria on which hiring, retention, and promotions will be based.

Both potential staff and employers must have a clear sense of the rather extreme demands that intermediate sanctions place on the kind of jobs involved and the type of difficulties encountered in the workplace. Therefore, the recruitment, screening, training, and performance review process needs to place emphasis on hiring and retaining individuals who are committed to the goals and approaches that characterize the unique aspects of the intermediate sanction working environment and culture. One problem frequently encountered in selecting qualified and committed staff relates to workplace and staff rules, regulations, and job protection. In some civil service and unionized environments, as well as in procurement and contracting procedures, there can be immutable or excessively rigid rules and policies regarding hiring, job responsibilities, transfer, and firing. However, intermediate sanctions, particularly with their implications for highly coordinated teamwork, require flexibility and accommodation. Operational issues that must be addressed include job classification; lines of authority; use of volunteers, paraprofessionals, and contract workers; performance reviews; and privatization.

It is clear from earlier research that smaller caseloads do not necessarily produce more contacts between POs and clients (see, e.g., Banks et al., 1977) and that increased contacts may have no bearing on either the level or type of treatment actually provided. Thus, intermediate sanction staffing strategies clearly need to consider caseload size, number of contacts, purpose of contacts and services provided, time and place of contacts, and the resulting skills and qualifications that staff will need. It is also imperative that interdisciplinary and interagency teams require a great deal of attention on how members will collectively function, share authority, and provide feedback. Staff qualifications may well vary depending on the role and responsibility of the particular team members. Requirements by way of credentials, training,

experience, and aptitude will likely differ by type of position. Personnel policy must accommodate such differences. Some team members may, in fact, be paraprofessionals or volunteers, and some needed services may be available through contract or agreement with various other public and private agencies. Regardless of the staffing and agency mix, however, the division of labor and sharing of authority must be carefully delineated to avoid confusion, discontinuity, and mixed messages.

■ Conclusion

It would be easy and a misreading of the evidence discussed in this chapter to conclude that it is not possible to craft an implementable intermediate sanction program that addresses directly the risk and protective factors, as well as the surveillance and control requirements, associated with SVJ offenders who are high risk. It does require, however, heeding the lessons learned and insights gained from existing research, analysis, and evaluation. Truly intervening with families, maintaining active participation in education and employment, keeping focus on the peer group, providing drug treatment (not just testing), incorporating various cognitive-behavioral and skill-oriented techniques, and handling all the transitions from facilities to community to facilitate information flow, consistency, and transferability are crucial.

Also critical is having ready access to information on the extent and quality of day-to-day implementation as well as outcome. Some very basic questions concerning implementation, impact, and costs associated with intermediate sanctions remain unanswered. Future research on intermediate sanctions needs to carefully examine these questions, which means that the research should be designed and initiated at the same time that the intermediate sanction program is designed and initiated. As noted, existing research on intermediate sanctions strongly suggests that treatment availability *and* participation are associated with lower recidivism, but three problems in particular have compelled researchers to present a less than definitive response. First, the lack of existing treatment and appropriate services in the community, the frequency with which offenders did not receive the prescribed treatment and services, the paucity of resources allocated specifically for treatment, and the generally subordinate role treatment has played in intermediate sanctions have led to programs exhibiting much less treatment than surveillance. The lack of treatment intensity can refer both to the percentage of offenders left untreated (Petersilia & Turner, 1993) and to the generally low level of treatment provided to those who receive it (Petersilia, Turner, & Deschenes, 1992). Future intermediate sanction programs and research on them would benefit from having risk-based treatment services playing a prominent role in philosophy, design, and implementation. Such risk-based treatment service, as noted in earlier chapters, would be directed toward family, peers, school and/or work, and neighborhood-based social institutions.

Second, the research on intermediate sanction programs has generally suffered from too few participants, so that it becomes exceedingly difficult to generate any statistically significant differences in the analysis. Stated differently, to conclude that one group of offenders has performed better than another, differences are required in small-sample studies that exceed those one might reasonably expect to find. The solution is to launch a large enough effort so that a sufficient number of participants will be assured.

Finally, disentangling the effect of particular program components can be crucial to determining the relative importance of different aspects of intermediate sanctions. The reviewed research was mostly designed to evaluate the effect, for example, of intermediate sanctions *to the extent* that they combined surveillance and treatment, or boot camps *to the extent* they may have included transition and intensive aftercare. It would be useful for future efforts, for example, to test specifically and systematically the impact of differential levels of treatment and surveillance and the effect of boot camps with and without intensive aftercare. Random assignment to surveillance-oriented and treatment-oriented intermediate sanctions or very different kinds of boot camps would represent a move in this direction. It would also be advisable to directly incorporate into future research and program efforts those offenders who are first screened on the basis of risk and then placed randomly into either an experimental intermediate sanction or a regular correctional program. In addition, focusing specifically on strategies designed to prevent and respond to technical violations is another aspect that would benefit from intermediate sanction research and programming.

■ *Note*

1. The combination is usually juvenile court administration in urban counties and a state executive system of probation in smaller counties.

PART III

Concluding Overview

CHAPTER 16

Serious and Violent Juvenile Offenders

Gaps in Knowledge and Research Priorities

■ *Nancy G. Guerra*

One approach to identifying gaps in knowledge about serious and violent juvenile (SVJ) offenders is to focus on "missing information" in the empirical literature. It would be quite easy, in fact, to compile a long list of research questions covering a diverse set of topics. This is an important task that is necessary in recommending future research priorities. However, I propose that future research questions are best viewed through a lens that frames the issues in terms of gaps in our approach to understanding the problem of serious juvenile crime.

In this chapter, I first attempt to provide this lens by identifying and discussing three key points related to how we think about SVJ offending. I propose that a framework for understanding this problem requires (a) a specific focus on SVJ offenders that incorporates issues of definition, heterogeneity, and co-occurrence with other behavior problems; (b) an understanding of the social ecology of serious juvenile crime in terms of the complex interaction between individual, situational, and contextual influences over time; and (c) an awareness of the relevance of research to services, systems, and policies that must include an appreciation of how research can be informed by the daily lives of people who experience or address problems of serious juvenile crime.

The overarching theme of this chapter is that research and practice must be interconnected in a feedback loop that allows each to inform the other. The research endeavor must be collaborative, and the common goal must be to forge an understanding of the dynamics of SVJ offending to formulate promising action strategies and develop responsive policies. Although there are endless possibilities for theoretical contemplation, the ultimate utility of research on social problems lies in its ability to inform practices so as to prevent or reduce the problem at hand.

Because any strategy to ameliorate serious juvenile crime rests on a complete picture of the nature and scope of the problem, gaps in knowledge about patterns and trends in youth crime are reviewed, particularly as this relates to SVJ offenders and available sources of data. Following this, limitations of the currently used risk assessment and classification instruments and methods are examined. Next, gaps in research on the causes and correlates of serious juvenile crime are reviewed, with particular emphasis on the strengths and limitations of a risk-focused approach and alternative models for use with SVJ offenders. Finally, needed research on the efficacy and effectiveness of prevention and intervention strategies is discussed.

Rather than conclude with a laundry list of gaps in research, I attempt to illuminate a set of research priorities and directions for future research that integrates gaps in how we approach the problem of SVJ crime with specific gaps in knowledge related to patterns and trends, prediction, etiology, and intervention. Drawing on relevant literature as well as comments by participants at the Office of Juvenile Justice and Delinquency Prevention (OJJDP) Study Group meetings, specific needs in each area and recommended actions are discussed. These are summarized in Table 16.1. It should be noted that these represent research priorities, and not recommendations for specific programs or services.

■ A Framework for Understanding Serious and Violent Juvenile Offending

Focusing on Serious and Violent Offenders

In Chapter 1 of this volume, Farrington and Loeber provide an overview of the mission of the OJJDP Study Group. They juxtapose what we know about recent trends in youth crime with what we know about etiology and intervention, and they highlight what could be considered a deep chasm. Against a backdrop of steep increases in juvenile violent crime over the past decade and public outcries for solutions, we are faced with an almost "generic" literature on juvenile delinquency that has not, to date, provided clear guidance for understanding serious, violent, and chronic offending. As they state, "It is likely that much of our knowledge about risk/protective factors and prevention/intervention programs does not apply specifically to SVJ juvenile offenders" (p. 6). Herein lies a basic problem in our approach to understanding serious juvenile offending. We must refocus research efforts toward understanding those individuals, events, and settings most connected to the true picture of youth violence and serious/violent offending at this time.

A prime example of this shortcoming can be found in the prevention and intervention literature. In a recent review of programs to prevent or reduce adolescent violence, Tolan and Guerra (1994b) noted the difficulty in finding programs that specifically measured impact on serious violence. In fact, it is common practice for programs to use outcomes such as attitudes about violence or delinquency, responses to hypothetical decision-making scenarios, or minor and age-normative problem behaviors as indexes of effectiveness

TABLE 16.1 Summary of Research Needs and Recommendations

	Need	*Recommendations*
Epidemiology	National data with oversampling in high-risk areas Assess SVJ offending in different age groups	Tie in surveys with existing national studies such as Department of Labor/OJJDP survey
Assessment	Develop assessment tools to predict future risk, guide placements, and assess needs Determine potential cultural biases	Field test instrument development projects that examine cultural influences and include positive features of youth and settings Refine prediction tools to increase accuracy
Causes and correlates	Incorporate qualitative and quantitative data to better understand causes of SVJ offending Focus research on why people stop offending and how individuals adapt to risk Assess situational factors in crime (time, place) Link data on youthful offenders with early adult records	Augment existing quantitative studies with narrative studies Conduct research with individuals and in settings where crime should be high but isn't Create databases that permit examination of youth to adult transitions related to SVJ offending
Prevention and intervention	Determine which programs are appropriate for SVJ offending versus general youth development Use randomized trials when appropriate and specify alternate methods of evaluation Determine optimal implementation and cost-benefits analyses	Conduct studies that match outcome assessments to expected benefits Study impact of different programs on SVJ offending and its developmental precursors Improve evaluation of community-based, local efforts Improve evaluation of multicomponent programs

NOTE: SVJ = serious and violent juvenile.

and to conclude that change in these proximal outcomes indicates that the program "works" as an antiviolence intervention. This is not to imply that changes in attitudes about violence are not an important component of a strategy to prevent or mitigate SVJ offending; however, it is unlikely that these programs alone will have an impact on actual offending.

Of course, there are several reasons why it is difficult to measure program impact vis-à-vis violent or serious delinquent behavior, particularly during the early years before such be-

havior is evident. Nevertheless, several accommodations are warranted both in terms of types of outcomes measured, long-term follow-up, and program impact on youth with the most extreme behavior problems. These issues are carefully examined later in this chapter and are presented at this time to highlight the need to focus efforts on understanding the causes and potential solutions to the problem of SVJ offending.

To begin, redirecting research efforts along these lines first requires some degree of consensus about the operational definition of this categorization as well as relevant subgroupings or classification typologies. In Chapter 2 of this volume, Loeber, Farrington, and Waschbusch underscore the need for unambiguous definitions while highlighting the difficulties inherent in setting some type of cut score or threshold for inclusion. Still, they offer a set of recommendations for distinguishing serious and violent offenders based on predetermined standards regarding type and/or number of offenses. Adopting a common definition would at the very least allow for comparability across studies and uniformity across policies.

It should be noted that adoption of categorical definitions of SVJ offenders and accompanying typologies (e.g., property vs. violent; life course persistent vs. adolescence limited) still results in an offense-based typology. Reporting is based on either official records of the crime an individual is arrested for or self-reported incidents of behavior, with each source of data presenting an incomplete picture of actual behavior (Huizinga, 1991). In addition to being offense based, the resulting categorizations may still be too crude to permit more fine-tuned analyses. Greater specificity may be needed, particularly when moving beyond documentation of patterns and trends toward an understanding of causes, correlates, and effective solutions. For instance, are factors leading to predatory violence such as robbery (when the victim is a stranger) similar to those leading to interpersonal violence (when the victim is an acquaintance, friend, or relative)? If not, should training youth in conflict resolution skills have any impact whatsoever on predatory violence? In any case, it is important to consider carefully the level of specificity needed to address different types of research questions and to refine definitions and classifications accordingly.

A related issue arises from the use of any classification scheme that defines and labels individuals based on commission of an offense. In other words, when the "problem" is labeled as understanding serious and violent "offenders" rather than the dynamics of serious and violent offending, co-occurring behavioral problems and situational and contextual factors that may have contributed greatly to this pattern of offending are easily overlooked. Clearly, there is a sizable literature suggesting that a small group of offenders repeatedly commit a large percentage of serious and violent crimes (see Chapter 2), and it is important to understand how these criminal career patterns develop (Blumstein, Cohen, & Farrington, 1988b; Farrington, 1986; Moffitt, 1993). However, any typology must permit consideration of the range of individual, contextual, and situational influences that affect onset, occurrence, and desistance of SVJ offending.

Understanding the Social Ecology of Crime

Theories of delinquent and criminal behavior range from those that focus largely on individual attributes (e.g., Moffitt, 1993) to others that emphasize situational factors or events (e.g., Felson, 1993), and still others that highlight the role of contextual influences (e.g., Sampson & Laub, 1993a). Regardless of their primary thrust, almost all recent theories of crime and delinquency at least acknowledge the interplay between individual, situational, and contextual factors, suggesting that an understanding of serious juvenile crime requires consideration of the full range of influences on an individual's behavior.

Most frequently, one or several contextual influences are postulated at different points in development. For example, there is a large body of research documenting the role of family factors such as coercive child management practices in the etiology of early aggressive behavior (Patterson, 1982). In developmental studies, this pattern has been shown to generalize from minor oppositional behavior at home to more serious noncompliance at home and in other settings (Patterson, Reid, & Dishion, 1992). Other studies have investigated the influence of peers. Several studies have documented a link between early aggression, rejection by peers, and subsequent escalation of problem behaviors (see Parker & Asher, 1987, for a review). During adolescence, association with antisocial peers rather than peer rejection has been found to be one of the strongest predictors of delinquent behavior (Lipsey and Derzon, Chapter 6, this volume).

Other research has focused on the role of contextual and systemic factors outside the family and peer group. Social, cultural, and economic forces have been implicated in the etiology of antisocial and criminal behavior, particularly as they can account for the higher crime rates among poor, urban minorities (Hammond & Yung, 1991). Several characteristics of distressed urban settings have been linked with crime and violence. For instance, the chronic and persistent poverty that characterizes some inner-city neighborhoods portends multiple stressors that, in turn, have been found to predict future problem behaviors (Guerra, Huesmann, Tolan, VanAcker, & Eron, 1995). In addition to multiple stressors, community-level social disorganization and social isolation, particularly as they affect informal social control and the development of illegitimate social organizations, have been implicated in the learning and escalation of crime and violence (Sampson & Laub, 1993a). Furthermore, the lack of economic opportunities coupled with variations in cultural history and cultural norms may promote involvement with gangs and other illegal acts (Anderson, 1990).

Not only do parents, peers, communities, and culture exert independent influences on children's antisocial behavior, these contexts are also interconnected and overlapping, making the picture even more complex. Children live in families that reside in specific neighborhoods with certain cultural and social opportunities and constraints. Because social contexts overlap, events taking place in one context such as the parent's workplace can affect parent-child interactions and indirectly affect the child, even though he or she has no direct participation in the parent's workplace.

The ecological organization of social contexts makes it difficult to ascertain the myriad potential interactions across contexts as they relate to individual antisocial behavior. In addition to multiple contextual influences, individuals also experience contexts differently. Thus, a simultaneous focus on the person and the context in which development and action occur is necessary to understand SVJ offending in terms of the dynamic interaction between individuals and the settings in which they live.

Such an approach stretches the limits of quantitative methodologies, and may be better served by a strategy that combines comparative longitudinal and ethnographic methods that consider the full range of contextual influences. At the very least, quantitative studies should be augmented by qualitative efforts that provide narrative accounts of how identified risk factors play out in daily life. Furthermore, these studies should incorporate situational and functional factors that contribute to SVJ offending, and describe how these interact with individual and contextual influences.

Relevance of the Research Enterprise to Services, Systems, and Policies Affecting SVJ Offenders

Given the truly lethal consequences of SVJ offending, there is an urgent need for research that is useful for prevention and intervention efforts in the field. A central issue confronting social scientists is the extent to which research simultaneously advances knowledge and informs policy and practice in this area. Toward this goal, researchers must pay attention to a number of issues including (a) the need for research to be informed by the daily lives of children and families, (b) the need for replication of findings, (c) building in sensitivity to the generalizability of findings across cultures and settings, (d) considering practical concerns such as costs and ease of implementation for interventions or system changes, and (e) developing methods of dissemination that are readily understood in the field.

Too often there has been a poor fit between researchers' assumptions about the dynamics of SVJ offending and the perspectives and voices of those who commit such crimes. For example, a primary focus of prevention science is the "systematic study of potential precursors of dysfunction" (Coie et al., 1993). Models such as this equate violence with psychopathology and disorder. Yet field studies using narrative interviews suggest that in some contexts violence may serve a number of practical functions including maintaining status and respect, acquisition of material goods, and management of conflicts (Fagan & Wilkinson, in press). Preventive interventions in these settings that do not acknowledge the functional aspects of violence for some youth will likely be doomed to failure.

In addition to grounding research in the daily lives of participants, it is important to promote replication studies. Policies and practices should not be driven by one or two studies with significant results. Unfortunately, studies that fail to replicate findings are often difficult to publish, particularly in intervention research. Consistent with a need for replication is a need to establish the generalizability of findings across cultures and settings.

Critics have often noted that many basic assumptions about human development and criminal behavior are rooted in research conducted with largely white, middle-class children (Rogoff & Morelli, 1989). More research is needed that carefully examines the role of culture in the etiology and prevention of SVJ offending (Laub & Lauritsen, 1993).

Research on SVJ offenders must be extended to include determinations of real-world feasibility. For example, rather than assessing a panoply of risk factors for SVJ offending, it would be useful to focus on those risk factors that are most readily modifiable. At the very least, it is important to distinguish risk factors useful for identification of populations (e.g., urban, economically disadvantaged), or subgroups of individuals (e.g., males), from risk factors to be targeted by an intervention (e.g., family management practices). Similarly, prevention and intervention studies must consider the extent to which such programs or strategies are easily implemented in the field, as well as associated costs. Field testing programs that are prohibitively costly to implement does not provide useful guidance for service providers. Along these lines, researchers must also incorporate mechanisms for dissemination of findings via user-friendly manuals and materials that can be useful for translating research into practice, and include dissemination plans in research grant applications.

■ Gaps in Research

Patterns and Trends in SVJ Offending

Given a perspective that emphasizes the need to focus on SVJ offenders, to consider offending within a social ecological framework, and to conduct studies that are most relevant for policy and practice, let us now turn to a discussion of current gaps in knowledge about patterns and trends in SVJ offending.

First, it is important to note that available national-level data on SVJ offending are derived primarily from either official records or victimization surveys and generally are not available for youth under age 12. There have been few systematic efforts to collect national data using self-report measures. Yet there are several problems with available data, particularly official records. As Loeber et al. (Chapter 2, this volume) point out, arrest or adjudication records reflect only a small percentage of actual SVJ offending when compared with self-reported offending. Such records are also extremely sensitive to changes in official law enforcement and judicial practices, and they do not provide a window into early delinquent involvement. Local policies for collecting information such as ethnicity (particularly as this relates to nuances in ethnic affiliation and how these are identified) and gang involvement also vary and limit the breadth of information available. Thus, large-scale, self-report surveys that include SVJ offending and that oversample in high-risk communities would be a necessary and much-needed complement to data based on official records. A practical strategy to accomplish this task would be to incorporate relevant questions in compatible survey research studies, such as is currently accomplished by the cofunding by OJJDP of a new Department of Labor study.

Still, although self-report measures have gained popularity as valid measures of delinquent behavior, they are also subject to potential biases in responding and administration (e.g., school-based surveys miss those who are not in school). Because of these limitations, another important step is to continue to develop and validate self-report measures and methods that are best suited to assessing SVJ offending and related characteristics of interest. Research is also needed that examines specific types of response biases and how best to increase accuracy of reporting. For example, some research has shown that compared to white youth, African American youth tend to agree in response to agree-disagree items and to favor the extreme ends of response scales (Bachman & O'Malley, 1984). More generally, there is some evidence of differential underreporting by African American youth (for a review of this and recent self-report of delinquency results, see Farrington, Loeber, Stouthamer-Loeber, Van Kammen, & Schmidt, 1996).

Data that document behavior problems that co-occur with SVJ offending would be particularly useful in determining prevention and intervention strategies. As Huizinga and Jakob-Chien (Chapter 4, this volume) noted, in studies where data are available on co-occurring problems, a significant number of SVJ offenders have been found to experience other problems, particularly school problems. In fact, school problems combined with other problems involve 80% of delinquent youth in some of the samples studied. This is quite important in that it suggests a potential mechanism for identifying at-risk youth in school settings (e.g., those having school problems and additional problems) as well as types of interventions recommended. However, as they note, more data are needed, particularly in terms of the overlap between SVJ offending and other areas of difficulty, such as mental health problems.

Risk Assessment and Classification of SVJ Offending

In Chapter 9 of this volume, Le Blanc reviewed the current state of the art regarding measures and methods of screening for serious, violent, and chronic offenders. He noted,

In summary, much technical work still needs to be done before we can develop appropriate screening instruments for the identification of potential SVJ offenders or the classification of SVJ offenders. Some screening strategies and instruments are promising, but none can be recommended for immediate use to policymakers and practitioners. (p. 193)

As he carefully points out, there are virtually no screening instruments to date that have been designed for and validated with SVJ offenders. Yet because of the widespread use of screening for assignment to prevention and intervention programs across multiple institutions (e.g., schools, juvenile justice), it is imperative that efforts be directed toward the improvement of assessment measures and techniques, particularly as related to SVJ offending. In addition to developing an array of intervention options, well-designed and validated assessment procedures are needed to assess and classify youth to maximize the impact of these interventions.

Risk assessments are used in different settings and for different purposes, and specialized measures must be developed and validated in each setting. At the prevention stage, techniques and strategies have been developed for both community-level assessment for universal, population-based programs and individual-level risk assessment for targeted programs. Known factors at the community level that are associated with higher rates of SVJ offending such as low income, social disorganization, and social isolation have been used to select specific communities for prevention programming. Within communities, strategies such as Communities That Care have been implemented to describe in more detail the specific risk factors at the community, family, and individual level and to document programmatic needs (Hawkins & Catalano, 1992).

It is generally easier to identify community factors that portend high risk than to screen for those individuals who are most likely to become SVJ offenders. The low base rate of SVJ offending makes it difficult to predict accurately future offending, particularly with younger children. Multiple gating methods have been advocated as a cost-effective screening mechanism to identify risk groups. This approach involves beginning with a relatively inexpensive screening (the first gate) for a designated population, followed by a more expensive and sophisticated screening with a pool of individuals identified at the first gate (Loeber, 1990). Such an approach is bolstered by the use of multiple informants and multiple-variable domains.

This procedure is widely used in prevention screening. However, as Le Blanc (Chapter 9, this volume) points out, four practical questions remain that suggest directions for future research: the number of gates to retain, the age at which to screen, the location of screening, and the best predictors to include. The age at which to screen and optimal location will, most likely, depend on the specific focus of the planned intervention or activities. Because of concern over relatively high rates of false positives and false negatives, however, more research is needed to examine various combinations of predictors and gates for children from diverse backgrounds and age groups. More gates and more variables do not necessarily increase prediction accuracy. For example, in one recent child screening study with kindergarten children, Lochman et al. (1995) found that a two-step procedure using teacher and parent behavior ratings effectively predicted negative behavioral outcomes over 1 year later, although an additional parenting practices screening measure did not add to prediction accuracy. Studies such as this provide important information for minimizing intrusiveness and maximizing accuracy of risk-screening procedures. However, the utility of screening measures (particularly for young children) for predicting SVJ offending still must be demonstrated.

Perhaps nowhere is there a more critical need to improve risk assessment and classification practices that affect SVJ offenders than in the juvenile justice system. Structured decision making for placement and services, based on formalized risk assessment tools, is now the norm in state juvenile corrections agencies. Several instruments have been developed that revolve around a core set of risk predictors complemented by different site-specific factors. Although progress has been made in empirical validation of these scales, several problems remain. In particular, because of the low base rates of SVJ offending, it is difficult to predict violent and serious future offending. Rather, scales typically predict general outcomes such as rearrest. Furthermore, although these general outcomes can be reasonably estimated at the aggregate level, a given individual's future behavior is extremely difficult to predict. Because risk factors often include static contextual variables (e.g., neighborhood violence, income level), minority youth from poor urban neighborhoods are likely to score higher on risk, which should also result in higher false positive rates for those groups of juveniles.

Beyond simply assessing likelihood of reoffending, screening instruments are used to predict the need for temporary detention, appropriate placements, custody needs within correctional facilities, and specific types of interventions and services recommended. In most cases, these instruments have been developed by state and local agencies and are typically not based on empirical research. However, the limited number of empirical studies support the utility of continuing to develop reliable and valid measures for all phases of justice system services.

Another area in need of further development concerns the use of assessment to determine appropriate services. Assignment to treatment generally is determined through either a classification system or checklist of individual needs from a needs assessment scale. Ease of implementation has been enhanced by keeping most scales short and simple. However, several limitations to this procedure should be addressed. In particular, most needs assessments focus on broadly defined deficits across multiple domains of functioning, with one or two questions in each domain. It is unlikely that a useful typology presenting a true picture of individual needs can emerge from such assessments. Even more troubling is the fact that such assessments rarely focus on strengths, that is, assets or supports that can be mobilized to promote healthy development. Perhaps a more useful approach would be to compile a developmental profile beginning with earliest justice system contacts that details an individual's specific strengths and weaknesses across multiple domains.

Causes and Correlates of SVJ Offending

A range of methodologies has been employed to examine causes and correlates of offending. Over the past several decades, a multitude of cross-sectional studies have identified and replicated correlates of offending, including those specific to SVJ offending. The causal role of these factors has also been implicated in longitudinal studies that in some cases have relied on relatively short windows of time such as a few years, and in other cases have followed the life course pathways of selected individuals for several decades. Still other studies have tested causality through experimental manipulation via interventions designed to affect proposed antecedent factors.

From this array of studies has come a unifying framework focused on risk factors and protective factors for delinquent behavior (i.e., a risk-focused approach) that has dominated the field over the past decade (Coie et al., 1993; Howell, Krisberg, Hawkins, & Wilson, 1995). Such a framework represents a clear advance over vague theories of criminal behavior that were often difficult to test empirically and provided little clear direction for prevention and intervention. However, although it has made many contributions, this framework has several limitations that need to be overcome so that we can advance our knowledge of the causal processes that contribute to SVJ offending. These limitations can be discussed while keeping in mind the three points mentioned earlier in this chapter related to the need to focus specifically on SVJ offending, to understand such behavior in terms of ecological influences, and to ground empirical studies in the practical experiences of those involved.

First, most variables studied in cross-sectional and longitudinal studies that measure SVJ as an outcome and are used to develop lists of risk factors are largely driven by deficit models of development. Although the notion of "protective factors" or conditions that counteract the effects of exposure to risk has surfaced repeatedly, empirical studies that link specific protective factors to specific domains of risk are virtually nonexistent for SVJ offending. It is important to distinguish protective factors that are the opposite of risk factors from those that interact with risk factors to counteract their effects.

A notable advance in this literature would be to enumerate protective factors vis-à-vis specific risk profiles and contexts. For example, what protective factors reduce risk for children living in high-violence and gang-ridden neighborhoods? Who have family problems? Who attend bad schools? Who display individual deficits such as impulsivity?

Who have combined risk profiles? Recent qualitative studies suggest that there may be tremendous individual variation in response to risk even within similar community contexts. For example, Gustin, Guerra, and Attar (in press) interviewed four children who were at risk for delinquency based on living in high-violence neighborhoods, attending schools with few resources, and experiencing multiple stressors, yet experienced highly successful and adaptive outcomes. For each child the protective factors were different and ranged from a supportive family and a close network of friends to an optimistic outlook on life.

Risk-focused approaches must also acknowledge and integrate information on the actual and perceived benefits of involvement in SVJ offending. It is naive to dismiss the potential benefits of criminal activity as well as the specific situational correlates that portend violent or criminal events (Fagan & Wilkinson, 1996). For instance, for children living in low-income, high-violence neighborhoods with high levels of gang activity, carrying a weapon or joining a gang may be motivated primarily out of fear and desire for self-protection. In addition, specific events may promote or inhibit offending.

In most cases, risk-focused approaches tend to be atheoretical, providing lists of risk and protective factors, although these are sometimes loosely woven together by a general theory. Unfortunately, these general theories are often tautological, for instance, proposing that children become involved in delinquent acts because they are not involved in nondelinquent acts. Such an orientation provides little clear guidance for distinguishing among risk factors, but rather tends to convey the idea that risk factors are generally independent of each other and of equal value. Thus, targeting any two presumably is better than targeting one alone. However, it is more likely the case that successfully addressing a single strong causal factor may be more effective than targeting three or four variables that have weak or spurious influences. Of course, this is the rationale behind multicomponent, multilevel interventions described by Wasserman and Miller (Chapter 10, this volume). However, even the most comprehensive interventions rarely evaluate adequately the relative contribution of different components related to types of risk factors.

Differentiating the impact of risk factors requires advances in both methodology and theory. For instance, as Lipsey and Derzon (Chapter 6, this volume) demonstrate, meta-analyses can be used to synthesize longitudinal research on risk factors to provide a ranking of influence based on effect size. Their research is enhanced by the addition of age groupings with quite different predictors emerging for children (ages 6-11) and adolescents (ages 12-14). Indeed, it is striking to note that antisocial parents but not antisocial peers contribute very significantly to the prediction of offending when measured between ages 6 and 11, but this relation virtually reverses between ages 12 and 14.

Still, such findings must be understood within the context of theoretical explanations that are sensitive to the heterogeneity of SVJ offending. It has become increasingly clear that no single theory is likely to account for as complex a phenomenon as delinquency. A focus on the social ecology of offending has illustrated the role of contextual influences as well as the need to account for person-in-context interactions. Clearly, theoretical advances are warranted that more clearly specify both indirect effects of variables as well as important interactions that are linked to particular patterns of offending or offender typologies among discrete populations.

One issue that has emerged in recent years is the need to incorporate developmental questions into theories of delinquent behavior (as is also evident from the results of the Lipsey and Derzon meta-analyses in Chapter 6). Although there is a large developmental literature on problem behavior in children and adolescence, and particularly on the development of aggressive and antisocial behavior, the developmental literature and the criminal justice literature have evolved in two separate strands that have only minimally informed each other. Only recently have researchers begun to reject the notion that the causes of offending do not vary with age. Loeber and Le Blanc (1990) have proposed a "developmental criminology" that examines the effects of identified variables on youth of different ages as well as the differential effects of these variables on processes of offending including initiation, escalation, and desistance. Similarly, Sampson and Laub (1993a) have described an age-graded theory of informal social control as applied to offending, and Williams, Guerra, and Elliott (1996) have put forth an ecological model of life course development that emphasizes developmental stages, life course transitions and pathways, and nested social contexts. As these developmental perspectives suggest, it is important to understand how individuals navigate their life course in relation to SVJ offending. This includes questions of when and why individuals begin offending patterns early or later in development, as well as when and why they outgrow them and how these changes can be maintained.

It is also important to study further how risk and protective factors and accompanying developmental processes vary as a function of other key characteristics such as gender, culture, and social class. This requires a more sophisticated operationalization of "sociocultural context" that goes beyond a checklist of ethnicity, a 5-point social class rating index, or a simple contrast of males versus females. Rather than attempting to make generalizations about specific groups of offenders, it is more useful to understand the key aspects of a given sociocultural context that influence the processes of involvement and desistance from SVJ offending.

A good example of the limitations of broad-stroke assessments is the complex relation between poverty and SVJ offending. Although crime rates are highest in low-income neighborhoods (Fingerhut & Kleinman, 1990) and relations have been found between poverty and aggression (Patterson, Kupersmidt, & Vaden, 1990), it is likely that the specific sociocultural conditions that exist in certain low-income settings rather than lack of money relate to increased offending. As Jencks (1992) notes, "If low incomes alone drove people to crime, graduate students and clergymen would also commit a lot of crimes" (p. 113). Thus, although there is a critical need to understand the concentration of SVJ offending in disadvantaged neighborhoods, it is clear that this must go beyond the assessment of income or social class.

Similarly, the role of gender has often been reduced to comparisons between males and females, with males outscoring females on SVJ offending. Yet further distinctions within each gender are also warranted. For instance, a critical issue is to make better distinctions between males who are SVJ offenders and males whose offending is more temporary, less serious, and less frequent than SVJ offenders.

In a recent review of longitudinal and comparative research on violent criminal behavior, Laub and Lauritsen (1993) propose a research agenda that examines carefully the sociocultural processes underlying the development of extreme antisocial and violent behavior. They argue for a strategy that combines comparative longitudinal and ethnographic methods to examine variations in the interactions between individuals and the sociocultural environment and how these variations influence offending. In particular, they point to the need to examine factors that influence the large within-individual changes in antisocial behavior, despite an overall picture of relative stability within a population. Methodologies that combine quantitative data with life histories of offenders (e.g., Farrington & West, 1993) are particularly illustrative.

Finally, research on causes and correlates of SVJ offending must be sensitive to the practical utility of such endeavors. For example, although the notion of conducting a community-wide risk assessment is consistent with a risk-focused approach, the community collaboratives that implement such assessments typically do not have the expertise to conduct the surveillance and assessments needed. Consequently, they often use lists of risk and protective factors based on research in other locations, involving groups, circumstances, or offending problems that may not match local community needs. Researchers must develop mechanisms to synthesize more clearly those findings about correlates and causes that could be considered universal and applicable in all settings, as well as influences that may be unique to particular settings.

Prevention and Intervention Strategies

As detailed in several recent reviews of the field (e.g., Guerra, Tolan, & Hammond, 1994; Tolan & Guerra, 1994b; Yoshikawa, 1995; Zigler, Taussig, & Black, 1992) as well as Chapters 10-15 of this volume, there is a large and growing empirical literature focused on the prevention and mitigation of antisocial behavior and its precursors. Parallel to this empirical literature, there is also a growing community response to serious youth crime that uses a range of programs (Guerra & Williams, 1996). A primary challenge is to increase the collaboration between researchers and practitioners so that community programs, system responses, and re-search efforts are synchronized. This requires that the scholarly community acknowledge the practical efforts of researchers and their attempts to convey findings in a user-friendly fashion that are responsive to community input. It also requires that service providers and agencies perceive the value of research to answer questions relevant to their concerns, and receive guidance in conducting sound evaluations. In either case, it is imperative to promote continued dialogue between researchers and practitioners to develop prevention and intervention strategies that are useful and effective in the field.

Research on the prevention and/or mitigation of SVJ offending can be broadly divided into studies that evaluate specific programs or combinations of programs (e.g., preschool enrichment, parent training) and studies that evaluate specific methods, practices, or policies (e.g., diversion, graduated sanctions, corrections). It is important to realize the constraints of this dichotomy, particularly because the impact of different practices may depend on the specific programs used, and this must be considered in evaluation. A good example of this can be found in the diversion literature. Whether or not diversion "works" cannot be answered independently of knowing what programs are provided through diversion (Guerra et al., 1994). Similarly, as Altschuler (Chapter 15, this volume) details, intermediate sanctions involve a range of different responses, and their effectiveness hinges on the amount of treatment received, although less is known about the unique contributions of different treatments, an area in need of further investigation.

When considering evaluations of specific prevention and intervention programs that target specific risk or protective factors, their impact on SVJ offending is often unclear. Many programs, particularly postnatal, preschool, or early-prevention programs, are de-signed to boost academic functioning, social competence, or parenting skills. Because SVJ offending does not occur during this age period, only a few studies with long-term follow-up data have been able to assess their ultimate impact on offending, with positive, albeit rather weak, results and limited information about the mediating role of changes in risk and protective factors (for reviews, see Wasserman and Miller, Chapter 10, this volume; Yoshikawa, 1995).

Furthermore, little is known about whether these programs must be extended in time through childhood and adolescence via continued programming or "booster" sessions, or whether they are effective alone if applied during certain optimal periods early in development. Because of the costs and resources involved in providing continuous programming, it is of both theoretical and practical significance to determine the ages during which specific types of interventions (e.g., family, social skills, academic competence) are maximally effective, and to specify the age-appropriate foci of booster sessions. Life course models of development and offending that detail critical developmental contexts and important transitions (e.g., Sampson & Laub, 1993a; Williams et al., 1996) provide a framework that can guide the development of programs and specify relevant contexts for children of different ages.

Even when interventions are conducted during developmental periods when SVJ offending is likely to be evident, they often fail to measure this outcome. In many cases, the "clinical" or real-world significance of group differences is negligible, particularly when all participants score relatively low on an outcome measure that is related to SVJ offending such as aggression or fighting. In other cases, change in age-normative behaviors (e.g., smoking cigarettes) is interpreted as evidence that a program reduces violence or delinquency (for a review, see Tolan & Guerra,

1994b). Thus, programs that make youth a little less aggressive or less likely to initiate cigarette smoking are often touted as effective delinquency prevention programs. Future research must specify SVJ offending outcomes, if appropriate, and use measures that directly assess these outcomes if they are to claim to be effective in preventing or reducing this behavior. Along these lines, it is unlikely that SVJ offending can be addressed without dealing with the issue of guns, and the increase in juvenile homicide related to an increase in the use of guns. Yet models of risk and preventive intervention studies do not adequately account for the role of guns and their relation to recent increases in SVJ offending among youth.

In fact, as offending becomes more serious, the effectiveness of intervention strategies tends to diminish. As Lipsey and Wilson (Chapter 13, this volume) demonstrate via meta-analyses of intervention studies, programs for serious juvenile offenders produce reductions in recidivism of a substantial magnitude only under optimal circumstances, and the effects are virtually eliminated under less than optimal conditions. There are also few effective strategies for preventing SVJ offending among gang-involved youth, with only "promising strategies" to recommend (Howell, Chapter 12, this volume). Thus, more research and development are needed in dealing with youth involved in serious violent and delinquent behavior. Because so many of these youth are involved in the justice system, research on effective intervention strategies must evaluate programs (e.g., job training) and juvenile justice responses (e.g., intensive probation supervision) to determine optimal responses.

This points to one of the most difficult issues in intervention research: how to determine the relative contributions of different intervention programs and practices and recommended combinations. On the one hand, given that no single factor is likely to cause SVJ offending, the impact of single-component, single-context programs is limited. On the other hand, long-term, multicomponent, multicontext programs can become difficult to manage with a number of unintended "interventions" (e.g., policy changes, demographic shifts) occurring, and some contexts (e.g., political and economic forces) unamenable to change via the planned intervention. One solution is to provide the most comprehensive intervention possible and to experimentally assess the contribution to change in outcome of each of the hypothesized mediators targeted by the intervention (to the extent that it is possible to measure each variable). Another approach is to use a step design, whereby each step adds an additional component, depending on the particular research questions.

In either case, an important issue for future intervention research involves a greater focus on determining the specific moderators of intervention impact. Rather than ask, "what works?" it is imperative to ask, "what works for whom and under what conditions and in what settings?" Given the multitude of causal mechanisms, their differential relevance at different stages of development, and the multiple social contexts to which individuals are exposed and experience differently, it is likely that most intervention effects will be interactions rather than main effects.

For example, in a recent analysis of data from the Metropolitan Area Child Study, a large-scale, multicomponent, multicontext intervention for urban elementary school children, Guerra et al. (1997) failed to find significant main effects for intervention condition when comparing three types of interventions that were progressively more extensive in scope. However, when the child's initial level of aggression was considered, the interventions were found to be increasingly more effective, but only for the most aggressive children. Thus, looking only for main effects would have obscured the impact of this program for some children. In a similar vein, it is likely that most programs work for some youth but not others, and more emphasis should be placed on determining the best "child-intervention match." This may also require a greater emphasis on process evaluations and participant interviews regarding program impact on their lives, as well as replication studies in similar and different populations.

■ *Directions for Future Research*

The focus of this chapter has been on identifying gaps in knowledge and research priorities in relation to serious, violent, and chronic juvenile offending. As discussed initially, I believe that setting a research agenda requires a careful examination of how we think about the problem of SVJ offending as well as a delineation of the most pressing research priorities.

First, as previously mentioned, it is critical that research focus more explicitly on SVJ offending as an identified outcome. This task would be facilitated by a consensus in the field regarding the operational definition of this classification, but would still require refinements specific to the nature and purpose of the research. In other words, the associated precursors or level of specificity of behavior would depend on the specific research questions. This focus on SVJ offending points to a methodological gap regarding how we measure SVJ offending. Given the limitations of official arrest and/or conviction data, it seems important to further refine and develop self-report measures that are appropriate at different ages and are sensitive to issues of gender and culture.

Second, researchers have tended to ignore the fact that the low base rates for SVJ offending mean that most children and youth are not involved in this behavior, or age out quite rapidly. In fact, although behaviors such as aggression are quite stable, it is a relative, not an absolute, stability, and is really only most apparent at the extremes of the distribution (Moffitt, 1993). Rather than focusing solely on why SVJ offending emerges as an outcome, we must focus on why it does not develop, and specifically on what individual and contextual influences affect nonparticipation and/or desistance. These questions are best addressed by research that combines quantitative and qualitative methods and provides for assessment of the variations in sociocultural contexts and how these influence behavior.

Third, researchers must respond to the practical issues faced by those who deal with SVJ offenders, including community agencies, schools, and juvenile justice agencies. Decisions that affect SVJ offenders are being made daily, often without the benefit of empirical support. A prime example of the need to forge partnerships between researchers and practitioners is in the area of assessment and classification. Although significant progress has been made in the use of structured assessments, there remains a hodgepodge of methods and measures that provide few useful typologies to assign placements or select appropriate services.

Fourth, a focus on practical issues must be extended to an increased emphasis on prevention and intervention research. Programs that are being conducted in the community are infrequently evaluated carefully, and programs developed by researchers are often difficult to infuse or sustain in community settings. These efforts would be greatly enhanced by a partnership between researchers and practitioners. Given a focus on the problem of SVJ offending, a program of research should be defined that evaluates carefully the most promising multicomponent programs and permits careful assessment of their "active" ingredients and appropriateness for different types of offenders. Programs targeted for evaluation should be those that are theoretically grounded, cost-effective, easy to implement, user-friendly, and most consistent with ongoing policies and practices.

Fifth, a program of intervention research with SVJ offenders must be complemented by continued efforts to prevent such behavior. To date, the impact of early prevention on SVJ offending has often been an afterthought rather than a carefully planned component focused on long-term outcomes. Questions about inoculation versus maintenance of effects should be answered through systematic efforts to prevent SVJ offending that begin early in development. Further attempts must be made to enhance screening accuracy when a subset of high-risk individuals are selected for targeted services.

To accomplish these goals and delineate a research agenda, we must adopt a framework that permits their consideration simultaneously in a manner that is sensitive to individual differences, contextual influences, and stability and change in SVJ offending. Rather than buying into a single theory of delinquency, it seems more fruitful to adopt a comprehensive model that permits consideration of the complexity of this behavior. This complexity can only be captured by models that provide for a life course or developmental perspective, whereby serious, violent, and chronic offending is seen as a "developmental outcome"—one of many potential developmental outcomes with a subset of common pathways. Thus, future research can be guided by efforts to identify prototypical pathways to nondelinquent and serious delinquent outcomes, and prevention and intervention studies can be guided by knowledge about age-specific precursors and relevant developmental contexts.

CHAPTER 17

Conclusions and the Way Forward

■ *Rolf Loeber &*
David P. Farrington

The final chapter summarizes the main points of the preceding chapters and then addresses the extent to which the juvenile justice system can deal with serious and violent juvenile (SVJ) offenders and the extent to which parents, schools, neighborhoods, and public health approaches can assist in prevention of SVJ offending. It then sets out an agenda for future research on SVJ offenders.

■ *Overview*

Major Aims of This Book
(Chapter 1 by David P. Farrington and Rolf Loeber)

The main aim of this volume is to review knowledge about SVJ offenders. Knowledge about risk and protective factors, prevention programs, and sanctions is reviewed, with specific attempts to integrate the risk factor and intervention literature. It is hoped that the policy and research recommendations will assist in the further implementation of the Office of Juvenile Justice and Delinquency Prevention's (OJJDP) Comprehensive Strategy.

The main focus of the Study Group is on serious juvenile offenders. Serious violent offenses include homicide, rape, robbery, aggravated assault, and kidnapping. Serious nonviolent offenses include burglary, motor vehicle theft, theft over $100, arson, drug trafficking, and extortion.

This volume was inspired by OJJDP's Comprehensive Strategy (Howell, 1995; Wilson & Howell, 1994), which is based on five general principles:

1. Strengthen the family in its primary responsibility to instill moral values and provide guidance and support to children.

2. Support core social institutions (schools, religious institutions, and community organizations) in their roles of developing capable, mature, and responsible youth.

3. Promote delinquency prevention as the most cost-effective approach to dealing with juvenile delinquency. When children engage in "acting out" behavior, such as status offenses, the family and community, in concert with child welfare services, must take primary responsibility for responding with appropriate treatment and support services. Communities must take the lead in designing and building comprehensive prevention approaches that address known risk factors and target youth at risk of delinquency.

4. Intervene immediately and effectively when delinquent behavior occurs to prevent delinquent offenders from becoming chronic offenders or progressively committing more serious and violent crimes. Initial intervention attempts should be centered on the family and other core social institutions.

5. Identify and control the small group of serious, violent, and chronic juvenile offenders who have failed to respond to intervention and nonsecure community-based treatment

and rehabilitation services offered by the juvenile justice system.

OJJDP's Comprehensive Strategy provided an excellent framework for understanding, preventing, and controlling SVJ offending. However, to assist in its widespread implementation, there is a need for more detailed quantitative analyses of risk and protective factors for serious, violent, or chronic juvenile offending; most previous reviews focused on delinquency in general rather than on SVJ offenders. Similarly, there is a need for more detailed quantitative analyses of the effectiveness (and cost-effectiveness) of prevention and intervention programs, again focusing on their effects on SVJ offenders. Unfortunately, we found little information on cost-effectiveness, apart from a few major interventions such as the Perry Preschool Program (Schweinhart, Barnes, & Weikart, 1993; see also Greenwood, 1995).

The present volume aims to provide reviews of risk and protective factors and prevention and intervention programs focusing especially on SVJ offenders. It also aims to integrate the two different areas, so that knowledge about risk and protective factors is linked to knowledge about prevention and intervention programs. Ideally, prevention/intervention programs should be based on research on risk/protective factors, and conversely, conclusions about causal effects of risk/protective factors should be drawn from knowledge about the effectiveness of prevention/intervention programs. Attempts were made to compare SVJ offenders with other offenders as well as with nonoffenders. Because we found little information specifically on SVJ offenders, contributors to this volume carried out special reanalyses of data.

This volume aims to specify the relative importance of different risk and protective factors in the development of SVJ offending, and the relative effectiveness of different prevention/intervention programs. It aims to specify what works best with what types of individuals, at what stages of development, and under what contextual conditions, but information about these topics was limited. It has a developmental focus, reviewing the effects of risk factors and interventions on different stages of development, including the onset, persistence, escalation, de-escalation, and desistance of serious offending. It also aims to study key transition points in the development of serious delinquency careers, and optimal points for intervention efforts. The volume also concentrates on the contribution of gang members to SVJ offending, on the effects of joining or leaving a gang on SVJ offending, and on prevention/intervention programs targeted on gangs. We will now briefly summarize each chapter.

■ *Part I: Developmental Course and Risk Factors*

Serious and Violent Juvenile Offenders *(Chapter 2 by Rolf Loeber, David P. Farrington, and Daniel A. Waschbusch)*

Several interrelated questions are addressed:

1. How can SVJ offenders best be defined?
2. How do SVJ offenders relate to past classification efforts for juvenile offenders?
3. How much overlap is there between serious juvenile offenders, violent juvenile offenders, and chronic juvenile offenders?
4. What are the major trends in the prevalence of SVJ offenders over the latest decades?
5. How well do official records and self-reports of SVJ offenders represent their actual delinquent involvement?
6. How much of the total volume of crime do chronic offenders account for?

7. What is the geographic distribution of SVJ offenders (and specially juvenile homicide) in the United States?

Studies show that there is considerable overlap between serious, violent, and chronic offenders, even when court or police records were used. About half of the violent juvenile offenders are also chronic offenders, and about a third of the chronic offenders are also violent offenders. Moreover, about a third of the serious offenders are also chronic offenders. Research by Snyder (Appendix, this volume) on youth referred to juvenile courts in a large southwestern county showed a substantial increase in the proportion of chronic juvenile offenders, especially in the period 1990-1995. The vast majority of chronic offenders committed at least one violent or serious nonviolent crime. Snyder also found that the typical chronic career contained more violent offenses in the 1990s than in the 1980s. However, the vast majority of violent offenders committed only one officially recorded violent crime. Two cohort studies in Philadelphia have also shown an increase in the proportion of chronic offenders (i.e., those with six or more arrests) over time. However, data from major metropolitan areas are needed to show trends in the proportion of chronic offenders.

Because much knowledge of serious, violent, and chronic offending is based on official records (i.e., police or court records), it is important to know to what extent self-reports of offending overlap with those of official records, and in what respects self-reports contain unique information. For example, one study showed that 86% of the juvenile career offenders did not have a record of arrest. The peak period of officially recorded offending for juveniles usually falls between the ages of 14 and 17 (Farrington, 1986). However, the majority of the self-reported male juvenile persisting serious offenders show an onset of serious offending between ages 8 and 14. Thus, given that most jurisdictions in the United States are reluctant to deal with offenders under age 12, this implies that the juvenile justice system is not likely to deal with many serious juvenile offenders at the beginning of their delinquent careers. However, offenders under age 12 could be dealt with by the juvenile justice system, and they are currently dealt with by human service agencies such as child welfare, mental health, and child protection. The fragmentation of services and the lack of comprehensive services for offenders under age 12 is of great concern.

Race, Ethnicity, and Serious Juvenile Offending *(Chapter 3 by Darnell F. Hawkins, John H. Laub, and Janet L. Lauritsen)*

This chapter examined what was known about the relationship between race and ethnicity and SVJ offending in the United States. Using data from the Uniform Crime Reports (UCR) and self-reports of offending and victimization, the chapter presented a descriptive account of the racial distribution of SVJ offending among juveniles. These sources of data reveal long-standing patterns of differential involvement by race, with black (African American) youths having disproportionately higher rates of SVJ offending. On the other hand, the extent of black-white differences and the degree of stability of the ratio varies over time according to the type of offense. Whereas black-white arrest ratios for the composite index of violent offending and robbery declined between 1983 and 1992, black and white juvenile arrest rates for homicide grew more disparate over these years. This increasing disparity was especially evident from the mid-1980s on. Data for several large U.S. cities also revealed comparatively high homicide rates among Latino youths during the 1980s.

Given the perennial debate regarding the potential for bias in the use of arrest data for examining ethnic and racial differences, the chapter examined recent findings from studies of self-reported offending by juveniles and victim reports of the perceived age characteristics of their assailants in the National Crime Victimization Survey (NCVS). These sources of data provided reasons to exercise caution in using arrest data alone as an estimate of the extent of racial differences in some serious types of delinquency, including violence. However, on the basis of findings reported from both self-report and victimization surveys it appears that race is an important correlate of SVJ offending.

The chapter also reviewed various explanations of ethnic and racial differences in SVJ offending. The dominant research tradition in the study of juvenile offending has depended largely on individual-level analyses. This theoretical and analytic orientation has tended to see ethnic and racial differences in SVJ offending and their causes as largely indistinguishable from individual-level explanations. In contrast to this research orientation, the chapter focused on social ecological explanations, which incorporate measures of broader social structural variation and community-specific contexts and cultures. To a large extent, social ecological factors appeared to be important influences on ethnic and racial differences, independently of individual-level factors. Hence, the ideal research design for the study of ethnic and racial differences in juvenile offending should combine traditional individual- and community-level measures of potential correlates. The chapter concluded that black-white comparisons alone were insufficient as a means of analyzing the extent of involvement in serious and violent offending by the nation's juveniles. As the nation's population grows more racially and ethnically diverse, so does the diversity of group involvement in SVJ offending.

The Contemporaneous Co-Occurrence of Serious and Violent Juvenile Offending and Other Problem Behaviors
(Chapter 4 by David Huizinga and Cynthia Jakob-Chien)

There is substantial co-occurrence or overlap between each of the problems considered in this chapter and serious violent and serious nonviolent juvenile offending. Included are drug use, problem drug use, mental health problems, school problems (poor academic achievement, truancy, suspension, and dropout), victimization, and different combinations of these problems. Almost all of these problems overlap with serious delinquency.

With the exception of multiple school problems and combinations of school and other problems, only about half or less of the serious delinquents are also contemporaneously involved in specific problems. Also, although serious offenders are disproportionately represented among the group of youth who have a particular problem, they often make up less than half of all those experiencing a problem. Thus, although there is clear co-occurrence between serious offending and these other problems, it would be incorrect to characterize serious delinquents as predominantly having a particular problem, and it would be incorrect to characterize the group having a given problem as being made up predominantly of serious delinquents.

The obvious exception to this rule is for those experiencing difficulty in some arena of school. School problems, especially when combined with other problems, characterize 80% or more of serious delinquent youth. It should be carefully observed, however, that

the converse is not true. The largest proportion of youth having school problems are not serious delinquents.

As this generalization and other findings indicate, serious offenders are likely to have multiple other problems. Over 90% have at least one other problem and about three quarters have two or more of the problems examined. In this sense, serious offenders are truly multiple-problem youth.

Development of Serious and Violent Offending Careers
(Chapter 5 by Patrick H. Tolan and Deborah Gorman-Smith)

This chapter focuses on the major parameters of involvement that relate to serious and violent offending (frequency, variety, seriousness level), the behavioral precursors to such offending, and the emerging understanding of such behavioral development. These parameters and related concepts such as age of onset, desistance, and career length are important aspects of a career perspective on criminal behavior. In particular, there is repeated evidence that such parameters aid in predicting the probability of sustained criminal and other antisocial behavior, including serious and violent acts.

The empirical evidence and related theory about the role of these parameters and important precursors (e.g. aggression, impulsive behavior, oppositional behavior) in distinguishing serious and violent offending from other delinquency and nonoffending were reviewed. In addition, developmental theories about the criminal behavior of adolescents were reviewed, and the current leading theory, the developmental pathways approach of Loeber and colleagues, was described (Loeber & Le Blanc, 1990). A test of the application of the theorized trajectories and sequences was undertaken with a sample drawn to be nationally representative of the United States and an inner-city high-risk sample. Results indicated that the model was quite consistent with the patterns seen in both samples and was an even better fit to the development of serious and violent offending than offending in general.

The consistency of promising findings about patterns of involvement and career trajectories has to be qualified in several ways. First, most studies focused on relations between variables. Few attempted to determine the probability of behavior patterns within individuals. Second, because violent and serious offending are such low-rate behaviors even among those most actively criminal, there is limited ability to translate these correlational findings into accurate prediction. Third, the bulk of the studies focused on Caucasian males, raising substantial concerns about the generalizability to females and other ethnic groups.

social characteristics of the juveniles or their families.

Differences among studies in their methodological characteristics and the samples used were associated with effect sizes in ways that made it difficult to assess the relative strength of the various predictors. A multiple regression procedure was, therefore, used to control for these secondary variables and estimate the magnitude of the effect sizes associated with each different predictor construct for a uniform set of conditions.

In predicting from age 6-11 risk factors to serious delinquency at age 15-25, the best predictors are (a) a prior delinquent offense, (b) substance use, (c) male gender, (d) low socioeconomic status, and (e) an antisocial parent. In predicting from age 12-14 risk factors to serious delinquency at age 15-25, the best predictors are (a) lack of strong social ties, (b) antisocial peers, and (c) prior delinquent offenses.

Predictors of Violent or Serious Delinquency in Adolescence and Early Adulthood: A Synthesis of Longitudinal Research *(Chapter 6 by Mark W. Lipsey and James H. Derzon)*

A meta-analysis was presented to synthesize longitudinal research on the predictive risk factors for adolescent and early adult serious criminal behavior. Its purpose was to identify those predictor variables measured on juveniles aged 6-11 and 12-14 that were correlated with the degree of their violent or serious delinquent behavior when they were 15-25 years old. Available longitudinal studies yielded sufficient information to permit examination of four broad categories of predictor variables: (a) early antisocial behavior, (b) personal characteristics of the juveniles, (c) parent and family characteristics, and (d)

A Review of Predictors of Youth Violence *(Chapter 7 by J. David Hawkins, Todd Herrenkohl, David P. Farrington, Devon Brewer, Richard F. Catalano, and Tracy W. Harachi)*

This chapter reviewed potentially malleable or changeable predictors of violence and focused on individual, contextual (family, school, peers), situational, and community factors. Among the individual factors, the following predict violence: pregnancy and delivery complications; hyperactivity, concentration problems, restlessness, and risk taking; aggressiveness; early initiation of violent behavior itself; involvement in other forms of antisocial behavior; and beliefs and attitudes favorable to deviant or antisocial behavior including violence.

Within the family, living with a criminal parent or parents, harsh discipline, physical abuse and neglect, poor family management practices, low levels of parental involvement with the child, high levels of family conflict, parental attitudes favorable to violence, and separation from the family are linked to later violence. As to school factors, academic failure, low commitment to schooling, truancy and early school leaving, and frequent school transitions predict violent behavior. Delinquent siblings, delinquent peers, and gang membership also predict violence, though the effects of these factors appear to be greatest in adolescence. Finally, poverty, community disorganization, availability of drugs, neighborhood adults involved in crime, and exposure to violence and racial prejudice in the community are all associated with an increased risk for later violence.

Violent behavior is a result of the interactions of individual, contextual (family, school, peers), situational, and neighborhood factors. Multivariate models that include these factors in theoretically linked causal sequences need to be tested to guide the development of multicomponent violence prevention interventions. In addition, more research is needed to identify those factors that function truly in a protective fashion against risk exposure, serving to mediate or moderate the effects of risk. Furthermore, more studies need to focus specifically on the prediction of SVJ offenders as opposed to the prediction of delinquency in general.

Membership in Youth Gangs and Involvement in Serious and Violent Offending *(Chapter 8 by Terence P. Thornberry)*

Adolescents who join juvenile street gangs are more frequently involved in serious and violent delinquency compared to adolescents who are not gang members. Indeed, gang membership is one of the strongest and most robust correlates of serious delinquency that researchers have uncovered. Moreover, in the past 10-15 years there has been a tremendous spread of gangs throughout American society. Gangs are now found in hundreds of cities, both large and small. Because of this, it is essential that any comprehensive examination of serious and violent delinquency should understand the role that gang membership plays in generating criminal involvement.

Several recent longitudinal studies have found that gang members, although representing a minority of the overall population, are responsible for the vast majority of delinquent acts. In the Rochester Youth Development Study, for example, about 30% of the sample were gang members but they accounted for about 70% to 80% of the instances of serious and violent delinquencies.

This chapter also reviewed the results of several longitudinal studies that examined the processes that might bring about the increased delinquency that gang members exhibit. Gang members have somewhat higher rates of involvement in violence prior to joining the gang but there appears to be a general drop-off in violent delinquency following the period of gang membership. These studies indicate that rates of violent delinquency are particularly high only during periods of active gang membership. The consistency and strength of these results suggest that the gang environment facilitates involvement in delinquency, especially violent delinquency.

The final issues reviewed in this chapter concerned the distinction between delinquent peer groups and street gangs. Longitudinal studies have recently compared gang members to nonmembers who associate with highly delinquent peer groups to see if gangs are simply another type of delinquent peer group. The results suggested that they are not, at least with respect to levels of offending. Uniformly, gang members report significantly higher rates of violent delinquency than do nonmembers, even those who associate with highly delinquent peers.

These findings highlight the importance of focusing on juvenile gangs as important targets for prevention and treatment programs. If gang members are indeed responsible for the majority of serious and violent delinquent acts, as suggested by all studies that have examined this topic, it is unlikely that the overall rate of serious delinquency can be reduced unless gangs are brought under control.

Screening of Serious and Violent Juvenile Offenders: Identification, Classification, and Prediction
(Chapter 9 by Marc Le Blanc)

Screening has two purposes, the identification of potential SVJ offenders for prevention and the classification of offenders for decisions or programming in the juvenile justice system. Operational definitions of SVJ offending are regularly used in the juvenile justice system, although many researchers prefer scales. The screening strategy for prevention has to be multistage because potential offenders have to be distinguished from nonoffenders and then SVJ offenders have to be distinguished among offenders.

Criminology and criminal justice have a long experience with the design and implementation of screening methods. From these traditions, there are many lessons that must be kept in mind. The criterion should be appropriate to the question, involve an adequate follow-up period, and use a cut-off point that does not excessively lower the base rate. The predictors should involve multiple infor-

mants in multiple settings and should rest on solid empirical evidence, as well as on theoretical significance. The reliability of predictors and outcome should be maximized. Research wisdom would recommend additive methods over multiplicative methods for the combination of predictors. Measuring and reporting predictive accuracy should be a common practice. Finally, the screening device should be validated in a different sample.

Whatever the age group studied for prevention, or the nature of the program envisaged, research indicates that multiple gating, multiple informants, multiple-variable domains, and multiple methods seem the best solution to the identification of potential SVJ offenders. A candidate screening instrument for chronic offending was identified, and meta-analysis results also suggested potential predictors. The Cambridge screening instrument can be applied only from late childhood and relies on four characteristics that distinguish chronic offenders: convicted at age 10-12, convicted sibling at 10, troublesome at 8-10, and poor elementary school attainment at 10. The meta-analysis results indicate predictor domains that vary by outcomes.

Over the past decades, risk and needs assessment instruments have been developed for detention, probation, parole, and placement decisions. Such classification devices are potentially useful at different stages, including court referrals and transfers to adult court. Some existing instruments display a sound face validity, but their reliability and empirical validity have rarely been tested, either for use in a particular jurisdiction or for implementation in another juvenile justice system. No screening devices exist specifically for the identification of SVJ offenders. Risk and needs assessments consider multiple-variable domains, but these classification instruments may be improved by testing the use of multiple informants, by increasing the variable domains considered, and by testing the usefulness of multiple methods of data gathering.

There is much technical work still to be done before adequate screening instruments can be used for the identification or classification of potential SVJ offenders. Some strategies and instruments are promising, but no specific instrument can be recommended to policymakers and practitioners. However, more efforts should be made to develop such instruments in community assessment centers.

■ Part II: Preventive Interventions and Graduated Sanctions

The Prevention of Serious and Violent Juvenile Offending (Chapter 10 by Gail A. Wasserman and Laurie S. Miller)

This chapter discussed programs that target risk factors for serious and violent offending, as well as those that target risk factors for its precursors. Many programs targeting antisocial behavior are relevant to the prevention of SVJ offending because early antisocial behavior tends to be a precursor of SVJ offending. Because antisocial behavior is likely to be multidetermined, it is unlikely that interventions directed only toward a single system (i.e., child, family, school, peer group) will be successful. The component "building blocks" of successful interventions were described, including those oriented toward parent and family (e.g., parent management, family preservation); those oriented toward child social and academic skills, and classroom-based programs; and those that make use of medication for various forms of child disruptive behavior disorders, as well as recently developed conflict resolution and peer mediation programs.

Gaps in knowledge are different at each developmental period. For example, during infancy and preschool, there are few programs testing behavioral parent management techniques, and there are few studies focusing specifically on child antisocial behavior or that carry evaluation into adolescence or beyond, when serious and violent offending is likely to occur. Limitations of programs implemented during the school years include the lowered importance placed on family components in comparison to school-directed components. This relative lack of attention to family-oriented treatments is greater when we examine programs for adolescents, which focus quite heavily on the peer group to the exclusion of other risks. Programs oriented toward parenting in the school years and in adolescence are likely to show good results, especially when behavioral change is consistently promoted in both home and school settings. Furthermore, despite great overlap between antisocial behavior and psychiatric diagnosis (especially attention-deficit hyperactivity disorder), most interventions fail to screen or refer for commonly treatable forms of psychopathology.

The chapter considered how successful, methodologically rigorous multisystemic programs have combined different components to prevent serious antisocial behavior, examining those programs that are oriented toward different developmental periods (before school entry, during school years, adolescence) and those that are offered at different levels of prevention—universal (for everyone), selected (for at-risk youth), or indicated (for identified problem youth). The chapter presented a comprehensive table, organized by developmental periods, that lists programs, the risk target, and the results of the intervention. Many multiple-component programs are effective. Where available, information about program implementation, attrition rates, and quantification of effectiveness is included.

Comprehensive Community- and School-Based Interventions to Prevent Antisocial Behavior
(Chapter 11 by Richard F. Catalano, Michael W. Arthur, J. David Hawkins, Lisa Berglund, and Jeffrey J. Olson)

Research suggests the effectiveness of interventions that reduce risk factors while enhancing protective factors in family, school, peer, and community environments in preventing health and behavior problems. Multifaceted interventions that support enduring community-level change are required to achieve sustained reductions in the prevalence of SVJ offending. The most promising current community prevention models have been adapted from the field of public health. Given the success of community interventions in reducing risk factors for heart disease, community interventions designed to reduce risk factors for SVJ offending and drug abuse are currently being implemented. However, intervention at the community level and measurement at the individual level pose key challenges in evaluation.

Experimental and quasi-experimental studies of schoolwide and community interventions indicate that the following interventions have shown positive effects on reducing risk and enhancing protection against adolescent antisocial behavior:

- Behavioral consultation for schools
- Schoolwide monitoring and reinforcement of prosocial behavior, attendance, and academic performance
- School organization interventions
- Situational crime prevention
- Comprehensive community intervention incorporating community mobilization, parent involvement and education, and classroom-based social/behavioral skills curricula

- Intensive police patrolling, especially targeting "hot spots"
- Policy and law changes affecting the availability and use of guns, tobacco, and alcoholic beverages
- Mandatory sentencing laws for crimes involving firearms
- Media interventions to change public attitudes

Generally, these interventions have targeted risk factors including easy availability of firearms and drugs, community disorganization, laws and norms favorable to antisocial behavior, low commitment to school, academic failure, family management problems, early initiation of problem behavior, and favorable attitudes toward antisocial behavior. They have also targeted the protective factors of social bonding and clear norms against SVJ offending.

Pilot work on a comprehensive community prevention strategy called Communities That Care (CTC), consisting of three phases, is highlighted. First, key community leaders are mobilized to become an oversight body and to appoint a prevention board of diverse members of their community. Second, the community prevention board is trained to assess risk and protective factors for adolescent health and behavior problems in the community and to prioritize specific factors to address through preventive action. Third, the board selects and implements preventive interventions that address the prioritized factors from a menu of programs and strategies that have shown positive effects in adequately controlled research studies. After these strategic interventions have been implemented, communities monitor their impact by periodically reassessing levels and trends in the targeted risk and protective factors and adjust the interventions as needed to achieve greater effects.

Promising Programs for Youth Gang Violence Prevention and Intervention
(Chapter 12 by James C. Howell)

Early in our nation's history, youth gang work emphasized prevention. These programs were followed by interventions designed to reintegrate particular gangs into conventional society. Then a major shift occurred as programs, led by the police, aimed to suppress youth gangs. Currently, a mixture of approaches is being tried across the nation, predominantly police suppression programs. None of these approaches has been demonstrated conclusively through rigorous research to be effective. Two factors appear to account for this: the difficulties associated with gang intervention work and the complexity of program evaluation in this area.

Three promising gang program models are recommended. The first one targets gang problems directly. The second one targets gang problems within a comprehensive strategy for dealing with serious, violent, and chronic juvenile delinquency. The third model targets gang-related homicides.

1. *The Comprehensive Community-Wide Approach to Gang Prevention, Intervention, and Suppression Program.* This comprehensive program model was designed specifically to target youth gang problems. It was developed as the product of a nationwide assessment of youth gang prevention, intervention, and suppression programs in the late 1980s. Twelve program components developed by Spergel and his colleagues involve the design and mobilization of community efforts by police, prosecutors, judges, probation and parole officers, corrections officers, schools, employers, community-based agencies, and a range of grassroots organizations. Technical assistance manuals are available to support local program development. Variations of these models are currently being implemented and tested in several cities.

The Chicago Gang Violence Reduction Program is a version of the comprehensive gang program that Spergel and his colleagues developed. It targets two of the most violent gangs in Chicago. The program consists of two coordinated strategies: (a) targeted control of violent or potentially hard-core violent youth gang offenders, in the form of increased probation department and police supervision and suppression, and (b) provision of a wide range of social services and opportunities for targeted youth. Preliminary evaluation of the program suggests that it is effective.

2. *OJJDP's Comprehensive Strategy for SVJ offenders.* Targeting gang problems within a community's comprehensive strategy for dealing with serious, violent, and chronic juvenile offenders is the second recommended approach. OJJDP's Comprehensive Strategy for Serious, Violent, and Chronic Juvenile Offenders provides a framework for strategic community planning and program development. OJJDP's *Guide for Implementing the Comprehensive Strategy for Serious, Violent, and Chronic Juvenile Offenders* is a resource for carrying out the OJJDP Comprehensive Strategy. It contains numerous promising and effective program models that will help prevent and reduce gang problems while targeting serious, violent, and chronic juvenile offenders. It is based on risk-focused prevention and graduated sanctions.

The 8% Early Intervention Program in Orange County, California implements the graduated sanctions component of the Comprehensive Strategy. The gang component of the 8% Early Intervention Program targets gang leadership and the most chronic recidivists. The Gang Incident Tracking System

(GITS) identifies and tracks gang members, providing the information base for the TARGET program, which supports gang interdiction, apprehension, and prosecution. TARGET uses intelligence gathering and information sharing to identify and select appropriate gang members and gangs for interventions.

A reduction in gun access and use is an essential component of a comprehensive strategy. Numerous excellent proposals for firearms reduction have been made that merit testing, including police seizures of illegally carried guns in hot spot areas, which have been found to reduce homicides and drive-by shootings. "Coerced use reduction" may be effective. Undercover purchases of firearms from adolescents, control of the supply channels, creation of ammunition scarcity, bilateral buy-back agreements, and nonuse treaties with financial compliance incentives hold promise. Interdicting supply channels may be more feasible than commonly assumed because of the newness of guns used in gang homicides and their purchase within the state.

3. *A strategy to prevent and reduce youth gang-related homicides.* Because of recent increases in gang homicides, a third gang program strategy for targeting them is recommended. Reducing youth gang-related homicides should be a priority wherever they occur. Studies in Chicago and Los Angeles indicate that these two cities disproportionately account for gang-related homicides in the United States. A strategy to prevent and reduce gang-related homicides is recommended. It should include the following program components:

- Chicago's Gang Violence Reduction Program appears to be a promising program model for targeting gang-motivated violence and homicides. It should be replicated and tested in other Chicago communities, in specific Los Angeles communities, and in

other cities experiencing significant levels of gang homicides.

- Hospital emergency room intervention may help break the cycle of violence.
- Counseling for drive-by shooting victims should help reduce the traumatic effects of victimization.
- Access to firearms by violent street gangs can be reduced by legislation, regulation, and community education and by removing illegal guns from the possession of gang members.
- A firearm injury and fatality reporting system should be established to determine the sources of weapons and assist interdiction efforts.
- Vertical prosecution of gang criminal activity has proven to enhance the application of criminal justice sanctions, particularly when combined with multiagency investigation, prosecution, and sanctioning.

Effective Intervention for Serious Juvenile Offenders: A Synthesis of Research *(Chapter 13 by Mark W. Lipsey and David B. Wilson)*

This chapter reports a meta-analysis of 200 experimental and quasi-experimental studies that investigated the effectiveness of various interventions for reducing the recidivism of serious juvenile offenders. Two broad categories of intervention were examined: (a) programs and treatments for serious juvenile offenders who were in the community, though possibly on probation or parole, and (b) programs and treatments for institutionalized juvenile offenders.

1. *Interventions for noninstitutionalized offenders.* The juvenile and intervention characteristics most closely associated with the size of the observed effects in the 117 studies involving noninstitutionalized serious offenders were as follows: Intervention effects were smaller for juvenile samples with only

prior property offenses than those with mixed priors (which included offenses against persons). Effects were larger where the duration of treatment was longer. Curiously, fewer contact hours per week were associated with larger effect sizes.

The different types of intervention programs were categorized into four groups on the basis of the magnitude of their mean positive effects on recidivism as follows:

- Largest effects: interpersonal skills training, behavioral approaches (mostly behavioral contracting), individual counseling, and drug abstinence programs.
- Moderate effects: multiple services and restitution programs.
- Small or no effects: wilderness challenge programs, deterrence programs (e.g., shock incarceration), early release probation and parole, and vocational programs (not involving work per se).

The best types of treatment for serious, noninstitutionalized offenders yield reductions in recidivism from around .50 to .30, a substantial 40% reduction.

2. Interventions for institutionalized offenders. The juvenile and intervention characteristics most closely associated with the size of the observed effects in the 83 studies involving institutionalized serious offenders were as follows: Intervention effects were greater where there was a longer duration of treatment. Studies in which there was a high level of monitoring of treatment implementation yielded larger effects than those in which implementation integrity was low. Larger effects were found for programs that were relatively well established (2 years or older) and that used mental health rather than criminal justice personnel to administer the treatment.

The treatments, ordered from those producing the largest effects to those producing the smallest, were as follows:

- Largest effects: interpersonal skills training, cognitive-behavioral programs, and teaching family homes programs.
- Moderate effects: group counseling, community residential programs, individual and multiple services, and guided group therapy.
- Small or no effects: employment-related programs, drug abstinence programs, and wilderness challenge programs.

The best types of treatment for serious, institutionalized offenders yield reductions in recidivism from around .50 to .30, a substantial 40% reduction.

The Impact of the Juvenile Justice System and Prospects for Graduated Sanctions in a Comprehensive Strategy *(Chapter 14 by Barry Krisberg and James C. Howell)*

This chapter examines the effectiveness of the juvenile justice system in handling SVJ offenders. Juvenile correctional facilities generally provide poor conditions of confinement and are becoming more crowded. Postrelease recidivism rates are often high, although the rate of offending is often lower after confinement than before. Most serious and high-rate offenders slow down their rate of offending after correctional interventions, although part of this decrease is attributable to maturation and regression to the mean.

It is unclear how far high-rate and low-rate offenders can be predicted in advance in priority prosecution programs. Because of the inadequacy of research designs, the effectiveness of targeted enforcement and suppression programs is also unclear. The effects of promising programs need to be vigorously evaluated.

Increasingly, serious juvenile offenders are being dealt with in the adult criminal justice system. Juveniles who are more likely to be incarcerated are also more likely to reoffend. Furthermore, juveniles in adult prisons are more likely to suffer violent victimization than those in juvenile correctional facilities. Unfortunately, the relative effectiveness of adult and juvenile court is unclear, because no study has been able to compare juveniles dealt with by the two systems.

Following OJJDP's Comprehensive Strategy, it is argued that a continuum of program options must be combined with a system of graduated sanctions, depending on risk and needs assessment. Juvenile Assessment Centers are useful in ensuring that the service needs of juvenile offenders are addressed in dispositional recommendations. Alternatives to secure confinement for serious and chronic juveniles are at least as effective as incarceration in suppressing recidivism, but considerably less costly.

More sophisticated self-report methods should be employed to throw more light on the data on desistance and continuity in criminal behavior. Experimental studies are essential to develop knowledge of what works with juvenile offenders, especially research that determines the most cost-effective length of stay, that measures the utility of immediate intervention, and that determines the appropriate mix of residential and home-based services for different offenders. Existing longitudinal studies of community samples should be enhanced by collecting data on the experiences of subjects in the child welfare, mental health, and justice systems.

Intermediate Sanctions and
Community Treatment for Serious
and Violent Juvenile Offenders
(Chapter 15 by David M. Altschuler)

Various intermediate sanctions such as electronic monitoring, house arrest, home detention, drug and alcohol testing, community tracking, intensive supervision, boot camps, split sentences, day treatment/reporting centers, community service, and restitution are increasingly being used across the country with juvenile offenders as alternatives to (a) institutionalization, (b) routine probation, and (c) routine parole or aftercare. Used as an alternative to institutionalization, intermediate sanctions are typically (though not exclusively) intended for nonviolent, as well as chronic but still relatively less serious, delinquents who are considered "incarceration bound." For the institution-bound class of offenders, the intent is generally to reserve limited and expensive bed space for those who most require it, and thus the strategy is one largely designed to address institutional crowding and save money. This is the classic use of intermediate sanctions: as an institutional population control mechanism.

Juvenile offenders who have committed serious, chronic, and even violent offenses, as well as those at risk of committing such offenses, are represented to various degrees in all three populations receiving intermediate type sanctions. This chapter clarifies how and in what ways intermediate sanctions could be used with serious, chronic, and violent offenders in each of the three populations, who should be included, and what are some of the major issues that must be addressed from the standpoint of program design, management, cost, implementation, and evaluation.

There are strong suggestions in the existing research on intermediate sanctions that treatment availability *and* participation in treatment are associated with lower recidivism, but three problems in particular have compelled researchers to present a less than definitive response. First, the lack of existing treatment and appropriate services in the community, the frequency with which offenders did not receive the prescribed treatment and services, the paucity of resources allocated specifically for treatment, and the generally subordinate role treatment has played in intermediate sanctions have led to programs exhibiting much less treatment than surveillance. The lack of treatment intensity has extended both to the percentage of offenders left untreated and the generally low level of treatment provided to those who receive it. Future intermediate sanction programs and research on them would benefit if risk-based treatment services played a prominent role in philosophy, design, and implementation.

Second, the research on intermediate sanction programs has generally suffered from too few participants, so that it becomes exceedingly difficult to generate any statistically significant differences in the analysis. Stated differently, to conclude that one group of offenders has performed better than another, differences are required in small-sample studies that exceed those one might reasonably expect to find. The solution is to launch a large enough effort so that a sufficient number of participants will be assured.

Third, disentangling the effect of particular program components can be crucial to determining the relative importance of different aspects of intermediate sanctions. The research was mostly designed to evaluate the effect, for example, of intermediate sanctions *to the extent* that they combined surveillance and treatment, or boot camps *to the extent* that they may have included intensive aftercare. It would be useful for future efforts, for example, to test specifically and systematically the impact of differential levels of treatment and surveillance-oriented and treatment-oriented intermediate sanctions or very different kinds of boot camps. It would also be advisable to incorporate into future research and program efforts those offenders who are first screened on the basis of risk and then placed randomly into either an experimental intermediate sanction or a regular correctional program. In addition, focusing specifically on strategies designed to prevent and respond to technical violations is another aspect that would benefit from intermediate sanction research and programming.

■ *Part III: Concluding Overview*

Serious and Violent Juvenile Offenders: Gaps in Knowledge and Research Priorities *(Chapter 16 by Nancy G. Guerra)*

This chapter examined gaps in knowledge and research priorities in the areas of patterns and trends, risk assessment and classification, causes and correlates, and prevention and intervention strategies. Three issues were detailed: (a) the need to focus specifically on SVJ offenders; (b) the need to understand the social ecology of SVJ offending in terms of the interaction between individual, situational, and contextual influences over time; and (c) the need to forge collaborations between researchers, practitioners, and individuals whose lives are affected by SVJ offending.

Several research gaps were identified in examining current data on patterns and trends of youth violence. Addressed were the relative lack of data for youth under age 12, as well as the overreliance on official records for epidemiological data about SVJ offending for adolescents and young adults. Repeated, large-scale self-reported delinquency studies are needed in high-risk areas. The need to improve self-report measures and increase their developmental and cultural sensitivity was discussed. In addition, the need for assessments that also carefully measure co-occurring behavior problems was underscored.

Although several advances in methodology for screening for prevention services involving at-risk youth have been made (e.g., multiple gating), continued research is warranted, particularly in terms of the ages at which to screen and most appropriate measures and gates to retain. Advances are needed in developing screening tools used to measure risk and classify offenders.

The research on causes and correlates of SVJ offending has occurred most recently using a risk-focused approach. Its strengths and limitations were discussed to the extent that they can guide future research. In particular, the lack of research on protective factors vis-à-vis specific risk profiles and contexts was highlighted. There is also a need to examine why most children do not engage in SVJ offending, and why many youth desist from offending during specific developmental periods. Risk factors need to be examined as they emerge and change in different sociocultural contexts. Instead of general theories of delinquency, frameworks that are sensitive to life course developmental and sociocultural issues are proposed.

In multiple areas, there is the need to forge partnerships between researchers and practitioners. In intervention research, it is necessary to specify outcomes of SVJ offending at the outset and to provide for appropriate (and sometimes long-term) follow-up. Intervention research would benefit from developmental models that specify appropriate risk factors, contexts, and outcomes for different age groups. The best combinations of risk factors can be investigated in intervention research through sophisticated designs that permit assessments of the independent and joint contributions to change of different variables. Because it is unlikely that change will be uniform across participants, it is also important to examine potential moderators of change such as age, gender, ethnicity, and initial level of risk.

■ Policy and Research Issues

Policy Implications

Parents, schools, and neighborhoods are the primary socializing agents to bring up children into nondelinquent individuals. Thus, the actions of parents, schools, and neighborhoods constitute the prime method of preventing juveniles' escalation to serious or violent delinquency. In contrast, the primary function of the juvenile justice system is to deal with those youth who do not benefit from this socialization.

In comparison to parents, schools, and neighborhoods, the juvenile justice system is in a worse position to prevent delinquency. There are several reasons for this. First, it usually deals with adolescent youth only, and not with younger children. Juveniles' malleability of behavior may be highest at an early compared to at a later age, although Lipsey and Wilson (Chapter 13, this volume) show that interventions with institutionalized offenders can be almost as successful as those carried out earlier. Also, the onset of serious persisting offending for a large proportion of youth takes place between ages 7 and 14. Given that the juvenile justice system largely focuses on adolescent populations, this provides too narrow a window for it to identify and respond effectively to many very young offenders.

Second, the juvenile justice system responds to delinquents arrested by the police for offenses thought to be sufficiently serious. Thus, it often does not deal with minor or status offenses that can constitute stepping-stones toward more serious offenses, particularly for the preadolescent population of juveniles. Third, the juvenile justice system is hampered by its restricted access only to detected delinquent youth and, therefore, has limited ability to influence community levels of juvenile delinquency. Because about two thirds of serious violent crime does not show up in juvenile justice records (Elliott, Huizinga, & Morse, 1986; Loeber, Farrington, and Waschbusch, Chapter 2, this volume), "community-based prevention [rather than prevention through the juvenile justice system] holds the most prospects for reducing the bulk of juvenile crime" (Howell & Krisberg, 1995, p. 275). Last, the juvenile justice system's concerns about the causes of SVJ offending are usually limited to the intentions, motivations, and characters of offenders (Moore, Prothrow-Smith, Guyer, & Spivak, 1994). Otherwise, it is reactive to juveniles' delinquent acts and is not geared to influence causes of serious delinquency in the juveniles' families, their schools, or their neighborhoods. In fact, the justice system's ability to address known risk and causal factors for serious juvenile offending is often extremely limited, although the 8% Early Intervention Program in California has shown how this might be achieved.

Having pointed out these limitations of the juvenile justice system, we must also acknowledge its strengths. For those youth who have not benefited from the socializing functions of the family, school, and neighborhood, the system acts as an arbiter and an administrator of justice and sanctions for serious transgressions. The usual functions of the juvenile justice system, such as diversion, adjudication, placement, and probation, need not be elaborated here. There are several ways that the impact of these actions can be gauged, first on the probability of reoffending of the offender, and second on the reduction of SVJ offenders in the community.

The effectiveness of the juvenile justice system can be greatly enhanced by providing intake officers with effective tools to discriminate between less and more serious offenders, and between occasional and frequent offenders, at the time of their first referral. Because the first known offense does not necessarily contain information about where the presenting offense fits in the juvenile's delinquent career, the task is to identify other information that can facilitate intake officers' discrimination. Better screening devices need to be developed and routinely used.

Optimizing intake officers' discrimination between occasional and repeat offenders, and between minor offenders and serious offenders (given that serious offenders also commit minor offenses at a high rate), can then be more effectively linked to graduated sanctions, that is, sanctions appropriate to juveniles' risks, needs, offense frequency, and seriousness. If such optimization is not in place, a substantial proportion of frequent juvenile offenders will be dealt with as either first or occasional offenders. The key question is whether it is feasible to apply graduated sanctions in such a way that predicted SVJ offenders are more intensively dealt with than predicted occasional offenders or predicted minor offenders.

OJJDP's Comprehensive Strategy links graduated sanctions to risk and needs assessments (Howell, 1995), which can facilitate juvenile justice personnel's screening of incoming cases in an economical and efficient manner. Risk assessments are based on the seriousness of the delinquent act and the potential for reoffending, as indicators of the risk to public safety. Needs assessments are to ensure that different types of problems are taken into account in the formulation of a case plan. In addition, needs assessments provide a baseline for monitoring a juvenile's progress over time and stimulate periodic reassessments for the evaluation of treatment effectiveness.

In the case of SVJ offenders, certain components of risk and needs assessment are essential. For juvenile justice personnel to become more efficient in identifying SVJ offenders, additional information is needed above that which is usually collected about the present offense(s), particularly information connected with increased risks of reoffending. Examples are information about gang membership and drug dealing. Research is badly needed to expand the options of legally and ethically permissible information used in screening devices by juvenile justice personnel to identify SVJ offenders on a routine basis.

Several options were reviewed for optimizing the impact of the juvenile justice system on juveniles' frequency and seriousness of offending after probation or release from incarceration (Altschuler, Chapter 15, this volume). This recidivism-reducing function of the juvenile justice system may address risk factors known to maintain offending, or enhance protective factors associated with a reduction in the frequency and seriousness of offending. It should be noted, though, that typically actions from juvenile justice personnel are restricted to factors that may affect individual juvenile delinquents rather than neighborhood or peer influences.

The role of the police in dealing with SVJ offenders needs to be strengthened. Programs are needed to remove handguns, especially among juveniles at risk (Howell, Chapter 12, this volume), and various ways in which police actions can reduce gangs have been suggested (Howell, Chapter 12, this volume; Thornberry, Chapter 8, this volume). In addition, geographic information systems can greatly aid police in identifying hot spots of criminal activities and, presumably, the concentration of SVJ offenders (Howell, Chapter 12, this volume). Finally, policymakers often express the need to "get tough" with SVJ offenders, based on ideas about retribution for delinquent acts committed and deterring other at-risk youth.

Public Health Approaches

There are major differences between public health and justice approaches to serious delinquency and violence (Moore et al., 1994; Reiss & Price, 1996; Shepherd & Farrington, 1993). Public health approaches aim to establish the prevalence and incidence of disease and psychopathology, in the present case, serious and violent offending. This assessment is not necessarily restricted to those youth detected by the juvenile justice system, which is primarily focused on those youth whose behavior fits within a legal classification of offenses (Shepherd & Farrington, 1993).

Public health, unlike most juvenile justice approaches, also focuses on the identification and reduction of risk factors and the identification and promotion of protective factors. Examples of immediate, proximal risk factors for SVJ offending are situational influences such as alcohol or firearms that facilitate violence. Examples of long-term, distal risk factors are poor supervision by parents and chronic conflict among family members. Immediate and long-term causes are approximated in a public health approach by analysis of risk in terms of social, physical, and community factors. In contrast, the justice system is primarily focused on the control of offenders and on deterrence (Moore et al., 1994).

Public health approaches to delinquency can potentially focus on universal populations, selected or at-risk populations, or indicated populations, including youth referred to the juvenile court for delinquency. In contrast, the juvenile justice system is virtually never concerned with primary prevention and, because of a lack of resources, is preoccupied mostly with the prevention of reoffending among those referred to the juvenile court. In recent years, the public health approach to universal prevention of delinquency has been increasingly studied and evaluated (Wasserman and Miller, Chapter 10, this volume). In contrast, the prevention of SVJ offending in selected, at-risk populations, or in indicated populations has been less the focus of systematic evaluations (Shepherd & Farrington, 1993). We will discuss briefly each of the three public health approaches in turn.

1. *Universal approaches.* Extensive reviews of primary prevention methods can be found in Hawkins, Catalano, and Brewer (1995b) and in Wasserman and Miller (Chapter 10, this volume). Promising targets for preventing future SVJ offenders are early education and parents' childrearing practices. Universal approaches can be aimed at reducing individuals' propensity to commit crime, and also at reducing the occurrence of criminological situations (Wikström, 1995b). Examples of the latter are various community mobilization efforts (Howell, Chapter 12, this volume; Catalano et al., Chapter 11, this volume; Hawkins & Catalano, 1992). Another example concerns routine guarding of school playgrounds to prevent bullying and physical fighting among schoolchildren. However, it should be understood that universal approaches target large populations and therefore cannot be expected to be highly efficient in preventing future SVJ offenders, as Le Blanc (Chapter 9, this volume) argues. Nevertheless, primary prevention can be cost-effective not only in preventing SVJ offenders but also in preventing all the associated problems.

2. *Selected approaches.* These approaches are of great importance because only a minority of youth are at risk of becoming SVJ offenders. Therefore, selected approaches aim to identify risk factors that distinguish youth at risk for SVJ offending as distinct from those at risk for less serious forms of delinquency or nondelinquency. On that basis, populations at high risk for SVJ offending can be identified and given interventions. Such interventions aim to reduce risk factors or enhance protective factors that are known to be associated with (a) a deceleration in the severity and frequency of offending, and/or (b) desistance in offending.

3. *Indicated approaches.* Potential targets for prevention in referred populations are deviant or delinquent activities that are known to increase the risk of repeated SVJ offending. Prime examples are the prevention of repeated victimization (Van Kammen & Loeber, 1995; Wikström, 1995b), gang membership (Thornberry, Chapter 8, this volume; Howell, Chapter 12, this volume), and drug dealing (Van Kammen & Loeber, 1994).

Wasserman and Miller (Chapter 10, this volume) point out that because SVJ offending is multidetermined, intervention approaches need to address its multiple causes. This implies that several modes of intervention need to be implemented concurrently, for example, parent training and improving academic attainment. Second, interventions addressing multiple risk factors often need to be implemented simultaneously in several settings. For example, home visits to improve family functioning may have to be combined with classroom management programs for teachers so that the same high-risk youth can be targeted in the two settings. One of the advantages of the multiple-setting approach to the reduction of future SVJ offending is a focus on the consistency across settings of child problem behaviors that often are characteristic of those youth most at risk for later serious offending (Loeber, 1982). Other examples of interventions in multiple settings are cooperative programs between schools and the juvenile justice system (Coordinating Council on Juvenile Justice and Delinquency Prevention, 1996), between community groups and the police, and the routine resolution of serious domestic disputes by the police.

Finally, better routine data collection that can shed light on SVJ offending is needed. Geographic clustering analyses of victimization surveys can probably help to identify communities in which SVJ offenders are concentrated, as can systematic data collection of injuries reported in hospital emergency rooms.

Police and court records can be better automated and linked across different jurisdictions so that cumulative delinquency records
of individual SVJ offenders can be compiled.
This will have the great advantage of eliminating the treatment of SVJ repeat offenders
as first offenders in one jurisdiction because
of their unknown offending elsewhere.

Who Is Accountable?

SVJ offending is similar to many other
problem behaviors in juveniles in that it persists in communities because new recruits
emerge within each generation of youth. Yes-
terday's 8-year-olds who become SVJ offenders are soon joined by today's and tomorrow's 8-year-olds, and so on from generation
to generation. To what extent do traditional
public institutions responsible for juveniles
cope with these persisting cycles of SVJ offenders?

Traditionally, the juvenile justice system
has been seen as the agency primarily responsible for dealing with SVJ offenders. Other
agencies, such as child protection or child
welfare services, have been assigned to deal
with child offenders, and with those juveniles
who repeatedly engage in status offenses. In
addition, the mental health system deals with
juvenile offenders of any age who have mental health problems.

We expressed major reservations about
how well the juvenile justice system in its
current form is suited to deal with SVJ offenders in general, and young SVJ offenders
in particular, and hence to have an impact on
levels of SVJ offending in the community.
Even less is known about the effectiveness of
child protection and welfare services in dealing with very young offenders. Mental health
services are not known to affect community
levels of SVJ offending. We will briefly dis-

cuss the role of these three institutions in preventing the development of SVJ offenders.

A very large proportion of the eventual
SVJ offenders start offending as children (under age 10). For that reason, the juvenile justice system typically does not intercept these
offenders at the beginning of their criminal
career. In 1994, only 25,000 out of about 1.5
million referrals to juvenile courts were of
children under age 10 (H. N. Snyder, personal
communication, March 1997). Child welfare
services, because of their mandate to concentrate on status offenders, are in a poor position to distinguish between those status offenders who commit few other forms of
delinquency and those who also engage in serious and violent offenses. Mental health
services also have little impact on SVJ offending in communities, because of (a) a lack
of any mandate to be responsible for SVJ offenders; (b) a focus on a medical individual-
treatment model rather than on community
needs and community-relevant interventions;
(c) inconsistent evidence of effectiveness of
dealing with known SVJ offenders or preventing SVJ offending in communities; (d)
recent reversals in insurance coverage of juveniles diagnosed with known precursor disorders, including oppositional defiant disorder, conduct disorder, and attention-deficit
hyperactivity disorder; and (e) a widespread
lack of mental health insurance among families in the most disadvantaged inner cities
who often are most at risk of producing SVJ
offenders. In fact, a survey of help seeking by
parents of seriously delinquent boys showed
that three quarters of the caretakers never
sought or received help from a mental health
professional, and this also applied to preadolescent, seriously delinquent boys (Stouthamer-
Loeber, Loeber, & Thomas, 1992).

All three systems—the juvenile justice
system, the child welfare system, and mental
health services—tend to be reactive in their
responses to multiple-problem youth, rather

than proactive in attempting to prevent their emergence. Thus, in each system, sanctions and treatment are more dominant than preventive efforts. Furthermore, the three systems often operate independently rather than in an integrated fashion and are not held collectively accountable for community levels of SVJ offending. Thus, fragmentation of services and separation of responsibilities among these institutions often is the rule rather than the exception. This state of affairs represents traditional roles of institutions dealing with youth and is largely based on old knowledge of developmental aspects of SVJ offending. Current knowledge about the background and developmental course of young SVJ offenders, presented in this volume, will eventually force a change in the division of responsibilities among the different institutions.

The boundaries between the juvenile justice system, child welfare services, and mental health services in dealing with SVJ offenders are often poorly defined and are more characterized by gaps than by integrated services. As a consequence, there is a lack of accountability of agencies who are responsible for the early offending of this group of juvenile offenders. We do not discount the important efforts played by other organizations, such as school, churches, and other community organizations. Often, schools have adopted programs to deal with high-risk youth in elementary classrooms, but in general schools have neither the mandate, resources, nor specialist knowledge to undertake this task on a routine basis from year to year and from generation to generation of youth.

There is more promise in the CTC program, which mobilizes efforts within communities to address known risk factors with proven prevention programs. The laudable efforts of CTC often include collaborating with the juvenile justice system, child welfare services, mental health services, and other agencies to divide the work in such a manner that SVJ offending in the community can be dealt with in a comprehensive manner. However, even with CTC there is no guarantee that the accountability of institutions in dealing with SVJ offenders at the level of prevention and intervention is defined, facilitated, enforced, and maintained from generation to generation of youth.

We recommend that juvenile justice, child welfare, and mental health services have clearly defined responsibilities for preventing the development of SVJ offenders and that they work in coordination rather than in isolation.

Developing a Research Agenda

There are many gaps in knowledge about the development of, and effective interventions for, SVJ offenders that might be filled by new research projects, by reanalyses of existing studies, or by additional data collection in existing studies. First, there is a need to focus specifically on SVJ offenders and to compare them with other types of offenders. Most existing research on risk/protective factors and prevention/intervention strategies provides information about delinquents versus nondelinquents rather than about SVJ offenders versus other types (or serious vs. nonserious, violent vs. nonviolent offenders).

The focus on juvenile offenders follows the legal boundary between juvenile delinquency and adult crime, which is somewhat arbitrary in the context of behavioral development. More research is needed on what are the most useful typologies of offenders for development, explanation, prevention, and intervention purposes. SVJ offenders are important for policy and practice, but other typologies related to them (e.g., life course persistent vs. adolescence-limited offenders) might be more useful for these other purposes. More research is also needed specifically on persistent or chronic juvenile offenders, and on the linkages among violent offending, serious offending, and frequent offending in the juvenile years. A key issue is how serious, violent, or chronic juvenile offenders differ in kind or in degree from other types of offenders.

Most existing typologies of offenders tend to be rather static and specific to a particular age. Dynamic typologies are needed that take account of developmental transitions between different classes of offenders. Research is needed to describe the usual course of developmental transitions over time, to investigate how far they can be predicted and to study how far they vary with such factors as gender, ethnicity, and community context. It is important to specify developmental pathways that begin with minor deviance in infancy or early childhood and that are likely to progress to SVJ offending. This will help to determine what SVJ offenders are like in childhood and how early and accurately they can be identified. In addition, it is important to specify the adult criminal careers and adult life experiences of SVJ offenders.

In the past, SVJ offenders have usually been measured using arrest or court data. More self-report research on serious or violent offenders is needed. Previously, such offenders have often been missing from school- or community-based samples. It is important to assess the concurrent and predictive validity of official and self-report measures of offending and to derive accurate estimates of the prevalence and incidence of serious and violent offenses in particular inner cities or areas, where SVJ offenders disproportionally reside and operate. A key issue centers on how much of the total crime problem is accounted for by SVJ offenders. Equally, it is important to study other social problems (e.g., mental health, educational, employment, welfare) of these individuals to derive

realistic estimates of their total burden on society. Such estimates are crucial in calculating the cost-effectiveness of prevention/intervention programs. A key question is how far all these problems are functionally related and how far they all have similar origins.

Another key research priority is to establish the most important risk factors for SVJ offenders, compared with other types of offenders and with nonoffenders. It is crucial to determine which individual, family, peer, school, neighborhood, and community factors are the strongest predictors, and how these different factors have independent, additive, interactive, or sequential effects on SVJ offending. It is also important to determine which factors have differential effects on the onset, persistence, escalation, de-escalation, or desistance of offending, and whether there are different effects at different ages. Results from these investigations should help in developing and improving theories of SVJ offending and screening devices to predict SVJ offenders. It is even more crucial to carry out research to identify protective factors, because these have been sorely neglected in the past and are likely to have important implications for prevention and intervention.

A key research priority is to assess the effects of interventions (from early prevention to aftercare) specifically on SVJ offenders (vs. nonserious and nonviolent offenders), and especially on their reoffending. It is important to investigate the relative effectiveness of different types of interventions with different types of offenders at different ages. Different effects within different population subgroups (e.g., males vs. females, African Americans vs. Caucasians) and in different communities also need to be studied. Promising interventions need to be evaluated in controlled experiments as far as possible. It seems likely that interventions containing several different components (e.g., individual social skills training, parent management training, peer resistance training) will prove to be the most effective.

Generally, longitudinal studies are needed to investigate developmental pathways and risk/protective factors, and experimental studies are required to investigate prevention/intervention strategies. It would be ideal to combine these two approaches and include experimental interventions in longitudinal, multiple-cohort studies (Farrington, Ohlin, & Wilson, 1986; Tonry, Ohlin, & Farrington, 1991), but the longitudinal-experimental design seems very difficult to mount in practice. Also, the low prevalence of SVJ offenders poses problems for the investigation of risk/protective factors and prevention/intervention strategies.

Some of the key questions about development and risk/protective factors could be addressed by carrying out reanalyses of existing longitudinal studies, as indeed contributors to this volume have done. Some of the key questions about prevention/intervention techniques could be addressed by collecting additional data on SVJ offending in existing experimental studies. However, the designs of many existing studies would not permit urgent questions to be addressed. Existing studies may include too few SVJ offenders, too few females, too few ethnic minorities, a too narrow age range, a too restricted range of risk/protective factors measured, unicomponent or too limited prevention/intervention techniques, too infrequent data collection, and so on.

What types of new projects are needed? New longitudinal studies should include multiple cohorts to draw conclusions about the development of different age groups from birth to the teenage years. Also, they should include both males and females and the major racial/ethnic groups. Also, they should measure a wide range of risk and especially protective factors (individual, family, peer, school, community, etc.). They should be based on large, high-risk samples, especially in inner-city areas, incorporating screening methods to maximize the yield of SVJ offenders while making it possible to draw conclusions about the total population. Also, they should include long-term follow-ups to permit conclusions about developmental pathways.

New experimental studies should include multiple-component interventions and should be designed to evaluate the success of the components as well as the complete package. Ideally, the components should be targeted on different age ranges, and the interventions should be applied to high-risk youth or high-risk communities. It would be useful to evaluate a very flexible, wide-ranging prevention program such as CTC (Hawkins & Catalano, 1992), although the evaluation of community programs raises special challenges for research (Farrington, 1997). In this program, major risk factors are first assessed in a community, and then prevention strategies are implemented to counteract specific risk factors. This type of program is promising. Evaluating it in high-risk communities or inner-city areas might significantly advance knowledge about the prevention of SVJ offending. Although it seems difficult to combine a multiple-cohort longitudinal study with multiple-component interventions, it would be possible to implement multiple-component interventions in a single-cohort longitudinal study. It would also be possible to follow up one or more cohorts of youth within a multiple-cohort intervention study such as CTC. Both of these types of longitudinal-experimental studies are worth implementing and evaluating.

To advance knowledge and reduce crime in the future, an integrated and coordinated program of data collection, intervention, and research specifically on SVJ offenders should be developed by appropriate federal agencies, advised by scholars from the juvenile delinquency and juvenile justice communities.

Appendix

Serious, Violent, and Chronic Juvenile Offenders—An Assessment of the Extent of and Trends in Officially Recognized Serious Criminal Behavior in a Delinquent Population

■ *Howard N. Snyder*

The nationwide growth in the juvenile violent crime arrest rate between 1986 and 1994, after more than a decade of relative stability, has fueled the public's concerns over the viability of the juvenile justice system. To respond to these concerns, most state legislatures have recently made substantial changes in their state's juvenile justice systems. Some legislation has even removed serious and violent offenders from the jurisdiction of the juvenile court and placed these youth under the jurisdiction of the criminal court. Clearly, the future of America's juvenile justice system is being molded by the public's perception of serious and violent juvenile offenders. Therefore, it is important for juvenile justice policymakers, practitioners, and the public to understand the volume of, and growth in, this segment of the juvenile offending population.

This research was designed to place the serious and violent offender in context of the general population handled by the juvenile justice system. Unlike other recent studies that have focused on self-reported delinquent behavior, this work focuses on youth with of-

AUTHOR'S NOTE: This research was supported in part by grants to the National Center for Juvenile Justice from the Office of Juvenile Justice and Delinquency Prevention (Grants 95-JN-FX-K008 and 95-JN-FX-0008).

ficial records of delinquency. Although information about self-reported law-violating behavior is essential to understand the development of law-violating careers, the juvenile justice system can respond only to officially recognized delinquent behavior. Therefore, a clear picture of serious and violent juvenile behavior from the perspective of the juvenile justice practitioner is necessary to support the development of policies that guide the justice system's response to juvenile offenders.

This descriptive study was designed to answer a set of basic questions often raised in the debates over juvenile justice policies and procedures:

1. What are the proportions of serious and violent offenders in the officially recognized delinquent population?
2. Are these proportions increasing?
3. Are serious and violent juvenile offenders in recent years being referred for more serious and violent crimes?
4. Are chronic offenders also serious and violent offenders?
5. Is the onset of officially recognized juvenile violence and serious offending occurring at younger ages?

■ *Method*

To explore officially recognized serious and violent juvenile offending, this study analyzes the juvenile court careers of all persons born between 1962 and 1977 who were referred to the juvenile court in Maricopa County, Arizona, for a delinquency offense prior to their 18th birthday.[1] Another way of classifying this population is to identify each cohort not by its birth year but by the year its members turned 18 years of age and aged out of the original jurisdiction of the juvenile justice system. From this perspective, this study investigates the officially recognized offend-

ing patterns of the juvenile justice "graduating classes" of 1980 through 1995.[2]

Maricopa County population in 1995 was 2.4 million persons, making it the sixth largest county in the United States. In 1995 the violent crime rate in Maricopa County was 12% greater than the national average, and its property crime rate was 75% above the national average. Maricopa County contains a populous central city (Phoenix) and a rapidly growing and ethnically varied population, and it faces the range of problems found in most large metropolitan areas in the United States. In many ways, it is typical of urban America.

When a youth is arrested in this jurisdiction, the youth (or paper on the incident) is sent to the juvenile court's intake screening office for processing. By policy, law enforcement does not screen the case before sending it to juvenile court intake. Therefore, in this jurisdiction, the juvenile court referral population is comparable to the juvenile arrest population in most other jurisdictions.

To characterize the nature of a juvenile court career, this study counted each of a youth's referrals to juvenile court intake and classified each referral by the most serious charge in the set of charges presented at intake. The most serious offense in each case was classified into one of three general offense categories:

1. *Violent offenses* include the offenses of murder and nonnegligent manslaughter, kidnapping, violent sexual assault, robbery, and aggravated assault.
2. *Serious nonviolent offenses* include burglary, serious larceny, motor vehicle theft, arson, weapons offenses, and drug trafficking.
3. *Nonserious delinquent offenses* include such crimes as simple assault, possession of a controlled substance, disorderly conduct, vandalism, nonviolent sex offenses, minor larceny, liquor law offenses, and all other delinquent offenses.

TABLE A1.a Trends in Number of Delinquent Careers and Referrals

	All Delinquents		
Class	Careers	Referrals	Referrals/ Career
All	151,209	325,259	2.15
1980	8,312	17,109	2.06
1981	8,160	17,215	2.11
1982	8,523	18,148	2.13
1983	8,385	17,473	2.08
1984	8,193	17,138	2.09
1985	8,191	16,674	2.04
1986	9,071	18,755	2.07
1987	10,100	20,374	2.02
1988	10,700	21,348	2.00
1989	10,312	20,890	2.03
1990	9,801	20,660	2.11
1991	9,678	21,367	2.21
1992	10,091	23,216	2.30
1993	10,019	23,725	2.37
1994	10,429	24,643	2.36
1995	11,244	26,524	2.36

If a referral contained only status offenses (e.g., running away from home, truancy, curfew, underage drinking) or traffic offenses, the referral was excluded from the analyses. All the remaining delinquency referral records were sorted by referral date (earliest referral first), and a rap sheet detailing the youth's juvenile court delinquent career was prepared.

■ Results

Size of the Graduating Classes

A total of 151,209 youth from the juvenile justice graduating classes of 1980 through 1995 had at least one referral to juvenile court intake in Maricopa County for a delinquent offense prior to their 18th birthday (Table A1.a). Thirty percent (or 46,108) of these youth were female (Table A1.b). The number of youth in each class generally increased over time;

however, the increases were not consistent from year to year. Overall, there were 35% more youth (28% more males and 54% more females) in the juvenile justice graduating class of 1995 than in the class of 1980. The sizes of the classes were rather constant between 1980 and 1985. Following a transition year in 1986, the 1987 graduating class was nearly 25% larger than the class of 1985. This class size was roughly maintained from 1987 through 1994. Once again, in 1995, the size of the graduating class abruptly changed, moving out of the range observed in the prior 8 years to a level about 10% above the average class size of the prior 8 years. Although these changes are somewhat related to the growth in the juvenile population within the county during this period, the consistent growth in the general juvenile population within the county cannot explain the abrupt changes in the sizes of the juvenile justice graduating classes between 1985 and 1987 and between 1994 and 1995.

Between 1980 and 1990, the membership in each birth cohort in Maricopa County increased substantially. For example, the decennial census in 1980 found that there were 22,100 seven-year-olds in the county; by 1990 this same birth cohort (who were now age 17) had 27,900 members—a 26% growth over the 10-year period. These figures indicate a substantial net in-migration (and relatively little out-migration) of young persons with this birth year in the county over the time period when these youth were at risk of juvenile court referral. Certainly, a large proportion of each juvenile justice graduating class lived in the county throughout their juvenile years, whereas others moved into the jurisdiction during their juvenile years (ages 7 through 17) and stayed until they aged out of juvenile court jurisdiction. With an unstable population base, the proportion of youth in a birth cohort that were referred to a juvenile court cannot be developed from these

TABLE A1.b　Trends in Number of Delinquent Careers and Referrals by Sex

| Class | Male Delinquents | | | Female Delinquents | | |
	Careers	Referrals	Referrals/ Career	Career	Referrals	Referrals/ Career
All	105,101	255,721	2.43	46,108	69,538	1.51
1980	5,975	13,969	2.34	2,337	3,140	1.34
1981	5,847	13,999	2.39	2,313	3,216	1.39
1982	6,016	14,595	2.43	2,507	3,553	1.42
1983	5,863	13,829	2.36	2,522	3,644	1.44
1984	5,720	13,617	2.38	2,473	3,521	1.42
1985	5,744	13,076	2.28	2,447	3,598	1.47
1986	6,263	14,619	2.33	2,808	4,136	1.47
1987	6,960	15,714	2.26	3,140	4,660	1.48
1988	7,294	16,277	2.23	3,406	5,071	1.49
1989	7,088	15,947	2.25	3,224	4,943	1.53
1990	6,826	16,270	2.38	2,975	4,390	1.48
1991	6,756	16,904	2.50	2,922	4,463	1.53
1992	7,048	18,440	2.62	3,043	4,776	1.57
1993	6,919	18,846	2.72	3,100	4,879	1.57
1994	7,135	19,267	2.70	3,294	5,376	1.63
1995	7,647	20,352	2.66	3,597	6,172	1.72

data with any precision. However, rough estimates (i.e., assuming the birth cohort was equal to the number of 18-year-olds in the county in the graduation year) indicate over the set of 16 birth cohorts that about one of every three youth had a juvenile court referral for a delinquent offense. Roughly 45% of males and 20% of females had at least one referral to the juvenile court for a delinquency offense prior to their 18th birthday. These estimates also show that the proportion of the birth cohort with a juvenile court referral increased somewhat over the 16-year period.

Age at Onset

It is often heard in many juvenile justice policy debates that juveniles are beginning their court careers at younger ages. Over the graduating classes, was there any evidence that members were referred to juvenile court at earlier ages for their first delinquency referral, their first serious nonviolent referral, or their first violent referral? On average,

across all 16 cohorts, the first delinquency referral occurred at age 15.2 years, the first serious nonviolent referral occurred at 15.2 years, and the first violent referral occurred at age 15.8 years. There is no evidence that any of these average entry ages changed from the class of 1980 through the class of 1995.

In addition, there is no evidence from court records that the proportion of the graduating class that began their court careers below age 14 has risen to extraordinary levels in recent years. Across the 16 graduating classes, 26.1% of all youth began their officially recognized delinquent careers below age 14. The class of 1988 had the smallest proportion of delinquent careers beginning below age 14 (21.9%), whereas the proportions in the graduating classes in the early 1980s and mid-1990s average about 28%.

Over the 16 graduating classes, 7.1% of referred youth (and 23.9% of those youth ever referred for a serious nonviolent offense) had their first referral for a serious nonviolent offense below age 14 (Figure A1). Over the graduating classes, these proportions fell and

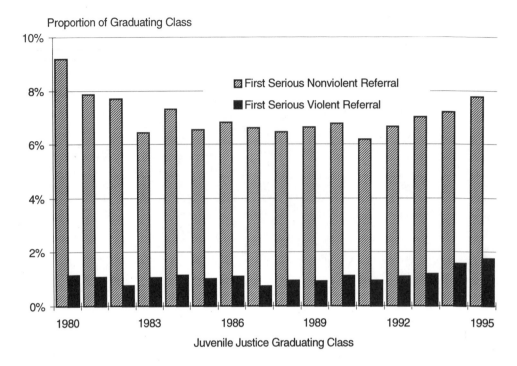

Figure A1. Proportion of Careers With First Serious Referral Prior to Age 14

then increased, staying within a limited range and giving little support for the notion that juveniles in recent years are entering the juvenile justice system at younger ages for serious nonviolent offenses. Over the 16 graduating classes, 1.1% of referred youth (and 13.5% of those youth ever referred for a violent offense) had their first referral for a violent offense below age 14. As with the serious nonviolent referrals, these proportions fluctuated within a limited range over the 16 graduating classes, giving no indication of earlier onset of violent referrals in recent years.

Number of Referrals

The 151,209 youth from the juvenile justice graduating classes of 1980 through 1995 were involved in a total of 325,259 delinquency referrals. Twenty-one percent of referrals involved females. The class of 1995 had 55% more delinquency referrals than the class of 1980. Between the class of 1980 and the class of 1995, the increase in court referrals was greater for females (97%) than for males (46%); however, the male and female increases between the classes of 1986 and 1995 were more consistent, with male referrals increasing 39% and female referrals increasing 49%.

The 55% increase in referrals between the classes of 1980 and 1995 is greater than the 35% increase in the sizes of the graduating cohorts. Thus, youth in the class of 1995 had a higher average number of referrals per career than did members of the class of 1980. Across all cohorts, the average career con-

TABLE A2 Trends in the Offense Characteristics of Delinquency Referrals

| | | No. of Referrals | | | Percentage of Referrals | | |
| | | | Serious | | | Serious | |
Class	All Referrals	Serious	Nonviolent	Violent	Serious	Nonviolent	Violent
All	325,259	90,467	75,366	15,101	27.8	23.2	4.6
1980	17,109	4,885	4,097	788	28.6	23.9	4.6
1981	17,215	5,124	4,312	812	29.8	25.0	4.7
1982	18,148	5,200	4,316	884	28.7	23.8	4.9
1983	17,473	4,866	4,111	755	27.8	23.5	4.3
1984	17,138	4,873	4,166	707	28.4	24.3	4.1
1985	16,674	4,728	4,026	702	28.4	24.1	4.2
1986	18,755	5,224	4,443	781	27.9	23.7	4.2
1987	20,374	5,092	4,363	729	25.0	21.4	3.6
1988	21,348	5,388	4,657	731	25.2	21.8	3.4
1989	20,890	5,267	4,514	753	25.2	21.6	3.6
1990	20,660	5,813	4,937	876	28.1	23.9	4.2
1991	21,367	6,287	5,177	1,110	29.4	24.2	5.2
1992	23,216	7,134	5,805	1,329	30.7	25.0	5.7
1993	23,725	7,077	5,689	1,388	29.8	24.0	5.9
1994	24,643	6,767	5,400	1,367	27.5	21.9	5.5
1995	26,524	6,742	5,353	1,389	25.4	20.2	5.2

NOTE: A career could be counted in more than one category.

tained 2.15 delinquent referrals, with 60% having only one referral in their court careers. Over the 16 birth cohorts, males averaged more delinquency referrals per career than females (2.43 vs. 1.51), and males had a smaller percentage of careers with only one referral (54% vs. 73%).

The average number of referrals per career increased significantly across the graduating classes. For the graduating classes in the 1980s, the average number of referrals per career was 2.06 (2.32 for males and 1.44 for females), whereas in the 1990s the average increased to 2.28 (2.60 for males and 1.58 for females). In addition, the proportion of each cohort with only one referral in their careers declined relatively consistently from 62% in the 1980 cohort to 56% in the 1995 cohort. Declines in the proportion of single-referral careers were observed in both the male (55% to 51%) and the female (79% to 68%) cohorts. Therefore, along with the growth in the number of youth in each birth

cohort referred to juvenile court intake, recent graduating classes also averaged more referrals per court career than did previous graduating classes.

Offense Characteristics of Graduating Classes

Compared to the class of 1980, the class of 1995 generated more referrals in each of the general offense categories (Table A2). The increases in the number of referrals for violent and for nonserious offenses were greater than the growth in the size of the juvenile justice graduating classes, whereas the increase in serious nonviolent referrals paralleled the growth in the size of the referral cohort (Table A3). As a result of these differential increases, the offense profile of the juvenile justice graduating classes changed in the recent years. Compared to the class of 1980, the class of 1995 not only had more referrals per

TABLE A3 Changes Between the Classes of
1980 and 1995 (in percentages)

Size of graduating class	35
Delinquency referrals	55
Nonserious referrals	62
Serious referrals	38
Serious nonviolent referrals	31
Violent referrals	76

career (2.36 vs. 2.06), it also had more nonserious (1.76 vs. 1.47) and more violent (0.124 vs. 0.095) referrals per career. In contrast, the average number of serious nonviolent referrals per career changed relatively little between the classes of 1980 and 1995 (0.493 vs. 0.476). Compared to earlier cohorts, the cohorts aging out of the juvenile court's jurisdiction most recently were, on average, brought to court more often for both violent and nonserious delinquent offenses; however, there was no difference in the average frequency with which cohort members were referred for a serious nonviolent (largely serious property) offense.

Delinquent Career Types

Serious nonviolent careers. Although graduating class averages may be useful in some discussions, the assessments of change may be most useful when focusing on individual careers. An individual career may have many attributes; for example, a youth may be a violent offender (with one or more violent referrals in his or her career) while also being a serious nonviolent offender and a chronic offender. One way to address questions concerning the changes in the character of individual juvenile careers is to study each of several career attributes independently.

Over all graduating classes, 29.5% of youth referred had at least one serious nonviolent referral in their careers (Table A4). The proportion of serious nonviolent offenders in each cohort (i.e., the percentage of the cohort with at least one serious nonviolent referral in their career) showed no consistent trend over the classes of 1980 through 1995 (Figure A2). Has the level of serious nonviolent offending changed within individual careers? That is,

TABLE A4 Trends in the Offense Attributes of Juvenile Court Delinquent Careers

Class	All Careers	No. of Careers			Percentage of Careers		
		Serious	Serious Nonviolent	Violent	Serious	Serious Nonviolent	Violent
All	151,209	50,859	44,669	12,212	33.6	29.5	8.1
1980	8,312	2,763	2,421	643	33.2	29.1	7.7
1981	8,160	2,791	2,462	649	34.2	30.2	8.0
1982	8,523	2,852	2,504	685	33.5	29.4	8.0
1983	8,385	2,738	2,455	594	32.7	29.3	7.1
1984	8,193	2,747	2,477	567	33.5	30.2	6.9
1985	8,191	2,723	2,462	554	33.2	30.1	6.8
1986	9,071	2,992	2,667	653	33.0	29.4	7.2
1987	10,100	3,113	2,751	627	30.8	27.2	6.2
1988	10,700	3,238	2,883	644	30.3	26.9	6.0
1989	10,312	3,216	2,857	650	31.2	27.7	6.3
1990	9,801	3,285	2,915	719	33.5	29.7	7.3
1991	9,678	3,504	3,057	888	36.2	31.6	9.2
1992	10,091	3,792	3,283	1,030	37.6	32.5	10.2
1993	10,019	3,704	3,178	1,091	37.0	31.7	10.9
1994	10,429	3,593	3,056	1,085	34.5	29.3	10.4
1995	11,244	3,808	3,241	1,133	33.9	28.8	10.1

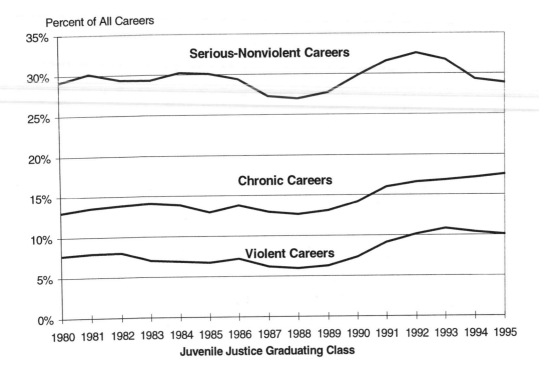

Percent of All Careers

Figure A2. Career Types Within Juvenile Justice Graduating Classes
NOTE: An individual career may be in more than one career type.

were those youth involved in serious nonviolent behavior referred for more of these acts in the later cohorts? To address this point, the career referral rate for serious nonviolent offenses (i.e., the average number of serious nonviolent referrals in careers that had at least one serious nonviolent referral) was developed for each cohort (Figure A3). Overall, youth referred for a serious nonviolent offense were referred an average of 1.69 times for such behaviors in their juvenile court careers. This rate did not change over the 16 cohorts. Therefore, the growth in serious nonviolent referrals observed from the class of 1980 through the class of 1995 was the result of more youth becoming involved in these behaviors and was not caused by an increase in the individual level of youth involvement in serious nonviolent crimes.

Violent careers. The court records show that over all graduating classes between 1980 and 1995, 8.1% of all youth referred had at least one referral for a violent offense in their career (Table A4). The data show, however, that the classes that graduated in the 1990s had a greater proportion of their members charged with a violent offense (Figure A2). A violent offense referral was found in 6% to 8% of the court careers of the classes of 1980 through 1990. After a transitional class in 1991, the proportion of violent offenders in the classes of 1992 through 1995 increased to the 10%-11% level. Therefore, from the juvenile court's perspective, a greater proportion of youth in the recent graduating classes were involved in violent crime.

Were the increases in violent offense referrals in the later graduating classes the result

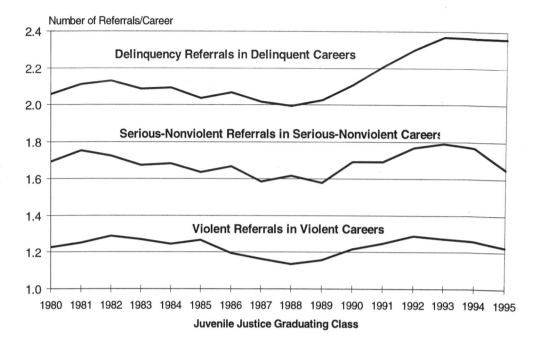

Figure A3. Rate of Offense-Specific Referrals Within Career Type

of increases in the number of referred youth with a violent act in their careers, or had the frequency of violent referrals within an individual career increased? Turning once again to the career referral rates, the average number of violent offense referrals in the careers of youth with a violent offense referral remained constant over the 16 graduating classes, averaging 1.24 violent referrals per career (Figure A3). Across all cohorts, 83% of violent careers (i.e., careers with at least one violent referral) had only one violent referral in the career. That is, 17% of all violent careers over all graduating classes (or 1.4% of all referred youth) had two or more referrals for a violent offense. Over the graduating classes of 1980 through 1995, the proportion of repeat violent offenders fluctuated, reaching a low point of 11% in the class of 1988 and high points of 20% in 1982 and 1992 (Figure A4). Therefore, the substantial increases in violent crime referrals between the classes of the 1980s and those of the 1990s were primarily the result of a greater number of youth being referred for a single violent offense and not the result of an increase in the level of repeat violent offending by members of the more recent graduating classes.

Very few of the individuals in the 16 cohorts could be characterized as chronically violent offenders. Of the 151,209 youth in these 16 cohorts, 168 had four or more violent referrals in their court records. This was 0.1% of all referred youth and 1.4% of those youth ever referred for a violent offense. Even those with three or more violent referrals in their careers represent just 0.4% of all referred juveniles and 4.8% of violent juvenile offenders.

Chronic offenders. Juvenile policymakers have been actively concerned since the mid-1970s with the chronic offender. Popularized by Wolfgang, Figlio, and Sellin (1972), their

Percent of All Violent Careers

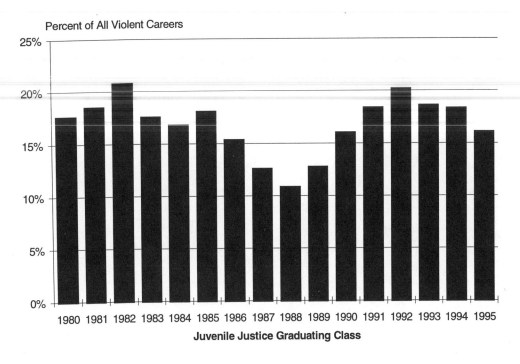

Figure A4. Violent Careers With More Than One Violent Referral

study of police contacts in Philadelphia defined chronic offenders as that small portion of a birth cohort who are responsible for the majority of serious crimes committed by the cohort. In the Philadelphia cohort, for example, 18% of all the males with police contacts were responsible for 52% of all delinquent acts committed by the cohort. In the Philadelphia study, chronic offenders were those youth with five or more police contacts in their juvenile careers. A corresponding definition can be developed using juvenile court referrals. A study of the referral patterns of the complete set of 16 graduating classes finds that 14.6% of youth (those with four or more delinquency referrals before their 18th birthdays) were responsible for a disproportionate number of the cohort's serious referrals. More specifically, these chronic offenders were involved in 44.6% of all referrals, 39.3% of all nonserious referrals, 58.2% of

serious nonviolent referrals, and 60.0% of violent referrals (Table A5).

The later graduating classes contained greater proportions of chronic offenders (Table A6). The court records show that the proportion of each graduating cohort that were chronic offenders (those with four or more referrals) remained constant throughout the classes of the 1980s, averaging 13% of all cohort members (Figure A2). The classes of the early 1990s, however, displayed an abrupt increase in their chronic offender proportions, averaging 17% of the careers in the 1992 through 1995 graduating classes. As a result, chronic offenders in the graduating classes of the 1990s were involved in a greater proportion of referrals in all offense categories.

However, although the number and proportion of chronic careers grew over the cohorts, it is important to realize that the nature of the individual chronic career remained the

TABLE A5 Proportion of Referrals Involving Chronic Offenders (in percentages)

Class	All Delinquency	Nonserious	Serious	Serious Nonviolent	Violent
All	44.6	39.3	58.5	58.2	60.0
1980	42.0	36.4	55.9	56.3	53.7
1981	43.8	37.8	57.9	57.8	58.3
1982	44.4	38.6	59.0	58.6	60.6
1983	43.2	37.5	57.7	56.8	62.6
1984	43.1	37.5	57.0	56.3	61.4
1985	40.7	35.3	54.4	53.5	60.1
1986	42.2	36.4	57.4	57.5	57.0
1987	39.4	34.8	53.2	53.7	50.3
1988	38.7	33.4	54.2	54.9	49.8
1989	39.7	35.1	53.4	53.0	55.5
1990	42.9	37.3	57.2	56.8	59.5
1991	46.7	41.2	59.8	59.3	61.9
1992	49.5	43.9	62.1	61.9	62.9
1993	50.4	44.8	63.4	63.3	63.9
1994	50.8	45.4	65.0	64.6	66.5
1995	50.4	46.5	62.1	62.0	62.4

same. Over the 16 graduating classes, chronic offenders averaged 6.56 referrals in their juvenile court career, were referred for 4.17 nonserious offenses, 1.98 serious nonviolent offenses, and 0.41 violent offenses (Table

TABLE A6 Trends in the Proportion of Chronic Careers

Class	All Careers	Chronic Careers	Percentage Chronic
All	151,209	22,115	14.6
1980	8,312	1,085	13.1
1981	8,160	1,106	13.6
1982	8,523	1,183	13.9
1983	8,385	1,183	14.1
1984	8,193	1,138	13.9
1985	8,191	1,066	13.0
1986	9,071	1,254	13.8
1987	10,100	1,310	13.0
1988	10,700	1,360	12.7
1989	10,312	1,358	13.2
1990	9,801	1,395	14.2
1991	9,678	1,548	16.0
1992	10,091	1,674	16.6
1993	10,019	1,690	16.9
1994	10,429	1,792	17.2
1995	11,244	1,973	17.5

A7). These offense-specific referral rates for chronic offenders did not vary in any consistent manner across the classes, although the number of nonserious offense referrals in these careers did increase somewhat in the classes of 1993 through 1995. In all, the court records show that the later classes contained more (not more active, or more serious, or more violent) chronic offenders and that chronic offenders were generally responsible for a greater proportion of all types of referrals in the classes of 1992 through 1995 compared to previous classes.

Career Attributes of Serious Juvenile Offenders

So far, we have largely been considering selected attributes of delinquent careers without considering their interrelationships. To help visualize the overlapping attributes of delinquent careers, it is useful to divide members of the referral cohorts into eight career categories, which can be labeled using a three-character career index. The first charac-

TABLE A7 Average Offense Profile of Chronic Careers

Class	Referrals/Chronic Career				
	All	*Nonserious*	*Serious*	*Serious Nonviolent*	*Violent*
All	6.56	4.17	2.39	1.98	0.41
1980	6.62	4.10	2.52	2.13	0.39
1981	6.81	4.13	2.68	2.25	0.43
1982	6.81	4.22	2.59	2.14	0.45
1983	6.38	4.00	2.38	1.98	0.40
1984	6.49	4.04	2.44	2.06	0.38
1985	6.37	3.95	2.41	2.02	0.40
1986	6.32	3.93	2.39	2.04	0.35
1987	6.13	4.06	2.07	1.79	0.28
1988	6.07	3.92	2.15	1.88	0.27
1989	6.11	4.04	2.07	1.76	0.31
1990	6.36	3.97	2.38	2.01	0.37
1991	6.44	4.01	2.43	1.98	0.44
1992	6.86	4.21	2.64	2.15	0.50
1993	7.07	4.42	2.66	2.13	0.52
1994	6.98	4.53	2.45	1.95	0.51
1995	6.78	4.66	2.12	1.68	0.44

ter of the career index is either a *C* or an *X*, indicating that the career has either four or more referrals (chronic, or *C*) or fewer than four referrals (not chronic, or *X*). The second character of the career index is either an *S* or an *X*, indicating whether the career contains a serious nonviolent offense (*S*) or not (*X*). The third character of the career index is either a *V* or an *X*, indicating whether the career contains a violent offense (*V*) or not (*X*). The career indexes are as follows:

XXX: Nonchronic careers with no serious offenses

XSX: Nonchronic careers with at least one serious nonviolent offense

XXV: Nonchronic careers with at least one violent offense

XSV: Nonchronic careers with at least one serious nonviolent and one violent offense

CXX: Chronic careers with no serious offenses

CSX: Chronic careers with at least one serious nonviolent offense

CXV: Chronic careers with at least one violent offense

CSV: Chronic careers with at least one serious nonviolent and one violent offense.

It should be noted that the entire chronic violent offender population is the combination of two groups: *CXV* and *CSV*.

Most youth referred to court were never charged with a serious offense (Table A8 and Figure A5). Nearly two thirds (63.9%) of juvenile court careers had fewer than four referrals and had no referrals for a serious offense (*XXX*). Another 2.5% of careers were chronic offenders with no serious offenses in their careers (*CXX*). In all, two thirds (66.4%) of all youth referred to juvenile court intake were never charged with a serious offense.

Chronic and violent offenders (*CXV* and *CSV*) were 4.2% of the graduating classes. Although 83.0% of chronic offenders had at least one serious (i.e., violent or serious nonviolent) referral, the large majority of chronic offenders did not have a violent referral. More than three fourths (76.7%) of all chronic offenders (i.e., *CXV, CSV, CSX,* and *CXX*) had at least one serious nonviolent referral in their careers, and 29.0% had at least one violent referral. More than half (52.6%) of all violent offenders were also chronic offenders, and this proportion changed little over the 16 gradu-

TABLE A8 Frequency of Career Types

Career Type	Career Index	No. of Careers	Percentage of All Careers
Nonchronic with no serious offenses	XXX	96,589	63.9
Nonchronic with at least one serious nonviolent offense	XSX	26,717	17.7
Chronic with at least one serious nonviolent offense	CSX	11,930	7.9
Chronic with at least one serious nonviolent and one violent offense	CSV	5,027	3.3
Nonchronic with at least one violent offense	XXV	4,793	3.2
Chronic with no serious offenses	CXX	3,761	2.5
Chronic with at least one violent offense	CXV	1,397	0.9
Nonchronic with at least one serious nonviolent and one violent offense	XSV	995	0.7
Total		151,209	100.0

NOTE: This information is visually displayed in Figure A5 using a Venn diagram with overlapping circles representing the nonserious, chronic, serious nonviolent, and violent career attributes.

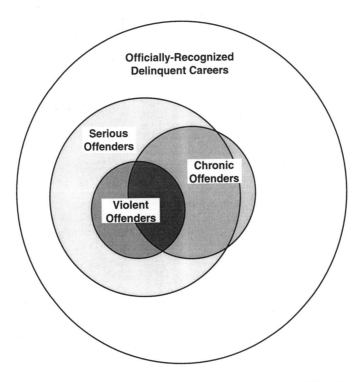

Figure A5. Anatomy of Delinquent Careers Highlighting the Joint Attributes of Chronicity, Serious Nonviolent, and Violent Referrals

NOTE: The outer circle represents all officially recognized delinquent careers. The portion of the large circle not covered by the chronic, serious, and violent offenders' circles represents careers with fewer than four referrals and no referrals for a serious offense. Overlaps represent careers with multiple attributes. The circles and their overlaps are drawn proportional to the number of careers with those attributes.

Percent of All Violent Careers

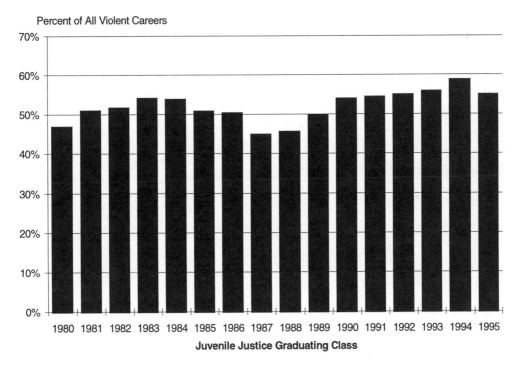

Figure A6. Proportion of Violent Careers That Were Also Chronic Careers

ating classes (Figure A6). Most (78.3%) of the chronic and violent offenders also had at least one serious nonviolent referral in their careers (*CSV*). In fact, the most common career type containing a violent offense referral was *CSV,* chronic offenders with both a violent and a serious nonviolent referral in their careers. Nearly 3 of every 5 careers containing a serious nonviolent offense were not chronic (59.8%), and almost 7 of every 8 serious nonviolent careers did not contain a violent offense (86.5%).

The existence of at least one serious nonviolent referral in a career was very common, even in relatively short careers (Figure A7). The court records show that 62% of careers with four referrals to juvenile court intake had at least one referral for a serious nonviolent offense. The likelihood of juveniles having a serious nonviolent offense in their careers was over 90% once the career reached nine re-

ferrals. In fact, over half of careers with nine referrals contain at least three separate referrals for a serious nonviolent offense.

The existence of a violent referral in a juvenile court career was directly related to the length of a career. As Figure A8 shows, the relation is almost linear, and the slope is far more gradual than that between serious nonviolent referrals and career length. It is as if each new referral to court increases a juvenile's likelihood of having a violent offense in his or her career. Youth with three referrals have a 5% greater likelihood of having a violent offense in their career than those with two referrals. Similarly, those with four referrals have a 5% greater likelihood than those with three referrals, as do careers with 12 referrals compared to those with 11 referrals. A similar linear relationship holds for the second violent referral.

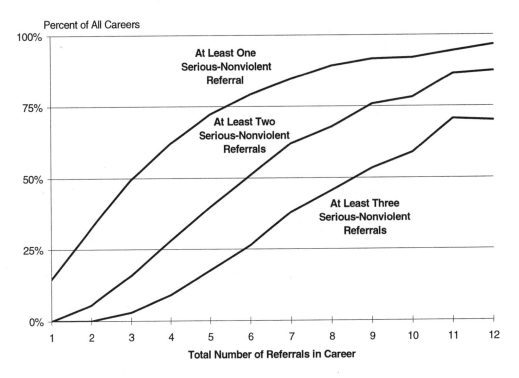

Figure A7. Proportion of Careers With Serious Nonviolent Referrals

■ *Conclusions*

If this study's community and its juvenile justice system are typical of other jurisdictions in this country, practitioners and policymakers can take some comfort in the fact that the juvenile justice system is largely achieving its goal of successfully intervening in the lives of delinquent youth. First, the large majority of youth referred to the juvenile justice system were referred only once. Although many of these youth may have desisted from delinquent behavior on their own and some may have committed additional delinquent acts that were not detected by law enforcement, the fact is that 60% of those youth referred to juvenile court intake never returned for a new offense. Even the 8% of all referred youth who were charged with a violent offense rarely returned to court charged with a

second violent act. In this community, five of every six of youth charged with a violent offense never returned on a new violent charge. If the public's concern is for repetitive violent youth, this study should help to put that concern in perspective—only 1% of all court-involved youth in the last 16 juvenile justice graduating classes were charged with two or more violent acts.

Practitioners and policymakers should also consider that the world may not be changing as rapidly as they believe. A larger proportion of youth are becoming involved in the juvenile justice system. However, it is not true that a new type of juvenile offender (e.g., a generation of *violent predators*) is emerging in our communities. Compared to the juvenile justice graduating classes of the early 1980s, those of the early 1990s had a somewhat greater proportion of referred youth charged with a violent offense, but the in-

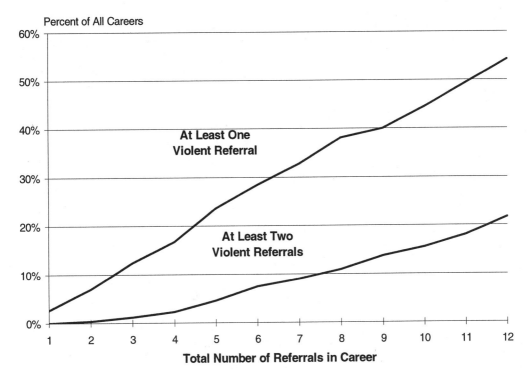

Figure A8. Proportion of Careers With Violent Referrals

crease was not dramatic. In this study the juvenile justice graduating classes in the first half of the 1980s had about 8% of their members charged with a violent offense, compared to 10% in the first half of the 1990s. This is not evidence of a new type of violent offender, especially when it is remembered that the vast majority of violent offenders in the more recent classes (as in previous classes) were charged with only a single violent act.

If there were a new breed of serious juvenile offenders, the court's workload in serious nonviolent crime should also have increased; however, the proportion of a graduating class charged with a serious but nonviolent offense did not change over the 16 classes studied. In fact, much of the growth in referrals for the more recent graduating classes was a growth in referrals for nonserious offenses, an indication that the juvenile

justice system may be spreading its net wider, bringing in more juveniles, not more serious juvenile offenders.

If our society were facing a new type of delinquent offender, this type of offender should be most apparent in the large urban areas in this country, such as the one studied in this research. Based on this study, the empirical evidence for a new type of offender is not there. Too often, changes in policy and practice are based on exceptions and rare events (e.g., the Willie Bosket case in New York or the 6-year-old charged with attempted murder in Richmond, California)—high-profile, unique cases that create the perceptions that drive change. With a growing population and the laws of probability, more of these outlandish events will occur. We must defend against having our understanding of juvenile crime and our evaluations of the juvenile justice system molded by these aberrations.

What we should remember is captured best in this study's finding of the relationship between career length and the existence of a violent crime referral in the career. From this study, it appears that each time a youth returns to court on a new charge there is a greater risk that it will be for a violent crime. To reduce juvenile violence, therefore, we must work to reduce the recidivism of juvenile offenders regardless of the act that has brought them to the attention of the juvenile justice system. And the earlier we successfully intervene in the career, the more effective the intervention will be in reducing the overall level of violence caused by the members of a juvenile justice graduating class. Waiting to intervene until the youth is officially labeled a violent offender will have little effect on the overall level of officially recognized violent crime because the large majority of this violence is tied to a youth who will commit only one officially recognized violent crime. By the time the label can be applied, the youth's officially recognized violence is over.

■ Notes

1. The data used in this chapter were housed in and made available by the National Juvenile Court Data Archive, which is maintained by the National Center for Juvenile Justice in Pittsburgh, Pennsylvania, and supported by grants from the Office of Juvenile Justice and Delinquency Prevention, U.S. Department of Justice. The data were originally collected by the Maricopa County Juvenile Court. The Maricopa County Juvenile Court bears no responsibility for the analyses or the interpretations presented herein, although the court has reviewed a draft of the chapter and has given its permission for the author to identify the source of the data.

2. Much of the significant research on the nature of juvenile law-violating careers describes the behavior of youth who passed through their juvenile law-violating years in the 1950s, 1960s, and 1970s. Many policymakers believe that children today are much different than children 20 years ago. This *graduating class* terminology emphasizes the timeliness of the information in this chapter.

References

Aber, J. L., Brown, J. L., Chaudry, N., Jones, S. M., & Samples, F. (1996). The evaluation of the Resolving Conflict Creatively Program: An overview. *American Journal of Preventive Medicine. Youth Violence Prevention: Descriptions and Baseline Data From 13 Evaluation Projects, 12,* 82-90.

Abikoff, H. (1991). Cognitive training in ADHD children: Less to it than meets the eye. *Journal of Learning Disabilities, 24,* 205-209.

Abikoff, H., & Gittelman, R. (1984). Does behavior therapy normalize the classroom behavior of hyperactive children? *Archives of General Psychiatry, 41,* 449-454.

Abikoff, H., & Hechtman, L. (1996). Multimodal therapy and stimulants in the treatment of children with ADHD. In P. Jensen & E. D. Hibbs (Eds.), *Psychosocial treatment for child and adolescent disorders: Empirically based approaches* (pp. 341-169). Washington, DC: American Psychological Association.

Abikoff, H., & Klein, R. G. (1992). Attention-deficit hyperactivity and conduct disorder: Comorbidity and implications for treatment. *Journal of Consulting and Clinical Psychology, 60,* 881-892.

Achenbach, T. M., & Edelbrock, C. S. (1983). *Manual for the Child Behavior Checklist and Revised Child Behavior Profile.* Burlington: University of Vermont, Department of Psychiatry.

Ageton, S. S. (1983). *Sexual assault among adolescents.* Lexington, MA: Lexington Books.

Akamine, T., O'Neill, B. A., & Haymond, C. J. (1980). *Effectiveness of Homebuilders' family counseling intervention.* Washington State University, Department of Education.

Akers, R. L., Krohn, M. D., Lanza-Kaduce, L., & Radosevich, M. (1979). Social learning and deviant behavior: A specific test of a general theory. *American Sociological Review, 44,* 636-655.

Alexander, J. F., Barton, C., Schiavo, R. S., & Parsons, B. V. (1976). Systems-behavioral intervention with families of delinquents: Therapist characteristics, family behavior and outcome. *Journal of Consulting and Clinical Psychology, 44,* 656-664.

Alexander, J. F., & Parsons, B. V. (1973). Short-term behavioral intervention with delinquent families: Impact of family process and recidivism. *Journal of Abnormal Psychology, 81,* 219-225.

Alinsky, S. D. (1946). *Reveille for radicals.* Chicago: University of Chicago Press.

Allen-Hagen, B. (1975). *Youth crime control project: A final report on an experimental alternative to incarceration of young adult offenders* (Research Rep. No. 75-1). Washington, DC: D.C. Department of Corrections.

Altschuler, D. M., & Armstrong, T. L. (1991). Intensive aftercare for the high-risk juvenile parolee: Issues and approaches in reintegration and community supervision. In T. L. Armstrong (Ed.), *Intensive interventions with high-risk youths: Promising approaches in juve-*

nile probation and parole (pp. 45-84). Monsey, NY: Criminal Justice Press.

Altschuler, D. M., & Armstrong, T. L. (1994a). *Intensive aftercare for high-risk juveniles: An assessment.* Washington, DC: U.S. Department of Justice, Office of Juvenile Justice and Delinquency Prevention.

Altschuler, D. M., & Armstrong, T. L. (1994b). *Intensive aftercare for high-risk juveniles: A community care model.* Washington, DC: Office of Juvenile Justice and Delinquency Prevention.

Altschuler, D. M., & Armstrong, T. L. (1995). Managing aftercare services for delinquents. In B. Glick & A. P. Goldstein (Eds.), *Managing delinquency programs that work* (pp. 137-170). Laurel, MD: American Correctional Association.

American Academy of Pediatrics. (1992). Firearms and adolescents. *Pediatrics, 89,* 784-787.

American Psychiatric Association. (1987). *Diagnostic and statistical manual of mental disorders* (3rd ed., rev.). Washington, DC: Author.

American Psychiatric Association. (1994). *Diagnostic and statistical manual of mental disorders* (4th ed.). Washington, DC: Author.

American Psychological Association, Commission on Violence and Youth. (1993). *Violence and youth: Psychology's response.* Washington, DC: American Psychological Association.

Anderson, E. (1990). *Streetwise: Race, class, and change in an urban community.* Chicago: University of Chicago Press.

Anderson, E. (1994, May). The code of the streets. *Atlantic Monthly,* pp. 81-94.

Andrews, D. A., & Bonta, J. (1994). *The psychology of criminal conduct.* Cincinnati, OH: Anderson.

Andrews, D. A., Zinger, I., Hoge, R. D., Bonta, J., Gendreau, P., & Cullen, F. T. (1990). Does correctional treatment work? A clinically-relevant and psychologically informed meta-analysis. *Criminology, 28,* 369-404.

Arbuthnot, J., & Gordon, D. A. (1986). Behavioral and cognitive effects of a moral reasoning development intervention for high-risk behavior-disordered adolescents. *Journal of Consulting and Clinical Psychology, 54,* 208-216.

Armstrong, T. L. (1988). National survey of juvenile intensive probation supervision, Part I. *Criminal Justice Abstracts, 20,* 342-348.

Armstrong, T. L. (1991). Introduction. In T. L. Armstrong (Ed.), *Intensive interventions with high-risk youths: Promising approaches in juvenile probation and parole* (pp. 1-26). Monsey, NY: Criminal Justice Press.

Armstrong, T. L., & Altschuler, D. M. (1994). Recent developments in programming for high-risk juvenile parolees: Assessment findings and program prototype development. In A. R. Roberts (Ed.), *Critical issues in crime and justice* (pp. 189-213). Newbury Park, CA: Sage.

Arthur, M. W., Ayers, C. D., Graham, K. A., & Hawkins, J. D. (1997). *Mobilizing communities to reduce risks for substance abuse: A comparison of two strategies.* Manuscript submitted for publication.

Arthur, M. W., Brewer, D. D., Graham, K. G., Shavel, D. A., Tremper, M., & Hawkins, J. D. (1996). *Assessing state and community readiness for prevention.* Unpublished manuscript, University of Washington, Seattle, Social Development Research Group.

Arthur, M. W., Hawkins, J. D., Catalano, F. R., Pollard, J. A., & Howze, T. H. (1997). *Six State Consortium for Prevention Needs Assessments Studies Project: Measurement validation results.* Final report submitted to the Kansas Department of Social and Rehabilitation Services, Alcohol and Drug Abuse Services. Seattle: University of Washington, Social Development Research Group.

Ary, D. V., Biglan, A., Glasgow, R., Zoref, L., Black, C., Ochs, L., Severson, H., Kelly, R., Weissman, W., Lichtenstein, E., Brozovsky, P., Wirt, R., & James, L. (1990). The efficacy of social-influence prevention programs versus "standard care": Are new initiatives needed? *Journal of Behavioral Medicine, 13,* 281-296.

Ashford, J. B., & LeCroy, C. W. (1990). Juvenile recidivism: A comparison of three prediction instruments. *Adolescence, 25,* 441-450.

Attar, B., Guerra, N., & Tolan, P. (1994). Neighborhood disadvantage, stressful life events, and adjustment in urban elementary-school children. *Journal of Clinical Child Psychology, 23,* 391-400.

Auerbach, A. W. (1978). *The role of the therapeutic community "Street Prison" in the rehabilitation of youthful offenders.* Doctoral dissertation, George Washington University. (University Microfilms No. 78-01086)

August, G. J., Realmuto, G. M., Crosby, R. D., & MacDonald, A. W. (1995). Community-based multiple-gate screening of children at risk for conduct disorder. *Journal of Abnormal Child Psychology, 23,* 521-544.

Austin, J., Elms, W., Krisberg, B., & Steele, P. (1991). *Unlocking juvenile corrections.* San Francisco: National Council on Crime and Delinquency.

Austin, J., Joe, K., Krisberg, B., & Steele, P. (1990, March). The impact of juvenile court sanctions: A court that works. In *Focus.* San Francisco: National Council on Crime and Delinquency.

Austin J., & Krisberg, B. (1982). The unmet promise of alternatives to incarceration. *Crime & Delinquency, 28,* 274-409.

Bachman, J. G., & O'Malley, P. M. (1984). Yea-saying, nay-saying, and going to extremes: Black-white differences in response styles. *Public Opinion Quarterly, 48,* 491-509.

Baird, S. C. (1984). *Classification of juveniles in corrections: A model system approach.* Madison, WI: National Council on Crime and Delinquency.

Baird, S. C. (1987). *The development of risk prediction scales for the California Youthful Offender Parole Board.* San Francisco: National Council on Crime and Delinquency.

Baird, S. C. (1991). *Validating risk assessment instruments in community corrections.* Madison, WI: National Council on Crime and Delinquency.

Baker, R. L. A., & Mednick, B. R. (1984). *Influences on human development: A longitudinal perspective.* Boston: Kluwer-Nijhoff.

Bandura, A. (1986). *Social foundations of thought and action: A social-cognitive view.* Englewood Cliffs, NJ: Prentice Hall.

Bank, L., Marlowe, J. H., Reid, J. B., Patterson, G. R., & Weinrott, M. R. (1991). A comparative evaluation of parent-training interventions for families of chronic delinquents. *Journal of Abnormal Child Psychology, 19,* 15-33.

Banks, J., Porter, A. L., Rardin, R. L., Silver, T. R., & Unger, V. E. (1977). *Phase I evaluation of intensive special probation projects.* Washington, DC: U.S. Department of Justice.

Barkley, R. A. (1987). *Defiant children: A clinician's manual for parent training.* New York: Guilford.

Barnes, H. E., & Teeters, N. K. (1945). *New horizons in criminology.* New York: Prentice Hall.

Barton, C., Alexander, J. F., Waldron, H., Turner, C. W., & Warburton, J. (1985). Generalizing treatment effects of functional family therapy: Three replications. *American Journal of Family Therapy, 13,* 16-26.

Barton, W., & Butts, J. (1988). *The Metro County intensive supervision experiment.* Ann Arbor, MI: Institute for Social Research.

Barton, W. H., & Butts, J. A. (1990). Viable options: Intensive supervision programs for juvenile delinquents. *Crime & Delinquency, 36,* 238-256.

Battin, S. R., Hill, K. G., Abbott, R. D., Catalano, R. F., & Hawkins, J. D. (in press). The contribution of gang membership to delinquency beyond delinquent friends. *Criminology.*

Battin, S., Hill, K. G., Hawkins, J. D., Catalano, R. F., & Abbott, R. (1996). *Testing gang membership and association with antisocial peers as independent predictors of antisocial behavior: Gang members compared to non-gang members of law-violating youth groups.* Paper presented at the annual meeting of the American Society of Criminology, Chicago.

Baumeister, R. F., Smart, L., & Boden, J. M. (1996). Relation of threatened egoism to violence and aggression: The dark side of high esteem. *Psychological Review, 103,* 5-33.

Baumer, T. L., & Mendelsohn, R. I. (1992). Electronically monitored home confinement: Does it work? In J. M. Byrne, A. J. Lurigio, & J. Petersilia (Eds.), *Smart sentencing: The emergence of intermediate sanctions* (pp. 54-67). Newbury Park, CA: Sage.

Bean, J. S. (1988). The effect of individualized reality therapy on the recidivism rates and locus of control

orientation of male juvenile offenders (Doctoral dissertation, University of Mississippi, 1988). *Dissertation Abstracts International, 49,* 2370B. (University Microfilms No. 88-18138)

Beasley, R. W., & Antunes, G. (1974). The etiology of urban crime: An ecological analysis. *Criminology, 11,* 439-461.

Bell, G. B., & Bennett, W. J. (Eds.). (1996). *The state of violent crime in America: First report of the Council on Crime in America.* Washington, DC: New Citizenship Project.

Berrueta-Clement, J. R., Schweinhart, L. J., Barnett, W. S., Epstein, A. S., & Weikart, D. P. (1984). *Changed lives: The effects of the Perry Preschool Program on youths through age 19.* Ypsilanti, MI: High/Scope.

Bickford, A., & Massey, D. (1991). Segregation in the second ghetto: Racial and ethnic segregation in American public housing, 1977. *Social Forces, 69,* 1011-1036.

Biglan, A. (1995). Translating what we know about the context of antisocial behavior into a lower prevalence of such behavior. *Journal of Applied Behavior Analysis, 28,* 479-492.

Biglan, A., & Ary, D. V. (1985). Current methodological issues in research on smoking prevention. In C. Bell & R. J. Battjes (Eds.), *Prevention research: Deterring drug abuse among children and adolescents* (NIDA Research Monograph No. 63, pp. 170-195). Washington, DC: Government Printing Office.

Biglan, A., Severson, H., Ary, D., Faller, C., Gallison, C., Thompson, R., Glasgow, R., & Lichtenstein, E. (1987). Do smoking prevention programs really work? Attrition and the internal and external validity of an evaluation of a refusal skills training program. *Journal of Behavioral Medicine, 10,* 159-171.

Binet, A., & Simon, T. (1907). *Les enfants anormaux: guide pour l'admission des enfants anormaux dans les classes de perfectionnement* [Abnormal children: A guide for the admission of abnormal children in special classes]. Paris: Armand Colin.

Bishop, D. M., Frazier, C. E., Lanza-Kaduce, L., & Winner, L. (1996). The transfer of juveniles to criminal court: Does it make a difference? *Crime & Delinquency, 42,* 171-191.

Bjerregaard, B., & Lizotte, A. J. (1995). Gun ownership and gang membership. *Journal of Criminal Law and Criminology, 86,* 37-58.

Bjerregaard, B., & Smith, C. (1993). Gender differences in gang participation, delinquency, and substance use. *Journal of Quantitative Criminology, 9,* 329-355.

Black, G. S. (1989). *Changing attitudes toward drug use.* Rochester, NY: Gordon S. Black.

Blackburn, R. (1993). *The psychology of criminal conduct: Theory, research and practice.* Toronto: John Wiley.

Block, C. (1993). Lethal violence in the Chicago Latino community. In A. V. Wilson (Ed.), *Homicide: The victim/offender connection* (pp. 267-342). Cincinnati, OH: Anderson.

Block, C. R. (1988). Lethal violence in the Chicago Latino community, 1965-1981. In J. F. Kraus, S. B. Sorenson, & P. D. Juarez (Eds.), *Proceedings of research conference on violence and homicide* (pp. 31-65). Los Angeles: University of California.

Block, C. R., & Block, R. B. (1991). Beginning with Wolfgang: An agenda for homicide research. *Journal of Crime and Justice, 14,* 31-70.

Block, C. R., & Christakos, A. (1995). Major trends in Chicago homicide: 1965-1994. *Research Bulletin.* Chicago: Illinois Criminal Justice Information Authority.

Block, C. R., Christakos, A., Jacob, A., & Przybylski, R. (1996). Street gangs and crime: Patterns and trends in Chicago. *Research Bulletin.* Chicago: Illinois Criminal Justice Information Authority.

Block, R. (1979). Community, environment, and violent crime. *Criminology, 17,* 46-57.

Block, R., & Block, C. R. (1993). Street gang crime in Chicago. *Research in brief.* Washington, DC: U.S. Department of Justice, National Institute of Justice.

Blumstein, A. (1995). Youth violence, guns, and the illicit-drug industry. *Journal of Criminal Law and Criminology, 86,* 10-36.

Blumstein, A., Cohen, J., & Farrington, D. (1988a). Criminal career research: Its value for criminology. *Criminology, 26,* 1-35.

Blumstein, A., Cohen, J., & Farrington, D. (1988b). Longitudinal and criminal career research: Further clarifications. *Criminology, 26,* 57-74.

Blumstein, A., Cohen, J., Roth, J. A., & Visher, C. A. (Eds.). (1986). *Criminal careers and "career criminals."* Washington, DC: National Academy Press.

Blumstein, A., Farrington, D. P., & Moitra, S. D. (1985). Delinquency careers: Innocents, desisters, and persisters. In M. Tonry & N. Morris (Eds.), *Crime and justice: An annual review of research* (Vol. 6, pp. 137-168). Chicago: University of Chicago Press.

Boland, B. (1996, August). What is community prosecution? *National Institute of Justice Journal,* pp. 233-238.

Bond, L. A., & Compas, B. E. (Eds.). (1989). *Primary prevention and promotion in the schools.* Newbury Park, CA: Sage.

Borduin, C. M., Cone, L. T., Mann, B. J., Henggeler, S. W., Fucci, B. R., Blaske, D. M., & Williams, R. A. (1995). Multisystemic treatment of serious juvenile offenders: Long-term prevention of criminality and violence. *Journal of Consulting and Clinical Psychology, 63,* 569-578.

Borduin, C. M., Henggeler, S. W., Blaske, D. M., & Stein, R. J. (1990). Multisystemic treatment of adolescent sexual offenders. *International Journal of Offender Therapy and Comparative Criminology, 34,* 105-113.

Borduin, C. M., Mann, B. J., Cone, L. T., Henggeler, S. W., Fucci, B. R., Blaske, D. M., & Williams, R. A. (1995). Multisystemic treatment of serious juvenile offenders: Long-term prevention of criminality and

violence. *Journal of Consulting and Clinical Psychology, 63,* 569-587.

Bosworth, K., Espelage, D., Dahlberg, L., Daytner, G., DuBay, T., & Karageorge, K. (in press). The effectiveness of a multimedia violence prevention program for early adolescents. *Adolescence.*

Bosworth, K., Espelage, D., & DuBay, T. (1997). *A multimedia tool for mediating conflict in young adolescents.* Manuscript under review.

Bosworth, K., Espelage, D., DuBay, T., Dahlberg, L., & Daytner, G. (1996). Using multimedia to teach conflict resolution skills to young adolescents. *American Journal of Preventive Medicine, 12,* 65-74.

Bottoms, A. E., & Wiles, P. (1988). Crime and housing policy: A framework for crime prevention analysis. In T. Hope & M. Shaw (Eds.), *Crime, policing and place.* London: HMSO.

Botvin, G. J., Baker, E., Renick, N. L., Filazzola, A. D., & Botvin, E. M. (1984). A cognitive behavioral approach to substance abuse prevention. *Addictive Behaviors, 9,* 137-147.

Bowker, L., & Klein, M. W. (1983). The etiology of female juvenile delinquency and gang membership: A test of psychological and social structural explanations. *Adolescence, 18,* 739-751.

Boydstun, J. E. (1975). *San Francisco field interrogation final report.* Washington, DC: Police Foundation.

Bracht, N., & Kingsbury, L. (1990). Community organization principles in health promotion: A five-stage model. In N. Bracht (Ed.), *Health promotion at the community level* (pp. 66-88). Newbury Park, CA: Sage.

Braithwaite, J. B., & Law, H. G. (1978). The structure of self-reported delinquency. *Applied Psychological Measurement, 2,* 221-238.

Brennan, R. T. (1992). *Project evaluation: ECSS program of the Lesson One Foundation beginners' curriculum (pre-kindergarten to third grade).* Boston: Lesson One Foundation.

Brennan, T. (1980). *Multivariate taxonomic classification for criminal justice research: Vol. 1. An evaluative overview of classification of criminal justice.* Final report to the National Institute of Justice. Boulder, CO: Behavioral Research Institute.

Brennan, T. (1987a). Classification: An overview of selected methodological issues. In D. M. Gottfredson & M. Tonry (Eds.), *Crime and justice: An annual review: Vol. 9. Prediction and classification: Criminal justice decision making* (pp. 201-248). Chicago: University of Chicago Press.

Brennan, T. (1987b). Classification for control in jails and prisons. In D. M. Gottfredson & M. Tonry (Eds.), *Crime and justice: An annual review: Vol. 9. Prediction and classification: Criminal justice decision making* (pp. 323-366). Chicago: University of Chicago Press.

Brewer, D. D., Hawkins, J. D., Catalano, R. F., & Neckerman, H. J. (1995). Preventing serious, violent, and chronic juvenile offending: A review of evaluations of selected strategies in childhood, adolescence, and the community. In J. C. Howell, B. Krisberg, J. D. Hawkins, & J. J. Wilson (Eds.), *Sourcebook on serious, violent, and chronic juvenile offenders* (pp. 61-141). Thousand Oaks, CA: Sage.

Brier, N. (1995). Predicting anti-social behavior in youngsters displaying poor academic achievement: A review of risk factors. *Developmental and Behavioral Pediatrics, 16,* 271-276.

Briggs, P. F., Wirt, R. D, & Johnson, R. (1961). An application of prediction tables to the study of delinquency. *Journal of Consulting Psychology, 25,* 46-50.

Bronfenbrenner, U. (1979). *The ecology of human development: Experiments by nature and design.* Cambridge, MA: Harvard University Press.

Browne, S. F. (1975). *Denver high-impact anti-crime program: Evaluation report.* Denver, CO: Denver Manpower Administration.

Bry, B. H. (1982). Reducing the incidence of adolescent problems through preventive intervention: One- and five-year follow-up. *American Journal of Community Psychology, 10,* 265-276.

Bry, B. H., & George, F. E. (1979). Evaluating and improving prevention programs: A strategy from drug abuse. *Evaluation and Program Planning, 2,* 127-136.

Bry, B. H., & George, F. E. (1980). The preventive effects of early intervention on the attendance and grades of urban adolescents. *Professional Psychology, 11,* 252-260.

Bry, B. H., McKeon, P., & Pandina, R. J. (1982). Extent of drug use as a function of number of risk factors. *Journal of Abnormal Psychology, 91,* 273-279.

Bryk, A. S., & Raudenbush, S. W. (1992). *Hierarchical linear models: Applications and data analysis methods.* Newbury Park, CA: Sage.

Buikhuisen, W., & Jongman, R. W. (1970). A legalistic classification of juvenile delinquents. *British Journal of Criminology, 10,* 109-123.

Burgess, E. W. (1928). Factors determining success or failure on parole. In A. A. Bruce, E. W. Burgess, & A. J. Arn (Eds.), *The working of the intermediate sentence law and the parole system in Illinois* (pp. 205-249). Springfield, IL: State Board Parole.

Burke, P. B. (1997). *Policy-driven responses to probation and parole violations.* Washington, DC: National Institute of Corrections.

Bursik, R., & Webb, J. (1982). Community change and patterns of delinquency. *American Journal of Sociology, 88,* 24-42.

Bursik, R. J. (1980). The dynamics of specialization in juvenile offenses. *Social Forces, 58,* 851-864.

Bursik, R. J., Jr., & Grasmick, H. G. (1993). *Neighborhoods and crime: The dimensions of effective community control.* New York: Lexington Books.

Butts, J. A., Snyder, H. N., Finnegan, T. A., Aughenbaugh, A. L., Poole, R. S. (1996). *Juvenile court statistics 1994.* Washington, DC: U.S. Department of Justice, Office of Juvenile Justice and Delinquency Prevention.

Byrne, J. M., & Kelly, L. (1989). *Restructuring probation as an intermediate sanction: An evaluation of the Massachusetts Intensive Probation Supervision Program.* Unpublished final report to the National Institute of Justice.

Byrne, J. M., Lurigio, A. J., & Baird, S. C. (1989). *The effectiveness of the new intensive supervision programs* (Research in Corrections No. 5). Washington, DC: National Institute of Corrections.

Byrne, J. M., & Pattavina, A. (1992). The effectiveness issue: Assessing what works in the adult community corrections system. In J. M. Byrne, A. J. Lurigio, & J. Petersilia (Eds.), *Smart sentencing: The emergence of intermediate sanctions* (pp. 281-303). Newbury Park, CA: Sage.

Cadoret, R. (1991). Genetic and environmental factors in initiation of drug use and transition to abuse. In M. Glantz & R. Pickens (Eds.), *Vulnerability to drug abuse* (pp. 99-113). Washington, DC: American Psychological Association.

Cadoret, R. J., & Stewart, M. A. (1991). An adoption study of attention deficit hyperactivity, aggression and their relationships to adult antisocial personality. *Comprehensive Psychiatry, 32,* 73-82.

Cairns, R. B., Cairns, B. D., & Neckerman, H. J. (1989). Early school dropout. *Child Development, 60,* 1437-1452.

Cairns, R. B., Cairns, B. D., Neckerman, H. J., Gest, S. D., & Gariepy, J. L. (1988). Social networks and aggressive behavior: Peer support or peer rejection? *Developmental Psychology, 24,* 815-823.

Cairns, R., Earls, F., Fisher, C., Linster, R., Massey, D., Moffitt, T., Ohlin, L., Raudenbush, S., Reiss, A. J., Sampson, R. J., Simcha-Fagan, O., Street, L., Sullivan, M., & Taub, R. (1990, November). *Community measures in the development of delinquent and criminal behavior.* Workshop sponsored by the Program on Human Development and Criminal Behavior, Harvard School of Public Health, Chicago.

California Department of Youth Authority. (1982). *Early identification of the chronic delinquent.* Sacramento: Author.

Campbell, A. (1990). Female participation in gangs. In C. R. Huff (Ed.), *Gangs in America* (pp. 163-182). Newbury Park, CA: Sage.

Campbell, S. B., & Ewing, L. J. (1990). Hard-to-manage preschoolers: Adjustment at age nine and predictors of continuing symptoms. *Journal of Child Psychology and Psychiatry, 31,* 871-889.

Capaldi, D. M., & Patterson, G. R. (1996). Can violent offenders be distinguished from frequent offenders? Prediction from childhood to adolescence. *Journal of Research in Crime and Delinquency, 33,* 206-231.

Capizzi, M., Cook, J. I., & Schumacher, M. (1995, Fall). The TARGET model: A new approach to the prosecution of gang cases. *The Prosecutor,* pp. 18-21.

Caplan, N. S., Deshaies, D. J., Suttles, G. D., & Mattick, H. W. (1967). The nature, variety, and patterning of street club work in an urban setting. In M. Klein & B. G. Myerhoff (Eds.), *Juvenile gangs in context* (pp. 194-202). Englewood Cliffs, NJ: Prentice Hall.

Carlson, C. L., Pelham, W. E., Milich, R., & Dixon, J. (1992). Single and combined effects of methylphenidate and behavior therapy on the classroom performance of children with attention-deficit hyperactivity disorder. *Journal of Abnormal Child Psychology, 20,* 213-232.

Cartwright, D. S., Tomson, B., & Schwartz, H. (1975). *Gang delinquency.* Monterey, CA: Brooks/Cole.

Caspi, A., Elder, G. H., & Bem, D. J. (1987). Moving against the world: Life-course patterns of explosive children. *Developmental Psychology, 23,* 308-313.

Casswell, S., Gilmore, L., Maguire, V., & Ransom, R. (1989). Changes in public support for alcohol policies following a community-based campaign. *British Journal of the Addictions, 84,* 515-522.

Catalano, R. F., & Hawkins, J. D. (1996). The social development model: A theory of antisocial behavior. In J. D. Hawkins (Ed.), *Delinquency and crime: Current theories* (pp. 149-197). New York: Cambridge University Press.

Cauce, A. M., Comer, J. P., & Schwartz, D. (1987). Long-term effects of a systems-oriented school prevention program. *American Journal of Orthopsychiatry, 57,* 127-131.

Center for Successful Child Development. (1993). *Beethoven's fifth: The first five years of the Center for Successful Child Development* (Executive summary). Chicago: Ounce of Prevention Fund.

Centers for Disease Control. (1990). Forum on youth violence in minority communities: Setting the agenda for prevention. *Public Health Report, 106,* 225-279.

Centerwall, B. (1984). Race, socioeconomic status, and domestic homicide, Atlanta, 1971-72. *American Journal of Public Health, 74,* 813-815.

Centerwall, B. (1995). Race, socioeconomic status, and domestic homicide. *Journal of the American Medical Association, 273,* 1755-1758.

Cernkovich, S. A., Giordano, P. C., & Pugh, M. D. (1983). *The chronic offender and self-report measures of chronic delinquency.* Paper presented at the annual meeting of the American Society of Criminology, Denver, CO.

Cernkovich, S. A., Giordano, P. C., & Pugh, M. D. (1985). Chronic offenders: The missing cases in self-reported delinquency research. *Journal of Criminal Law and Criminology, 76,* 705-732.

Chaiken, J., & Chaiken, M. (1987). *Selecting "career criminals" for priority prosecution.* Cambridge, MA: Abt.

Chaiken, J., Chaiken, M., & Rhodes, W. (1994). Predicting violent behavior and classifying violent offenders. In A. J. Reiss & J. A. Roth (Eds.), *Understanding and preventing violence: Vol. 4. Consequences and control* (pp. 217-295). Washington, DC: National Academy Press.

Chaiken, M. R., & Chaiken, J. M. (1984). Offender types and public policy. *Crime & Delinquency, 30,* 195-226.

Chambliss, W. (1994). Policing the ghetto underclass: The politics of law and law enforcement. *Social Problems, 41,* 177-194.

Chandler, M. J. (1973). Egocentrism and antisocial behavior: The assessment and training of social perspective-taking skills. *Developmental Psychology, 9,* 326-333.

Charlebois, P., Le Blanc, M., Gagnon, C., & Larivée, S. (1994). Methodological issues in multiple-gating procedures for antisocial behaviors in elementary students. *Remedial and Special Education, 15,* 44-55.

Charlebois, P., Le Blanc, M., Gagnon, C., Larivée, S., & Tremblay, R. E. (1993). Age trends in early behavioral predictors of serious antisocial behaviors. *Journal of Psychopathology and Behavioral Assessment, 15,* 23-41.

Chavez, E. L., Oetting, E. R., & Swaim, R. (1994). Dropout and delinquency: Mexican-American and Caucasian Non-Hispanic youth. *Journal of Clinical Child Psychology, 23,* 47-55.

Chesney-Lind, M., Leisen, M. B., Allen, J., Brown, M., Rockhill, A., Marker, N., Liu, R., & Joe, K. (1995a). *Crime, delinquency, and gangs in Hawaii: Evaluation of Hawaii's Youth Gang Response System: Part I.* Honolulu: University of Hawaii, Manoa, Social Science Research Institute, Center for Youth Research.

Chesney-Lind, M., Leisen, M. B., Allen, J., Brown, M., Rockhill, A., Marker, N., Liu, R., & Joe, K. (1995b). *The Youth Gang Response System. A process evaluation: Part II.* Honolulu: University of Hawaii, Manoa, Social Science Research Institute, Center for Youth Research.

Chesney-Lind, M., Marker, N., Stern, I. R., Song, V., Reyes, H., Reyes, Y., Stern, J., Taira, J., & Yap, A. (1992). *An evaluation of Act 189: Hawaii's response to youth gangs.* Honolulu: University of Hawaii, Manoa, Social Science Research Institute, Center for Youth Research.

Chesney-Lind, M., Marker, N., Stern, I. R., Yap, A., Song, V., Reyes, H., Reyes, Y., Stern, J., & Taira, J. (1992). *Gangs and delinquency in Hawaii.* Honolulu: University of Hawaii, Manoa, Social Science Research Institute, Center for Youth Research.

Children's Research Center. (1993). *A new approach to child protection: The CRC model.* Madison, WI: National Council on Crime and Delinquency.

Clarke, R. V. (1983). Situational crime prevention: Its theoretical basis and practical scope. In M. Tonry & N. Morris (Eds.), *Crime and justice: An annual review of research* (Vol. 4, pp. 225-256). Chicago: University of Chicago Press.

Clarke, R. V. (1995). Situational crime prevention. In M. Tonry & D. P. Farrington (Eds.), *Crime and justice: A review of research: Vol. 19. Building a safer society: Strategic approaches to crime prevention* (pp. 91-150). Chicago: University of Chicago Press.

Clarke, R. V., & McGrath, G. (1990). Cash reduction and robbery prevention in Australian betting shops. *Security Journal, 1,* 160-163.

Clear, T. (1988). Statistical prediction in correction. *Research in Correction, 1,* 1-39.

Clear, T. R. (1991). Juvenile intensive probation supervision: Theory and rationale. In T. L. Armstrong (Ed.), *Intensive interventions with high-risk youths: Promising approaches in juvenile probation and parole* (pp. 29-44). Monsey, NY: Criminal Justice Press.

Clear, T. R., & Byrne, J. M. (1992). The future of intermediate sanctions: Questions to answer. In J. M. Byrne, A. J. Lurigio, & J. Petersilia (Eds.), *Smart sentencing: The emergence of intermediate sanctions* (pp. 319-331). Newbury Park, CA: Sage.

Clear, T. R., & Hardyman, P. L. (1990). The new intensive supervision movement. *Crime & Delinquency, 36,* 42-60.

Cloward, R. A., & Ohlin, L. B. (1960). *Delinquency and opportunity: A theory of delinquent gangs.* New York: Free Press.

Coates, R., Miller, A., & Ohlin, L. (1978). *Diversity in a youth correctional system.* Cambridge, MA: Ballinger.

Cohen, B. (1969). The delinquency of gangs and spontaneous groups. In T. Sellin & M. E. Wolfgang (Eds.), *Delinquency: Selected studies* (pp. 61-111). New York: John Wiley.

Cohen, J. (1986). Research on criminal careers: Individual frequency rates and offense seriousness. In A. Blumstein, J. Cohen, J. A. Roth, & C. A. Visher (Eds.), *Criminal careers and "career criminals"* (Vol. 1, pp. 292-418). Washington, DC: National Academy Press.

Cohen, J. (1988). *Statistical power analysis for the behavioral sciences* (2nd ed.). Hillsdale, NJ: Lawrence Erlbaum.

Cohen, M. I., Williams, K., Bekelman, A. M., & Crosse, S. (1994). Evaluation of the National Youth Gang Drug Prevention Program. In M. W. Klein, C. Maxson, & J. Miller (Eds.), *The modern gang reader* (pp. 266-275). Los Angeles: Roxbury.

Coie, J. D., & Dodge, K. A. (1983). Communities and changes in children's sociometric status: A five-year longitudinal study. *Merrill-Palmer Quarterly, 29,* 261-282.

Coie, J. D., & Jacobs, M. R. (1993). The role of social context in the prevention of conduct disorder. *Development and Psychopathology, 5,* 263-275.

Coie, J. D., Watt, N. F., West, S. G., Hawkins, J. D., Asarnow, J. R., Markman, H. J., Ramey, S. L. Shure, M. B., & Long, B. (1993). The science of prevention: A conceptual framework and some directions for a national research program. *American Psychologist, 48,* 1013-1022.

Comer, J. P. (1988). Educating poor minority children. *Scientific American, 259,* 42-48.

Committee for Children. (1990). *Second Step: A violence prevention curriculum.* Seattle, WA: Author.

Conduct Problems Prevention Research Group. (1992). A developmental and clinical model for the prevention of conduct disorders: The FAST Track program. *Development and Psychopathology, 4,* 509-527.

Conduct Problems Prevention Research Group. (1996, May). *An initial evaluation of the FAST Track program.* Paper presented at the National Conference on Prevention, Washington, DC.

Connell, J. P., Kubisch, A. C., Schorr, L. B., & Weiss, C. H. (Eds.). (1995). *New approaches to evaluating community initiatives: Concepts, methods, and contexts.* Washington, DC: Aspen Institute.

Cook, P. (1985). The case of the missing victims: Gunshot woundings in the National Crime Survey. *Journal of Quantitative Criminology, 1,* 91-102.

Cook, P., & Laub, J. (in press). The unprecedented epidemic in youth violence. In M. Tonry & M. Moore (Eds.), *Crime and justice: A review of research.* Chicago: University of Chicago Press.

Cook, P. J. (Ed.). (1981a). Gun control. *Annals of the American Academy of Political and Social Science, 455,* 1-167.

Cook, P. J. (1981b). The "Saturday night special": An assessment of alternative definitions from a policy perspective. *Journal of Criminal Law and Criminology, 72,* 1735-1745.

Cook, P. J. (1991). The technology of personal violence. In M. Tonry (Ed.), *Crime and justice: An annual review* (Vol. 14, pp. 1-71). Chicago: University of Chicago Press.

Cook, P. J., & Nagin, D. (1979). *Does the weapon matter?* Washington, DC: Institute of Law and Social Research.

Cook, P. J., & Tauchen, G. (1982). The effect of liquor taxes on heavy drinking. *Bell Journal of Economics, 13,* 379-390.

Cooper, H., & Hedges, L. V. (Eds.). (1994). *The handbook of research synthesis.* New York: Russell Sage.

Coordinating Council on Juvenile Justice and Delinquency Prevention. (1996). *Combatting violence and delinquency: The National Juvenile Justice Action Plan.* Washington, DC: Office of Juvenile Justice and Delinquency Prevention.

Copas, J. B., & Loeber, R. (1990). Relative improvement over chance (RIOC) for 2 × 2 tables. *British Journal of Mathematical and Statistical Psychology, 43,* 293-307.

Copas, J. B., & Tarling, R. (1986). Some methodological issues in making predictions. In A. Blumstein, J. Cohen, J. Roth, & C. A. Visher (Eds.), *Criminal careers and "career criminals"* (Vol. 2, pp. 291-313). Washington, DC: National Academy Press.

Corsica, J. Y. (1993). Employment training interventions. In A. Goldstein & C. R. Huff (Eds.), *The gang intervention handbook* (pp. 301-317). Champaign, IL: Research Press.

Coulton, C. J. (1995). Using community-level indicators of children's well-being in comprehensive community initiatives. In J. P. Connell, A. C. Kubisch, L. B. Schorr, & C. H. Weiss (Eds.), *New approaches to evaluating community initiatives: Concepts, methods, and contexts.* Washington, DC: Aspen Institute.

Cowles, E. L., & Castellano, T. C. (1995). *Boot camp, drug treatment and aftercare intervention: An evaluation review.* Washington, DC: National Institute of Justice.

Cox, S. M., Davidson, W. S., & Bynum, T. S. (1995). A meta-analytic assessment of delinquency related outcomes of alternative education programs. *Crime & Delinquency, 41,* 219-234.

Craig, M. M., & Glick, S. J. (1963). Ten years' experience with the Glueck Social Prediction Table. *Crime & Delinquency, 9,* 249-261.

Crick, N. R., Bigbee, M., & Howes, C. (1996). Gender differences in children's normative beliefs about aggression: How do I hurt thee? Let me count the ways. *Child Development, 67,* 1003-1014.

Crick, N. R., & Grotpeter, J. K. (1995). Relational aggression, gender, and social-psychological adjustment. *Child Development, 66,* 710-722.

Cristoffel, K. K. (1991). Toward reducing pediatric injuries from firearms: Charting a legislative and regulatory course. *Pediatrics, 88,* 294-305.

Cronin, R. (1994). *Innovative community partnerships: Working together for change.* Washington, DC: U.S. Department of Justice, Office of Juvenile Justice and Delinquency Prevention.

Cronin, R., Bourque, B., Gragg, F., Mell, J., & McGrady, A. (1988). *Evaluation of the habitual serious and violent juvenile offender program.* Washington, DC: American Institutes of Research.

Cronin, R. C. (1996). *Office of Juvenile Justice and Delinquency Prevention Assessment Center Fact Finding Project: Final report.* Washington, DC: U.S. Department of Justice, Office of Juvenile Justice and Delinquency Prevention.

Cullen, F. T., & Gilbert, K. E. (1982). *Reaffirming rehabilitation.* Cincinnati, OH: Anderson.

Curry, G. D. (1990). *Client evaluation of youth gang services.* Report to the U.S. Department of Justice, Office of Juvenile Justice and Delinquency Prevention.

Curry, G. D., Ball, R. A., & Decker, S. H. (1996a, August). Estimating the national scope of gang crime from law enforcement data. *Research in brief.* Washington, DC: U.S. Department of Justice, National Institute of Justice.

Curry, G. D., Ball, R. A., & Decker, S. H. (1996b). Estimating the national scope of gang crime from law en-

forcement data. In C. R. Huff (Ed.), *Gangs in America* (2nd ed., pp. 266-275). Thousand Oaks, CA: Sage.

Curry, G. D., & Spergel, I. A. (1988). Gang homicide, delinquency, and community. *Criminology, 26,* 381-405.

Curry, G. D., & Spergel, I. A. (1992). Gang involvement and delinquency among Hispanic and African-American adolescent males. *Journal of Research in Crime and Delinquency, 29,* 273-291.

Curry, G. D., Williams, K., & Koenemann, L. (1996, November). *Structure, culture, and delinquency in female gang involvement.* Paper presented at the annual meeting of the American Society of Criminology, Chicago.

Curry, G. D., Williams, K., & Koenemann, L. (1997, March). *Race and ethnic differences in female gang involvement.* Paper presented at the annual meeting of the Academy of Criminal Justice Sciences, Lexington.

Dade County Grand Jury. (1985). *Dade youth gangs.* Final report of the Grand Jury, Miami.

Dade County Grand Jury. (1988). *Dade County gangs.* Final report of the Grand Jury, Miami.

Dahmann, J. (1981). *Operation Hardcore, a prosecutorial response to violent gang criminality: Interim evaluation report.* Washington, DC: Mitre Corporation. Reprinted in M. W. Klein, C. L. Maxson, & J. Miller (Eds.). (1995). *The modern gang reader* (pp. 301-303). Los Angeles: Roxbury.

DeBaryshe, B. D., Patterson, G. R., & Capaldi, D. M. (1993). A performance model for academic achievement in early adolescent boys. *Developmental Psychology, 29,* 795-804.

Decker, S. H., & Van Winkle, B. (1996). *Life in the gang: Family, friends, and violence.* New York: Cambridge University Press.

Delinquency Research Group. (1986). *An evaluation of the delinquency of participants in the Youth at Risk program.* Claremont, CA: Claremont Graduate School, Center for Applied Social Research.

Dembo, R., & Rivers, J. E. (1996, December). *Juvenile assessment centers: The Florida experience.* Paper presented at the Office of Juvenile Justice and Delinquency Prevention National Conference, Baltimore.

Dembo, R., Turner, G., Schmeidler, J., Sue, C. C., Borden, P., & Manning, D. (1996). Development and evaluation of a classification of high risk youths entering a juvenile assessment center. *Substance Use and Misuse, 31,* 303-322.

Dembo, R., Williams, L., Getreu, A., Genung, L., Schmeidler, J., Berry, E., Wish, E. D., & LaVoie, L. L. (1991). A longitudinal study of the relationships among marijuana/hashish use and delinquency in a cohort of high risk youths. *Journal of Drug Issues, 21,* 271-312.

Denno, D. W. (1990). *Biology and violence: From birth to adulthood.* Cambridge, UK: Cambridge University Press.

Department of Justice. (1996). *Youth violence: A community-based response.* Washington, DC: U.S. Department of Justice.

Derzon, J. H. (1996). A meta-analysis of the efficacy of various antecedent behaviors, characteristics, and experiences for predicting later violent behavior (Doctoral dissertation, Claremont Graduate School, 1996). *Dissertation Abstracts International, 57,* 748.

Deschenes, E. P., Greenwood, P. W., & Marshall, G. (1996). *The Nokomis challenge program evaluation.* Santa Monica, CA: RAND.

Developmental Research and Programs. (1996). *Promising approaches to prevent adolescent problem behaviors.* Seattle, WA: Author.

Dicken, C., Bryson, R., & Kass, N. (1977). Companionship therapy: A replication in experimental community psychology. *Journal of Consulting and Clinical Psychology, 45,* 637-646.

Didier, L. (1990, March). *Fred Meyer final report: Preparing for the drug (free) years.* Salem: Oregon Prevention Resource Center.

DiIulio, J. (1995, Fall). Arresting ideas. In *Policy review.* Washington, DC: Heritage.

Dishion, T., Patterson, G. R., Stoolmiller, M., & Skinner, M. L. (1991). Family, school, and behavioral antecedents to early adolescent involvement with antisocial peers. *Developmental Psychology, 2,* 172-180.

Dodge, K. A. (1993). The future of research on the treatment of conduct disorder. *Development and Psychopathology, 5,* 311-319.

Dodge, K. A., Bates, J. E., & Pettit, G. S. (1990). Mechanisms in the cycle of violence. *Science, 250,* 1678-1683.

Dodge, K. A., & Frame, C. L. (1982). Social cognitive biases and deficits in aggressive boys. *Child Development, 53,* 620-635.

Dodge, K. A., Murphy, R. R., & Buchsbaum, K. (1984). The assessment of intention-cue detection skills in children: Implications for developmental psychopathology. *Child Development, 55,* 163-173.

Dootjes, I. (1972). Predicting juvenile delinquency. *Australian and New Zealand Journal of Criminology, 5,* 157-171.

Dorfman, L., & Wallack, L. (1993). Advertising health: The case for counter-ads. *Public Health Reports, 108,* 716-726.

Dryfoos, J. G. (1990). *Adolescents at risk: Prevalence and prevention.* New York: Oxford University Press.

Dryfoos, J. G. (1991). Adolescents at risk: A summation of work in the field: Programs and policies. *Journal of Adolescent Health, 12,* 630-637. [Special issue: Adolescents at risk]

Dryfoos, J. G. (1994). *Full service schools: A revolution in health and social services for children, youth, and families.* San Francisco: Jossey-Bass.

Dryfoos, J. G. (1995). Full service schools: Revolution or fad? *Journal of Research on Adolescence, 5* 157-172.

Dumas, J. E. (1989). Treating antisocial behavior in children: Child and family approaches. *Clinical Psychology Review, 9,* 197-222.

Duncan, O. D., Ohlin, L. E., Reiss, A. J., & Stanton, H. R. (1952). Formal devices for making selection decisions. *American Journal of Sociology, 58,* 573-584.

Dunford, F. W., & Elliott, D. S. (1984). Identifying career offenders using self-reported data. *Journal of Research in Crime and Delinquency, 21,* 57-86.

Durlak, J. A. (1995). School-based prevention programs for children and adolescents. In *Developmental clinical psychology and psychiatry* (Vol. 34). Thousand Oaks, CA: Sage.

Dwyer, J. H., MacKinnon, D. V., Pentz, M. A., Flay, B. R., Hansen, W. B., Wang, E. Y. I., & Johnson, C. A. (1989). Estimating intervention effects in longitudinal studies. *American Journal of Epidemiology, 130,* 781-795.

Edelman, C., & Mandle, C. L. (1986). *Health promotion throughout the lifespan.* St. Louis, MO: C. V. Mosby.

Eisenhower Foundation. (1990). *Youth investment and community reconstruction: Street lessons on drugs and crime for the nineties.* Washington, DC: Author.

Elliott, D., & Ageton, S. (1980). Reconciling race and class differences in self-reported and official estimates of delinquency. *American Sociological Review, 45,* 95-110.

Elliott, D., & Voss, H. (1974). *Delinquency and dropout.* Lexington, MA: Lexington Books.

Elliott, D. S. (1994). Serious violent offenders: Onset, developmental course, and termination—The American Society of Criminology 1993 presidential address. *Criminology, 32,* 1-21.

Elliott, D. S., Dunford, F. W., & Huizinga, D. (1987). The identification and prediction of career offenders utilizing self-reported and official data. In J. D. Burchard & S. N. Burchard (Eds.), *Prevention of delinquent behavior.* Newbury Park, CA: Sage.

Elliott, D. S., & Huizinga, D. H. (1984). *The relationship between delinquent behavior and ADM problems.* National Youth Report No. 28. Boulder, CO: Behavioral Research Institute.

Elliott, D. S., Huizinga, D., & Ageton, S. S. (1985). *Explaining delinquency and drug use.* Beverly Hills, CA: Sage.

Elliott, D. S., Huizinga, D., & Menard, S. (1989). *Multiple problem youth: Delinquency, substance use and mental health problems.* New York: Springer-Verlag.

Elliott, D. S., Huizinga, D., & Morse, B. (1986). Self-reported violent offending. *Journal of Interpersonal Violence, 1,* 472-514.

Empey, L., & Erickson, M. (1972). *The Provo experiment.* Lexington, MA: Lexington Books.

Empey, L., & Lubeck, S. (1971). *The Silverlake experiment.* Chicago: Aldine.

Eron, L. D., Gentry, J. H., & Schlegel, P. (Eds.). (1994). *Reasons to hope: A psychological perspective on violence & youth.* Washington, DC: American Psychological Association.

Eron, L. D., Walder, L. O., & Lefkowitz, M. M. (1971). *Learning of aggression in children.* Boston: Little, Brown.

Erwin, B. S. (1987). New dimensions in probation: Georgia's experience with intensive probation supervision. *Research in brief.* Washington, DC: U.S. Department of Justice, National Institute of Justice.

Esbensen, F., & Huizinga, D. (1991). Juvenile victimization and delinquency. *Youth & Society, 23,* 202-228.

Esbensen, F., & Huizinga, D. (1993). Gangs, drugs, and delinquency in a survey of urban youth. *Criminology, 31,* 565-589.

Esbensen, F., Huizinga, D., & Weiher, A. W. (1993). Gang and non-gang youth: Differences in explanatory factors. *Journal of Contemporary Criminal Justice, 9,* 94-116.

Esbensen, F., & Osgood, D. W. (1997). National evaluation of G.R.E.A.T. *Research in brief.* Washington, DC: U.S. Department of Justice, National Institute of Justice.

Espiritu, R., & Huizinga, D. H. (1996). Developmental gender differences in delinquency and victimization. In R. Loeber, D. H. Huizinga, & T. Thornberry, *Program of research on the causes and correlates of delinquency.* Annual report, 1995-1996, presented to the Office of Juvenile Justice and Delinquency Prevention. Pittsburgh, PA: Western Psychiatric Institute and Clinic.

Ethiel, N. (Ed.). (1996). *Saving our children: Can youth violence be prevented?* Cambridge, MA: Harvard Law School, Center for Criminal Justice.

Eyberg, S. M., & Boggs, S. R. (1989). Parent training for oppositional-defiant preschoolers. In C. E. Schaefer & J. M. Briemeister (Eds.), *Handbook of parent-training: Parents as cotherapists for children's behavior problems* (pp. 105-132). New York: John Wiley.

Facella, C. A. (1983). *Female delinquency in a birth cohort.* Doctoral dissertation, University of Pennsylvania, Philadelphia.

Fagan, J. (1989). The social organization of drug use and drug dealing among urban gangs. *Criminology, 27,* 633-669.

Fagan, J. (1990a). Social processes of delinquency and drug use among urban gangs. In C. R. Huff (Ed.), *Gangs in America* (pp. 266-275). Newbury Park, CA: Sage.

Fagan, J. (1990b). Treatment and reintegration of violent juvenile offenders: Experimental results. *Justice Quarterly, 7,* 233-263.

Fagan, J. (1996). Gangs, drugs, and neighborhood change. In C. R. Huff (Ed.), *Gangs in America* (2nd ed., pp. 39-74). Thousand Oaks, CA: Sage.

Fagan, J., & Pabon, E. (1990). Contributions of delinquency and substance use to school dropout among inner-city youths. *Youth & Society, 21,* 306-354.

Fagan, J., Piper, E., & Moore, M. (1986). Violent delinquents and urban youths. *Criminology, 24,* 439-471.

Fagan, J., Weis, J. G., & Cheng, Y. (1990). Delinquency and drug use among inner city students. *Journal of Drug Issues, 20,* 351-402.

Fagan, J., & Wilkinson, D. (in press). The functions of adolescent violence. In D. S. Elliott & B. Hamburg (Eds.), *Violence in American schools.* Cambridge, UK: Cambridge University Press.

Fagan, J. A. (1995). Separating the men from the boys: The comparative advantage of juvenile versus criminal court sanctions on recidivism among adolescent felony offenders. In J. C. Howell, B. Krisberg, J. D. Hawkins, & J. J. Wilson (Eds.), *Sourcebook on serious, violent, and chronic juvenile offenders* (pp. 238-274). Thousand Oaks, CA: Sage.

Fagan, J. A., & Hartstone, E. (1984). Strategic planning in juvenile justice—Defining the toughest kids. In R. Mathias, P. DeMuro, & R. S. Allinson (Eds.), *Violent juvenile offenders* (pp. 31-51). San Francisco: National Council on Crime and Delinquency.

Family Services Research Center. (1995, October). Multisystemic therapy using home-based services: A clinically effective and cost effective strategy for treating serious clinical problems in youth. Charleston: Medical University of South Carolina, Department of Psychiatry and Behavioral Sciences.

Farquhar, J. W., Fortmann, S. P., & Flora, J. A. (1990). Effects of community-wide education on cardiovascular disease risk factors: The Stanford Five-City Project. *Journal of the American Medical Association, 264,* 359-365.

Farrell, A. D., & Meyer, A. L. (1997). *Effectiveness of a school-based prevention program for reducing violence among urban adolescents: Differential impact on girls and boys.* Manuscript under review.

Farrington, D. P. (1973). Self-reports of deviant behavior: Predictive and stable? *Journal of Criminal Law and Criminology, 64,* 99-110.

Farrington, D. P. (1979). Environmental stress, delinquent behavior, and convictions. In I. G. Sarason & C. D. Spielberger (Eds.), *Stress and anxiety* (Vol. 6., pp. 93-107). Washington, DC: Hemisphere.

Farrington, D. P. (1983). Offending from 10 to 25 years of age. In K. T. Van Dusen & S. A. Mednick (Eds.), *Prospective studies of crime and delinquency* (pp. 17-37). Boston: Kluwer-Nijhoff.

Farrington, D. P. (1985). Predicting self-reported and official delinquency. In D. P. Farrington & R. Tarling (Eds.), *Prediction in criminology.* Albany: State University of New York Press.

Farrington, D. P. (1986). Age and crime. In M. Tonry & N. Morris (Eds.), *Crime and justice: An annual re-*

view of research* (Vol. 7, pp. 189-250). Chicago: University of Chicago Press.

Farrington, D. P. (1987). Early precursors of frequent offending. In J. Q. Wilson & G. C. Loury (Eds.), *From children to citizens* (pp. 27-50). New York: Springer-Verlag.

Farrington, D. P. (1989a). Early predictors of adolescent aggression and adult violence. *Violence and Victims, 4,* 79-100.

Farrington, D. P. (1989b). Self-reported and official offending from adolescence to adulthood. In M. Klein (Ed.), *Cross-national research in self-reported crime and delinquency* (pp. 399-423). Dordrecht, Netherlands: Kluwer.

Farrington, D. P. (1991). Childhood aggression and adult violence: Early precursors and later-life outcomes. In D. J. Pepler & K. H. Rubin (Eds.), *The development and treatment of childhood aggression* (pp. 5-29). Hillsdale, NJ: Lawrence Erlbaum.

Farrington, D. P. (1993). *Protective factors in the development of juvenile delinquency and adult crime.* Unpublished manuscript, Cambridge University, Institute of Criminology.

Farrington, D. P. (1995). Key issues in the integration of motivational and opportunity-reducing crime prevention strategies. In P.-O. H. Wikström, R. V. Clarke, & J. McCord (Eds.), *Integrating crime prevention strategies: Propensity and opportunity* (pp. 333-357). Stockholm, Sweden: National Council for Crime Prevention.

Farrington, D. P. (1996a). The explanation and prevention of youthful offending. In J. D. Hawkins (Ed.), *Delinquency and crime: Current theories* (pp. 68-148). Cambridge, UK: Cambridge University Press.

Farrington, D. P. (1996b). *Understanding and preventing youth crime.* York, England: Joseph Rowntree Foundation.

Farrington, D. P. (1997a). Evaluating a community-based prevention program. *Evaluation, 3,* 157-173.

Farrington, D. P. (1997b). Early prediction of violent and nonviolent youthful offending. *European Journal on Criminal Policy and Research, 5,* 51-66.

Farrington, D. P. (in press). Predictors, causes and correlates of male youth violence. In M. Tonry & M. H. Moore, *Youth violence, crime and justice* (Vol. 24). Chicago: University of Chicago Press.

Farrington, D. P., & Loeber, R. (in press). Transatlantic replicability of risk factors in the development of delinquency. In P. Cohen, C. Slomkowski, & L. N. Robins (Eds.), *Where and when: The influence of history and geography on aspects of psychopathology.* Mahwah, NJ: Lawrence Erlbaum.

Farrington, D. P., Loeber, R., Elliott, D. S., Hawkins, J. D., Kandel, D. B., Klein, M. W., McCord, J., Rowe, D. C., & Tremblay, R. E. (1990). Advancing knowledge about the onset of delinquency and crime. In B. Lahey & A. E. Kazdin (Eds.), *Advances in clinical child psychology* (Vol. 13, pp. 283-342). New York: Plenum.

Farrington, D. P., Loeber, R., Stouthamer-Loeber, M., Van Kammen, W. B., & Schmidt, L. (1996). Self-reported delinquency and a combined delinquency seriousness scale based on boys, mothers, and teachers: Concurrent and predictive validity for African-Americans and Caucasians. *Criminology, 34,* 501-525.

Farrington, D. P., Ohlin, L. E., & Wilson, J. Q. (1986). *Understanding and controlling crime: Toward a new research strategy.* New York: Springer-Verlag.

Farrington, D. P., Snyder, H. S., & Finnegan, T. A. (1988). Specialization in juvenile court careers. *Criminology, 26,* 461-488.

Farrington, D. P., & Tarling, R. (1985). *Prediction in criminology.* Albany: State University of New York Press.

Farrington, D. P., & West, D. J. (1993). Criminal, penal and life histories of chronic offenders: Risk and protective factors and early identification. *Criminal Behaviour and Mental Health, 3,* 492-523.

Farrington, D. P., & Wikström, P.-O. (1994). Criminal careers in London and Stockholm: A cross-national comparative study. In E. G. M. Weitekamp & H. J. Kerner (Eds.), *Cross-national longitudinal research on human development and criminal behavior* (pp. 65-89). Boston: Kluwer-Nijhoff.

Fattah, D. (1987). The House of Umoja as a case study for social change. *Annals of the American Academy of Political and Social Science, 494,* 37-41.

Fawcett, S. B., Paine, A. L., Francisco, V. T., & Vliet, M. (1993). *Promoting health through community development.* New York: Haworth.

Federal Bureau of Investigation. (1993). *Age-specific arrest rates and race-specific arrest rates for selected offenses, 1965-1992.* Washington, DC: Government Printing Office.

Feldhusen, J. F., Aversano, F. M., & Thurston, J. R. (1976). Prediction of youth contacts with law enforcement agencies. *Criminal Justice and Behavior, 3,* 235-253.

Feldhusen, J. F., Thurston, J. R., & Benning, J. J. (1973). A longitudinal study of delinquency and other aspects of children's behavior. *International Journal of Criminology and Penology, 1,* 341-351.

Feldman, L. H. (1991). Evaluating the impact of intensive family preservation services in New Jersey. In K. Wells & D. Biegel (Eds.), *Family preservation services: Research and evaluation* (pp. 47-71). Newbury Park, CA: Sage.

Felson, R. B. (1993). Predatory and dispute-related violence: A social interactionist approach. In R. V. Clark & M. Felson (Eds.), *Routine activity and rational choice, advances in criminological theory* (pp. 103-126). New Brunswick, NJ: Transaction.

Fergusson, D. M., Lynskey, M. T., & Horwood, L. J. (1996). Alcohol misuse and juvenile offending in adolescence. *Addiction, 91,* 483-494.

Fetzer Institute. (1994). Resolving conflict creatively program. In *Connections, the newsletter of the Collaborative for the Advancement of Social and Emotional Learning.* New Haven, CT: Yale Child Study Center.

Feyerherm, W., Pope, C., & Lovell, R. (1992). *Youth gang prevention and early intervention programs.* Report to the U.S. Department of Justice, Office of Juvenile Justice and Delinquency Prevention.

Fife, D., & Abrams, W. R. (1989). Firearms' decreased role in New Jersey homicides after a mandatory sentencing law. *Journal of Trauma, 29,* 1548-1551.

Fingerhut, L., Ingram, D., & Feldman, J. (1992). Firearm and nonfirearm homicide among persons 15 through 19 years of age: Differences by level of urbanization, United States, 1979 through 1989. *Journal of the American Medical Association, 267,* 3048-3053.

Fingerhut, L. A., & Kleinman, J. D. (1990). International and interstate comparisons of homicide among young males. *Journal of the American Medical Association, 263,* 3292-3295.

Firestone, P., Kelly, M. J., Goodman, J. T., & Davey, J. (1981). Differential effects of parent training and stimulant medication with hyperactives. *Journal of the American Academy of Child and Adolescent Psychiatry, 20,* 135-147.

Flay, B. R., Koepke, D., Thomson, S. J., Santi, S., Best, J. A., & Brown, K. S. (1989). Six-year follow-up of the first Waterloo school smoking prevention trial. *American Journal of Public Health, 79,* 1371-1376.

Flynn, B. S., Worden, J. K., Secker-Walker, R. H., Badger, G. J., & Geller, B. M. (1995). Cigarette smoking prevention effects of mass media and school interventions targeted to gender and age groups. *Journal of Health Education, 26* S-45–S-51.

Flynn, B. S., Worden, J. K., Secker-Walker, R. H., Badger, G. J., Geller, B. M., & Costanza, M. C. (1992). Prevention of cigarette smoking through mass media intervention and school programs. *American Journal of Public Health, 82,* 827-834.

Fo, W. S., & O'Donnell, C. R. (1975). The Buddy System: Effect of community intervention on delinquent offenses. *Behavior Therapy, 6,* 522-524.

Forehand, R., Furey, W. M., & McMahon, R. J. (1984). The role of maternal distress in parent training to modify child noncompliance. *Behavioral Psychotherapy, 12,* 93-108.

Forehand, R., & McMahon, R. J. (1981). *Helping the noncompliant child: A clinician's guide to parent training.* New York: Guilford.

Forst, M., Fagan, J., & Vivona, T. S. (1989). Youth in prisons and state training schools. *Juvenile and Family Court Journal, 39,* 1-14.

Fortmann, S. P., Flora, J. A., & Winkleby, M. A. (1995). Community intervention trials: Reflections on the Stanford Five-City Project experience. *American Journal of Epidemiology, 142,* 576-586.

Foshee, V., & Bauman, K. E. (1992). Parental and peer characteristics as modifiers of the bond-behavior relationship: An elaboration of control theory. *Journal of Health and Social Behavior, 33*(1), 66-76.

Fox, J. A. (1996). *Trends in juvenile violence. A report to the United States attorney general on current and future rates of juvenile offending.* Washington, DC: Bureau of Justice Statistics, Department of Justice.

Fox, J. R. (1985). Mission impossible? Social work practices with Black urban youth gangs. *Social Work, 30,* 25-31.

Fréchette, M., & Le Blanc, M. (1987). *Délinquances et délinquants* [Delinquencies and delinquents]. Montreal: Gaétan Morin.

Frick, P. J., Lahey, B. B., Loeber, R., Tannenbaum, L., Van Horn, Y., Christ, M. A. G., & Hanson, K. (1992). Familial risk factors to oppositional defiant disorder and conduct disorder: Parental psychopathology and maternal parenting. *Journal of Consulting and Clinical Psychology, 60,* 49-55.

Friedman, C. J., Mann, F., & Friedman, A. S. (1975). A profile of juvenile street gang members. *Adolescence, 10,* 563-607.

Fritsch, E., & Hemmens, C. (1995). Juvenile transfer in the United States 1979-1995: A comparison of state waiver statutes. *Juvenile and Family Court Journal, 17,* 105-123.

Gabor, T. (1986). *The prediction of criminal behavior: Statistical approaches.* Toronto: University of Toronto Press.

Gabriel, R. M. (1996). *Self-Enhancement, Inc. violence prevention program.* Portland, OR: RMC Research.

Gabriel, R. M., Hopson, T., Haskins, M., & Powell, K. E. (1996). Building relationships and resilience in the prevention of youth violence. *American Journal of Preventive Medicine, 12*(Suppl. 5). [Youth violence prevention: Descriptions and baseline data from 13 evaluation projects]

Gadow, K. D., Nolan, E. E., Sverd, J., Sprafkin, J., & Paolicelli, L. (1990). Methylphenidate in aggressive-hyperactive boys: I. Effects on peer aggression in public school settings. *Journal of the American Academy of Child and Adolescent Psychiatry, 29,* 710-718.

Gainer, P. S., Webster, D. W., & Champion, H. R. (1993). A youth violence prevention program: Description and preliminary evaluation. *Archives of Surgery, 128,* 303-308.

Gandossy, R. P., Williams, J. R., Cohen, J., & Harwood, H. J. (1980). *Drugs and crime: A survey and analysis of the literature.* Owings Mill, MD: National Health.

Garmezy, N. (1985). Stress-resistant children: The search for protective factors. In J. E. Stevenson (Ed.), *Recent research in developmental psychopathology* (pp. 213-233). New York: Pergamon.

Garrett, C. J. (1985). Effects of residential treatment on adjudicated delinquents: A meta-analysis. *Journal of Research in Crime and Delinquency, 22,* 287-308.

Geis, G. (1965). *Juvenile gangs.* Report to the President's Committee on Youth Crime. Washington, DC: Government Printing Office.

Gendreau, P., Little, T., & Goggin, C. (1996). A meta-analysis of the predictors of adult offender recidivism: What works. *Criminology, 34,* 575-607.

Gendreau, P., & Ross, R. R. (1987). Revivification of rehabilitation: Evidence from the 1980s. *Justice Quarterly, 4,* 349-407.

Genelin, M. (1993). Gang prosecution: The hardest game in town. In A. Goldstein & C. R. Huff (Eds.), *The gang intervention handbook* (pp. 417-426). Champaign, IL: Research Press.

General Accounting Office. (1996). *Juvenile justice: Status of delinquency prevention programs and description of local projects.* Report to the Committee on Economic and Educational Opportunity, House of Representatives (GAO/GGD-96-147). Washington, DC: Author.

George, W. H., Crowe, L. C., Abwender, D., & Skinner, J. B. (1989). Effects of raising the drinking age to 21 years in New York State on self-reported consumption by college students. *Journal of Applied Social Psychology, 19,* 623-635.

Gibbons, D. C. (1962). Prospects and problems of delinquent typology. *Sociological Inquiry, 32,* 235-244.

Gibbons, D. C. (1975). Offender typologies—Two decades later. *British Journal of Criminology, 15,* 140-156.

Giesbrecht, N., & Ferris, J. (1993). Community-based research initiatives in prevention. *Addiction, 88*(Suppl.), 83S-93S.

Ginsberg, C., & Loffredo, L. (1993). Violence-related attitudes and behaviors of high school students—New York City 1992. *Journal of School Health, 63,* 438-439.

Gittelman, R. (1982). A controlled study of methylphenidate in combination with academic instruction. *Psychopharmacology Bulletin, 18,* 112-113.

Gittelman, R., Abikoff, H., Pollack, E., Klein, D., Katz, S., & Mattes, J. (1980). A controlled trial of behavior modification and methylphenidate in hyperactive children. In C. C. K. Whalen & B. Henker (Eds.), *Hyperactive children: The social ecology of identification and treatment* (pp. 221-243). New York: Academic Press.

Glaser, D. (1987). Classification for risk. In D. M. Gottfredson & M. Tonry (Eds.), *Crime and justice: An annual review: Vol. 9. Prediction and classification: Criminal justice decision making* (pp. 249-292). Chicago: University of Chicago Press.

Glick, B., & Goldstein, A. P. (1987). Aggression replacement training. *Journal of Counseling and Development, 65,* 356-362.

Glueck, S., & Glueck, E. (1950). *Unraveling juvenile delinquency.* New York: Commonwealth Fund.

Gold, M. (1970). *Delinquent behavior in an American city.* Belmont, CA: Brooks/Cole.

Gold, M., & Mann, D. W. (1984). *Expelled to a friendlier place: A study of alternative schools.* Ann Arbor: University of Michigan Press.

Gold, M., & Mattick, H. (1974). *Experiment in the streets: The Chicago Youth Development project.* Ann Arbor: University of Michigan, Institute for Social Research.

Goldstein, A. P. (1993). Interpersonal skills training interventions. In A. Goldstein & C. R. Huff (Eds.), *The gang intervention handbook* (pp. 87-157). Champaign, IL: Research Press.

Goldstein, A. P., & Glick, B. (1994). *The prosocial gang: Implementing aggression replacement training.* Thousand Oaks, CA: Sage.

Goleman, D. (1995). *Emotional intelligence.* New York: Bantam.

Goodman, G. (1972). *Companionship therapy: Studies in structured intimacy.* San Francisco: Jossey-Bass.

Goodstadt, M. S. (1989). Substance abuse curricula vs. school drug polices. *Journal of School Health, 59,* 246-250.

Goodstein, L., & Sontheimer, H. (1987). *A study of the impact of ten Pennsylvania residential placements on juvenile recidivism.* Shippensburg, PA: Center for Juvenile Justice, Training and Research.

Gordon, D. A., Graves, K., & Arbuthnot, J. (1987). *Prevention of adult criminal behavior using family therapy for disadvantaged juvenile delinquents.* Unpublished manuscript, Ohio University, Athens, OH.

Goring, C. (1913). *The English convict: A statistical study.* London: Darling & Son.

Gorman-Smith, D., Tolan, P. H., Zelli, A., & Huesmann, L. R. (1996). The relation of family functioning to violence among inner-city minority youth. *Journal of Family Psychology, 10,* 115-129.

Gottfredson, D., & Barton, W. (1992). *Deinstitutionalization of juvenile offenders.* College Park: University of Maryland.

Gottfredson, D. C. (1986). An empirical test of school-based environmental and individual interventions to reduce the risk of delinquent behavior. *Criminology, 24,* 705-731.

Gottfredson, D. C. (1987). An evaluation of an organization development approach to reducing school disorder. *Evaluation Review, 11,* 739-763.

Gottfredson, D. C., & Gottfredson, G. D. (1992). Theory-guided investigation: Three field experiments. In J. McCord & R. E. Tremblay (Eds.), *Preventing antisocial behavior* (pp. 311-329). New York: Guilford.

Gottfredson, D. C., Gottfredson, G. D., & Hybl, L. G. (1993). Managing adolescent behavior: A multiyear, multischool study. *American Educational Research Journal, 30,* 179-215.

Gottfredson, D. C., Gottfredson, G. D., & Skroban, S. (1996). A multimodel school based prevention demonstration. *Journal of Adolescent Research, 11,* 97-115.

Gottfredson, D. C., Karweit, N. L., & Gottfredson, G. D. (1989). *Reducing disorderly behavior in middle schools* (Rep. No. 47). Baltimore: Johns Hopkins University, Center for Research on Elementary and Middle Schools.

Gottfredson, D. M. (1987). Prediction and classification in criminal justice decision making. In D. M. Gottfredson & M. Tonry (Eds.), *Crime and justice: An annual review: Vol. 9. Prediction and classification: Criminal justice decision making* (pp. 1-20). Chicago: University of Chicago Press.

Gottfredson, D. M., & Tonry, M. (Eds.). (1987). *Crime and justice: An annual review: Vol. 9. Prediction and classification: Criminal justice decision making.* Chicago: University of Chicago Press.

Gottfredson, G. D. (1975). Organizing crime: A classificatory scheme based on offense transitions. *Journal of Criminal Justice, 3,* 321-332.

Gottfredson, G. D. (1981). Schooling and delinquency. In S. W. Martin, L. B. Sechrest, & R. Rednez (Eds.), *New directions in the rehabilitation of criminal offenders* (pp. 424-469). Washington, DC: National Academy Press.

Gottfredson, M. R., & Gottfredson, D. M. (1985). *Decision making in criminal justice: Toward the rational exercise of discretion.* Cambridge, MA: Ballinger.

Gottfredson, M. R., & Hirschi, T. (1986). The true value of lambda would appear to be zero: An essay on career criminals, criminal careers, selective incapacitation, cohort studies, and related topics. *Criminology, 24,* 213-234.

Gottfredson, M. R., & Hirschi, T. (1990). *A general theory of crime.* Stanford, CA: Stanford University Press.

Gottfredson, S. D., & Gottfredson, D. M. (1985). Screening for risk among parolees: Policy, practice, and method. In D. J. Farrington & R. Tarling (Eds.), *Prediction in criminology.* Albany: State University of New York Press.

Gottfredson, S. D., & Gottfredson, D. M. (1986). Accuracy of prediction models. In A. Blumstein, J. Cohen, J. A. Roth, & C. A. Visher (Eds.), *Criminal careers and "career criminals"* (Vol. 2, pp. 212-290). Washington, DC: National Academy Press.

Gove, W., Hughes, M., & Geerken, M. (1985). Are the Uniform Crime Reports a valid indicator of the index crimes? An affirmative answer with minor qualifications. *Criminology, 23,* 451-501.

Graham, J. W., & Donaldson, S. I. (1993). Evaluating interventions with differential attrition: The importance of nonresponse mechanisms and use of follow-up data. *Journal of Applied Psychology, 78,* 119-128.

Green, B. C. (1980). *An evaluation of a Big Brothers' program for father-absent boys: An eco-behavioral analysis.* Unpublished doctoral dissertation, New York University.

Greenberg, B. (1974). School vandalism: Its effect and paradoxical solutions. *Crime Prevention Review, 1,* 105.

Greenberg, M. T., Kusche, C. C. A., Cook, E. T., & Quamma, J. P. (1995). Promoting emotional competence in school-aged children: The effects of the PATHS curriculum. *Development and Psychopathology, 7,* 117-136.

Greenhill, L. L. (1995). Attention-deficit hyperactivity disorder: The stimulants. *Child and Adolescent Psychiatric Clinics of North America, 4,* 123-167.

Greenwood, P. W., Deschenes, E. P., & Adams, J. (1993). *Chronic juvenile offenders: Final results from the Skillman Aftercare Experiment.* Santa Monica, CA: RAND.

Greenwood, P. W., Model, K. E., Rydell, C. P., & Chiesa, J. (1996). *Diverting children from a life of crime: Measuring costs and benefits.* Santa Monica, CA: RAND.

Greenwood, P. W., & Turner, S. (1987). *The VisionQuest Program: An evaluation.* Santa Monica, CA: RAND.

Grossman, M., Coate, D., & Arluck, G. M. (1987). Price sensitivity of alcoholic beverages in the United States: Youth alcohol consumption. *Advances in substance abuse: Behavioral and biological research: Suppl. 1. Control issues in alcohol abuse prevention: Strategies for state and communities.* Greenwich, CT: JAI.

Groves, B. M., Zuckerman, B., Marans, S., & Cohen, D. J. (1993). Silent victims: Children who witness violence. *Journal of the American Medical Association, 269,* 262-264.

Gruenewald, P. J., Ponicki, W. R., & Holder, H. D. (1993). The relationship of outlet densities to alcohol consumption: A time series cross-sectional analysis. *Alcoholism: Clinical and Experimental Research, 17,* 38-47.

Grunhut, M. (1955). Juvenile delinquents under punitive detention: A study of the first hundred Campsfield House boys. *British Journal of Delinquency, 5,* 191-213.

Guerra, N. G., Eron, L. D., Huesmann, L. R., Tolan, P. H., & VanAcker, R. (1996). A cognitive/ecological approach to the prevention and mitigation of violence and aggression in inner-city youth. In K. Bjorkquist & D. P. Fry (Eds.), *Styles of conflict resolution: Models and applications from around the world* (pp. 199-213). New York: Academic Press.

Guerra, N. G., Huesmann, L. R., Tolan, P. H., VanAcker, R., & Eron, L. D. (1995). Stressful event and individual beliefs as correlates of economic disadvantage and aggression among urban children. *Journal of Consulting and Clinical Psychology, 63,* 518-528.

Guerra, N. G., Huesmann, L. R., Tolan, P. H., VanAcker, R., Henry, D., & Eron, L. D. (1997). *Proximal outcomes for a large scale preventive intervention.* Manuscript under review.

Guerra, N. G., & Slaby, R. G. (1990). Cognitive mediators of aggression in adolescent offenders: 2. Intervention. *Developmental Psychology, 26,* 269-277.

Guerra, N. G., Tolan, P. H., & Hammond, R. (1994). Prevention and treatment of adolescent violence. In L. D. Eron, J. Gentry, & P. Schlegel (Eds.), *Reason to hope: A psychological perspective on violence and youth* (pp. 383-404). Washington, DC: American Psychological Association.

Guerra, N. G., & Williams, K. R. (1996). *Building effective strategies to address youth violence in your community: Program guide*. Miami, FL: John S. and James L. Knight Foundation.

Gustin, J., Guerra, N. G., & Attar, B. (in press). Resilience in urban children: Four kids who could. In G. Brookins (Ed.), *Exits from poverty*. Washington, DC: American Psychological Association.

Haapanen, R. (1990). *Selective incapacitation and the serious offender*. New York: Springer-Verlag.

Hagan, J., & Peterson, R. (1995). Criminal inequality in America: Patterns and consequences. In J. Hagan & R. Peterson (Eds.), *Crime and inequality* (pp. 14-36). Stanford, CA: Stanford University Press.

Hagedorn, J. (1988). *People and folks: Gangs, crime and the underclass in a rustbelt city*. Chicago: Lake View.

Haglund, B., Weisbrod, R. R., & Bracht, N. (1990). Assessing the community: Its services, needs, leadership, and readiness. In N. Bracht (Ed.), *Health promotion at the community level* (pp. 91-108). Newbury Park, CA: Sage.

Hall, J. (1952). *Theft, law and society*. New York: Bobbs-Merrill.

Hammond, W. R., & Yung, B. R. (1991). Preventing violence in at-risk African American youth. *Journal of Health Care for the Poor and Underserved, 2*, 359-373.

Hammond, W. R., & Yung, B. R. (1992). *Evaluation and activity report: Positive Adolescents Choices Training (PACT) program*. Dayton, OH: Wright State University, School of Professional Psychology.

Hamparian, D., Estep, L., Muntean, S., Priestino, R., Swisher, R., Wallace, P., & White, J. (1982). *Youth in adult courts: Between two worlds*. Washington, DC: U.S. Department of Justice, Office of Juvenile Justice and Delinquency Prevention.

Hamparian, D. (1984). *The young criminal years of the violent few*. Cleveland, OH: Federation for Community Planning.

Hamparian, D. M., Davis, J. M., Jacobson, J. M., & McGraw, R. E. (1985). *The young criminal years of the violent few*. Report prepared for the National Institute of Juvenile Justice and Delinquency Prevention. Washington, DC: U.S. Department of Justice.

Hamparian, D. M., Schuster, R., Dinitz, S., & Conrad, J. P. (1978). *The violent few: A study of dangerous juvenile offenders*. Lexington, MA: D. C. Heath.

Hansen, W. B., Johnson, C. A., Flay, B. R., Graham, J. W., & Sobel, J. (1988). Affective and social influences approaches to the prevention of multiple substance abuse among seventh-grade students: Results from Project SMART. *Preventive Medicine, 17*, 135-154.

Harachi, T. W., Ayers, C. D., Hawkins, J. D., Catalano, R. F., & Cushing, J. (1995). Empowering communities to prevent adolescent substance abuse: Results from a risk- and protection-focused community mobilization effort. *Journal of Primary Prevention, 16*, 233-254.

Harachi Manger, T. (1991). *Empowering communities for the prevention of adolescent substance abuse*. Unpublished doctoral dissertation, University of Washington, Seattle.

Harachi Manger, T., Hawkins, J. D., Haggerty, K. P., & Catalano, R. F. (1992). Mobilizing communities to reduce risks for drug abuse: Lessons on using research to guide prevention practice. *Journal of Primary Prevention, 13*, 3-22.

Harden, (1997). Boston's approach to juvenile crime encircles youths, reduces slayings. *The Washington Post,D October 23, p. A3.

Harrell, A. (1996)., Findings of the evaluation of the Children at Risk program. Paper presented at the University of Maryland, College Park.

Harries, K. (1990). *Serious violence: Patterns of homicide and assault in America*. Springfield, IL: Charles C Thomas.

Harris, M. B. (1996). Aggression, gender, and ethnicity. *Aggression and Violent Behavior, 1*, 123-146.

Harrison, L., & Gfroerer, J. (1992). The intersection of drug use and criminal behavior: Results from the National Household Survey on drug abuse. *Crime & Delinquency, 38*, 422-443.

Hathaway, S. R., & Monachesi, E. D. (1953). *Analyzing and predicting juvenile delinquency with the MMPI*. Minneapolis: University of Minnesota Press.

Havighurst, R. J., Bowman, P. H., Liddle, G. P., Matthews, C. V., & Pierce, J. V. (1962). *Growing up in River City*. New York: John Wiley.

Hawkins, D. (in press). Racial and ethnic differences in rates of homicide: What can we learn from data disaggregation? In M. D. Smith & M. Zahn (Eds.), *Homicide studies: A sourcebook of social research*. Thousand Oaks, CA: Sage.

Hawkins, D. F. (1983). Black and white homicide differentials: Alternatives to an inadequate theory. *Criminal Justice and Behavior, 10*, 407-440.

Hawkins, D. F. (1993). Crime and ethnicity. In B. Forst (Ed.), *The socio-economics of crime and justice* (pp. 89-120). Armonk, NY: M. E. Sharpe.

Hawkins, D. F. (1994). The analysis of racial disparities in crime and justice: A double-edged sword. In *Enhancing capacities and confronting controversies in criminal justice* (pp. 48-49). Washington, DC: U.S. Department of Justice.

Hawkins, D. F. (1995). Ethnicity, race, and crime: A review of selected studies. In D. F. Hawkins (Ed.), *Ethnicity, race, and crime: Perspectives across time and place* (pp. 11-45). Albany: State University of New York Press.

Hawkins, J. D. (1995). Controlling crime before it happens: Risk-focused prevention. *National Institute of Justice Journal,* 10-18.

Hawkins, J. D., Abbott, R., Catalano, R. F., & Gillmore, M. R. (1991). Assessing effectiveness of drug abuse prevention: Long-term effects and replication. In C. Leukfeld & W. Bukoski (Eds.), *Drug abuse prevention research: Methodological issues* (NIDA Research Monograph No. 107, DHHS Publication No. ADM 91-1761, pp. 195-212). Washington, DC: Government Printing Office.

Hawkins, J. D., Arthur, M. W., & Catalano, R. F. (1995). Preventing substance abuse. In M. Tonry & D. P. Farrington (Eds.), *Building a safer society: Strategic approaches to crime prevention: Vol. 19. Crime and justice: A review of research* (pp. 343-427). Chicago: University of Chicago Press.

Hawkins, J. D., Arthur, M. W., & Olson, J. J. (1997). Community interventions to reduce risks and enhance protection against anti-social behavior. In D. S. Stoff, J. Breiling, & J. D. Masers (Eds.), *Handbook of antisocial behaviors* (pp. 365-374), New York: NIMH/John Wiley.

Hawkins, J. D., & Catalano, R. F. (1992). *Communities that care.* San Francisco: Jossey-Bass.

Hawkins, J. D., & Catalano, R. F. (1993). *Risk-focused prevention using the social development strategy.* Seattle, WA: Developmental Resources and Programs.

Hawkins, J. D., Catalano, R. F., & Associates. (1992). *Communities That Care: Action for drug abuse prevention.* San Francisco: Jossey-Bass.

Hawkins, J. D., Catalano, R. F., & Brewer, D. D. (1995a). Preventing serious, violent, and chronic delinquency and crime. In J. C. Howell (Ed.), *Guide for implementing the comprehensive strategy for serious, violent, and chronic juvenile offenders* (pp. 57-131). Washington, DC: U.S. Department of Justice, Office of Juvenile Justice and Delinquency Prevention.

Hawkins, J. D., Catalano, R. F., & Brewer, D. D. (1995b). Preventing serious, violent, and chronic offending: Effective strategies from conception to age 6. In J. C. Howell, B. Krisberg, J. D. Hawkins, & J. J. Wilson (Eds.), *Sourcebook on serious, violent, and chronic juvenile offenders* (pp. 36-60). Thousand Oaks, CA: Sage.

Hawkins, J. D., Catalano, R. F., & Kent, L. A. (1991). Combining broadcast media and parent education to prevent teenage drug abuse. In L. Donohew, H. E. Sypher, & W. J. Bukoski (Eds.), *Persuasive communication and drug abuse prevention* (pp. 283-342). Hillsdale, NJ: Lawrence Erlbaum.

Hawkins, J. D., Catalano, R. F., & Miller, J. Y. (1992). Risk and protective factors for alcohol and other drug problems in adolescence and early adulthood: Implications for substance abuse prevention. *Psychological Bulletin, 112,* 64-105.

Hawkins, J. D., Catalano, R. F., Kosterman, R., Abbott, R., & Hill, K. G. (1997). *Promoting academic success and preventing crime in urban America: Six year follow up effects of the Seattle Social Development Project.* Manuscript under review.

Hawkins, J. D., Catalano, R. F., Morrison, D. M., O'Donnell, J., Abbott, R. D., & Day, L. E. (1992). The Seattle Social Development Project: Effects of the first four years on protective factors and problem behaviors. In J. McCord & R. E. Tremblay (Eds.), *Preventing antisocial behavior: Interventions from birth through adolescence* (pp. 139-161). New York: Guilford.

Hawkins, J. D., Doueck, H. J., & Lishner, D. M. (1988). Changing teaching practices in mainstream classrooms to improve bonding and behavior of low achievers. *American Educational Research Journal, 25,* 31-50.

Hawkins, J. D., Farrington, D. P., & Catalano, R. F. (in press). Reducing violence through the schools. In D. S. Elliott, B. A. Hamburg, & K. R. Williams (Eds.), *Youth violence: New perspectives for schools and communities.* Cambridge: Cambridge University Press.

Hawkins, J. D., & Lam, T. (1987). Teacher practices, social development and delinquency. In J. D. Burchard & S. N. Burchard (Eds.), *Primary prevention of psychopathology: Vol. 10. Prevention of delinquent behavior* (pp. 241-274). Newbury Park, CA: Sage.

Hawkins, J. D., Von Cleve, E., & Catalano, R. F. (1991). Reducing early childhood aggression: Results of a primary prevention program. *Journal of the American Academy of Child and Adolescent Psychiatry, 30,* 208-217.

Hawkins, J. D., & Weis, J. G. (1985). The social development model: An integrated approach to delinquency prevention. *Journal of Primary Prevention, 6(2),* 73-97.

Hechtman, L., & Weiss, G. (1986). Controlled prospective fifteen year follow-up of hyperactives as adults: Non-medical drug and alcohol use and anti-social behaviour. *Canadian Journal of Psychiatry, 31,* 557-567.

Hedges, L. V. (1981). Distribution theory for Glass's estimator of effect size and related estimators. *Journal of Educational Statistics, 6,* 107-128.

Hedges, L. V., & Olkin, I. (1985). *Statistical methods for meta-analysis.* New York: Academic Press.

Heinicke, C. C., Beckwith, L., & Thompson, A. (1988). Early intervention in the family system: A framework and review. *Infant Mental Health Journal, 9,* 111-141.

Henggeler, S. W., & Blaske, D. M. (1990). An investigation of systemic conceptualizations of parent-child coalitions and symptom change. *Journal of Consulting and Clinical Psychology, 58,* 336-344.

Henggeler, S. W., & Borduin, C. M. (1990). *Family therapy and beyond: A multisystemic approach to treating the behavior problems of children and adolescents.* Pacific Grove, CA: Brooks/Cole.

Henggeler, S. W., Cunningham, P. B., Pickrel, S. G., Schoenwald, S. K., & Brondino, M. J. (1996). Multisystemic therapy: An effective violence prevention approach for serious juvenile offenders. *Journal of Adolescence, 19,* 47-61.

Henggeler, S. W., Melton, G. B., & Smith, L. A. (1992). Family preservation using multisystemic therapy: An effective alternative to incarcerating serious juvenile offenders. *Journal of Consulting and Clinical Psychology, 60,* 953-961.

Henggeler, S. W., Melton, G. B., Smith, L. A., Schoenwald, S. K., & Hanley, J. H. (1993). Family preservation using multisystemic treatment: Long-term follow-up to a clinical trial with serious juvenile offenders. *Journal of Child and Family Studies, 2,* 283-293.

Henry, B., Avshalom, C., Moffitt, T. E., & Silva, P. A. (1996). Temperamental and familial predictors of violent and nonviolent criminal convictions: Age 3 to age 18. *Developmental Psychology, 32,* 614-623.

Hewitt, L. E., & Jenkins, R. L. (1946). *Fundamental patterns of maladjustment and the dynamics of their origin.* Springfield: State University of Illinois.

Hill, K. G., Hawkins, J. D., Catalano, R. F., Kosterman, R., Abbott, R., & Edwards, T. (1996, November). *The longitudinal dynamics of gang membership and problem behavior: A replication and extension of the Denver and Rochester gang studies in Seattle.* Paper presented at the annual meeting of the American Society of Criminology, Chicago.

Hill, K. G., Hawkins, J. D., Catalano, R., Maguin, E., & Kosterman, R. (1995, November). *The role of gang membership in delinquency, substance use, and violent offending.* Paper presented at the annual meeting of the American Society of Criminology, Boston.

Hill, K. G., Howell, J. C., Hawkins, J. D., & Battin, S. R. (1996, November). *Risk factors in childhood for adolescent gang membership: Results from the Seattle Social Development Project.* Manuscript under review.

Hindelang, M. (1974). The Uniform Crime Reports revisited. *Journal of Criminal Justice, 2,* 1-18.

Hindelang, M. (1978). Race and involvement in common law personal crimes. *American Sociological Review, 43,* 93-109.

Hindelang, M. (1981). Variations in sex-race-age-specific incidence rates of offending. *American Sociological Review, 46,* 461-474.

Hindelang, M., Hirschi, T., & Weis, J. (1981). *Measuring delinquency.* Beverly Hills, CA: Sage.

Hingson, R., Heeren, T., Howland, J., & Winter, M. (1983). Reduced BAC limits for young people: Impact on night fatal crashes. *Alcohol, Drugs and Driving, 7*(2), 117-127.

Hinshaw, S. P. (1991). Stimulant medication and the treatment of aggression in children with attentional deficits. *Journal of Clinical Child Psychology, 20,* 301-312.

Hinshaw, S. P., & Erhardt, D. (1991). Attention-deficit hyperactivity disorder. In P. C. Kendall (Ed.), *Child and adolescent therapy: Cognitive-behavioral perspectives* (pp. 98-128). New York: Guilford.

Hinshaw, S. P., Heller, T., & McHale, J. P. (1992). Covert antisocial behavior in boys with attention-deficit hyperactivity disorder: External validation and effects of methylphenidate. *Journal of Consulting and Clinical Psychology, 60,* 274-281.

Hinshaw, S. P., Klein, R. G., & Abikoff, H. (in press). Childhood attention-deficit hyperactivity disorder: Nonpharmacologic and combination treatments. In P. Nathan & J. Gorman (Eds.), *Treatments that work.* New York: Oxford University Press.

Hirschi, T. (1969). *Causes of delinquency.* Berkeley: University of California Press.

Hodge, E. F., & Tait, C. D. (1963). A follow-up study of potential delinquents. *American Journal of Psychiatry, 120,* 449-453.

Hoge, R. D., & Andrews, D. A. (1996). *Assessing the youthful offender: Issues and techniques.* New York: Plenum.

Hogh, E., & Wolf, P. (1983). Violent crime in a birth cohort: Copenhagen 1953-1977. In K. T. Van Dusen & S. A. Mednick (Eds.), *Prospective studies of crime and delinquency* (pp. 249-267). Boston: Kluwer-Nijhoff.

Holder, H. D., & Blose, J. O. (1987). Impact of changes in distilled spirits availability on apparent consumption: A time series analysis of liquor-by-the-drink. *British Journal of Addiction, 82,* 623-631.

Home Office. (1989a). Criminal and custodial careers of those born in 1953, 1958, and 1963. In *Home Office Statistical Bulletin.* London: Author.

Home Office. (1989b). Criminal and custodial careers of those born in 1953, 1958 and 1963: Variations in sentencing with the number of court appearances. In *Home Office Statistical Bulletin.* London: Author.

Hope, T. (1991). Crime information in retailing: Prevention through analysis. *Security Journal, 2,* 240-245.

Hope, T. (1995). Community crime prevention. In M. Tonry & D. P. Farrington (Eds.), *Crime and justice: A review of research: Vol. 19. Building a safer society: Strategic approaches to crime prevention* (pp. 21-89). Chicago: University of Chicago Press.

Horn, W. F., Ialongo, N. S., Pascoe, J. M., Greenberg, G., Packard, T., Lopez, M., Wagner, A., & Puttler, L. (1991). Additive effects of psychostimulants, parent training, and self-control therapy with ADHD children. *Journal of the American Academy of Child and Adolescent Psychiatry, 30,* 233-240.

Horne, A. M. (1993). Family-based interventions. In A. Goldstein & C. R. Huff (Eds.), *The gang intervention handbook* (pp. 189-218). Champaign, IL: Research Press.

Howell, J. C. (Ed.). (1995). *Guide for implementing the comprehensive strategy for serious, violent, and chronic juvenile offenders.* Washington, DC: U.S. Department of Justice, Office of Juvenile Justice and Delinquency Prevention.

Howell, J. C. (1996). Juvenile transfers to the criminal justice system: State-of-the-art. *Law and Policy, 18,* 17-60.

Howell, J. C. (1997). Youth gang homicides, drug trafficking, and program interventions. In J. C. Howell, *Juvenile justice and youth violence* (pp. 115-132). Thousand Oaks, CA: Sage.

Howell, J. C., & Krisberg, B. (1995). Conclusion. In J. C. Howell, B. Krisberg, J. D. Hawkins, & J. J. Wilson (Eds.), *Sourcebook on serious, violent, and chronic juvenile offenders* (pp. 275-278). Thousand Oaks, CA: Sage.

Howell, J. C., Krisberg, B., Hawkins, J. D., & Wilson, J. J. (1995). *Sourcebook on serious, violent, and chronic juvenile offenders.* Thousand Oaks, CA: Sage.

Howell, J. C., Krisberg, B., & Jones, M. (1995). Trends in juvenile crime and youth violence. In J. C. Howell, B. Krisberg, J. D. Hawkins, & J. J. Wilson (Eds.), *Sourcebook on serious, violent, and chronic juvenile offenders* (pp. 1-35). Thousand Oaks, CA: Sage.

Howells, K., McEwan, M., Jones, B., & Mathews, C. (1983). Social evaluations of mental illness in relation to criminal behavior. *British Journal of Social Psychology, 22,* 165-166.

Hudley, C. C. A. (1994). The reduction of childhood aggression using the Brainpower program. In M. Furlong & D. Smith (Eds.), *Anger, hostility, and aggression: Assessment, prevention, and intervention strategies for youth* (pp. 313-344). Brandon, VT: Clinical Psychology Publishing.

Huesmann, L. R., Eron, L. D., Lefkowitz, M. M., & Walder, L. O. (1984). Stability of aggression over time and generations. *Developmental Psychology, 20,* 1120-1134.

Huesmann, L. R., Guerra, N. G., Miller, L. S., & Zelli, A. (1992). The role of social norms in the development of aggressive behavior. In A. Fraczek & H. Zumkley (Eds.), *Socialization and aggression* (pp. 139-152). New York: Springer.

Huff, C. R. (1996a). The criminal behavior of gang members and nongang at-risk youth. In C. R. Huff (Ed.), *Gangs in America* (2nd ed., pp. 75-102). Thousand Oaks, CA: Sage.

Huff, C. R. (Ed.). (1996b). *Gangs in America* (2nd ed.). Thousand Oaks, CA: Sage.

Huizinga, D. (1979). *Dynamic typologies.* Paper presented at the 10th annual meeting of the Classification Society (NAB), Gainesville, FL.

Huizinga, D. (1991). Assessing violent behavior with self-reports. In J. S. Milner (Ed.), *Neuropsychology of aggression* (pp. 47-66). Boston: Kluwer.

Huizinga, D. (1996). *The influence of delinquent peers, gangs, and co-offending on violence.* Fact sheet prepared for the U.S. Department of Justice, Office of Juvenile Justice and Delinquency Prevention.

Huizinga, D. (1997, February). *Gangs and the volume of crime.* Paper presented at the annual meeting of the Western Society of Criminology, Honolulu, HI.

Huizinga, D., & Elliott, D. (1986). Reassessing the reliability and validity of self-report delinquency measures. *Journal of Quantitative Criminology, 2,* 293-327.

Huizinga, D., Esbensen, F.-A., & Weiher, A. (1994). Examining developmental trajectories in delinquency using accelerated longitudinal research design. In E. G. M. Weitekamp & H. J. Kerner (Eds.), *Cross-national longitudinal research on human development and criminal behavior* (pp. 203-216). Boston: Kluwer-Nijhoff.

Huizinga, D., Esbensen, F.-A., & Weiher, A. W. (1991). Are there multiple paths to delinquency? *Journal of Criminal Law and Criminology, 82,* 83-118.

Huizinga, D., Loeber, R., & Thornberry, T. P. (1993). Longitudinal study of delinquency, drug use, sexual activity, and pregnancy among children and youth in three cities. *Public Health Reports: Journal of the U.S. Public Health Service,108*(Suppl. 1), 90-96.

Huizinga, D., Loeber, R., & Thornberry, T. P. (1994). *Urban delinquency and substance abuse: Initial findings.* Washington, DC: Office of Juvenile Justice and Delinquency Prevention.

Huizinga, D., Loeber, R., & Thornberry, T. P. (1995). *Recent findings from the program of research on the causes and correlates of delinquency.* Washington, DC: Office of Juvenile Justice and Delinquency Prevention.

Huizinga, D. H. (1995). Developmental sequences in delinquency. In L. Crockett & A. Crouter (Eds.), *Pathways through adolescence* (pp. 15-34). Mahwah, NJ: Lawrence Erlbaum.

Huizinga, D. H., Esbensen, F., & Weiher, A. (1996). The impact of arrest on subsequent delinquent behavior. In R. Loeber, D. H. Huizinga, & T. P. Thornberry (Eds.), *Program of research on the causes and correlates of delinquency: Annual report 1995-1996* (pp. 82-101). Washington, DC: Office of Juvenile Justice and Delinquency Prevention.

Hunsaker, A. (1981). The behavioral-ecological model of intervention with Chicano gang delinquents. *Hispanic Journal of Behavioral Sciences, 3,* 225-239.

Hunzeker, D. (1993). Ganging up against violence. *State legislatures.* Denver, CO: National Conference of State Legislatures.

Hurst, H., IV, & Torbet, P. M. (1993). *Organization and administration of juvenile services: Probation, aftercare, and state institutions for delinquent youth.* Pittsburgh, PA: National Center for Juvenile Justice.

Hutson, H. R., Anglin, D., & Eckstein, M. (1996). Drive-by shootings by violent street gangs in Los Angeles: A five-year review from 1989 to 1993. *Academic Emergency Medicine, 3,* 300-303.

Hutson, H. R., Anglin, D., Kyriacou, D. N., Hart, J., & Spears, K. (1995). The epidemic of gang-related homicides in Los Angeles County from 1979 through 1994. *Journal of the American Medical Association, 274,* 1031-1036.

Hutson, H. R., Anglin, D., & Mallon, W. (1992). Injuries and deaths from gang violence: They are preventable. *Annals of Emergency Medicine, 21,* 1234-1236.

Hutson, H. R., Anglin, D., & Pratts, M. J. (1994). Adolescents and children injured or killed in drive-by shootings in Los Angeles. *New England Journal of Medicine, 330,* 324-327.

Hyndman, B., Giesbrecht, N., Bernardi, D. R., Coston, N., Douglas, R. R., Ferrence, R. G., Gliksman, L., Godstadt, M. S., Graham, D. G., & Loranger, P. D. (1992). Preventing substance abuse through multi-component community action research projects: Lessons from past experiences and challenges for future initiatives. *Contemporary Drug Problems, 19,* 133-164.

Ialongo, N. S., Horn, W. F., Pascoe, J. M., Greenberg, G., Packard, T., Lopez, M., Wagner, A., & Puttler, L. (1993). The effects of a multimodal intervention with attention-deficit hyperactivity disorder children: A 9-month follow-up. *Journal of the American Academy of Child and Adolescent Psychiatry, 32,* 182-189.

Inciardi, J. A. (1990). The crack-violence connection within a population of hard-core adolescent offenders. In M. De La Rosa, E. Y. Lambert, & B. Gropper (Eds.), *Drugs and violence: Causes, correlates, and consequences* (pp. 92-111). NIDA Research Monograph No. 103. Rockville, MD: U.S. National Institute on Drug Abuse.

Inciardi, J. A., Horowitz, R., & Pottieger, A. E. (1993). *Street kids, street drugs, street crime: An examination of drug use and serious delinquency in Miami.* Belmont, CA: Wadsworth.

Institute of Medicine, Committee on Prevention of Mental Disorders. (1994). In *Reducing risks for mental disorders: Frontiers for preventive intervention research* (P. J. Mrazek & R. J. Haggerty, Eds.). Washington, DC: National Academy Press.

Jackson, R. K., & McBride, W. (1985). *Understanding street gangs.* Plackerville, CA: Custom.

Jankowski, M. S. (1995). Ethnography, inequality, and crime in the low-income community. In J. Hagan & R. Peterson (Eds.), *Crime and inequality* (pp. 80-94). Stanford, CA: Stanford University Press.

Janosz, M., Le Blanc, M., Boulerice, B., & Tremblay, R. E. (1996). *Disentangling the weight of school dropout predictors: A test on two longitudinal samples.* Unpublished manuscript.

Jarjoura, G. R. (1996). The conditional effect of social class on the dropout-delinquency relationship. *Journal of Research in Crime and Delinquency, 33,* 232-255.

Jencks, C. (1992). *Rethinking social policy.* Cambridge, MA: Harvard University Press.

Jenkins, E., & Bell, C. (1994). Violence exposure, psychological distress, and high risk behaviors among inner-city high school students. In S. Friedman (Ed.), *Anxiety disorders in African Americans* (pp. 76-88). New York: Springer.

Jenkins, R. L. (1973). The runaway reaction. In R. L. Jenkins (Ed.), *Behavior disorders of childhood and adolescence* (pp. 86-95). Springfield, IL: Charles C Thomas.

Jensen, G., & Brownfield, D. (1986). Gender, lifestyles, and victimization. *Violence and Victims, 1,* 85-99.

Jessness, C. F., Allison, F. S., McCormic, P. M., Wedge, R. F., & Young, M. L. (1975). *Evaluation of the effectiveness of contigency contracting with delinquents.* Sacramento: California Youth Authority.

Jessness, C. F., & Haapanen, R. A. (1982). *Early identification of chronic offenders.* Sacramento, CA: Department of Youth Authority.

Jessness, C. F., & Wedge, R. F. (1983). *Classifying offenders: The Jessness Inventory Classification System technical manual.* Sacramento, CA: Department of Youth Authority.

Jessor, R. (1993). Successful adolescent development among youth in high-risk settings. *American Psychologist, 48,* 117-126.

Johnson, B. D., Wish, E. D., Schmeidler, J., & Huizinga, D. (1991). Concentration of delinquent offending: Serious drug involvement and high delinquency rates. *Journal of Drug Issues, 21,* 205-291.

Johnson, C., Webster, B., & Connors, E. (1995). Prosecuting gangs: A national assessment. *Research in brief.* Washington, DC: U.S. Department of Justice, National Institute of Justice.

Johnson, C. A., Pentz, M. A., Weber, M. D., Dwyer, J. H., Baer, N. A., MacKinnon, D. P., Hansen, W. B., & Flay, B. R. (1990). Relative effectiveness of comprehensive community programming for drug abuse prevention with high-risk and low-risk adolescents. *Journal of Consulting and Clinical Psychology, 58,* 447-456.

Johnson, D. L., & Walker, T. (1987). Primary prevention of behavior problems in Mexican-American children. *American Journal of Community Psychology, 15,* 375-385.

Join Together. (1992). *Who is really fighting the war on drugs?* Boston: Trustees of Boston University.

Jonassen, C. (1949). A reevaluation and critique of the logic and some methods of Shaw and McKay. *American Sociological Review, 14,* 608-614.

Jones, M. B., & Offord, D. R. (1989). Reduction of antisocial behavior in poor children by nonschool skill development. *Journal of Child Psychology and Psychiatry and Allied Disciplines, 30,* 737-750.

Jung, R. S., & Jason, L. A. (1988). Firearm violence and the effects of gun control legislation. *American Journal of Community Psychology, 16,* 515-524.

Kandel, E., Brennan, P. A., Mednick, S. A., & Michelson, N. M. (1989). Minor physical anomalies and recidivistic adult violent criminal behavior. *Acta Psychiatrica Scandinavia, 79,* 103-107.

Kandel, E., & Mednick, S. A. (1991). Perinatal complications predict violent offending. *Criminology, 29,* 519-529.

Kantrowitz, R. E. (1980). Training nonprofessionals to work with delinquents: Differential impacts of varying training/supervisions/intervention strategies (Doctoral dissertation, Michigan State University, 1980). *Dissertation Abstracts International, 40,* 5007B. (University Microfilms No. 80-06139)

Kaplan, S. L., Busner, J., Kupietz, S., Wassermann, E., & Segal, B. (1990). Effects of methylphenidate on adolescents with aggressive conduct disorder and ADHD: A preliminary report. *Journal of the American Academy of Child and Adolescent Psychiatry, 29,* 719-723.

Kasarda, J. (1993). Inner-city concentrated poverty and neighborhood distress: 1970-1990. *Housing Policy Debate, 4,* 253-302.

Kawaguchi, R., & Butler, E. W. (1982). Impairments and community adjustment of young adults: Alcohol use, drug abuse and arrest. *Chemical Dependencies: Behavioral and Biomedical Issues, 4,* 209-219.

Kawaguchi, R. M. (1975). *Camp Fenner Canyon evaluation: Final report.* Los Angeles: Los Angeles County Probation Department. (NCJRS Document Reproduction Service No. NCJ036121).

Kazdin, A. (1987a). *Conduct disorders in children and adolescents.* Newbury Park, CA: Sage.

Kazdin, A. (1987b). Treatment of antisocial behavior in childhood: Current status and future directions. *Psychological Bulletin, 102,* 187-203.

Kazdin, A. E. (1993). Adolescent mental health: Prevention and treatment programs. *American Psychologist, 48,* 127-141.

Kazdin, A. E., Bass, D., Siegel, T., & Thomas, C. C. (1989). Cognitive-behavioral treatment and relationship therapy in the treatment of children referred for antisocial behavior. *Journal of Consulting and Clinical Psychology, 57,* 522-535.

Kazdin, A. E., Esveldt-Dawson, K., French, N. H., & Unis, A. S. (1987a). Effects of parent management training and problem-solving skills training combined in the treatment of antisocial child behavior. *Journal of the American Academy of Child and Adolescent Psychiatry, 26,* 416-424.

Kazdin, A. E., Esveldt-Dawson, K., French, N. H., & Unis, A. S. (1987b). Problem-solving skills training and relationship therapy in the treatment of antisocial child behavior. *Journal of Consulting and Clinical Psychology, 55,* 76-85.

Kazdin, A. E., Siegel, T. C. C., & Bass, D. (1992). Cognitive problem-solving skills training and parent management training in the treatment of antisocial behavior in children. *Journal of Consulting and Clinical Psychology, 60,* 733-747.

Kelder, S. H., Orpinas, P., McAlister, A., Frankowski, R., Parcel, G. S., Friday, J. (1996). The Students for Peace project: A comprehensive violence-prevention program for middle school students. *American Journal of Preventive Medicine, 12*(Suppl. 5). [Youth violence prevention: Descriptions and baseline data from 13 evaluation projects]

Kellam, S. G., Mayer, L. S., Rebok, G. W., & Hawkins, W. E. (in press). Effects of improving achievement on aggressive behavior and of improving aggressive behavior on achievement through two preventive interventions: An investigation of causal paths. In B. Dohrenwend (Ed.), *Adversity, stress, and psychopathology.* Washington, DC: American Psychiatric Press.

Kellam, S. G., & Rebok, G. W. (1992). Building developmental and etiological theory through epidemiologically based preventive intervention trials. In J. McCord & R. E. Tremblay (Eds.), *Preventing antisocial behavior: Interventions from birth through adolescence* (pp. 162-195). New York: Guilford.

Kellam, S. G., Rebok, G. W., Ialongo, N., & Mayer, L. S. (1994). The course and malleability of aggressive behavior from early first grade into middle school: Results of a developmental epidemiologically-based preventive trial. *Journal of Child Psychology and Psychiatry, 35,* 259-281.

Kellam, S. G., Werthamer-Larsson, L., Dolan, L. J., Brown, C. C. H., Mayer, L. S., Rebok, G. W., Anthony, J. C. C., Laudolff, J., & Edelsohn, G. (1991). Developmental epidemiologically based preventive trials: Baseline modeling of early target behaviors and depressive symptoms. *American Journal of Community Psychology, 19,* 563-584.

Keller, M. B., Lavori, P. W., Beardslee, W. R., Wunder, J., Schwartz, C. C. E., Roth, J., & Biederman, J. (1992). The disruptive behavioral disorder in children and adolescents: Comorbidity and clinical course. *Journal of the American Academy of Child and Adolescent Psychiatry, 31,* 204-209.

Kellerman, A. L., Lee, R. K., Mercy, J. A., & Banton, J. (1991). The epidemiologic basis for the prevention of firearm injuries. *Annual Review of Public Health, 12,* 17-40.

Kelling, G. L., Pate, T., Dieckman, D., & Brown, C. E. (1974). *The Kansas City Prevention Patrol Experiment: A summary report.* Washington, DC: Police Foundation.

Kemp, M., & Lee, R. (1975). *Project Crest: A third year experimental study.* Gainesville, FL: Project Crest.

Kempf, K. (1993). Hirschi's theory of social control: Is it fecund but not yet fertile? *Advances in Theoretical Criminology, 4,* 143-186.

Kennedy, D. M., Piehl, A. M., & Braga, A. A. (1996). Youth violence in Boston: Gun markets, serious youth offenders, and a use-reduction strategy. *Law and Contemporary Problems, 59,* 147-196. [Special issue]

Kent, D. R., & Smith, P. (1995). The Tri-Agency Resource Gang Enforcement Team: A selective approach to reduce gang crime. In M. W. Klein, C. L. Maxson, & J. Miller (Eds.), *The modern gang reader* (pp. 292-296). Los Angeles: Roxbury.

Kirigin, K. A., Braukmann, C. J., Atwater, J. D., & Worl, M. M. (1982). An evaluation of teaching family (Achievement Place) group homes for juvenile offenders. *Journal of Applied Behavior Analysis, 15,* 1-16.

Klein, M. W. (1968). *The Ladino Hills Project: Final report.* Los Angeles: University of Southern California, Youth Studies Center.

Klein, M. W. (1969). Gang cohesiveness, delinquency, and a street-work program. *Journal of Research in Crime and Delinquency, 6,* 135-166.

Klein, M. W. (1971). *Street gangs and street workers.* Englewood Cliffs, NJ: Prentice Hall.

Klein, M. W. (1993). Attempting gang control by suppression: The misuse of deterrence principles. *Studies on Crime and Prevention, 2,* 88-111.

Klein, M. W. (1995). *The American street gang: Its nature, prevalence, and control.* New York: Oxford University Press.

Klein, M. W., Gordon, M. A., & Maxson, C. L. (1986). The impact of police investigation on police-reported rates of gang and nongang homicides. *Criminology, 24,* 489-512.

Klein, M. W., & Maxson, C. L. (1989). Street gang violence. In N. A. Weiner & M. E. Wolfgang (Eds.), *Violent crime, violent criminals* (pp. 198-234). Newbury Park, CA: Sage.

Klein, M. W., Maxson, C. L., & Cunningham, L. C. (1991). Crack, street gangs, and violence. *Criminology, 29,* 623-650.

Klein, M. W., Maxson, C. L., & Miller, J. (1995). *The modern gang reader.* Los Angeles: Roxbury.

Klein, N. C. C., Alexander, J. F., & Parsons, B. V. (1977). Impact of family systems intervention on recidivism and sibling delinquency: A model of primary prevention and program evaluation. *Journal of Consulting and Clinical Psychology, 45,* 469-474.

Klein, R. G. (1987). Pharmacotherapy of childhood hyperactivity: An update. In H. Y. Meltzer (Ed.), *Psychopharmacology: The third generation of progress* (pp. 1215-1224). New York: Raven.

Klinteberg, B. A., Andersson, T., Magnusson, D., & Stattin, H. (1993). Hyperactive behavior in childhood as related to subsequent alcohol problems and violent offending: A longitudinal study of male subjects. *Personality and Individual Differences, 15,* 381-388.

Kobrin, S. (1959). The Chicago Area Project—A twenty-five year assessment. *Annals of the American Academy of Political and Social Science, 322,* 19-29.

Kodluboy, D. W., & Evenrud, L. A. (1993). School-based interventions: Best practices and critical issues. In A. Goldstein & C. R. Huff (Eds.), *The gang intervention handbook* (pp. 257-299). Champaign, IL: Research Press.

Koepsell, T. D., Martin, D. C., Diehr, P. H., Psaty, B. M., Wagner, E. H., Perrin, E. B., & Cheadle, A. (1991). Data analysis and sample size issues in evaluations of community-based health promotion and disease prevention programs: A mixed model analysis of variance approach. *Journal of Clinical Epidemiology, 44,* 701-713.

Kohn, G., & Shelly, C. (1991, August). *Juveniles and gangs.* Paper presented at the annual convention of the American Psychological Association, Washington, DC.

Krisberg, B. (1996). The historical legacy of juvenile corrections. In *Juvenile justice programs and trends* (pp. 45-50). Correctional Issues series. Lanham, MD: American Correctional Association.

Krisberg, B., & Austin, J. (1978). *The children of Ishmael: Critical perspectives on juvenile justice.* Palo Alto, CA: Mayfield.

Krisberg, B., & Austin, J. (1993). *Reinventing juvenile justice.* Newbury Park, CA: Sage.

Krisberg, B., DeComo, R., Rudenstine, S., & Del Rosario, D. (1995). *Juveniles Taken Into Custody FY 1994.* San Francisco: National Council on Crime and Delinquency.

Krisberg, B., DeComo, R., Wordes, M., & Del Rosario, D. (1996). *Juveniles Taken Into Custody FY 1995.* San Francisco: National Council on Crime and Delinquency.

Krisberg, B., Litsky, P., & Schwartz, I. (1984). Youth in confinement: Justice by geography. *Journal of Research in Crime and Delinquency, 21,* 153-181.

Krisberg, B., Neuenfeldt, D., Wiebush, R., & Rodriguez, O. (1994). *Juvenile intensive supervision: Planning guide.* Washington, DC: U.S. Justice Department, Office of Juvenile Justice and Delinquency Prevention.

Krisberg, B., Onek, D., Jones, M., & Schwartz, I. (1993). *Juveniles in state custody: Prospects for community-based care of troubled adolescents.* San Francisco: National Council on Crime and Delinquency.

Krisberg, B., Rodriguez, O., Bakke, A., Neuenfeldt, D., & Steele, P. (1989). *Demonstration of post-adjudication non-residential intensive supervision programs: Assessment report.* San Francisco: National Council on Crime and Delinquency.

Krohn, M. D., Lizotte, A. J., Thornberry, T. P., Smith, C., & McDowall, D. (1996). Reciprocal causal relationships among drug use, peers, and beliefs: A five wave panel model. *Journal of Drug Issues, 26,* 405-428.

Krohn, M. D., Thornberry, T. P., Collins-Hall, L., & Lizotte, A. J. (1995). School dropout, delinquent behavior, and drug use: An examination of the causes and consequences of dropping out of school. In H. B. Kaplan (Ed.), *Drugs, crime, & other deviant adaptations—Longitudinal studies* (pp. 163-183). New York: Plenum.

Kulik, J. A., Stein, K. B., & Sarbin, T. R. (1968). Dimensions and patterns of adolescent antisocial behavior. *Journal of Consulting and Clinical Psychology, 32,* 378-382.

Kurz, G. A., & Moore, L. E. (1994). *The "8% problem": Chronic juvenile offender recidivism.* Santa Ana, CA: Orange County Probation Department.

Kvaraceus, W. C. (1953). *KD Proneness Scale and Check List.* Yonkers, NY: World Book.

LaFree, G. (1995). Race and crime trends in the United States, 1946-1990. In D. F. Hawkins (Ed.), *Ethnicity, race, and crime: Perspectives across time and place* (pp. 169-193). Albany: State University of New York Press.

Lally, J. R., Mangione, P. L., & Honig, A. S. (1988). The Syracuse University Family Development Research Project: Long-range impact of an early intervention with low-income children and their families. In D. R. Powell (Ed.), *Annual advances in applied developmental psychology* (Vol. 3, pp. 79-104). Norwood, NJ: Ablex.

Lam, J. A. (1989). *The impact of conflict resolution programs on schools: A review and synthesis of the evidence.* Amherst, MA: National Association for Mediation in Education.

Land, K., McCall, P., & Cohen, L. (1990). Structural covariates of homicide rates: Are there any invariances across time and space? *American Journal of Sociology, 95,* 922-963.

Land, K. C. (1992). Models of criminal careers: Some suggestions for moving beyond the current debate. *Criminology, 30,* 149-155.

Larson, C. C. P. (1980). Efficacy of prenatal and postpartum home visits on child health and development. *Pediatrics, 66,* 191-197.

Larson, J. D. (1992). Anger and aggression management techniques through the "Think First" curriculum. *Journal of Offender Rehabilitation, 18,* 101-117.

Laub, J. (1983). Urbanism, race, and crime. *Journal of Research in Crime and Delinquency, 20,* 183-198.

Laub, J. (1987). Data for positive criminology. In M. Gottfredson & T. Hirschi (Eds.), *Positive criminology* (pp. 56-70). Newbury Park, CA: Sage.

Laub, J. H., & Lauritsen, J. L. (1993). Violent criminal behavior over the life course: A review of the longitudinal and comparative research. *Violence and Victims, 8,* 235-252.

Laub, J., & McDermott, M. J. (1985). An analysis of serious crime by young black women. *Criminology, 23,* 81-98.

Lauritsen, J., Sampson, R., & Laub, J. (1991). The link between offending and victimization among adolescents. *Criminology, 29,* 265-291.

Le Blanc, M. (1995). Common, temporary, and chronic delinquencies: Prevention strategies during compulsory school. In P.-O. Wikström, J. McCord, & R. W. Clarke (Eds.), *Integrating crime prevention strategies: Motivation and opportunity* (pp. 169-205). Stockholm: National Council for Crime Prevention.

Le Blanc, M. (1996). Changing patterns in the perpetration of offenses over time: Trajectories from early adolescence to the early 30's. *Studies on Crime and Crime Prevention, 5,* 151-165.

Le Blanc, M. (1997). Socialization or propensity: A test of an integrative control theory with adjudicated boys. *Studies in Crime and Crime Prevention, 6,* 200-224.

Le Blanc, M., Côté, G., & Loeber, R. (1991). Temporal paths in delinquency: Stability, regression and pro-

gression analyzed with panel data from an adolescent and a delinquent sample. *Canadian Journal of Criminology, 33,* 23-44.

Le Blanc, M., & Fréchette, M. (1989). *Male criminal activity, from childhood through youth: Multilevel and developmental perspectives.* New York: Springer-Verlag.

Le Blanc, M., & Kaspy, N. (in press). Trajectories of delinquency and problem behavior: Comparison of synchronous and nonsynchronous paths on social and personal control characteristics of adolescents. *Journal of Quantitative Criminology.*

Le Blanc, M., & Lanctot, N. (in press). Social and psychological characteristics of gang members according to the gang structure and its subcultural and ethnic makeup. *Journal of Gang Research.*

Le Blanc, M., Marineau, D., Fréchette, M., Limoges, T. (1971). Quelques résultats d'un projet de prévention spécifique [Some results of a preventive intervention]. *Revue Canadienne de Criminologie, 13,* 232-250.

Le Blanc, M., McDuff, P., Charlebois, P., Gagnon, C., Lariveé, S., & Tremblay, R. E. (1991). Social and psychological consequences, at 10 years old, of an earlier onset self-reported delinquency. *Psychiatry, 54,* 133-147.

Lee, R., & Haynes, N. M. (1978a). Counseling delinquents: Dual treatment revisited. *Rehabilitation Counseling Bulletin, 22,* 130-133.

Lee, R., & Haynes, N. M. (1978b). Counseling juvenile offenders: An experimental evaluation of Project Crest. *Community Mental Health Journal, 14,* 267-271.

Lee, R., & Olejnik, S. (1981). Professional outreach counseling can help the juvenile probationer: A two-year follow-up study. *Personnel and Guidance Journal, 59,* 445-449.

Lefebvre, R. C., Lasater, T. M., Carleton, R. A., & Peterson, G. (1987). Theory and delivery of health programming in the community: The Pawtucket Heart Health Program. *Preventive Medicine, 16,* 80-95.

Lemert, E. (1951). *Social pathology.* New York: McGraw-Hill.

Lerman, P. (1975). *Community treatment and social control.* Chicago: University of Chicago Press.

Levy, D., & Sheflin, N. (1985). The demand for alcoholic beverages: An aggregate time-series analysis. *Journal of Public Policy and Marketing, 4,* 47-54.

Liang, K. Y., & Zeger, S. L. (1986). Longitudinal data analysis using generalized linear models. *Biometrika, 73,* 13-22.

Lindsay, B., & McGillis, D. (1986). Citywide community crime prevention: An assessment of the Seattle program. In D. P. Rosenbaum (Ed.), *Community crime prevention: Does it work?* (pp. 46-67). Beverly Hills, CA: Sage.

Lipsey, M. W. (1992). Juvenile delinquency treatment: A meta-analytic inquiry into the variability of effects. In T. D. Cook, H. Cooper, D. S. Cordray, H. Hartmann, L. V. Hedges, R. J. Light, T. A. Louis, & F. Mosteller

(Eds.), *Meta-analysis for explanation: A casebook* (pp. 83-127). New York: Russell Sage.

Lipsey, M. W. (1995). What do we learn from 400 research studies on the effectiveness of treatment with juvenile delinquents? In J. McGuire (Ed.), *What works? Reducing reoffending* (pp. 63-78). New York: John Wiley.

Lipsey, M. W., & Derzon, J. H. (1992, November). *Prediction, prevention, programming, and meta-analysis.* Paper presented at the meeting of the American Evaluation Association, Chicago.

Lipsey, M. W., & Wilson, D. B. (1996). *A toolkit for practical meta-analysis.* Cambridge, MA: Human Services Research Institute.

Lipton, D., Martinson, R., & Wilks, J. (1975). *The effectiveness of correctional treatment: A survey of treatment evaluation studies.* New York: Praeger.

Lizotte, A. J., Howard, G. J., Krohn, M. D., & Thornberry, T. P. (1997). Patterns of carrying firearms among juveniles. *Valparaiso University Law Review, 31,* 375-393.

Lizotte, A. J., Tesoriero, J. M., Thornberry, T. P., & Krohn, M. D. (1994). Patterns of adolescent firearms ownership and use. *Justice Quarterly, 11,* 51-73.

Lochman, J. E. (1987). Self- and peer-perceptions and attributional biases of aggressive and nonagressive boys in dyadic interactions. *Journal of Consulting and Clinical Psychology, 55,* 404-410.

Lochman, J. E. (1992). Cognitive-behavioral intervention with aggressive boys: Three-year follow-up and preventive effects. *Journal of Consulting and Clinical Psychology, 60,* 426-432.

Lochman, J. E., and the Conduct Problems Research Group. (1995). Screening of child behavior problems for prevention programs at school entry. *Journal of Consulting and Clinical Psychology, 63,* 549-559.

Lochman, J. E., & Curry, J. F. (1986). Effects of social problem-solving training and self-instruction with aggressive boys. *Journal of Clinical Child Psychology, 15,* 159-164.

Lochman, J. E., Burch, P. R., Curry, J. F., & Lampron, L. B. (1984). Treatment and generalization effects of cognitive-behavioral and goal-setting interventions with aggressive boys. *Journal of Consulting and Clinical Psychology, 52,* 915-916.

Loeber, R. (1982). The stability of antisocial and delinquent child behavior: A review. *Child Development, 53,* 1431-1446.

Loeber, R. (1988). Natural histories of conduct problems, delinquency, and associated substance use: Evidence for developmental progressions. In B. B. Lahey & A. E. Kazdin (Eds.), *Advances in clinical child psychology* (Vol. 11, pp. 73-124). New York: Plenum.

Loeber, R. (1990). Development and risk factors of juvenile antisocial behavior and delinquency. *Clinical Psychology Review, 10,* 1-41.

Loeber, R. (1996). Developmental continuity, change, and pathways in male juvenile problem behaviors and delinquency. In J. D. Hawkins (Ed.), *Delinquency and crime: Current theories* (pp. 1-27). Cambridge, UK: Cambridge University Press.

Loeber, R., DeLematre, M. M., Keenan, K., & Zhang, Q. (in press). A prospective replication of developmental pathways in disruptive and delinquent behavior. In R. B. Cairns (Ed.), *The individual as a focus in developmental research.* Thousand Oaks, CA: Sage.

Loeber, R., & Dishion, T. J. (1983). Early predictors of male delinquency: A review. *Psychological Bulletin, 94,* 68-99.

Loeber, R., & Dishion, T. J. (1987). Antisocial and delinquent youths: Methods for their identification. In J. D. Burchard & S. N. Burchard (Eds.), *Prevention of delinquent behavior* (pp. 75-89). Newbury Park, CA: Sage.

Loeber, R., Dishion, T. J., & Patterson, G. R. (1984). Multiple gating: A multistage assessment procedure for identifying youths at risk for delinquency. *Journal of Research in Crime and Delinquency, 21,* 7-32.

Loeber, R., Green, S. M., Lahey, B. B., Christ, M. A. G., & Frick, P. J. (1992). Developmental sequences in the age of onset of disruptive child behaviors. *Journal of Child and Family Studies, 1,* 21-41.

Loeber, R., & Hay, D. F. (1994). Developmental approaches to aggression and conduct problems. In M. Rutter & D. F. Hay (Eds.), *Development through life: A handbook for clinicians* (pp. 488-515). Oxford: Blackwell Scientific.

Loeber, R., & Hay, D. F. (1996). Key issues in the development of aggression and violence from childhood to early adulthood. *Annual Review of Psychology, 48,* 371-410.

Loeber, R., Keenan, K., & Zhang, Q. (1997). Boys' experimentation and persistence in developmental pathways toward serious delinquency. *Journal of Child and Family Studies, 6,* 321-357.

Loeber, R., & Le Blanc, M. (1990). Toward a developmental criminology. In M. Tonry & N. Morris (Eds.), *Crime and justice: A review of research* (Vol. 12, pp. 375-473). Chicago: University of Chicago Press.

Loeber, R., & Schmaling, K. (1985). Empirical evidence for overt and covert patterns of antisocial conduct problems. *Journal of Abnormal Child Psychology, 13,* 337-352.

Loeber, R., & Stouthamer-Loeber, M. (1986). Family factors as correlates and predictors of juvenile conduct problems and delinquency. In M. Tonry & N. Morris (Eds.), *Crime and justice: An annual review of research* (Vol. 7, pp. 219-339). Chicago: University of Chicago Press.

Loeber, R., & Stouthamer-Loeber, M. (1987). Prediction. In H. C. Quay (Ed.), *Handbook of juvenile delinquency* (pp. 325-382). New York: John Wiley.

Loeber, R., & Stouthamer-Loeber, M. (in press). Development of juvenile aggression and violence: Some common misconceptions and controversies. *American Psychologist.*

Loeber, R., Stouthamer-Loeber, M., Van Kammen, W., & Farrington, D. P. (1989). Development of a new measure of self-reported antisocial behavior for young children: Prevalence and reliability. In M. W. Klein (Ed.), *Cross-national research in self-reported crime and delinquency* (pp. 203-225). Dordrecht, Netherlands: Kluwer-Nijhoff.

Loeber, R., Stouthamer-Loeber, M., Van Kammen, W. B., & Farrington, D. P. (1991). Initiation, escalation and desistance in juvenile offending and their correlates. *Journal of Criminal Law and Criminology, 82,* 36-82.

Loeber, R., Van Kammen, W. B., & Fletcher, M. (1996). *Serious, violent and chronic offenders in the Pittsburgh Youth Study: Unpublished data.* Western Psychiatric Institute and Clinic, Pittsburgh, PA.

Loeber, R., Van Kammen, W. B., Krohn, M. D., & Huizinga, D. (1991). The crime-substance use nexus in young people. In D. Huizinga, R. Loeber, & T. P. Thornberry (Eds.), *Urban delinquency and substance abuse.* Washington, DC: Office of Juvenile Justice and Delinquency Prevention and Department of Justice.

Loeber, R., Wung, P., Keenan, K., Giroux, B., Stouthamer-Loeber, M., Van Kammen, W. B., & Maughan, B. (1993). Developmental pathways in disruptive child behavior. *Development and Psychopathology, 5,* 101-133.

Loftin, C., Heumann, M., & McDowall, D. (1983). Mandatory sentencing and firearms violence: Evaluating an alternative to gun control. *Law and Society Review, 17,* 287-318.

Loftin, C., & McDowall, D. (1984). The deterrent effects of the Florida Felony Firearm law. *Journal of Criminal Law and Criminology, 75,* 250-259.

Loftin, C., McDowall, D., & Wiersema, B. (1993). Evaluating effects of changes in gun laws. *American Journal of Preventive Medicine, 9*(Suppl.), 39-43.

Loftin, C., McDowall, D., Wiersema, B., & Cottey, T. I. (1991). Effects of restrictive licensing of handguns on homicide and suicide in the District of Columbia. *New England Journal of Medicine, 325,* 1615-1620.

Loftin, C., & Mercy, J. (1995). Estimating the incidence, causes, and consequences of interpersonal violence for children and families. In *Integrating federal statistics on children: Report of a workshop.* Washington, DC: National Academy Press.

Loftus, A. P. T. (1974). Predicting recidivism using the Glueck Social Prediction Scale with male first offender delinquents. *Australian and New Zealand Journal of Criminology, 7,* 31-43.

Lombroso, C. (1911). *Crime: Its causes and remedies.* Boston: Little, Brown.

Loney, J., Kramer, J., & Milich, R. (1983). The hyperkinetic child grows up: Predictors of symptoms, delinquency, and achievement at follow-up: Birth and childhood cohorts. In S. A. Mednick, M. Harway, &

K. M. Finello (Eds.), *Handbook of longitudinal research* (Vol. 1, pp. 426-447). New York: Praeger.

Loney, J., & Milich, R. (1982). Hyperactivity, inattention, and aggression in a clinical practice. In M. Wolraich & D. K. Routh (Eds.), *Advances in behavioral pediatrics* (pp. 88-147). Greenwich, CT: JAI.

Loney, J., Whaley-Klahn, M. A., Kosier, T., & Conboy, J. (1983). Hyperactive boys and their brothers at 21: Predictors of aggressive and antisocial outcomes. In K. T. Van Dusen & S. A. Mednick (Eds.), *Prospective studies of crime and delinquency* (pp. 181-207). Boston: Kluwer-Nijhoff.

Lorion, R. P., Tolan, P. H., & Wahler, R. G. (1987). Prevention. In H. C. Quay (Ed.), *Handbook of juvenile delinquency* (pp. 383-416). New York: John Wiley.

Lowry, P., Hassig, S., Gunn, R., & Mathison, J. (1988). Homicide victims in New Orleans: Recent trends. *American Journal of Epidemiology, 128,* 1130-1136.

Luepker, R. V., Murray, D. M., Jacobs, D. R., Mittelmark, M. B., Bracht, N., Carlaw, R., Crow, R., Elmer, P., Finnegan, J., Folsom, A. R., Grimm, R., Hannan, P. J., Jeffrey, R., Lando, H., McGovern, P., Mullis, R., Perry, C. L., Pechacek, T., Pirie, P., Sprafka, M., Weisbrod, R., & Blackburn, H. (1994). Community education for cardiovascular disease prevention: Risk factor changes in the Minnesota Heart Health Program. *American Journal of Public Health, 84,* 1383-1393.

Lurigio, A. J., & Petersilia, J. (1992). The emergence of intensive probation supervision programs in the United States. In J. M. Byrne, A. J. Lurigio, & J. Petersilia (Eds.), *Smart sentencing: The emergence of intermediate sanctions* (pp. 3-17). Newbury Park, CA: Sage.

Lynam, D. R. (1996). Early identification of chronic offenders: Who is the fledgling psychopath? *Psychological Bulletin, 120,* 209-234.

MacKenzie, D. L., & Hebert, E. E. (Eds.). (1996). *Correctional boot camps: A tough intermediate sanction.* Washington, DC: National Institute of Justice.

MacKenzie, D. L., & Parent, D. (1992). Boot camp prisons for young offenders. In J. M. Byrne, A. J. Lurigio, & J. Petersilia (Eds.), *Smart sentencing: The emergence of intermediate sanctions* (pp. 103-119). Newbury Park, CA: Sage.

MacKenzie, D. L., & Souryal, C. (1994). *Multisite evaluation of shock incarceration.* Washington, DC: National Institute of Justice.

Magnusson, D., Stattin, H., & Dunér, A. (1983). Antecedents of aggression and antisocial behavior. In K. T. Van Dusen & S. A. Mednick (Eds.), *Aggression and criminality in a longitudinal perspective* (pp. 277-302). Boston: Kluwer-Nijhoff.

Maguin, E., Hawkins, J. D., Catalano, R. F., Hill, K., Abbott, R., & Herrenkohl, T. (1995, November). *Risk factors measured at three ages for violence at age 17-18.* Paper presented at the American Society of Criminology, Boston.

Maguin, E., & Loeber, R. (1996). Academic performance and delinquency. In M. Tonry (Ed.), *Crime and justice: A review of research* (Vol. 20, pp. 145-264). Chicago: University of Chicago Press.

Maguire, K., & Pastore, A. L. (Eds.). (1996). *Sourcebook of criminal justice statistics, 1995*. Washington, DC: Government Printing Office.

Mahoney, A. R. (1987). *Juvenile justice in context*. Boston: Northeastern University Press.

Maloney, D., Romig, D., & Armstrong, T. (1988). *Juvenile probation: The balanced approach*. Reno, NV: National Council of Juvenile and Family Court Judges.

Maltz, M. (1984). *Recidivism*. New York: Academic Press.

Mann, C. R. (1993). *Unequal justice: The question of color*. Bloomington: Indiana University Press.

Mannuzza, S., Klein, R. G., Bessler, A., Malloy, P., & LaPadula, M. (1993). Adult outcome of hyperactive boys: Educational achievement, occupational rank, and psychiatric status. *Archives of General Psychiatry, 50,* 565-576.

Mannuzza, S., Klein, R. G., Konig, P. H., & Giampino, T. L. (1989). Hyperactive boys almost grown up: IV. Criminality and its relationship to psychiatric status. *Archives of General Psychiatry, 46,* 1073-1079.

Martinson, R. (1974). What works? Questions and answers about prison reform. *Public Interest, 10,* 22-54.

Marzuk, P. M. (1996). Violence, crime and mental illness: How strong a link? *Archives of General Psychiatry, 53,* 481-488.

Massey, D. (1996). The age of extremes: Concentrated affluence and poverty in the twenty-first century. *Demography, 33,* 395-412.

Massey, D., & Denton, N. (1993). *American apartheid: Segregation and the making of the underclass*. Cambridge, MA: Harvard University Press.

Mathias, R., DeMuro, P., & Allinson, R. S. (1984). *Violent juvenile offenders*. San Francisco: National Council on Crime and Delinquency.

Mattick, H., & Caplan, N. S. (1962). *Chicago Youth Development Project: The Chicago boys club*. Ann Arbor, MI: Institute for Social Research.

Maxfield, M. G., & Widom, C. S. (1996). The cycle of violence: Revisited 6 years later. *Archives of Pediatrics and Adolescent Medicine, 150,* 390-395.

Maxson, C. L. (1995, September). Street gangs and drug sales in two suburban cities. *Research in brief*. Washington, DC: U.S. Department of Justice, National Institute of Justice.

Maxson, C. L. (in press). Gang homicide. In M. D. Smith & M. A. Zahn (Eds.), *Homicide studies: A sourcebook of social research*. Thousand Oaks, CA: Sage.

Maxson, C. L., Gordon, M. A., & Klein, M. W. (1985). Differences between gang and nongang homicides. *Criminology, 23,* 209-222.

Maxson, C. L., & Klein, M. W. (1990). Street gang violence: Twice as great, or half as great? In C. R. Huff (Ed.), *Gangs in America* (pp. 71-100). Newbury Park, CA: Sage.

Maxson, C. L., Woods, K., & Klein, M. W. (1996. February). Street gang migration: How big a threat? *National Institute of Justice Journal, 230,* 26-31.

Mayer, G. R., & Butterworth, T. W. (1979). A preventive approach to school violence and vandalism: An experimental study. *Personnel and Guidance Journal, 57,* 436-441.

Mayer, G. R., Butterworth, T. W., Nafpaktitis, M., & Sulzer-Azaroff, B. (1983). Preventing school vandalism and improving discipline: A three-year study. *Journal of Applied Behavior Analysis, 16,* 355-369.

McArdle, J. J., & Hamagami, F. (1991). Modeling incomplete longitudinal and cross-sectional data using latent growth structural models. In L. M. Collins & J. L. Horn (Eds.), *Best methods for the analysis of change: Recent advances, unanswered questions, future directions* (pp. 276-304). Washington, DC: American Psychological Association.

McAuliffe, W. E., Dembling, B., Wilson, R., LaBrie, R., Geller, S., & Mulvaney, N. (1993, November). *Social indicator modeling for substance abuse treatment allocation*. Proceedings from the National Technical Center for Substance Abuse Needs Assessment 1993 Social Indicator Workshop, Cambridge, MA.

McCord, J. (1978). A thirty-year follow-up of treatment effects. *American Psychologist, 33,* 284-289.

McCord, J. (1979). Some child-rearing antecedents of criminal behavior in adult men. *Journal of Personality and Social Psychology, 37,* 1477-1486.

McCord, J. (1988). L'évaluation des interventions: en premier lieu, ne pas nuire [Evaluating interventions: First, do no harm]. In P. Durning (Ed.), *Éducation familiale, un panorama des recherches internationales*. Paris: Édition Matrice.

McCord, J., & Ensminger, M. (1995, November). *Pathways from aggressive childhood to criminality*. Paper presented at the American Society of Criminology, Boston.

McCord, J., Tremblay, R. E., Vitaro, F., & Desmarais-Gervais, L. (1994). Boys' disruptive behaviour, school adjustment, and delinquency: The Montreal Prevention Experiment. *International Journal of Behavioural Development, 17,* 739-752.

McCord, W., McCord, J., & Zola, I. K. (1959). *Origins of crime: A new evaluation of the Cambridge-Somerville Youth Study*. New York: Cambridge University Press.

McDowall, D., Lizotte, A. J., & Wiersema, B. (1991). General deterrence through civilian gun ownership: An evaluation of the quasi-experimental evidence. *Criminology, 29,* 541-559.

McDowall, D., Loftin, C., & Wiersema, B. (1992). A comparative study of the preventive effects of mandatory sentencing laws for gun crimes. *Journal of Criminal Law and Criminology, 83,* 378-394.

McKinlay, S. M., Stone, E. J., & Zucker, D. M. (1989). Research design and analysis issues. *Health Education Quarterly, 16,* 307-313.

McPartland, J. M., & Nettles, S. M. (1991). Using community adults as advocates or mentors for at-risk middle school students: A two-year evaluation of Project RAISE. *American Journal of Education, 99,* 568-586.

Mednick, S. A., & Kandel, E. S. (1988). Congenital determinants of violence. *Bulletin of the American Academy of Psychiatry and the Law, 16,* 101-109.

Meehan, P. J., & O'Carroll, P. W. (1992). Gangs, drugs, and homicide in Los Angeles. *American Journal of the Disabled Child, 146,* 683-687.

Megargee, E. I., & Bohn, M. J. (1979). *Classifying criminal offenders: A new system based on the MMPI.* Beverly Hills, CA: Sage.

Meredith, C., & Paquette, C. (1992). Crime prevention in high rise rental apartments: Findings of a demonstration project. *Security Journal, 3,* 161-169.

Messner, S., & Tardiff, K. (1986). Economic inequality and levels of homicide: An analysis of urban neighborhoods. *Criminology, 24,* 297-318.

Miethe, T., & Meier, R. (1994). *Crime and its social context: Toward an integrated theory of offenders, victims, and situations.* Albany: State University of New York Press.

Miller, A., & Ohlin, L. (1985). *Delinquency and community.* Beverly Hills, CA: Sage.

Miller, B. C. (1995). Risk factors for adolescent nonmarital childbearing. In K. A. Moore (Ed.), *Report to Congress on out-of-wedlock childbearing* (pp. 201-216). Hyattsville, MD: U.S. Department of Health and Human Services.

Miller, G. H. (1995). *Evaluation of Michigan's Families First program.* Lansing, MI: University Associates.

Miller, J. (1991). *Last one over the wall: The Massachusetts experiment in closing reform schools.* Columbus: Ohio State University Press.

Miller, L. S. (1994a). Preventive interventions for conduct disorders: A review. *Child and Adolescent Psychiatric Clinics of North America, 3,* 405-419.

Miller, L. S. (1994b). Primary prevention of conduct disorder. *Psychiatric Quarterly, 65,* 273-285.

Miller, L. S., & Klein, R. (1996). *Early primary prevention of conduct problems.* (NIMH Grant IRIMH-55188-OIAZ-MPPN3810)

Miller, W. B. (1962). The impact of a "total community" delinquency control project. *Social Problems, 10,* 168-191.

Miller, W. B. (1966). Violent crimes by city gangs. *Annals of the American Academy of Political and Social Science, 364,* 96-112.

Miller, W. B. (1974). American youth gangs: Past and present. In A. Blumberg (Ed.), *Current perspectives on criminal behavior* (pp. 410-420). New York: Knopf.

Miller, W. B. (1982). *Crime by youth gangs and groups in the United States.* Washington, DC: U.S. Department of Justice, Office of Juvenile Justice and Delinquency Prevention. (Rev. 1992)

Miller, W. B. (1990). Why the United States has failed to solve its youth gang problem. In C. R. Huff (Ed.), *Gangs in America* (pp. 263-287). Newbury Park, CA: Sage.

Miller, W. B. (1993). *Critique of "Weed and Seed" project with a proposal for a new prevention initiative.* Report to the U.S. Department of Justice, Office of Juvenile Justice and Delinquency Prevention.

Miller, W. B. (1994). *Boston assaultive crime* [Memorandum].

Minnesota Governor's Commission on Crime Prevention and Control. (1973). *An evaluation of the Group Residence Program for juvenile girls: June 1972 through April 1973.* St. Paul: Minnesota Department of Corrections.

Mitchell, S., & Rosa, P. (1979). Boyhood behaviour problems as precursors of criminality: A fifteen-year follow-up study. *Journal of Child Psychology & Psychiatry 22,* 19-33.

Mladenka, K., & Hill, K. (1976). A reexamination of the etiology of urban crime. *Criminology, 13,* 491-506.

Moffitt, T. E. (1987). Parental mental disorder and offspring criminal behavior: An adoption study. *Psychiatry, 50,* 346-360.

Moffitt, T. E. (1990a). Juvenile delinquency and attention deficit disorder: Boys' developmental trajectories from age 13 to age 15. *Child Development, 61,* 893-910.

Moffitt, T. E. (1990b). The neuropsychology of juvenile delinquency: A critical review. In M. Tonry & N. Morris (Eds.), *Crime and justice: A review of research* (Vol. 12, pp. 99-169). Chicago: University of Chicago Press.

Moffitt, T. E. (1993). Adolescence-limited and life-course-persistent antisocial behavior: A developmental taxonomy. *Psychological Review, 100,* 674-701.

Monahan, J. (1981). *Predicting violent behavior: An assessment of clinical techniques.* Beverly Hills, CA: Sage.

Monahan, J., & Klassen, D. (1982). Situational approaches to understanding and predicting violent behavior. In M. E. Wolfgang & N. A. Weiner (Eds.), *Criminal violence* (pp. 292-319). Beverly Hills, CA: Sage.

Montgomery, I. M., Torbet, P. M., Malloy, D. A., Adamcik, L. P., Toner, M. J., & Andrews, J. (1994). *What works: Promising interventions in juvenile justice.* Washington, DC: U.S. Department of Justice, Office of Juvenile Justice and Delinquency Prevention.

Moore, C. B. (1978). Ego strength and behavior: A study of a residential treatment program for delinquent girls (Doctoral dissertation, California School of Professional Psychology, 1977). *Dissertation Abstracts International, 38,* 5033B. (University Microfilms No. 78-02837)

Moore, J. W. (1978). *Homeboys: Gangs, drugs and prison in the barrios of Los Angeles.* Philadelphia: Temple University Press.

Moore, J. W. (1991). *Going down to the barrio: Homeboys and homegirls in change.* Philadelphia: Temple University Press.

Moore, M. H. (1986). Purblind justice: Normative issues in the use of prediction in the criminal justice system. In A. Blumstein, J. Cohen, J. A. Roth, & C. A. Visher (Eds.), *Criminal careers and "career criminals"* (Vol. 2, pp. 314-355). Washington, DC: National Academy Press.

Moore, M. H. (1995). Public health and criminal justice approaches to prevention. In M. Tonry & D. P. Farrington (Eds.), *Crime and justice: A review of research: Vol. 19. Building a safer society: Strategic approaches to crime prevention* (pp. 237-262). Chicago: University of Chicago.

Moore, M. H., Prothrow-Smith, D., Guyer, B., & Spivak, H. (1994). Violence and intentional injuries: Criminal justice and public health perspectives on an urgent national problem. In A. J. Reiss & J. A. Roth (Eds.), *Understanding and preventing violence* (Vol. 4, pp. 167-216). Washington, DC: National Academy Press.

Moore, R. H. (1987). Effectiveness of citizen volunteers functioning as counselors for high-risk young male offenders. *Psychological Reports, 61,* 823-830.

Moore, R. H., & Levine, D. (1974). *Evaluation research of a community-based probation program.* Lincoln: University of Nebraska at Lincoln, Department of Psychology.

Morales, A. (1992). A clinical model for the prevention of gang violence and homicide. In R. C. Cervantes (Ed.), *Substance abuse and gang violence* (pp. 105-118). Newbury Park, CA: Sage.

Morris, J. A. (1970). *First Offender: A volunteer program for youth in trouble with the law.* New York: Funk & Wagnalls.

Morris, N., & Tonry, M. (1990). *Between prison and probation: Intermediate punishments in a rational sentencing system.* New York: Oxford University Press.

Mossman, D. (1994). Assessing predictors of violence: Being accurate about accuracy. *Journal of Consulting and Clinical Psychology, 62,* 783-792.

Mulvey, E. P., & Phelps, P. (1988). Ethical balances in juvenile justice research practice. *American Psychologist, 43,* 65-69.

Murphy, H. A., Hutchinson, J. M., & Bailey, J. S. (1983). Behavioral school psychology goes outdoors: The effect of organized games on playground aggression. *Journal of Applied Behavioral Analysis, 16,* 29-35.

Murray, C., & Cox, L. (1979). *Beyond probation.* Beverly Hills, CA: Sage.

Murray, D. M., & Hannan, P. J. (1990). Planning for the appropriate analysis in school-based drug-use prevention studies. *Journal of Consulting and Clinical Psychology, 58,* 458-468.

Murray, D. M., & Wolfinger, R. D. (1994). Analysis issues in the evaluation of community trials: Progress toward solutions in SAS/STAT MIXED. *Journal of*

Community Psychology, pp. 140-154. [CSAP special issue]

Muscat, J. (1988). Characteristics of childhood homicide in Ohio, 1974-84. *American Journal of Public Health, 78,* 822-824.

Nagin, D. S., & Farrington, D. P. (1992a). The onset and persistence of offending. *Criminology, 30,* 501-523.

Nagin, D. S., & Farrington, D. P. (1992b). The stability of criminal potential from childhood to adulthood. *Criminology, 30,* 235-260.

Nagin, D. S., Farrington, D. P., & Moffitt, T. E. (1995). Life-course trajectories of different types of offenders. *Criminology, 33,* 111-139.

National Conference of State Legislatures. (1995). *Special analysis of 1995 juvenile justice gang related enactments for the National Youth Gang Center.* Denver, CO: Author.

National Drug Intelligence Center. (1994). *NDIC Street Gang Symposium* [Proceedings]. Washington, DC: Author.

National Institute of Corrections. (1995). Offenders under age 18 in state adult corrections systems: A national picture. In *Special issues in corrections* (Vol. 1). Washington, DC: U.S. Department of Justice.

National Youth Gang Center. (1997). *The 1995 National Youth Gang Survey.* Washington, DC: U.S. Department of Justice, Office of Juvenile Justice and Delinquency Prevention.

Needle, J., & Stapleton, W. V. (1983). *Police handling of youth gangs.* Washington, DC: U.S. Department of Justice, Office of Juvenile Justice and Delinquency Prevention.

Neithercutt, M. G., & Gottfredson, D. M. (1973). *Caseload size variation and difference in probation/parole performance.* Pittsburgh, PA: National Center for Juvenile Justice.

New York City Youth Board. (1960). *Reaching the fighting gang.* New York: Author.

Newcomb, M. D., Maddahian, E., & Bentler, P. M. (1986). Risk factors for drug use among adolescents: Concurrent and longitudinal analyses. *American Journal of Public Health, 76,* 525-530.

Newton, G. D., & Zimring, F. E. (1969). *Firearms and violence in American life: A staff report to the National Commission on the Causes and Prevention of Violence.* Washington, DC: Government Printing Office.

Nirdorf, B. J. (1988). *Gang alternative and prevention program. Program policy and procedure handbook.* Los Angeles: County of Los Angeles Probation Department.

O'Brien, R. (1985). *Crime and victimization data.* Beverly Hills, CA: Sage.

O'Carroll, P. W., Loftin, C., Waller, J. B., McDowall, D., Bukoff, A., Scott, R. O., Mercy, J. A., & Wiersema, B. (1991). Preventing homicide: An evaluation of the efficacy of a Detroit gun ordinance. *American Journal of Public Health, 81,* 576-581.

O'Donnell, J., Hawkins, J. D., Catalano, R. F., Abbott, R. D., & Day, L. E. (1995). Preventing school failure, drug use, and delinquency among low-income children: Long-term intervention in elementary schools. *American Journal of Orthopsychiatry, 65,* 87-100.

O'Malley, P. M., & Wagenaar, A. C. (1991). Effects of minimum drinking age laws on alcohol use, related behaviors and traffic crash involvement among American youth: 1976-1987. *Journal of Studies on Alcohol, 52,* 478-491.

Oetting, E. R., Donnermeyer, J. F., Plested, B. A., Edwards, R. W., Kelly, K., & Beauvais, F. (1995). Assessing community readiness for prevention. *International Journal of the Addictions, 30,* 659-683.

Office of Justice Programs, Working Group on Gangs. (1996). *A report to the assistant attorney general.* Washington, DC: U.S. Department of Justice, Office of Justice Programs.

Office of Juvenile Justice and Delinquency Prevention. (1995a). *Community assessment centers: A discussion of the concept's efficiency.* Washington, DC: U.S. Department of Justice, Office of Juvenile Justice and Delinquency Prevention.

Office of Juvenile Justice and Delinquency Prevention. (1995b). *Delinquency prevention works.* Washington, DC: Author.

Office of Juvenile Justice and Delinquency Prevention. (1995c). *Matrix of community-based initiatives.* Washington, DC: Author.

Office of Juvenile Justice and Delinquency Prevention. (1996a). *Combating violence and delinquency: The national juvenile justice action plan.* Washington, DC: U.S. Department of Justice, Office of Juvenile Justice and Delinquency Prevention.

Office of Juvenile Justice and Delinquency Prevention. (1996b, December). *Innovative local law enforcement and community policing programs for the juvenile justice system* [Information brief]. Washington, DC: U.S. Department of Justice, Office of Juvenile Justice and Delinquency Prevention.

Offord, D. R. (1990). Conduct disorder: Risk factors and prevention. In D. Shaffer, I. Philips, & N. Enzer (Eds.), *Prevention of mental disorder, alcohol, and drug use in children and adolescents* (Office of Substance Abuse Prevention Monograph No. 2). Rockville, MD: Department of Health and Human Services.

Olds, D. L. (1996, November). *Reducing risks for childhood-onset conduct disorder with prenatal and early childhood home visitation.* Paper presented at a preconference workshop at the annual meeting of the American Public Health Association, New York.

Olds, D. L., Henderson, C. C. R., Chamberlin, R., & Tatelbaum, R. (1986). Preventing child abuse and neglect: A randomized trial of nurse home visitation. *Pediatrics, 78,* 65-78.

Olds, D. L., Henderson, C. C. R., Phelps, C. C., Kitzman, H., & Hanks, C. C. (1993). Effects of prenatal and infancy nurse home visitation on government spending. *Medical Care, 31,* 155-174.

Olds, D. L., Henderson, C. C. R., Tatelbaum, R., & Chamberlin, R. (1988). Improving the life-course development of socially disadvantaged mothers: A randomized trial of nurse home visitation. *American Journal of Public Health, 78,* 1436-1445.

Olweus, D. (1977). Aggression and peer acceptance in adolescent boys: Two short-term longitudinal studies of rating. *Child Development, 48,* 1301-1313.

Olweus, D. (1979). Stability of aggressive reaction patterns in males: A review. *Psychological Bulletin, 86,* 852-875.

Olweus, D. (1991). Bully/victim problems among schoolchildren: Basic facts and effects of a school based intervention program. In D. J. Pepler & K. H. Rubin (Eds.), *The development and treatment of childhood aggression* (pp. 411-448). Hillsdale, NJ: Lawrence Erlbaum.

Olweus, D. (1992). Bullying among school children: Intervention and prevention. In R. D. Peters, R. J. McMahon, & V. L. Quinsey (Eds.), *Aggression and violence throughout the life span* (pp. 100-125). Newbury Park, CA: Sage.

Orange County Probation Department. (1995). *8% Early Intervention Program: Program design and preliminary field test results.* Santa Ana, CA: Author.

Orange County Probation Department. (1996). *8% Early Intervention Program field test results (12 months).* Santa Ana, CA: Author.

Orpinas, P., Parcel, G. S., McAlister, A., & Frankowski, R. (1995). Violence prevention in middle schools: A pilot evaluation. *Journal of Adolescent Health, 17,* 360-371.

Osborn, S. G., & West, D. J. (1978). The effectiveness of various predictors of criminal careers. *Journal of Adolescence, 1,* 101-117.

Osofsky, J. (1995). The effects of exposure to violence on young children. *American Psychologist, 50,* 782-788.

Palmer, T. (1971). California's Community Treatment Program for delinquent adolescents. *Journal of Research on Crime and Delinquency, 8,* 74-92.

Palmer, T. (1992). *The re-emergence of correctional intervention.* Newbury Park, CA: Sage.

Palmer, T. (1994). *A profile of correctional effectiveness and new directions for research.* Albany: State University of New York Press.

Parent, D., Leiter, V., Livens, L., Wentworth, D., & Stephen, K. (1994). *Conditions of confinement: Juvenile detention and corrections facilities.* Washington, DC: U.S. Department of Justice, Office of Juvenile Justice and Delinquency Prevention.

Parker, J., & Asher, S. (1987). Peer relations and later personal adjustment. *Psychological Bulletin, 102,* 357-389.

Paschall, M. J. (1996, June). *Exposure to violence and the onset of violent behavior and substance use among black male youth: An assessment of independent ef-*

fects and psychosocial mediators. Paper presented at the Society for Prevention Research, San Juan, PR.

Pate, A. M., Skogan, W. G., Wycoff, M. A., & Sherman, L. W. (with Annan, S., & the Newark Police Department). (1985). *Reducing the signs of crime: The Newark experience, executive summary.* Washington, DC: Police Foundation.

Patterson, C. J., Kupersmidt, J. B., & Vaden, N. A. (1990). Income level, gender, ethnicity, and household compositions as predictors of children's school-based competence. *Child Development, 61,* 485-494.

Patterson, G. R. (1979). A performance theory of coercive family interaction. In R. B. Cairns (Ed.), *The analysis of social interactions: Methods, issues, and illustrations* (pp. 119-162). Hillsdale, NJ: Lawrence Erlbaum.

Patterson, G. R. (1982a). *Coercive family processes.* Eugene, OR: Castalia.

Patterson, G. R. (1982b). *A social learning approach to family intervention: III. Coercive family process.* Eugene, OR: Castalia.

Patterson, G. R. (1984). Siblings: Fellow travelers in coercive family processes. *Advances in the Study of Aggression, 1,* 173-215.

Patterson, G. R., Capaldi, D., & Bank, L. (1991). An early starter model for predicting delinquency. In D. J. Pepler & K. H. Rubin (Eds.), *The development and treatment of childhood aggression* (pp. 139-168). Hillsdale, NJ: Lawrence Erlbaum.

Patterson, G. R., Reid, J. B., & Dishion, T. J. (1992). *Antisocial boys: A social interactional approach* (Vol. 4). Eugene, OR: Castalia.

Patterson, G. R., Reid, J. B., Jones, R. R., & Conger, R. E. (1975). *A social learning approach to family intervention: Families with aggressive children.* Eugene, OR: Castalia.

Pearson, F. S. (1988). Evaluation of New Jersey's intensive supervision program. *Crime & Delinquency, 34,* 437-448.

Peeples, F., & Loeber, R. (1994). Do individual factors and neighborhood context explain ethnic differences in juvenile delinquency? *Journal of Quantitative Criminology, 10,* 141-158.

Pelham, W. E., Carlson, C. C., Sams, S. E., Vallano, G., Dixon, M. J., & Hoza, B. (1993). Separate and combined effects of methylphenidate and behavior modification on boys with attention deficit-hyperactivity disorder in the classroom. *Journal of Consulting and Clinical Psychology, 61,* 506-515.

Pennell, S. (1983). *San Diego Street Youth Program: Final evaluation.* San Diego, CA: Association of Governments.

Pennell, S., Curtis, C., Henderson, J., & Tayman, J. (1989). Guardian Angels: A unique approach to crime prevention. *Crime & Delinquency, 35,* 378-400.

Pennell, S., Curtis, C., & Scheck, D. D. (1990). Controlling juvenile delinquency: An evaluation of an interagency strategy. *Crime & Delinquency, 36,* 257-275.

Pentz, M. A., Brannon, B. R., Charlin, V. L., Barrett, E. J., MacKinnon, D. P., & Flay, B. R. (1989). The power of policy: The relationship of smoking policy to adolescent smoking. *American Journal of Public Health, 79,* 857-862.

Pentz, M. A., Dwyer, J. H., MacKinnon, D. P., Flay, B. R., Hansen, W. B., Wang, E. Y. I., & Johnson, C. A. (1989). A multi-community trial for primary prevention of adolescent drug abuse: Effects on drug use prevalence. *Journal of the American Medical Association, 261,* 3259-3266.

Pentz, M. A., MacKinnon, D. P., Flay, B. R., Hansen, W. B., Johnson, C. A., & Dwyer, J. H. (1989). Primary prevention of chronic diseases in adolescence: Effects of the Midwestern Prevention Project on tobacco use. *American Journal of Epidemiology, 130,* 713-724.

Pepler, D. J., & Rubin, K. H. (Eds.). (1991). *The development and treatment of childhood aggression.* Hillsdale, NJ: Lawrence Erlbaum.

Perkins, D. D., Florin, P., Rich, R. C., Wandersman, A., & Chavis, D. M. (1990). Participation and the social and physical environment of residential blocks: Crime and community context. *American Journal of Community Psychology, 18,* 83-115.

Perry, C. L., Kelder, S. H., Murray, D. M., & Klepp, K.-I. (1992). Communitywide smoking prevention: Long-term outcomes of the Minnesota Heart Health Program and Class of 1989 study. *American Journal of Public Health, 82,* 1210-1216.

Perry, C. L., Klepp, K.-I., & Sillers, C. (1989). Community-wide strategies for cardiovascular health: The Minnesota Heart Health Program youth program. *Health Education Research, 4,* 87-101.

Perry, C. L., Williams, C. L., Forster, J. L., Wolfson, M., Wagenaar, A. C., Finnegan, J. R., McGovern, P. G., Veblen-Mortenson, S., Komro, K. A., & Anstine, P. S. (1993). Background, conceptualization and design of a community-wide research program on adolescent alcohol use: Project Northland. *Health Education Research, 8,* 125-136.

Perry, C. L., Williams, C. L., Veblen-Mortenson, S., Toomey, T. L., Komro, K. A., Anstine, P. S., McGovern, P. G., Finnegan, J. R., Forster, J. L., Wagenaar, A. C., & Wolfson, M. (1996, July). Project Northland: Outcomes of a community-wide alcohol use prevention program during early adolescence. *American Journal of Public Health, 86,* 956-965.

Peters, M., Albright, K., Gimbel C., Thomas, D., Laxton, G., Opanga, M., & Afflerbach, M. (1996). *Evaluation of the impact of boot camps for juvenile offenders: Denver interim report.* Fairfax, VA: Caliber.

Peters, M., Bullman, S., Gimbel C., Thomas, D., Laxton, G., Opanga, M., Afflerbach, M., & Croan, G. (1996). *Evaluation of the impact of boot camps for juvenile offenders: Mobile interim report.* Fairfax, VA: Caliber.

Petersilia, J. (1987). *Expanding options for criminal sentencing.* Santa Monica, CA: RAND.

Petersilia, J., Lurigio, A. J., & Byrne, J. M. (1992). Introduction: The emergence of intermediate sanctions. In J. M. Byrne, A. J. Lurigio, & J. Petersilia (Eds.), *Smart sentencing: The emergence of intermediate sanctions* (pp. ix-xv). Newbury Park, CA: Sage.

Petersilia, J., & Turner, S. (1990). Comparing intensive and regular supervision for high-risk probationers: Early results from an experiment in California. *Crime & Delinquency, 36,* 87-111.

Petersilia, J., & Turner, S. (1991). An evaluation of intensive probation in California. *Journal of Criminal Law and Criminology, 82,* 610-658.

Petersilia, J., & Turner, S. (1993). Evaluating intensive supervision probation/parole: Results of a nationwide experiment. *Research in brief.* Washington, DC: U.S. Department of Justice, National Institute of Justice.

Petersilia, J., Turner, S., & Deschenes, E. P. (1992). The costs and effects of intensive supervision for drug offenders. *Federal Probation, 56,* 12-17.

Peterson, E. (1996). *Juvenile boot camps: Lessons learned* (Fact Sheet No. 36). Washington, DC: Office of Juvenile Justice and Delinquency Prevention.

Peterson, P. L., Hawkins, J. D., Abbott, R. D., & Catalano, R. F. (1994). Disentangling the effects of parental drinking, family management, and parental alcohol norms on current drinking by black and white adolescents. *Journal of Research on Adolescence, 4,* 203-227.

Peterson, P. L., Hawkins, J. D., & Catalano, R. F. (1992). Evaluating comprehensive community drug risk reduction interventions: Design challenges and recommendations. *Evaluation Review, 16,* 579-602.

Pfiffner, L. J., & O'Leary, S. G. (1993). School-based psychological treatments. In J. L. Matson (Ed.), *Handbook of hyperactivity in children* (pp. 234-255). Boston: Allyn & Bacon.

Piercy, F., & Lee, R. (1976). Effects of a dual treatment approach on the rehabilitation of habitual juvenile delinquents. *Rehabilitation Counseling Bulletin, 19,* 482-492.

Piper, E. (1985). Violent recidivism and chronicity in the 1958 Philadelphia cohort. *Journal of Quantitative Criminology, 1,* 319-344.

Podkopacz, M., & Feld, B. C. (1995). Juvenile waiver policy and practice: Persistence, seriousness and race. *Law and Inequality, 14,* 101-207.

Polk, K., Alder, C., Basemore, G., Blake, G., Cardray, S., & Coventry, G. (1981). *Becoming an adult: An analysis of maturational development from age 16-30.* Final report, Grant MH 14806, Center for Studies of Crime and Delinquency, National Institute of Mental Health. Washington, DC: U.S. Department of Health and Human Services.

Pollard, J., Catalano, R. F., Hawkins, J. D., & Arthur, M. (1997). *Development of a school-based survey measuring risk and protective factors predictive of substance abuse in adolescent populations.* Manuscript under review.

Poorkaj, H., & Bockelman, C. (1973). The impact of community volunteers on delinquency prevention. *Sociology and Sociological Research, 57,* 335-341.

Pope, C., & Feyerherm, W. (1993). *Minorities and the juvenile justice system.* Washington, DC: Office of Juvenile Justice and Delinquency Prevention.

Porteus, S. D. (1942). *Qualitative performance in the maze test.* New York: Psychological Corporation.

Poyner, B. (1993). What works in crime prevention: An overview of evaluations. In R. V. Clarke (Ed.), *Crime prevention studies.* Monsey, NY: Criminal Justice Press.

Poyner, B., & Webb, B. (1987). *Successful crime prevention: Case studies.* London: Tavistock Institute of Human Relations.

Price, R. H., & Lorion, R. P. (1989). Prevention programming as organizational reinvention: From research to implementation. In D. Shaffer, I. Philips, & N. B. Enzer (Eds.), *Prevention of mental disorders, alcohol and other drug use in children and adolescents* (pp. 99-121) (OSAP Prevention Monograph No. 2). Rockville, MD: Office for Substance Abuse Prevention.

Prochaska, J. O., DiClemente, C. C., & Norcross, J. C. (1992). In search of how people change: Applications to addictive behaviors. *American Psychologist, 47,* 1102-1114.

Provence, S., & Naylor, A. (1983). *Working with disadvantaged parents and their children: Scientific and practice issues.* New Haven, CT: Yale University Press.

Provence, S., Naylor, A., & Patterson, S. (1977). *The challenge of day care.* New Haven, CT: Yale University Press.

Pulkkinen, L. (1983). Predictability of criminal behavior. *Psykolgia, 18,* 3-10.

Puska, P., Tuomilehto, J., Nissinen, A., Salonen, J. T., Vartiainen, E., Pietinen, P., Koskela, K., & Korhonen, H. J. (1989). The North Karelia Project: 15 years of community-based prevention of coronary heart disease. *Annals of Medicine, 21,* 169-173.

Pynoos, R. S., & Nader, K. (1988). Psychological first aid and treatment approach to children exposed to community violence: Research implications. *Journal of Traumatic Stress, 1,* 445-473.

Quay, H. C. (1964). Dimensions of personality in delinquent boys as inferred from the factor analysis of case history data. *Child Development, 35,* 479-484.

Quay, H. C. (1979). Classification. In H. C. Quay & J. S. Werry (Eds.), *Psychopathological disorders of childhood* (2nd ed., pp. 1-42). New York: John Wiley.

Quay, H. C. (1986). Conduct disorders. In H. C. Quay & J. S. Werry (Eds.), *Psychopathological disorders of childhood* (3rd ed., pp. 35-72). New York: John Wiley.

Quay, H. C., & Parsons, L. B. (1971). *The differential classification of juvenile offender.* Washington, DC: U.S. Bureau of Prisons.

Rae-Grant, N., Thomas, B. H., Offord, D. R., & Boyle, M. H. (1989). Risk, protective factors, and the prevalence of behavioral and emotional disorders in children and adolescents. *Journal of the American Academy of Child and Adolescent Psychiatry, 28,* 262-268.

Raine, A., Brennan, P., & Mednick, S. A. (1994). Birth complications combined with early maternal rejection at age 1 year predispose to violent crime at age 18 years. *Archives of General Psychiatry, 51,* 984-988.

Raine, A., Brennan, P., Mednick, B., & Mednick, S. A. (1996). High rates of violence, crime, academic problems, and behavioral problems in males with both early neuromotor deficits and unstable family environments. *Archives of General Psychiatry, 53,* 544-549.

Raine, A., & Jones, F. (1987). Attention, autonomic arousal, and personality in behaviorally disordered children. *Journal of Abnormal Child Psychology, 15,* 583-599.

Ramsay, M. (1991). *The influence of street lighting on crime and fear of crime* (Crime Prevention Unit Paper No. 28). London: Home Office.

Rasmussen, D., & Yu, Y. (1996). *An evaluation of juvenile justice innovations in Duval County, Florida.* Tallahassee: Florida State University.

Raymond, M. R. (1987). Missing data in evaluation research. *Evaluation and the Health Professions, 9,* 395-420.

Reid, J. B. (1993). Prevention of conduct disorder before and after school entry: Relating interventions to developmental findings. *Development and Psychopathology, 5,* 243-262.

Reiss, A. J., Miczek, K. A., & Roth, J. A. (Eds.). (1994). *Understanding and preventing violence: Vol. 2. Biobehavioral influences.* Washington, DC: National Academy Press.

Reiss, A. J., & Roth, J. A. (Eds.). (1993). *Understanding and preventing violence.* Washington, DC: National Academy Press.

Reiss, D., & Price, R. H. (1996). National research agenda for prevention research. National Institute of Mental Health Report. *American Psychologist, 51,* 1109-1115.

Rescarla, L. A., Provence, S., & Naylor, A. (1982). The Yale Child Welfare Research Program: Description and results. In E. F. Zigler & E. W. Gordon (Eds.), *Day care: Scientific and social policy issues* (pp. 183-199). Boston: Auburn.

Rhine, E. (1996). Something works: Recent research on effective correctional programming. In American Correctional Association, *The state of corrections: 1995 proceedings.* Lanham, MD: American Correctional Association.

Ribisl, K. M., & Davidson, W. S., II. (1993). Community change interventions. In A. Goldstein & C. R. Huff (Eds.), *The gang intervention handbook* (pp. 333-355). Champaign, IL: Research Press.

Rice, R. (1963, October 19). A reporter at large: The Persian Queens. *The New Yorker, 39.*

Richman, N., Stevenson, J., & Graham, P. J. (1982). *Preschool to school: A behavioural study.* London: Academic Press.

Riggs, W. C., & Joyal, A. E. (1938). A validation of the Loofbourrow-Keys Personal Index of problem behavior in junior high schools. *Journal of Educational Psychology, 14,* 194-201.

Ringwalt, C. C. L., Graham, L. A., Pascall, M. J., Flewelling, R. L., & Browne, D. C. C. (1996). Supporting adolescents with guidance and employment. *American Journal of Preventive Medicine, 12,* 31-38.

Rivers, J., & Trotti, T. (1995). *South Carolina delinquent males: An 11-year follow-up into adult probation and prison* Report to the U.S. Department of Justice, Office of Juvenile Justice and Delinquency Prevention.

Robins, L. (1986). Changes in conduct disorder over time. In D. C. Farren & J. D. McKinney (Eds.), *Risk in intellectual and psychosocial development* (pp. 227-259). New York: Academic Press.

Robins, L. N. (1966). *Deviant children grown up: A sociological and psychiatric study of sociopathic personality.* Baltimore: Williams & Wilkins.

Robins, L. N., & Price, R. K. (1991). Adult disorders predicted by childhood conduct problems: Results from the NIHM Epidemiologic Catchment Area project. *Psychiatry, 54,* 116-132.

Robins, L. N., & Ratcliff, K. S. (1979). Risk factors in the continuation of childhood antisocial behavior into adulthood. *International Journal of Mental Health, 7,* 96-116.

Rodriguez, O. (1988). Hispanics and homicide in New York City. In J. F. Kraus, S. B. Sorenson, & P. D. Juarez (Eds.), *Proceedings of research conference on violence and homicide in Hispanic communities* (pp. 67-84). Los Angeles: University of California.

Roebuck, J. B. (1967). *Criminal typology.* Springfield, IL: Charles C Thomas.

Rogers, E. (1995). *Diffusion of innovations* (4th ed.). New York: Free Press.

Rogoff, B., & Morelli, G. (1989). Perspectives on children's development from cultural psychology. *American Psychologist, 44,* 343-348.

Rose, H., & McClain, P. (1990). *Race, place, and risk: Black homicide in urban America.* Albany: State University of New York Press.

Rosenbaum, D. P., Lewis, D. A., & Grant, J. A. (1986). Neighborhood-based crime prevention: Assessing the efficacy of community organization in Chicago. In D. P. Rosenbaum (Ed.), *Community crime prevention: Does it work?* (pp. 109-133). Beverly Hills, CA: Sage.

Rosenberg, M. L., & Fenley, M. A. (1991). *Violence in America: A public health approach.* New York: Oxford University Press.

Rosenberg, M. L., & Mercy, J. A. (1986). Homicide epidemiologic analysis at the national level. *Bulletin of the New York Academy of Medicine, 62,* 382-390.

Rosenthal, R. (1991). *Meta-analytic procedures for social research* (Rev. ed.). Newbury Park, CA: Sage.

Ross, R. R., & McKay, B. (1976). A study of institutional treatment programs. *International Journal of Offender Therapy and Comparative Criminology: An Interdisciplinary Journal, 20,* 167-173.

Rothman, J., & Tropman, J. E. (1987). Models of community organization and macro practice perspective: Their mixing and phasing. In F. Lox, T. Erlich, T. Rothman, & T. Tropman (Eds.), *Strategies of community organization* (pp. 3-26). Itasca, IL: Peacock.

Rowe, D., & Gulley, B. L. (1992). Sibling effects on substance use and delinquency. *Criminology, 30,* 217-233.

Rowland, R. G. (1992). An evaluation of the effects of a mentoring program on at-risk students in selected elementary schools in the North East Independent School District (Doctoral dissertation, Texas A&M University). *Dissertation Abstracts International, 53*(1A), 30.

Rubin, K. H., & Krasnor, L. R. (1986). Social-cognitive and social behavioral perspectives on problem-solving. In M. Perlmutter (Ed.), *Minnesota Symposium on Child Psychology* (Vol. 18., pp. 1-68). Hillsdale, NJ: Lawrence Erlbaum.

Rutter, M. (1979). Protective factors in children's responses to stress and disadvantage. In M. W. Kent & J. E. Rolf (Eds.), *Primary prevention of psychopathology: Vol. 3. Social competence in children* (pp. 49-74). Hanover, NH: University Press of New England.

Rutter, M. (1985). Resilience in the face of adversity: Protective factors and resistance to psychiatric disorder. *British Journal of Psychiatry, 147,* 598-611.

Rutter, M., & Garmezy, N. (1983). Developmental psychopathology. In P. Mussen (Ed.), *Handbook of child psychology* (Vol. 4, pp. 775-911). New York: John Wiley.

Rutter, M., Maughan, B., Mortimore, P., Ouston, J., & Smith, A. (1979). *Fifteen thousand hours: Secondary schools and their effects on children.* Cambridge, MA: Harvard University Press.

Safer, D. (1996). A school intervention for aggressive adolescents. In J. Hertzberg, G. F. Ostrum, & J. R. Field (Eds.), *Violent behavior: Vol. 1. Assessment and intervention* (pp. 243-256). Baltimore: University Park.

Saffer, H., & Grossman, M. (1987). Beer taxes, the legal drinking age, and youth motor vehicle fatalities. *Journal of Legal Studies, 16,* 351-374.

Sahagun, L. (1990, November 11). Fight against gangs turns to social solution. *Los Angeles Times,* p. A3.

Sampson, R. (1987). Urban black violence: The effect of male joblessness and family disruption. *American Journal of Sociology, 93,* 348-382.

Sampson, R., & Groves, W. B. (1989). Community structure and crime: Testing social disorganization theory. *American Journal of Sociology, 94,* 774-802.

Sampson, R., & Laub, J. (1993a). *Crime in the making: Pathways and turning points through life.* Cambridge, MA: Harvard University Press.

Sampson, R., & Laub, J. (1993b). Structural variations in juvenile court processing: Inequality, the underclass, and social control. *Law and Society Review, 27,* 285-311.

Sampson, R., & Lauritsen, J. (1990). Deviant lifestyles, proximity to crime and the offender-victim link in personal violence. *Journal of Research in Crime and Delinquency, 27,* 7-40.

Sampson, R., & Lauritsen, J. (1994). Violent victimization and offending: Individual-, situational-, and community-level risk factors. In A. J. Reiss & J. A. Roth (Eds.), *Understanding and preventing violence: Vol. 3. Social influences* (pp. 1-115). Washington, DC: National Academy Press.

Sampson, R., & Lauritsen, J. (1997). Racial and ethnic disparities in crime and criminal justice in the United States. In M. Tonry (Ed.), *Crime and justice: A review of research* (pp. 311-374). Chicago: University of Chicago Press.

Sampson, R. J., & Wilson, W. J. (1995). Toward a theory of race, crime, and urban inequality. In J. Hagan & R. Peterson (Eds.), *Crime and inequality.* Stanford, CA: Stanford University Press.

San Diego County Probation Department. (1996). *Juvenile correctional intervention program.* San Diego, CA: Author.

Saner, H., & Ellickson, P. (1996). Concurrent risk factors for adolescent violence. *Journal of Adolescent Health, 19,* 94-103.

Satterfield, J. H., Satterfield, B. T., & Schell, A. M. (1987). Therapeutic interventions to prevent delinquency in hyperactive boys. *Journal of the American Academy of Child and Adolescent Psychiatry, 26,* 56-64.

Schilling, R., & McAlister, A. (1990). Preventing drug use in adolescents through media interventions. *Journal of Consulting and Clinical Psychology, 58,* 416-424.

Schlicter, K. J., & Horan, J. J. (1981). Effects of stress inoculation on the anger and aggression management skills of institutionalized juvenile delinquents. *Cognitive Therapy and Research, 5,* 359-365.

Schlossman, S., & Sedlak, M. (1983a). *The Chicago Area Project revisited.* Report prepared for the U.S. National Institute of Education. Santa Monica, CA: RAND.

Schlossman, S., & Sedlak, M. (1983b). The Chicago Area Project revisited. *Crime & Delinquency, 29,* 398-462.

Schneider, A. L. (1990). *Deterrence and juvenile crime: Results from a national policy experiment.* Research in Criminology series. New York: Springer-Verlag.

Schnelle, J. F., Kirchner, R. E., Jr., Casey, J. D., Uselton, P. H., Jr., & McNees, M. P. (1977). Patrol evaluation research: A multiple-baseline analysis of saturation police patrolling during day and night hours. *Journal of Applied Behavioral Analysis, 10,* 33-40.

Schnelle, J. F., Kirchner, R. E., McNees, M. P., & Lawler, J. M. (1975). Social evaluation research: The evaluation of two police patrolling strategies. *Journal of Applied Behavior Analysis, 8,* 353-365.

Schwartz, A. J. (1989). Middle-class educational values among Latino gang members in East Los Angeles County high schools. *Urban Education, 24,* 323-342.

Schweinhart, L. J., Barnes, H. V., & Weikart, D. P. (1993). *Significant benefits: The High/Scope Perry Preschool study through age 27.* Ypsilanti, MI: High/Scope.

Schwitzgebel, R., & Kolb, D. A. (1964). Inducing behaviour change in adolescent delinquents. *Behavior Research and Therapy, 1,* 297-304.

Scottish Council on Crime. (1975). *Crime and the prevention of crime.* Scottish Home and Health Department. Edinburgh: HMSO.

Sechrest, L. (1987). Classification for treatment. In D. M. Gottfredson & M. Tonry (Eds.), *Crime and justice: An annual review: Vol. 9. Prediction and classification: Criminal justice decision making* (pp. 293-322). Chicago: University of Chicago Press.

Seckel, J. P., & Turner, J. K. (1985). *Assessment of Planned Re-Entry Programs (PREP).* Sacramento: California Youth Authority.

Seitz, V., & Apfel, N. H. (1994). Parent-focused intervention: Diffusion effects on siblings. *Child Development, 65,* 677-683.

Seitz, V., Rosenbaum, L. K., & Apfel, N. H. (1985). Effects of family support intervention: A ten-year follow-up. *Child Development, 56,* 376-391.

Seitz, V., Rosenbaum, L. K., & Apfel, N. H. (1991). Effects on an intervention program for pregnant adolescents: Educational outcomes at two years postpartum. *American Journal of Community Psychology, 15.*

Sellin, T. (1931). The bias of a crime index. *Journal of Criminal Law and Criminology, 22,* 335-356.

Shadish, W. R., & Haddock, C. K. (1994). Combining estimates of effect size. In H. Cooper & L. V. Hedges (Eds.), *The handbook of research synthesis* (pp. 261-281). New York: Russell Sage.

Shannon, L. W. (1988). *Criminal career continuity: Its social context.* New York: Human Science Press.

Shaw, C. R. (1930). *The Jack Roller: A delinquent boy's own story.* Chicago: University of Chicago.

Shaw, C. R., & McKay, H. D. (1931). *Social factors in juvenile delinquency: Report on the causes of crime* (Vol. 2). National Commission on Law Observance and Enforcement. Washington, DC: Government Printing Office.

Shaw, C. R., & McKay, H. D. (1969). *Juvenile delinquency and urban areas* (Rev. ed.). Chicago: University of Chicago Press.

Shaw, C., & McKay, H. (1949). Rejoinder. *American Sociological Review, 14,* 614-617.

Shearing, C. D., & Stenning, P. C. (1986). From the panoptican to Disney World: The development of discipline. In A. N. Doob & E. L. Greenspen (Eds.), *Perspectives in criminal law: Essays in honour of John L. J. Edwards.* Aurora, Ontario: Canada Law Book.

Shelden, R. G., & Chesney-Lind, M. (1993). Gender and race differences in delinquent careers. *Juvenile and Family Court Journal, 44,* 73-90.

Sheley, J. F., & Wright, J. D. (1993). Gun acquisition and possession in selected juvenile samples. *Research in brief.* Washington, DC: National Institute of Justice, Office of Juvenile Justice and Delinquency Prevention.

Shepherd, J. P., & Farrington, D. P. (1993). Assault as public health problem. *Journal of the Royal Society of Medicine, 86,* 89-92.

Sherman, L. W. (1990, March-April). Police crackdowns. In *National Institute of Justice reports.* Washington, DC: U.S. Department of Justice, National Institute of Justice.

Sherman, L. W. (1992). Attacking crime: Police and crime control. In M. Tonry & N. Morris (Eds.), *Crime and justice* (Vol. 15, pp. 159-200). Chicago: University of Chicago Press.

Sherman, L. W., Gottfredson, D., MacKenzie, D., Eck, J., Reuter, P., & Bushway, S. (1997). *Preventing crime: What works, what doesn't, what's promising.* Washington, DC: Office of Justice Programs, U. S. Department of Justice.

Sherman, L. W., Shaw, J. W., & Rogan, D. P. (1995, January). The Kansas City gun experiment. *Research in brief.* Washington, DC: U.S. Department of Justice, National Institute of Justice.

Sherman, L. W., & Weisburd, D. (1992). *Does patrol prevent crime? The Minneapolis Hot Spots Experiment.* Paper presented at the 47th International Society of Criminology Course, Urban Crime Prevention, Tokyo.

Shivrattan, J. L. (1988). Social interactional training and incarcerated juvenile delinquents. *Canadian Journal of Criminology, 30,* 145-163.

Shorstein, H. L. (1995, December). *Statement on juvenile justice.* Paper presented at the Leadership Forum: Systems Reform and Juvenile Justice, National Conference on State Legislatures, Sanibel Island, FL.

Short, J. F., Jr. (1969). Introduction to the revised edition. In C. Shaw & H. McKay, *Juvenile delinquency and urban areas* (pp. xxv-liv). Chicago: University of Chicago Press.

Short, J. F., Jr. (1963). Street corner groups and patterns of delinquency: A progress report. *American Catholic Sociological Review, 28,* 13-32.

Short, J. F., Jr. (1990). New wine in old bottles? Change and continuity in American gangs. In C. R. Huff (Ed.), *Gangs in America* (pp. 223-239). Newbury Park, CA: Sage.

Short, J. F., Jr. (1995a). *Poverty, ethnicity, and violence.* Boulder, CO: Westview.

Short, J. F., Jr. (1995b, November). *Youth collectives (including gangs) and adolescent violence.* Paper presented at the annual meeting of the American Society of Criminology, Boston.

Short, J. F., Jr. (1996). *Gangs and adolescent violence.* Boulder, CO: Center for the Study and Prevention of Violence.

Short, J. F., Jr., & Strodtbeck, F. L. (1965). *Group process and gang delinquency.* Chicago: University of Chicago Press.

Shure, M. B., & Spivack, G. (1980). Interpersonal problem-solving as a mediator of behavioral adjustment in preschool and kindergarten children. *Journal of Applied Developmental Psychology, 1,* 29-44.

Shure, M. B., & Spivack, G. (1982). Interpersonal problem-solving in young children: A cognitive approach to prevention. *American Journal of Community Psychology, 10,* 341-356.

Shure, M. B., & Spivack, G. (1988). Interpersonal cognitive problem-solving. In R. H. Price, E. L. Cowen, R. P. Lorion, & J. Ramos-McKay (Eds.), *Fourteen ounces of prevention: A casebook for practitioners* (pp. 69-82). Washington, DC: American Psychological Association.

Sickmund, M., Snyder, H. N., & Poe-Yamagata, E. (1997). *Juvenile offenders and victims: 1997 update on violence.* Washington, DC: Office of Juvenile Justice and Delinquency Prevention.

Simcha-Fagan, O., & Schwartz, J. E. (1986). Neighborhood and delinquency: An assessment of contextual effects. *Criminology, 24,* 667-702.

Simons, R., Wu, C.-I., Conger, R., & Lorenz, F. (1994). Two routes to delinquency: Differences between early and late starters in the impact of parenting and deviant peers. *Criminology, 32,* 247-275.

Singer, S. I. (1981). Homogeneous victim-offender populations: A review and some research implications. *Journal of Criminal Law and Criminology, 72,* 779-778.

Singer, S. I. (1986). Victims of serious violence and their criminal behavior: Subcultural theory and beyond. *Victims and Violence, 1,* 61-71.

Six State Consortium for Prevention Needs Assessment Studies. (1994). *State needs assessment studies: Alcohol and other drugs: General protocol* (Grant proposal funded by the Center for Substance Abuse Prevention, Contract No. 277-94-1014).

Skogan, W. (1981). *Issues in the measurement of victimization.* Washington, DC: Bureau of Justice Statistics.

Skogan, W. (1984). Reporting crimes to the police: The status of world research. *Journal of Research in Crime and Delinquency, 21,* 113-138.

Skogan, W. G., & Wycoff, M. A. (1986). Storefront police officers: The Houston field test. In D. P. Rosenbaum (Ed.), *Community crime prevention: Does it work?* (pp. 179-199). Beverly Hills, CA: Sage.

Skolnick, J. H., & Bayley, D. H. (1988). Theme and variation in community policing. In M. Tonry & N. Morris (Eds.), *Crime and justice* (Vol. 10, pp. 1-37). Chicago: University of Chicago Press.

Slicker, E. K., & Palmer, D. J. (1993). Mentoring at-risk high school students: Evaluation of a school-based program. *School Counselor, 40,* 327-334.

Sloan, J. H., Kellerman, A. I., Reay, D. T., Ferris, J. A., Koepsell, T., Rivara, F. P., Rice, C., Gray, L., & LoGerfo, J. (1988). Handgun regulations, crime, assaults, and homicide: A tale of two cities. *New England Journal of Medicine, 319,* 1256-1262.

Sloan-Howitt, M., & Kelling, G. (1990). Subway graffiti in New York City: "Gettin' up" vs. "meanin' it and cleanin' it." *Security Journal, 1,* 131-136.

Small, S. A., & Luster, T. (1994). Adolescent sexual activity: An ecological risk-factor approach. *Journal of Marriage and the Family, 56,* 181-192.

Smith, C., & Thornberry, T. P. (1995). The relationship between childhood maltreatment and adolescent involvement in delinquency. *Criminology, 33,* 451-481.

Smith, C. S., Farrant, M. R., Marchant, H. J. (1972). *The Wincroft Youth Project.* London: Tavistock.

Smith, D. R., & Jarjoura, G. R. (1988). Social structure and criminal victimization. *Journal of Research in Crime and Delinquency, 25,* 27-52.

Smith, D. R., Smith, W. R., & Noma, E. (1984). Delinquent career-lines: A conceptual link between theory and juvenile offenses. *Sociological Quarterly, 25,* 155-172.

Snyder, H. N. (1988). *Court careers of juvenile offenders.* Washington, DC: Office of Juvenile Justice and Delinquency Prevention.

Snyder, H. N., & Sickmund, M. (1995). *Juvenile offenders and victims: A national report.* Washington, DC: U.S. Department of Justice, Office of Juvenile Justice and Delinquency Prevention.

Snyder, H. N., Sickmund, M., & Poe-Yamagata, E. (1996). *Juvenile offenders and victims: 1996 update on violence.* Washington, DC: Office of Juvenile Justice and Delinquency Prevention.

Sontheimer, H., & Goodstein, L. (1993). An evaluation of juvenile intensive aftercare probation: Aftercare versus system response effects. *Justice Quarterly, 10,* 197-227.

Soriano, F. I. (1993). Cultural sensitivity and gang intervention. In A. Goldstein & C. R. Huff (Eds.), *The gang intervention handbook* (pp. 441-461). Champaign, IL: Research Press.

Sorrentino, A. (1959). The Chicago Area Project after twenty-five years. *Federal Probation, 23,* 40-45.

Sorrentino, A., & Whittaker, D. W. (1994, May). The Chicago Area Project: Addressing the gang problem. *FBI Law Enforcement Bulletin,* pp. 7-12.

Spence, S. H., & Marzillier, J. S. (1981). Social skills training with adolescent male offenders: II. Short-term, long-term and generalized effects. *Behavior Research and Therapy, 19,* 349-368.

Spencer, T., Biederman, J., Wilens, T., Harding, M., O'Donnell, D., & Griffin, S. (1996). Pharmacotherapy of attention-deficit hyperactivity disorder across the life cycle. *Journal of the American Academy of Child and Adolescent Psychiatry, 35,* 409-432.

Spergel, I. A. (1964). *Slumtown, racketville, haulburg.* Chicago: University of Chicago Press.

Spergel, I. A. (1966). *Street gang work: Theory and practice.* Reading, MA: Addison-Wesley.

Spergel, I. A. (1972). Community action research as a political process. In I. A. Spergel (Ed.), *Community organization: Studies in constraint* (pp. 231-262). Beverly Hills, CA: Sage.

Spergel, I. A. (1986). The violent youth gang in Chicago: A local community approach. *Social Service Review, 60,* 94-131.

Spergel, I. A. (1991). *Youth gangs: Problem and response.* Report to the U.S. Department of Justice, Office of Juvenile Justice and Delinquency Prevention.

Spergel, I. A. (1995). *The youth gang problem: A community approach.* New York: Oxford University Press.

Spergel, I. A., Chance, R. L., Ehrensaft, K. E., Regulus, T., Kane, C., & Alexander, A. (1992). *Prototype/models for gang intervention and suppression.* Report to the U.S. Department of Justice, Office of Juvenile Justice and Delinquency Prevention.

Spergel, I. A., Chance, R. L., Ehrensaft, K., Regulus, T., Kane, C., & Laseter, R. (1992). *Technical assistance manuals.* Report to the U.S. Department of Justice, Office of Juvenile Justice and Delinquency Prevention.

Spergel, I. A., Chance, R., Ehrensaft, K., Regulus, T., Kane, C., Laseter, R., Alexander, A., & Oh, S. (1994). *Gang suppression and intervention: Community models.* Washington, DC: U.S. Department of Justice, Office of Juvenile Justice and Delinquency Prevention.

Spergel, I. A., & Curry, G. D. (1990). Strategies and perceived agency effectiveness in dealing with the youth gang problem. In C. R. Huff (Ed.), *Gangs in America* (pp. 288-309). Newbury Park, CA: Sage.

Spergel, I. A., & Curry, G. D. (1993). The National Youth Gang Survey: A research and development process. In A. Goldstein & C. R. Huff (Eds.), *The gang intervention handbook* (pp. 359-400). Champaign, IL: Research Press.

Spergel, I. A., Curry, D., Chance, R., Kane, C., Ross, R., Alexander, A., Simmons, E., & Oh, S. (1994). *Gang suppression and intervention: Problem and response.* Washington, DC: U.S. Department of Justice, Office of Juvenile Justice and Delinquency Prevention.

Spergel, I. A., & Grossman, S. F. (1994, November). *Gang violence and crime theory: Gang Violence Reduction Project.* Paper presented at the American Society of Criminology Annual Meeting, Miami, FL.

Spergel, I. A., & Grossman, S. F. (1995, July). *Little Village Gang Violence Reduction Program.* Paper presented at the annual conference on Criminal Justice Research and Evaluation, Washington, DC.

Spergel, I. A., & Grossman, S. F. (1996). *Evaluation of a gang violence reduction project: A comprehensive and integrated approach.* Chicago: University of Chicago, School of Social Service Administration.

Spergel, I. A., & Grossman, S. F. (1997). *Evaluation of the Little Village Gang Violence Reduction Project.* Chicago: University of Chicago, School of Social Service Administration.

Spergel, I. A., Turner, C., Pleas, J., & Brown, P. (1969). *Youth manpower: What happened in Woodlawn.* Chicago: University of Chicago, School of Social Service Administration.

Spivack, G., & Shure, M. B. (1989). Interpersonal cognitive problem-solving (IPCS): A competence-building primary prevention program. *Prevention in the Human Services, 6,* 151-178.

Stanwyck, D. J., & Anson, C. A (1989). *The Adopt-a-Student evaluation project, final report.* Submitted to the W. T. Grant Foundation. Atlanta: Georgia State University.

Stattin, H., & Magnusson, D. (1989). The role of early aggressive behavior in the frequency, seriousness, and types of later crime. *Journal of Consulting and Clinical Psychology, 57,* 710-718.

Steffensmeier, D., & Allan, E. A. (1995). Age-inequality and property crime: The effects of age-linked stratification and status-attainment processes on patterns of criminality across the life course. In J. Hagan & R. D. Peterson (Eds.), *Crime and inequality* (pp. 95-115). Stanford, CA: Stanford University Press.

Stein, D. B., & Smith, E. D. (1990). The "REST" program: A new treatment system for the oppositional defiant adolescent. *Adolescence, 25,* 891-904.

Stodgill, R. M. (1950). *Behavior cards: A test-interview for delinquent children.* New York: Psychological Corporation.

Stott, D. H. (1960). A new delinquency prediction instrument using behavioral indications. *International Journal of Social Psychiatry, 6,* 195-205.

Stouthamer-Loeber, M., & Loeber, R. (1988). The use of prediction data in understanding delinquency. *Behavioral Sciences and the Law, 6,* 333-354.

Stouthamer-Loeber, M., Loeber, R., Huizinga, D., & Porter, P. (1997). *The early onset of persistent serious offending.* Unpublished report to the Office of Juvenile Justice and Delinquency Prevention, Washington, DC.

Stouthamer-Loeber, M., Loeber, R., & Thomas, C. (1992). Caretakers seeking help for boys with disruptive and delinquent behavior. *Comprehensive Mental Health Care, 2,* 159-178.

Strain, P. S., Young, C. C., & Horowitz, J. (1981). Generalized behavior change during oppositional child training: An examination of child and family demographic variables. *Behavior Modification, 5,* 15-26.

Sullivan, C., Grant, J. D., & Grant, M. Q. (1957). The development of interpersonal maturity: Application to delinquency. *Psychiatry, 20,* 373-385.

Sullivan, M. (1989). *"Getting paid": Youth crime and work in the inner city.* Ithaca, NY: Cornell University Press.

Sulzer-Azaroff, B., & Mayer, G. R. (1994). *Achieving educational excellence: Behavior analysis for achieving classroom and schoolwide behavior change.* San Marcos, CA: Western Image.

Szasz, T. S., & Alexander, G. J. (1968). Mental illness as an excuse for civil wrongs. *Journal of Nervous and Mental Disease, 147,* 113-123.

Taggart, R. (1995). *Quantum Opportunity Program.* Philadelphia: Opportunities Industrialization Centers of America.

Taylor, C. S. (1990). Gang imperialism. In C. R. Huff (Ed.), *Gangs in America* (pp. 103-115). Newbury Park, CA: Sage.

Taylor, R. B., & Gottfredson, S. (1986). Environmental design, crime and prevention: An examination of community dynamics. In A. J. Reiss, Jr. & M. Tonry (Eds.), *Crime and justice: A review of research: Vol. 8. Communities and crime.* Chicago: University of Chicago Press.

Tebes, J. K., Snow, D. L., & Arthur, M. W. (1992). Panel attrition and external validity in the short-term follow-up study of adolescent substance use. *Evaluation Review, 16,* 151-170.

Tebes, J. K., Snow, D. L., Ayers, T. S., & Arthur, M. W. (1996). Panel accretion and external validity in adolescent substance use research. *Evaluation Review, 20,* 470-484.

Teret, S. P., Wintemute, G. J., & Beilenson, P. L. (1992). The firearm fatality reporting system: A proposal. *Journal of the American Medical Association, 267,* 3073-3074.

Thambidurai, G. A. (1980). A comparative outcome study of a contract parole program for individuals committed to the youth correctional complex in the state of New Jersey (Doctoral dissertation, Rutgers University, State University of New Jersey, 1980). *Dissertation Abstracts International, 41,* 371B. (University Microfilms No. 80-16503)

Thomas, C. R. (1996, June). *The Second Chance Program.* Paper presented at the National Youth Gang Symposium. Dallas, TX.

Thomas, C. W., & Bilchik, S. (1985). Prosecuting juveniles in criminal courts: A legal and empirical analysis. *Journal of Criminal Law and Criminology, 76,* 439-479.

Thomas, D., Peters, M., Gimbel, C., Laxton, G., Opanga, M., Afflerbach, M., & Croan, G. (1996). *Evaluation of the impact of boot camps for juvenile offenders: Cleveland interim report.* Fairfax, VA: Caliber.

Thompson, B., & Kinne, S. (1990). Social change theory: Applications to community health. In N. Bracht (Ed.), *Health promotion at the community level* (pp. 45-65). Newbury Park, CA: Sage.

Thompson, D. W., & Jason, L. A. (1988). Street gangs and preventive interventions. *Criminal Justice and Behavior, 15,* 323-333.

Thornberry, T. P. (1976). The once and future promise of the rehabilitative idea. *Journal of Criminal Law and Criminology, 67,* 117-122.

Thornberry, T. P. (1987). Toward an interactional theory of delinquency. *Criminology, 25,* 863-891.

Thornberry, T. P. (1996). *The contribution of gang members to the volume of delinquency.* Fact sheet prepared for the U.S. Department of Justice, Office of Juvenile Justice and Delinquency Prevention.

Thornberry, T. P., & Figlio, R. M. (1974). Victimization and criminal behavior in a birth cohort. In T. P. Thornberry & E. Sagarin (Eds.), *Images of crime: Offenders and victims* (pp. 102-112). New York: Praeger.

Thornberry, T. P., Esbensen, F., & Van Kammen, W. (1991). Commitment to school and delinquency. In D. Huizinga, T. Thornberry, & R. Loeber, *Urban delinquency and drug use.* Unpublished report to the Office of Juvenile Justice and Delinquency Prevention.

Thornberry, T. P., Huizinga, D., & Loeber, R. (1995). The prevention of serious delinquency and violence: Implications from the Program of Research on the Causes and Correlates of Delinquency. In J. C. Howell, B. Krisberg, J. D. Hawkins, & J. J. Wilson (Eds.), *Sourcebook on serious, violent, and chronic juvenile offenders* (pp. 213-237). Thousand Oaks, CA: Sage.

Thornberry, T. P., & Krohn, M. D. (1997). Peers, drug use, and delinquency. In D. Stoff, J. Breiling, & J. D. Maser (Eds.), *Handbook of antisocial behavior* (pp. 218-233). New York: John Wiley.

Thornberry, T. P., Krohn, M. D., Lizotte, A. J., & Chard-Wierschem, D. (1993). The role of juvenile gangs in facilitating delinquent behavior. *Journal of Research in Crime and Delinquency, 30,* 55-87.

Thornberry, T. P., Moore, M., & Christenson, R. L. (1985). The effect of dropping out of high school on subsequent criminal behavior. *Criminology, 23,* 3-18.

Thrasher, F. M. (1936). The boys' club and juvenile delinquency. *American Journal of Sociology, 41,* 66-80.

Thrasher, F. M. (1963). *The gang: A study of 1,313 gangs in Chicago.* Chicago: University of Chicago Press. (Original work published 1927)

Thurman, Q. C., Giacomazzi, A. L., Reisig, M. D., & Mueller, D. G. (1996). Community-based gang prevention and intervention: An evaluation of the Neutral Zone. *Crime & Delinquency, 42,* 279-295.

Tilley, N. (1993). Crime prevention and the Safer Cities Story. *Howard Journal of Criminal Justice, 32,* 40-57.

Tolan, P. H. (1987). Implications of age of onset for delinquency risk identification. *Journal of Abnormal Child Psychology, 15,* 47-65.

Tolan, P. H., Blitz, C., & Davis, L. (1992, November). *Discriminators of drug use vs. violent delinquency.* Paper presented at the annual meeting of the American Society for Criminology, New Orleans, LA.

Tolan, P. H., & Gorman-Smith, D. (1997). Treatment of juvenile delinquency: Between punishment and therapy. In D. Stoff, J. Breiling, & J. D. Maser (Eds.), *Handbook of antisocial behavior* (pp. 405-416). New York: John Wiley.

Tolan, P. H., Gorman-Smith, D., Huesmann, L. R., & Zelli, A. (1997). Assessment of family relationship characteristics: A measure to explain risk for antisocial behavior and depression in youth. *Psychological Assessment, 9,* 212-223.

Tolan, P. H., & Guerra, N. G. (1994a). Prevention of delinquency: Current status and issues. *Applied and Preventive Psychology, 3,* 251-273.

Tolan, P. H., & Guerra, N. G. (1994b). *What works in reducing adolescent violence: An empirical review of the field.* Monograph prepared for the Center for the Study and Prevention of Youth Violence. Boulder: University of Colorado.

Tolan, P. H., & Guerra, N. G. (in press). Societal causes of violence towards children. In P. K. Trickett & C. Schellenbach (Eds.), *Violence against children in the family and the community.* Washington, DC: American Psychological Association.

Tolan, P. H., Guerra, N. G., & Kendall, P. (1995). A developmental-ecological perspective on antisocial behavior in children and adolescents: Towards a unified risk and intervention framework. *Journal of Consulting and Clinical Psychology, 63,* 579-584.

Tolan, P. H., Henry, D., Guerra, N. G., VanAcker, R., Huesmann, L. R., & Eron, L. (1996). *Patterns of psychopathology among urban-poor children: I. Community, age, ethnicity, and gender effects.* Manuscript submitted for publication.

Tolan, P. H., & Loeber, R. (1993). Antisocial behavior. In P. H. Tolan & B. J. Cohler (Eds.), *Handbook of clinical research and practice with adolescents* (pp. 207-331). New York: John Wiley.

Tolan, P. H., .& Lorion, R. P. (1988). Multivariate approaches to the identification of delinquency-proneness in males. *American Journal of Community Psychology, 16,* 547-561.

Tolan, P. H., & McKay, M. M. (1996). Preventing serious antisocial behavior in inner-city children: An empirical based family intervention program. *Family Relations, 45,* 148-155.

Tolan, P. H., & Thomas, P. (1995). The implications of age of onset for delinquency risk: II. Longitudinal data. *Journal of Abnormal Child Psychology, 23,* 157-181.

Tollett, T. (1987). *A comparative study of Florida delinquency commitment programs.* Tallahassee, FL: Department of Health and Rehabilitative Services.

Tolson, E. R., McDonald, S., & Moriarty, A. R. (1992). Peer mediation among high school students: A test of effectiveness. *Social Work in Education, 14,* 86-93.

Tonry, M. (1987). Prediction and classification: Legal and ethical issues. In D. M. Gottfredson & M. Tonry (Eds.), *Crime and justice: An annual review: Vol. 9. Prediction and classification: Criminal justice decision making* (pp. 367-423). Chicago: University of Chicago Press.

Tonry, M. (1994). Racial politics, racial disparities, and the war on crime. *Crime & Delinquency, 40,* 475-494.

Tonry, M. (1995). *Malign neglect: Race, crime, and punishment in America.* New York: Oxford University Press.

Tonry, M., Ohlin, L. E., & Farrington, D. P. (1991). *Human development and criminal behavior.* New York: Springer-Verlag.

Torbet, P., Gable, R., Hurst, H., Montgomery, I., Szymanski, L., & Thomas, D. (1996). *State responses to serious and violent juvenile crime.* Washington, DC: U.S. Department of Justice, Office of Juvenile Justice and Delinquency Prevention.

Torbet, P. M. (1996). Juvenile probation: The workhorse of the juvenile justice system. In *Juvenile Justice Bulletin.* Washington, DC: Office of Juvenile Justice and Delinquency Prevention.

Torres, D. M. (1981). *Gang Violence Reduction Project 3rd evaluation report.* Sacramento: California Department of the Youth Authority.

Torres, D. M. (1985). *Gang Violence Reduction Project: Update.* Sacramento: California Department of the Youth Authority.

Towberman, D. B. (1992). National survey of juvenile needs assessment. *Crime & Delinquency, 38,* 230-238.

Tracy, P. E. (1979). *Subcultural delinquency: A comparison of the incidence and seriousness of gang and non-gang member offensivity.* Unpublished manuscript, University of Pennsylvania, Center for Studies in Criminology and Criminal Law.

Tracy, P. E., & Kempf-Leonard, K. (1996). *Continuity and discontinuity in criminal careers.* New York: Plenum.

Tracy, P. E., Wolfgang, M. E., & Figlio, R. M. (1985). *Delinquency in two birth cohorts.* Executive summary. Washington, DC: Office of Juvenile Justice and Delinquency Prevention.

Tracy, P. E., Wolfgang, M. E., & Figlio, R. M. (1990). *Delinquency careers in two birth cohorts.* New York: Plenum.

Tremblay, R. E., & Craig, W. M. (1995). Developmental crime prevention. In M. Tonry & D. P. Farrington (Eds.), *Crime and justice: An annual review: Vol. 19. Building a safer society: Strategic approaches to crime prevention* (pp. 151-236). Chicago: University of Chicago Press.

Tremblay, R. E., Mâsse, B., Perron, D., Le Blanc, M., Schwartzman, A. E., & Ledingham, J. E. (1992). Early disruptive behavior, poor school achievement, delinquent behavior and delinquent personality: Longitudinal analyses. *Journal of Consulting and Clinical Psychology, 60,* 64-72.

Tremblay, R. E., McCord, J., Boileau, H., Charlebois, P., Gagnon, C. C., Le Blanc, M., & Larivée, S. (1991). Can disruptive boys be helped to become competent? *Psychiatry, 54,* 148-161.

Tremblay, R. E., Pagani-Kurtz, L., Vitaro, F., Mâsse, L. C., & Pihl, R. O. (1995). A bimodal preventive intervention for disruptive kindergarten boys: Its impact through mid-adolescence. *Journal of Consulting and Clinical Psychology, 63,* 560-568.

Tremblay, R. E., Pihl, R. O., Vitaro, F., & Dobkin, P. L. (1994). Predicting early onset of male antisocial behavior from preschool behavior. *Archives of General Psychiatry, 51,* 732-739.

Tremblay, R. E., Vitaro, F., Bertrand, L., Le Blanc, M., Beauchesne, H., Boileau, H., & David, L. (1992). Parent and child training to prevent early onset of delinquency: The Montreal Longitudinal-Experimental Study. In J. McCord & R. E. Tremblay (Eds.), *Preventing antisocial behavior: Interventions from birth through adolescence* (pp. 117-138). New York: Guilford.

Trevvett, N. B. (1965). Identifying delinquency-prone children. *Crime & Delinquency, 11,* 186-191.

Trickett, P. K., Apfel, N. H., Rosenbaum, L. K., & Zigler, E. F. (1982). A five-year follow-up of participants in the Yale Child Welfare Research Program. In E. F. Zigler & E. W. Gordon (Eds.), *Day care: Scientific and social policy issues* (pp. 200-222). Boston: Auburn.

Turner, S., & Petersilia, J. (1992). Focusing on high-risk parolees: An experiment to reduce commitments to the Texas Department of Corrections. *Journal of Research in Crime and Delinquency, 29,* 34-61.

Valdez, R., Nourjah, B., & Nourjah, P. (1988). Homicide in southern California, 1966-1985: An examination based on vital statistics data. In J. F. Kraus, S. B. Sorenson, & P. D. Juarez (Eds.), *Proceeding of research conference on violence and homicide in Hispanic communities* (pp. 85-100). Los Angeles: University of California.

Van Kammen, W. B., & Loeber, R. (1994). Are fluctuations in delinquent activities related to the onset and offset of juvenile illegal drug use and drug dealing? *Journal of Drug Issues, 24,* 9-24.

Van Kammen, W. B., & Loeber, R. (1995, November). *Adolescents and their guns: Relationship to delinquency and victimization.* Paper presented at the meeting of the American Society of Criminology, Boston.

Van Kammen, & W. B., Loeber, R.(1994). Are fluctuations in delinquent activities related to the onset and offset of juvenile illegal drug use and drug dealing? *Journal of Drug Issues, 24,* 9-24.

Vartiainen, E., Pallonen, U., McAlister, A., Koskela, K., & Puska, P. (1986). Four-year follow-up results of the smoking prevention program in the North Karelia Youth Project. *Preventive Medicine, 15,* 692-698.

Vartiainen, E., Pallonen, U., McAlister, A., & Puska, P. (1990). Eight-year follow-up results of an adolescent smoking prevention program: The North Karelia Youth Project. *American Journal of Public Health, 80,* 78-79.

Vaughn, J. B. (1991). Use of electronic monitoring with juvenile intensive supervision programs. In T. L. Armstrong (Ed.), *Intensive interventions with high-risk youths: Promising approaches in juvenile probation and parole* (pp. 189-210). Monsey, NY: Criminal Justice Press.

Veno, A., & Veno, E. (1993). Situational prevention of public disorder at the Australian Motorcycle Grand Prix. In R. V. Clarke (Ed.), *Crime prevention studies* (Vol. 2). Monsey, NY: Criminal Justice Press.

Veverka, M. (1971). The Gluecks' Social Prediction Table in a Czechoslovak research. *British Journal of Criminology, 11,* 187-189.

Vigil, J. D. (1988). *Barrio gangs: Street life and identity in Southern California.* Austin: University of Texas Press.

Vitaro, F., & Tremblay, R. E. (1994). Impact of a prevention program on aggressive children's friendships and social adjustment. *Journal of Abnormal Child Psychology, 22,* 457-475.

Wadsworth, M. E. J. (1976). Delinquency, pulse rates and early emotional deprivation. *British Journal of Criminology, 16,* 245-256.

Wadsworth, M. E. J. (1978). Delinquency prediction and its uses: The experience of a 21-year follow-up study. *International Journal of Mental Health, 7,* 43-62.

Wagenaar, A. C., & Holder, H. D. (1991). A change from public to private sale of wine: Results from natural experiments in Iowa and West Virginia. *Journal of Studies on Alcohol, 52,* 162-173.

Wahler, R. G. (1980). The insular mother: Her problems in parent-child treatment. *Journal of Applied Behavioral Analysis, 13,* 207-219.

Wahler, R. G., & Dumas, J. E. (1984). Changing the observational coding styles of insular and noninsular mothers: A step toward maintenance of parent training effects. In R. F. Dangel & R. A. Polster (Eds.), *Parent training: Foundations of research and practice* (pp. 379-416). New York: Guilford.

Waldo, G. P., & Griswold, D. (1979). Issues in the measurement of recidivism. In L. Sechrest, S. O. White, & E. D. Brown (Eds.), *The rehabilitation of criminal offenders: Problems and prospects* (pp. 225-250). Washington, DC: National Academy of Sciences.

Walker, H. M., Severson, H. H., Nicholson, F., Kehle, T., Jenson, W. R., & Clark, E. (1994). Replication of the Systematic Screening for Behavior Disorders (SSBD) procedure for the identification of at-risk children. *Journal of Emotional and Behavioral Disorders, 2,* 66-77.

Wandersman, A., Florin, P., Friedmann, R., & Meier, R. (1987). Who participates, who does not, and why? An analysis of voluntary neighborhood associations in the United States and Israel. *Sociological Forum, 2,* 534-555.

Wang, A. Y. (1994). Pride and prejudice in high school gang members. *Adolescence, 29,* 279-291.

Washburne, J. W. (1929). An experiment on character measurement. *Journal of Juvenile Delinquency, 13,* 1-8.

Wasik, B. H., Ramey, C. T., Bryant, D. M., & Sparling, J. J. (1990). A longitudinal study of two early intervention strategies: Project CARE. *Child Development, 61,* 1682-1696.

Wasserman, G. A. (1996, October). *Is there an alternate pathway for girls' anti-social behavior?* Paper presented at the annual meeting of the American Academy of Child and Adolescent Psychiatry, Philadelphia.

Wasserman, G. A., Miller, L., Pinner, E., & Jaramillo, B. S. (1996). Parenting predictors of the development of conduct problems in high-risk boys. *Journal of the American Academy of Child and Adolescent Psychiatry, 35,* 1227-1236.

Watt, A., & Rodmell, S. (1988). Community involvement in health promotion: Progress or panacea? *Health Promotion, 2,* 359-367.

Watts, R. J. (1991, June). *Manhood development for African-American boys: Program and organization development.* Paper presented at the American Society for Community Research and Action, Tempe, AZ.

Watts, R. K., & Rabow, J. (1983). Alcohol availability and alcohol-related problems in 213 California cities. *Alcoholism: Clinical and Experimental Research, 7,* 47-58.

Webb, B. (1994). Steering column locks and motor vehicle theft: Evaluations from three countries. In R. V. Clarke (Ed.), *Crime prevention studies* (Vol. 2). Monsey, NY: Criminal Justice Press.

Webb, B., & Laycock, G. (1992). *Tackling car crime: The nature and extent of the problem* (Crime Prevention Unit Paper No. 32). London: Home Office.

Webster, D. W. (1993). The unconvincing case for school-based conflict resolution programs for adolescents. *Health Affairs, 12,* 126-141.

Webster-Stratton, C. (1984). Randomized trial of two parent-training programs for families with conduct-disordered children. *Journal of Consulting and Clinical Psychology, 52,* 666-678.

Webster-Stratton, C. (1989). Long-term follow-up of families with young conduct problem children: From preschool to grade school. *Journal of Clinical Child Psychology, 19,* 144-149.

Webster-Stratton, C. (1990). Enhancing the effectiveness of self-administered videotape parent training for families with conduct-problem children. *Journal of Abnormal Child Psychology, 18,* 479-492.

Webster-Stratton, C. (1991). Annotation: Strategies for helping families with conduct disordered children. *Journal of Child Psychology and Psychiatry, 32,* 1047-1062.

Webster-Stratton, C. (1997). *Preventing conduct problems in young children: A partnership between Head Start and schools.* Manuscript under review.

Webster-Stratton, C., & Hammond, M. A. (1997). Treating children with early-onset conduct problems: A comparison of child and parent training interventions. *Journal of Consulting and Clinical Psychology, 65,* 93-109.

Wehby, J. H., Dodge, K. A., & Valente, E. (1991). School behavior of first grade children identified as at-risk for development of conduct problems. *Behavioral Disorders, 19,* 67-78.

Weiner, N. (1996). *The priority prosecution of the serious habitual offender: Roadblocks to early warning, early intervention and maximum effectiveness.* Philadelphia: Sellin Center for Studies in Criminology and Criminal Law.

Weissberg, R. P., & Greenberg, M. T. (1997). School and community competence-enhancement and prevention programs. In W. Damon (Series Ed.) & I. E. Sigel & K. A. Renninger (Vol. Eds.), *Handbook of child psychology: Vol. 5. Child psychology in practice* (5th ed.). New York: John Wiley.

Weisz, J. R., Walter, B. R., Weiss, B., Fernandez, G. A., & Mikow, V. A. (1990). Arrests among emotionally disturbed violent and assaultive individuals following minimal versus lengthy intervention through North Carolina's Willie M Program. *Journal of Consulting and Clinical Psychology, 58,* 720-728.

Weitekamp, E. G. M., Kerner, H. J., Schindler, V., & Schubert, A. (1995). On the "dangerousness of chronic/habitual offenders": A re-analysis of the 1945 Philadelphia birth cohort data. *Studies on Crime and Crime Prevention: Annual Review, 4,* 159-175.

Wells, L. E., & Rankin, J. H. (1988). Direct parental controls and delinquency. *Criminology, 26,* 263-285.

Werner, E. E., & Smith, R. S. (1982). *Vulnerable but invincible: A longitudinal study of resilient children and youth.* New York: McGraw-Hill.

Werner, E. E., & Smith, R. S. (1992). *Overcoming the odds: High risk children from birth to adulthood.* Ithaca, NY: Cornell University Press.

West, D. J., & Farrington, D. P. (1973). *Who becomes delinquent? Second report of the Cambridge Study in Delinquent Development.* London: Heinemann.

Weston, J. (1995). Community policing: An approach to youth gangs in a medium-sized city. In M. W. Klein, C. L. Maxson, & J. Miller, *The modern gang reader* (pp. 297-300). Los Angeles: Roxbury.

White, H. R. (1990). Drug-use delinquency connection in adolescence. In R. Weisheit (Ed.), *Drugs, crime, and criminal justice* (pp. 215-256). Cincinnati, OH: Anderson.

White, H. R. (1992). Early problem behavior and later drug problems. *Journal of Research in Crime and Delinquency, 29,* 412-429.

White, H. R., Pandina, R. J., & LaGrange, R. L. (1987). Longitudinal predictors of serious substance use and delinquency. *Criminology, 25,* 715-740.

White, J. (1985). *The comparative dispositions study.* Report to the U.S. Department of Justice, Office of Juvenile Justice and Delinquency Prevention.

White, J. L., Moffitt, T. E., Earls, F., Robins, L., & Silva, P. A. (1990). How early can we tell? Predictors of childhood conduct disorder and adolescent delinquency. *Criminology, 28,* 507-533.

White, J., Moffitt, T. E., Caspi, A., Bartusch, D. J., Needles, D. J., & Stouthamer-Loeber, M. (1994). Measuring impulsivity and examining its relation to delinquency. *Journal of Abnormal Psychology, 103,* 192-205.

Widom, C. S. (1989). The cycle of violence. *Science, 244,* 160-166.

Wiebush, R. G., Baird, C., Krisberg, B., & Onek, D. (1995). Risk assessment and classification for serious, violent, and chronic juvenile offenders. In J. C. Howell, B. Krisberg, J. D. Hawkins, & J. J. Wilson (Eds.), *Sourcebook on serious, violent, and chronic juvenile offenders* (pp. 171-212). Thousand Oaks, CA: Sage.

Wikström, P.-O. (1995a). Preventing city-center street crimes. In M. Tonry & D. Farrington (Eds.), *Crime and justice: A review of research: Vol. 19. Building a safer society: Strategic approaches to crime prevention* (pp. 429-468). Chicago: University of Chicago Press,

Wikström, P.-O. (1995b). Self-control, temptations, frictions and punishment. An integrated approach to crime prevention. In P.-O. Wikström, R. V. Clarke, & J. McCord (Eds.), *Integrating crime prevention strategies: Propensity and opportunity* (pp. 7-38). Stockholm, Sweden: National Council for Crime Prevention.

Wikström, P.-O. H. (1985). *Everyday violence in contemporary Sweden.* Stockholm: National Council for Crime Prevention.

Wilbanks, W. L. (1985). Predicting failure in parole. In D. P. Farrington & R. Tarling (Eds.), *Prediction in criminology* (pp. 78-95). Albany: State University of New York Press.

Wilkins, L. T. (1985). The politics of prediction. In D. P. Farrington & R. Tarling (Eds.), *Prediction in criminology* (pp. 34-53). Albany: State University of New York Press.

Williams, C. L., Perry, C. L., Dudovitz, B., Veblen-Mortenson, S., Anstine, P. S., Komro, K. A., & Toomey, T. L. (in press). A home-based prevention program for sixth grade alcohol use: Results from Project Northland. *Journal of Primary Prevention.*

Williams, J. H. (1994). *Understanding substance use, delinquency involvement, and juvenile justice system involvement among African-American and European-American adolescents.* Unpublished dissertation, University of Washington, Seattle.

Williams, K. W., Guerra, N. G., & Elliott, D. E. (1996). *Human development and violence prevention: A focus on youth.* Baltimore: Annie E. Casey Foundation.

Williams, T. P., & Lillis, R. P. (1986). Changes in alcohol consumption by 18-year-olds following an increase in New York State's purchase age to 19. *Journal of Studies on Alcohol, 47,* 290-296.

Wilson, J. J., & Howell, J. C. (1993). *A comprehensive strategy for serious, violent, and chronic juvenile offenders: Program summary.* Washington, DC: U.S. Department of Justice, Office of Juvenile Justice and Delinquency Prevention.

Wilson, J. J., & Howell, J. C. (1994). Serious and violent juvenile crime: A comprehensive strategy. *Juvenile and Family Court Journal, 45,* 3-14.

Wilson, J. J., & Howell, J. C. (1995). Comprehensive strategy for serious, violent, and chronic juvenile offenders. In J. C. Howell, B. Krisberg, J. D. Hawkins, & J. J. Wilson (Eds.), *Sourcebook on serious, violent, and chronic juvenile offenders* (pp. 36-47). Thousand Oaks, CA: Sage.

Wilson, W. J. (1987). *The truly disadvantaged: The inner city, the underclass, and public policy.* Chicago: University of Chicago Press.

Wilson, W. J., Aponte, R., Kirschenman, J., & Wacquant, L. (1988). The ghetto underclass and the changing structure of American poverty. In F. Harris & R. W. Wilkins (Eds.), *Quiet riots: Race and poverty in the United States.* New York: Pantheon.

Winfree, L. T., Jr., Backstrom, T., & Mays, G. L. (1994). Social learning theory, self-reported delinquency, and youth gangs: A new twist on a general theory of crime and delinquency. *Youth and Society, 26,* 147-177.

Winner, L., Lanza-Kaduce, L., Bishop, D. M., & Frazier, C. E. (1997). *The transfer of juveniles to criminal court: Re-examining recidivism over the long term.* Gainesville: University of Florida, Department of Statistics.

Wolf, M. M., Phillips, E. L., & Fixson, D. L. (1974). *Achievement Place: Phase II* (Vol. 1). Rockville, MD: National Institute of Mental Health, Center for Studies of Crime and Delinquency.

Wolfgang, M. E. (1983). Delinquency in two birth cohorts. In K. T. Van Dusen & S. A. Mednick (Eds.), *Prospective studies of crime and delinquency* (pp. 7-16). Boston: Kluwer-Nijhoff.

Wolfgang, M. E., Figlio, R. M., & Sellin, T. (1972). *Delinquency in a birth cohort.* Chicago: University of Chicago Press.

Wolfgang, M., Thornberry, T. P., & Figlio, R. M. (1987). *From boy to man, from delinquency to crime.* Chicago: University of Chicago Press.

Woodson, R. L. (1981). *A summons to life: Mediating structures and the prevention of youth crime.* Cambridge, MA: Ballinger.

Woodson, R. L. (1986). *Gang mother: The story of Sister Falaka Fattah.* Elmsford, NY: Pergamon.

Woolard, J. L., Gross, S. L., Mulvey, E. P., & Repucci, N. D. (1992). Legal issues affecting mentally disordered youth in the juvenile justice system. In J. J. Cocozza (Ed.), *Responding to the mental health needs of youth in the juvenile justice system.* Seattle, WA: National Coalition for the Mentally Ill in the Criminal Justice System.

Wright, J. D. (1995, March-April). Ten essential observations on guns in America. *Society,* pp. 63-68.

Wycoff, M. A. (1982). Evaluating the crime-effectiveness of municipal police. In J. R. Greene (Ed.), *Managing police work: Issues and analysis.* Beverly Hills, CA: Sage.

Wycoff, M. A., Skogan, W. G., Pate, A. M., & Sherman, L. W. (with Annan, S.). (1985a). *Citizen contact patrol: The Houston field test, executive summary.* Washington, DC: Police Foundation.

Wycoff, M. A., Skogan, W. G., Pate, A. M., & Sherman, L. W. (with Annan, S.). (1985b). *Police as community organizers: The Houston field test, executive summary.* Washington, DC: Police Foundation.

Yoshikawa, H. (1994). Prevention as cumulative protection: Effects of early family support and education on chronic delinquency and its risks. *Psychological Bulletin, 115,* 28-54.

Yoshikawa, H. (1995). Long-term effects of early childhood programs on social outcomes and delinquency. *Future of Children, 5,* 51-75.

Zhang, Q., Loeber, R., & Stouthamer-Loeber, M. (1997). Developmental trends of delinquency attitudes and delinquency: Replication and synthesis across time and samples. *Journal of Quantitative Criminology, 13,* 181-216.

Zigler, E., & Finn-Stevenson, M. (1997). Policy efforts to enhance child and family life: Goals for 2010. In R. P. Weissberg, T. P. Gullotta, R. L. Hampton, & G. R. Adams (Eds.), *Healthy children 2010: Strategies to enhance social, emotional, and physical wellness.* Thousand Oaks, CA: Sage.

Zigler, E., Taussig, C., & Black, K. (1992). Early childhood intervention: A promising preventive for juvenile delinquency. *American Psychologist, 47,* 997-1006.

Zigler, E., & Valentine, J. (Eds.). (1979). *Project Head Start: A legacy of the war on poverty.* New York: Free Press.

Zimring, F. E. (1976). Street crime and new guns: Some implications for firearms control. *Journal of Criminal Justice, 4,* 95-107.

Zimring, F. E. (1985). Violence and firearms policy. In L. A. Curtis (Ed.), *American violence and public policy* (pp. 133-152). New Haven, CT: Yale University Press.

Zimring, F. E. (1993). Policy research on firearms and violence. *Health Affairs, 12,* 109-121.

Zimring, F. E. (1996). Kids, guns, and homicide: Policy notes on an age-specific epidemic. *Law and Contemporary Problems, 59,* 25-37. [Special issue]

Zimring, F. E., & Hawkins, G. (1987). *The citizen's guide to gun control.* New York: Macmillan.

Zingraff, M. T., Leiter, J., Myers, K. A., & Johnson, M. C. (1993). Child maltreatment and youthful problem behavior. *Criminology, 31,* 173-202.

Zins, J., & Forman, S. G. (1988). Mini-series on primary prevention: From theory to practice. *School Psychology Review, 17,* 539-634.

Zoccolillo, M. (1993). Gender and the development of conduct disorder. *Development and Psychopathology,* pp. 65-78.

Index

About the Contributors

David M. Altschuler, Ph.D., is Principal Research Scientist at the Johns Hopkins Institute for Policy Studies, Baltimore, Maryland, and Adjunct Associate Professor in Sociology. He is also co-principal investigator on the Intensive Juvenile Aftercare Demonstration Initiative, which is funded by the Office of Juvenile Justice and Delinquency Prevention.

Michael W. Arthur, Ph.D., is Research Associate Professor in the School of Social Work at the University of Washington and a project director at the Social Development Research Group, Seattle Washington. His research and practice interests include prevention research methodology, state and community prevention systems, and community-based interventions to prevent adolescent behavior problems and promote social competence.

Lisa Berglund, Ph.D., is Project Director for the DHHS-funded evaluation study Positive Youth Development, at the Social Development Research Group at the University of Washington, Seattle. Her expertise is in adolescent and family psychology, and her research interests include risk and protective factors for prevention of youth violence, and parent and adolescent training interventions.

Devon Brewer, Ph.D., is Research Scientist at the Alcohol and Drug Abuse Institute, University of Washington, Seattle. His research specialties include research methods, social networks, memory, and cognition.

Richard F. Catalano, Ph.D., is Professor in the School of Social Work at the University of Washington, Seattle, and Associate Director of the Social Development Research Group. His interests include research and program development in substance abuse and delinquency. He is principal investigator for the Focus on Families, Raising Healthy Children, and Minority Youth Health projects.

James H. Derzon, Ph.D., is Research Associate at the Center for Evaluation Research and Methodology at Vanderbilt Institute for Public Policy, Nashville, Tennessee. His interests include the research methods and the antecedent prediction of drug use, delinquency, and other antisocial behaviors.

David P. Farrington, Ph.D., is Professor of Psychological Criminology at the Institute of Criminology, University of Cambridge, Cambridge, England. He is Director of the Cambridge Study in Delinquent Development and coinvestigator on the Pittsburgh Youth Study. He is currently President of the European Association of Psychology and Law and President-Elect of the American Society of Criminology. His extensive publications cover numerous aspects of juvenile delinquency and crime in general.

Deborah Gorman-Smith, Ph.D., is Assistant Professor, Department of Psychiatry, and is with the Families and Communities Research Group, Institute for Juvenile Research, Department of Psychiatry, University of Illinois at Chicago. She is a collaborator with Drs. David Henry and Patrick Tolan on the Chicago Youth Development Study, a longitudinal study of adolescent development in the inner city, and SAFE Children, a prevention program for families living in high-risk urban neighborhoods.

Nancy G. Guerra, Ph.D., is Associate Professor of Psychology at the University of Illinois at Chicago. Her research interests focus on cognitive-behavioral interventions with aggressive youth, community-based responses to youth violence, and application of child development research in Latino and African American populations. She has published numerous articles, chapters, and books in these areas. Currently, she is principal investigator on a large-scale, multiyear preventive intervention research trial funded by the National Institute of Mental Health. This research involves the evaluation of a multicomponent, multisystem, school-based intervention to prevent antisocial behavior in urban youth. She is also a member of the President's Advisory Council on Juvenile Justice, chaired by Attorney General Janet Reno.

Tracy W. Harachi, Ph.D., M.S.W., is Research Associate Professor at the Social Development Research Group, University of Washington, Seattle. Her research interests include comprehensive prevention programming for children and families, family management, parenting and adaptation among ethnic minority and immigrant families, cross-cultural measurement, and multilevel methodology.

Darnell F. Hawkins, Ph.D., is Professor of African-American Studies and Sociology, Department of African-American Studies, University of Illinois at Chicago. Research interests include the study of racial and ethnic difference in crime and the administration of justice.

J. David Hawkins, Ph.D., is Professor in the School of Social Work and Director of the Social Development Research Group, University of Washington, Seattle. He is cofounder of Developmental Research and Programs. His research focuses on understanding and preventing child and adolescent health and behavior problems. He seeks to identify risk and protective factors for health and behavior problems across multiple domains; to understand how these factors interact in the development or prevention of problem behavior; and to test comprehensive prevention strategies that seek to reduce risk through the enhancement of protective factors in families, schools, peer groups, and communities. He is committed to translating research into effective practice and policy to improve adolescent health and development.

Todd Herrenkohl, M.S.W., is a doctoral student in social welfare at the University of Washington, Seattle. His research is focused on the etiology of youth violence and its prevention. His practice background is in mental health services for families and adolescents.

James C. Howell, Ph.D., is Adjunct Researcher, National Youth Gang Center, Tallahassee, Florida. He formerly was Director of the Research and Program Development Division of the Office of Juvenile Justice and Delinquency Prevention, U.S. Department of Justice. He is coauthor (with John Wilson) of the OJJDP *Comprehensive Strategy for Serious, Violent, and Chronic Juvenile Offenders,* and lead editor of *A Sourcebook: Serious, Violent, and Chronic Juvenile Offenders* (Sage).

David Huizinga, Ph.D., is Senior Research Associate at the Behavioral Research Institute, University of Colorado, Boulder. He holds graduate degree in mathematics and psychology and is currently the principal investigator of two long-term longitudinal studies that focus on developmental lifespan issues related to delinquency, crime, drug use, and mental health.

Cynthia Jakob-Chien, Ph.D., is Assistant Professor in the Department of Sociology and Anthropology at the University of Northern Iowa, Cedar Falls. Her current research focuses on social learning theories of crime and delinquency.

Barry Krisberg, Ph.D., has been President of the National Council on Crime and Delinquency, San Francisco, California, for 14 years. He received both his master's and doctorate degrees in criminology and sociology from the University of Pennsylvania. Prior to joining NCCD, he held several academic positions. He was a faculty member at the University of California at Berkeley and an adjunct professor with Hubert Humphrey Institute of Public Affairs at the University of Minnesota. He was the recipient of the August Vollmer Award of the American Society of Criminology in 1993.

John H. Laub, Ph.D., is Professor in the College of Criminal Justice at Northeastern University, Boston, Massachusetts, and Visiting Scholar at the Henry A. Murray Research Center at Radcliffe College. His research interests include theories of crime and deviance over the life course, juvenile justice, and the history of criminology. He has published widely, including *Crime in the Making: Pathways and Turning Points Through Life* (1993), coauthored with Robert J. Sampson.

Janet L. Lauritsen, Ph.D., is Associate Professor of Criminology and Criminal Justice at the University of Missouri, St. Louis. Her research interests include victimization and offending, adolescent sexual behavior, and quantitative research methods.

Marc Le Blanc, Ph.D., is Professor in the École de Psycho-Éducation, University of Montreal, Quebec, Canada. He is a member of the Royal Society of Canada and is also the recipient of the Marcel Vincent medal for achievement in social sciences. He has published 10 books, 80 book chapters, and 140 articles. He is a member of several expert groups for the governments of Quebec and Canada.

Mark W. Lipsey, Ph.D., is Professor of Public Policy, Department of Psychology and Human Development, Vanderbilt University, Nashville, Tennessee. He is Codirector of the Center for Evaluation Research and Methodology, Vanderbilt Institute of Public Policy Studies (VIPPS).

Rolf Loeber, Ph.D., is Professor of Psychiatry, Psychology, and Epidemiology at the Western Psychiatric Institute and Clinic, School of Medicine, University of Pittsburgh, Pittsburgh, Pennsylvania, U.S.A., and Professor of Developmental Psychotherapy, Free University, Amsterdam, Netherlands. He is Codirector of the Life History Studies Program and principal investigator of two longitudinal studies, the Pittsburgh Youth Study and the Developmental Trends Study. He has published widely in the fields of juvenile antisocial behavior and delinquency, substance use, and mental health problems.

Laurie S. Miller, Ph.D., is Assistant Professor of Clinical Psychology in Psychiatry, Columbia University, and Research Scientist, New York State Psychiatric Institute, New York. She is director of the Disruptive Behavior Disorder Clinic at Babies Hospital, New York. Research interests include the development and prevention of antisocial behavior.

Jeffrey J. Olson, M.S.W., is currently working toward his doctorate degree at the School of Social Work, University of Washington, Seattle. His interests include prevention research in substance abuse and delinquency, social work practice theory, and social work ethics.

Howard N. Snyder, Ph.D., is Director of Systems Research at the National Center for Juvenile Justice, Pittsburgh, Pennsylvania. His research and publications reflect his interest in the improvement of available information on juvenile crime, victimization, and the justice system; the development of, and changes in, juvenile delinquent careers;

the nature of violent crime against young children; temporal cycles of violent crime by and against juveniles; and the impact of court processing on juvenile careers.

Terence P. Thornberry, Ph.D., is Professor in the School of Criminal Justice, University at Albany State University of New York. He is Director of the Rochester Youth Development Study, an ongoing longitudinal study of delinquency and drug use.

Patrick H. Tolan, Ph.D., is with the Families and Communities Research Group, Institute for Juvenile Research, Department of Psychiatry, University of Illinois at Chicago. He is Director of Research at the Institute for Juvenile Research and Professor in the Department of Psychiatry and Psychology. He is a collaborator with Drs. Deborah Gorman-Smith and David Henry on the Chicago Youth Development Study, a longitudinal study of adolescent development in the inner city, and SAFE Children, a prevention program for families living in high-risk urban neighborhoods.

Daniel A. Waschbusch, M.S., is a graduate student researcher working toward a doctorate degree in clinical and developmental psychology. He will complete clinical internship at the University of Mississippi Medical Center during the academic year 1997-1998. His research interests include attention-deficit hyperactivity disorder, conduct problems, peer relationships of elementary-aged children, and methodology.

Gail A. Wasserman, Ph.D., is Professor of Clinical Psychology in Child Psychiatry, Department of Child Psychiatry, College of Physicians and Surgeons, Columbia University, New York State Psychiatric Institute. At Columbia, she directs a multidisciplinary center for the study of child disruptive behavior disorders. Her research interests concern the ways in which risk factors operate at many levels in vulnerable children.

David B. Wilson, Ph.D., is Research Associate at the Center for Evaluation Research and Methodology at Vanderbilt Institute for Public Policy Studies, Nashville, Tennessee. His primary research interest is in intervention research with emphasis on juvenile delinquency interventions and the role of method in influencing outcomes research. Also included in his interests are the advancement of meta-analytic methodology and the application of research synthesis to policy-relevant issues.